Foundations of Programming Languages

Design and Implementation

Seyed H. Roosta

University of South Carolina Spartanburg

THOMSON

BROOKS/COLE

Australia • Canada • Mexico • Singapore • Spain • United Kingdom • United States

THOMSON

BROOKS/COLE

Editor: Kallie Swanson
Senior Editorial Assistant: Carla Vera
Technology Project Manager: Burke Taft
Executive Marketing Manager: Tom Ziolkowski
Marketing Assistant: Darcie Pool
Advertising Project Manager: Laura Hubrich
Project Manager, Editorial Production: Kelsey McGee
Print/Media Buyer: Vena M. Dyer

Permissions Editor: Sue Ewing
Production Service: Forbes Mill Press
Cover Designer: Denise Davidson
Cover Image: Ryuichi Okano/Photonica
Compositor: Wolf Creek Press
Cover Printing, Printing and Binding:
    Phoenix Color Corp.

For more information about our products, contact us at:
Thomson Learning Academic Resource Center
1-800-423-0563
For permission to use material from this text, contact us by:
Phone: 1-800-730-2214
Fax: 1-800-730-2215
Web: http://www.thomsonrights.com

Library of Congress Control Number: 2002108051

ISBN 0-534-39303-9

Brooks/Cole–Thomson Learning
511 Forest Lodge Road
Pacific Grove, CA 93950
USA

Asia
Thomson Learning
5 Shenton Way #01-01
UIC Building
Singapore 068808

Australia
Nelson Thomson Learning
102 Dodds Street
South Melbourne, Victoria 3205
Australia

Canada
Nelson Thomson Learning
1120 Birchmount Road
Toronto, Ontario M1K 5G4
Canada

Europe/Middle East/Africa
Thomson Learning
High Holborn House
50/51 Bedford Row
London WC1R 4LR
United Kingdom

Latin America
Thomson Learning
Seneca, 53
Colonia Polanco
11560 Mexico D.F.
Mexico

Spain
Paraninfo Thomson Learning
Calle/Magallanes, 25
28015 Madrid, Spain

Contents

16 ADDITIONAL PROGRAMMING METHODS   562

Preface

Motivation

Design is an important concept for all computer science students regardless of whether they will ever have to design and create a programming language. One who understands the motivation for various programming language facilities will be able to practice them more intelligently. *Implementation* is also an important issue because the language designer must be aware of the costs of the facilities provided for that particular programming language. Both issues are important to all computer scientists because they all use programming languages and because there is an increasing demand for the design of languages that require new skills in their development. Thus, this textbook treats the design and implementation of programming languages as fundamental skills that all computer science students and computer scientists should possess. We believe that a command of the essentials provides enough information for programming language users to practice in this area of computer science.

Relative to the several existing books, which informally survey a selection of programming languages for the formal specification of applications, this book covers significant material on design and implementation issues and the theoretical foundations of programming languages. This is not a feature-by-feature examination of programming languages. Rather, it is a study of programming languages organized by concepts.

All programming language users require some kind of *descriptive skills* to express their ideas. The book aims to teach the descriptive tools important to programming language design and implementation. Besides, it is important to be informed of the designs tried in the past and why they succeeded or failed. Thus, we aim to present language facilities and styles. To accomplish this objective, we present an informal survey of a selection of *metalanguages* for formally specifying programming languages. The book covers the important area of techniques and metalanguages for the formal specification of the syntax and semantics of computer programming languages. This book is specifically designed for use as a textbook in undergraduate programming language survey courses by senior students studying the structure, design, or theory of programming language and covers most of the material specified in *ACM/IEEE-CS Curriculum Task Force Report*. This is in agreement with the recommendations of the ACM Task Force on the Core of Computer Science.

Foundations of Programming Languages

There are several advantages to concentrating on the foundations of programming languages rather than on the details of an assortment of fashionable computer languages. More important is the advantage for students: Their knowledge will be useful throughout their careers, and they can experience using a variety of actual programming languages. Nevertheless, after much consideration, we have concentrated on different language design principles, such as *declarative, imperative, applicative, object-oriented*, and *parallel* programming approaches because, in my experience, their goals should be articulated in the design and implementation of any programming language. Thus, we emphasize the fundamental features and concepts common to all programming languages. By using this strategy, we are able to provide students with several paradigms ranging from a very high-level (formal semantics) to a very low-level (lambda calculus) of design and implementation and to demonstrate a clear connection between the models. Generally speaking, we look at the principles underlying the major paradigms of programming languages. Thus, readers are equipped with a broad base of knowledge applicable to many programming languages.

In accord with the goals of emphasizing broad principles rather than details, no language is presented in full consideration. Only the language manual or the official definition can serve that purpose. Furthermore, one basic skill that the students should acquire in a programming language course is the ability to learn and evaluate a language solely on the basis of its design, implementation, and applicability.

Book Organization

This book advocates the concepts of programming languages. Abstraction principles are emphasized throughout the book as the core to understand and manage complex paradigms. The text contains more material than can be covered in a one-semester course. We have provided a wide variety of topics so that instructors may choose materials to suit the particular needs of their students. We have tried to allow as much flexibility as possible with respect to the order in which the various sections may be read.

The prerequisite structure relating all the chapters is shown in Figure P.1, meaning that a particular chapter should not be read until all earlier chapters connected to it with lines leading downward have been read.

Dependencies between the chapters are indicated in the graph. We have purposely attempted to minimize mutual interdependencies and to make our presentation as broad as possible. Chapter 1 provides a historical background for programming languages.

The next two chapters provide the foundations for a careful study of programming language design and implementation. In this sense, Chapters 2 and 3 are devoted to the principles of programming languages, including data types, type binding, type checking, type conversion, abstraction, parameters, exceptions, and expressions.

FIGURE **P.1**   **Prerequisites for the text chapters**

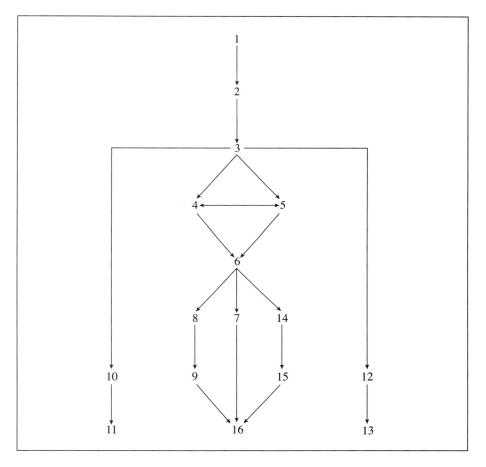

Chapter 4 deals primarily with the *syntax* of programming languages and treats grammars in the guise of *BNF* metalanguage and their variants. Chapter 5 studies *semantic* formalisms that can be classified as *axiomatic, operational, denotational,* and *translational* semantics. Denotational semantics is one of the most complete and successful methods of specifying a programming language, and axiomatic semantics has become an important component of software development by means of proofs of correctness for algorithms.

The *imperative* programming language design is treated in Chapter 6. The term imperative comes from command or action in which the language mimics the Von Neumann computational model, including global variables and side effects with explicitly specified processing operations. Chapter 7 is devoted to the discussion of the core of imperative programming embodied in two languages, C and Modula.

Chapter 8 describes the design of *object-oriented* programming languages, which are based on grouping of data and operations. The concepts of such grouping can be modeled in terms of modules, objects, and classes. C++, which is an extension of C, is expressed in Chapter 9 along with Smalltalk, which consists of a powerful user interface and environment in addition to its language features. In addition, Java as a programming language with characteristics such as simple, general-purpose, object-oriented, distributed, interpreted, robust, secure, architecture-neutral, portable, high-performance, multi-threaded, and dynamic primitives is discussed in this chapter. Java supports programming for the Internet in the form of platform-independent Java *applets*.

Chapter 10 is dedicated to *declarative* programming languages including *logic* languages. A declarative language is concerned with expressing what a program does rather than how. A declarative language has no implicit state that can be modified by assignment statements and other constructs in the language, so the emphasis is placed entirely on programming with expressions or terms. *Prolog* as a logic programming language is introduced in Chapter 11 by describing the terms of logic grammars and procedures associated with logic deduction.

Chapter 12 introduces the *applicative* programming language method that more closely resemble mathematics, where the function application is the only control structure. There are no conditional, assignment, explicit sequencing, or looping structures, which lead the program with "if you give me that, then I'll give you this" style of programming. The lambda calculus, which is the intellectual ancestor of functional languages, is expressed in this chapter by describing its syntax and the evaluation of lambda expressions by reduction rules. Chapter 13 is devoted to LISP as the pioneer of functional programming language in which the programs and data are both represented by lists. In addition, Scheme and ML, as two variations of functional programming languages, are discussed in this chapter.

The emphasis in Chapter 14 is on *parallel* programming languages. The execution of a parallel program forms a set of concurrently executing processes, which communicate and synchronize by reading and sharing variables. Chapter 15 introduces three parallel programming approaches, parallel programming with *UNIX*, with *Ada*, and with *C**. Chapter 16 deals with some of the new programming language methods, such as *data flow*, *database*, *network*, and *Internet* programming languages. VAL as a data flow programming language is expressed by its expressions and functions, which take input values and produce a result without side effects. We study the most influential commercially marketed product language, SQL as a language for database systems. SQL uses a combination of relational-algebra and relational-calculus constructs. Although we refer to SQL as a query language, it contains many other capabilities besides querying a database. Also in this chapter, we briefly discuss the client/server network-programming model with Sockets and Internet programming with Hypertext Markup Language (HTML). Sockets are abstractions that serve as endpoints of communication within a networking domain. HTML is a coding language that allows users to create Web pages. In addition, in this chapter we briefly discuss Windows programming with Visual Basic. Visual Basic programs are created in an Integrated Development Environment (IDE), in which the programmer can create, run, and debug Visual Basic programs conveniently. There are brief guides to sources of further information at the end of each chapter. Whenever possible, we have referenced publications that are readily accessible. In some cases, more references may be found in those publications. Exercises are a vital part of the textbook and are scattered throughout. They range in difficulty from being trivial to requiring references. We regard certain exercises as fundamental to mastery of the material.

Features

Some distinctive features of the book are that it

▶ Provides an overview of the key paradigms used in developing different programming languages.

▶ Explores the implementation of each programming language in sufficient detail to provide the reader an understanding of the relationship between design concepts and its implementation.

▶ Provides sufficient formal theory to understand where programming language fits within the general computer science agenda.

▶ Provides a sufficient knowledge and alternative references to allow readers the opportunity to extend their enthusiasm in this important topic.

▶ Raises a number of research issues. Thus, the book may serve as a source of inspiration for students and researchers who want to be engaged in the area of programming language design and implementation.

▶ Combines a general presentation of principles with considerable detail about different programming language representatives, including some of the newest logic, functional, data flow, parallel and object-oriented languages.

▶ Draws together the basic information and examples of a wide variety of definitional methods used in programming languages.

Audience

The intended audience includes advanced undergraduate and beginning graduate students in computer science. Readers are expected to have a general knowledge of programming languages, preferably experience with at least one high-level programming language, and the related aspects of computer science such as trees and other data structures and the concept of recursion. Some basic knowledge of other areas in computer science such as compiler construction, set theory, functions, logic, discrete mathematics, and modern algebra would be helpful in some places, but are not necessary. Some knowledge of design and analysis of algorithms is desirable. The book provides many references from which such necessary background can be obtained.

Acknowledgments

I want to express my gratitude to the staff at Brooks/Cole, including Bill Stenquist, my publisher, and especially to Kallie Swanson, my editor, for her encouragement and support of this project, and to the rest of her in-house team, including Carla Vera and Kelsey McGee. I have benefited by the diligence and help of Robin Gold, of Forbes Mill

Press, who not only was the production editor, but improved both the syntax and the semantics of the book, and of Linda Weidemann, of Wolf Creek Press, the compositor. I am grateful for their valuable assistance and professional support. I give my personal thanks to my family members: my wife, Sima, and my children, Nasim, Maryam, and Mahsa, for their reliable and unconditional love and understanding. The University of South Carolina at Spartanburg and its Department of Computer Science provided an active and nurturing environment to conduct this project. I reserve special thanks for professors Jerome Lewis and Gamal Elnagar for providing valuable support at various stages. Finally, the organization of this book has benefited greatly from the comments and especially the criticism of the then-anonymous reviewers, to whom I express my appreciation:

Claude W. Anderson, Rose-Hulman Institute of Technology
Jim Ball, Indiana State University
Susan Gerhard, Embry-Riddle Aeronautical University
Shriram Krishnamurthi, Brown University
Paul A. Nagin, Hofstra University
Bryan Morse, Brigham Young University
Xindong Wu, University of Vermont

Seyed H. Roosta

▶   *This book is dedicated with affection and respect to the memory of my father, Seyed Abolghasem Roosta; to my mother for her generosity; to my brother for his understanding; and to my wife for her affectionate support and encouragement: She endured the long hours I spent on this book, and without her support, this book would not be a reality.*

Introduction

A **programming language** is a notational system for describing computations in both machine readable and human readable form. Computations can be defined by using the mathematical concepts of a Turing Machine—a kind of computer whose operations are simple enough to be described with great precision. In general, computations include all kinds of computer operations, including data manipulation, text processing, and information storage and retrieval. The study of programming languages is sometimes called *programming linguistics,* an analogy to *natural linguistics,* which is the study of natural languages. Both types of language have syntax (form) and semantics (meaning), but neither type of language is static. Numerous language concepts have been invented, tested, improved, and incorporated into successive languages. Programming languages should be

► Universal, meaning that every problem to be addressed must have a solution that can be programmed in that language. Even a very small language can meet this strict requirement.

► Reasonably natural for solving problems within an intended class of applications, meaning that a language whose only data types are numbers would best be used for solving numeric problems but would not be especially useful for solving word processing, commercial data processing, or artificial intelligence problems.

► Capable of being implemented on a computer, meaning that every well-formed program in the language must be executable. For example, mathematical notations are not implementable because problems can be formulated that can't be solved by a computer, which lacks direct representations of mathematical symbols.

► Capable of efficient implementation, meaning that it must adhere to acceptable language design principles such as readability, writability, maintainability, orthogonality, and portability.

▶ Portable, meaning that it must be usable not only on the computer system on which it was developed but also on other computer systems. A language that is widely available and whose definitions and syntax are independent of the characteristics of a particular platform architecture is a useful base for developing transportable languages.

▶ Verifiable, meaning that someone can prove that a program correctly performs its required functions. A language that makes program verification difficult might be more troublesome to use than would one that supports and simplifies verification, even though the former might provide many more features that superficially appear to make programming easier.

▶ Understandable in its underlying structure, meaning that the language can be learned quickly and easily. A thorough knowledge of a variety of programming language constructs and implementation techniques further enables a programmer to learn a new programming language more easily.

As important as these individual concepts are, more important are how they can be put together to form complete programming language and the styles of programming that the language can support (e.g., imperative programming, declarative programming, applicative programming, and object-oriented programming). In this textbook, we introduce the major principles and concepts underlying these paradigms.

Section 1.1 is devoted to the language design concept, in which we briefly discuss the concept of the design as an important criterion of any programming language. Section 1.2 deals with language processing, which means steps required to prepare a program for execution associated with a programming language. Language processing can be classified as language interpretation or language translation. Programming languages may be divided into three general types: *machine, low-level,* and *high-level* languages. In Section 1.3, we discuss machine language, which is the only notation that the computer can understand and respond to directly. Section 1.4 deals with assembly language as a representative of low-level languages, which is directly influenced by a machine's instruction set and hardware architecture level. Finally, in Section 1.5, we discuss high-level languages with a brief description of some programming languages.

1.1 PROGRAMMING LANGUAGE DESIGN

A programming language is intended to describe programs. In general, the design of each new programming language has been strongly influenced by experience with earlier languages. Often a program is expressed in a programming language so that it can be executed on a computer. People use many programming languages to control and interact with computers. A language is called a **special-purpose language** if it is designed for a specific class of applications (e.g., editing text, report generation, graphics, or database maintenance). Most of these languages have now vanished, and only a few significantly affected the development of programming languages. A language is called a **general-purpose language** if it can be applied to a wide range of applications. For example, Fortran was created for scientific applications, COBOL for business applications, LISP for artificial intelligence applications, Simula for simulation applications, Prolog for natural language processing applications, Ada for embedded military applications, and C for solving general-purpose problems. Because special-purpose languages are not programming languages that can be used for general programming, we reserve the term *programming language* for a computer language that can be used, at least in principle, to express any computer program.

The challenge of programming language design is achieving the power, expressiveness, and comprehensibility that human readability requires while retaining the precision and simplicity that is needed for language translation. A programming language provides facilities for the natural expression of the structure of data (data abstraction) and for the structure of the computational process for solving the problem (control abstraction). Fortunately, beneath the surface details, most languages are very similar. Therefore, the study of programming languages will enable you to see more that is familiar in any new language that you encounter, which will speed your learning of new languages.

Some reasons for the success or failure of a programming language are external to the language itself. For example, use of COBOL or Ada in the United States was enforced in certain areas of programming by government mandate. Likewise, part of the reason for the success of Fortran might be attributed to the strong support of various computer manufacturers that have expended large efforts to provide sophisticated implementations and extensive documentation for these languages. The success of SNOBOL can be attributed to an excellent publication describing the language (Griswold, 1975). Pascal and LISP have benefited from their use as objects of theoretical study by students of language design as well as from actual practical use. Despite the importance of these external influences, the programmer ultimately determines the popularity of a language. Programmers might prefer one language to another for many reasons. Let us consider some of the important criteria in a good language design.

▶ **Writability:** The quality of a language that enables a programmer to use it to express a computation clearly, correctly, concisely, and quickly.

▶ **Readability:** The quality of a language that enables a programmer to understand and comprehend the nature of a computation easily and accurately.

▶ **Orthogonality:** The quality of a language that the features provided have as few restrictions as possible and can be combined in any meaningful way. For example, suppose a language provides for an expression that can produce a value, and it provides for a conditional statement that evaluates an expression to get a true or false value. These two features of the language, expression and conditional statement, are orthogonal if any expression can be used within the conditional statement. Another example that addresses the lack of orthogonality is that in Modula-2 strings can be assigned to string variables of greater length, but not vice versa. In Pascal, file types have a special status and thus cause a number of non-orthogonalities. For example, files cannot be passed by value to procedures, and assignment to file variables is prohibited. In many other languages, files are part of a library instead of the language definition, thus avoiding such non-orthogonalities.

▶ **Reliability:** The quality of a language that ensures a program will not behave in unexpected or disastrous ways while running.

▶ **Maintainability:** The quality of a language that allows errors to be found easily and corrected and new features to be added.

▶ **Generality:** The quality of a language that avoids special cases in the availability or use of constructs and by combining closely related constructs into a single, more general one. For example, C and Ada have variable-length arrays, and Modula-2 and Fortran have the ability to pass variable-length array parameters, but Pascal does not have variable-length arrays that can address the arrays' lack of generality.

▶ **Uniformity:** The quality of a language that similar features should look similar and have similar meaning and, inversely, that different constructs should look different. For example, in Pascal, *repeat structure* opens its own statement blocks, but *while* requires begin-end pairs, which addresses non-uniformities of the loop structures in the language. Another example of non-uniformity is the semicolon that is used in Modula-2 and Ada as a statement separator and as a declaration terminator. In C, the semicolon is used more consistently as a terminator.

▶ **Extensibility:** The quality of a language that provides some general mechanism so the user can add new constructs to a language. It could mean simply being able to define new data types, which most languages permit. At a different level, it could mean adding new functions from a library. It could also mean being able to add keywords and constructs to the language definition.

▶ **Standardability:** The quality of a language that allows programs to be transported from one computer to another without significant changes in the language structure.

▶ **Implementability:** The quality of a language that allows a translator or interpreter to be written. This is related to efficiency of translation, but it is also a function of the capacity of the language definition. One of the reasons that ALGOL-60 was not used more may have been that the stack-based structure needed for the run-time system was not widely known at that time. And the size and complexity of Ada has been a problem to the development of compilers and has impaired its availability and use.

Although there are many predecessors of what we consider as the modern computer—reaching as far back as the early 19th century, when Joseph Marie Jacquard created a loom programmed to weave cloth and Charles Babbage created the first full modern computer design (which he could never get to work)—the Computer Age did not really begin until the first computer was made available to the public in 1951. A common argument in programming language design has been to classify different stages of development into generations of computer technology. This has been done for hardware for some time now, with fifth-generation architectures now in use. Each generation is marked by a significant advancement in technology. Programming languages have also been classified according to this scheme:

1. **First-generation** (1951–1957) languages are essentially machine languages.

2. **Second-generation** (1958–1963) languages are the unstructured high-level languages such as assembly languages.

3. **Third-generation** (1964–1969) languages include most of the current procedural languages such as Pascal, C, Modula, and Ada. Attempts were made to improve the reliability of programs by introducing mathematical definitions for constructs and providing a language with mechanisms that would permit a translator to prove the correctness of a program as it performed the translation.

4. **Fourth-generation** (1970–1990) languages are considered those languages with the following five properties:

   ▶ Database structures and programming

   ▶ A centralized data dictionary containing information about system components

   ▶ Visual programming, such as using a mouse with icons

   ▶ A graded-skill user interface allowing novices as well as database experts to use the programs

   ▶ An interactive, integrated, multifunction programming environment

   Accordingly, fourth-generation languages have developed into languages as a solution to the software crisis. They include powerful commands like FINDALL and SORT, which act on files of data or whole databases, and are usually embedded in an environment with many development tools such as editors, debuggers, and document preparation and control utilities. A common example of such a language is Structured Query Language (SQL). Generally speaking, these languages solve the software crisis in data processing applications by allowing naive programmers to write applications quickly.

5. **Fifth-generation** (1991–2000 and beyond) languages usually include the so-called very high-level languages such as logical and mathematical languages including Prolog and SETL (SET-Oriented Language). Whereas functional languages (exemplified by LISP) are based on the mathematical notions of function, function decomposition, and function application (i.e., ML [MetaLanguage], Miranda, and Scheme), logic languages (exemplified by Prolog) have their roots in logic, particularly predicate calculus.

   Where will programming language design be in the next 10 years? The unfulfilled dreams of the past should make us cautious in trying to answer such a question. The development of new programming languages will depend partially on hardware and architecture developments and partially on the interests of large corporations. But it seems now as though there will be a steady process of increasing understanding and refinement based primarily on existing languages, rather than overwhelming new developments.

FIGURE **1.1** **The interpretation process**

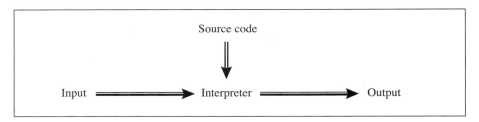

▼ 1.2 PROGRAMMING LANGUAGE PROCESSING

Any system that processes, prepares for execution (by adding more features), and executes programming languages is called a language processor. Language processors include compilers, interpreters, and auxiliary tools such as syntax-directed editors. In general, a translator accepts programs written in the language and either runs them directly or transforms them into a form suitable for execution. A translator that immediately carries out a program is called an *interpreter,* whereas a translator that changes a program into a form suitable for execution is called a *compiler.* In other words, interpretation is a one-step process, in which both the program and the input are provided to the interpreter, and the output is the result of the interpretation as shown in Figure 1.1.

More precisely, an interpreter is a program that repeatedly runs the following sequence:

▶ Retrieve the next statement.
▶ Determine the actions to be performed.
▶ Perform the actions.

This sequence is very similar to the pattern of actions carried out by a traditional computer:

▶ Fetch the next instruction whose address is specified by the instruction pointer register.
▶ Advance the instruction pointer register, meaning set the address of the next instruction to be fetched.
▶ Decode the instruction.
▶ Execute the instruction.

This similarity shows that interpretation can be viewed as a simulation of a special-purpose machine. In contrast, compilation is at least a two-step process, in which the original program (source program) is entered into the compiler, which writes a new

FIGURE **1.2**   **The compilation process**

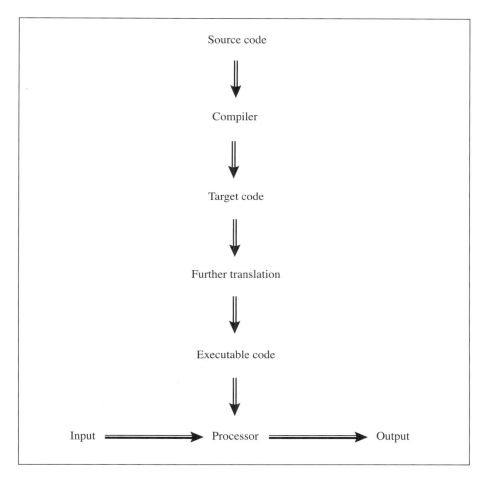

program (target program). More commonly, the target program is an assembly language program, and must be translated by an assembler into an object program, then linked with other object programs, and loaded into memory locations before it can be carried out. The compilation steps can be visualized as shown in Figure 1.2.

It is also possible to have translators between interpreters and compilers. A translator translates a source program into an intermediate language and then interprets the intermediate language. Such translators could be called *pseudointerpreters* because they run the program without producing a target program, but they process the entire source program before execution begins.

The properties of a programming language that can be determined before execution are called *static properties,* and properties that can be determined only during execution are called *dynamic properties.* This distinction is not very useful for interpreters, but it is for compilers because a compiler can only use the static properties of a language. Typical static properties of a language are its syntactic structure, which is discussed in Chapter 4.

1.3 MACHINE LANGUAGES

Regardless of the programming language that you are using, a symbolic language still has to be translated into a form that the computer can execute. This encoded form is called the **machine language,** or *natural language,* of a computer; it is the only notation that the computer can understand and respond to directly. Machine language consists of binary numbers, which can be interpreted by a computer's Central Processing Unit (CPU). A CPU usually has a small program, called a **microcode,** embedded directly in the chip. The microcode translates machine instructions directly into hardware signals. In other words, machine language is the set of microprocessor instructions encoded as binary numbers. For example, for the assignment statement

```
B = A + 2
```

a typical sequence of machine code instructions might be as shown in the following table:

	Operation	Register	Tag	Memory Address
0001 01 00 0000 0000	(load) 0001	01	00	0000 0000
0011 01 10 0000 0010	(add) 0011	01	10	0000 0010
0010 01 00 0000 0100	(store) 0010	01	00	0000 0100

where load and store instructions (the first 4 bits) move data from memory into registers and vice versa. The next two bits designate a register, with 01 referring to register 1 in each of the three instructions. The two bits after that represent a tag, with 00 representing the ordinary address, so the last eight bits of the first instruction refer to a memory address associated with a variable (e.g., the memory address of variable A is 0). The tag 10 identifies a constant, so the last eight bits of the second instruction represent the constant 2. The last instruction stores the value of register 1 in a memory location associated with the variable B (the memory address of B is 4, as represented by the last eight bits of the instruction). Although the microprocessor uses machine language, no one actually programs in this language any more.

1.4 LOW-LEVEL LANGUAGES

In programs written in a **low-level programming language,** each symbolic instruction can generate *one* machine instruction. An assembly language is a mnemonic version of a machine language, or source code, in which names are used instead of binary codes for operations and for memory addresses. Multiple assembly languages exist

FIGURE **1.3**   **The assemble–link–execute cycle**

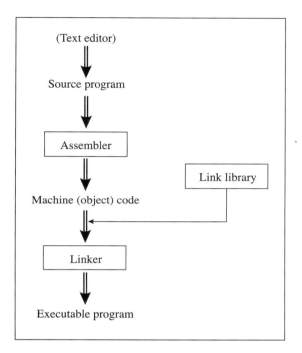

because of the various types of computers in use. Each assembly language is directly influenced by a machine's instruction set and hardware architecture. In other words, to program in assembly language you need to provide a lot of descriptive detail about the program's components. The exact level of detail necessary varies among computers, but working with assembly language brings you closer to the machine. Even though coding in a low-level language is not particularly productive or easy, it has some advantages:

▶   Provides more control over handling particular hardware requirements

▶   Generates smaller and more compact executable modules

▶   Often results in faster execution

For example, for the assignment statement

```
B = A + 2
```

the following is a hypothetical assembly code into which the machine instructions might be translated:

```
MOV   R1, A
ADD   R1, #2
MOV   B, R1
```

FIGURE **1.4**   An assembly language program

```
; Pologue comments
; constants
   ConName    equ    value
DOSSEG
_STACK    SEGMENT    para stack    'stack'
   dw    nnn    dup (?)
_STACK ENDS
_DATA    SEGMENT    word public    'data'
   VarInit    dw    vale
   VarUnInit db    ?
_DATA ENDS
_TEXT    SEGMENT    word public    'code'
   assume    cs:_TEXT
Shell:
   . . .
   . . .
   . . .
- TEXT ENDS
END    Shell
```

This code moves the content of the address associated with variable A into register R1, adds the constant 2 to it (treating the contents of register R1 as a fixed-point number), and then stores the result in the location denoted B. Thus, the statements compute B=A+2. An **assembler** is a translator program that converts assembly language source code into machine language. The most popular assemblers for the Intel family are the Microsoft Assembler (MASM™) and the Borland Turbo Assembler (TASM™). Figure 1.3 shows the stages that an assembly program goes through before it can be run. The assembler reads the source code and produces an object code—that is, a machine language translation of the program. The object code may contain calls to subroutines in an external link library. The **linker** then copies the needed subroutines from the link library into the object code to create a special header record at the beginning of the program, and produces an **executable** version of the program. Output can be produced by running the executable program, which is similar to the machine code of the source program.

Figure 1.4 shows a general assembly language program for the Intel-based PC computers. Although the program doesn't contain all the information you would need to start writing programs, it does provide a framework you can build on. Each program consists of three segments: *stack, data,* and *text* segments.

❧   1.5   HIGH-LEVEL LANGUAGES

A **high-level programming language** has the following characteristics:

- ▶ Elementary data types and structures with primitive operations for manipulating data
- ▶ Sequence control to regulate the execution of primitive operations
- ▶ Data control to manage how data are supplied to the operations for execution
- ▶ Storage management to allocate memory for programs and data
- ▶ Operating environment to communicate with the external environment
- ▶ Machine architecture independence to ensure portability
- ▶ Availability of program libraries to increase efficiency as size increases

Programmers writing in a high-level language such as C use powerful commands, each of which may generate *many* machine language instructions. A Pascal program, roughly equivalent to the assembly language presented in Figure 1.4, is shown in Figure 1.5.

Hypothetical C code into which the assembly instructions for B=A+2 might be converted is as follows:

```
#include <stdio.h>
main()    {
   int A = 3, B = 0;
   B = A + 2;
   }
```

FIGURE **1.5**   **A Pascal program**

```
PROGRAM Shell (Input, Output)
( * Prologue comments * )
CONST
   ConName = value;
VAR
   VarInit : WORD;
   VarUnInit : BYTE;
BEGIN   ( * Shell * )
   . . .
   . . .      ( * executable statements * )
   . . .
END.   ( * Shell * )
```

FIGURE **1.6**   **The compile–link–execute cycle**

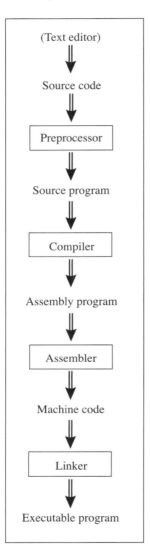

The program that converts a high-level language to a machine language is called a **compiler,** as shown in Figure 1.6. An alternative approach is to use an **interpreter,** which converts source code to machine language one line at a time. Thus, with a high-level language a compiler is used to translate the source code into machine (object) code, whereas with a low-level language, an assembler is used for the translation. Then a linker program for both high-level and low-level languages completes the process by converting the object code into an executable code to produce output. Because of the speed of low-level assembly programs and the efficiency of high-level programs, a common practice was to combine the benefits of both programming levels. The bulk of the program is coded in a high-level language, and critical modules (those that cause noticeable delay) are coded in assembly language.

Several high-level programming languages have been designed, but only a few have significantly affected the development of new programming languages. Following are brief descriptions of some high-level programming languages, in order of development.

- **Fortran** (**For**mula **Tran**slator), developed by IBM as the first high-level programming language, introduced features such as symbolic expressions and subprograms with parameters. Fortran can be used for scientific and engineering applications that require complex mathematical computations.

- **COBOL** (**Co**mmon **B**usiness-**O**riented **L**anguage), a highly structured language, was specifically designed for business applications and emphasized data representation. COBOL is used primarily for commercial applications that require precise and efficient manipulation of large amounts of data.

- **ALGOL** (**Algo**rithmic **L**anguage) was designed with a well-defined and machine-independent structure and inspired most of the subsequent theoretical work in programming languages. ALGOL-60 introduced the concept of block structure, whereby variables and procedures could be declared in a program wherever they were needed. ALGOL-68 contained additional features for parallel processing.

- **LISP** (**Lis**t **P**rocessing) was designed for problems with irregular data structures that are well represented as *lists*. LISP has been used for symbolic calculations in differential and integral calculus, electrical circuit theory, mathematical logic, game playing, and artificial intelligence. The proliferation of LISP prompted creation of Common LISP by 1984 with an object-oriented extension named CLOS (Common LISP Object System). An extension of LISP designed for parallel processing is called MultiLISP.

- **APL** (**A** **P**rogramming **L**anguage) is geared toward arrays but is a much higher level language than Fortran. APL supports numerous powerful aggregate operators that act on arrays. APL has 66 high-level operators compared with 6 in Fortran.

- **PL/I** (**P**rogramming **L**anguage **I**) is a large language that combines many features of Fortran, ALGOL, and COBOL. The IBM version contains parallelization primitives that allow the creation and termination of parallel tasks for parallel processing.

- **Simula** was developed at the Norwegian Computing Center by the Royal Norwegian Council for Scientific and Industrial Research. Simula was a system descriptive language for discrete event networks and was designed to simulate situations such as queues at a supermarket, response times of emergency services, and chain reactions of nuclear reactors. Developed for simulation, Simula contributed to the understanding of abstraction and computation through its introduction of the class concept, which is fundamental to most object-oriented programming languages.

▶ **SNOBOL** (**St**ring-**O**riented Sym**bol**ic Language, pronounced "snowball") was developed by David Farber, Ralph Griswold, and Ivan Polonsky at Bell Laboratories and was designed primarily to process string data. The successor to SNOBOL, called Icon, was developed by Griswold.

▶ **Pascal,** named after the seventeenth-century mathematician and philosopher Blaise Pascal, was designed for teaching structured programming in an academic environment. Pascal became the preferred introductory programming language at most universities and has influenced nearly all recent languages. Pascal emphasizes safety with a simple input/output (I/O) mechanism and strong typing component. Concurrent Pascal is a parallel version that uses shared memory parallel architectures and features *processes* and *monitors* for describing and coordinating concurrency. Parallel Pascal is a parallel extension developed for shared memory and distributed memory parallel architectures.

▶ **C** evolved from two earlier languages, BCPL (**B**asic **C**ombined **P**rogramming **L**anguage) and B. BCPL was developed in 1967 by Martin Richards as a language for writing operating systems and compilers. Ken Thompson modeled many features of his language B after their counterparts in BCPL. Both BCPL and B were typeless languages, and every data item occupied one word in memory. Treating a data item as an integer or a real number was the programmer's responsibility. Developed by Dennis Ritchie at Bell Laboratories in 1972 as a general-purpose language, C is commonly used for systems programming. The emphasis in C is on flexibility and lack of restrictions. Its ability to access hardware makes it a better choice than other programming languages for writing operating systems (e.g., UNIX is written in C). With the popularity of UNIX on parallel architectures, several variants of C have been developed for use in parallel applications.

▶ **Smalltalk** was designed to be a self-contained, interactive programming language, in which programs would be characterized by a high degree of modularity and dynamic extensibility. The environment consists of windows, several of which can be on the screen at one time. Smalltalk is a pure object-oriented language.

▶ **Ada** was developed under the sponsorship of the U.S. Department of Defense as a general-purpose programming language for numerical computations, system programming, and applications with real-time and concurrency requirements. Pascal was influential as the basis of the language, which supports both shared memory and message passing for parallel computation. Ada is the best available example of a state-of-the-art concurrent programming language.

▶ **Modula** combined the block-and-type structure of Pascal with *module* constructs for defining abstract data types. Modula is a general-purpose language that has enough of the underlying hardware visible to be useful in operating system design.

▶ **Prolog** (**Pro**gramming in **Log**ic) is a high-level language whose heritage is logic notation and automatic theorem proving. Concurrent Prolog is a well-known parallel variant used in expert systems.

▶ **Scheme** is a version of LISP developed by Gerald Sussman and Guy Steele at MIT. This version of LISP is more uniform than the original and was designed to resemble lambda calculus more closely. Like any other functional programming language, Scheme relies on recursion to perform loops and other repetitive operations. It has been used to write text editors, optimizing compilers, operating systems, graphic packages, expert systems, and numeric applications.

▶ **ML** was developed as a functional programming language by Robin Milner at Edinburgh University in the 1970s with a syntax and a mechanism for type checking similar to that of Pascal—but much more flexible. In ML, the basic program is the same as in Scheme in defining and applying functions. Unlike Scheme, however, ML has a rich set of data types, from enumeration types to records to lists. It supports higher order functions—that is, functions that take functions as arguments. In contrast, languages such as Pascal or C support functions as arguments only in limited ways. The recent revision is called ML97 and has even more powerful features.

▶ **C++** is a popular object-oriented programming language. Bjarne Stroustrup, motivated by Simula, added classes to C in a preprocessing compiler step. The success and widespread use of C, coupled with the lack of any sort of support for abstract data types in C, has prompted widespread use of C++. Even more important, C++ provides object-oriented programming capabilities. Unlike Smalltalk, which is a pure object-oriented language, C++ is a hybrid language, meaning that programming can be done in a C-like style, an object-oriented style, or both.

▶ **Miranda,** developed by David Turner in the early 1980s, is a functional language that has adopted many features of ML, particularly the type system and pattern matching. Miranda has no variable or assignment features, so it is completely referentially transparent, unlike every other functional language, including ML and Scheme.

▶ **Haskell** (Hudak and Fasel, 1992) is largely based on Miranda. Like Miranda, Haskell is a purely functional language, having no variables and no assignment statement. Another characteristic of Haskell is its use of lazy evaluation (no expression is evaluated until its value is required). This leads to some surprising capabilities in the language, in which computation proceeds by replacing expressions with their value until the value is required. The language is named for logician Haskell B. Curry, whose work provided much of the logical basis for the language.

▶ **HTML** (**H**yper**T**ext **M**arkup **L**anguage), developed to build a Web address or Web page by Tim Berners-Lee in 1989 in Switzerland, is an easy-to-understand language. HTML controls the appearance of a Web page and consists of hypertext and hypermedia. In hypertext, pointers or links are used to jump to other parts of a document or to other files or Web sites. Hypermedia allows the addition of other items to text documents, including images, animation, and sound.

▶ **Visual Basic** evolved from BASIC (**B**eginner's **A**ll-**P**urpose **S**ymbolic **I**nstruction **C**ode), which was developed in the 1960s. Development of the Microsoft Windows graphical user interface (GUI) in the late 1980s and the early 1990s spurred

TABLE **1.1** A summary of some of the major programming languages

Language	Year	Originator	Predecessor Language	Intended Purpose
Fortran	1954	J. Backus		Numeric computation
ALGOL-60	1958	Committee	Fortran	Numeric computation
COBOL	1959	Committee		Business data processing
APL	1956	K. Iverson		Array processing
LISP	1956	J. McCarthy		Symbolic computation
SNOBOL4	1962	R. Griswold		String processing
PL/I	1963	Committee	Fortran	General purpose
Simula-67	1967	O. J. Dahl	ALOGOL-60	Simulation purpose
ALGOL-68	1963	Committee	ALOGOL-60	General purpose
BCPL	1970	Committee	ALGOL-60	General purpose
Forth	1970	C. Moore	Fortran	General purpose
ML	1970	R. Milner	LISP	Functional programming
Bliss	1971	W. Wulf	ALGOL-68	System programming
Pascal	1971	N. Wirth	ALGOL-60	Educational purpose
Prolog	1972	A. Colmerauer		Artificial intelligence
C	1974	D. Ritchie	ALGOL-68	System programming
Mesa	1974	Xerox PARC	Pascal	System programming
SETL	1974	J. Schwartz		Very high-level programming
Concurrent Pascal	1975	P. B. Hansen	Pascal	Concurrent programming
CLU	1974	B. Liskov	Simula-67	Methodology abstraction
Euclid	1977	Committee	Pascal	Verification programming
Gypsy	1977	D. Good	Pascal	Verification programming
Modula-2	1977	N. Wirth	Pascal	Real-time programming
Ada	1979	J. Ichbiah	Pascal	Real-time programming
Fortran-77	1979	J. Backus	Fortran	Numeric computation
Icon	1980	Committee	C	General purpose
Elf	1980	Committee	Prolog	Logic Programming
Miranda	1980	D. Turner	LISP	Functional programming

the evolution of Visual Basic by Microsoft in 1991. Visual Basic greatly simplifies Windows application development, and the latest version, Visual Basic 6, was released in 1998.

▶ **Java** emerged as the name of a C and C++ based language when a group of Sun Microsystems programming language designers visited a local coffee shop. Sun formally announced Java at a major conference in 1995, and it generated imme-

TABLE **1.1**   (*continued*)

Language	Year	Originator	Predecessor Language	Intended Purpose
REBOL	1980	Committee	LISP	Functional programming
Scheme	1980	G. L. Steele	LISP	Functional programming
VAL	1980	W. Ackerman		Data-flow programming
C++	1980	B. Stroustrap	C	Object-based programming
Smalltalk	1980	A. Kay	Simula-67	Personal computing
SR	1982	G. R. Andrews	C	Concurrent programming
CLOS	1984	Committee	LISP	Object-based functional
Common LISP	1984	Committee	LISP	Functional programming
Blue	1985	Committee	C++	Object-based programming
Eiffel	1987	B. Meyer	C++	Object-based programming
Oberon	1988	N. Wirth	Modula-2	General purpose
Haskell	1989	Yale University	LISP	Functional programming
Ada 95	1989	J. Ichbiah	Ada	Concurrent programming
HTML	1989	Committee		Web programming
Occam	1989	Inmoc Company	Ada	Distributed programming
Java	1980	Sun Microsystems	C++	Object-based programming
Visual Basic	1990	Microsoft		Windows programming
Fortran-90	1990	Committee	Fortran	Scientific computing
Linda	1991	Scientific Computing	C	Concurrent programming
C*	1991	Thinking Machine	C++	Concurrent programming
Concurrent Prolog	1992	Committee	Prolog	Concurrent logic for AI
MultiLISP	1992	Committee	LISP	Parallel functional language
Perl	1994	Committee	C++	Object-based programming
Python	1995	G. V. Rossum	C	Object-based programming
UML	1998	G. Booch	C++	Modeling language
Modula-3	1999	Committee	Modula	Concurrent programming
Ruby	2000	Y. Matsumoto	Python	Object-based scripting
Dylan	2000	Apple	C++	Object-based dynamic

diate interest in the business community because of the phenomenal commercial interest in the World Wide Web. Designed for commercial reasons, Java is not an academic language like Pascal or a language designed by one person or a small group for its own local use like C or C++.

Table 1.1 summarizes the evolution of several important classes of programming languages, but is not intended to be a comprehensive list.

Summary

Numerous language concepts have been invented, tested, and improved by being incorporated in successive languages. As important as the individual concepts are the ways in which they may be put together to form a complete programming language and the style of programming that the language can support, such as imperative, declarative, applicative, and object-oriented programming. In this chapter, we briefly discussed some important criteria in the language design. In addition, we classified programming languages according to computer technology development by generation. Language translation is an important step in preparing programs to run. A translator accepts programs written in the language and either runs them directly or transforms them into a form suitable for execution. We briefly explained the language translation. Finally, we briefly outlined three general types of programming languages: machine, low-level, and high-level languages. Machine language consists of binary numbers, which can be interpreted by a computer's CPU. Low-level language is a super version of machine language, in which each symbolic instruction can generate one machine instruction. A programming language is high-level if it is independent of the underlying machine architecture and closely resembles a language with characteristics such as elementary data types, sequential control, storage management, operating environment, and availability of program libraries.

Data Types

Conventional computers are based on the notion of a main memory consisting of elementary cells, each of which is identified by an address. The contents of a cell constitute its value. The value of a cell can be read or modified. Modification implies replacing a value with a new value. Furthermore, hardware allows for access to cells on a one-at-a-time basis. In addition, any programming language may be viewed as specifying a set of operations that are to be applied to certain data in a certain sequence. Basic differences among languages exist in the types of data allowed, in the types of operations available, and in the mechanisms provided for controlling the sequence in which the operations are applied to the data. These three areas—*data, operations,* and *controls*—form the basis of the next two chapters and also provide the framework for much of the discussion and comparison of different languages outlined in this book.

In every programming language, built-in data types are classified as *primitive, composite,* and *recursive* data types. We briefly discuss different data types, including integer, real, Boolean, character, array, string, enumeration, pointer, structure, function, list, stacks, and queues in Section 2.1. The determination of one of the components of a data object is called binding, which is known as the process of associating an attribute to a variable. In Section 2.2, we discuss type binding, which can occur at three specific times: *compile-time binding, load-time binding,* and *run-time binding.* Type checking is the process a translator goes through to verify that all constructors in a program are valid types of entities such as constants, variables, and functions. Type checking can be classified as *static type checking,* in which type information is maintained and checked at translation time, and *dynamic type checking,* in which type information is performed at run time. In Section 2.3, we explain type checking as one of the important concepts of designing and implementing programming languages. Type conversion deals with two different data types in the evaluation of an expression. Section 2.4 illustrates two classifications of type conversions: *implicit* and *explicit.*

◸ 2.1 DATA TYPES

Data inside a computer are just a collection of bits, and any programming language can be based on this property. A **data object,** also known as a **variable** or **identifier,** can be characterized by four components: L, N, V, and T.

▶ L is the *location* and holds the value of a data object. The action that allocates a location for a data object is called *allocation.* An allocation performed before execution is called static allocation; if performed at run time, it is called *dynamic allocation.*

▶ N is the *name* of an identifier and is used to refer to the data object.

▶ V is the *value* of the data object and is represented in coded form in the allocated location of the data object.

▶ T is the data *type* and represents the possible form of values that a data object can hold.

In other words, a fundamental abstraction in a programming language is the use of a name or a variable to denote language entities. A name should be informative, concise, memorable, and pronounceable. The meaning of a name is determined by the properties or attributes associated with the name. For example, the C declaration

```
int    n=5;
```

declares n as a variable and associates two attributes with n: *int* (integer) as its data type and 5 as its value. Similarly, the Pascal declaration

```
function    add (X:integer) : Boolean;
begin
 . . .
 . . .
end
```

declares add as an identifier and associates:

▶ The attribute function with add

▶ One parameter with name x and data type integer with add

▶ Boolean as the data type of the returned value with add

A **local variable** is a variable that is declared within a block for use only within that block. A **global variable** is a variable that is declared in the outermost block of the program and can be used anywhere in a program. In the following C fragment, x and y are declared as global and local variables, respectively.

```
#include <stdio.h>
int    x=10;
main    ( )    {
int    y=20;
}
```

A property of every variable is that it is created (or allocated) at some definite time and may be deleted (or deallocated) at some later time when it is no longer needed. The interval between creation and deletion is called the *lifetime* of a variable. The concept of lifetime is important for the pragmatic reason that a variable needs to occupy storage only while it is alive. After the variable is deleted, the memory locations it formerly occupied may be reallocated for some other purposes. This allows memory to be used economically. In any programming language, data and operations are related through a mechanism known as a **data type,** which usually has a set of operations that can be applied to values. Often these operations aren't mentioned explicitly with the data type but are part of its definition. Examples include the arithmetic operations involved on integers and real numbers and string manipulation operations applied to character data types. In general, a programming language translator can use type information to check for the validity of operations and actions, thus providing error detection capabilities. In other words, the type of a variable can be viewed as a specification of the values that can be associated with the variable together with the operations that can be legally used to create, access, and modify such values. For example, an assignment statement such as

    x=y;

is valid only when the types of x and y are consistent.

Design and Implementation: For each data type, four important elements must be considered:

1. The set of values associated with that data type
2. The operations performed on that data type
3. The internal representation of values of that data type in the program
4. The external representation of values of that data type when they are output

We use the term *value* to classify anything that can be evaluated, stored, incorporated in a data structure, passed as an argument to a function, returned as function results, and so on. In other words, we define a value to be any entity that exists during a computation. For example, in Pascal we can use

▶ Primitive values (e.g., characters, integers, and real numbers)
▶ Composite values (e.g., arrays, records, and files)
▶ Pointer values as references
▶ Reference values to variables passed as arguments

When we say that v is a value of data type T, we mean simply that $v \in T$ (or, v belongs to T). When we say that an expression E is of type T, we are asserting that the result of evaluating E will be a value of type T. Type information can be categorized as *implicit type information* and *explicit type information*. **Implicit type information** includes *types of constants* and *types of variables* that might not be given in a declaration. In this case, the type must be inferred by the translator, either from context information or from standard rules. For example, 10 is implicitly an integer, true is a Boolean, and I is an integer data object in the Fortran programming language. **Explicit type information** is contained in declarations. Variables can be declared to be a specific data type, such as

```
int     x;
float   y;
```

where x and y are two variables of integer and real types, respectively. From the user's point of view, type information can be classified as the following:

▶ **Built-in data types,** which are included within the language definition and can be used through the declaration of the data objects

▶ **User-defined data types,** which are defined through a declaration of the type before its use in a data object declaration

In every programming language, built-in data types are classified as the following:

1. Primitive data types, whose values are atomic and therefore are not divisible
2. Composite data types, whose values are composed of simpler values
3. Recursive data types, whose values may be composed of other values of the same type

2.1.1 Primitive Data Types

Primitive data types, sometimes called *unstructured data types,* have elements consisting of indivisible entities and therefore cannot be decomposed into simple values (e.g., integer, real, Boolean, and character). The choice of primitive data types is important in programming language design. For example, a language intended for commercial data processing, such as COBOL, is likely to have primitive types whose values are fixed-length strings and fixed-point numbers. A language intended for numerical computation, such as Fortran, is likely to have primitive types whose values are real numbers. A language intended for string processing, such as SNOBOL, is likely to have a primitive type whose values are strings of any length. In Scheme, numbers are classified as integers, rational numbers, real numbers, or complex numbers. This classification is hierarchical in that all integers are rational, all rational numbers are real, and all real numbers are complex. Java contains all the primitive data types that you would expect to find in a modern programming language. Data type lengths in Java are fixed to ensure portability across implementations of the language. In the following, we examine the most common primitive built-in data types.

Integer Type

The **integer type** (*int*) has as its domain the set of integers that can be represented on the computer.

Design and Implementation: The domain of the integer data type in some languages is implementation dependent. For example, on small computers, 2 bytes are often used for storing integers, and the integers range from –32,768 to 32,767. If we dedicate

TABLE **2.1**   Integer type variables

Declaration	Fortran	C	C++	Java	Scheme
integer data object	integer sum	int sum;	int sum;	int sum;	(integer? sum)
integer data object with initial value 10	integer sum sum=10	int sum=10;	int sum=10;	int sum=10;	(define sum 10)
integer data object and then initialize with 10	integer sum sum=10	int sum; sum=10;	int sum; sum=10;	int sum; sum=10;	(integer? sum) (define sum 10)

the leftmost bit for sign representation, 0111111111111111 can represent 32,767, the maximum positive integer, and 1000000000000000 can represent −32,768, the minimum negative integer. Typical implementation allocates 2 or 4 bytes for integer numbers in the 2s complement system. With regard to the 2s complement notation, a positive integer x in the range 0 to $2^{n-1} - 1$ is usually given by its n-bit binary representation; all such integers have a leading 0 to identify them as positive. A negative integer x in the range −1 to -2^{n-1} is given by its n-bit binary representation of $2^n - x$; all such integers have a leading 1 to identify them as negative. Thus, the first bit functions as the sign bit—0 as positive and 1 as negative. Then, for example, if $n = 6$, we can represent numbers between −32 and +31. The number 6 is represented by 000110, whereas −6 is represented by writing the integer $2^6 - 6 = 58$ in binary, or 111010. We can convert 6 to −6 by changing 0 to 1 and 1 to 0 in the positive representation of the number and adding 1 to the result:

$+6 \Rightarrow 000110$ (change 0 to 1 and 1 to 0) $\Rightarrow 111001$ (add 1) $\Rightarrow 111010 \Rightarrow -6.$

To write an integer constant that will be treated as long integer in C++, insert either an *l* or an *L* at the end of the number. In Java, four integer numeric data types—*byte, short, int,* and *long*—correspond to stored integers of a maximum length 8 bits, 16 bits, 32 bits, and 64 bits, respectively. In addition, in Java we can denote integers by writing them in octal or hexadecimal form. To specify an integer in octal, precede the integer with a 0; in hexadecimal, precede the integer number with a 0 followed by an *x*. Scheme supports integer numbers using the predicate `integer?` as

    (integer? object)

which returns true, if the object is an integer, and false otherwise. Table 2.1 shows examples of integer type variables in different programming languages.

Real Type

Real type (*real*) variables or *floating-point* numbers are used to store data containing a decimal point and a fractional part.

Design and Implementation: Floating-point numbers are denoted either by writing them as *integerpart.fractionpart,* or by using scientific notation where the character *e* or *E* indicates that the number is to be raised to the power of the integer following the *e* or *E*. Examples are 3.1415, −15.0, 0.000123, 12,345.90, 1.56e2 (156.), 1.56e−2 (0.0156), 2.34E4 (23,400.) and 2.34E−4 (0.000234). In addition to its ability to store fractions, the real type format can represent a considerably larger range of numbers than can the integer format. For example, on Control Data Corporation Cyber (CDC™) series computers, real numbers range in value from 10^{-294} (a very small fraction) to 10^{+322} (a very large number), whereas the range of positive integers extends only from 1 to approximately 10^{15}. A common *real* type representation consists of four components: *sign, mantissa* (or coefficient), *radix* (or exponent base), and *exponent.* For a floating-point number F, let S be the value of the sign bit (0 if positive, and 1 if negative), M the mantissa, E the exponent, and R the radix. The value of F is then $(-1)^S \times M \times R^E$. For example, 34.0 as a decimal real number can be represented as $(-1)^0 \times 34 \times 10^0$ or $(-1)^0 \times 0.34 \times 10^2$, and −34.0 can be represented as $(-1)^1 \times 0.34 \times 10^2$. Scheme supports real numbers using the predicate `real?` as

```
(real? object)
```

for which it returns true if the object is a real number and false otherwise. For example,

```
(real? 3.0) ⇒ true    (real? 2.345) ⇒ true    (real? −2/3) ⇒ true
```

ANSI C provides three floating types—*float, double,* and *long double*—to deal with real numbers. A floating constant without a suffix denotes the type double; an appended suffix specifies a different type. C++ also provides several ways of writing floating-point numbers. The type is *always* double unless otherwise specified; a different floating type can be specified with the letters f or F for type float and l or L for type long double as suffixes. There are two real number types in Java. The first is float, which represents 32-bit floating-point numbers, and the second is double, which represents 64-bit floating-point numbers. In general, typical implementation allocates 4 or 8 bytes for real numbers. Table 2.2 shows examples of *real* type variables in different programming languages.

Boolean Type

A data type for representing true or false is usually called a *Boolean* or *logical data type.*

Design and Implementation: The domain of a Boolean type (*Boolean* or *bool*) consists of two values, representing *true* and *false.* The operators on Boolean types are logical operators, including AND, OR, and NOT. Values are bound to a certain machine representation when the language is implemented. For example, true might be bound to bit string 00000001 and false to 00000000 in a machine when 1 byte is used to represent the Boolean type. In general, typical implementation allocates 1 byte for Boolean type representation. In Java, variables can hold either the value true or the value false, as in

```
boolean flag=true;   boolean index=false;
```

TABLE **2.2**   **Real type variables**

Declaration	Fortran	C	C++	Java
real data object	real sum	float sum;	float sum;	float sum;
real data object with initial value 9.5	real sum sum=9.5	float sum=9.5;	float sum=9.5;	float sum=9.5;
real data object and then initialize with 9.5	real sum sum=9.5	float sum; sum=9.5;	float sum; sum=9.5;	float sum; sum=9.5;
real data object and then initialize with 105 in scientific notation	real sum sum=1.05E2	float sum; sum=1.05E2;	float sum; sum=0.105E3;	float sum; sum=0.0105E4;

The C++ language is still evolving. Older versions of C++ had no Boolean type but, instead, used the integers 1 and 0 for true and false representations. One change proposed by the ANSI Standards Committee—and implemented with surprising speed in most compilers—was the addition of the Boolean type *bool,* whose two values are true and false. Boolean expressions now return values of type *bool,* rather than values of type *int.* In other words, in C++ a Boolean expression evaluates to the *bool* value true when it is satisfied and to the *bool* value false when it is not satisfied, as in

```
bool flag=true;   bool index=false;
```

Scheme supports the Boolean type, using the predicate `boolean?`, as in

```
(boolean? object)
```

which returns `true` if the object is either true or false, and `false` otherwise. For example,

(boolean? #t) ⇒ true   (boolean? #f) ⇒ true   (boolean? 'x) ⇒ false

Character Type

A character data type provides data objects that have a single character as their value.

Design and Implementation: Character type variables store values consisting of combinations of letters, digits, and special characters. Fortran uses *character* to declare such variables. For example,

```
character *7 object
```

identifies object as a variable that can contain a string of exactly seven characters, such as

```
object='ABCDEFG'
```

In C, variables of any type can be used to represent characters. In particular, *char* is used for this purpose, as in

```
char object='A';
```

In addition to representing characters, a variable of type *char* can be used to hold small integer values. Each *char* is stored in 1 byte. Other than being large enough to hold all the characters in the character set, the size of a byte isn't specified in C. However, in most computers, a byte comprises 8 bits and is capable of storing 2^8, or 256, distinct values. C++ follows the same rule regarding this data type. In Java, *char* uses 16 bits (ISO Unicode character set), with characters being identified by the value enclosed within single quotes. For example,

```
char object='A';
```

declares a variable initialized to contain the character A.

Scheme supports the character type, using the predicate `char?`, as in

```
(char? object)
```

which returns `true` if object is a character and `false` otherwise. For example,

```
(char? 10) ⇒ false    (char? #\a) ⇒ true
```

2.1.2 Composite Data Types

Composite data types, sometimes called *structured data types,* are compound types such as arrays, records, tuples, lists, sets, functions, strings, pointers, linked lists, stacks, queues, and serial and direct files. Composite data types are classified as *heterogeneous,* when elements are of different types (e.g., records and structures), and *homogeneous,* when elements are of the same type (e.g., arrays). Here, we examine two groups of composite data types: fixed-size data types—arrays, strings, pointers, structures, functions, and lists—and dynamic-size data types—linked lists, stacks, and queues.

Array Type

An **array** is a collection of two or more adjacent memory cells, called *array elements,* that are associated with a particular symbolic name and that are all of the same data type. An array index set is a range of consecutive values.

Design and Implementation: An array variable is a mapping from an index set to a collection of component variables. In a *static array,* the index set is fixed at compile time—that is, upon declaration of the array variable. In a *dynamic array,* the index set is fixed at run time. In a *flexible array,* the index set is not fixed, allowing a new array value to be assigned to the array variable at any time. To set up an array in Fortran, we must declare both the name of the array and the number of elements associated with it. For example,

```
REAL class(8)
```

instructs the compiler to associate eight adjacent memory cells with the name *class*. Each element of an array may contain a single real value. To reference a particular element, we must specify the array name and identify the element desired. Thus, we may use class(1) to reference the first element of the array, class(2) the second element, and so on. The integer enclosed in parentheses is the array subscript. In C and C++, the declaration

```
int    class[5];
```

allocates space for the five-element array *class*. The elements of the array are of type integer and are accessed with class[0], class[1], class[2], class[3], and class[4]. The index or subscript of an array always starts at 0. For example,

```
int    class[ ]={10,20,30,40,50};
```

declares an array having five elements initialized 10, 20, 30, 40, and 50. In Java, the definition

```
int    class[ ]=new int[10];
```

declares the variable *class* to be an array of integers that will have space for 10 integer values. The declaration

```
char    stream[ ]=new char[20];
```

declares an array called *stream* that will contain 20 characters. One important feature of Java is that some data types, which in other languages would be treated as basic or primitive data types, are regarded as objects and, hence, can be sent messages. In Java, the computing system can be viewed as consisting of objects that cooperate with each other to carry out a task by a means of mechanism of message sending. A message is essentially procedure invocation and consists of an arbitrary number of arguments ranging from zero to some arbitrary number imposed by the Java interpreter. For example, to get the number of items in an array, a message *length* can be sent to an array. In this sense, the expression

```
stream.length();
```

consists of a message (length()), resulting in an integer that represents the number of items in the array.

String Type

A variable of type **string** is one in which the values consist of sequences of characters.

Design and Implementation: All modern programming languages support the type *string*. One possibility, adopted for the ML programming language, is to provide data type strings with values that are strings of any length. Another approach, adopted for the C and C++ programming languages, is to define a string to be an array of characters. That allows selection of any character of a string by array indexing. Another approach, adopted for the Miranda and Prolog programming languages, is to define a string to be a list of characters, which makes all the usual list operations automatically applicable to strings.

The Scheme programming language provides operations for creating strings, extracting characters from strings, obtaining substrings, concatenating strings, and altering the contents of strings. Strings are indexed by exact nonnegative integers, and the index of the first element of any string is 0. The following are examples of string manipulations:

```
(string=? string₁ string₂ string₃ . . . )
(string<? string₁ string₂ string₃ . . . )
(string>? string₁ string₂ string₃ . . . )
(string<=? string₁ string₂ string₃ . . . )
(string>=? string₁ string₂ string₃ . . . )
```

Each predicate returns true if the relation holds and false otherwise. Predicates express relationships among all the arguments. For example, *string=?* determines whether the lexicographic ordering of its arguments is monotonically decreasing. Two strings are lexicographically equivalent if they are the same length and consist of the same sequence of characters. If two strings differ only in length, the shorter string is considered to be lexicographically less than the longer string. The comparisons are based on the character predicate `char?`. In Java, strings can be defined in the same way that primitive data types can be defined. For example, the declaration

```
string   object="Nasim Maryam Mahsa";
```

declares a string variable object that contains the string `"Nasim Maryam Mahsa"`. Just as arrays are regarded in Java as objects, so are strings. For example,

```
string   object;
object="Nasim Maryam Mahsa";
```

would initialize the value of `object` to the string `"Nasim Maryam Mahsa"`.

Enumeration Type

We often want a variable to take on only one of the possible values representing the variable. For example, a variable *day* might have only seven possible values represented by "Monday", "Tuesday", "Wednesday", "Thursday", "Friday", "Saturday", and "Sunday". In some languages, such as Fortran or COBOL, such a variable is given the data type integer, and the values are represented as distinct integers. For example, Monday=1, Friday=5, and so forth. The program then accesses the values as represented. However, in such cases, the programmer is responsible for ensuring that no operations are applied to the integers represented for the intended meaning. Languages such as C, Pascal, and Ada include an *enumeration* data type that allows the programmer to define such variables more directly.

Design and Implementation: In an enumeration type, we list all the values that can be taken by that type. The declaration

```
type months = (Jan, Feb, Mar, Apr, May, Jun, Jul, Aug, Sep, Oct, Nov, Dec);
```

makes *months* an enumeration with 12 elements. In enumeration type, names like `Feb` are treated as constants (`Feb=2`), meaning that enumeration data type is a set of integer constants represented by identifiers. The listing of the enumeration literals provide an ordering of the discrete values; that is,

```
Jan < Feb < . . . < Dec
```

In other words, the programmer defines both the literal names to be used for the values and their ordering. The Boolean type is essentially treated as a predefined enumeration type; that is,

```
type Boolean = (true, false);
```

In C, an enumeration introduced by keyword `enum` starts with 0, unless specified otherwise, and increments by 1. For example, the enumeration

```
enum months {Jan, Feb, Mar, Apr, May, Jun, Jul, Aug, Sep, Oct, Nov, Dec};
```

creates a new type, `enum months`, in which the identifiers are set automatically to the integers 0 to 11. To number the `months` 1 to 12, use the following enumeration:

```
enum months {Jan=1, Feb, Mar, Apr, May, Jun, Jul, Aug, Sep, Oct, Nov, Dec};
```

In addition, the value of each enumeration constant of an enumeration can be set explicitly in the definition by assigning a value to the identifier. In this sense, we can write

```
if (months == May)    then    . . .
```

instead of the

```
if (months == 5)      then    . . .
```

The identifiers in an enumeration must be unique.

Pointer Type

Normally, a variable contains a specific value. However, a variable of type **pointer** contains the address of another variable. Hence, a pointer variable lets one memory location contain the address of another memory location. In other words, a variable name directly references a value, and a variable of type *pointer* indirectly references a value. In addition, such addresses can be manipulated as if they were arithmetic entities: They can be added to, subtracted from, multiplied, and even divided. An important issue associated with pointer variables is that once a programming error has been committed with a pointer, various unacceptable events could occur, depending on the nature of the error. Some such events include memory being made unusable and memory becoming corrupt, leading to a crash of the application or even the host operating system. In general, the ability to access and change the value of a data object using another data object of pointer type is the characteristic that makes pointer variables so powerful.

FIGURE **2.1**   Representation of `rank` and `aptr` in memory with designated addresses

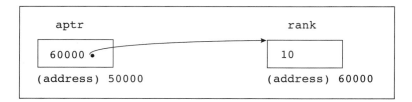

Design and Implementation: Variables of type *pointer,* like any other variables, must be declared before they can be used. For example, the following declaration in C,

```
int    rank,    *aptr;
```

declares the variable `aptr` to be of type *pointer* to *int* (a pointer to an integer value). Variable `rank` is also declared to be an integer. When used in this manner in a declaration, ∗ indicates that the variable being declared is a pointer. Pointers can be declared to point to objects of any data type. Pointers should be initialized either when they are declared or with an assignment statement. For example, for the declaration

```
int    rank=10,    *aptr;
```

the statement

```
aptr =&rank;
```

assigns the address of the variable `rank` to pointer variable `aptr`. In other words, `aptr` can access to variable `rank` (is pointing to a location of memory associated with variable `rank` because the address of `rank` is stored as the content of `aptr`), as illustrated in Figure 2.1.

For example, the following print statements display the value of variable `rank` on the screen, which is 10.

```
printf(" %d ", rank);
printf(" %d ", *aptr);
```

Pointer variables are allowed to point only to data objects of the same type in C, Pascal, and Ada, wherein type declarations and static type checking (types that are checked at compile time) are used. Without this restriction, we cannot determine during translation the type of variable that a pointer will designate at run time, and dynamic type checking (types that are checked at run time) would be necessary. In addition, C++ allows pointer types whose objects are pointers to pointers, pointer types whose objects are pointers to pointers to pointers, and so on. The following declaration defines a pointer object that points to another object of type pointer to integer.

```
int    **ptrptr;
```

Each asterisk in a definition indicates another level of indirection. Thus, the two asterisks in front of `ptrptr` indicate a pointer to a pointer. In the following, `ptrptr` points to an object (`ptr`) that is a pointer to variable `rank` of type integer.

```
int    rank=10;
int    *ptr=&rank;
ptrptr = &ptr;
```

In this example, the following print statements display 10 on screen.

```
printf(" %d ", rank);
printf(" %d ", *ptr);
printf(" %d ", **ptrptr);
```

As the result of this assignment, the objects `rank`, `ptr`, and `ptrptr` have the following relationship:

```
(points to)    (points to)
ptrptr    ⇒    ptr    ⇒    rank
```

Pointers were not adopted in the Java programming language.

Structure Type

Structures are *derived data types;* that is, they are constructed by using data objects of different data types (in contrast to arrays, which contain only elements of the same data type).

Design and Implementation: Structures are commonly used to define records to be stored in files. In the following definition in the C programming language,

```
struct    course
{
int    number;
char    grade;
};
```

the keyword `struct` introduces the structure definition, and the identifier `course` is the *structure tag*. The structure tag names the structure definition and is used with the keyword `struct` to declare variables of type *structure*. Variables declared within the braces of the structure definition are called members. Variables of type *structure* can be declared like variables of other types. For example, the declaration

```
struct    course    programming;
```

declares `programming` to be a variable of the type structure `course`. A member of any variable of type structure (in this example *programming*) can be accessed by placing a period between the name of variable and the name of the member. In the following, `number` and `grade` members of variable `programming` are assigned 344 and A, respectively.

```
programming.number = 344;
programming.grade = 'A';
```

A change in the order of the members of a structure has no effect on the meaning of a program because the members are accessed by name, not by relative position (as in an array). The `struct` construct in C permits the use of public data members but not member functions or operators. The *class* construct in C++ is a generalization of the *struct* construct of C. In addition, the C++ *class* permits the use of data members, member functions and operators, and access specifiers. The *struct* construct differs from the *class* construct only in that the default access specification is public.

Function Type

Some languages (e.g., Pascal) permit you to pass procedures and functions as parameters to other procedures and functions.

Design and Implementation: To specify that a parameter is a function requires stating only the return type and nothing about the types of the arguments. For example,

```
Procedure    p(X: integer;    procedure F; Y: real);
```

defines a procedure whose second argument is a function parameter. The C code that describes what a function does is called the **function definition,** and takes the general form

```
type    function_name(paramter_list)
{
/*   declarations    */

/*   statements      */
}
```

Everything before the first brace constitutes the *header* of the function definition, and everything between the braces constitutes the *body* of the function definition. The parameter list is a comma-separated list of declarations. For example, in the following C code

```
int    factorial(int n)
{
        int i, product=1;
        for (i=2; i <= n; i++)
            product *=i;
        return product;
}
```

the first `int` indicates that the value returned by the function will be converted to an integer. The parameter list consists of the declaration of a variable, which informs the compiler that the function takes a single argument of type `int`. An expression such as factorial(5) causes the function to be invoked, the effect of which is to run the code that constitutes the function definition, with *n* having the value 5. For example, in C++,

```
bool    IsVowl(char CurrentCharacter)
```

indicates that the function `IsVowl` returns a Boolean value, in which the function expects to be passed a variable of type character.

List Type

Lists consist of an ordered sequence of objects; that is, we can refer to the first element of the list, the second element, and so forth. Lists have the following characteristics:

▶   Lists are variable length and may have any number of components. Lists typically grow and shrink during program execution. A list with no component is called the *empty* list.

▶   Lists are homogeneous if all the members are of the same data type and heterogeneous if the members are of different data types.

▶   The entries in lists can be either single objects or other lists.

The usual operations permitted on lists are insertions and deletions of elements in arbitrary places, finding the length of a list, and determining whether or not a list is empty.

Design and Implementation: Lists are the original data structures of functional programming languages. For example, the languages LISP, ML, and Prolog provide a list data type. A list has the form (`x :: y`), where element `x` is the head of the list, and the subset `y` is the tail of the list.

Most operations of lists include the ability to explore the structure of a list. For example, a list in ML is a sequence of zero or more elements of the same type (homogeneous). List elements are written between brackets [and], and commas separate the elements from each other. Thus, `[1, 2, 3, 4]` is a list of integers, and `["ab", "cd", "ef"]` a list of strings.

Most operations in LISP take list arguments and return list values. For example, the cons operation in LISP language takes two list arguments and returns a list whose first argument is appended to the beginning of the second argument:

```
(cons '(1 2 3) '(A B C) ) = ( (1 2 3) (A B C) )
```

In this example, the first element is the sublist (1 2 3), the second element is the object A, the third is the object B, and the fourth is the object C.

Lists are a predefined data type in Prolog with a special notation. They are built of functors (the terms that directly precede a set of brackets). Just two functors are needed for all list objects. One is the functor [ ], which denotes the empty list. The other, represented by a dot (.), builds lists from other lists. The dot corresponds to *cons* in LISP language. So, the list with the single element A is written as A.[ ], or (A, [ ]). The list consisting of the elements A, B, and C is written as A.B.C.[ ], or, because the dot functor is right associative (an operator is said to be *right associative* when subexpressions with multiple occurrences of the operator are grouped from right to left) as (A, B, C). Here is an example of a list containing another list as an element in Prolog.

```
A. X. B. (Y. Z. [ ]). C. [ ] = [A, X, B, [Y, Z], C]
```
In Prolog, the notation [X | Y] stands for X.Y, and [A, X | Y] stands for A.X.Y.

Variations on Lists

One way to represent lists is to pack the list items next to one another in a sequential structure such as an array. When list items are stored next to one another, we say they are stored contiguously. However, to insert a new item or to delete an item, we might have to shift all the items beyond the point of insertion or deletion so we can maintain the contiguous sequential arrangement of items in the underlying list. This is inherently inefficient. Another potential difficulty is the predetermined size of the list. Some of these disadvantages can be overcome by using the dynamic data structures that we explain in the following. However, these data structures have disadvantages of their own, such as inefficient access to the *i*th list element and storage penalties for the space needed to store the data structure.

Linked Lists

A **linked list** is a linear collection of self-referential structures, called *nodes*, connected by pointer links.

Design and Implementation: Each node of linked list contains a pointer member that points to a node of the same structure type. A linked list can be accessed via a pointer to the first node of the list. Subsequent nodes are accessed by using the link pointer member stored in each node. By convention, the link pointer in the last node of the list is assigned to NULL to mark the end of the linked list. Data are stored in a linked list dynamically, meaning that each node is created as necessary. For example, the following C declaration

```
struct    node
          {
          int    number;
          char   grade;
          struct node  *nextptr;
          };
```

defines a type as struct node. A variable of type struct node contains three members: integer data type member number, character data type member grade, and pointer type member nextptr. Member nextptr points to a variable of type struct node, which is a structure of the same type as the one being declared here—hence, the term *self-referential* structure. The member nextptr is referred to as a *link* because it can be used to link a structure to another structure of the same type. The functions *malloc* and *free* and the operator *sizeof* are essential to create a linked list. Function *malloc* takes as an argument the number of bytes to be allocated and returns a pointer of type *void* * (pointer to void) to the allocated memory. A *void* * pointer

FIGURE **2.2**   **A graphic representation of a node of linked list**

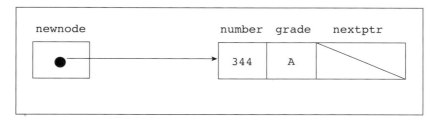

may be assigned to a variable of any pointer type. The function *malloc* is normally used with the *sizeof* operator. For example, the statement

```
newnode = malloc(sizeof(struct node));
```

evaluates `sizeof(struct node)` to determine the size in bytes of `struct node`, and allocates a new area in memory of `sizeof(struct node)` bytes and stores a pointer to the allocated memory in the variable newnode. If no memory is available, the *malloc* function returns a NULL pointer. The *free* function deallocates memory— that is, the memory is returned to the system so that it can be reallocated. To free memory allocated by the preceding *malloc* call, we use the statement

```
free(newnode);
```

The following program creates a node by calling *malloc* and assigning the values to the members of the node, as shown in Figure 2.2. Invoking the *free* function deallocates the memory associated with the node.

```
#include   <stdio.h>
#include   <stdlib.h>
     struct node
          {
          int    number;
          char   grade;
          struct node    *nextptr;
          };
     struct   node    *newnode;
main()
     {
     newnode = malloc(sizeof(struct node));
     newnode -> number=344;
     newnode -> grade='A';
     newnode -> nextptr=NULL;
     free(newnode);
     }
```

FIGURE **2.3**   **Push and Pop operations performed on a stack**

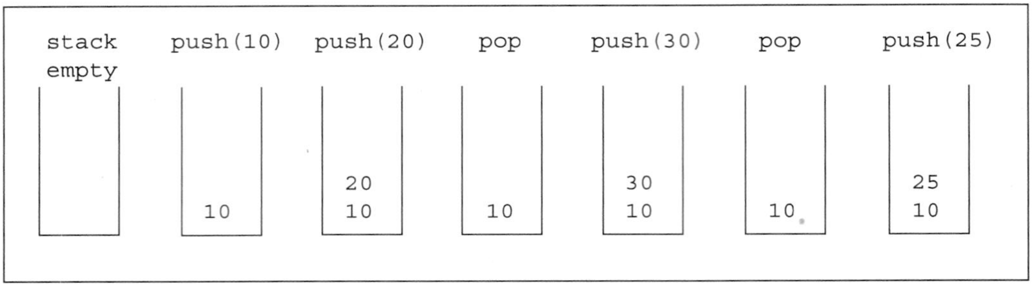

stack empty	push(10)	push(20)	pop	push(30)	pop	push(25)
		20		30		25
	10	10	10	10	10	10

Stacks

A **stack** is a linear data structure that can be accessed only from the top for storing and retrieving data.

Design and Implementation: The stack is called a Last-In First-Out (LIFO) data structure. A stack is defined in terms of operations that change its status and operations that check this status. The operations are as follows, and a series of Push() and Pop() operations is shown in Figure 2.3.

Clear()	Clear the stack
IsEmpty()	Check to see if the stack is empty
IsFull()	Check to see if the stack is full
Push(element)	Put the item *element* on top of the stack
Pop()	Remove the *element* from the top of the stack

Queues

A **queue** is a linear data structure that grows by adding elements to its top and shrinks by taking elements from its bottom.

Design and Implementation: The queue is called a First-In First-Out (FIFO) structure, and operations are similar to stack operations. The operations are as follows, and a series of Enqueue() and Dequeue() operations is shown in Figure 2.4.

Clear()	Clear the queue
IsEmpty()	Check to see if the queue is empty
IsFull()	Check to see if the queue is full
Enqueue(element)	Put the item *element* on top of the queue
Dequeue()	Remove the *element* from the bottom of the queue

FIGURE **2.4**   **Enqueue and Dequeue operations performed on a queue**

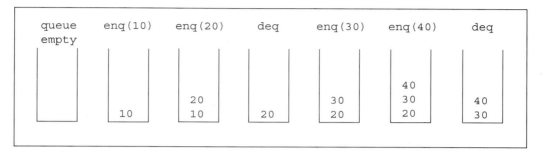

2.1.3   Recursive Data Types

Recursive data types, sometimes referred to as *circular data types,* have values that are composed from values of the same type. In other words, a recursive type is defined in terms of itself. For example, the type *list* is a recursive type. A list is a sequence of values and may have any number of components. For example, suppose that we want to define a type whose values are integer lists. We may define recursively an integer list to be a value that is either empty or a pair consisting of an integer (its head) and a further integer list (its tail). The following ML declaration defines a type whose values are lists of integers.

```
datatype   intlist =nil    |   cons of int * intlist
```

The following ML declaration defines a recursive type `inttree`, whose values are binary trees containing integers at their leaves:

```
datatype   inttree = leaf of int | branch of inttree * inttree
```

Some values of type `inttree`, expressed in ML notation, are as follows:

```
leaf = 11
branch (leaf 11, leaf 5)
branch ( branch (branch (leaf 5, leaf 7), leaf 9),
         branch (leaf 12, leaf 18) )
```

Pointers are most useful in the creation of recursive data types in procedural languages. Recursive types are extremely important in data structures and algorithm design and represent data whose size and structure is not known in advance, but may change as completion proceeds. Recursive data types occur only through pointer types in Pascal and C programming languages. For example, consider the following declaration in Pascal

```
type link = ↑ cell;
```

where type `link` is defined in terms of type `cell`. Furthermore, type `cell` is defined in terms of `link` because a `cell` is a record with a field holding a `link`:

```
type link = record
            info: integer;
            next: link;
            end;
```

Thus, `link` and `cell` are defined recursively in terms of each other. Two typical examples of recursive data types in procedural languages are linked-lists and binary trees.

2.2 TYPE BINDING

The determination of one of the components of a data object (name, location, value, and type)—that is, the process of associating an attribute to a variable—is called **binding**. We say that a declaration produces an association or binding between the declared identifier and the entity that it will denote. Here is an example of a declaration in C programming language:

```
int A;
```

The declaration is interpreted as the following: A location able to hold an integer number is created and a reference to it is given the name A. In this example, the identifier A is bound to some locations (known to compiler, but not to the programmer) and to the type integer. Similarly, running an assignment statement binds a value to a location.

Design and Implementation: Binding to attributes happen at different and invisible points after the programmer submits a program for execution. An attribute can be classified according to the time during *translation* or *execution* at which it is computed and bound to a name. This is called the *binding time* of the attributes. For example, a simple assignment statement such as

```
A=B+C;
```

can be interpreted and established with various bindings:

▶   A binding between names and locations must be performed to obtain the addresses of A, B, and C.

▶   A binding between locations and values must be performed to retrieve the data from the addresses of B and C.

▶   Compute the value of expression B+C.

▶   A new binding between the location and its computed value must be established to store the resulting value in the address of A.

A schematic view of a data object and its bindings is shown in Figure 2.5.

In this view, *memory space* is a collection of memory locations that are not visible to the programmer and is used to select the location bindings. *Identifier space* is the collection of all possible names that can be given to data objects. *Type space* is the set of all

FIGURE **2.5**   **A data object and its bindings**

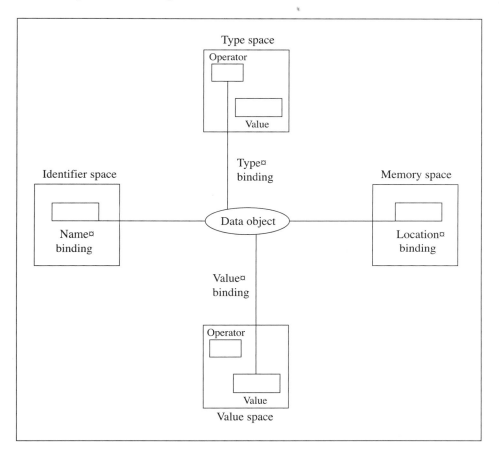

possible types that can be assigned to a data object. Each type is a space of possible values to which a data object can be bound and a set of operations can be applied to an object of that type. *Value space* is the set of all possible values to which an object can be bound. Programming languages differ in the number of entities that they can handle, in the number of attributes to be bound to those entities, and in the time at which such binding occurs. Binding can occur at three specific times, which give them their names:

▶ **Compile-time binding,** also known as *static binding* and sometimes referred to as *early bindings,* occurs when the program is translated into machine language; name and type bindings take place at compile time when declarations are encountered by the compiler and cannot be changed later.

▶ **Load-time binding** occurs when the machine code generated by the compiler is being stored to memory locations; location binding occurs at load time. At this time, all the hypothetical addresses used by the compiler are actually bound to physical locations in the computer. Depending on the language, load-time bind-ing can be performed statically or dynamically.

▶ **Run-time binding,** also known as *dynamic binding* and sometimes referred to as *late bindings,* occurs when the program is being executed; value binding occurs at run time. Run-time decisions are the choices made during the execution of the program, for example, when a value is equal to zero.

Generally speaking, the later the binding, the more flexible the language, the ear-lier the binding, the more efficient the language. Languages differ substantially in which attributes are bound statically and which are bound dynamically. Functional languages often have more dynamic binding than do imperative languages. For exam-ple, in the declaration

```
int    x=2;
```

the value 2 and the data type int are bound statically to the name x. Similarly, in the C program segment

```
#include    <stdio.h>
main( )
   {
   int    x;
   x = 10;
   }
```

the assignment binds the value 10 dynamically to x when the statement is carried out. In general, type binding is static in languages that require declaration of variables. Languages such as Pascal, C, and Ada require explicit declarations. BASIC and For-tran, however, have some implicit typing. BASIC variable names like A are real, A% is integer, A$ is string. Fortran variables starting with I through N default to integer type, while others default to real. APL, SNOBOL4, and SETL2 are among the lan-guages that support dynamic type binding. In SETL2, for example, a program may contain statements like the following:

```
class := {1, 3, "HELLO", 6};
class := 5;
```

indicating that, the variable class initially contains a set and later is bound to the in-teger 5. Binding times can also depend on the translator. Interpreters by definition perform all bindings dynamically, whereas compilers will perform many bindings statically. Dynamic binding can be changed according to some specified rules. It is easy to implement but has the disadvantages of strict programming discipline re-quirements and inefficient implementation. Programs are hard to read because the identity of the particular declaration to which a given variable is bound depends on the particular point of execution and, thus, cannot be determined statically. Bindings must be maintained by a translator so that appropriate bindings are given to names during translation (statically) and execution (dynamically). A translator performs this by creating a data structure to maintain the information. From the abstract point of view, we can think of it as a function that expresses the binding of attributes to names.

FIGURE **2.6**   **Binding of attributes to names**

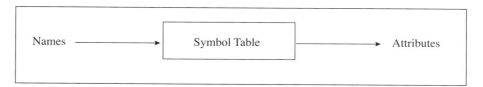

FIGURE **2.7**   **Symbol table maintained by a compiler**

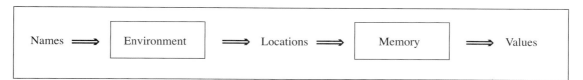

This function is a fundamental part of the language design and implementation and is usually called the *symbol table*. Mathematically speaking, the symbol table is a function from names to attributes, which can be written as

```
Symbol Table : Names ⇒ Attributes
```

and represented as shown in Figure 2.6.

As translation and execution proceeds, this function is changed to reflect additions and deletions of bindings. There is a fundamental distinction between the way a symbol table is maintained by an interpreter and a compiler. During the execution of a compiled program, a compiler generates code that maintains program attributes such as locations and values. This process consists of two parts:

▶   The memory allocation process, which is the binding of names to storage locations and is called the *environment*.

▶   The binding of storage locations to values, which is called the *memory* and known as *store* or *state* because it abstracts the memory of an actual computer.

A schematic view of a symbol table maintained by a compiler is shown in Figure 2.7.

In an interpreter because static and dynamic attributes are both computed during execution, the memory allocation and binding of storage locations to values are combined in one process, as shown in Figure 2.8.

FIGURE **2.8**   **Symbol Table maintained by an interpreter**

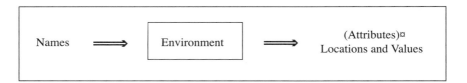

2.3 TYPE CHECKING

Type checking is the process a translator goes through to verify that all constructs in a program are valid for the types of its constants, variables, functions, and other entities. For example, in the following statements in C language:

```
Z = X + 5 * Y;
Switch (X+2, 2.5, Y);
```

Y must be of a type that permits multiplication by an integer, (5*Y). Similarly, the types of the actual parameters for the call to function Switch must be checked for compatibility with the types of the formal parameters. Type checking by the translator can help detect and prevent errors. Type checking can occur at compile time, at run time, or not at all.

Design and Implementation: The type checking process involves the application of a type equivalence test that consists of rules for determining whether two types are the same; it is used to detect and prevent execution errors. If this test isn't used, type checking is the programmer's responsibility, which often leads to numerous undetected errors. The test can be used to check and change types at the following times.

1. **Compile-time checking:** The types can be checked at compile time, indicating that type checking must be performed by the compiler with regard to the declaration of data objects. It can be viewed as *static type checking,* in which type information is maintained and checked at translation time. In this sense, the types of expressions and objects are determined from the text of the program. This type of checking is easy to implement and inexpensive in memory and run time, but it requires rather complicated and restrictive rules.

2. **Run-time checking:** The types can be checked at run time, which means that type checking must be performed every time a data object is accessed. It can be viewed as *dynamic type checking,* in which type information is maintained and checked at run time. This method of checking can be expensive in memory use and run time because a check must be performed every time a data object is referenced and a type indicator must be part of every data value.

A language is said to be *strongly typed language* if all feasible type checking is performed at compile time and all other type checking is done at run time. In this case, all objects must have well-defined types, along with a complete set of rules for type checking that can be performed at translation time. In general, strong typing provides a level of security to our programs. Ada is a strongly typed language, whereas C is not a very strongly typed language because of exceptions made for conditions that are difficult or impossible to check at translation time. Pascal is nearly a strongly typed language, but it is not quite because of two exceptions: subrange types and variant records. Languages with no complete static type systems (e.g., APL, LISP, SNOBOL, and Bliss) are *weakly typed programming languages.* The Scheme dialect of LISP is a weakly, dynamically typed language. There are two kinds of types in Scheme declarations. Variables and other symbols have no predeclared type, but have the type of the value they possess at each moment of execution. Thus, type checking in Scheme is restricted to generating errors for functions requiring certain values to perform their operations. For example, *car* and *cdr* as two functions require their operands to be a list, indicating that (car 2) generates an error. Another alternative is that the types might not be checked at all, which is what typically happens in the preceding cases for Pascal. This situation places the burden of type checking on the programmer and can lead to serious undetected errors.

An essential part of type checking is *type inference,* where the types of expressions are inferred from the types of their subexpressions. For example, an expression (A+B) might be declared as correct type, if A and B have the same type, that type has a "+" operation (type checking), and the result type of the expression is of the type A and B (type inference). Where possible, ML infers the type of an expression. The inferred type *int* for integer is included in the ML interpreter in response to the expressions such as the following.

```
2 + 2;
        val it = 4 : int
```

An error is reported if the type of the expression cannot be inferred. It is worth noting that type checking of operands for operators (A and B for +) is complicated by the practice of *operator overloading,* which is the use of one operator for several operations. For example, 2 has type integer, so + denotes integer addition for 2+2; however, 2.0 has type real, so + denotes real addition in 2.0+2.0. In Pascal, for example, the "+" operator is used for both integer and real arithmetic, as well as set union. A further complication is the use of the "−" operator in both unary form (one operand involved such as −A) and binary form (two operands involved such as A−B). Ada further complicates this by permitting additional overloading by the programmer. As another example, in a function call, the types of the actual parameters or arguments must match the types of the formal parameters (type checking), and the result type of the call is the result type of the function (type inference). In general, type checking and type inference rules are the most complex and important parts of the language design. To summarize this discussion, the following are some fundamental questions to be asked about type checking in the language design process:

▶   Is the type checking system done statically or dynamically?

▶   Is the type checking system strong or weak?

▽ 2.4 TYPE CONVERSION

Operators involved in the evaluation of expressions require one or more than one operand. **Type conversion** deals with two different data types in the evaluation of an expression. For example, in the assignment statement

```
A = B + C;
```

the right operand of the assignment operator "=" is the expression B+C that assigns a value to the left operand A as the result of the execution. Now, consider the operands A and B to be of type *real* and C to be of type *integer*. Because many integers have an equivalent *real* representation, converting the integer operand C to a *real* of equivalent value may be possible to obtain the *real* value for A. In other words, in some situations two different types may be combined in certain ways to form a type that still may be correct. The types of this form are called **compatible types.** For example, in C programming language the statement

```
A = B + 3.15;
```

could be interpreted as the following steps:

▶ Variable B is converted to a real and the type of the result of B+3.15 is real.

▶ Then the real value is truncated to an integer and assigned to A.

In contrast, in a more strongly typed language like Modula-2, reals and integers cannot be mixed in arithmetic expressions, and reals cannot be assigned to integers, so the above statement would generate a type error. In this case, the statement in Modula-2 would have to be written as the following:

```
A = TRUNC (FLOAT(B) + 3.15);
```

The original Fortran type system rejected expressions like X+I and 2*3.15 because one operand is an integer and the other is a real (I represents an integer variable in Fortran). This restriction was lifted in later versions of Fortran. Most programming languages treat the expression 2*3.15 as if it were 2.0*3.15, which is the product of two real numbers. This process is called **coercion,** meaning that the integer 2 is coerced to a real number before the multiplication is performed. Converting data types may be done either implicitly or explicitly.

2.4.1 Implicit Data Type Conversion

Programming languages that allow implicit data type conversions provide a list of all pairs of types for which data type conversion is permitted. For example, in Pascal the assignment statement x:=y is legal when y is of type *int* and x is of type *real,* indicating that the integer value y is converted to a real value to be stored in x. The assignment statement is not valid in Modula-2, but in Modula-2, the INTEGER and CARDINAL types are compatible. Thus,

```
x:=y
```

is of a correct type if x is type CARDINAL and y is type INTEGER. In C, mixed types are permitted. For instance, the assignment statement

```
x=y+2.5;
```

where x and y are type *int,* can be performed with conversion types. In this case, y is converted to a *real,* and the real value of y+2.5 is truncated to an integer and can be assigned to x. Generally speaking, in every programming language, converting one type to another under certain conditions is necessary, and this implicit type conversion is also called *type coercion.* C++ and Java have integer types that are smaller than the *int* type. In C++, these are *char* and *short int;* whereas in Java, they are *byte, short,* and *char.* Operands of all of these types are coerced to *int* implicitly, whenever any operator is applied to them. So although data can be stored in variables of these types, it cannot be manipulated before conversion to a larger type. For example, consider the following statements in Java language.

```
byte   A, B, C;
A = B + C;
```

In this case, the values of B and C are coerced to *int* and an integer addition is performed. Then the sum (B+C) is converted to *byte* and stored in variable A.

The advantage of automatic type conversion is that you aren't required to write extra code to perform an obvious type conversion that could affect the simplicity of the design. However, the disadvantage of type conversion is that errors might not be detected, which can affect reliability of the programming language. For example, the expression 1/3+15 in PL/I is converted to the value 5.33333333333333 on a system with 15-digit precision. The leading 1 is lost to overflow because the precision of the fractional value is to be maintained. The result is unpredictable behavior; you might expect a conversion to be performed in one way, but the translator performs it in a different way.

2.4.2 Explicit Data Type Conversion

When specific functions are called to perform the conversion from one type to another, the data type conversion is explicit. For example, in Ada, the function FLOAT can convert any type to an equivalent type *float.* Such conversions are normally permitted between numeric data types. Examples include *trunc* and *round* in Pascal and TRUNC and FLOAT in Modula-2. Another kind of explicit type conversion is with a *cast,* meaning that a value or an object of one type can be converted to an equivalent value of another type. For example, the C fragment

```
int    a;
float   b=12.5;
a = (int) b;
```

truncates the real value 12.5 to 12, thus performing an actual conversion with 12 as the value of the variable a.

Summary

A data object known as variable can be characterized by four components as: location, name, value, and type. From the declaration point of view, type information can be categorized as implicit and explicit type information. From the implementation point of view, type information can be categorized as built-in and user-defined types. We briefly discussed different data types, including integer, real, Boolean, character, array, string, pointer, structure, function, stack, and queue. Determining one component of a data object is called binding, which is the process of associating an attribute to a variable. Binding can occur at three specific times: compile-time binding, load-time binding, and run-time binding. Binding is one of the important concepts of design and implementation of any programming language.

Type checking is the process a translator uses to verify that all constructors in a program are valid for the types of entities. Type checking can be classified as static type checking, in which type information is maintained and checked at translation time, and dynamic type checking, in which type information is performed at run time. We discussed type checking relative to the static and dynamic type checking. Type conversion deals with two different data types in evaluating an expression. Implicit data type conversion and explicit data type conversion are two important concepts of type conversion in designing and implementing any programming language.

Design Specification Principles

An abstraction is a representation of an object and is categorized as procedural, modular, object, and user-defined forms. Data abstraction is involved with the program components that are subject to computation, such as character strings or numbers. Data abstraction is divided into three categories: basic data abstraction, which refers to the internal representation of data values; structured data abstraction, which is the principal method for abstracting collections of data values; and unit data abstraction, which is the principal method for collecting all the information needed to create and use a particular data type. Control abstraction describes the order in which statements are to be executed. Basic control abstraction performs the computation and storage of a value to the location given by a variable. Structured control abstraction is referred to as subprogram invocation or activation, and unit control abstraction represents a collection of routines that provide services to other parts of a program.

In Section 3.1, we introduce the abstraction concept with a different approach to address this important issue in design and implementation of languages. Expressions are formed from operators and operands, in which operators are known as functions and operands as parameters. In Section 3.2, we briefly discuss the formal and actual parameters and three distinct semantics models of parameter passing: In Mode, Out Mode, and InOut Mode models. Then, we introduce five different parameter passing mechanisms—parameter passing by constant-value, parameter passing by reference, parameter passing by name, parameter passing by result, and parameter passing by value-result—to address data transmission between subprograms. Section 3.3 describes the fundamental concepts of exceptions, exception handling, and raising of exceptions. The remainder of the section describes and illustrates the exception-handling facilities in different programming languages: PL/I, Ada, ML, C++, and Java.

Section 3.4 contains the various fundamental forms of expressions, such as infix, prefix, postfix, and mixfix. In general, each programming language has rules for the evaluation of expressions, such as applicative order, normal order, short circuit, lazy, and block order evaluation. Applicative order evaluation corresponds to a bottom-up evaluation of the values of vertices of the tree representing an expression. Normal order evaluation corresponds to the evaluation of each operand when it is needed for computing the result. Short circuit evaluation performs the evaluation of an expression without evaluating all its subexpressions, and block order evaluation occurs when an expression contains a declaration. In addition, in Section 3.4, we discuss the expression evaluation mechanisms to provide enough background knowledge for upcoming topics where different programming languages are discussed. A clear understanding of execution environment is often necessary to understand fully the behavior of programs because the program execution is embedded in this environment. In Section 3.5, we discuss the static and dynamic environments to address the lifetime and access path of data objects by operations in the program execution. We also want to show that static environment is no longer adequate to deal with dynamic creation of data objects. A more serious situation occurs if the language designer wants to extend the expressiveness and flexibility of the languages by allowing functions to be dynamically created, that is, allowing function to be returned from other functions via returned value or referenced parameters. This kind of flexibility is usually desired in a functional programming language, and such languages become what are called first-class values languages. One undesirable situation of execution environments supported by dynamic storage management is that a program could run out of storage if it makes heavy use of dynamic storage. An approach provided to storage management is *garbage collection,* which keeps track of allocated but inaccessible storage called *garbage* and permits it to be reallocated. We discuss garbage and garbage collections as one important property associated with languages supported by fully dynamic memory environments. Object-oriented programming languages also fall into this category, and the discussion on garbage and garbage collections applies to them as well.

3.1 ABSTRACTIONS

An **abstraction** is a representation of an object that ignores what could be considered as irrelevant details of that object, thus making use of the object easier. Abstractions include the procedural, modular, objects, and user-defined forms. Procedural abstraction allows you to concentrate on one section of a program at a time without having to deal with the overall details of the program. *Modular abstraction* is defined as a collection of related declarations. A **module** is a grouping of related declarations that can include types, variables, and procedures and can be thought of as the relation between variables and procedures. In general, programming language abstraction falls into two general categories: *data abstraction* and *control abstraction*. With data, you can work more effectively by using simpler abstractions that do not include many irrelevant details of data objects. With procedures, you can concentrate on good design practices and modularity. Abstractions are further classified as three levels: *basic, structured,* and *unit,* which can be thought of as measures of the amount of information contained in the abstraction. In other words, basic abstractions collect the most localized machine information, structured abstractions collect global information about program structure, and unit abstractions collect information about the entire program. The level to which a language supports these kinds of abstractions is important to its effective use in the design, implementation, and modification of programs.

3.1.1   Data Abstraction

Data abstraction deals with the program components that are subject to computation, such as character strings or numbers. In other words, data abstraction is based on the properties of the data objects and operations on those objects, and is a fundamental part of a programming language. Data abstraction leads to consideration of abstract data types, which allow development of programs that are independent of how data are represented in them. One advantage of abstract representation is that data first represented as one data type may later be represented as other, more specialized types. Data abstraction techniques involve defining a small set of procedures that create and operate on a given type of data and allow only these procedures direct access to the data. This set of procedures and the chosen data representation constitute an abstract data type (ADT). Because access to data of an ADT is possible only through ADT procedures, the rest of a program is independent of the representation chosen for the data. This property is called **representation independence** and ensures that if the representation is changed, only the ADT procedure is affected.

Basic Data Abstraction

The higher-level programming languages provide a set of basic data types, including a bit string representing a real number, a bit string representing a character, or a bit string representing an integer. **Basic data abstraction** refers to the internal representation of common data values in a computer system. In general, locations in computer memory that contain data values are called variables, and the kind of data value in memory locations is called data types. Data types of basic data values are given as the names of their corresponding mathematical values, such as *integer* and *real*. A declaration statement is used to specify the variables' names and data types. For example, in the following declarations in C programming language,

```
int     x;
float   y;
char    z;
```

x is declared as the name of a variable with the data type *int,* y is declared as the name of a variable with the data type *float,* and z is declared as the name of a variable with the data type *char.* Each declaration then can address a variable and define its type. In general, a data type can define a type as a set of values that a variable might take on.

Structured Data Abstraction

Structured data abstraction is the principal method for abstracting collections of data values that are related. For example, a personnel record may consist of a name,

address, phone number, and salary, each of which may be a different data type but together represent the record as a whole. In this case, the record type is a low-level abstraction. Such an abstraction is useful when you want to assign one entire record to
another or pass an entire record as a parameter. This form permits the user to manipulate a record by name, ignoring such details as component names and types. In other
words, the implementation of records hides details of how they are implemented and
provides an example of data abstraction. Variables can be given a data structure via a
declaration, as in the C programming language declaration

```
int    list[10];
```

which establishes the variable `list` as an array of 10 integer values. Some languages
permit a further abstraction of data structures as new data type names that aren't internal but that you can construct when needed by using a *type declaration.* For example, in C the statement

```
typedef    struct    card    Card;
```

defines the new type name `Card` as a synonym for type `struct  card`. Such data
types are called **structured types,** and you can use them to define a structure type so
that you don't have to provide a structure tag. For example, the definition

```
typedef    struct    {
      char    grade;
      int     course;
      }       Card;
```

creates the structure type `Card` without the need for a separate `typedef` statement.
`Card` can now be used to declare a variable of type `struct card`. The declaration

```
Card    deck[52];
```

declares an array of 52 `Card` structures (i.e., variables of type `struct  Card`). Note
that creating a new name with `typedef` doesn't create new type; `typedef` simply
creates a new type name, which may be used as an alias for an existing type name.

Unit Data Abstraction

Unit data abstraction is the principal method for collecting all the information
needed to create and use a particular data type in one unit location. The typical scope
of unit data abstraction is a module, which is a set of statements formed as a block to
carry out a specific process. Blocks commonly comprise procedures or functions, are
useful for implementing top-down design of programs, and provide reusability of the
modules. Such data encapsulation restricts access to the details of the data type. In
other words, unit data abstraction ensures that changes in the structure of the data
type do not affect other areas of the program. Advantages of using unit data abstraction include the following:

1. The simplicity of program units makes them easier to read, write, and modify.
    By ignoring lower levels of detail, a program unit can concentrate on a single

task. This property is crucial to the top-down design approach to programming languages.

2.   The reusability of program units allows a block to be used in many different programming environments. This capability eliminates redundant programming effort and reduces the number of errors.

3.   The independence of program units ensures that the actions of a block are independent of its use. This characteristic indicates that a program based on the abstraction is not affected by the details of its implementation.

Two programming languages that support unit data abstraction are Modula-2 and Ada, which do so through module and package, respectively.

3.1.2   Control Abstraction

Control abstraction describes the order in which statements or groups of statements (program blocks) are to be executed. It deals with the components of the program that transfer control (e.g., loops, conditional statements, and procedure calls). In other words, control abstraction can be thought of as the modification of a program's execution path. Control abstraction may be classified as *basic, structured,* and *unit control* abstractions.

Basic Control Abstraction

A typical *basic control abstraction* is an assignment statement that abstracts the computation and storage of a value to the location given by a variable, as in

```
x=x+5;
```

which indicates that the old value of x is increased by 5 to obtain the new value of the variable. In general, two mechanisms can be used to accomplish the flow of control over individual instructions: sequencing and branching. Normally, instructions in a program are executed one after the other in the order in which they are written, which is called sequencing or *sequential execution.* Sequencing is accomplished by automatically increasing the program counter (a register in the hardware) after carrying out each instruction. Thus, instructions stored in consecutive memory locations can be fetched and run one after the other.

Alternatively, you may specify that the next instruction to be run could be other than the next one in sequence. This is called branching or *transfer of control.* Thus, the program counter can be altered explicitly to provide control transfer to a specific location. In programming languages, branching can be represented by a *jump* or *goto* instruction, known as an unconditional branch. For example, in C the goto statement changes the program's flow of control to the first statement after the label specified in the goto statement. A *label* is an identifier followed by a colon. The following program uses the goto statement to loop 10 times and print the counter value each time. The program tests count to determine whether it is greater than 10. If so, control is transferred from the goto statement to the first statement after the label end.

Otherwise, `count` is printed and incremented and control is transferred from the `goto` statement to the first statement after the label `start`.

```
#include <stdio.h>
main()
{
     int count=1;
   start:
     if (count>10)
         goto end;
     printf(" %d ", count);
     count=count+1;
     goto start;
   end:
     printf(" \n End of the Program ");
}
```

Structured Control Abstraction

Suppose that a program block is outlined as

```
. . .
Z1 = X1 - Y1
IF   (Z1 .LE. 0)    Z1= -Z1
. . .
. . .
. . .
C1 = A1 - B1
IF   (C1 .LE. 0)    C1= -C1
```

Note that the same program segment is repeated, although with different variables. If we abstract this fragment from the particular variable, we can express it as

```
Z= X - Y
IF   (Z .LE. 0)    Z = -Z
```

which means that Z, X, and Y represent Z1, X1, and Y1 and C1, A1, and B1 in the first and second occurrences, respectively. Instead of repeating this fragment every time when it is needed, we can define a structured control abstraction once and then call it to be used every time it is required. We do so with a subprogram declaration called a procedure, sometimes referred to as a *subprogram, function,* or *subroutine.* For example, in the following subroutine declaration:

```
Subroutine   Name (Parameters)
. . .
{body of the subroutine}
. . .
Return
End
```

`Name` is the identification name of the subroutine, and `Parameters` is a list of the names of variables that represent different values each time the subroutine is called. A subroutine that defines this control abstraction can be expressed as

```
Subroutine   CALC (X, Y, Z)
             Z= X - Y
             IF   (Z .LE. 0)   Z = -Z
Return
End
```

A call statement within the program can invoke this subroutine. For example, we can rewrite the program fragment as

```
. . .
CALL   CALC(X1, Y1, Z1)
. . .
. . .
CALL   CALC(A1, B1, C1)
```

where running CALL passes control from the caller to the callee, which is the subroutine being called. This method is sometimes referred to as *subprogram invocation* or *activation.* The Return statement in the callee passes control back to the caller, which resumes execution at the statement following CALL. Thus, the variables in the caller's environment can be accessed by referring to the parameters in the callee's environment. Generally speaking, this method allows you to consider a sequence of actions as a single action and to control the instruction of these actions with other parts of the program.

In addition, structured control mechanisms come in many forms, including the *while* and *for* loops in C, the *repeat* loops in Pascal, and the *loop-exit* mechanism in Modula-2. For example, the following program fragment computes x to be the greatest common divisor of u and v in Modula-2 and C, respectively. For instance, the greatest common divisor of 8 and 20 is 4, and for 3 and 11 it is 1.

```
(* Modula-2 example of greatest common divisor of two numbers *)
x := u;
y := v;
LOOP
   IF   y ≤ 0   THEN
      EXIT
   END;
   t := y;
   y := x mod y;
   x := t;
END;

/* C example of greatest common divisor of two numbers */
x := u;
y := v;
while ( y > 0)
```

```
{
t := y;
y := x % y;
x := t;
}
```

Subroutine or function calls are more complex than selection or looping because they require storing information about the condition of the program at the point of the call and the way the callee operates. One advantage of structured control abstractions is that they can be nested within other control structures, usually to any desired depth.

Unit Control Abstraction

A **unit control abstraction** represents a collection of procedures that provide logically related services to other parts of a program. For example, the procedures that provide the mean, median, and standard deviation can be collected into a program unit that computes the values of these statistical terms. This control unit can be used by other parts of the program, which, generally speaking, allows the program to be defined as a whole without your needing to know the details of the services provided by the unit. An example of the unit control abstraction is found in Ada programming language.

◥ 3.2 PARAMETERS AND PARAMETER TRANSMISSION

The terms *parameter* and *parameter transmission* apply to data sent to and returned from the subprograms through a variety of language mechanisms. Parameter transmission is the major alternative method for sharing data objects among subprograms. In this concept, the terms *actual parameter* and *formal parameter* become central. A formal parameter is a particular kind of local data object within a subprogram. The subprogram definition lists the names and declarations for formal parameters as part of the specification part of the subprogram. A formal parameter name is a simple identifier, and the declaration gives the type and other attributes as for an ordinary local variable declaration. For example, the C subprogram (function) definition

```
int    Max(int X, int Y)
   {
   if   (X > Y)
      return X;
   else
      return Y;
   }
```

defines two formal parameters named X and Y and declares the type of each one. In other words, a formal parameter is the specification of the parameter within *the invoked subprogram,* sometimes named *called subprogram.* The declaration of a formal parameter does not mean the same as declaration for a local variable in a subprogram.

The specification of the parameter in the *invoking subprogram,* sometimes named *calling subprogram,* is known as an actual parameter. An actual parameter is a data object that is shared with the caller subprogram. An actual parameter can be classified as any of the following:

▶   A local data object belonging to the caller

▶   A formal parameter of the caller

▶   A nonlocal data object visible to the caller

▶   A result returned by a subprogram invoked by the caller and immediately transmitted to the called subprogram

For example, in the C program

```
#include <stdio.h>
main ( )
   {
   int   A, B, C;
   int Max(int, int);
   A = 10;
   B = 20;
   C = Max(A, B);
   printf(" The Maximum of %d and %d is %d ", A, B, C);
   }
int   Max(int X, int Y)
   {
   if   (X > Y)
      return X;
   else
       return Y;
   }
```

A and B in the *main* program are called actual parameters, and X and Y in subprogram Max are called formal parameters. Formal parameters do not take on any value until Max is called, then they are replaced by the arguments from the calling subprogram, as in

```
Z = Max( A, B);
```

where the formal parameter X is replaced by the value of the actual parameter A, and the parameter Y is replaced by the B. In general, an actual parameter is represented at the point of call of the subprogram by an expression, termed an *actual-parameter expression.* For example, the subprogram defined

```
Max(int X, int Y)
```

might be called with any of the types of actual parameter expressions shown in Table 3.1.

In this sense, when a subprogram is called with an actual-parameter expression of any of these forms, the expression is evaluated at the time of the call, before the subprogram is invoked. The data objects that result from evaluating the actual parameter expressions then become the actual parameters transmitted to the subprogram.

TABLE **3.1**   Subprograms and corresponding parameters

Subprogram call in main program	Actual parameter in main program
Max(X, Y)	X and Y as local variables of main program
Max(G, H)	G and H as global variables declared
Max(20, 30)	20 and 30 as constant values
Max(I+2,Switch(X, Y))	results of an expression and defined functions
Max(A+10, B+5)	results of two expressions evaluations
Max(A[2], Class.Name)	member of an array and a structure declared

To emphasize the fact that formal parameters have no value until they are replaced by actual parameters, formal parameters are sometimes called *parameters,* whereas actual parameters are called *arguments.* The formal parameters, depending on the parameter transmission mechanism to be discussed shortly, may be an alias to the actual parameter data object or may simply contain a copy of the value of that data object.

3.2.1 Semantics Models of Parameter Passing

In general, the relation between formal parameters and actual parameters can be characterized by one of the following distinct semantics models: *In Mode, Out Mode,* and *InOut Mode.* In the following, we briefly discuss the three semantics models when physical moves are used.

▶ *In Mode* parameter, in which the formal parameter receives data from the corresponding actual parameter as illustrated in the following:

Calling subprogram   Called subprogram
Max(A, B)   {Call A ⇒ X }   Max(X, Y)

▶ *Out Mode* parameter, in which the formal parameter transmits data to the actual parameter as illustrated in the following:

Calling subprogram   Called subprogram
Max(A, B)   {Call A ⇒ X}   Max(X, Y)
{Return B ⇐ Y}

▶ *InOut Mode* parameter, in which the formal parameter can behave as In Mode and Out Mode as illustrated in the following:

Calling subprogram   Called subprogram
Max(A, B)   {Call A ⇒ X}   Max(X, Y)
{Return A ⇐ X}

In general, a call to a subprogram such as `Max` binds the arguments to the parameters of the subprogram declaration, while transferring control to the body of the subprogram. How these bindings are provided depends on the parameter passing mechanisms used for the call. Programming language designers have developed a variety of models to guide the implementation of the parameter passing. However, all mechanisms—pass by constant-value, pass by reference, pass by name, pass by result, and pass by value-result—have differences that can lead to similar programs having different semantics, as we discuss in the following section.

3.2.2 Parameter Passing by Constant-Value

If a parameter is transmitted by a constant value, the value of the actual parameter is passed to the called subprogram. In other words, in this parameter passing mechanism, the arguments are expressions that are evaluated at the time of the call, and their values become the values of the parameters while the subprogram runs. This mechanism is an implementation for the *In Mode* semantics model. In this method, no change or other modification in the value of the actual parameter is possible while the subprogram is running, and the formal parameter may not be transmitted to another subprogram except as a constant value parameter. In this sense, the formal parameter acts as a local constant during execution of the subprogram. Generally speaking, call by constant value has the effect of protecting the calling program from changes in the actual parameter. Thus, from the calling program point of view, the actual parameter is only an input argument for the subprogram. Its value cannot be modified by the subprogram execution, either inadvertently or to transmit results back. For example, we can think of the call `Max(10, 2+3)` of the preceding `Max` subprogram (function in C) as executing the body of `Max` with `A` replaced by `10` and `B` replaced by `5` as the result of the evaluation of `2+3`. Pass by value is the default parameter passing mechanism in Ada, Pascal, Modula-2, and C. The parameter passing by value implementation mechanisms are the following:

▶ Upon invoking a subprogram, the actual parameter passes its value.

▶ Upon reference in the subprogram, formal parameter contains the value that is used.

Pass by constant value is normally implemented by actual data transmission because accesses are usually more efficient with this method. The main disadvantage of the pass by constant value mechanism is that additional storage is required for the formal parameters in the called subprogram. In addition, the actual parameter value must be physically moved to the storage area for the corresponding formal parameters, indicating that if the parameter is of a large aggregate type (i.e., a large array), sufficient space must be made for the copy passed to the formal parameter. In this case, the time needed for the transfer can also be costly.

3.2.3 Parameter Passing by Reference

Pass by reference is perhaps the most common parameter passing mechanism. To transmit an actual parameter as a call by reference parameter means that a pointer to the memory location of the data object is made available to the called subprogram. In other words, instead of passing the value of a variable, the method passes the location of the variable, so that the formal parameter becomes an alias for the actual parameter and any changes made to the formal parameter apply to the actual parameter as well. In this method, at the beginning of the called subprogram execution, the actual parameter value is used to initialize the local storage location for the formal parameter. This mechanism is an implementation model for the *InOut Mode* semantics model. From the implementation point of view, parameter passing occurs in four stages:

1. In the calling subprogram, each actual parameter expression is evaluated to provide a pointer to the actual parameter data object. A list of these pointers is stored in a common storage area that is also accessible to the called subprogram.

2. The activation record for the subprogram is created, the return point is established, and the flow of control is transferred to the called subprogram.

3. In the called subprogram, the list of pointers to actual parameters is accessed so that the appropriate value of the actual parameters can be retrieved.

4. On transmission of the called subprogram, the results are returned to the calling subprogram through the actual parameter data objects.

While the called subprogram is running, reference to formal parameter name is treated as ordinary local variable reference, except that there is a pointer selection attribute. In Fortran, pass by reference is the only parameter passing mechanism. In Pascal and Modula-2, pass by reference can be achieved by using the VAR keyword. For example, the Pascal subprogram

```
procedure    change(var x:integer);
begin
      x : = x + 1;
end;
```

might be invoked by change(y), in which y is an actual parameter declared in calling subprogram. In this approach, the value of y is increased by 1. C can achieve pass by reference by passing a reference or location explicitly. C uses the operator & to indicate the location of a variable and the operator * to dereference a variable. Thus, the C subprogram

```
void    change(int *x)
        {
        *x = *x + 1;
        }
```

might be invoked by change(y), in which the value of y is increased by 1. In effect, the actual parameter is shared with the called subprogram. The advantage of pass by reference is that the passing process is efficient, in both time and space, when duplicate memory locations are not required. The main disadvantage is that access to the formal parameters will be slower because one more level of indirect addressing is required. In addition, if only one-way communication to the called subprogram is required, inadvertent and erroneous changes may be made to the actual parameter.

Another problem associated with pass by reference is that aliases can be created. This should be expected because pass by reference makes access to actual parameters available, thereby broadening their access as nonlocal variables. For example, if the C subprogram

```
void   Max(int *first, int *second)
       {
        . . .
        . . .
       }
```

is invoked by Max(&X, &X), then first and second variables in Max become aliases. The problem with this kind of aliasing (two expressions denoting the same location are said t ʲ be aliases for each other) is the same as in other circumstances, meaning that it ʲs harmful to readability and, thus, to reliability. It also makes program verificatioꞁ extremely difficult. In contrast, for parameters of aggregate type (an array), the reference parameter is more efficient because the entire aggregate is not copied, only its address, which results in both storage and time savings.

3.2.4   Parameter Passing by Name

Parameter passing by name is the most difficult parameter-passing mechanism. It views a subprogram call as a substitution for the entire body of the subprogram. This mechanism is an implementation for the *InOut Mode* semantics model that does not correspond to a single implementation model. In this method, the actual parameter is textually substituted for the corresponding formal parameter in all its occurrences in the called subprogram. In other words, the formal parameter is bound to an access method at the time of the subprogram call, but the actual binding to a value or an address is delayed until the formal parameter is assigned or referenced. From the implementation point of view, the formal parameter is not evaluated until it is actually used in the called subprogram. Thus, the name of the formal parameter, or its textual representation at the point of call, replaces the name of the actual parameter it corresponds to. This can lead to unsuspected complications. For example, the subprogram

```
void   Change(int A, int B)
       {
       int Temp;
       Temp = A;
       A = B;
       B = Temp;
       }
```

which is intended to change the value of A and B, can produce unexpected and incorrect results when invoked by the call

```
Change(X, Y[X]);
```

where X is an integer index and Y is an array of integers. In this example, the replaced rule specifies that the statements to be run are

```
Temp = X;
X = Y[X];
Y[X] = Temp;
```

Now, if X=3 and Y[3]=4 before the subprogram is invoked, X=4 and Y[4]=3 is produced after the subprogram is executed, in which Y[3] is unaffected and contradicts the objective. Note that by the time the address of Y[X] is computed in the third line, X has been assigned the value of Y[X] in the previous line, and this will not assign Temp to the array Y subscripted at the original X.

The basic implementation technique consists of replacing each reference to a formal parameter with a call to a subprogram that evaluates a reference to the actual parameter in the appropriate environment. The main disadvantage of the pass by name is that it can easily lead to programs that are hard to read and understand. In addition, the burden of run-time calls to the called subprogram makes the call costly. Despite these disadvantages, pass by name can be a powerful mechanism in certain circumstances. One of the earliest examples is called Jensen's Device after its inventor J. Jensen. It uses the pass by name mechanism to apply an operation to an entire array. For example, the C program

```
#include <stdio.h>
main ( )
        {
        int Sum(int, int, int, int);
        int I=0, Total=0;
        int X[10] = {1, 2, 3, 4, 5, 6, 7, 8, 9, 10};
        Total = Sum(X, I, 0, 10);
        printf(" The sum of all elements is %d : ", Total);
        }
int   Sum(int A[ ], int Index, int Lower, int Upper)
        {
        int Temp = 0;
        for   (Index = Lower; Index < Upper; Index++)
              {
              Temp =Temp + A[Index];
              }
        return Temp;
        }
```

computes the sum of all the elements X[0] through X[9], if A and Index are pass by name parameters. The main objective of this mechanism is flexibility. For example, binding a variable to a type occurs at a later point in APL than it does in Fortran, which yields more flexibility of using variables. Recently, pass by name has enjoyed a resurgence of interest in functional programming languages, where it is called delayed evaluation, which we'll discuss shortly.

3.2.5 Parameter Passing by Result

If a parameter is transmitted by result, no value is passed to the called subprogram. In this method, the formal parameter acts as a local variable and does not receive a value on entry to its subprogram but, rather, is assigned a value during the subprogram execution, and just before control is transferred back to the calling subprogram, its value is passed back to the corresponding actual parameter. In other words, when the called subprogram terminates, the final value of the formal parameter is assigned as the new value of the actual parameter, just as in parameter passing by value. The sole purpose of parameter passing by result is to change something in the calling subprogram through called subprogram execution. For example, the C program

```
#include <stdio.h>
main ( )
      {
      void Init(int [ ], int, int);
      int Index, A[5];
      Init(A, 0, 5);
      For   (Index = 0; Index < 5; Index++)
            printf(" %d ", A[Index]);
      }
void  Init(int A[ ], int Lower, int Upper)
      {
      int I;
      for   (I = Lower; I < Upper; I++)
            X[I] = I * 2;
      }
```

computes the value of each element of the array as two times of the subscript of the array element (0, 2, 4, 6, and 8).

This mechanism provides an implementation for the *Out Mode* semantics model. This implementation requires local storage for the formal parameters, which are copied back to the actual parameters on exit from the called subprogram. Thus, we have the same storage and transfer disadvantages as for parameter passing by value. In this case, the address of the return value can be set either at the time of call or just before returning from the called subprogram. Consequently, the problem is to ensure that the initial value of the actual parameter is not used in the called subprogram. In addition, one problem with the passing parameter by result is that there can be an actual parameter collision, such as the one created with the call

```
Change(X, X);
```

In this case, whichever of the two formal parameters is assigned to their corresponding actual parameter last becomes the value of the actual parameter. This indicates that, the order in which the actual parameters are assigned determines their value. Because the order is usually implementation-dependent, portability problems can occur that are difficult to diagnose.

3.2.6   Parameter Passing by Value-Result

In pass by value-result, the actual parameters are initially copied into the formal parameters at the subprogram call and the formal parameters are eventually copied back to the location of the actual parameters upon termination of the called subprogram. This mechanism achieves a similar result to pass by reference, except that no actual alias is established (two expressions denoting the same location are said to be aliases for each other). For example, consider the following pseudocode:

```
(calling subprogram)
    {
    void Change(int);
    int A= 10;
    Change(A);
    printf(" %d ", A);
    }
(called subprogram)    Change(int X)
    {
    X = 5;
    A = 2;
    }
```

Variable A has value 5 after Change is called if pass by value-result is used, whereas A has the value 2 if pass by reference is used. In this case, as a reference parameter, X and A refer to the same address; hence, the value 2 is printed. For value-result, X is changed to 5 within the subprogram, and this value is passed back to actual parameter A upon completion; hence, 5 is printed. The passing parameter mechanism needs to be implemented to achieve the corresponding result. Pass by value-result is sometimes called *pass by copy* because the actual parameter is copied to the formal parameter at subprogram call and then copied back at subprogram termination. This mechanism provides an implementation for the *InOut Mode* semantics model. The implementation mechanism of parameter passing by value-result is the following:

1. Both the value and the locations of the actual parameters are computed (*In Mode*).

2. The value of actual parameters is assigned to the corresponding formal parameters and the locations are saved.

3. After the called subprogram is executed, the final values of the formal parameters are copied back to the actual parameter locations (*Out Mode*).

This mechanism is in effect a combination of pass by value and pass by result, indicating that it shares the disadvantage of requiring multiple storage for parameters and time for coping values. In addition, issues left unspecified by this mechanism, and possibly differing in different languages or implementations, are the order in which results are copied back to the actual parameters and whether the locations of the actual parameters are calculated only on entry and stored or whether they are recalculated on exit. In other words, this mechanism shares with pass by result the disadvantage associated with the order in which actual parameters are assigned.

3.3 EXCEPTIONS AND EXCEPTION HANDLING

In general, the events or conditions that a program encounters during its execution can be classified as either *expected,* when its execution produces an expected result, or *unexpected,* when its execution produces an unexpected result. An *exception* is any unexpected or infrequent event detectable either by hardware or software and that might require special attention. For example, assume that running some values of parameters can cause an illegal operation, which produces unexpected results. Typical examples of exceptions include run-time errors, disk read errors, out-of-range array subscripts, division by zero, or arithmetic overflow (when an integer is computed that is larger than can be supported by the particular hardware involved). For example, Pascal and Java compilers must generate code to check the correctness of every subscript expression. In C, subscript ranges are not checked because the cost of such checking was not believed to be worth the benefit of detecting such errors.

An exception is *raised* or *signaled* when its association event occurs. To distinguish the expected and unexpected events, programmers want to be able to divide the program into several units. In this case, the occurrence of an exception might implicitly transfer control to an appropriate unit, called an *exception handler,* that deals with that particular exception. In other words, an exception handler is a subprogram or code sequence that is designed to be run when a particular exception is raised and that is supposed to allow normal execution to resume. This indicates that programs are required to behave *reasonably* under a wide range of circumstances, even in the presence of a failure of the underlying hardware/software, or events that happen so infrequently that they are considered exceptions, or invalid input data. Raising an exception does not necessarily mean that we are in the presence of a *catastrophic* error but, rather, that the program is unable to proceed in a manner that leads to normal termination or a correct produced result.

Traditional programming languages (except PL/I) offer no special help in properly handling exceptions, or provide little help in dealing with exceptions. Perhaps the most important reason is the complexity handling exceptions impose to the language. In general, when an exception occurs, a standard system action is invoked. In this sense, the central issues raised by exception-handling schemes are the following:

- How is a user-defined exception specified, and what is its scope?

- How is an exception raised?

- How do we specify the units to be run when exceptions are raised?

- How is a raised exception bound to an exception handler?

- Are hardware-detectable errors treated as exceptions that can be handled?

- Should it be possible to disable exceptions?

- Where does control flow after an exception is transferred?

The implicit invocation of an exception is commonly referred to as *raising the exception.* Most languages provide a facility for explicitly invoking exceptions as well. This facility is in the general form of raising the exception consisting of the name of the exception. This kind of method permits the program virtually to raise a language-defined exception to invoke the exception handler at that specific point of the program execution. In addition to the language-defined exceptions provided by a language, the language may also permit user-defined exceptions. Such exceptions can be declared like any other data object and will exist within the scope of their declarations. In this case, user-defined exceptions must be raised explicitly because they have no associated condition. A subprogram that may raise the exception could be coded by introducing an additional return parameter (e.g., an integer) denoting an exception code (i.e., 0 indicating no exception, and 1 to address exception number one, and so on). In this case, the calling subprogram explicitly tests the exception code after each call and then transfers control to the appropriate exception handler. These exceptions must behave much like user-defined subprogram invocation and may even be permitted to accept parameters. The major difference between user-defined exceptions and user-defined subprograms lies in the flow of control on termination of the invoked subprogram. User-defined subprograms will always return to the statement immediately after the point of invocation, whereas an explicitly invoked subprogram exception handler may proceed differently, such as terminating program execution. In some situations, it may be desirable to ignore certain exceptions for a time. This could be done by disabling the exception. A disabled exception could be enabled again at a later time.

Example: One simple exception-handling mechanism is that provided by the BASIC programming language. For example, the statement

```
ON ERROR GOTO 100
```

transfers control to line number 100, if any error occurs. At line 100, an error handler is written, which ends with one of three following statements.

▶ RESUME: transfers control back to the beginning of the line where the error occurred.

▶ RESUME NEXT: transfers control to the line following the line where the error occurred.

▶ RESUME Line-Number: transfers control to the specified line number.

BASIC's exception handling is rudimentary because it lacks a number of features. Only one error handler can exist at any one time, only predefined errors can be handled, and no user-defined exceptions can be declared. Programming languages need more complex exception-handling mechanisms. Some programming languages with exception handling include Ada, C++, CLU-OOL, Eiffel, Java, Mesa, ML, and PL/I. There are advantages to having exception-handling mechanisms supported in a language:

▶ Without exceptions, handling the code required to detect unexpected events can considerably complicate a program. For example, suppose a subprogram includes expressions that contain five division operations, and each could have a zero division. In this case, without language-defined exceptions, each of these operations would have to be preceded by a selection construct to detect the possible division-by-zero error. In contrast, the presence of exception handling in the language could permit the compiler to insert such checks in the code when required by the programs.

▶ Exception-handling mechanisms allow a single exception handler to be used for a large number of different program units. For example, exception propagation allows an exception raised in one subprogram to be handled in some other subprogram with the same exception handler.

▶ With exceptions, a language encourages its users to consider all the events that could occur during program execution and how they can be handled. This is better than not considering such possibilities and simply hoping nothing will go wrong. For example, this is required by Ada to include multiple selector construct to support actions for all possible values of the control expression.

▶ Exception handling separates error-handling code from normal programming tasks, thus making programs easier to read and to modify. However, you should be aware that exception handling usually requires more time and resources because in some cases it requires propagating errors to the invoking subprogram.

3.3.1   Design and Implementation

A language might permit the enabling or disabling of exceptions. Whether these conditions are permitted is a philosophical decision that the language designer must decide. Suppressing an exception through disabling might be valuable when testing for the exception is expensive in time and space and the value of the resulting reliability is not worth that cost to the programmer. Indexed-bound testing for arrays is an example of an exception whose cost might exceed its value in some circumstances. In these cases, some languages permit specified exceptions to be disabled during a subprogram activation. This suppression occurs at compile time and prevents the generation of the code needed to implement the exception. In general, each exception handler is a block of statements that is bound to an exception. For language-defined exceptions, the name binding is a permanent part of the language. In contrast, user-defined exceptions are bound to their name at the point of declaration, and that binding holds within the scope of that declaration. The binding of the exception to its exception handler is either one of two following models:

▶ The exception handler block is bound to the exception in the scope of a subprogram through a declaration attached to that subprogram. This is illustrated in the following pseudocode, in which exceptions are declared and are separately assigned handlers in the declaration section of the subprogram. In this model, binding a handler to an exception holds throughout the scope of the subprogram.

```
Subprogram   A
   E₁, E₂ : Exception
   Exception Handler E₁ is
      { H₁    block-of-statements    }
   Exception Handler E₂ is
      { H₂    block-of-statements    }
   Subprogram   B
```

```
            E₁, E₃ : Exception
            Exception Handler E₁ is
                { H₃    block-of-statements    }
            Exception Handler E₃ is
                { H₄    block-of-statements    }
        begin
           { block-of-statements    }
           E₁ Exception-Handler is H₃
           E₂ Exception-Handler is H₂
           E₃ Exception-Handler is H₄
        End; B
    begin
       { block-of-statements    }
       E₁ Exception-Handler is H₁
       E₂ Exception-Handler is H₂
       Subprogram B
    End; A
```

In this design choice, the exception handler is embedded in the subprogram that raises the exception; thus, it simplifies communication between the two subprograms. In this model, the exception handler for exception E_1 is redeclared in subprogram B, introducing a new exception handler for the H_1 handler within B. Here, we see that the name binding E_1 holds through A, although the handler binding changes within B. This model of exception handling is implemented in Ada.

▶ In this model, the exception handler is a separate subprogram outside the scope of the subprogram that can raise its associated exception; thus, communication can be through parameters. The exception handler binding is based on the data object value binding, in which statements run within the subprogram can modify the exception. This is illustrated in the following pseudocode, in which the exception handler is bound to the exception by an executable statement. The statement we provide to do this, *Bind Exception-Handler,* acts much like an assignment statement by binding an exception handler to an exception at run time.

```
Subprogram    A
    E₁, E₂ : Exception
    Subprogram    B
        E₃ : Exception
    begin
    E₁ Exception-Handler is H₁ (first call) or H₄ (second call)
    E₂ Exception-Handler is H₂ (first call) or H₅ (second call)
        Bind Exception-Handler E₃ to
            { H₃    block-of-statements    }
    E₃ Exception-Handler is H₃
    End; B
begin
    Bind Exception-Handler E₁ to
    { H₁    block-of-statements    }
```

```
    E₁ Exception-Handler is H₁
    Bind Exception-Handler E₂ to
    { H₂    block-of-statements    }
    E₂ Exception-Handler is H₂
    Subprogram B
    E₁ Exception-Handler is H₄
    Bind Exception-Handler E₂ to
    { H₅    block-of-statements    }
    E₂ Exception-Handler is H₅
    Subprogram B
End; A
```

In this example, exceptions E_1 and E_2 have different initial bindings for the first and second call of subprogram B.

After an exception has been raised and the corresponding exception handler has been carried out, either control can transfer to somewhere in the program outside of the handler code or program execution can simply be terminated. This environment, under which execution continues after exception, is called the *continuation of the exception*. The two approaches to deal with the continuation of the exception are as follows:

▶ **Resumption model:** Resume the subprogram execution that invoked the exception. In this case, after running the appropriate exception handler, control is returned back to the subprogram where the exception was raised. In such a case, the exception handler can perform some repairs, so that normal execution can continue. There are two alternatives in this approach: re-run the statement that caused the exception occurred in subprogram, or resume running at the statement immediately following the statement that caused the exception occurred. The implementation is thus powerful and flexible. Nevertheless, it can promote the unsafe programming practice of removing the symptom of an error without removing the cause. For example, the exception raised for an unacceptable value of an operand could be handled by arbitrarily generating an acceptable value. The choice to return to the statement that raised the exception might seem like a good one, but in the case of an error exception, it is only useful if the handler somehow is able to modify the values or operations that caused the exception to be raised. Otherwise, the exception would simply be reraised. The required modification for an error exception is often very difficult. This implementation has been adopted by PL/I and Mesa.

▶ **Termination model:** Terminate the subprogram execution that invoked the exception and return to the calling environment. This solution consists of terminating the execution of the subprogram that raises the exception and then transferring control to the exception handler. Accordingly, this implementation means that the action that raised the exception cannot be resumed, indicating that the execution of the raising subprogram can be deleted. Termination is obviously the simplest choice, and in many error exception conditions, it is the best. Bliss, CLU, ML, and Ada adopted this simpler scheme.

Binding exceptions to exception handlers and continuing execution is illustrated in Figure 3.1.

FIGURE **3.1**   Exception handling flow of control

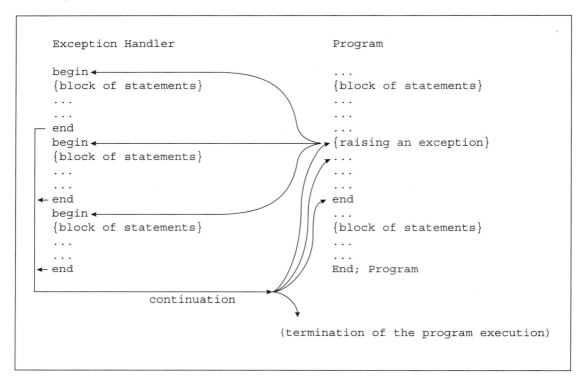

A related issue is raising an exception for which no exception handler is defined. In this case, there might be a default exception handler associated with every exception whose exception handler has not been explicitly defined. We will now examine exception-handling features provided by PL/I, Ada, ML, C++, and Java as representative of this trend, using an example of each.

3.3.2   Exception Handling in PL/I, Ada, ML, C++, and Java

PL/I pioneered the concept of allowing user programs to be directly involved in exception handling. The language provides exception handlers for a list of language-defined exceptions. After PL/I, a substantial amount of work has been done to design alternative methods of exception handling. In particular, Mesa (Mitchell, Maybury, & Sweet, 1979), Ada and Common LISP (Steele, 1984), Modula-3 and C++ (Cardelli et al., 1989), ML (Milner, Tofte, & Harper, 1990), and Java (Liang, 1998) include exception-handling facilities. In the following, we examine the exception-handling facilities of programming languages PL/I, Ada, ML, C++, and Java.

Exception Handling in PL/I

PL/I provides built-in exceptions and allows users to define their own exceptions. In PL/I, the exception is called CONDITION, and the exception handler is declared by ON statement with the following syntax.

```
ON CONDITION    Begin
 . . .
End;
```

where CONDITION is the exception name and Begin . . . End; can be a simple statement or a block of statements for exception handler. Then, the statement can explicitly raise an exception:

```
SIGNAL CONDITION;
```

The PL/I provides 22 conditions for abnormal events such as overflow, conversion errors, dividing by zero, and so forth. When an exception is encountered during execution, the flow of control is transferred to exception handler. Once this association is established, it remains valid until it is overridden by running another exception, or until termination of the block in which the ON statement is carried out. The language also provides a number of predefined exceptions and predefined exception handlers for them. For example, ZERODIVIDE exception is raised when a divide by zero is attempted.

Example: When the following code runs, the first statement would assign to DATA the value −9999 whenever an attempt was made to divide by zero (the ZERODIVIDE exception is raised). In the second part, a message is printed and the MOREDATA flag is set when the input is at the end of the file.

```
ON ZERODIVIDE DATA := −9999;
ON ENDFILE(SYSIN)
BEGIN
PUT PAGE LIST('END OF PRINTING');
MOREDATA = 'NO';
END;
```

We can also raise an exception such as

```
IF DATA < 0.0001 THEN SIGNAL ZERODIVDE;
```

where the exception handler associated with ZERODIVIDE would be invoked whenever the variable DATA became less than 0.0001 and DATA would then be assigned the value −9999.

Continuation of the Exception in PL/I

In PL/I, different exceptions provide different continuation schemes. For some exceptions, execution returns to the statement that caused the exception, other exceptions cause program termination. User-defined handlers can cause control to be passed to any part of the program after handling an exception, but there is no mechanism to transfer the control to the statement that caused the exception. In general, the PL/I continuation design is often confusing for programmers.

Exception Handling in Ada

Ada provides five predefined exceptions, which are listed with a brief description:

1. The CONSTRAINT_ERROR exception is raised if constraints are violated, such as exceeding array bounds, a variant record component not being available under the current values, or an access value being unreachable.

2. The NUMERIC_ERROR exception is raised if the result of a numeric operation is outside the range of its type or is attempting to divide a number by zero.

3. The PROGRAM_ERROR exception is raised when an unavailable subprogram is invoked.

4. The STORAGE_ERROR exception is raised when storage that is dynamically allocated is not available; memory is exhausted.

5. The TASKING_ERROR exception is raised when an error occurs during the concurrent running tasks; when two or more tasks attempt unsuccessfully to communicate.

In addition, user-defined exceptions are also provided, in which their declaration is similar to that of any other data object, with the data type name being *exception*. In this case, user-defined exceptions must be raised explicitly by a *raise* statement. Predefined exceptions can be raised explicitly through a *raise* statement, in addition to being raised implicitly through the occurrence of that particular exception.

Example: The following Ada block illustrates a language-defined and a user-defined exception named NUMERIC_ERROR and Singular, respectively.

```
Block:
declare
   I, J, K:   INTEGER;
   Singular:  exception;   -- declare user-defined exception
begin
   I : = J * K;   -- overflow could cause NUMERIC_ERROR
   if Result = 0 then raise Singular;
                  -- user-defined exception is raised
exception
   when NUMERIC_ERROR  =>   -- deal with NUMER_ERROR
   when Singular  =>   -- deal with Singular exception
end Block;
```

When an exception is raised in Ada, the exception handler for the exception in the current subprogram is executed, after which the subprogram is terminated, indicating that Ada follows the termination model for exceptions. The designers of Ada extended the exception mechanism in two ways. First, one can define, raise, and handle exceptions. Second, exceptions may be propagated through the dynamic chain of execution path until a handler is found. This happens if the subprogram has no exception part, or if no exception handler for the exception exists; the subprogram is exited and the exception is reraised in the controlling subprogram in the execution path. In other words, execution continues down the dynamic chain, going from each subprogram to its caller, until the execution path finds an environment that defines an exception handler for the exception. In this respect, exceptions are bound dynamically, although, all other names in Ada are bound statically.

Example: In the following code, Block begins running by calling the function X, where an exception called E is raised in the execution of the function. Because X has no exception handler for E, X is terminated and control is returned to Block. This indicates that E is propagated to Block, its exception handler deals with the exception, and execution continues at the code marked as *continue Block*. In this example, the exception is handled by Block because X was called from Block. Of course, the exception handler for E could have been included at the end of the function X itself, where it would always be handled in the same way.

```
Block:
declare
   A:    INTEGER;
   Function X return Integer is
   E:    exception;   -- declare user-defined exception
   B:    INTEGER;
   begin
      . . .
         raise E;   -- user-defined exception is raised
      . . .
         return B;
   end X;
begin
   A := X;   -- function X is called
   . . .      -- continue Block
   exception
      when E   =>   -- deal with exception E
      put (" Something is Wrong ");
      return 0;
   end exception;
end Block;
```

In the case of a user-defined exception, the system cannot automatically raise the exception, and the exception must be raised manually using raise statement.

Continuation of the Exception in Ada

After an exception handler has run, the block that raises an exception and all blocks to which the exception was propagated are always terminated. In this case, control never returns implicitly to the raising block after the exception is handled. Control simply continues at the end of a block, which causes an immediate return to a higher level of control.

Exception Handling in ML

In ML, we may also define our own exceptions and raise them in program when an exceptional condition is discovered. The simplest form of an exception declaration is

```
exception Winput;
```

where `Winput` is declared to be the name of an exception. In the definition of a function F, we can use an expression

```
raise Winput
```

to raise exception `Winput` when we find an erroneous input or other condition that we associate in our mind with `Winput`. In this case, if function F raises exception `Winput` during the running of a program, then F returns no value. Rather, ML will terminate execution and print the following message:

```
uncaught exception Winput
```

Example: Consider a function `Comb(n, m)` that computes $\binom{n}{m}$. The program will not behave correctly in situations where either n is negative or m is outside of the range 0 to n. One approach to the problem is to define some exceptions and raise them when the input is improper. In this case, we begin by defining two exceptions, `WrongN` and `WrongM`. These exceptions are used to check for the erroneous input possibilities. When carried out, the expressions, `raise WrongN` and `raise WrongM` cause the function `Comb` to terminate abnormally, without returning an integer.

```
exception WrongN, WrongM;
fun   Comb(n, m) =
   if n < 0 then raise WrongN
   else   if m < 0 orelse m > n then raise WrongM
      else   if m = 0 orelse m = n then 1
         else Comb(n-1, m) + Comb(n-1, m-1);
```

The first call of the function

```
Comb(5, 2);
```

returns an integer 10, normally. The second call of the function

```
Comb(-1, 0);
```

returns `uncaught exception WrongN`, indicating that an exception is raised and the function `Comb` does not return an integer. The third call

```
Comb(5, 6);
```

returns `uncaught exception WrongM`, indicating that an exception is raised and the function Comb does not return an integer. Raising an uncaught exception always terminates computation. We might prefer that when an exception is raised, there is an attempt to produce an appropriate value and continue the computation. In this case, we may use an expression of the form

```
<expression>   handle   <match>
```

to help in this process. Here, the <expression> is one in which we consider that one or more exceptions may be raised. The <match> takes exceptions as patterns and associates them with expressions of the same type as <expression>. If <expression> produces a value *v* and does not raise an exception, then the <match> is not applied to *v*, and *v* is the result of the *handle* expression. However, if <expression> raises an exception, perhaps with arguments, then the <match> is applied. The first pattern that matches the exception causes its associated expression to be evaluated, and this value becomes the value of the *handle* expression. If none of the patterns match, then the exception is uncaught at this point. The exception may be handled by another, surrounding handle expression, or it may remain uncaught, propagated to the top level, and result in termination of the computation.

Example: Let us reconsider the function Comb(n, m), where we attempted to compute $\binom{n}{m}$ and catch situations where n≤0, m<0, or m>n. In this example, our only response when we found an error in the arguments was to raise one of two exceptions, BadN and BadM, and cause computation to halt.

```
Exception OutOfRange of int*int;
fun   CombX(n, m) =
   if n ≤ 0 then raise OutOfRange(n, m)
   else if m < 0 orelse m > n then raise OutOfRange(n, m)
   else if m = 0 orelse m = n then 1
   else CombX(n-1, m) + CombX(n-1, m-1);
fun   Comb(n, m) = CombX(n, m)    handle
   OutOfRange(0, 0) => 1 |
   OutOfRange(n, m) => (
       print(" Out Of Range: n = ");
       print(Int.toString(n));
       print(" m = ");
       print(Int.toString(m));
       print(" \n ");
       0   );
```

With regard to this example, the first call of the function

```
Comb(4, 2);
```

returns an integer 6, normally. The second call of the function

```
Comb(3, 4);
```

raises the exception OutOfRange(3, 4) with the following messages

```
Out Of Range: n = 3 m = 4
```

and returns 0. This integer is the value returned by Comb because 0 is the last expression. The third call of the function

```
Comb(0, 0);
```

raises an exception where the OutOfRange(0, 0) is matched and the value 1 is produced.

Continuation of the Exception in ML

After an exception handler is carried out, the control returns to the statement that an exception is raised. The normal action in ML is to terminate the function, but if a handler is provided, the exception handler is run, and flow of control returns to the point of the error.

Exception Handling in C++

The exception-handling features provided in C++ enable programmers to write clearer, more robust, and more fault-tolerant programs. The design is similar to that of the exception handling of Ada and ML: Binding exceptions to handlers is static, and unhandled exceptions are propagated to the caller. But in other ways, the C++ design is quite different: There are no built-in hardware-detectable exceptions that can be handled by the user, and exceptions are not named. This leads to the design issue that exceptions are connected to handlers through a parameter type. Also, exceptions cannot be disabled. The style of exception handling presented here is based on the work of Andrew Koenig (Koenig & Stroustrup, 1990). C++'s exception-handling features enable the programmers to remove the error-handling code from the main program, which improves program readability and modifiability. The C++ style of exception handling allows programmers to handle all kinds of exceptions, to handle all exceptions of a certain type, or to handle all exceptions of related types. C++ exception handling is designed for situations where the function that detects an error is unable to deal with it. Such a function will *throw* (raise) an exception, but there is no guarantee that an exception handler will be specifically defined to process that kind of exception. If there is, the exception will be *caught* (handled) by exception handler. If there is no exception handler for that particular kind of exception, the program terminates. C++ uses a special construct that is introduced with the reserved word *try*. A *try* construct includes a compound statement called the *try block* and a list of exception handlers defined with reserved word *catch*. The compound statement in *try block* is expected to raise an exception, and the *catch block*, treated as a function, is expected to handle each exception. A *catch* function can have only a single formal parameter. When information about the exception is to be passed to the exception handler, the parameter includes a type name and a variable name that is used for that purpose. The general form of the *try block* and *catch* functions is as follows:

```
try   {
( statements that are expected to raise an exception )
}
catch (single parameter)   {
( exception handler code )
}
   . . .
catch (single parameter)   {
( exception handler code )
}
```

where the exception handlers for a *try* block are listed immediately following the *try* block. Each exception handler starts with the keyword *catch* followed by parentheses containing a type (indicating the type of exception that *catch* function handles) and an optional parameter name. This is followed by braces to specify the exception-handling code. When an exception is raised, the code in the *catch* block is carried out. The C++ exception-handling method is based on two features:

▶   Throwing an exception

▶   Catching an exception

The keyword *throw* is used to indicate that an exception has occurred; the general form of throwing an exception is

```
throw[expression];
```

where the brackets are used to specify that the expression is optional. A *throw* without an operand can only appear in an exception handler to address that the handler reraises the exception, in which it is then handled elsewhere. A *throw* normally specifies one operand (parameter). The operand of *throw* can be of any type, and it selects the particular handler, which must have a matching type with formal parameter. If the operand is an object, we call it an *exception object*. The exception will be handled by the closest exception handler (*catch* function), indicating that control exits the current *try* block and proceeds to an appropriate *catch* function (if one exists). The exception handler can be in a deeply nested scope within a *try* block; control will still proceed to the *catch* function. The exception handler can also be in a deeply nested function call; control will still proceed to the handler. As part of throwing an exception, a temporary copy of the *throw* operand is created and initialized. This object then initializes the parameter in the exception handler. The temporary object is destroyed when the exception handler completes execution and exits. If the parameter in *throw* is unnamed—that is, only a type is listed for purposes of matching with the thrown object type—then information is not conveyed from the thrown point to the handler and control only passes from the thrown point to the handler. An exception whose thrown object type matches the type of the argument in the *catch* header causes the *catch* block, the exception handler for exceptions of that type, to execute. In this case, the *catch* handler is the first one listed after the currently active *try* block that matches the type of the thrown object.

Example: The following program illustrates using the *try, throw,* and *catch* features to detect a division by zero, to address a divide-by-zero exception, and to handle exceptions.

```
#include <iostream>
using std::cout;
using std::cin;
using std::endl;
  // class DivideByZeroException to be used in exception handling
  // for raising an exception on a division by zero.
class DivideByZeroException {
public:
```

```
      DivideByZeroException( )
         : message( " attempted to divide by zero " ) { }
      const char *what( ) const { return message; }
private:
   const char *message;
};
   // definition of function quotient, illustrating raising an exception
   // when a divide-by-zero exception is encountered.
double quotient (int numerator, int denominator )
{
   if (denominator == 0)
      throw DivideByZeroException( );
   return static_cast< double > (numerator) / denominator;
}
int main( )
{
   int number1, number2;
   double result;
   cout << " Enter two integers (end-of-file to end): ";
   while (cin >> number1 >> number2 ) {
   // the try block associates the code that may raise an exception and
   // the code that should not be executed if the exception occurs
      try   {
         result = quotient (number1, number2 );
         cout << " The quotient is: "<< result << endl;
      }
      catch ( DivideByZeroException ex ) {    // exception handler
         cout << " Exception occurred: " << ex.what( ) << " \n ";
      }

      cout << " \n Enter two integers (end-of-file to end):";
   }
   cout << endl;
   return 0;    // terminates normally
}
```

In this example, the program contains a try block, which provides the code that may raise an exception. Note that the actual division that may cause the exception is not explicitly listed inside the *try* block; instead, the call to function quotient contains the code that attempts the actual division. Function quotient actually raises the divide-by-zero exception. The *try* block is immediately followed by a catch block containing the exception handler for the divide-by-zero exception. The catch block specifies that it will handle exception objects of type DivideByZeroException, which matches the type of the object thrown in function quotient. The body of this exception handler prints the error message returned by calling function. A sample output of this program execution is as the following:

```
Enter two integers (end-of-file to end): 100 7
The quotient is: 14.2857

Enter two integers (end-of-file to end): 100 0
Exception occurred: attempted to divide by zero

Enter two integers (end-of-file to end): 33 9
The quotient is: 3.66667

Enter two integers (end-of-file to end):
```

Continuation of the Exception in C++

After an exception handler is carried out, control flows to the first statement following the *try* construct, meaning the statement immediately after the last exception handler in the *try* block. An exception handler may reraise an exception, using a *throw* without an expression, in which case, that exception is propagated to the caller.

Exception Handling in Java

Java's exception-handling mechanism is based on that of C++, but it is designed to be more within the concept of object-oriented programming. Java provides exception-handling features to respond to exceptional situations so that the program can continue its normal execution. A Java exception is an instance of a class derived from the Throwable class. The Throwable class is contained in the Java.lang package, and subclasses of Throwable are contained in various packages. For example, numeric exceptions are included in the Java.lang package because they are related to the Java.lang.Number class. Figure 3.2 shows some pre-defined exception classes in Java.

The Error class and its descendants are related to errors that are raised by the Java interpreter, such as running out of heap memory. These exceptions are never raised by user programs, and they should never be handled there. If such an error occurs, there is little you can do beyond notifying the user and trying to terminate the program gracefully. The Exception class describes the errors caused by your program and external circumstances. These errors can be caught and handled by your program. IOException, one of the direct descendants of Exception class, is raised when an error has occurred in an input or output operation, all exception handlers are defined as methods in the various classes defined in the package `java.io`. The `RuntimeException` class describes programming errors such as bad casting, accessing an out-of-bound array, and numeric errors. Examples of the subclasses of `RuntimeException` are `ArithmeticException`, `NullPointerException`, `IllegalArgumentException`, `ArrayStoreException`, and `IndexOutOfBoundsException`. You can create your own exception classes by extending Throwable or a subclass of Throwable. The convention in Java is that user-defined exceptions are subclasses of Exception. The exception-handling model in Java is based on three operations:

► Claiming an exception

► Throwing an exception

► Catching an exception

FIGURE **3.2** Pre-defined exception classes in Java

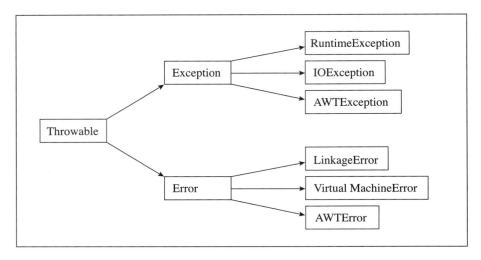

In Java, the statement currently being run belongs to a method; the statement be-longs either to `main( )` or to a method invoked by another method. In general, every method must state the types of exceptions it can encounter. This process is called *claiming an exception* and simply tells the compiler what possibly can go wrong. To claim an exception in a method, you use the *throws* keyword in the method declara-tion, as in the following:

```
public void myMethod( ) throws IOException
```

where the `throws` keyword indicates that `myMethod( )` might raise an exception named `IOException`. If the method might raise multiple exceptions, you can add a list of the exceptions, separated by commas after *throws:*

```
MethodDeclaration throws Exception₁, Exception₂, . . . , Exception_N
```

When a statement causes errors, the method containing the statement creates an exception object and passes it to the system. The exception object contains informa-tion about the exception, including its type and the state of the program when the error occurred. This process is called *throwing an exception.* The following is the syn-tax for raising an exception:

```
throw new TheException( );
```

Or, if you prefer, you can use the following:

```
TheException e = new TheException( );
throw e;
```

The keyword to claim an exception is *throws,* and the keyword to raise an excep-tion is *throw.* After a method raises an exception, the Java run-time system begins the process of finding the code to handle the error (exception handler) by searching backward through a chain of method calls, starting from the current method. The handler must match the type of exception raised. If no such handler is found, the program terminates. This process of finding a handler is called *catching an exception.* We use the try-catch block to specify the exception handlers as shown in the following:

```
try
{
   ( statements that may raise exceptions )
}
catch    (Exception₁ e)
{   handler for Exception₁   }
catch    (Exception₂ e)
{   handler for Exception₂   }
   . . .
catch    (Exceptionₙ e)
{   handler for Exceptionₙ   }
```

If no exception arises during the execution of the `try` block statements, the `catch` blocks are skipped. If one of the statements inside the `try` block raises an exception, Java skips the remaining statements of the `try` block and starts to search for a handler for the exception. If the exception type matches one listed in a `catch` block, the code in the `catch` block is carried out. If the exception type does not match any exception in the `catch` blocks, Java exits this method (called method) and passes the exception to the method that invoked this method (calling method) and continues the same process to find a handler. If no handler is found in the chain of the calling methods, the program terminates and prints an error message on the screen.

Example: This example demonstrates catching exceptions, using the Rational class. The class provides constructors and addition, subtraction, multiplication, and division methods. A rational number is a number with numerator and a denominator in the form X/Y, where X is a numerator and Y is a denominator; for example ⅓, ¾, and ¹⁰⁄₄. A rational number cannot have a denominator of 0, but a numerator of 0 is fine. The program follows.

```
public   class   TestRationalException
{   public static void main (String[ ] args)
   {   Rational r1 = new Rational(4, 2);
      Rational r2 = new Rational(2, 3);
      Rational r3 = new Rational(0, 1);
      try
      {   System.out.Println(r1+ " + " + r2 + " = " + r1.add(r2));
         System.out.Println(r1+ " - " + r2 + " = " + r1.subtract(r2));
         System.out.Println(r1+ " * " + r2 + " = " + r1.multiply(r2));
         System.out.Println(r1+ " / " + r2 + " = " + r1.divide(r2));
         System.out.Println(r1+ " / " + r3 + " = " + r1.divide(r3));
      }
```

```
            catch (Exception e)
            {   System.out.Println(e); }
            System.out.Println(r1+ " - " + r2 + " = " + r1.subtract(r2));
    }
}
class   Rational
{   private   long numer, denom;
    Rational(long n, long d)
    {   long k = gcd(n, d);
        numer = n/k;
        denom = d/k;    }
    Rational( )
    { this(0, 1);    }
    private long gcd(long n, long d)
    {   long t1 = Math.abs(n);
        long t2 = Math.abs(d);
        long remainder = t1%t2;
        while (remainder != 0)
        {   t1 = t2;
            t2 = remainder;
            remainder = t1%t2;    }
        return t2;
    }
    public   long numerator( )
    {   return numer;    }
    public   long denominator( )
    {   return denom;    }
    public Rational add(Rational r)
    {   long n = numer * r.denom + denom * r.numer;
    long d = denom * r.denom;
    return new Rational(n, d);    }
    public Rational subtract(Rational r)
    {   long n = numer * r.denom - denom * r.numer;
        long d = denom * r.denom;
        return new Rational(n, d);    }
    public Rational multiply(Rational r)
    {   long n = numer * r.numer;
        long d = denom * r.denom;
        return new Rational(n, d);    }
    public Rational divide(Rational r)
    {   long n = numer * r.denom;
        long d = denom * r.numer;
        return new Rational(n, d);    }
    public   String toString( )
    {   return numer + "/ " + denom;    }
}
```

To reduce a rational number to its lowest terms, you need to find the greatest common divisor (GCD) of the absolute values of its numerator and denominator, then divide both numerator and denominator by this value. Here is the classic Euclid's algorithm for finding the great common divisor of two integer values X and Y.

```
t1 <- abs(X);    // get absolute value of X and Y
t2 <- abs(Y);
r = t1 % t2;     // r is the remainder of t1 and t2
while (r != 0)
{    t1 = t2;
t2 = r;
r = t1 % t2;    }
// when r is 0, t2 is the common divisor between t1 and t2
return t2;
```

The program creates two rational numbers, r1 and r2, to test numeric methods (add( ), subtract( ), multiply( ), and divide( )) on rational numbers. Invoking the divide( ) method with divisor 0 causes the method to raise an exception object. In the catch block, the type of the object e is *Exception(catch Exception e)*, which matches the object raised by the divide( ) method. So the catch block catches this exception. The exception handler simply prints a short message about the exception using System.out.Println(e). A sample output that the exception raises when the divisor is zero is the following:

```
2/1 + 2/3 = 8/3
2/1 - 2/3 = 4/3
2/1 * 2/3 = 4/3
2/1 / 2/3 = 3/1
java.lang.ArithmeticException: / by zero
```

In this example, the main class creates two rational numbers, r1 and r2, and displays the results of r1+r2, r1−r2, r1*r2, and r1/r2. The rational number is encapsulated in a rational object. Internally, a rational number is represented in its lowest terms, which is the greatest common divisor between the numerator and denominator. The gcd( ) method as a private method is only for internal use by the Rational class. The abs(X) method is defined in the Math class that returns the absolute value of X. The equation r1+r2 is called in the form of r1.add(r2), which returns

(r1.numer*r2.denom+r1.denom*r1.numer) / (r1.denom*r2.denom).

The numerator data field of the object r1 is r1.numer and the denominator data field of object r1 is r1.denom. The return value of r1+r2 is a new rational object. Note that the execution continues in the event of the zero denominator. If the handlers had not caught the exception, the program would have terminated.

Continuation of the Exception in Java

After an exception handler is carried out, flow of execution continues with the statement following the try construct. If no exception handler is found, the handlers of enclosing `try` constructs are searched, innermost first. If no handler is found in this process, the exception is propagated to the caller of the method. If the method call was in a `try` block, the search for a handler continues in the attached collection of handlers in the block. Propagation continues until the original caller is found, which is the *main* function. Finally, if no matching handler is found anywhere, the program is terminated.

3.4 EXPRESSIONS

Expressions are formed from operators and operands. **Operators** are known as functions, and **operands** are known as arguments or parameters. Operators can be classified as *predefined* or *user-defined* and can have one or more operands. An operator that takes one operand is called a *monadic* or *unary* operator, and an operator that takes two operands is known as a *dyadic* or *binary* operator. For example, in −a + b + c, the + is a binary operator because it applies to two operands a and b, and − is a unary operator because it applies only to one operand a. **Functions** are another form of operator, but they can have different numbers of operands.

3.4.1 Expression Notations

Expressions are composed of various fundamental forms: infix, prefix, postfix, and mixfix. We consider notations along with certain attributes useful in the design of programming languages. Prefix and postfix notations are sometimes called parenthesis-free because operations can be performed without the operands being enclosed in parentheses. In other words, in prefix and postfix notations, the operands of each operator can be found unambiguously, without the need for parentheses.

Infix Notation

In **infix notation,** the operator symbol appears between the operands and has the following syntax.

```
Operand₁    Operator    Operand₂
```

The infix notation has been widely adopted for use with most programming languages. For example, 3*2 is in the infix notation where the operands of * are 3 and 2, respectively. But how can the expression 5−3*2+4 be evaluated? Is the result the value of (5−3)*(2+4), is it the result of 5−(3*2)+4, or is it the result of 5−(3*2+4)? Expression evaluation rules, which we discuss shortly, answer these questions. In general, an operator at a higher precedence level takes its operands before an operator at a lower precedence level. Parentheses may be used to specify precisely the grouping of operators and operands as (5−3)*(2+4), indicating that (5−3) and (2+4) are the operands of the operator *. An expression can be represented by a tree, with

▶ Each internal node corresponding to an operator

▶ Each external node (terminal or leaf) corresponding to an operand

FIGURE **3.3**   Tree representation for expression (5–3)*(2+4)

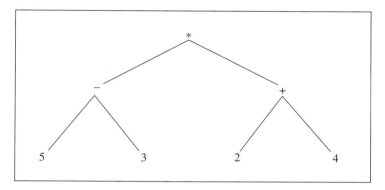

For example the tree representation of (5–3)*(2+4) is shown in Figure 3.3, where two internal nodes correspond to the operators – and + and four external nodes correspond to the operands 5, 3, 2, and 4. Infix evaluation corresponds to an in-order traversal of the tree representation of the expression.

In general, the infix notation is suitable for binary operations. Infix notation with implicit precedence and associativity rules and explicit use of parentheses provides a natural representation for most arithmetic, relational, and logical expressions. Here are some examples of infix notation:

```
(10+20)*40  =  30 * 40  =  1200
2 + 3 * 5 + 8 = 2 + 15 + 8 = 25
(20 / 10) + (2 * 5) = 12
```

Prefix Notation

In **prefix notation**—also known as *Polish Prefix* in honor of Polish mathematician Jan Lukasiewicz, who invented this notation—the operator appears before the operands and has the following syntax.

```
Operator    Operand₁    Operand₂
```

Prefix notation is read from left to right; that is, the next term after the operator is the first operand and the term after the first term is the second operand of the operator. If an operand is itself an operation with operands, the same rule applies. For example, the expression (5–3)*(2+4) can be represented as * – 5 3 + 2 4. The – operator requires two operands, 5 and 3. Similarly, the operands for + are 2 and 4, and the operands for * are the (5–3) and (2+4) subexpressions. This notation is parenthesis-free.

A variant of prefix notation used in the LISP programming language is *Cambridge Polish* notation, in which all operators and operands must be enclosed in parentheses. For instance, the expression (5–3)*(2+4) with * – 5 3 + 2 4 in Polish Prefix becomes (* (– 5 3) (+ 2 4)) in Cambridge Polish notation. Similarly, 4+5*2 and

(4+5)*2 can be expressed as $(+\ 4\ (*\ 5\ 2))$ and $(*\ (+\ 4\ 5)\ 2)$, respectively. The reason is that, in LISP, operations can apply to a variable number of operands. An example of a user-defined prefix notation is `read(x)` and `max(x,y)`, in which the operators are written first and the operands are enclosed in parentheses and, as in the latter case, are separated by a comma. Although prefix notation generally does not require the use of parentheses, you need to know the required number of operands for each operator. However, that's difficult to determine when user-defined operations are involved. Here are some examples in prefix notation:

```
*  +  10  20  40  =  *  30  40  =  1200
*  20  +  25  15  =  *  20  40  =  800
+  /  20  10  *  2  5  =  +  2  *  2  5  =  +  2  10  =  12
*  15  +  2  *  -  10  8  *  2  5  =  *  15  +  2  *  2  10  =  *  15  +  2  20  =  *  15  22  =  330
```

In general, the decoding of prefix notation extends to operators with a fixed number $k \geq 0$ of operands. The application of an operator Op^k of $k \geq 0$ to $E_1, E_2, \ldots E_k$ is written in prefix notation as $Op^k\ E_1\ E_2\ \ldots E_k$. During a left-to-right decoding, the ith expression to the right of Op^k is the ith operand of Op^k, for $1 \leq i \leq k$.

Postfix Notation

In **postfix notation,** also known as *Suffix* or *Reverse Polish* notation, the operator appears after the list of operands and has the following syntax:

```
Operand₁    Operand₂    Operator
```

For example, the expression $(5-3)*(2+4)$ can be represented as $5\ 3\ -\ 2\ 4\ +\ *$, where the operator symbol follows the list of operands. Postfix corresponds to a postorder traversal of the tree representation of the expression. In postfix notation, when an operator is examined, its operands have already been evaluated, making the evaluation strategy straightforward and easy to implement. An advantage of postfix expressions is that they can be evaluated by use of a stack data structure. Here are some examples in Postfix notation.

```
10  20  +  40  *  =  30  40  *  =  1200
20  25  15  +  *  =  20  40  *  =  800
20  10  /  2  5  *  +  =  2  2  5  *  +  =  2  10  +  =  12
2  10  8  -  2  5  *  *  +  15  *  =  2  2  10  *  +  15  *  =  2  20  +  15  *  =  22  15  *  =  330
```

In general, the decoding of postfix notation extends to operators with a fixed number $k \geq 0$ of operands. The application of an operator Op^k of $k \geq 0$ to $E_1, E_2, \ldots E_k$ is written in postfix notation as $E_k \ldots E_2\ E_1\ Op^k$. During a right-to-left decoding, the ith expression to the left of Op^k is the ith operand of Op^k, for $1 \leq i \leq k$.

Mixfix Notation

In **mixfix notation,** the operations are defined as a combination of prefix, postfix, and infix notations. For example,

```
if    condition    then    expression₁    else    expression₂
```

FIGURE **3.4**   Tree representation of the expression A*B+5*C*D

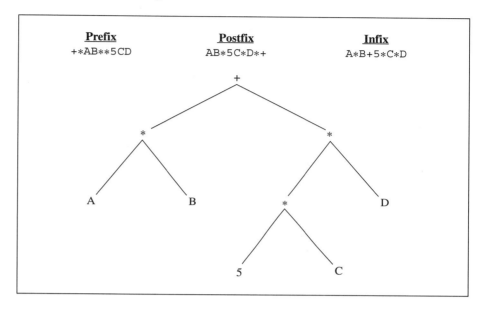

specifies a mixfix notation containing a condition, condition, and two expressions, expression$_1$ and expression$_2$. If condition evaluates to true, expression$_1$ is the evaluated value of the if statement; otherwise, it is expression$_2$. Here are some examples in Mixfix notation:

```
if      a > b
        then    a=2*5
        else    b=3*5

while (a > b)
        a=b*5

for (a=2*5;    a < 10;    a=a+1)
        b=b*5
```

In summary, the expression A*B+5*C*D can be represented in prefix, postfix, and infix notation as follows.

Prefix	Postfix	Infix
+*AB**5CD	AB*5C*D*+	A*B+5*C*D

The tree representation of the expression is depicted in Figure 3.4.

3.4.2   Expression Evaluations

Each programming language has rules for evaluating expressions. Here, we discuss briefly the fundamental kinds of expression evaluations: applicative order, normal order, short circuit, and block.

FIGURE **3.5** Alternative evaluations of the expression 2*5+4

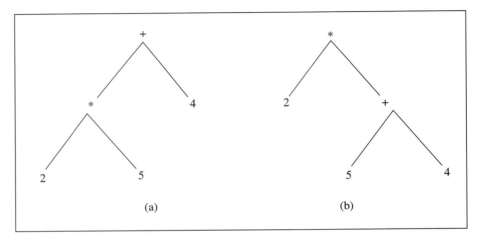

(a)   (b)

Applicative Order Evaluation

Applicative order evaluation, sometimes called *strict evaluation* or *eager evaluation,* corresponds to a bottom–up evaluation of the values of nodes of the tree representing an expression. In other words, in strict evaluation, all operands are evaluated individually and then operators are applied to the respective operand values. For example, in the tree representation of the expression (5−3)*(2+4) (see Figure 3.3), the − and + operators representing the first internal nodes of the tree (bottom-up) are applied to 5 and 3 and 2 and 4, respectively, the external nodes, to obtain 2 and 6. Then the * operator is used, giving the result, 12. In some languages, however, there is no specific order for the evaluation of operands. One reason is that a translator may rearrange the order of partial calculations to increase efficiency. For example, in evaluating the user-defined function Add(2,3+4), a translator may evaluate 3+4 before 2 because evaluating more complicated expressions first is more efficient. A further consideration is the order in which operations are performed. In general, when more than one operator appears in an expression, the expression is inherently ambiguous unless the concepts of precedence and associativity of operators are applied. For example, an expression 2*5+4 can be interpreted alternatively as follows.

▶ Perform the multiplication first and addition next, which produces the value 14, as shown in Figure 3.5(a).

▶ Perform the addition first and multiplication next, which produces the value 18, as shown in Figure 3.5 (b).

Generally, the operators that appear in expressions must be given an order of precedence to fix the sequence of their execution. The extensive set of precedence rules used in the C programming language is summarized in Table 3.1, in which operator priority is from top to bottom.

TABLE **3.1**   Operator precedence

Operator	Associativity	Type
( )	Left to right	Parentheses
++ — + − !	Right to left	Unary
* / %	Left to right	Multiplicative
+ −	Left to right	Additive
< <= > >=	Left to right	Relational
<< >>	Left to right	Shift
== !=	Left to right	Equality
&	Left to right	Bitwise AND
∧	Left to right	Bitwise exclusive OR
|	Left to right	Bitwise OR
&&	Left to right	Logical AND
||	Left to right	Logical OR
?:	Left to right	Conditional
=+ =− =* =/ =% =	Right to left	Assignment
,	Left to right	Sequential

In expressions involving operators from more than one level, the operator with highest level of precedence is to be applied first. An operator is said to be *left associative* if subexpressions containing multiple occurrences of the operator are scanned from left to right. Similarly, an operator is said to be *right associative* when subexpressions with multiple occurrences of the operator are grouped from right to left. Without rules specifying the relative precedence of operators, parentheses would be needed to make the operands of an operator explicit. For example, if the correct value of the expression 2*5+4 is 18, indicating that we must perform (5+4) first and multiplication next, we need to write the expression as 2*(5+4). Although this precedence convention is common among programming languages, some languages use other strategies for evaluating expressions. For example, APL, Smalltalk, and Forth handle the hierarchy of operators differently.

One of the advantages of the postfix and prefix notations is that parentheses aren't necessary to express the order in which operations are performed, so precedence rules aren't required to clarify an unparenthesized expression. For instance, the expression (2+3)*4 can be written as *+234 and 23+4* in postfix and prefix notations, respectively. In addition, associativity of operators can be expressed without the need for a particular rule. As a result, in some programming languages the infix notation is combined with the prefix or postfix notations, which makes the translator considerably more complex. Also, several languages, including Ada and ML, explicitly recognize the analogy between operators and functions. For instance, a+b is exactly equivalent to +(a,b), indicating that operators and functions may be defined in exactly the same way. Such languages are intended to be easier to learn, as separate rules for operators and functions aren't required. In addition, such languages are notationally more convenient because they allow you to define new operators.

Normal Order Evaluation

Normal order evaluation of expressions corresponds to the evaluation of each operand when it is needed in the computation of the result. For example, consider the following function defined in C when it is called with Add(2+3).

```
Add(X)
    int X;    {
    X= X+10;
    }
```

The result is obtained by substituting the expression 2+3 into X without first evaluating it. Then, the expression 2+3 is evaluated and used in the function. In other words, 2+3, not 5, is passed as the value of X to the function.

Short Circuit Evaluation

Short circuit evaluation of Boolean, or logical, expressions corresponds to evaluation of an expression without evaluating all its subexpressions. For example, the Boolean expressions

```
X or True
```

and

```
True or X
```

are true regardless of whether X is true or false. Similarly,

```
False and X
```

is evaluated as false relative to any value for X. In this form, the Boolean expression is to be evaluated from left to right to the point at which the truth value of the entire expression is deduced, indicating the end of the evaluation. For example, in C, the logical operators && and || are short circuits. In Modula-2, the corresponding Boolean operators AND and OR are also short circuits. The conditional *if-then-else* can be used to define the short circuit Boolean operator as shown here:

```
if    test-expression    then-expression    else-expression
```

that is, if the value of test-expression is true, the value of the entire *if-then-else* condition should be the value of the then-expression; otherwise, it should be the value of the else-expression. For example, a test for the validity of an array index can be written in the same expression as a test of its subscripted value, as long as the range test occurs first:

```
if   ( i <= lastindex) and (a[i] = x) then . . .
```

without short-circuit evaluation, the test `i<=lastindex` will not prevent an error from occurring if `i>lastindex` because the expression `a[i]` in the second part of the expression will still be evaluated. Without short-circuit evaluation, the test must be written using nested if statements as shown here:

```
if   ( i <= lastindex) then if   (a[i] = x) then . . .
```

Ada has both short-circuit and non–short-circuit Boolean operators, in which the usual *and* and *or* operators are not short-circuit, whereas the corresponding short-circuit operators are written *and then* and *or else*. The following test in Ada language follows the short-circuit evaluation.

```
if   ( i <= lastindex) and then (a[i] = x) then . . .
```

Some languages, other than C++, use *complete evaluation*. In complete evaluation, when two expressions are joined by an `&&` or an `||`, both subexpressions are always evaluated and then the truth tables are used to obtain the value of the final expression.

Lazy Evaluation

An evaluation rule frequently adopted in functional languages is *lazy evaluation*, sometimes called *delayed evaluation*. This evaluation rule refers to a method that eliminates unnecessary evaluation of expressions that

▶ Postpones evaluation of an expression until it is needed

▶ Eliminates the reevaluation of the same expression more than once

In other words, an expression subject to lazy evaluation is not evaluated until its value is required and, once evaluated, is never reevaluated. The conditional statements suggest the use of lazy evaluation, indicating that they never evaluate operands before applying the operation; instead, conditional statements always pass the operands un-evaluated, and let the operation decide if evaluation is needed. The best example is the case of expressions containing conditionals. For example, the C expression

```
Z + (Y = 0 ? X : X / Y)
```

has an embedded if statement that computes `X/Y` if `Y` is not `0`. But, if we evaluate the operands of the conditional operator, we produce the effect of doing exactly what the conditional statement is set up to avoid—dividing `X` by `Y` even if `Y` is zero. Clearly, in this case, we are not interested in evaluating all the operands before the operation is applied. Instead, we need to pass the operands to the conditional operation unevaluated and let the operation determine the order of evaluation.

Block Order Evaluation

Block order evaluation corresponds to evaluating an expression containing a declaration. For example, in Pascal, a block expression is a function body involving variable declaration. In ML "let *declaration* in *expression* end" forms a block expression, where the subexpression *expression* is evaluated and the bindings produced by *declaration* are used for evaluating *expression*. For example, the following program fragment is an ML block expression that computes the area of a triangle in which X, Y, and Z are the lengths of its sides.

```
let    val    S=(X+Y+Z) * 0.5
in     sqrt (S *(S-X) * (S-Y) * (S-Z))
end
```

In this form, the entire let—end is an expression, or its body, indicating that expressions may be nested. Ada has no block expressions or conditional expressions.

▼ 3.5 STATIC AND DYNAMIC ENVIRONMENTS

The *lifetime* of any data object begins when the data object is bound to a particular storage location (i.e., when a block of storage is allocated and the storage representation for the data object is initialized). The lifetime of a data object ends when this binding of object to storage block is dissolved (i.e., when the locations can no longer be accessed from the program). For a data structure of variable size, individual components of the structure have their own lifetime, determined by the time at which they are created and inserted into the structure and by the time at which they are deleted from the data structure. When a data object is created, an *access path* to the data object must also be created so that the data object can be accessed by operations in the program execution. In other words, an access path ordinarily leads to the location of a data object, (i.e., to the beginning of the block of storage for the object). An access path can be created in two ways:

▶ Through association of the data object with a name

▶ Through association of the data object with a pointer

At the end of the lifetime of the data object, this block of storage must be recovered for reallocation to another data object at some later time. In a language like Fortran, all memory allocation is performed at load time, and the location of all variables are fixed for the duration of program execution, Functions and subroutines cannot be nested, and recursion is not allowed. Thus, all the information associated with a function or subroutine can be statically allocated. In this approach, each function has a fixed activation record, which contains space for the local variables and parameters, and possibly for return calls. Global variables are defined by COMMON statement and are determined by pointers to a common area. The general form of each activation record is shown in Figure 3.6.

In this situation, when a call to a subroutine S occurs, the parameters are evaluated and their locations are stored in the parameter space of the activation record of S. Then, the current instruction pointer is stored as the return address, and a jump is performed to the instruction pointer of S. When S exits, a jump is performed to the return address. If S is a function, special arrangements must be made for the returned value.

FIGURE **3.6**   General form of an activation record

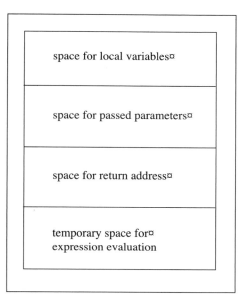

In procedural languages, the dynamic allocation and deallocation of storage occurs only for stack-based access operations (PUSH and POP). This is a relatively easy implementation, in which storage is allocated for the stack when a procedure is called and deallocated when the procedure is exited. Pointers are particularly interested in procedural languages, in which they provide a means of dynamic memory allocation from a special area of storage called the *heap*. Usually a programming language allocates dynamic storage in a separate area called the heap. The term *heap* indicates that we have a pool of memory, in which space can be dynamically allocated and deallocated during program execution. Space can be created when needed, and when no longer needed it may be returned to the heap for later use. In these languages, dynamic storage may be explicitly allocated and deallocated by the programmer system calls during program execution. Examples are *new* and *dispose* in Pascal and *malloc* and *free* in C for allocation and deallocation of storage, respectively.

A more serious situation occurs if the language designer wants to extend the expressiveness and flexibility of the languages by allowing functions to be dynamically created, that is, allowing function to be returned from other functions via returned value or referenced parameters. This kind of flexibility is usually desired in a functional programming language, and such languages become what are called first-class values languages. Automatic memory management actually falls into two categories: *maintaining free space* and *garbage collection,* as we discuss in the following sections.

FIGURE **3.7**   Allocated space to an executing program

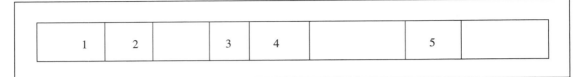

FIGURE **3.8**   New block allocated to an executing program

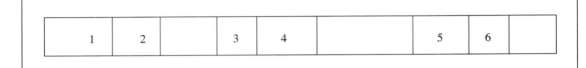

3.5.1 Maintaining Free Space

In the process of maintaining the free space available for allocation, a contiguous block of memory is generally provided by the operating system for the use of a running program. The free space within this block is maintained by a list of free blocks. One way to do this is via a lined-list as shown in Figure 3.7, which indicates that the total available space with allocated blocks numbered and free blocks blank.

When a block of certain size needs to be allocated, the memory management system searches the list for a free block with enough space, and then adjusts the free list to remove the allocated space, as illustrated in Figure 3.8 with block number 6 allocated.

When memory is reclaimed, blocks are returned to the free list. For example, if the blocks numbered 2 and 5 are stored to be reclaimed, then the new free list after reclamation would be as Figure 3.9.

In this respect, when blocks of memory are returned to the free list, they must be joined with immediately adjacent blocks to form the largest contiguous block of free memory. This process is called *coalescing*. In the preceding example, the blocks numbered 2 and 5 were coalesced with the free blocks adjacent to them on the right and left, respectively. Through coalescing, a free list can become fragmented, meaning that the free list of blocks consist of a number of small sized blocks. In this case, it is not possible to allocate large blocks. To prevent this, memory must occasionally be compacted by moving all free blocks together and coalescing them into one large block. For example, the free blocks of the preceding example could be compacted as shown in Figure 3.10.

In general, compaction involves considerable overhead because the locations of most of the allocated blocks will change and data structures and tables in the run-time environment will have to be modified to reflect these new locations.

FIGURE **3.9**   Reclaiming blocks allocated to an executing program

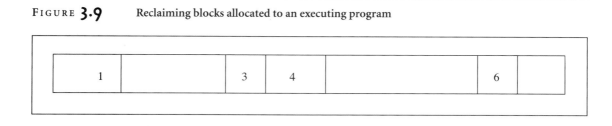

FIGURE **3.10**   Coalescing free blocks into one large block

3.5.2 Garbage and Garbage Collections

The process called **reclamation of storage** reclaims storage allocated but no longer used. One important property associated with storage management is the lifetime and access path of a data object during program execution. Two important issues in dynamic memory management arise because of the interplay between the lifetime of a data object and the access path that exists to it. This is an undesirable situation of execution environments supported by dynamic storage management that might allow a program to run out of heap storage, if it heavily uses dynamic storage. An alternative heap management approach is *garbage collection,* which keeps track of allocated but inaccessible storage called *garbage* and permits it to be reallocated. The storage allocated here is not commonly associated with variables directly but is accessible only by pointers and first-class value functions. The Ada language provides a garbage collector called *unchecked-deallocation,* which periodically returns allocated and unreferenced storage to the available storage pool, similar to Pascal's *dispose* procedure. Similarly, some of the well-known garbage collectors adopted in functional languages are *mark-scan, copying,* and *reference-counting,* which we discuss in the following sections. Object-oriented programming languages also fall into this category and the following discussion on garbage and garbage collections applies to them as well.

Garbage

When all access paths to a data object are destroyed but the data object continues to exist, the data object is said to be *garbage.* In this case, the data object can no longer be accessed from other parts of the program, meaning that it is of no further use. In addition, the binding of data object (name of the data object) to storage location has not

FIGURE **3.11**   Dynamic memory allocation can result in garbage and dangling references

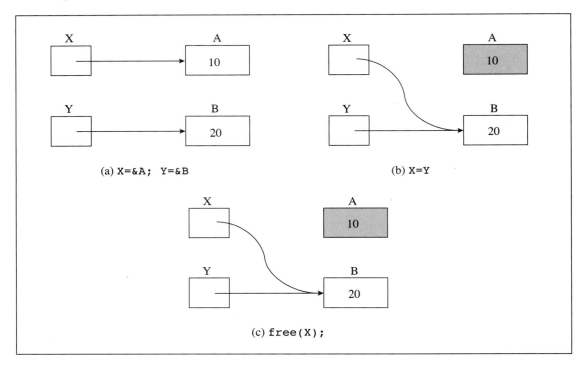

(a) X=&A; Y=&B

(b) X=Y

(c) free(X);

been broken; thus, the storage is not available for reallocation. In other words, garbage is memory that has been allocated in the program execution but that has become inaccessible to the other parts of the program.

Dangling References

When an access path continues to exist after the lifetime of the associated data object, the data object is said to be a *dangling reference*. An access path ordinarily leads to the location of a data object (i.e., to the beginning of the block of storage for the object). At the end of the lifetime of the data object, this block of storage is recovered for reallocation. However, the recovery of the storage does not necessarily destroy the existing access path to the block; thus, it may continue to exist, as a dangling reference. Storage is finite, even in large-scale machines, so a program that produces dangling references and garbage may fail to run if it exceeds the allocated memory associated with the program execution. In the following examples, we illustrate the situation that these two important issues raise during program execution.

Consider the following code in C language, in which X and Y as two pointer variables are pointing to different memory locations, as is shown in Figure 3.11(a).

```
int A=10, B=20, *X, *Y;
X = &A;
Y = &B;
```

The following statement

```
X = Y;
```

leaves X and Y pointing to the same storage, the storage that Y was pointing to, as shown in Figure 3.11(b). In this situation, the storage that X was pointing to is still allocated in the program execution environment, but it is inaccessible, thus there is garbage produced associated with A location. Consequently, in this situation, the statement

```
free(X);
```

deallocates the storage that X points to, leaves X as a dangling reference, and leaves Y as a dangling reference because they were both pointing to the same storage location, as is shown in Figure 3.11(c).

In the following C code, when function Add is exited, the pointer variable X is deallocated and the memory allocated to X is no longer accessible by the program outside of the function, which means that the memory allocated to X is garbage.

```
Add ( )
{
   int *X;
   X = (int *) malloc (sizeof (int) );
. . .
. . .
}
```

This is a typical way for garbage to develop—we failed to call *free,* a function in C used to reclaim the allocated memory. A similar situation occurs in Pascal, as shown in the following, in which we fail to call *dispose* to reclaim the allocated memory:

```
var X: ^ integer;
. . .
new(X);
. . .
```

Dangling references are a particularly serious problem for memory management because they may compromise the integrity of the entire run-time behavior of the program execution. For example, an assignment to a nonexistent data object through a dangling reference can modify storage that has already been allocated to another data object of an entirely different type, thus violating the security of the type checking mechanism, or it can modify housekeeping data that has been stored there temporarily by the storage management system, thus destroying the integrity of the memory management system. Garbage is a less serious problem. Storage that is allocated but is inaccessible becomes garbage that might otherwise be reallocated for another purpose. Programs that create garbage are said to have *memory leaks.* As a consequence, it is desirable to automatically reclaim garbage for further use. Programming languages that automatically reclaim garbage are said to perform *garbage collection*. A garbage collector is a run-time system that reclaims the portions of storage that have previously been allocated but are no longer used by the program. An example is the stack-based management of memory in the environment of a block-structured language, which provides a kind of simple garbage collection: the environment reclaims the location allocated to the top of the stack by POP operation. Garbage collection is needed for languages that support dynamic variables and is vital for languages like LISP that cause a large amount of dynamic memory activity because the graph structure method is adopted for implementation and passing the functions. Some of the well-known garbage collection methods adopted in functional languages are mark-scan, copying, and reference-counting, as we briefly explain in the following. We will not discuss the merit of the methods, so interested readers can refer to Peyton Jones (1987).

Mark-Scan Method

In this method sometimes called *mark-sweep*, each node of the graph represented by the program execution must contain an extra bit for marking. This method runs automatically when storage is about to run out and consists of two phases:

▶ **Mark phase:** During the *mark* phase, the entire graph associated with program execution is examined, marking each storage location that is encountered; thus, a storage location remains unmarked if it is not referenced in program execution. In other words, in *mark* phase, the garbage collector identifies all those storage locations that are accessible—that is, that are not garbage.

▶ **Scan phase:** The entire graph is checked and all unmarked storage locations are returned to the heap, meaning that unreferenced storage locations are treated as garbage and are reclaimed. In other words, in the scan phase, the garbage collector places all the inaccessible storage locations in the free storage area, often by placing them on the free-list.

The mark-scan algorithm is as follows.

```
Mark Phase:
   For each root R, Mark (R)
   Mark (R):
      If R is not marked then;
         Set mark bit of R;
         Mark (R ↑ .left);
         Mark (R ↑ .right);
      Endif.
Scan Phase:
   For each storage C
      If C is marked then reset C's mark bit
      Else   link C onto the free-list.
```

FIGURE **3.12**   Example of the mark phase of garbage collection

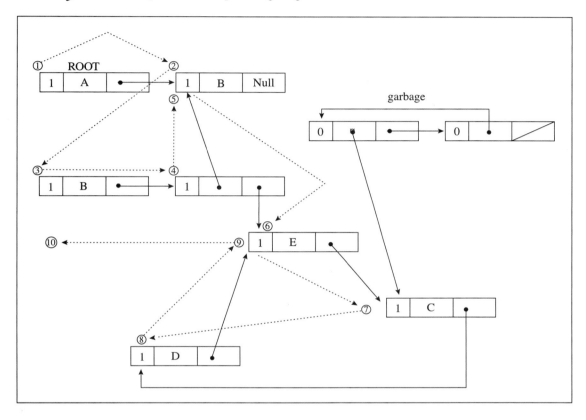

At the beginning of the garbage collection process, all storage is unmarked. Whenever the marking process encounters a storage location that is already marked, it will not continue checking that location. In particular, this guarantees that cycles in the storage list will not put the garbage collector into an infinite loop. Marking is depicted by dotted lines in Figure 3.12, which shows the path traced by the garbage collector. The second phase of garbage collection is the scan phase, when all of the inaccessible storage is returned to free storage.

Copying Method

In the copying method, the available memory is divided into two sections:

▶   **From-space (working half):** Memory is allocated to a running program.

▶   **To-space (free half):** When the copying method is invoked.

In this method, the entire structure is examined, in which each storage location is copied from from-space to to-space. When the working half fills up, the reachable locations are copied into consecutive locations in the free half. What is inaccessible remains in from-space and is thus garbage. When the copying is finished, from-space and to-space are exchanged. This exchange operation provides the opportunity to reallocate the memory locations from the from-space that were associated with garbage.

Reference-Counting Method

This method requires an extra field in each node of the graph structure represented by the program execution to count references to the node. In this method, when a node is created, the count is set to 1.

▶ **Count-increment:** If the node is referenced, count is increased by 1.

▶ **Count-decrement:** If the node is not referenced, count is decreased by 1.

Consequently, when the count is set to 0, the memory of the node is returned to available storage pool.

To sum up this discussion, in large-size storage, a garbage collection can be quite expensive because it necessitates tracking down and checking every memory location. The result is that a program runs along well until it runs out of storage, then it invokes garbage collection. After the garbage collection and assuming an adequate amount of storage was reclaimed, the program resumes high-speed execution until the next garbage collection. This is quite apparent in an interactive system because, periodically, the system will stop while a garbage collection is in progress. In another approach, garbage collection can take place continuously and in parallel with normal program execution.

Finally, a new method called generation scavenging adds a permanent storage area to the reclamation scheme. In this method, allocated objects that survive long enough are simply copied into permanent space and are never deallocated during subsequent storage reclamation. This means that the garbage collector needs to search only a very small section of memory for newer storage allocations, and the time for memory allocation is reduced. Of course, it is possible for permanent memory still to become exhausted with unreachable storage, but this is a much less severe problem than before because temporary storage tends to disappear quickly, whereas storage that stays allocated for some time is small and tends to persist anyway. This dynamic memory management has been proved to work very well, especially in combination with virtual memory systems.

SUMMARY

An abstraction is a representation of an object and is categorized as procedural, modular, object, and user-defined forms. Data abstraction is involved with the program components that are subject to computation, such as character strings or numbers.

Data abstraction is divided into three categories: basic data abstraction, which refers to the internal representation of data values; structured data abstraction, which is the principal method for abstracting collections of data values; and unit data abstraction, which is the principal method for collecting all the information needed to create and use a particular data type. Control abstraction describes the order in which statements are to be carried out. Basic control abstraction performs the computation and storage of a value to the location given by a variable. Structured control abstraction is referred to as subprogram invocation or activation, and unit control abstraction represents a collection of routines that provide services to other parts of a program. In this chapter, we outlined the abstraction concept with different examples to address this important issue in design and implementation of languages.

Parameter transmission is the major alternative method for sharing data objects among subprograms. A formal parameter is a particular kind of local data object within a subprogram. The subprogram definition lists the names and declarations for formal parameters as part of the specification part of the subprogram. A formal parameter name is a simple identifier, and the declaration gives the type and other attributes as for an ordinary local variable declaration. An actual parameter is a data object declared in the calling subprogram and is shared with the called subprogram. In this chapter, we briefly discussed the formal and actual parameters and three distinct semantics models of parameter passing: In Mode, Out Mode, and InOut Mode models. Then, we outlined five different parameter passing mechanisms: parameter passing by constant-value, parameter passing by reference, parameter passing by name, parameter passing by result, and parameter passing by value-result to address data transmission between subprograms.

Expressions are formed from operators and operands; operators are known as functions and operands as parameters. We briefly discussed the various fundamental forms of expressions, such as infix, postfix, prefix, and mixfix. In general, each programming language has rules for the evaluation of expressions, such as applicative order, normal order, short circuit, and block order evaluation. Applicative order evaluation corresponds to a bottom-up evaluation of the values of vertices of the tree representing an expression. Normal order evaluation corresponds to the evaluation of each operand when it is needed for computing the result. Short circuit evaluation performs the evaluation of an expression without evaluating all its subexpressions, and block order evaluation occurs when an expression contains a declaration. We also discussed the expression evaluation concepts to provide enough background knowledge for upcoming topics that different programming languages will discuss.

A clear understanding of execution environments is often necessary to understand fully the behavior of programs because the program execution is embedded in this environment. We discussed the static and dynamic environments to address the lifetime and access path of data objects by operations in the program execution. A more serious situation occurs if the language designer wants to extend the flexibility of the languages by allowing functions to be dynamically created. This kind of flexibility is usually desired in a functional or object-oriented language. We discussed maintaining free space and garbage collection as important properties associated with languages supported by fully dynamic memory environments.

EXERCISES

1. Give your own examples of features in any programming language that promote or violate the following design principles.
   a. Efficiency
   b. Expressiveness
   c. Maintainability
   d. Readability
   e. Reliability
   f. Security
   g. Simplicity
   h. Writability

2. What is the difference between *low-level* and *high-level* programming languages?

3. Explain the *local* and *global* variables.

4. Briefly explain the attributes of a *vector*.

5. Briefly explain the attributes of a *record*.

6. Lists and vectors are different from several important respects. Explain the differences.

7. Explain the two concepts of type compatibility: *Name* equivalence, and *Structural* equivalence.

8. What is the difference between *statically* typed and *dynamically* typed programming languages?

9. A structured type is a compound type, such as arrays, records, lists, sets, functions, and pointers. Describe two kinds of structured types: *heterogeneous* and *homogeneous*.

10. What is the environment at each *numbered point* in the following program?

```
program   test;
const x = 999;
❶    type   Nat = 0 . . x;
❷    var   m, n : Nat;
❸    function f(n : Nat) : Nat;
begin
❹    . . .
end.
```

11. Discuss the difficulties in a language that adopts *static typing* and *dynamic scooping*.

12. What is the *recursive* data type?

13. A queue can be represented as an array `queue[Maxsize]`. Define an equation to access the elements of the queue using the size of the queue. Define the queue size with regard to front and rear of the queue.

14. Explain the following three methods for binding the domain of the function to a specific subset of values.
    a. Compile-time binding
    b. Object creation-time binding
    c. Object manipulation-time binding

15. Briefly explain the following parameter passing mechanisms and the difference between them.
    a. Parameter passing by constant-value
    b. Parameter passing by reference
    c. Parameter passing by name
    d. Parameter passing by result
    e. Parameter passing by value-result

16. What is the output of the following program written in Pascal syntax using the five parameter passing mechanisms discussed?

```
program    test;
var    I: integer;
       A: array[1 . . 2] of integer;
procedure P(X, Y: integer;) ;
begin
       X := X + 1;
       I := I + 1;
       Y := Y + 1;
end;
begin
       A[1] := 1;
       A[2] := 1;
       I := 1;
       P(A[I], A[I]);
       Writeln(A[1]);
       Writeln(A[2]);
end;
```

17. Two-way linked lists are formed from nodes that have pointers to both their left and right neighbors in the list. Sketch a diagram to address a two-way linked list with 3 nodes.

18. Convert the following *infix* expressions to *postfix* expressions.
    a. (a + b)
    b. (x − y − z)
    c. (x − y − z) / (u + v)
    d. $(a^2 + b^2)*(m - n)$

19. Show the tree representation of each expression.

    a. `4 - 2 - 1`

    b. `9 + 7 - 5 - 3`

    c. `a * b + c * d`

    d. `a * b + 3 * b * c`

20. Find at least one example of a parameterless abstraction that does not perform exactly the same computation every time it is called. Under what circumstances will a parameterless abstraction behave like this?

21. Rewrite the following expressions in *prefix* and *postfix* notation. Consider the *sqrt* as an operator with one argument.

    a. `a * b + c`

    b. `a * b + c * d`

    c. `a * (b + c) * d`

    d. `a * b + 3 * b * c`

    e. `(a/2 + sqrt((b/2) * (a/2) - a*b)) / b`

    f. `(3-4)/5+6*7`

22. Consider the precedence relations among operators. Show the order of evaluation of the following expressions by parenthesizing all subexpressions.

    a. `a * b - 1 + c`

    b. `(a - b) / c && (d * e / a - 3)`

    c. `a * (b - 1) / c mod d`

    d. `a * b + 3 * b * c`

    e. `x - y - z / u + v`

23. Draw the *abstract trees* for the expressions in the previous exercise.

24. Explain the *applicative, short circuit, normal,* and *block* order evaluations. Use an example to explain the difference between them.

25. What is the sequence of the evaluation of operators in the expression `(3+4)*(5-6)` using the applicative order evaluation?

26. Would it make sense to apply the abstraction principle to *literals* and *types?*

27. Design each of the following as an abstract type with values *yes, no,* and *unknown,* and logical operations such as *and* and *or.*

    a. Complex

    b. Money

    c. Date

    d. Fuzzy

Give at least one possible representation in each case.

REFERENCE-NEEDED EXERCISES

To answer the following exercises, you might need to consult the following references: Hopcroft and Ullman, 1979; Knuth, 1997; Mitchell, 1998; Pratt and Zelkowitz, 1999; Riley, 1987; Standish, 1995; Watt, 1990.

1. What is the *lifetime* of a variable?

2. What is a *polytype?* Give one example of polytype.

3. What is *coercion?* Give one example of coercion.

4. Programs that obtain certain types of resources must explicitly return those resources to the system to avoid so-called *resource leaks.* In programming languages like C and C++, the most common kind of resource leak is a memory leak. Java performs automatic garbage collection of memory no longer needed, thus avoiding most memory leaks. In a program, demonstrate the try-catch-finally exception-handling mechanism.

5. One characteristic of a programming language is the kind of entities that may be bound to variables. These variables are called *bindables* of the language. Specify the bindables of Pascal language and the kinds of declarations in which they may be bound.

6. What is a *collateral* declaration?

7. Make a diagram showing the *lifetime* of the variables in the following program. Note that R will be activated three times, and N is in effect as a local variable in R.

```
Program   P;
var   N : Integer;
procedure   R( N : Integer);
   begin
      if N>0 then R(N-1)
   end;
   begin
      R(2)
   End.
```

8. Consider two sets X and Y. Let R be a *relation* in X⇔Y. Define its *inverse.*

9. Let A be a subset of set X, that is to say A∈ P(X). Define its *image.*

10. Define *composite* types and give an example of the following:
    a. Cartesian Products
    b. Disjoint Unions
    c. Mapping
    d. Powersets
    e. Recursive types

FIGURE **3.13**

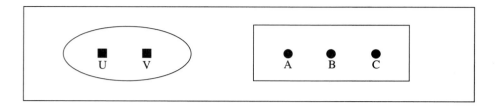

11. Suppose T={1, 5, 9} and S={A, B}. Answer the following questions.
    a. What is type T∗S?
    b. What is type S∗T?

12. Explain *Powerset,* variables of this type, and operations permitted on such variables.

13. Explain *Slice* as a substructure of an array that is itself an array.

14. Explain three different conventions for data parameter passing as *call by reference, call by copy,* and *call by name.*

15. We can view an array variable as a mapping from an index set to a collection of component variables. Consider how and when a given array variable's index set can be determined?

16. Explore the *relationship* between S → (T → U) and (S×T) → U.

17. Another kind of value composition is the *disjoint union,* whereby a value is chosen from either of two (usually different) types. Assume we use the notation S+T to stand for the set of values in which each value is chosen from either set S or set T, and in which each value is tagged to indicate which set it was chosen from. What is the disjoint union of the two sets shown in Figure 3.13?

18. Consider a *mapping* M that maps every value X in set S to a value in set T. Show the set of all different mappings from S={U, V} to T={A,B,C}.

19. Define some rules to illustrate how we can decide whether types T and S, defined in terms of *Cartesian Products, Disjoint Unions,* and *Mappings* are structurally equivalent or not?

20. Consider the function definition "fun F(X : T) = E" and the function call F(E'). *Normal-order* evaluation might be characterized by:

    F(E') ≡ subset(E, X, E')

    where subset(E, X, E') is the expression obtained by substituting E' for all free occurrences of X in E.
    a. Characterize *eager evaluation* in an analogous fashion.
    b. Show that *subset* has to be defined carefully because of the possibility of confusing the scopes of an identification with more than one declaration. Consider, for example, the following code in ML language.

```
let
    val   n = 2;
        fun f(X : int) = let val n = 7 in n * x end
    in
        f(n + 1)
    end
```

21. Consider the following block definitions. For each block, determine the bindings of every bound name. Label each one as local or global variable.

```
Program    P;
  Block    B1;
      Declare A, B, C;
      Block    B2;
          Declare C, D;
          Block    B3;
              Declare B, D, F;
          Begin
          . . .
          End B3;
      Begin
      . . .
      End B2;
      Block    B4;
          Declare B, C, D;
      Begin
      . . .
      End B4;
  Begin
  . . .
  End B1;
End P.
```

22. Consider the following program.

```
Program    Test(Input, Output);
  Type    T1 = array[1 . . 10] of char;
          T2 = array[1 . . 10] of T1;
  Var     A,B : T1;
          C : array[1 . . 10] of array[1 . . 10] of char;
          D : T2;
          E : char;
          F : T2;
  Begin
❶     A : = B;
❷     D[2] : = A;
❸     C : = D;
```

```
❹    D : = F;
❺    C[2][1] : = E;
❻    C[5] : = B;
❼    F : = C;
    End;
End.
```

Fill in the following table with Y if the statement number is legal and N if the statement number is illegal relative to the kind of type specified in the program.

	(1)	(2)	(3)	(4)	(5)	(6)	(7)
Domain Equivalence							
Name Equivalence							
Declaration Equivalence							

Syntax Specifications

Precise specification of a programming language is essential for describing the computational behavior of the language. Without a clear notation of the effect of language constructs, we have no idea of the computation being performed. In addition, without a formal definition of the language reasoning mathematically about the behavior of a program isn't possible. Apart from its other benefits, the act of writing a formal description provides insight into the elements the programmer is specifying. In general, formal specification of a programming language can serve several purposes:

- ▶ Helps language comprehension
- ▶ Supports language standardization
- ▶ Guides language design
- ▶ Aids compiler and language system writing
- ▶ Supports program correctness verification
- ▶ Models software specification

In this chapter, we do not formally describe any realistic language in its entirety; instead, we introduce the basic techniques for developing the specification of programming languages. A formal language is any set of character strings with characters chosen from a fixed, finite set of an alphabet of symbols. The strings that belong to the language are called its **constructs,** or phrases. For example, some of the languages associated with the symbols $\{a, b\}$ are

$L_1 = \{a, b, ab, ba\}$,

$L_2 = \{aa, abab, aabbaa, aaabbb, bbaa\}$, and

$L_3 = \{ab, bb, abab, aabba, aaabbb, bbaa\}$.

The only restriction on a language is that each string must be of finite length and must contain characters chosen from some fixed finite alphabet of symbols. We may include keywords that comprise more than one symbol in the phrase. For example, we can include the keywords *if, fi, else,* and *then* in a phrase of that particular language relative to the symbols {*a, b, x, y*} as in

```
if   a < b    then    x    else    y    fi.
```

Any programming language description can be classified according to its

▶ Syntax, which deals with the formation of phrases

▶ Semantics, which deals with the meaning of phrases

▶ Pragmatics, which deals with the practical use of phrases

In general, a programming language definition should enable us to determine whether the program is valid and, if the program is valid, to understand its underlying meaning or effect. For example,

```
A=B*10
```

can be interpreted as an assignment statement consisting of a variable followed by the operator "=" followed by an expression—all of which refer to syntax. The **syntax** of a programming language is similar to the grammar of a natural language, or a mechanism used to form different constructs of the language. In the preceding assignment statement, the variable on the left side corresponds to the subject of a sentence (noun), the equals sign corresponds to the verb, and the expression on the right side corresponds to the object of the verb. Running the assignment statement involves evaluating the expression on its right side and assigning the resulting value to the variable on its left side. The **semantics** of a language is much more complex and difficult to express because it involves defining what is happening during the execution of a phrase or a program, the meaning of which may involve interactions with other constructs in the language. Finally, a translator needs to provide user options for debugging, for interfacing with the operating system, and perhaps with a software development environment. These options are the **pragmatics** of a programming language translator. In general, facilities for pragmatic directives are part of the language definition.

Three mechanisms describe the design and implementation of programming languages: regular expressions, formal grammars, and attribute grammars. In Section 4.1, we explain regular expressions defined by alternation, concatenation, Kleene closure, and positive closure rules to represent a programming language. In Section 4.2, we discuss formal grammars as a set of symbols and rules used to represent a programming language. Formal grammars describe the structure of the language constructs without addressing their meaning. We briefly discuss the specification of the grammar of a language, consisting of four components: a set of terminal symbols, a set of variable symbols, a set of production rules, and start symbol. Section 4.3 deals with syntax specification, which defines the formal relations between the constituents of a language, thereby providing a structural description of the various constructs in the language. In Section 4.4, we classify grammars into four categories according to the structure of their production rules as type 0 or unrestricted grammar, type 1 or context-sensitive grammar, type 2 or context-free grammar, and type 3 or regular grammar. The syntactic structure of a construct as generated by a grammar can be represented with a syntax tree sometimes called derivation tree or parse tree as is described in Section 4.5. In Section 4.6, we address the ambiguity as a property of a language, in which a construct can be represented with two distinct derivation trees.

A grammar written in BNF (type 2 grammar) may be expressed in many other notational variations of BNF. In Section 4.7, we discuss Extended BNF and Syntax Diagram as two popular notational variations of BNF. Extended BNF enhances the descriptive power of BNF, which increases the readability and writability of the production rules. In Syntax Diagram, each production rule is represented as a directed graph to address the graphical notation of each production rule. Attribute grammar is a powerful and elegant mechanism of formalizing both the context-free and context-sensitive aspects of the syntax of a language. In this sense, attribute grammar can be used to determine whether a variable has been declared and whether the use of the variable is consistent with its declaration. In Section 4.8, we deal with the attribute grammars with several examples to address its efficiency in the design of a programming language.

4.1   REGULAR EXPRESSIONS

Invented by Stephen Kleene, regular expressions appeared in a Rand Corporation report in about 1950 and represent a form of language definition. Each regular expression E denotes some language $L(E)$ defined over the alphabet of the language. The alphabet of the language is a finite set of symbols that are assembled to form the strings or sentences of the language. A regular expression is defined by the following set of rules and can be used to represent a regular language.

Alternation: If a and b are regular expressions, then so is $(a + b)$. That is, the language defined by $(a + b)$ has all the strings from the language identified by a and all the strings from the language identified by b.

Concatenation (or *Sequencing*): If a and b are regular expressions, then so is $(a \bullet b)$. That is, the language defined by $(a \bullet b)$ has all the strings formed by concatenating a string from the set of strings identified by a to the end of a string in the set identified by b.

Kleene closure: If a is a regular expression, then so is a^*. That is, the defined language of a^* consists of all the strings formed by concatenating zero or more strings in the language identified by a.

Positive closure: If a is a regular expression, then so is a^+. That is, the defined language of a^+ consists of all the strings formed by concatenating one or more strings in the language identified by a. Thus a^+ is the same as a^*, but the case of zero strings whose concatenation is defined to be ε, is excluded.

Empty: The symbol $\varnothing$ is a regular expression and defined language consisting of no strings.

Atom: Any single symbol such as a or ε is a regular expression with a defined language consisting of the single string $\{a\}$ or $\{\varepsilon\}$.

TABLE **4.1**	Regular expressions
	Regular Expression **Denoted Language**

Regular Expression   **Denoted Language**

$\varnothing$ $L^{\varnothing} = \{ \ \}.$

ε $L^0 = \{\varepsilon\}.$

a $L^1 = \{a\}.$

$(A \bullet B)$ $L(A) \bullet L(B) = \{ab \mid a \in L(A) \text{ and } b \in L(B)\}.$

$(A + B)$ $L(A) + L(B) = \{a \mid a \in L(A) \text{ or } a \in L(B)\}.$

(A^*) $L^* = \{a_1 a_2 \ldots a_n \mid a_1, a_2, \ldots, a_n \in L(A) \text{ and } n \geq 0\} \bigcup_{i=0}^{\infty} = L^i.$

(A^+) $L^+ = \{a_1 a_2 \ldots a_n \mid a_1, a_2, \ldots, a_n \in L(A) \text{ and } n > 0\} \bigcup_{i=0}^{\infty} = L^i.$

Table 4.1 shows the defined language of the regular expressions.

Example 4.1: Let $L_1 = \{01, 1001\}$ and $L_2 = \{11, 00, 1\}$ be sets of strings consisting of 0 and 1. Then

$L_1 L_2 = \{0111, 0100, 011, 10011, 100100, 10011\}$

$L_1 + L_2 = \{01, 1001, 11, 00, 1\}$

Example 4.2: 00 is a regular expression representing $\{00\}$; the expression $(0 + 1)^*$ denotes all strings of 0s and 1s. Thus, $(0 + 1)^* 00 (0 + 1)^*$ denotes all strings of 0s and 1s with at least two consecutive 0s. The regular expression $(1 + 10)^*$ denotes all strings of 0s and 1s beginning with 1 and not having two consecutive 0s. The regular expression $(0 + 1)^* 011$ denotes all strings of 0s and 1s ending in 011. Also, $0^* 1^* 2$ denotes any number of 0s followed by any number of 1s followed by any number of 2s. We may use the shorthand $0^+ 1^+ 2^+$ for $00^* 11^* 22^*$.

◤ 4.2 FORMAL GRAMMARS

Each programming language has a vocabulary of symbols and rules for how these symbols may be put together to form phrases (e.g., declarations, expressions, commands, statements, and a complete program). Because syntax refers to the formation of constructs in the language and defines relations between them, it describes the structure of the language without addressing the meaning of the constructs of the language. For example, a `while` command in Pascal consists of the symbol `while` followed by an expression followed by the symbol `do`, followed by a command, as in

```
while  expression  do  command
```

Another example is the *if-else* structure in C with the following form:

```
if    (expression)
    statement1
else
    statement2
```

which means that the *if-else* statement is the concatenation of the keyword *if* comprising an opening parenthesis, an expression, a closing parenthesis, a statement, the keyword *else*, and another statement. These examples address the syntax of the `while` command in Pascal and the *if-else* structure in C, indicating how the symbols are used in forming these phrases. Another example is the assignment statement

```
X=Y+Z;
```

which represents a valid sequence of symbols, in contrast to the statement `X==Y+Z;`, which is invalid in C programming language. This indicates that the syntax of a programming language is concerned only with the formation of constructs. Moreover, syntax provides information needed for understanding a program and translation of the source program into an object program. The vocabulary and the rules for forming phrases vary from one language to another.

4.3   SYNTAX SPECIFICATION

The use of a formal grammar to define the syntax of a programming language is important to both the language user and the language implementer. The programmer can consult the grammar to get help for program formation, structure, and punctuation and with writing a syntactically correct program. For example, the syntax of the *if-then-else* structure can quickly settle any doubts. The implementer may consult the grammar to determine all the possible cases of eligible input program structures with which the translator may have to deal. For example, to design a compiler, one can use the grammar to write syntactic analyzer code that can recognize all valid programs. In general, by studying the grammar of a programming language a programmer and an implementer can gain direct insights into various structures that can be combined to form correct programs from different perspectives. Basically, a grammar is a notation that you can use to specify a structural description of the various constructs in the language. A grammar defines the set of all possible phrases that constitute programs in the subject language together with their syntactic structures. In addition to specifying the legal constructs of a language, a grammar permits construction of infinitely many possible programs. The grammar of a programming language consists of four components:

1. A set of symbols known as **terminal symbols** that are the atomic (nondivisible) symbols in the language. These symbols are the alphabet of the language and are combined to form valid constructs in the language. By convention, terminal symbols are represented by a set of lowercase characters.

2. A set of nonterminal symbols known as **variable symbols,** or syntactic categories, that are the constructs in the language. These symbols are used to represent

intermediate definitions within the language. By convention, variable symbols are represented by a set of uppercase characters.

3. A set of rules known as **production rules** that are used to define the formation of the constructs. A production rule describes how each variable symbol can be defined in terms of terminal symbols and nonterminal symbols.

4. A variable symbol, or distinguished symbol, called the **start symbol,** that specifies the principal category being defined, for example, assignment statement or program.

Each production rule has symbols as its left side, the symbol $\Rightarrow$ and a string over the set of terminals, and variables as its right side. A production rule indicates that the left-side symbols drive or simply imply the right-side symbols. Derivation begins with the start symbol, with each successive string in the sequence derived from the preceding string by replacing the variable with one of the production rules associated with that variable. Each string in the derivation is called a **sentential form,** and a language is formally defined as the set of sentential forms wherein each form consists solely of terminal symbols that can be derived from the initial symbol of a grammar. Hence, the derivation continues until the sentential form contains no variable. The sentential form, then, consists only of terminal symbols of the grammar and is the generated construct of the language. In general, once we have defined a basic set of production rules, we can use them to construct more complex sentential forms. In other words, by choosing alternative production rules with which to replace variable symbols in the derivation, we can form different sentences in the language or generate an entire language. A grammar for a programming language might contain hundreds of production rules; for example, the definition of the C programming language, which is inherently a context sensitive grammar, contains more than 150 rules. In the following list, we briefly explain some definitions that are useful for classification of grammars and upcoming topics.

▶ The length of a string is the number of symbols in it. The empty string, denoted ε, has length 0.

▶ The notation S^n is used for the set of strings over S with length n ($n \geq 0$). For example,

$S^0 = \{\varepsilon\}$ is the singleton set containing only the empty string

$S = \{\}$ is the empty set containing no strings

▶ The notation S^* is used for the set of all finite strings over S of any length, or

$$S^* = S^0 \cup S^1 \cup S^2 \cup \ldots$$

▶ The notation S^+ is used for the set of nonempty strings over S of any length, or

$$S^+ = S^1 \cup S^2 \cup S^3 \cup \ldots = S^* - \{\varepsilon\}.$$

▶ A string $\alpha_1 \alpha \alpha_2 \in (V \cup T)^+$ is said to drive directly another string $\alpha_1 \beta \alpha_2 \in (V \cup T)^*$ if and only if $\alpha \Rightarrow \beta$ is a production in grammar and can be rewritten as $\alpha_1 \alpha \alpha_2 \Rightarrow \alpha_1 \beta \alpha_2$.

▶ A string α_1 is said to drive α_m, $(\alpha_1 \Rightarrow \alpha_m)$ if and only if:

$$\alpha_1 \Rightarrow \alpha_2 \Rightarrow \alpha_3 \Rightarrow \ldots \Rightarrow \alpha_m.$$

▶ The grammar of a programming language can be defined as a quadruple, $G = (T, V, P, S)$ where:

T is a finite set of terminal symbols ($V \cap T = \phi$)

V is a finite set of variable symbols ($V \cap T = \phi$)

P is a finite set of production rules of the form $\alpha . X.\beta \Rightarrow \delta$, where $\alpha, \beta,$ and δ $\in (V \cup T)^*$ and $X \in V$

$S \in V$ is the start symbol of the phrase

▶ The language of a grammar G is $L(G) = \{W \mid W \in T^* \text{ and } S \Rightarrow^* W\}$.

▶ Two grammars, $G1$ and $G2$, are equivalent if and only if $L(G1) = L(G2)$.

In the following section, we classify the grammars according to their production rules.

4.4 Classification of Grammars

In the mid 1950s, Noam Chomsky classified grammars according to the structure of their production rules and suggested four types of grammars, 0, 1, 2, and 3. Two of these grammars—context-free (type 2) and regular (type 3)—became useful tools for describing the syntax of programming languages.

4.4.1 Type 0 Grammar

Type 0, or **unrestricted grammar** (sometimes called recursively enumerable, or phrase structured, grammar) requires at least one nonterminal symbol on the left side of a production rule. Each production rule takes the form $\alpha \Rightarrow \beta$, where $\alpha \in (V \cup T)^+$ and $\beta \in (V \cup T)^*$. For example,

```
a   Thing   b  ⇒  b   Else
```

is a production rule in which `a` and `b` are the terminal symbols and `Thing` and `Else` are the variable symbols of the grammar.

Example 4.3: An unrestricted grammar for describing string *aaaa* can be defined as $G = (V, T, P, S)$, where

$V = \{S, A, B, C, D, E\}$

$T = \{a, \varepsilon\}$

$S = \{S\}$

The production rules are as follows:

1. $S \Rightarrow ACaB$

2. $Ca \Rightarrow aaC$

3. $CB \Rightarrow DB$

4. $CB \Rightarrow E$
5. $aD \Rightarrow Da$
6. $AD \Rightarrow AC$
7. $aE \Rightarrow Ea$
8. $AE \Rightarrow \varepsilon$

The language generated by this grammar consists of string a^i, where i is a positive power of 2. For example, *aaaa* can be represented with the following derivation sequences.

$S \Rightarrow ACaB$	By rule 1
$\Rightarrow AaaCB$	By rule 2
$\Rightarrow AaaDB$	By rule 3
$\Rightarrow AaDaB$	By rule 5
$\Rightarrow ADaaB$	By rule 5
$\Rightarrow ACaaB$	By rule 6
$\Rightarrow AaaCaB$	By rule 2
$\Rightarrow AaaaaCB$	By rule 2
$\Rightarrow AaaaaE$	By rule 4
$\Rightarrow AaaaEa$	By rule 7
$\Rightarrow AaaEaa$	By rule 7
$\Rightarrow AaEaaa$	By rule 7
$\Rightarrow AEaaaa$	By rule 7
$\Rightarrow aaaa$	By rule 8

4.4.2 Type 1 Grammar

Type 1, or **context-sensitive grammar,** requires that the right side of a production rule have no fewer symbols than the left side. Each production rule takes the form $\alpha \Rightarrow \beta$, where $\alpha = \delta_1 A \delta_2$, $\beta = \delta_1 \omega \delta_2$, $A \in V$, $\delta_1, \delta_2 \in (V \cup T)^*$, and $\omega \in (V \cup T)^+$. These rules are called context sensitive because the replacement of a variable by its definition depends on the surrounding symbols. An example of a production rule is

```
a  Thing  ⇒  Thing  a  b.
```

Example 4.4: A context-sensitive grammar for describing a string consisting of characters a, b, and c can be defined as: G = (V, T, P, S), where

V = {Sentence, Thing, Other}
T = {a, b, c}
S = { Sentence}

The production rules are as follows:

1. Sentence $\Rightarrow a \ b \ c$

2. Sentence $\Rightarrow a$ Thing $b \ c$

3. Thing $b \Rightarrow b$ Thing

4. Thing $c \Rightarrow$ Other $b \ c \ c$

5. a Other $\Rightarrow a \ a$

6. a Other $\Rightarrow a \ a$ Thing

7. b Other $\Rightarrow$ Other b

The language generated by this grammar consists of strings with equal numbers of *a*'s, *b*'s, and *c*'s (e.g., *aabbcc* or *abc*). For example, *aabbcc* can be represented with the following derivation sequences.

Sentence	$\Rightarrow a$ Thing $b \ c$	By rule 2
	$\Rightarrow a \ b$ Thing c	By rule 3
	$\Rightarrow a \ b$ Other $b \ c \ c$	By rule 4
	$\Rightarrow a$ Other $b \ b \ c \ c$	By rule 7
	$\Rightarrow a \ a \ b \ b \ c \ c$	By rule 5

4.4.3   Type 2 Grammar

In type 2, or **context-free grammar**, each production rule takes the form $A \Rightarrow \alpha$, where $A \in V$ and $\alpha \in (V \cup T)^*$. In other words, the left side of a production rule is a single variable symbol, and the right side is a combination of terminal and variable symbols. Peter Naur later introduced a new notation for syntax description of programming languages, the Backus-Naur Form (BNF) grammar. John Backus's notation is equivalent to Chomsky's type 2 grammar, so the BNF and context-free grammars are equivalent; they differ only in the notation used. In BNF notation, nonterminal symbols are enclosed by angle brackets, < >, and the symbol ::= is used for the derivation of the left side to the right side. An example of a production rule in context-free notation is

```
Expression   ⇒  Value  +  Expression,
```

with the equivalent representation in BNF being

```
<expression>  ::= <value>  +  <expression>.
```

Example 4.5: A context-free grammar for describing real numbers is defined as $G = (V, T, P, S)$, where

$V = \{$Real-Number, Integer-Part, Fraction, Digit$\}$

$T = \{0,1,2,3,4,5,6,7,8,9\}$

$S = \{$Real-Number$\}$

The production rules are as follows:

1. Real-Number ⇒ Integer-Part . Fraction
2. Integer-Part ⇒ Digit
3. Integer-Part ⇒ Integer-Part Digit
4. Fraction ⇒ Digit
5. Fraction ⇒ Digit Fraction
6. Digit ⇒ 0 | 1 | 2 | 3 | 4 | 5 | 6 | 7 | 8 | 9

For example, the real number 125.78 in this grammar can be represented as the following derivation sequences.

Real-Number ⇒ Integer-Part . Fraction		By rule 1
⇒ Integer-Part Digit . Fraction		By rule 3
⇒ Integer-Part Digit Digit . Fraction		By rule 3
⇒ Digit Digit Digit . Fraction		By rule 2
⇒ Digit Digit Digit . Digit Fraction		By rule 5
⇒ Digit Digit Digit . Digit Digit		By rule 4
⇒ Digit Digit Digit . Digit 8		By rule 6
⇒ Digit Digit Digit . 7 8		By rule 6
⇒ Digit Digit 5 . 7 8		By rule 6
⇒ Digit 2 5 . 7 8		By rule 6
⇒ 1 2 5 . 7 8		By rule 6

Example 4.6: The following is the grammar for a calculator language in BNF notation, where

$T = \{0\ 1\ 2\ 3\ 4\ 5\ 6\ 7\ 8\ 9 + - * / = \}$

$V = \{$Calculation, Expression, Value, Number, Unsigned, Sign, Digit, Operator$\}$

$S = \{$Calculation$\}$

The production rules represented in BNF notation are as follows:

```
<calculation> ::= <expression>  =
<expression> ::=  <value>
<expression> ::=  <value>    <operator>    <expression>
<value>      ::=  <number>
<value>      ::=  <sign>  <number>
<number>     ::=  <unsigned>
<number>     ::=  <unsigned>  .  <unsigned>
<unsigned>   ::=  <digit>
<unsigned>   ::=  <digit>  <unsigned>
<digit>      ::=  0 | 1 | 2 | 3 | 4 | 5 | 6 | 7 | 8 | 9
<sign>       ::=  + | -
<operator>   ::=  + | - | * | /
```

To verify that 12 + 25= is a valid expression in this grammar, we need to construct a tree in which the internal nodes correspond to the variable symbols and external

FIGURE **4.1**   Tree representation for 12 + 25 =

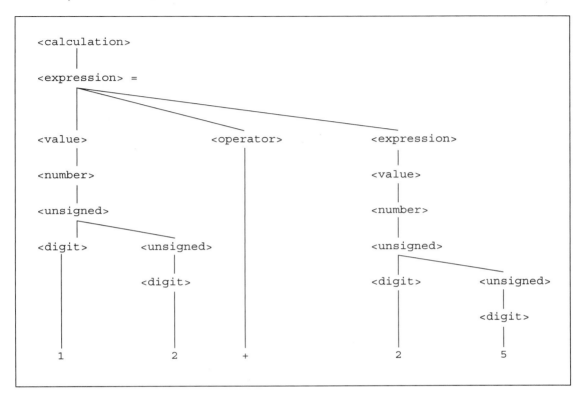

nodes to the terminal symbols, as shown in Figure 4.1. The root of the tree is the start symbol of the grammar.

Example 4.7: The string 011101011 belongs to the following grammar, as represented by the following sequence of derivations.

$$S \Rightarrow 0S \mid 1A$$
$$A \Rightarrow 0S \mid 1B$$
$$B \Rightarrow 0S \mid 1C \mid 1$$
$$C \Rightarrow 1C \mid 0C \mid 1 \mid 0$$

$$S \Rightarrow 0S \Rightarrow 01A \Rightarrow 011B \Rightarrow 0111C \Rightarrow 01110C \Rightarrow 011101C \Rightarrow 0111010C$$
$$\Rightarrow 01110101C \Rightarrow 011101011$$

Example 4.8: Consider the following grammar represented by the BNF notation.

$$V = \{\text{Sentence, Subject, Verb, Object}\}$$
$$T = \{\text{I, see, the, cat, sees, me}\}$$
$$S = \{\text{Sentence}\}$$

The production rules represented in BNF notation are as follows.

```
<sentence> ::= <subject>  <verb>  <object>
<subject>  ::= I | the <noun>
<object>   ::= me | the <noun>
<noun>     ::= cat
<verb>     ::= see | sees
```

The sentences **I see the cat** and **the cat sees me** are two possible representations in this grammar.

Example 4.9: Consider the grammar G = ({S, A}, {0, 1}, P, S) represented by the following production rules.

$$S \Rightarrow 0A1$$
$$A \Rightarrow 0A1$$
$$A \Rightarrow \varepsilon$$

Strings such as 000111, 0011, and 00001111 can be accepted by this grammar, indicating that the language of this grammar is $L(G) = \{0^n 1^n \mid n \geq 1\}$, which is any string consisting of an equal number of 0s and 1s.

4.4.4 Type 3 Grammar

In type 3, or **regular grammar** (sometimes called *restrictive grammar*), each production rule is restricted to only one terminal or one terminal and one variable on the right side of the production rules. These grammars are classified as *right-linear* or *left-linear* grammars. Each production rule of a right-linear grammar is formed as

$$A \Rightarrow xB \quad \text{or} \quad A \Rightarrow x$$

where $A \in V$, $B \in V$, and $x \in T$. Consequently, each production rule of a left-linear grammar is formed as

$$A \Rightarrow Bx \quad \text{or} \quad A \Rightarrow x$$

where $A \in V$, $B \in V$, and $x \in T$. An example of a production rule of right-linear grammar is

```
Thing ⇒  a  Thing
```

whereas an example of a production rule of left-linear grammar is

```
Thing ⇒  Thing  a
```

Example 4.10: A rightmost regular grammar for describing a binary numeral can be defined as G = (V, T, P, S), where

V = {Binary-Numeral}

T = {0, 1}

S = {Binary-Numeral}

The production rules are as follows:

1. Binary-Numeral $\Rightarrow$ 0
2. Binary-Numeral $\Rightarrow$ 1
3. Binary-Numeral $\Rightarrow$ 0 Binary-Numeral
4. Binary-Numeral $\Rightarrow$ 1 Binary-Numeral

A rightmost derivation of a binary number as 001010 in this grammar can be represented as follows:

Binary-Numeral $\Rightarrow$ 0 Binary-Numeral	By rule 3
$\Rightarrow$ 0 0 Binary-Numeral	By rule 3
$\Rightarrow$ 0 0 1 Binary-Numeral	By rule 4
$\Rightarrow$ 0 0 1 0 Binary-Numeral	By rule 3
$\Rightarrow$ 0 0 1 0 1 Binary-Numeral	By rule 4
$\Rightarrow$ 0 0 1 0 1 0	By rule 1

In this example, the replaced variable is always the rightmost variable in the previous sentential form. A leftmost regular grammar for describing binary numeral can be defined as $G = (V, T, P, S)$, where

$V = \{$Binary-Numeral$\}$

$T = \{0, 1\}$

$S = \{$Binary-Numeral$\}$

The production rules are as follows:

1. Binary-Numeral $\Rightarrow$ 0
2. Binary-Numeral $\Rightarrow$ 1
3. Binary-Numeral $\Rightarrow$ Binary-Numeral 0
4. Binary-Numeral $\Rightarrow$ Binary-Numeral 1

A leftmost derivation of a binary number as 001010 in this grammar can be represented as follows, in which the replaced variable is always the leftmost variable in the previous sentential form.

Binary-Numeral $\Rightarrow$ Binary-Numeral 0	By rule 3
$\Rightarrow$ Binary-Numeral 1 0	By rule 4
$\Rightarrow$ Binary-Numeral 0 1 0	By rule 3
$\Rightarrow$ Binary-Numeral 1 0 1 0	By rule 4
$\Rightarrow$ Binary-Numeral 0 1 0 1 0	By rule 3
$\Rightarrow$ 0 0 1 0 1 0	By rule 1

Such variations present no difficulty as far as understanding is concerned, provided the notational conventions are unambiguous and have been clearly explained. When Chomsky developed a mathematical theory of these classes of grammars, the connection between BNF and the Chomsky hierarchy enabled the mathematical analysis of the syntax and grammar of programming languages.

In the representation of production rules, when a variable has several alternatives, the symbol | is used to denote "or." The terms BNF grammar and context-free grammar are usually interchangeable in the discussion of syntax; in accordance with the traditional notation for programming language grammars, we use the BNF notation in this textbook. A complete grammar is a set of production rules that together define a hierarchy of constructs leading to a syntactic category, which for a programming language is called a **program**. For example, Figure 4.2 represents a grammar defining the programming language Pam.

4.5   SYNTAX TREE

The syntax of a programming language is commonly divided into two parts: the *lexical syntax* that describes the smallest units with significance, called *tokens,* and *the phrase-structure syntax* that explains how tokens are arranged into programs. In general, the lexical structure can be considered separately from syntactic structure, but it is closely related to and, in some cases can be an inextricable part of the syntax. The syntactic structure of a phrase as generated by a grammar can be represented with a **syntax tree** (sometimes called a *derivation tree* or a *parse tree*). Deriving the parse tree is called *parsing*. In a syntax tree all the terminal nodes are labeled with terminal symbols, all the internal nodes are labeled with variable symbols, and the root is labeled with the distinguished phrase or start symbol. Parsing was a crucial advance in language processing. It permitted the development of parser generators, thus overcoming one of the most difficult obstacles in compiler construction. In general, a grammar-oriented compiling technique, known as **syntax-oriented translation**, accepts a program as a string of characters when it satisfies the syntax of the language and converts the program to a derivation tree using the production rules of the language. This technique usually consists of two components:

1. A **lexical analyzer** (sometimes called a *scanner*), which converts the stream of input characters to a stream of tokens that becomes the input to the second phase of the process, as illustrated in Figure 4.3

2. A **syntactic analyzer,** which is a combination of a parser and an intermediate code generator and forms a derivation tree from the token list based on the syntax definition of the programming language, as shown in Figure 4.3

Either of two basic approaches to deriving parse trees may be used: **top-down parsers** or **bottom-up parsers**. A top-down parser begins with the start symbol as the root of the tree. It repeatedly replaces variable symbols, which are the left side of the production rules of the grammar, with a string of terminal symbols, which are the right side of the same production rules.

A bottom-up parser begins with a string of terminal symbols and repeatedly replaces sequences in the string, which correspond to the right side of the production rules of the grammar, with variable symbols, which correspond to the left side of the

FIGURE **4.2**   Grammar for the Pam programming language

```
V={Program, Series, Statement, Input-Statement, Output-Statement, Variable-
List, Assignment-Statement, Conditional-Statement, Definite-Loop,
Indefinite-Loop, Comparison, Expression, Term, Element, Constant, Variable,
Relation, Weak-Operator, Strong-Operator, Digit, Letter}
T={; read write  , := if then fi else to do end while ( ) = =< < > >= <> + - * /
0 1 2 3 4 5 6 7 8 9 a b c d e f g h i j k l m n o p q r s t u v w x y z }
S={ Program }
```
Production Rules:

Program	⇒	Series
Series	⇒	Series ; Statement | Statement
Statement	⇒	Input-Statement
Statement	⇒	Output-Statement
Statement	⇒	Assignment-Statement
Statement	⇒	Conditional-Statement
Statement	⇒	Definite-Loop
Statement	⇒	Indefinite-Loop
Input-Statement	⇒	**read** Variable-List
Output-Statement	⇒	**write** Variable-List
Variable-List	⇒	Variable
Variable-List	⇒	Variable-List , Variable
Assignment-Statement	⇒	Variable := Expression
Conditional-Statement	⇒	**if** Comparison **then** Series **fi**
Conditional-Statement	⇒	**if** Comparison **then** Series **else** Series **fi**
Definite-Loop	⇒	**to** Expression **do** Series **end**
Indefinite-Loop	⇒	**while** Comparison **do** Series **end**
Comparison	⇒	Expression Relation Expression
Expression	⇒	Term
Expression	⇒	Expression Weak-Operator Term
Term	⇒	Term Strong-Operator Element
Term	⇒	Element
Element	⇒	Constant
Element	⇒	Variable
Element	⇒	(Expression)
Constant	⇒	Digit
Constant	⇒	Constant Digit
Variable	⇒	Letter
Variable	⇒	Variable Digit
Variable	⇒	Variable Letter
Relation	⇒	= | =< | < | > | >= | < >
Weak-Operator	⇒	+ | −
Strong-Operator	⇒	* | /
Digit	⇒	0 | 1 | 2 | 3 | 4 | 5 | 6 | 7 | 8 | 9
Letter	⇒	a | b | c | d | e | f | g | h | i | j |
	⇒	k | l | m | n | o | p |
	⇒	q | r | s | t | u | v | w | x | y | z

FIGURE **4.3**   Program translation by scanner and parser

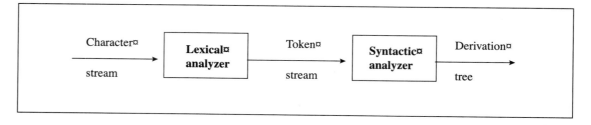

FIGURE **4.4**   A top-down parse tree for the real number 125.78

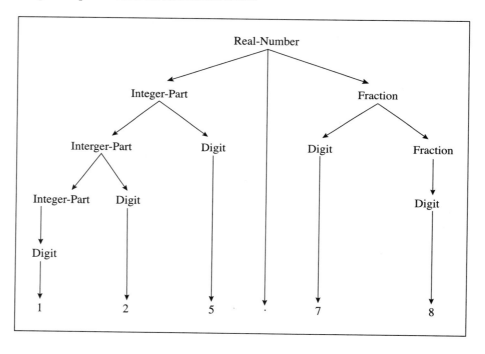

same production rules. This process continues until the start symbol is produced. An example of a top-down parse tree is presented in Figure 4.4, where the variable symbols have been replaced to show the derivation of the phrase constituting the real number 125.78. An example of a bottom-up parse tree is illustrated in Figure 4.5, where the terminal symbols corresponding to elements of the phrase 125.78 have been replaced to produce the start symbol of the grammar. In both cases, the tree is the result of a syntactic analysis of the real-number grammar. LEX and YACC are two well-known UNIX tools that generate lexical and syntax analyzers from the grammar of the language.

FIGURE **4.5**   **A bottom-up parse tree for the real number 125.78**

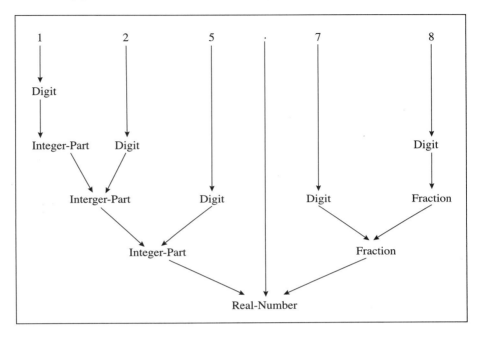

Relative to the grammar of a language, a derivation tree has the following properties:

▶   Each terminal node is labeled with a terminal symbol.

▶   Each internal node is labeled with a variable symbol.

▶   The label of an internal node is the left side of the production rule, and the labels of the children of the node, from left to right, are the right side of that production rule.

▶   The root of the tree is labeled with the start symbol.

To determine whether a phrase represents a syntactically valid structure in the language defined by a grammar, we need to use the production rules to construct a syntax tree of the phrase. If the phrase can be successfully represented, it belongs to the language. If the phrase can't be represented with the defined production rules, the phrase does not belong to the language. If the phrase doesn't belong to the language, new production rules might be added to make it do so. Determining whether the phrase is valid is called *recognition* or *representation*.

4.6 AMBIGUITY

A grammar that represents a phrase associated with its language in two or more distinct derivation trees is known as a **syntactically ambiguous grammar,** or simply an *ambiguous grammar.* Consider the grammar associated with some assignment statements in which the right sides are arithmetic expressions having addition and multiplication operations and the basic operands x, y, and z.

```
Assignment   ⇒  Identifier   =  Expression
Expression   ⇒  Expression   +  Expression
Expression   ⇒  Expression   *  Expression
Expression   ⇒  Identifier
Identifier   ⇒  x  |  y  |  z
```

Because the assignment statement x = x + y * z has two derivation trees, as shown in Figure 4.6 (a) and (b), the grammar is ambiguous. In this case, the two possible derivation trees have different meanings in that they imply that the two operators are applied in the opposite order when the assignment statement is evaluated. Regarding the two derivation trees, the first one implies that multiplication of y and z should be the first operation performed. The second derivation tree implies that addition of x and y should be the first operation performed. As a result, the overall result will be different in the two cases. For example, if the statement is *4 + 2 * 3*, the first derivation tree produces a calculation whose result is 10, whereas the second derivation tree produces a calculation whose result is 18.

The grammar is ambiguous because of a lack of syntactic structure. It can be resolved if we establish conventions that rule out one of the two derivation trees for that particular phrase. Generally speaking, deciding whether grammar is ambiguous is a theoretically difficult task, but in practice, ambiguities can be avoided. Sometimes the ambiguity is harmless, as when a grammar is being used only to determine whether a phrase is valid, but you should eliminate ambiguity whenever possible. For example, if we take the actual meaning of the preceding assignment statement from mathematics, we would choose the first derivation tree over the second because multiplication has a higher precedence than addition. This choice is the usual one for most programming languages, although a different choice is made for some languages (e.g., APL). To express the fact that multiplication takes precedence over addition and remove the ambiguity, either the grammar must be revised or a disambiguity rule must be introduced to establish the correct derivation tree. For example, we can remove the ambiguity of the grammar associated with the assignment statement by revising the grammar as follows and as shown in Figure 4.7.

```
Assignment   ⇒  Identifier   =  Expression
Expression   ⇒  Identifier   +  Expression
Expression   ⇒  Identifier   *  Expression
Expression   ⇒  Identifier
Identifier   ⇒  x  |  y  |  z
```

An alternative way to revise the grammar is to introduce a new variable in order to remove the ambiguity, as in

```
Assignment   ⇒  Identifier  =  Expression
Expression   ⇒  Element     +  Expression
Expression   ⇒  Element     *  Expression
```

FIGURE **4.6**   Two derivation trees for the assignment statement x = x + y * z

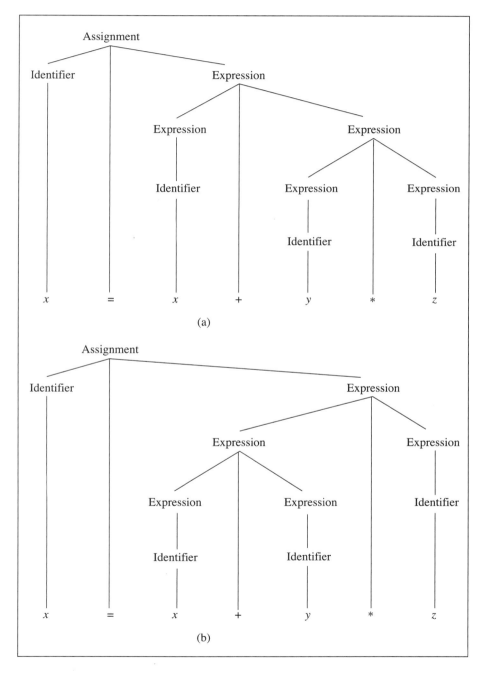

FIGURE **4.7**   **Revision of the grammar for the assignment statement** x = x + y * z

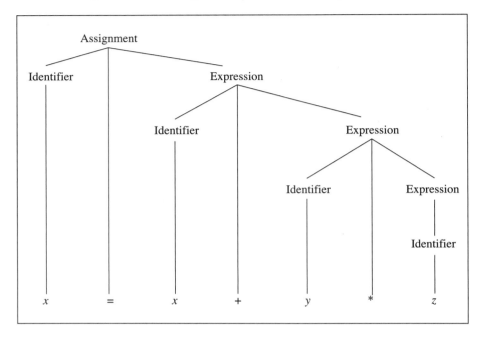

Expression	⇒	Element
Element	⇒	Identifier
Identifier	⇒	x │ y │ z

where x = x + y * z has a unique derivation tree, as shown in Figure 4.8.

4.7 BNF VARIATIONS

A grammar written in BNF may be expressed in many other notational variations of BNF. For example, the syntax of an identifier in Fortran can be represented as

```
<identifier> ::=  <letter>  |  <letter><alphabet>  |
    ::=  <letter><alphabet><alphabet>  |
    ::=  <letter><alphabet><alphabet><alphabet>  |
    ::=  <letter><alphabet><alphabet><alphabet><alphabet>  |
    ::=  <letter><alphabet><alphabet><alphabet><alphabet><alphabet>
```

A variation of BNF may be used to denote any number of occurrences of a sequence of symbols. For example, the notation $\{\cdots\}_i^j$ can be used to express any number n of occurrences of the enclosed sequence of symbols, for $i \le n \le j$. In this example, the identifier notation in Fortran can be defined simply as

FIGURE **4.8**   **Introducing a new variable for the assignment statement** x = x + y * z

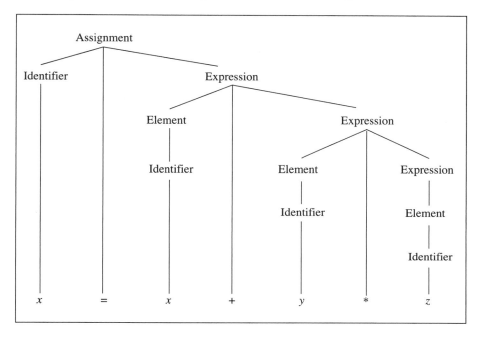

$$\text{<identifier> ::= <letter>\{< alphabet >\}}_0^5$$

Two popular notational variations of BNF are the Extended BNF (EBNF) grammar and Syntax Diagram.

Extended BNF Grammar

Despite the power and simplicity of the BNF grammar, it isn't an ideal notation for describing and reading the production rules of a programming language syntax. We can add some extra notations to extend the BNF grammar to allow for easier description of languages. Then, anything that can be specified with BNF can also be specified with the Extended BNF (EBNF) grammar. This extension doesn't enhance the descriptive power of BNF; it merely increases the readability and writability of the production rules. For example, to express an integer as a sequence of digits we can write in BNF a recursive rule such as:

```
<integer> ::= <digit>  |  <integer> <digit>
```

Although we can use this recursive definition to address an integer number, having notations that directly express the formation of a sequence of one or more of digits would be much more convenient. We can also use notations that effectively compress the production rules so we can describe the language more easily. In extending BNF, we recommend use of the notational extensions of

FIGURE **4.9**   Grammar for the assignment statement in (a) BNF and (b) EBNF

```
<assignment>    ::= <variable> = <expression>
<expression>    ::= <term>  |      <expression> + <term>  |  <expression> - <term>
<term>          ::= <primary>  |      <term> * < primary>  |  < term> / < primary>
<primary>       ::= <variable>  |  <number>  |  (<expression>)
<variable>      ::= <identifier>  |  <identifier>  <variable>
<number>        ::= <digit>  |  <digit>  <number>
<identifier>    ::= x  |  y  |  z
<digit>         ::= 0  |  1  |  2  |  3  |  4  |  5  |  6  |  7  |  8  |  9
(a)

<assignment>    ::= <variable> = <expression>
<expression>    ::= <term> {[+ | -] <term>}*
<term>          ::= <primary>{[* | /] <primary>}*
<primary>       ::= <variable>  |  <number>  |  '('<expression>')'
<variable>      ::= <identifier>{<identifier>  <variable>}*
<number>        ::= <digit>{<digit>  <number>}*
<identifier>    ::= <letter>{<letter>}*
<digit>         ::= {<digit>}+  |
                    0  |  1  |  2  |  3  |  4  |  5  |  6  |  7  |  8  |  9
(b)
```

▶ Braces { }, which are used to represent a sequence of zero or more instances of elements;

▶ Brackets [ ], which are used to represent an optional element; and

▶ Parentheses ( ), which are used to represent a group of elements.

For example, the BNF grammar associated with the assignment statement having the basic operands x, y, and z, as represented in Figure 4.9(a), can be restated in extended BNF, as given in Figure 4.9(b).

Syntax Diagram

In 1970, Niklaus Wirth used a different approach, called Syntax Diagram, to express grammars in his definition of the Pascal programming language. In this approach, each production rule is represented as a directed graph whose vertices are symbols. In this graph, terminal symbols are represented by circles and variables by rectangles. Syntax Diagram is a pictorial technique for syntax description and is equivalent to the BNF grammar. Figure 4.10 represents the syntax diagram for the Real-Number gram-

F I G U R E **4.10**   Syntax Diagram representation for the Real-Number grammar

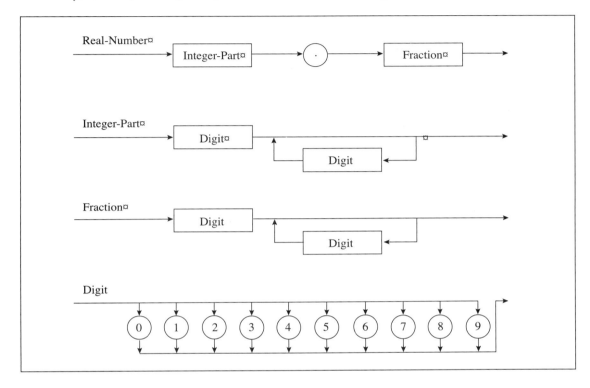

mar, where the variable symbols are represented in a transition diagram having one entry and one exit edge.

◩ 4.8 ATTRIBUTE GRAMMARS

Developed by Donald Knuth in 1968, attribute grammars are powerful and elegant mechanisms that formalize both the context-free and context-sensitive aspects of a language's syntax. For example, an attribute grammar can be used to determine whether a variable has been declared and whether the use of the variable is consistent with its declaration. Basically, an attribute grammar is an extension to a context-free grammar with certain formal primitives (e.g., attributes, evaluation rules, and conditions) that enable syntax aspects of a language to be specified more precisely. In general, for each distinct symbol of grammar, there is a finite set of attributes, each having an associated domain of values (e.g., integers, characters, and string values), or more complex structures. In addition, each attribute associated with the symbol has a logical condition expressing a constraint that has to be met by the attribute values involved. A general approach is to augment a production rule with attributes that will be set to true if the production rule is used correctly. Regarding the parse tree of a construct, attribute grammars can pass values from a node to its parent (above each node), or from the current node to a child (below each node). In addition to passing attribute values up or down the parse tree, the attribute values may be assigned, modified, and checked at any node in the derivation tree. Suppose that $A = \{a_1, a_2, \dots, a_n\}$ is a set of attributes associated with each grammar symbol. The set A consists of two disjoint sets of primitives.

▶   Synthesized attributes $S = \{s_1, s_2, \dots, s_n\}$ are used to pass information up a syntax tree. In other words, a synthesized attribute is a function that relates the left-side variable to values of the right-side variables.

▶   Inherited attributes $I = \{i_1, i_2, \dots, i_n\}$ are used to pass information down a syntax tree. In other words, an inherited attribute is a function that relates variable values in a tree with variable values higher in the tree. A corollary follows: $A = S \cup I$ and $S \cap I = \emptyset$.

In general, to every grammar symbol $x \in V \cup T$ we associate a set of attributes $A(x) \subset A$. We view $A(x)$ as additional information about the symbol x and set

$$I(x) = \{a \in A(x) \mid a \in I\}$$
$$S(x) = \{a \in A(x) \mid a \in S\}$$

The start symbol is the root of the syntax tree and inherits no information, so we require that $I(\text{start}) = \emptyset$. In addition, for all $t \in T$ we require that $S(t) = \emptyset$ because there is no subtree below a terminal node to synthesize information. The following is a simple example of how attribute grammars are used to describe a semantic model of a programming language—in this case, a simple grammar for an arithmetic expression.

```
Assignment    ⇒    Identifier    =    Expression
Expression    ⇒    Identifier    +    Expression
Expression    ⇒    Identifier    *    Expression
Expression    ⇒    Identifier
Identifier    ⇒    a  |  b    |  c
```

We define the attribute grammar of this language by an attribute named *value*, which represents the relationship among the grammar's variables as shown in Table 4.2.

The grammar involves the use of a synthesized attribute *value* associated with the variables. We now add the conditions and rules to the attribute grammar to specify the inherited attributes associated with the variables, as shown in Table 4.2.

Figure 4.11 illustrates an attributed syntax tree expressing the value of the arithmetic expression $x = 3 + 4 * 5$.

Example 4.11: Consider the grammar that recognizes sentences of the form $a^n b^m$.

$V = \{<\text{letter\_sequence}> <a\_\text{sequence}> <b\_\text{sequence}>\}$

$T = \{a, b\}$

$S = \{<\text{letter\_sequence}>\}$

TABLE **4.2**   Attribute grammar for an arithmetic expression

Production Rule	Attribute
Assignment $\Rightarrow$ Identifier = Expression	$value$(Identifier) $= value$(Expression)
Expression $\Rightarrow$ Identifier + Expression	$value$(Expression$_1$) $= value$(Identifier) $+ value$(Expression$_2$)
Expression $\Rightarrow$ Identifier * Expression	$value$(Expression$_3$) $= value$(Identifier) $* value$(Expression$_4$)
Expression $\Rightarrow$ Identifier	$value$(Expression) $= value$(Identifier)
Identifier $\Rightarrow a$	$value$(Identifier) $= value$ of number a
Identifier $\Rightarrow b$	$value$(Identifier) $= value$ of number b
Identifier $\Rightarrow c$	$value$(Identifier) $= value$ of number c

TABLE **4.3**   Attribute grammar for an arithmetic expression with conditions

Production Rule	Attribute
Assignment $\Rightarrow$ Identifier = Expression	$actual\text{-}type$(Identifier) $\Leftarrow expected\text{-}type$ (Expression)
Expression $\Rightarrow$ Identifier + Expression	$actual\text{-}type$(Expression$_1$) $\Leftarrow$ if ($actual\text{-}type$(Identifier)$=integer$)
	and ($actual\text{-}type$(Expression$_2$)$=integer$)
	then integer
	else real
	end-if
Expression $\Rightarrow$ Identifier * Expression	$actual\text{-}type$(Expression$_3$) $\Leftarrow$ if($actual\text{-}type$(Identifier)$=integer$)
	and ($actual\text{-}type$(Expression$_4$)$=integer$)
	then integer
	else real
	end-if
Expression $\Rightarrow$ Identifier	$actual\text{-}type$(Expression) $\Leftarrow expected\text{-}type$ (Identifier)
Identifier $\Rightarrow a$	$actual\text{-}type$(Identifier) $\Leftarrow search$(type of number a)
Identifier $\Rightarrow b$	$actual\text{-}type$(Identifier) $\Leftarrow search$(type of number b)
Identifier $\Rightarrow c$	$actual\text{-}type$(Identifier) $\Leftarrow search$(type of number c)

The production rules are as follows

```
<letter_sequence> :: =    <a_sequence> <b_sequence>
<a_sequence>      :: =    a | <a_sequence> a
<b_sequence>      :: =    b | <b_sequence> b
```

FIGURE **4.11**   (a) An attributed syntax tree expressing the *value* attribute; (b) an attributed syntax tree expressing the *actual-type* attribute

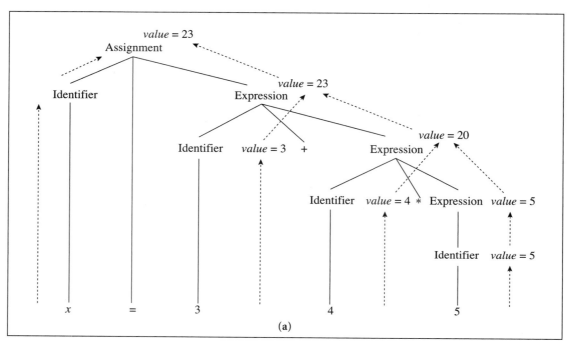

(a)

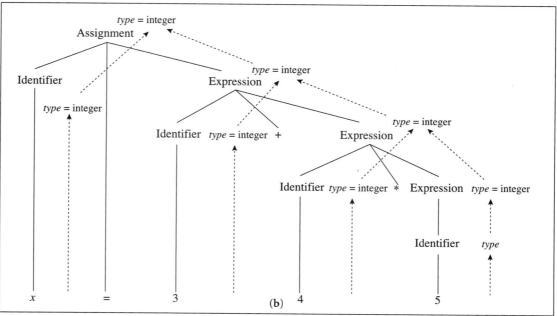

(b)

FIGURE **4.12**   Syntax tree for string *aaabbb*

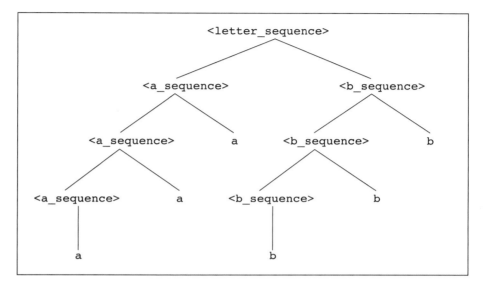

FIGURE **4.13**   Syntax tree for string *aabbb*

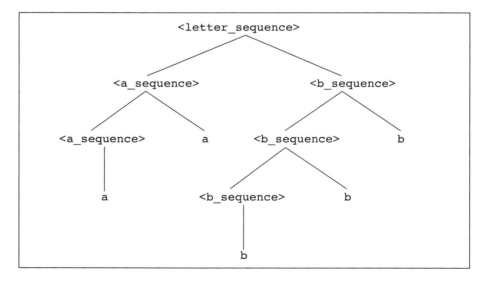

As Figure 4.12 shows, this grammar can accept the string aaabbb with an equal number of a's and b's (n=m). It can also generate the string aabbb (n≠m), as shown in Figure 4.13. In other words, there is no restriction that the number of a and b characters

FIGURE **4.14**   Attributed syntax tree for the string *aaabbb*

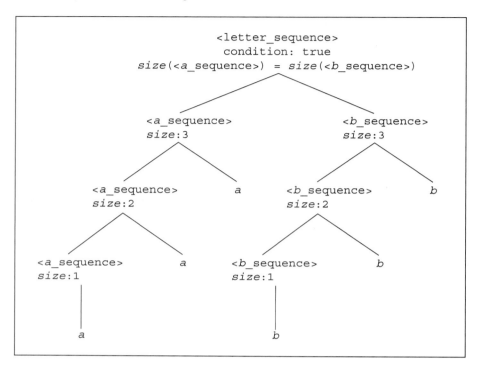

in represented strings be the same. However, we can provide a restriction that the number of a and b characters must be equal. To do so, we augment the grammar with an attribute describing the length of a letter sequence. To satisfy this restriction, we use an attribute size associated with the variable a_sequence and the variable b_sequence, adding a condition to provide that size for each sequence has the same value. We state this condition as

> if a character sequence consists of a single character then
>   size = 1; and
> if a character sequence is followed by a single character then
>   size = size of the sequence character + 1.

We represent the production rules of the attributed grammar as follows, where we differentiate a parent sequence from a child sequence by adding the subscript x to the variable.

    <letter_sequence> :: =   <a_sequence>   <b_sequence>
    condition
    size(<a_sequence>) = size(<b_sequence>)

```
<a_sequence> :: = a
    size(<a_sequence>) ⇐ 1
| <a_sequence>ₓ a
    size(<a_sequence>) ⇐ size(<a_sequence>ₓ) + 1
<b_sequence> :: = b
    size(<b_sequence>) ⇐ 1
    | <b_sequence>ₓ b
    size(<b_sequence>) ⇐ size(<b_sequence>ₓ) + 1
```

This attribute grammar successfully represents the sequence `aaabbb` because the sequence obeys the production rules and satisfies all the conditions of the attribute grammar. The attributed syntax tree for `aaabbb` is shown in Figure 4.14. Any string such as `aabbb` in which the total number of a's and b's are not the same cannot be accepted by this grammar.

SUMMARY

Without a clear notation of the effect of language constructs and formal definition of the language, we cannot reason mathematically about the behavior of the program. In this chapter, we discussed the specification of programming languages with regard to design and implementation. In general, three mechanisms were used to describe the design and implementation of programming languages: regular expressions, formal grammars, and attribute grammars. Regular expressions can be defined by alternation, concatenation, Kleene closure, and positive closure rules to represent any programming language. Formal grammars or syntax specification refers to a set of symbols and rules used to form constructs of the language and describes the structure of the language without addressing their meaning. We briefly discussed the specification of the grammar of a language, which consisted of four components: a set of terminal symbols, a set of variable symbols, a set of production rules, and start symbol.

We classified grammars into four categories according to the structure of their production rules as type 0 or unrestricted grammar, type 1 or context-sensitive grammar, type 2 or context-free grammar, and type 3 or regular grammar. The syntactic structure of a construct as generated by a grammar can be represented with a syntax tree sometimes called a derivation tree or parse tree. A grammar written in BNF (type 2 grammar) may be expressed in many other notational variations of BNF. We discussed Extended BNF and Syntax Diagram, two popular notational variations of BNF. Attribute grammar is a powerful and elegant mechanism that formalizes both the context-free and context-sensitive aspects of the syntax of a language. In this sense, attribute grammar can be used to determine whether a variable has been declared and whether the use of the variable is consistent with its declaration. We discussed the attribute grammar with several examples to address its efficiency in designing a programming language.

EXERCISES

1. Specify a grammar to recognize *odd-length* sequence of 0 and 1 over the alphabet 0 and 1. Represent the recognition of the valid string 00100.

2. Sketch the *abstract syntax tree* for (a+b)*(c−a) expression.

3. Define the *syntactic specification* of a grammar to accept 1+1*1 as an expression such that the grammar is *ambiguous.*

4. Describe the English language rules that a sentence may consist of a *subject, verb,* and *object* followed by a *period.*

5. Specify the syntactic specification of a *context-free* grammar to accept sentences such as "the girl sang a song" and "the cat surprised the boy with a song."

6. Sketch the syntax tree for the "the girl sang a song" using the grammar represented in the previous exercise.

7. Specify the syntactic specification of a *context-sensitive* grammar to accept strings having equal numbers of *a, b,* and *c* in that order. Using this grammar, derive the string aaabbbccc.

8. Assume the following grammar:

```
<assign>   ::= <id>   := <expr>
<id>       ::=  A | B | C
<expr>     ::= <id> + <expr>
<expr>     ::= <id> * <expr>
<expr>     ::=  (<expr> )
<expr>     ::= <id>
```

Show a parse tree and a *left-most* derivation of the following statement:

```
A := A * ( B + ( C * A ) )
```

9. Prove that the following grammar is *ambiguous.*

```
<S>    ::= <A>
<A>    ::= <A> + <A>
<A>    ::= <id>
<id>   ::=  a | b | c
```

10. Assume that we introduce the following production rules:

```
<expression>  ::= <number>
<expression>  ::= <expression> + <expression>
<expression>  ::= <expression> - <expression>
<expression>  ::= <expression> * <expression>
<number>      ::=  40| 3 | 9
```

Is the expression 40-3-9 ambiguous? If yes, why?

11. Write a grammar for the language consisting of strings that have n copies of the letter "a" followed by the same number of copies of the letter "b" where n>0. For example, the strings ab and aabb are in the language but a and abb are not.

12. Construct a grammar to accept an expression represented in the form of real numbers.

    ```
    145.56 + 65.84 − 45.35
    ```

    Show the syntax tree to represent this expression.

13. Consider the following production rules:

    ```
    <pop>  ::=  [<bop>, <pop>]
    <pop>  ::= <bop>
    <bop>  ::= <boop>
    <bop>  ::=  (<pop>)
    <boop> ::=  x
    <boop> ::=  y
    <boop> ::=  z
    ```

    For each of the following strings, prove that the string belongs to the grammar.

    ```
    z
    (x)
    [y]
    [(x),y]
    [(x),[y,x]]
    ```

14. Consider the grammar of calculator language described in this chapter. The user enters the expressions as the following:

    ```
    3*9+5  =
    40−3*9 =
    ```

    Draw the syntax tree of each expression.

15. Using the following syntactic specifications, demonstrate its ambiguity by displaying two derivation trees for the expression a+b+c.

    ```
    <expression>  ::=   <element>|<expression><operator><expression>
    <element>     ::=   <numeral>|<variable>
    <operator>    ::=   +|−
    <variable>    ::=    a|b|c
    ```

16. A useful graphical representation for a grammar rule is the syntax grammar, which indicates the sequence of terminals and nonterminals encountered in the right-hand side of the rule. Sketch the syntax diagram for the simple arithmetic expressions represented as following.

    ```
    <expression>    ::=      <term>{+ <term>}
    <term>          ::=      <factor>{* <factor>}
    <factor>        ::=      (<expression>)|<number>
    <number>        ::=      (<digit>){<digit>}
    <digit>         ::=      0|1|2|3|4|5|6|7|8|9
    ```

17. Define the syntactic specification of *conditional instructions* in some programming language using the standard BNF notations.

18. Construct a BNF grammar to represent the number 234.

19. Give a BNF specification for the language that consists of an even number of a's followed by an odd number of b's.

20. Consider the following grammar specification:

    ```
    <E>    ::=    <E> * <E>
    <E>    ::=    <E> & <E>
    <E>    ::=    c
    ```

    a. Give a derivation and parse tree for the string c*c&c*&c.
    b. Give a proof of the grammar ambiguity.

21. Consider an *aggregate production* rule as the following form.

    ```
    Program  ≡  decpart : Declaration_list;  body : Instruction
    ```

    Elaborate the meaning of this production rule by an example.

22. Consider a choice production rule as the following.

    ```
    Instruction ≡ Skip | Assignment | Compound | Conditional | Loop
    ```

    What do you need to construct a specimen of *Instruction?*

    Assume that v is a variable and e is an expression. Define a production rule to describe an `Assignment`.

23. Consider the following program given in a concrete notation.

    ```
    program
       declare
          X: integer;
       begin
          X = 0;
          X = X+1;
    end
    ```

    Define the syntactic specification of the *attribute grammar* representing this program.

24. What is the syntax production rule of the following form?

    ```
    Compound ⇒ Instruction*
    ```

25. Construct a grammar to recognize sentences of the form $a^n b^n c^n$.

26. Augment the grammar in the previous exercise with an *attribute* describing the length of a letter sequence to ensure that the sequences of a, b, and c all have the same length.

27. *Regular expressions* constitute a language. Write a context-free grammar for this language. Make the grammar reflect the different priorities of "*", "|", and "•".

REFERENCE-NEEDED EXERCISES

To answer the following exercises, you might need to consult the references: Best, 1996; Gunter, 1992; Pagan, 1981; Slonneger and Kurtz, 1995; Stansifer 1995; Tennent, 1991.

1. Deductive systems are rarely presented as grammars instead, they are more often given as *Post Systems,* named after Emil Post, who first used them. Describe a Post System and the components associated with them.

2. A binary numeral is a sequence of binary digits followed by a binary point and another sequence of binary digits; for example, 100.001 and 0.001101. Construct an attribute grammar defining the meaning of binary numerals that involves only synthesized attributes.

3. How does Pascal programming language resolve the dangling *else ambiguity?*

4. Consider the following program segment.

```
Program  P  is
   Var  x, y:  integer
   Var  a: boolean
begin
   .
   .
   .
end
```

   a. Introduce attribute grammar rules and associated conditions for this program.
   b. Construct an attributed syntax tree for this program fragment.

5 Semantic Specifications

The word *semantics*, introduced in 1893, originally referred to the study of what words mean. Subsequently, semantics also came to mean the study of the relation of words to sentences of a language, their significance, and changes in their meaning. In computer science, the investigation of semantics focuses on developing ways to express the meaning of programming languages. Designers, implementers, and users of programming languages need a complete and accurate understanding of the **syntax** (the formation) as well as the **semantics** (the meaning) of every construct of that language. The syntactic aspects of programming languages are supported by a well-defined and widely known mathematical theory of formal languages, which provides accurate descriptions of the syntax of various programming languages (e.g., context-free grammars).

Semantics also involves a description of what happens during execution of a program or a phrase of a program that refers to rules specifying its meaning. In other words, at run time, semantics can address the behavior of any syntactically valid program or construct written in the language. A rigorous definition of the semantics of programming languages can support

▶ Correct description and implementation of programming languages

▶ Systematic development and verification of program

▶ Analysis of existing programming languages

▶ Design of new languages that are simpler

One way of expressing the semantics of a language is by describing each of its constructs in a sentence. Such a description can provide a reasonably intuitive view of the language. For example, the syntax of the following conditional statement in C language

```
if  (a>b)  max=a;  else  max=b;
```

illustrates the formation of this construct (e.g., where to put a semicolon ";"), whereas the semantic rules express the effect of the statement (e.g., depending on the value of expression a>b, one of the two assignment statements is carried out). From another point of view, the meaning of each phrase in a program is the computation that it describes. For example, the meaning of a C expression such as x+1 is a computation that yields a value of 6 if the value of x is 5. Another example is a declaration, in which the meaning is a computation that produces bindings; for example, the C declaration

```
int    x=5;
```

would produce a binding of x to 5. Although no generally accepted method for semantic definition exists, there are many different approaches to semantic definition, such as the use of the context-free grammars for syntax specification. Indeed, formally defining the semantics of a programming language is still not customary. Nevertheless, several notational systems for formal definition have been developed and are increasingly in use:

▶ **By language reference manual,** which is the common method of describing programming languages. However, the manuals still suffer from the lack of precision associated with natural language descriptions. Programmers and language designers usually base their explanations of language features on underlying models of execution that are more implied than explicit. In general, semantic descriptions in reference manuals and language standards are largely inadequate because they are based primarily in implementation techniques and intuition.

▶ **By translator,** which is the common method of questioning the behavior of programming languages interactively. In this approach, the program is run to discover its behavior. In addition, the translator is machine dependent, thus may not be portable to all machines.

▶ **By formal definition,** which is a common method of questioning the behavior of programming languages by mathematical methods that are precise but complex and abstract. The advantage of such methods is that they define a programming language so precisely that programs can be proven correct mathematically and the translation can be validated to produce exactly the behavior described in the language definition. A number of formal methods have been developed to describe programming language behaviors, but they differ in their formation. These methods include operational semantics, axiomatic semantics, and denotational semantics. From the programming point of view, we might call the first two *proof systems* and the third *model theory*.

In this chapter, we will survey different formal semantic methods, which are important for several reasons:

▶ They provide an unambiguous language definition.

▶ They provide standards so that a language will not vary from implementation to implementation.

▶ They provide a basis for correctness proofs by both compilers and programs.

Our purpose is to illustrate the spirit of how language semantics can be defined and how styles differ from each other. We concentrate on the formal semantics of imperative languages, first discussing axiomatic semantics in Section 5.1 as a mathematical logic to specify the semantics of a programming language and its components. Axiomatic semantics describes the meaning of each syntactically correct program and program construct by associating with it properties of variables that hold before execution starts and after the program or construct halts. In this approach, the computation is described by a logical statement called a predicate or assertion. There are two kinds of assertions: *precondition* and *postcondition*. We extended the class of assertions to include logical expressions called formulas. The application for which axiomatic semantics is most useful is constructing program correctness.

Operational semantics appears in Section 5.2 as a tool to define programming language behavior by describing its actions in terms of the operations of an abstract or hypothetical machine. In this approach, the data structure of the modeling machine can be used to describe the effects of each programming language construct. The most famous abstract machine language used for operational semantics is the Vienna Definition Language (VDL). The VDL consists of a formal system that models the interpretation of a program, and its specification consists of two parts: a translator and an interpreter.

In Section 5.3, we discuss denotational semantics. In this approach, programs are translated to functions and we can prove their properties by using the standard mathematical theory of functions known as functional calculus. In this sense, we deal with denotational semantics components including semantic domains, semantic functions, auxiliary functions, and semantic equations.

5.1 AXIOMATIC SEMANTICS

The word *axiomatic* is used because elements of mathematical logic are used to specify the semantics of a programming language and its components. The first significant work on this approach was done by Hoare and Wirth (1980), and an axiomatic definition exists for the Pascal programming language. Axiomatic semantics describes the meaning of each syntactically correct program and program construct by associating with it properties of variables that hold before execution starts and after the program or construct halts. This approach defines programming language behavior by applying mathematical logic to language constructs, in which the state of the computation is described by a logical statement called a **predicate** or an **assertion.** Predicate logic is used as the metalanguage of axiomatic semantics to describe the initial assumptions and desired results for programs and program components. Specifications are somewhat analogous to the axioms and rules of inference of a logical calculus and constitute a formal system in which there is no explicit notion of the state of a machine. They prescribe a minimal set of constraints that any implementation of the subject language must satisfy in its treatment of the various types of constructs but say nothing about the details of how that might be achieved. After introducing the semantic concepts and mathematical techniques needed to describe the axiomatic semantics of conventional high-level programming languages, we apply them to

▶ Verify the correctness of operational descriptions

▶ Demonstrate the soundness of axiomatic descriptions

▶ Analyze and design programming languages

Thus, axiomatic semantics determine the result (or output or observable effect) of any program or any construct of the program. In general, there are no theoretical limits to the axiomatic approach for verifying software.

5.1.1   Principles of Axiomatic Semantics

The axiomatic approach defines each program construct in terms of its accomplishments when carried out. *Accomplishment* is defined by describing the state of the computation before and after the execution of the construct. The execution of a construct S in a programming language can be described by the state obtained before and after the execution of S. There is no single, comprehensive, or standard notation for axiomatic semantics, but the notational conventions adopted by different authors have many properties in common. They include all the standard notations for logical expressions:

▶ Logical operators ($\land, \lor, \lnot, \supset$, and $\equiv$)

▶ Logical quantifiers ($\exists$ and $\forall$)

▶ Logical constants (true and false)

Axiomatic semantics uses logical assertions, which are statements that are either true or false. In general, an assertion is a logical statement constructed with the individual variables, individual constants, and logical notations of applied predicate calculus. For each program construct, such as an assignment statement, an expression, a read statement, a write statement, and the like, the axiomatic method specifies the assertions that are assumed to be true before and after the program construct runs. In other words, we consider logical assertions to be statements about the behavior of a program that are true or false at any moment during the execution. There are two kinds of assertions:

1. A **precondition assertion** is an assertion about a construct that is true before the construct runs.

2. A **postcondition assertion** is an assertion about a construct that is true after the construct runs.

For example, given the assignment statement

    x=x+5

we would expect that, whatever value **x** has before the statement runs, its value after the assignment is carried out is 5 more than its previous value. In this sense, if **x=3** is the precondition assertion before execution, the postcondition assertion is **x=3+5** after execution. Standard notation for axiomatic semantics assertions is to write the precondition assertion inside braces before the construct and to write the postcondition assertion inside braces just after the construct, as represented in the following.

{x=3} x=x+5 {x=8}

Preconditions and postconditions are used to specify the behavior of programs at each step of execution and are often capable of being tested for validity during program execution. We can extend the class of assertions to include **logical expressions,** called **formulas,** as in

{P} S {Q}

where P and Q are logical assertions and S is a construct of the subject language. The interpretation of such a logical expression is

if P is true before the execution of S and if the execution of S terminates,
then Q is true after the execution of S.

P and Q are said to be *precondition* and *postcondition* of the logical expression, respectively. In other words, {P} S {Q} is valid if execution of the program construct S is begun in any state satisfying P, and if S terminates, it terminates in a state satisfying Q. Therefore, the meaning of construct S can be viewed as the ordered pair <{P},{Q}>, called a **specification** of S. We say that the construct S is correct with respect to the specification given by the precondition and postcondition provided that, if the construct is run with values that make the precondition true, the construct halts and the resulting values make the postcondition true. Furthermore, for an assertion Q, many assertions P with the property {P} S {Q} hold. However, one precondition is the most general or weakest assertion with the property {P} S {Q}—called the *weakest precondition* of postcondition Q and construct S. For example, y=3 is one possible precondition for statement x=y+1, which leads to postcondition (x=4 ⟹ x>0). In addition, y≥0 is also a precondition for statement x=y+1 with postcondition x>0. In this case, y≥0 is called a weakest precondition, or the necessary and sufficient precondition for statement x=y+1 that leads to postcondition x>0. The following are some sample valid logical expressions.

```
{x=2}      x=x+3      {x=5}
{x=3 ∧ y=4}      x=x+y      {x=7 ∧ y=4}
{y=5}      x=y+1      {x=6  ∧ y=5}
{2=2}      x=3      {x=3}
{true}      if B then x=1 else x=2 {x=1  or  x=2}
```

In the first logical expression, the knowledge of the semantics for assignment ensures that, after execution of x=x+3, the resulting state satisfies x=5 with regard to the previous value of x=2. In the last logical expression, regardless of the Boolean condition B, both assignments establish the postcondition. We can also use logical expressions to determine the value of one or more program constructs or the relationship between such constructs. For example, we expect the logical expression

{x=2}   x=x+3   {x=5}

to be true, but

```
{y=5}    x=y+1    {x=5  ∧ y=5}
```

to be false. The following are some sample invalid logical expressions.

```
{x=3 ∧ y=4}    x=x+y    {x=6 ∧ y=4}
{2=2}    x=3    {y=3}
{true}    if B then x=1 else x=2 {x=1  and  x=2}
```

5.1.2 Proof Rules

Statements and expressions of programming languages contain terms, formulas, and variables. For example, the test in a conditional statement is a formula, and the assignment statement assigns the value of an expression (term) to a variable. The goal of axiomatic semantics is to provide logical statements that capture the intended meaning of each construct in a programming language. These logical statements are formed so that a specification for a construct can be deduced. In addition to assertions and formulas, an axiomatic specification of a programming language includes a number of **inference rules,** also called *proof rules* or *deduction rules*, which enable the truth of certain assertions to be deduced from the truth of certain other assertions. In general, a rule of inference of the form:

$$\frac{R_1, R_2, \ldots, R_n}{R}$$

where $R_1, R_2, \ldots, R_n$, and R are all assertions, has the following interpretation:

> *given that $R_1, R_2, \ldots, R_n$ are true, then R is true can be deduced.*

In other words, when two expressions are equivalent according to axiomatic semantics, we may safely substitute one for the other in any specification. Further, an inference rule of the form:

$$\frac{R_1, R_2, \ldots, R_n \Rightarrow R_{n+1}}{R}$$

expresses that

> *if the truth of R_{n+1} is deduced by assuming the truth of $R_1, R_2, \ldots, R_n$, then the truth of R can be deduced.*

In general, such a deduction consists of a finite sequence of logical expressions, each of which is a rule of inference whose premises have already been established. For example, the axiomatic specification of the Pam language, summarized in Table 5.2, is based on the rules of syntax definition shown in Table 5.1. The general inference rules are independent of the language being defined, and any program submitted for semantic analysis has already been verified as syntactically correct.

The input and output rules are based on the existence of input and output files, as IN and OUT indicate the contents of these two files in assertions. The specification of input rules (*read* command) involves removing the first element from the input file and assigning it to the variable that appears in the *read* command. The output rule (*write* command) appends the current value identified by the expression to the end of the output file. In the assignment rule, Q stands for any formula, E for any term, and V

TABLE **5.1**   Rules of syntax definition

```
<series>        ::=      <statement₁>;<statement₂>  |

                         <read variable-list>  |

                         <write variable-list>

<variable>   ::=      <expression>   |

                         if <comparison>  then  <statement> fi  |

                         if <comparison>  then  <statement₁> else

                                      <statement₂> fi  |

                         to <expression>  do  <statement> end  |

                         while <comparison>  do  <statement> end

<variable-list>::=   <variable>  |  <variable-list>, <variable-list>
```

---

for any variable. This rule indicates that Q can be obtained by substituting E for any V is P. Selection rule 2 (*if* command) involves a choice between two alternatives. If we can prove that each alternative is true for the value of the Boolean expression given, the *if* command can be deduced. Note that the Boolean expression B is used as part of the precondition assertions in logical expressions. Selection rule 1 is the single alternative *if* and is similar to selection rule 2, except that for the false alternative we need to show that the final assertion can be derived directly from the initial assertion P when condition B is false. Repetition rule 1 of the form *to E do S end* is equivalent to a statement sequence consisting of K copies of S, where K is the initial value of expression E. Thus, we should be able to infer the truth of an assertion $\{P\}$ *to E do S end* $\{Q\}$ from the truth of the K assertions

$$\{P\}\,S\,\{P_1\},\ \{P_1\}\,S\,\{P_2\},\ldots,\{P_{k-1}\}\,S\,\{Q\}.$$

The value of K is crucial here, and we assume that it will be determined from the first precondition P. The final construct to be defined is the iteration rule of the form *while B do S end*. In this rule, P is an invariant condition whose truth is unaffected by the execution of the loop body S and hence by any number of runs S. Because S is carried out only as long as B is true, both B and P appear in its precondition. When execution of the entire construct is complete, P still holds, but B is necessarily false.

5.1.3 Program Correctness

Axiomatic semantics is commonly associated with proving a program to be correct using a purely static analysis for the text of the program. This static approach contrasts with the dynamic approach that tests a program by focusing on how the values of variables change as a program runs. Indeed, a set of axiomatic specifications for a particular language is said to constitute a **proof theory** for that language. Logical

TABLE **5.2**   Axiomatic specification of the semantics of Pam

Definition	Rule
$\dfrac{\{P\}\,S\,\{Q\},\,Q\Rightarrow R}{\{P\}\,S\,\{R\}}$	Consequence rule 1
$\dfrac{P\Rightarrow Q,\,\{Q\}\,S\,\{R\}}{\{P\}\,S\,\{R\}}$	Consequence rule 2
$\dfrac{\{P\}\,S\,\{Q\},\,\{P'\}\,S\,\{Q'\}}{\{P\wedge P'\}\,S\,\{Q\wedge Q'\}}$	And rule
$\dfrac{\{P\}\,S\,\{Q\},\,\{P'\}\,S\,\{Q'\}}{P\vee P'\}\,S\,\{Q\vee Q'\}}$	Or rule
$\dfrac{\{P\}\,S_1\,\{Q\},\,\{Q\}\,S_2\,\{R\}}{\{P\}\,S_1;\,S_2\,\{R\}}$	Composition rule
$\dfrac{\{P\}\,readW_1;\,readW_2\,\{Q\}}{\{P\}\,readW_1;W_2\,\{Q\}}$	Input composition rule
$\dfrac{\{P\}\,writeW_1;\,writeW_2\,\{Q\}}{\{P\}\,writeW_1;W_2\,\{Q\}}$	Output composition rule
$\{IN = <K>\,L\ \wedge P_K^V\}\,read\,V\,\{IN = L \wedge P\}$	Input rule
$\{OUT = L \wedge P \wedge V = K\}\,write\,V\,\{OUT = L<K> \wedge P \wedge V = K\}$	Output rule
$\{P_E^V\}\,V = E\,\{Q\}$	Assignment rule
$\dfrac{\{P \wedge B\}\,S\,\{Q\},\,P \wedge \neg B \Rightarrow Q}{\{P\}\,if\,B\,then\,S\,fi\,\{Q\}}$	Selection rule 1
$\dfrac{\{P \wedge B\}\,S_1\,\{Q\},\,\{P \wedge \neg B\}\,S_2\,\{Q\}}{\{P\}\,if\,B\,then\,S_1\,else\,S_2\,fi\,\{Q\}}$	Selection rule 2
$\dfrac{P \Rightarrow E \le 0}{\{P\}\,to\,E\,do\,S\,end\,\{P\}}$	Repetition rule 1
$\dfrac{P_0 \Rightarrow (E > 0 \wedge E = K),\,\{P_{i-1}\}\,S\,\{P_i\}\,for\,i = 1,\ldots K}{\{P_0\}\,to\,E\,do\,S\,end\,\{P_K\}}$	Repetition rule 2
$\dfrac{\{P \wedge B\}\,S\,\{P\}}{\{P\}\,while\,B\,do\,S\,end\,\{P \wedge \neg B\}}$	Iteration rule

expressions are useful in proving programs correct because proof systems exist for deriving valid logical expressions from existing expressions. A **correct program** is one that meets its specification. In other words, a program is correct with respect to a precondition and a postcondition provided that, if the program is started with assumptions that make the precondition true, the resulting values make the postcondition true when the program terminates. In other words, the correctness requirements of the program must be specified formally by giving two predicates:

▶ A precondition (input assertion) on input variables, and

▶ A postcondition (output assertion) on input and output variables.

The aim of verification, or correctness, is to show that if input holds before the program runs, execution terminates in a state where output holds. The entire proof is very large but can be summarized compactly by annotating the program with the conditions that hold between every statement. We use the proof rules to prove the correctness of the following program segments. In doing so, we consider a program S consisting of the statements

```
read    a, b
if      a >b    then    x=a    else    x=b
write x
```

and intend to prove that the assertion

$$\{IN=<-2, 7, 1> \land OUT=<>\} \quad S \quad \{OUT=<7>\}$$

is correct. In other words, we prove that the following is an axiom and can address the program proof regarding the input provided and output obtained.

```
{IN=<-2, 7, 1> ∧ OUT=<>} read    a, b;
                          if    a >b    then    x=a    else    x=b;
                          write x       {OUT=<7>}
```

Proof: The composition rule indicates that we need to establish the validity of

```
{IN=<-2, 7, 1> ∧ OUT=<>}    read    a, b    {Q}
```

for some logical expression Q, and of

```
{Q}    if    a >b    then    x=a    else    x=b    {R}
```

for some logical expression R, and of

```
{R}    write x       {OUT=<7>}
```

for the same logical expression R. Using the decomposition rule, we can deduce

```
{IN=<-2, 7, 1> ∧ OUT=<>}    read    a    {P}
{P}                         read    b    {Q}
```

which can address the following deduction regarding the input rule.

```
{P} = {IN=<7, 1> ∧ OUT=<> ∧ a=-2}
{Q} = {IN=<1> ∧ OUT=<> ∧ a=-2 ∧ b=7}
```

We now only need to prove

```
{IN=<1> ∧ OUT=<> ∧ a=-2 ∧ b=7}
    if    a >b    then    x=a    else    x=b;    write x
{OUT=<7>}
```

As the assertions

```
{Q ∧ a>b} ⇒ false ⇒{Q ∧ a>b}    x=a    {Q ∧ a>b ∧ x=a}
{Q ∧ ¬(a>b)} ⇒ true ⇒{Q ∧ ¬(a>b)}   x=b    {Q ∧ ¬(a>b) ∧ x=b}
```

both hold by virtue of the assignment and consequence rules, the inference rule for the if-statement addresses

```
{IN=<1> ∧ OUT=<> ∧ a=−2 ∧ b=7}
if   a >b   then   x=a   else   x=b;
{IN=<1> ∧ OUT=<> ∧ a=−2 ∧ b=7 ∧ ¬(a>b) ∧ x=7}
```

Now, we only need to prove the assertion

```
{IN=<1> ∧ OUT=<> ∧ a=−2 ∧ b=7 ∧ ¬(a>b) ∧ x=7}  write x   {OUT=<7>}
```

which, according to the output rule, can be deduced from

```
{IN=<1> ∧ OUT=<> ∧ a=−2 ∧ b=7 ∧ ¬(a>b) ∧ x=7}
write x
{IN=<1> ∧ OUT=<7> ∧ a=−2 ∧ b=7 ∧ ¬(a>b) ∧ x=7} ⇒ {OUT=<7>}
```

and holds by virtue of the consequence rule. We have proved that, with regard to the provided input, the output can be obtained, verifying the correctness of execution of the program.

Example: Consider the following program fragment in which all the variables are assumed to be integers.

```
{IN= <5> ∧ OUT= <10>}
read k;  sum=k;
while   k>1   do
   k=k − 1;   sum=sum+k;
end
write sum;
{OUT= <10,15>}
```

We are interested in proving that the program fragment is correct with respect to the IN and OUT assertions. We can rewrite the program as the following.

```
{IN=<5> ∧ OUT= <10>}    read k;  sum=k;   {Q}
{Q}    while   k>1   do
       k=k − 1;   sum=sum+k;
       end            {R}
{R}    write sum        {OUT= <10,15>}
```

In this example, the termination of the loop is ensured by the iteration rule because variable k is altered only by instruction k=k−1. This decreasing sequence of values would eventually make k >1 false. Starting the execution of the loop with the state satisfying {k=5 ∧ sum=5 ∧ OUT= <10>} ensures termination in a state satisfying {sum=15 ∧ OUT= <10>}. The precondition assertion of the output rule {sum=15 ∧ OUT= <10>} ensures termination in a state satisfying OUT. We can also easily prove that the assertion {k=5 ∧ sum=5 ∧ OUT= <10>} holds after execution of the instructions

```
read k;   sum=k;
```

using the input and assignment rules, respectively. Further discussion of this topic is beyond the scope of this text and can be pursued in books on programming methodology.

5.2 Operational Semantics

Operational semantics defines programming language behavior by describing its actions in terms of the operations of an abstract or hypothetical machine. This method requires that the operations of the machine used in the semantic notations be precisely defined. In general, a simple hypothetical machine similar to an actual computer is often used. It can be a **Turing machine,** called a *reduction machine* or an *abstract machine.* Such a machine is a collection of actions described in mathematical notation to represent programs by applying their operations to values to show the run-time behavior of a program rather than to carry it out efficiently. An example of an abstract machine is the SECD proposed by Peter Landin (1964) for the mechanical evaluation of lambda expressions. In this approach, the data structure of the modeling machine is used to describe the effects of each programming language construct. The SECD machine manipulates four stacks:

▶   S = the stack of intermediate answers
▶   E = the stack of environment
▶   C = the stack of control
▶   D = the stack of dump that holds the state for recursive calls

Pushing information on and off the stacks of the SECD machine is controlled by five instructions:

1. LDV I: Load the value of the variable at depth I.
2. LDC X: Load the constant X directly.
3. LDF L: Load the function represented by the list of instructions L.
4. APP: Apply a function to its arguments.
5. RTN: Return from a subroutine call.

The most famous abstract machine used for operational semantics was VDL developed by Peter Wegner (1972). In this approach, the abstract machine interprets a program by passing through a sequence of discrete states, in which state transitions are defined by a set of instruction definitions written in a specific notation.

5.2.1 Principles of Operational Semantics

Specifying a programming language by the operations through which each program construct is carried out is called **operational semantics.** Focusing on the individual steps through which each program construct is carried out gives useful insights into how programs are implemented. For example, the operational semantics of the *while* structure in C programming language as

```
while    (expression)
     statement
```

might be defined as the following operations:

▶ Evaluate the expression, yielding a value.

▶ If the evaluated value is true, run statement and repeat step 1.

▶ If the evaluated value is false, terminate the `while` command.

The operational semantics of a *for* structure in C programming language as

```
for    (expr₁; expr₂; expr₃)  {
       statement
       }
```

can be described in terms of the following operations:

```
          expr₁
loop:   if    expr₂=false
        goto  exit
        statement
        expr₃
        goto  loop
exit:   ...
```

In a mathematical expression such as $(3+4)*5$, one view of operational semantic definition can be described as the following sequence of operations:

```
(3+4)*5    ⇒ (7)*5    /* 3 and 4 are added to make 7 */
           ⇒ 7*5      /* parentheses are dropped */
           ⇒ 35       /* 7 and 5 are multiplied to make 35 */
```

In general, we can describe the operational semantics of a programming language using an actual machine with the behavior of the programming language specified by a **translator** or an **interpreter** for the language written in the machine code of the chosen computer. The lowest-level language in this sense is machine language because its semantics are completely defined by the architecture of the machine. However, this approach has some shortcomings as the following that makes it unsuitable for semantic specification:

▶ The complexities of the computer hardware and operating system used to run the interpreter would make the actions very difficult to understand.

▶ A semantic specification provided in this way works only for identical computer systems.

▶ For complex languages, correct interpreters are difficult to write. Moreover, these definitions are too machine-dependent to serve as formal specifications for a programming language.

FIGURE **5.1**   Organization of an abstract machine

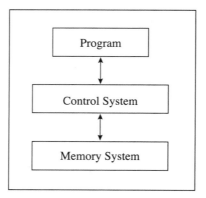

These problems can be avoided by substituting an abstract machine implemented as a software simulation for the real computer. In this case, the registers, memory allocation and deallocation, and information processing would all be simulated with discrete states and explicit sequences of computational operations. The abstract machine operations must be independent of the subject language. However, its states and transitions from one state to another must be explicitly defined. Thus, the virtual machine interprets a program by passing through a sequence of discrete states, in which state transitions are defined by a set of instruction definitions written in specific notation. As illustrated in Figure 5.1, this abstract machine consists of three components:

▶ Program
▶ Control system
▶ Memory system

In this approach, then, we define an abstract machine with primitive instructions — not necessarily realistic—but so simple that no misunderstanding can arise. The semantic description of the programming language specifies a translation to a metalanguage.

5.2.2 VDL Metalanguage

The first experiment involving operational semantics was to describe the semantics specification of PL/I (Lucas & Walk, 1969). However, one of the best known metalanguages used for describing the operational semantics specification of programming languages is the VDL designed at IBM's Vienna Laboratory (Wegner, 1972). The VDL consists of a formal system that models the interpretation of a program, and its specification consists of two parts:

1. A translator that specifies the translation of each program into an abstract syntax tree, converting each construct to the chosen low-level language

FIGURE **5.2**   A VDL configuration

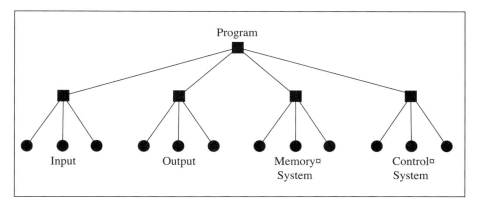

2. An interpreter that specifies how the program in this form could be carried out, corresponding to a virtual machine that supports the chosen low-level language

The objective of VDL is to define an abstract machine for interpreting programs
of the subject language. All the nonprimitive objects in VDL are modeled as syntax
trees, including the program being interpreted, memory, input and output lists, environment, and even the control mechanism that performs the interpretation. Figure
5.2 shows a typical VDL structure represented as a collection of subtrees.

An initial configuration contains all the components. The input subtree represents a list of input values, the output subtree represents an empty list, and the control
system subtree represents a single instruction to run the entire program. The transition functions given by the instructions of the VDL interpreter perform the steps of
the computation. A computation consists of selecting a terminal node of the control
tree and evaluating it according to the specific definitions and producing a new state
with a modified control tree. Interpretation of the program terminates when all the
nodes of the control tree have been evaluated, concluding evaluation of the program.
In other words, the VDL interprets a program by passing through a sequence of transition states to model the operations. The structure of its states are precisely defined,
as are the allowable transitions from one state to another by a set of the instruction
definitions written in a special notation. Note that the tree structure of the VDL does
not relate to any actual implementation.

5.2.3   Notations for Abstract Syntax Trees

The VDL uses a general notation for describing and manipulating structures, which
are depicted as trees with labeled edges and without left to right ordering. A node of
the tree known as an *object* can be characterized as one of the following forms.

Elementary Objects: An **elementary object** has no internal structure of its own; that
is, it corresponds to a terminal node of a tree representing a structure that contains

F I G U R E **5.3**   Tree representation of composite object,
A={ `<s-left:L>,<s-middle:M>,<s-right:R>`}

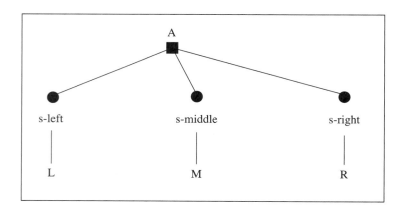

the object. We denote an elementary object by a sequence of one or more uppercase letters or by a sequence of characters enclosed in single quotes; A and + are two elementary objects. The null object is a special elementary object, indicating that the object is empty, and is denoted Ω.

Composite Objects: A **composite object** is represented by a set of one or more pairs of the form `<s : o>`, where "`s`" denotes a **selector** and "`o`" denotes an object, either elementary or composite. Selectors are arbitrary names consisting of lowercase characters. By convention, selector names begin with "`s-`". For example,

    A={`<s-left : L>, <s-middle : M>, <s-right : R>`}

represents a composite object comprising three components, as shown in Figure 5.3.
Similarly, the object

O={`<s-left:{<s-head:A>,<s-tail:B>}>,<s-middle:M>,<s-right:{<s-head:C>,<s-tail:D>}>`}

can be represented as Figure 5.4.
If the object consists of a null object, such as O={`<s-head:A>,<s-tail:Ω>`}, as depicted in Figure 5.5, the null object and the associated selector have no corresponding branch in the tree diagram.
In general, a selector may be defined as a function that takes an object as an argument and yields the corresponding component of the object. In other words, the function yields the subtree below the branch labeled by the selector.

Lists: An object may be regarded as a **list** of other objects, with any number of objects in the list. The convention is to use

    `elem(1), elem(2), elem(3), ... , elem(n)`

FIGURE **5.4**   Another tree representation of a composite object

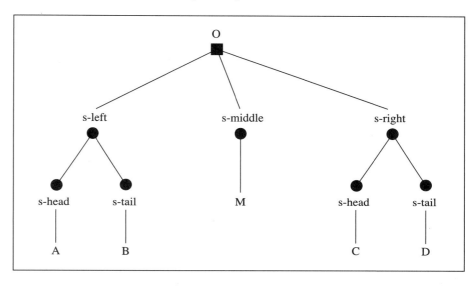

FIGURE **5.5**   An object with a null component

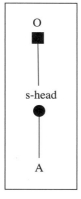

as the selectors of the list components. The subscripts start at 1 and go to the number of elements in the list. For example, the list

```
L={<elem(1):FIRST>,<elem(2):SECOND>,<elem(3):THIRD>}
```

can be depicted as in Figure 5.6.

In this case, the function head is equivalent to `elem(1)`, meaning that `head(L)` yields `FIRST`. The function tail yields a list consisting of all but the first element, or

```
Tail(L)=<SECOND,THIRD>={<elem(1):SECOND>,<elem(2):THIRD>}.
```

FIGURE **5.6**   Representation of a list with three elements

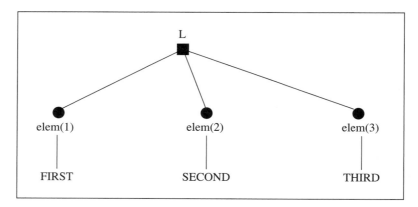

Finally, the function length provides the number of elements in a list so that length(L)=3.

Predicates: A predicate is a function that takes an object as an argument and yields an elementary object as True or False. By convention, predicates begin with "`is-`". Examples are `is-PLUS`, for an object that is +, or `is-intg`, for an object that is an integer.

Equations: An **equation** defines a predicate for a class of objects, the selectors involved, and the kinds of objects they select. For example, the equation

```
is-asmt-st = (<s-lhs : is-var>, <s-rhs : is-expr>)
```

states that an object satisfies the predicate `is-asmt-st` if and only if it consists of a component satisfying `is-var` with the selector as `s-lhs`, and a component satisfying `is-expr`, with the selector as `s-rhs`. Similarly, the equation

```
is-char=is-x ∨ is-y ∨ is-z
```

states that an object will satisfy `is-char` if and only if it satisfies one of the three predicates `is-x`, `is-y`, or `is-z`. Similarly, the following equation states that an object satisfies `is-expr` if and only if it satisfies one of the three predicates on the right.

```
is-expr = is-infix-expr ∨ is-var ∨ is-intg
```

For example, the VDL abstract syntax rules of the language Pam are outlined in the following lines of code.

```
is-series = is-st-list
is-st = is-read-st ∨ is-write-st ∨ is-asmt-st ∨ is-cond-st ∨ is-def-loop ∨ is-indef-loop
is-read-st = (<s-r : is-var-list>)
is-write-st = (<s-w : is-var-list>)
is-asmt-st = (<s-lhs : is-var>, <s-rhs : is-expr>)
```

```
is-cond-st = (<s-ifpart : is-comp>,<s-thenpart : is-series>,<s-elsepart : is-series>)
is-def-loop = (<s-limit : is-expr>,<s-body : is-series>)
is-indef-loop = (<s-test : is-comp>,<s-body : is-series>)
is-comp = (<s-left-opd : is-expr>,<s-right-opd : is-expr>,
          <s-rel : is-EQ ∨ is-GT ∨ is-LE ∨ is-LT ∨ is-GE ∨ is-NE>)
is-expr = is-inix-expr ∨ is-var ∨ is-intg
is-infix-expr = (<s-left-opd : is-expr>,<s-right-opd : is-expr>,
                <s-opr : is-PLUS ∨ is-MINUS ∨ is-TIMES ∨ is-OVER>)
is-var = (<s-addr : is-intg>)
```

Predicates that test for lists end with `–list` and are not explicitly defined by equations. For example, the predicate `is-st-list` is satisfied by any list of objects that all satisfy `is-st`. Similarly, the predicate `is-expr-list` can be satisfied by any list of objects that all satisfy `is-expr`. For example, an object satisfying a definite loop as

```
To   5   do   Sum = 40*Sum
```

would be represented as Figure 5.7, in which memory location 200 is associated with the variable `Sum`.

For an object that satisfies `is-series` of the Pam language abstract syntax rules, we can verify that the program segment

```
read     k;
while    k>0    do
         k=k−1
end
```

would be represented as shown in Figure 5.8, in which the memory location 100 is associated with the variable `k`.

5.3 DENOTATIONAL SEMANTICS

The word *denotational* comes from the verb *denote*. **Denotational semantics,** sometimes called *mathematical semantics*, was developed in the early 1970s by Christopher Strachey and Dana Scott on a purely mathematical basis. In this approach, programs can be translated to functions and their properties can be proved by using the standard mathematical theory of functions known as **functional calculus.** Although originally intended as a mechanism for the analysis of programming languages, denotational semantics has become a powerful tool for language design and implementation. Here, we illustrate denotational semantics by mapping a program and program components onto some abstract but precise domain of objects.

5.3.1 Principles of Denotational Semantics

Denotational semantics defines a programming language behavior by applying mathematical functions to programs and program components to represent their *meaning*. In general, several kinds of meaning can be associated with a construct; for example, an

FIGURE **5.7**   The VDL syntax tree representation of definite loop

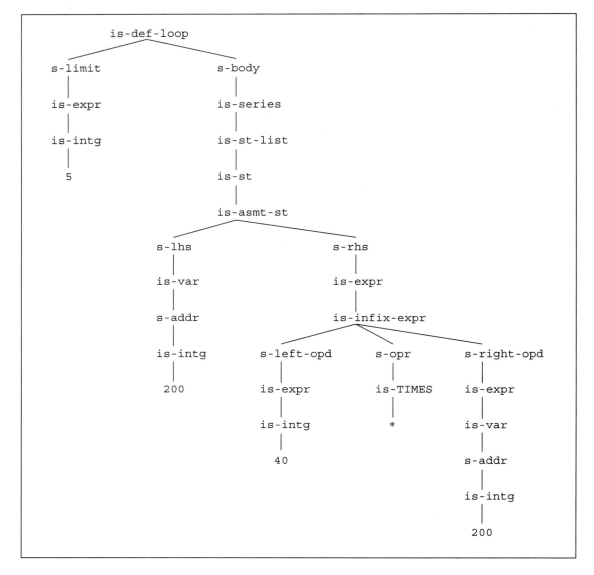

expression such as E=(a+b) can have types as well as values. The kind of meaning can be identified by attaching a tag such as Value and Type to that particular expression. In this case, Value(E) and Type(E) address the value and type of expression E, respectively. A characteristic feature of denotational semantics is that it not only assigns a meaning to a complete program, but also to every phrase in the programming language—every expression, every command, every declaration, and the like. Moreover, the meaning of

FIGURE **5.8**   The VDL syntax tree representation of the given program segment

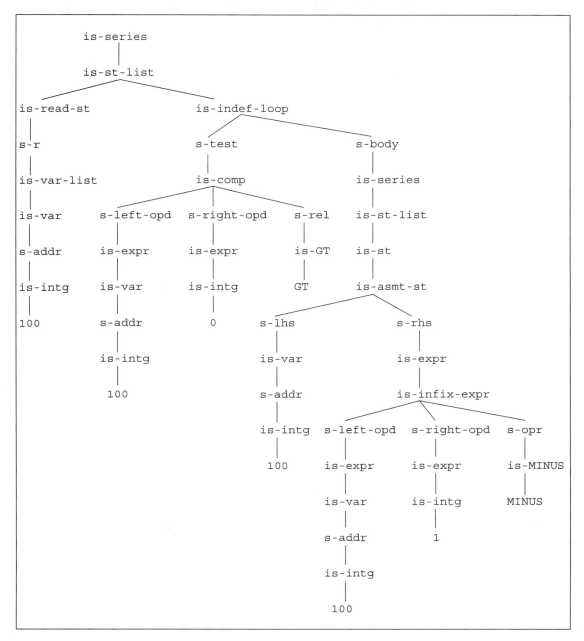

each phrase is defined in terms of the meaning of its subphrases. The meaning of each phrase is called its *denotation*, giving rise to the name *denotational semantics*. Denotational definitions are enclosed by double brackets [[ ]] to separate the syntactic definition from the semantic definition. For example, if *p* is a syntactic phrase in a programming language, a denotational specification of the language can define an abstract mathematical entity that models the semantic of *p* as `meaning`[[*p*]]. The double brackets indicate that the argument is a syntactic entity of the programming language. In this sense, the expressions 2*4, 5+3, 008 are syntactic phrases that all denote the same abstract object, the integer 8. Thus,

```
meaning[[2*4]] = meaning[[5+3]] = meaning[[008]] = meaning[[8]]
```

One advantage of denotational semantics is that we can predict the behavior of a program without actually running it on a computer. Similarly, we can understand the semantics of the programming language as a whole without having to try to visualize how programs run on a computer. Another benefit is that we can reason about programs—for example, to prove whether one program is equivalent to another. In other words, denotational semantics focus on the net effect of running a program or construct and ignore the steps by which that effect is achieved. They concentrate on what the program does as opposed to how it achieves that effect. A fundamental contribution of the work on denotational semantics is the concept of mathematical foundation for semantic domains, semantic functions, semantic equations, and auxiliary functions.

5.3.2 Semantic Domains

Domains identify the semantic objects relevant to a language. A domain is simply a set of values (called the elements of the domain). **Semantic domains** are sets of mathematical objects of a particular form. A denotational definition of a semantic domain lists its set of elements and operations but usually omits the properties of the operations. An example of a specification of a semantic domain consists of a set of integer elements and three operations: +, −, and *.

Domain

```
Int:    Integer={..., -2, -1, 0, ..., 1, 2, ...}
```

Operations

```
+   :   Integer+Integer ⇒ Integer
−   :   Integer−Integer ⇒ Integer
*   :   Integer*Integer ⇒ Integer
```

The symbol `Int` indicates that the name `Int` can be used for a general element from the domain—that is, an arbitrary integer number. In denotational semantics, we use the domain characteristics as follows:

▶ **A primitive domain** is one whose elements are primitive values that are not composed from simpler values. Primitive domain elements are classified as *character,* whose elements are taken from a character set

integer, whose elements are the positive integers, zero, and negative integers

natural, whose elements are the nonnegative integers

Boolean, whose elements are the truth values *true* and *false*

unit, whose only element is the 0-tuple

▶ **A function domain** is one whose elements are functions or mappings. Each element as $A \Rightarrow B$ is a function that maps elements of A to elements of B. For example, the element of the domain Integer $\Rightarrow$ Boolean are the functions that map integers to truth values, such as odd, even, positive, and negative numbers. Another example is

```
Store = (Variable ⇒ Integer)
```

which consists of sets binding variable names to values.

▶ **A Cartesian product domain** is one whose elements are ordered pairs. Each element $A \times B$ is an ordered pair (x, y) such that $x \in A$ and $y \in B$. This relation can be generalized to a domain as $D_1 \times \ldots \times D_n$, whose elements are ordered n-tuples $(x_1, \ldots, x_n)$.

▶ **A disjoint union domain** is one whose elements are chosen from either component domain. Each element $A + B$ is either x, where $x \in A$, or y, where $y \in B$. In other words, each element is tagged to indicate the component domain from which it was chosen: Left tags are elements chosen from A, and right tags are elements chosen from B.

▶ **A sequence domain** is one whose elements are homogeneous sequences. Each element of the sequence domain D^* is a finite sequence of zero or more elements chosen from D. For example, the domain

```
D = String = Character*
```

has as its elements the finite sequences of zero or more characters.

5.3.3   Semantic Functions

Functions play a prominent role in denotational semantics, modeling the bindings of variables in programming languages. Semantic functions synthesize the meaning of constructs; that is, they map syntactic objects onto objects in semantic domains. These functions are specified by giving their domains, called their *signatures*. A simple example is a function that maps an integer arithmetic expression onto its value, which we could call the `Value` function, as in

```
Value :      Expression ⇒ Integer
```

For `Value(4+2*3)=10` the semantic function `Value` maps the syntactic construct `(4+2*3)` onto the semantic value `10`. Thus, `(4+2*3)` is said to *denote* the value `10`. A semantic function mapped from the syntactic domain `Digit` onto the integer numbers of domain `Integer` is written as

```
Dig :       Digit ⇒ Integer
```

A program can be viewed as an entity that receives input and produces output. Thus, the semantic definition of a program can be represented by a function from input to output domains as

```
Program :   Program ⇒ (Input ⇒ Output)
```

Generally speaking, each semantic domain has one semantic function.

5.3.4 Semantic Equations

Equations specify how the semantic functions act on each construct of the programming language by using the structure of the grammar rules. For example, the grammar rule for `Digit`,

```
Digit :: =   '0' | '1' | ... | '9'
```

and the semantic function `Dig`,

```
Dig  :   Digit ⇒ Integer
```

can be combined to form the semantic equations

```
Dig(Digit⇒'0' ) = 0
Dig(Digit⇒'1' ) = 1
...
Dig(Digit⇒'9' ) = 9.
```

We can shorten this notation to

```
Dig[['0']] = 0,   Dig[['1']] = 1,    . . .   Dig[['9']] = 9.
```

The following is an example of a semantic equation for integer numbers based on the production rules

```
Number   :: =   Number Digit | Digit
```

and the semantic function

```
Num  :            Number ⇒ Integer
```

which can be written as

```
Num[[Number Digit]] = 10 * Num[[Number]] + Num[[Digit]]
Num[[Digit]] = Dig[[Digit]].
```

Here, `[[Number  Digit]]` refers to a syntactic object corresponding to numerals such as 165, in which 16 is referred to as `Number` and 5 as `Digit`. Using the production rules, this object can be decomposed as 1, 6, and 5 to be treated by a second semantic equation. Similarly,

```
Evaluate[[E₁+E₂]] Store = plus(Evaluate[[E₁]] Store, Evaluate[[E₂]] Store)
```

illustrates that the value of an expression (E_1+E_2) is the mathematical sum of the value of its components. The value of the expression depends on the binding of the variables, in this case represented by `Store`. Here, the semantic function `Evaluate` maps the syntactic expression onto semantic values, using mathematical operations such as plus. Generally speaking, each production rule in the syntax of the programming language has one semantic equation.

5.3.5   Auxiliary Functions

The predefined mathematical operations *plus*, *times*, *minus*, and *divide* in semantic functions are called auxiliary functions. For example,

```
plus:    Number + Number ⇒ Number
times:   Number * Number ⇒ Number
```

define two auxiliary functions, where `Number×Number` is an element of Cartesian product domain and `Number` is an element of the primitive domain `Integer`. The following list is a complete denotational specification of a language of nonnegative integer numerals:

Production rules

```
Number  :: = N D  |  D
```

Semantic domain

```
Number ={0,1,2,3, ...}
```

Semantic functions

```
Value:   Number ⇒ Number
Digit:   Digit ⇒ Number
```

Auxiliary functions

```
plus:    Number + Number ⇒ Number
times:   Number * Number ⇒ Number
```

Semantic equations

```
Value[[N D]] = plus(times(10, Value[[N]]), Digit[[D]])
Value[[D]] = Digit[[D]]
Digit[[0]] = 0          Digit[[5]] = 5
Digit[[1]] = 1          Digit[[6]] = 6
Digit[[2]] = 2          Digit[[7]] = 7
Digit[[3]] = 3          Digit[[8]] = 8
Digit[[4]] = 4          Digit[[9]] = 9
```

For example, we can evaluate 065 as a numeral according to this denotational definition as

```
Value[[065]] = plus(times(10, Value[[06]]), Digit[[5]])
             = plus(times(10, plus(times(10, Value[[0]]), Digit[[6]])), 5)
```

```
= plus(times(10, plus(times(10, Digit[[0]]), 6)), 5)
= plus(times(10, plus(times(10, 0), 6)), 5)
= plus(times(10, 6), 5)
= plus(60, 5)  = 65
```

The following is a description of the syntax and semantics of the language of binary numerals, or the representation of natural numbers using the base 2. For example, 1101 is the binary numeral that denotes the decimal number 13.

Production rules

```
Number  :: = N D  |  D
```

Semantic domain

```
Number ={0,1,2,3, ...}
```

Semantic functions

```
Value:   Binary - Number ⇒ Number
Digit:   Digit ⇒ Number
```

Auxiliary functions

```
plus:    Number + Number ⇒ Number
times:   Number * Number ⇒ Number
```

Semantic equations

```
Value[[N D]] = plus(times(2, Value[[N]]), Digit[[D]])
Value[[D]] = Digit[[D]]
Digit[[0]] = 0          Digit[[1]] = 1
```

Now, we can evaluate the denotated value of a binary numeral 1101, which is the decimal number 13.

```
Value[[1101]] =plus(times(2,Value[[110]]),Digit[[1]])
=plus(times(2,plus(times(2,Value[[11]]),Digit[[0]])),Digit[[1]])
=plus(times(2,plus(times(2,plus(times(2,Value[[1]]),Digit[[1]])),Digit[[0]])),Digit[[1]])
=plus(times(2,
 plus(times(2, plus(times(2, Digit[[1]]),Digit[[1]])),Digit[[0]])),Digit[[1]])
=plus(times(2,plus(times(2,plus(times(2,1),1)),0)),1)
=plus(times(2,plus(times(2,plus(2,1)),0)),1)
=plus(times(2,plus(times(2,3),0)),1)
=plus(times(2,plus(6,0)),1)
=plus(times(2,6),1)
=plus(12,1) = 13
```

The following are the denotational semantics of integer arithmetic expressions:

Production rules

```
Number      :: = N D  |  D
Digit       :: = 0 | 1 | ... | 9
Expression  :: = E₁ + E₂ | E₁ − E₂ | E₁ * E₂ | E₁ ÷ E₂ | (E) | N
```

Expression ::= $E_1 + E_2$ | $E_1 - E_2$ | $E_1 * E_2$ | $E_1 \div E_2$ | (E) | N

Semantic domain

Integer ={...−2, −1, 0, 1, 2, ...}

Semantic functions

```
Value:  Number ⟹ Number
Digit:  Digit ⟹ Number
Expr:   Expression ⟹ Integer
```

Auxiliary functions

```
plus:    Number + Number ⟹ Number
times:   Number * Number ⟹ Number
minus:   Number − Number ⟹ Number
divide:  Number ÷ Number ⟹ Number
```

Semantic equations

```
Expr[[E₁+E₂]]    = plus(Expr[[E₁]] , Expr[[E₂]])
Expr[[E₁−E₂]]    = minus(Expr[[E₁]] , Expr[[E₂]])
Expr[[E₁*E₂]]    = times(Expr[[E₁]] , Expr[[E₂]])
Expr[[E₁÷E₂]]    = divide(Expr[[E₁]] , Expr[[E₂]])
Expr[[(E)]]      = Expr[[E]]
Expr[[(N)]]      = Value[[N]]
Value[[N D]]     = plus(times(10, Value[[N]]), Digit[[D]])
Value[[D]]       = Digit[[D]]
Digit[[0]] = 0            Digit[[5]] = 5
Digit[[1]] = 1            Digit[[6]] = 6
Digit[[2]] = 2            Digit[[7]] = 7
Digit[[3]] = 3            Digit[[8]] = 8
Digit[[4]] = 4            Digit[[9]] = 9
```

For example, we can obtain the semantic value of the expression (4+2*3) as

```
Expr[[(4+2*3)]] = plus(Expr[[4]],Expr[[2*3]])
                = plus(Expr[[4]],times(Expr[[2]],Expr[[3]]) )
                = plus(Value[[4]],times(Value[[2]],Value[[3]]) )
                = plus(Digit[[4]],times(Digit[[2]],Digit[[3]]) )
                = plus(4, times(2, 3) ) = plus(4, 6) = 10.
```

◤ # SUMMARY

Semantics involves a description of what happens during execution of a program or a phrase of a program that refers to rules specifying its meaning. In other words, semantic rules express the effect of the constructs of the program. In this chapter, we reviewed the formal semantics of imperative languages. First, we discussed the axiomatic semantics, then operational semantics, and finally denotational semantics. Denotational, operational, and axiomatic semantics are all useful in various ways and complement each other. A good design criterion for a programming language is that it should be elegantly describable in each of these styles of semantic descriptions. Such a language should be simple to use, simple to reason and simple to implement. Axiomatic semantics described the meaning of each syntactically correct program construct by associating with it properties of variables that hold before execution starts and after the program construct halts. This approach defines a programming language behavior by applying mathematical logic to language constructs, in which a logical statement called a predicate or assertion described the state of the computation. There are two kinds of assertion: precondition and postcondition. We extended the class of assertions to include logical expressions called formulas. Axiomatic semantics is most useful for constructing programs correctly.

Operational semantics defines programming language behavior by describing its actions relative to the operations of an abstract or hypothetical machine. In this approach, the data structure of the modeling machine was used to describe the effects of each programming language construct. The most famous abstract machine used for operational semantics was the Vienna Definition Language (VDL). The VDL consisted of a formal system that models the interpretation of a program, and its specification consisted of two parts: a translator and an interpreter. In the denotational semantics approach, programs are translated to functions and their properties are proved by using the standard mathematical theory of functions known as functional

TABLE **5.3** Semantics specification of some programming languages

Language	Informal Specification	Formal Specification	Semantic Specification
Ada	Ichbiah (1983)	Donzeau-Gouge (1980)	Denotational
ALGOL-60	Naur (1963)	Mosses (1974)	Denotational
ML	Milner (1987)	Milner (1990)	Operational
ML		Watt (1987)	Action
Pascal	Jensen (1974)	Hoare (1973)	Axiomatic
Pascal	BSI (1982)	Tennent (1978)	Denotational
Scheme	Rees (1986)	Rees (1986)	Denotational
Pascal		Mosses (1986)	Action

calculus. We discussed the denotational semantics components including semantic domains, semantic functions, auxiliary functions, and semantic equations.

A number of semantics specifications of programming languages have been published. Table 5.3 provides references to informal and formal specification of some major programming languages used in different semantics definitions.

EXERCISES

1. Using the axiomatic definition of the semantics of the language called Pam, verify the following assertions:

```
{OUT = <>} N=2 ; To N Do
                          Write N;
                          N = N + 1
                   End    {OUT = <2,3>}


{N ≥0}
      P = 1; I = N;
      while I > 0 Do P = P * X; I = I - 1 end
{P = X^N }


{M=10 and N=20}
   X=M;   Y=N;   Sum=0;
   while  Y >= 5  do
           if 2*(Y/2) = Y  then Sum = Sum+X
   X = 2*X;    Y=Y/2;
   endwhile
{Sum+X=110}
```

2. Using the specification of the semantics of numerals, prove that `value[[008]]=8`.

3. Specify the components of a denotational semantics to represent the denotated value of the following *Commands* with regard to Calculator Language.

```
65 + 25 - 10 =
15 * 3 + 15 =
```

4. Show the abstract syntax tree that reflects the derivation of `value[[008]]`.

5. According to the specification of the semantics of Calculator Language, prove that `meaning[2+3]=5`.

6. Using the VDL notations, sketch a tree as the representation of the following program:

```
Read K;
While  K > 0    do
        K = K - 1
End
```

7. Prove the *correctness* of the following assertions:

```
{J=3 and K=4} J=J+K {J=7 and K=4}
{X=A and Y=B} Z=X;   X=Y;   Y=Z {X=B and Y=A}
{Y=0, Z=0, X=5} X=Y+3;   Z=X+Y;   X=X+5;   Y=Y+2 {X=10, Y=4, Z=7}
```

8. Compute the weakest *pre-condition* or *post-condition* of the following assertions:

```
{Y=0, Z=0, X=5} X=Y+3;   Z=X+Y;   X=X+5;   Y=Y+2 {X=?, Y=?, Z=?}
{2Y+X>12}   X=2Y+X−1 {Y=?, X=?}
{X=?, Y=?, Z=?} X=Y+1;   Z=X+Y;   X=X+3;   Y=Y+2 {Z=?, X=6, Y=4}
{Y>3/2}   X=2*(Y−1) −1 {X=?}
```

9. Assume the input of the following program as `[5, 25, -1]`:

```
program Test is
   var  Sum, Num  : integer
begin
   Sum :=20;
   read Num;
   while  Num >= 0    do
      if  Num > 9   and Num  < 100
          then   Sum := Sum + Num
      endif
      read Num
   endwhile
   write Sum
end
```

Define the denotational semantic components of this program, and specify the denotated output value of this program.

10. Assume that S_1 is X=A and S_2 is X=X+B, prove that `{true} S₁;S₂ {X=A+B}` holds.

11. Let *digits* be the set of three symbols {0, 1, 2}.
    a. Enumerate the sets `digits0`, `digits1`, and `digits2`.
    b. How many strings are in `digitsⁿ`?

12. Consider a language allows expressions such as E_1+E_2 to be evaluated in any order. What are the semantics implications of this design in the presence of side effects?

13. Consider the specification of a language insists on *left-to-right* evaluation of expressions such as E_1+E_2. State two aspects of this design that would otherwise prevent it from guaranteeing a unique result for every expression evaluation.

14. Prove the semantic equivalence of the following language phrases:
    a. `while E do C and if E then (C; while E do C) else skip`
    b. `if E then C₁ else C₂ and if not(E) then C₂ else C₁`
    c. `X :=5; Y := 2*X and Y := 10; X := Y/2`
    d. `E₁ + E₂ and E₂ + E₁`
    e. `if E then (if E then C₁ else C₂) else C₃ and if E then C₁ else C₂`
    f. `(while E do C₁); if E then C₂ else C₃ and (while E do C₁); C₂`

15. Draw a tree diagram of a VDL object satisfying "is-series" and corresponding to the Pam program:

```
Read  a;
If  a = 0    Then    read b;      write b;
             Else    write a;
End-if
```

16. Using the specification of the axiomatic semantics, prove that the following statements are intended to assign the quotient of x÷5 to q and the corresponding remainder to r.

```
r  : =  X;
q  : =  0;
while    5 =<  r
         do   r : = r - 5;
         q : = q + 1;
end
```

> # REFERENCE-NEEDED EXERCISES

To answer the following exercises, you might need to consult the references: Best, 1996; Gunter, 1992; Pagan, 1981; Slonneger, 1995; Stansifer, 1995; Tennent, 1991.

1. A hypothetical text editor TEXTEDIT works as follows. First, an input file is read into a text buffer, then the text buffer is updated in response to a sequence of commands issued by the user, and finally the contents of the text buffer are written to an output file. The commands available to the user include the following (where N is a numeral and S is any sequence of characters).

   mN   move to the Nth line.

   m"S"   move to the next line that has S as a substring.

   S"S_1""S_2"   substitute S_2 for the string S_1 in the current line.

   d   delete the current line and move to the next line.

   I "S"   insert a line S just before the current line.

   Write a denotational semantics of TEXTEDIT. In what respect is the informal specification imprecise? Hint: The current line is the last line moved to, and a command that cannot be carried out has no effect on the text buffer.

2. Using the axiomatic definition of the semantics of the language called *Eva*, show that the following two programs are semantically equivalent:

```
begin                begin
char c               string s
input c              proc p = begin
output c                  char c
end                      input c
```

```
                              cons c, s
                       end
                 call p
                 output head s
                 end
```

3. Using the denotational definition of the semantics of the language called *Wren*, determine the denotated value of the following program, in which the input list is [5, 22, −1].

```
program     sample      is
      var   sum,  num :  integer;
begin
      sum := 0;
      read  num;
      while  num >= 0  do
            if  num > 9  and  num < 100
            then  sum  := sum + num
         end if;
         read num
      end while;
      write  sum
end
```

4. The rule of inference for repeat statement may be formulated as

$$\frac{\{P\}\, S\, \{Q\},\ Q \wedge \neg B \Rightarrow P}{\{P\}\ \textit{repeat } S \textit{ until } B \textit{ end }\{Q \wedge B\}}$$

If this construct is added to Pam language, verify that the following assertion may be deduced:

```
{X ≥5} r := X;   q := 0;
       repeat   r := r − 5;
          q := q + 1;
       until   r < 5
       end
{X = r + 5 * q  ∧  r < 5}
```

Imperative Programming Specifications

The differences among programming languages revolve around what they make *convenient* to express, rather than what they can express. Computer languages are similar to *natural languages* in this respect. The major difference between computer and natural languages is that computer languages have been designed for particular tasks, whereas natural languages have evolved around what human beings most need to say to each other. Nevertheless, both natural and computer languages share the characteristic that, almost any language can express anything. Each computer language is designed to make particular tasks convenient. Some languages are designed to be easy to learn; others are designed to make simulating the real world as easy as possible; a group of languages is designed to do mathematical tasks; some are designed for functional tasks; some are designed for logic programming; and some are designed for object-oriented programming.

New computer languages are being designed all the time, and old languages are being revised. We may investigate a particular programming method by exploring the features of one or more representative languages. A programming language and its examples are most useful when it is clearly distinguished from another language. For example, block-structured programming can be described as the set of all programming languages that support nested block structures, including procedures and modules. We may say that Ada is a block-structured programming language. The object-based programming language describes languages that support interacting objects. For example, in Ada objects are called packages. Thus, Ada belongs to both the block-structured and object-based programming languages.

In previous chapters, we discussed the characteristics of the programming language design and the concepts of imperative programming languages generally. In the rest of the book we will view programming languages from a different perspective. We examine how these concepts are selected and put together to design complete programming languages. It is as important for the language designer to decide which concepts to omit as to decide which ones to include. Often the language designer is forced to compromise, because a particular combination of concepts would make the language hard to use, to understand or to implement. In general, the language designer has in mind a particular style of programming for which the language is intended to be suitable and applicable. A minor design decision like including or omitting a particular data type can significantly influence the way the language is used. Similarly, a major design decision—such as omitting the concept of storage allocation or basing the whole language on the concept of encapsulation—must imply a distinctive programming style or paradigm of programming language.

In this chapter, we look at imperative programming paradigm, which is the oldest but still dominant programming language method. In Section 6.1, we identify the key characteristics of imperative programming paradigm from the implementation point of view. The basic unit of imperative programming is the action that can be classified into three categories: computational, control-flow, and input-output actions. Imperative actions all have access to a common storage that consists of an arbitrary number of memory locations. Section 6.2 deals with actions as the design principles for imperative programming. Imperative programming was motivated by the structured control flow programming principle. We discuss the statement-oriented structured and block-oriented structured programming in Section 6.3 to address the concept of control flow through the execution of the program. In Section 6.4, we briefly talk about the steps of program execution that consist of compile, load, and run stages. It is important to know that imperative programming has some undesirable characteristics such as difficulty in reasoning, referential transparency, side effects, indiscriminate access, vulnerability access, and no overlapping definition. We briefly outline these characteristics in Section 6.5. Then, we discuss the desirable characteristics for imperative programming in Section 6.6.

6.1 Implementing Programming Languages

Milulinovic (1989) introduced the following taxonomy based on what drives the computational flow of the architectures:

1. Control-driven or control-flow architectures:
   - Reduced Instruction Set Computers (RISC)
   - Complex Instruction Set Computers (CISC)
   - High-Level Language Architectures (HLL)
2. Data-driven or data-flow architectures
3. Demand-driven or reduction architectures

In control-driven or control-flow architectures, the instruction sequence (i.e., the program) guides the processing activity. The flow of computation is determined by the instruction sequence, and data are gathered as an instruction needs them. A data-driven or data-flow architecture is controlled by the readiness or the availability of data. This indicates that an instruction is carried out (i.e., the control activity is invoked) when the data required by that instruction are ready to be operated upon. In demand-driven or reduction architectures, an instruction is enabled for execution when its results are required as operands for another instruction that has already been enabled for execution. The experimental languages associated with data-driven and demand-driven architectures are introduced and described further in the following chapters.

This classification indicates that programming languages began by imitating and abstracting the operations of a computer system. It is not surprising that the kind of computer for which they were written significantly affected their design. In most cases, the computer in question was the Von Neumann model consisting of a single CPU that sequentially carries out instructions that operate on values stored in memory locations. The design principles for imperative languages are motivated by the control flow concept of the program execution using the Von Neumann model of computation. Thus, imperative programming languages reflect the architecture of the underlying Von Neumann machine, meaning that programs consist of instructions stored in memory locations, and a register known as *program counter* determines which instruction is to be run next. In general, a programming language that is characterized by the following three properties is called an imperative language because its primary feature is a sequence of statements that represent commands (the Latin word *imperative* means "to command").

▶   The sequential execution of instructions

▶   The use of variables representing memory location values

▶   The use of assignment statements to change the values of variables and to allow the program to operate on these memory location values

In general, these properties deal with the notion of flow of control through program constructs, which refers to the run sequence of the program statements. This paradigm has a relatively long history: As early as the 1950s, language designers realized that variables and assignment commands constitute a simple but useful abstraction form of memory fetch and memory update. Imperative programming still dominates. Most commercial software programs currently in use or under development are written in imperative languages. Sometimes imperative languages are also called *procedural languages,* but this has nothing explicitly to do with the concept of procedures discussed in Chapter 2. Because of the close relationship with machine architecture, imperative programming languages can be implemented very efficiently. Imperative programming sometimes allows problems to be solved in a more efficient and straightforward way than is possible using other programming languages, such as logic and functional programming.

6.2   DESIGN PRINCIPLES FOR IMPERATIVE PROGRAMMING

Imperative programming languages describe how a given sequence of operations computes the result of a given problem. In the imperative approach, we are more concerned with how to formulate the solution in terms of our primitive operations. The basic unit of imperative programming is *action* that can be classified into three categories:

1. Computational actions such as arithmetic operations
2. Control-flow actions such as comparisons and looping statements
3. Input-output actions such as read and write operations

Imperative actions all have access to a common storage, which consists of an arbitrary number of memory locations. Each memory location can be characterized by the following state:

▶ It may contain a data, meaning that the location is allocated and containing data.

▶ It may be undefined, meaning that the location is allocated but not yet containing data.

▶ It may be unused, meaning that the location is not allocated.

Data stored in memory locations are stable. In other words, data contained in a memory location remains undisturbed and available for inspection until that memory location is deallocated or has a new data stored on it. An imperative action works by making changes in memory. Possible changes are

▶ Store data in a location. This action stores data in a memory location.

▶ Deallocate a memory location. This action changes the state of memory location to unused.

▶ Allocate a memory location. This action finds an unused memory location and changes its status to allocated.

▶ Retrieve a memory location. This action yields the data currently contained in a memory location.

It is sometimes helpful to think of computer memory as a sequence of snapshots, each one capturing the values in all the memory locations at a particular time. In the following, we outline some characteristics of imperative programming language design. Then, we thoroughly examine variables, assignment statements, and selection constructs, including those for single-way and multiple-way selections. We then discuss conditional and looping constructs that have been developed and used in programming languages. We then take a close look at the control flow and execution steps involved in imperative programming. Finally, we describe the desirable and undesirable attributes for imperative programming.

Variables

A major component of a computer system is the memory that comprises numerous memory cells (locations). The memory is where the data can be stored. The memory cells must be named, so that one can access the data stored in memory locations. In other words, values are stored in memory locations and can be accessed by naming such locations. In higher-level programming languages, the underlying notions of memory locations and names are represented by the concept of a *variable* definition and naming. A programming language variable is essentially a named memory location in which values are stored. A variable name should be informative, concise, memorable, and pronounceable, if possible. Much information comes from context and scope, the broader the scope of a variable, the more information should be conveyed by its name.

In variable declaration, we consider the memory locations in which the values of interest reside. The variable declaration performs the following three functions:

1. It allocates an area of memory of a specified size.
2. It attaches a symbolic name to the allocated area of memory. This is called binding a name to memory locations.
3. It initializes the contents of the memory locations if there is any initialization.

These are three important functions of variable declarations in most imperative programming languages, in which we keep track of the value of variables by associating a location and maintaining a map from locations to values. The value stored in the location of a variable is called its r-value (for right-side value), whereas the location of a variable is its l-value (for left-side value). However, this distinction is obvious from the assignment statement, in which the right-side stands for the value of the variable, while the left side stands for the location of the variable. In general, we can think of variables as being bound directly to values instead of to locations. In this sense, variable references refer to the values contained in these locations. The environment maintains the binding of names to locations. Depending on the language, the environment may be constructed statically (at load-time), dynamically (at execution-time), or a mixture of the two. In a language, such as Fortran, that uses a completely static environment, all locations are bound statically at load time. A language that uses a completely dynamic environment is LISP, in which all locations are bound during execution. Pascal, C, and Modula-2 are in the middle, meaning that some allocations are performed statically, while other allocations are performed dynamically. Not all names in a program are bound to locations. In a compiled language, names of constants and data types may represent purely compile-time quantities that have no existence at load or run time. For example, the following declaration

```
CONST    max = 10;
```

can be used by a compiler to replace all occurrences of max by the value 10. The name max is never allocated a location and indeed has disappeared altogether from the program when it runs. Because of this, a constant differs from a variable in two important ways:

▶ The value of the constant is known when the program is written (at compile time).

▶ The value of a constant does not change during program execution.

Programmer-defined constants are named by identifiers.

Data Types

The data type used in programming languages can be classified into either of two categories:

▶ Scalar data type, which is the simplest possible data type.

▶ Structured data type, which consists of some combination of scalar data types.

Any data type has three associated components:

▶ Type name, which is the identifier used to designate the type in declaration.

▶ A set of constants of that type, which is a symbol for a value that may be assigned to a variable of compatible type.

▶ A set of operations on that type, which are used to construct expressions for the type.

Every programming language provides a set of predefined data types from which all other types can be constructed. These are generally specified using predefined keywords such as integer, real, Boolean, and character. Sometimes predefined numeric types with specified precision are included, such as long real, double, long integer, short, short real, and so on. Some languages also have specified type constructors. An example is the *file type* in Pascal and C programming languages. An additional data type that is predefined in some languages is the string type: a sequence of characters of arbitrary length. String type can be defined in two ways:

▶ With unspecified maximum length (i.e., array in Module-2)

▶ With specified maximum length (i.e., array in Fortran or PL/I)

Finally, it is often useful to be able to specify a *notype* type, which is distinct from all other types. Such a type could be thought of as a set containing a single value distinct from all other values. Such a type is the *void* type in C or ALGOL and the *unit* type of ML. Arrays are the most widely used type constructors, in which space is allocated sequentially in memory, and indexing is performed by an offset calculation from the starting address of the memory. In multidimensional arrays, allocation is still linear and can be formed in two categories. For example, if **x** is a two-dimensional array with 10 elements in each row, then

▶ **Row-major form:** x can be started as $x[0,0], x[0,1], x[0,2], \ldots, x[0,9]$, $x[1,0], x[1,1]$, and so on.

▶ **Column-major form:** x can be started as $x[0,0], x[1,0], x[2,0], \ldots$, $x[9,0], x[0,1], x[1,1]$, and so on.

Pointers and Recursive Types

A type constructor that constructs the set of all addresses of a specific type is the reference or pointer. Pointers are most useful for creating recursive types, which is a type that uses itself in its declaration. Recursive types are important in data structures and algorithms because they naturally correspond to recursive algorithms and represent data whose size and structure is not known in advance, but may change as computation proceeds.

Type Equivalence

An important question in the application of type-to-type checking is type equivalence, meaning, *when are two types the same?* This question can be answered in three different ways: structural equivalence, name equivalence, and declaration equivalence.

1. **Structural Equivalence:** Two data types are the same if they have the same structure, meaning that they are built in exactly the same way using the same type constructors from the same simple types. In other words, two sets are the same if they contain the same values. For example, the types t1 and t2 defined as follows are structurally equivalent, if we were only concerned about the size of the index set.

```
t1 = array [1 . . 11]  of integer;
t2 = array [0 . . 10]  of integer;
```

Similarly, in the following, rec1 and rec2 are structurally equivalent, but rec1 and rec3 are not, since the boolean and integer fields are reversed in the definition of rec3.

```
range = 0 . . 10;
list = array[range] of boolean;
rec1 = record
        a : boolean;
        b : integer;
        c: list;
end;
rec2 = record
        a : boolean;
        b : integer;
        c: array [0 . . 10] of boolean;
end;
rec3 = record
        a : integer;
        b : boolean;
        c: list;
end;
```

2. **Name Equivalence:** Two named types are equivalent if they have the same name. This is a stronger condition than structural equivalence because a name can refer only to a single type declaration. Name equivalence is adopted in Ada. For example, the types array1 and array2 defined as follows are name equivalent, as are age and INTEGER.

```
type array1  is array (1 . . 10)  of INTEGER;
type array2  is new  array1;
type age   is   new INTEGER;
```

In Ada, the keyword *new* enforces the name equivalence.

3. **Declaration Equivalence:** Two type names that go back to the same original structure declaration by a series of redeclarations are considered to be equivalent types. Modula-2 supports declaration equivalence, but in C, a mixture of structural and declaration equivalence is used. For example, in the following declarations name1, name2, and name3 are all declaration equivalent, but not name equivalent.

```
type
   name1 = array[1 . . 10]  of integer;

   name2 = name1;
   name3 = name2;
```

Similarly, in the following Modula-2 declaration x and y are declaration equivalent variables.

```
VAR   x, y :  ARRAY[1 . . 10]  of  INTEGER;
```

Assignment Statements

The notion that every value computed must be assigned to a memory location is performed by an assignment statement. In general, the notions of memory locations and assignment statements are essential to every programming language. These notions force the programmer into a style of thinking that is shaped by the details of the computer system. For example, the following assignment statement is a typical action in which the value of a variable (memory location value) known as class is *changed*.

```
class = 10;
```

The assignment symbol "=" appears between the right and left sides. This assignment statement sets class to 10 and the old value of class is discarded. A similar example is the assignment statement

```
class = 4+5;
```

where the value 9 of the expression 4+5 is assigned as the value of class variable by ignoring the old value of variable. In general, the unit of work in a program written in imperative languages is a statement. The effects of individual statements combine to achieve the desired results in a program. Variables appearing on the left side of assignment statements denote locations, rather than the value of locations.

Operand Evaluation

An important design characteristic is the order of evaluation of operands in expressions. In Chapter 3, we indicated that the flow of control within expressions was governed by operator associativity and precedence rules. In general, variables as operands in expressions are evaluated by retrieving their values from memory locations. Constant values are evaluated the same way. For example, in the expression

```
A = 10;
B = A + 10;
```

the value of B is computed by taking the content of a memory location associated with variable A; thus, B takes the value 20. If an operand is a parenthesized expression, then all operators it contains must be evaluated before its value can be used as an operand. For example, in the evaluation of the expression

```
A = 10;
B = 20;
C = (A + B) * 10;
```

the value of C is computed by evaluating the value of the subexpression (A+B), in which two operands A and B and one operator "+" are involved. Thus, C takes the value 30*10 as the computed value. The important issue in imperative programming language design is the side effects from the evaluation of the expressions. If neither of the operands of an operator has side effects, then operand evaluation order is irrelevant. For example, no side effects are associated with evaluating the following subexpressions:

```
A = 10;
B = 20;
C = (A + 5) * (B + 10);
```

In contrast, sometimes evaluation of an operand has side effects. For example, the following C expression illustrates the situation where the stored value of A in memory is to be increased by 10 first, and the second subexpression then takes this new stored value as its value. In this example, the side effect of the evaluation of the first subexpression causes the value of B to be evaluated to 50.

```
A = 10;
B = (A = A + 10) * (A + 10);
```

A similar problem is a *functional side effect*. Functional side effects occur when the function changes either one of its parameters or a global variable involved in running the function. In this sense, a global variable is declared outside the function but is accessible in the function. For example, consider the following expression:

```
B = A + check(A);
```

If check does not have the side effect of changing A, then the evaluation order of expression, A and check(A), has no effect on the value of the B variable. However, if check changes the value of A, there is an effect on B. Consider the situation in which the function returns the value of A divided by 2. In this sense, suppose we have the following:

```
A = 20;
B = A + check(A);
```

Then, if the value of A is fetched first in the expression evaluation, its value is 20 and the function returns 10, indicating that the value of B is 30 as the result of the whole expression evaluation. But if the function is evaluated first, then the returned value of the function is 10, which will be the value of the A variable; thus, the value of the expression is 20. This issue can address the functional side effects that are related to the operand evaluation order. In general, there are two solutions to this problem:

1. The language designer can prevent function evaluation from affecting the value of expressions by simply disallowing functional side effects.

2. The language designer can state in the language definition that operands in expressions are to be evaluated in a specific order. Essentially, the implementor has to guarantee that particular order.

Disallowing functional side effects is a difficult issue because it eliminates some flexibility for the programmers. For example, optimization techniques used by compilers involve reordering operand evaluations. A strict evaluation order disallows those optimization methods when function calls are involved. In addition, using access to global variables to avoid parameter passing is an important method of increasing run speed, thus increasing the efficiency. An alternative adopted by Fortran 77 is that function calls are legal only if the functions do not change the values of other operands in the expression. This is the case when the language definition specifies the conditions under which a construct is legal but leaves it to the programmer to ensure that such restrictions are legally specified in the programs. In contrast, Pascal and Ada allow the operands to be evaluated in any order, so side effect evaluation problems can occur.

Selection Constructs

In general, the design of the data structures is the central decision in creating a program. Once the data structures are defined, the algorithms tend to fall into place and the coding is comparatively easy to do. In the last two chapters, we examined the basic data structures that are the building blocks of most programs. In the following sections we will combine such structures as we work through the design and implementation of programming languages. For example, an array data structure supports random access to a sequence of elements of the same type. Random access means that elements can be selected by their position in the data structure. An assignment

```
x = A[i];
```

assigns to x the value of the ith element of array A. The assignment

```
A[i] = x;
```

changes the value of ith element of array A to x. It is common in programming to come to a point where an N-way (N-choice) decision must be made. This indicates that occasionally an algorithm will contain a series of decisions in which a variable or expression is tested separately for each of the constant integral values it may assume, and different actions must be taken. For example, we may accept a character from a keyboard and, depending on what it is, take some appropriate action. We might think of the character as a command that causes one of several possible actions to be taken. One way of making such an effect is by using a list of if-statements like the following:

```
if  (condition₁)   action₁;
if  (condition₂)   action₂;
  .
  .
  .
if  (conditionₙ)   actionₙ;
```

In this form, a selection statement uses the value of a conditional expression to select one of several substatements for execution. For example, consider the following code

```
if   A > B
   Sum = Sum + A;
   Acount = Acount + 1;
if   B > A
   Sum = Sum + B;
   Bcount = Bcount + 1;
```

An alternative is using the *switch* multiselection structure to handle such decision making. The *switch* structure as a multiway conditional statement generalizing the *if-structure* consists of a series of *case* labels, and an optional *default* case is outlined in the following. In other words, *switch* structure is just a special type of control statement that combines some of the features of the `if` and `goto` constructs in a special form.

```
switch    (expression)
   {
   case 1:        action₁;
         break;
   case 2:        action₂;
         break;
   .
   .
   .
   case N:        action_N;
         break;
   default:       action_X;
         break;
   }
```

Selection structures vary from language to language, but they tend to agree on the following issues:

▶   Case selections can appear in any order.

▶   Case selections do not have to be consecutive, meaning that it is valid to have case-1 and case-4 without case-2 and case-3.

▶   Case selections must have distinct actions for each case; otherwise, we need to combine the actions to avoid any conflict.

To sum up, the effect of a *switch* structure is as follows:

1.   Evaluate the switch expression.

2.   Go to the case label having a constant value that matches the value of the expression found in Step 1; if a match is not found, go to the default label; if there is no default label, terminate the switch.

3.   Terminate the switch when a break statement is encountered.

The following example illustrates the `switch` structure in C language, in which the value of `index` variable is checked with 1, 2, 3, and 4 for appropriate action; otherwise, a message can address the wrong value of `index`.

```
switch   (index)
   {
   case 1:      Odd = 0;
        break;
   case 3:      Odd = Odd  + 1;
        break;
   case 2:      Even = 0;
        break;
   case 4:      Even = Even + 1;
        break;
   default:  printf(" Error in index value, index = %d \n", index);
        break;
   }
```

Conditional Constructs

A conditional statement describes control flow through the syntax of the construct, meaning that the conditional statement can be described in terms of the components of the construct. For example, in this conditional statement

```
if   <expression>   then   <statement₁>   else   <statement₂>
```

control flows through statement$_1$ or statement$_2$ if expression is true or false, respectively. A variant of this conditional statement is

```
if   <expression>   then   <statement>
```

with no else component. In this form, the statement is run only if expression is true. The conditionals can be nested as a general form that avoids nesting the parts.

```
if   <expression₁>    then    <statement₁>
else   if   <expression₂>  then    <statement₂>
   else   if   <expression₃>  then    <statement₃>
      else   . . .
```

For example, the following definitions can define a leap year:

1. After every fourth year, there is a leap year, so if 1956 is a leap year, the years 1960, 1964, . . . are leap years, too.

2. The years divisible by 100 are not leap years, so 1700, 1800, . . . are not leap years.

3. The years divisible by 400 are leap years, so 2000, 2400, 2800, . . . are leap years.

The rules for determining leap years were introduced by Pope Gregory XIII in the sixteenth century. A corresponding conditional form of leap year can be outlined as follows:

```
if   (Year mod 400) = 0   then   Leap-Year = true
else   if   (Year mod 100) = 0   then   Leap-Year = false
   else   if   (Year mod 4) = 0   then   Leap-Year = true
      else   Leap-Year = false
```

in which conditional statements assign *true* to variable `Leap-Year` if the value of variable `Year` satisfies a leap year definition.

Looping Constructs

A program in an imperative programming language usually performs its task by carrying out a sequence of elementary steps repeatedly. Looping constructs can be classified into two categories:

1. Definite iteration loops, in which the number of iterations is predetermined when control flows through construct.

2. Indefinite iteration loops, in which the number of iterations is not known when control flows through construct.

In other words, the looping constructs are divided depending on whether or not we can predict the number of times the loop will be carried out. The syntax for indefinite iteration construct is

```
while    <conditional-expression>
   do    <statement>
```

where the `statement` is called in the body of the construct and the control flows through the execution of the `statement` as soon as the `conditional-expression` is evaluated to true. If the expression evaluates to false, control leaves the construct. For example, in the following, the loop is carried out with `index` taking the values $0, 1, 2, \ldots, 9$ to initialize the corresponding array element with zero:

```
index = 0;
while    (index < 10)
         {
         A[index] = 0;
         index = index + 1;
         }
```

The syntax for definite iteration construct is

```
for    (expression₁;    expression₂;    expression₃)
       body-of-loop;
```

where control flows through the execution of the `body-of-loop` depending on the value of the `expression`$_2$. For example, in

```
for    (index = 0;    index < 10;    index++)
       A[index] = 0;
```

the assignment `A[index] = 0;` is carried out with `index` taking the values $0, 1, 2, \ldots, 9$ on successive executions, meaning that `index` is increased by 1 after each run. Treating the limit of the control variable in this example as `index` depends on the following issues:

▶   Are the step and the limit computed once, just before loop entry, or are they recomputed each time control flows through the loop?

▶   Is the limit tested at the beginning or at the end of each loop iteration?

▶   Can the value of the control variable be changed (i.e., by an assignment statement) within the loop?

The answers for C language are as follows:

▶   `Expression`$_1$ and `expression`$_2$ are evaluated only once.

▶   `Expression`$_2$ is tested at the beginning of each iteration, and if the test fails, the statements within the body are skipped without being run.

▶   `Expression`$_3$ is evaluated after each iteration to change the value of the control variable involved in `expression`$_2$.

Because of these characteristics of the imperative programming languages, we could design the program in abstract and then code it in C, Modula-2, Java, C++, Awk, Perl, or any other programming language. Comparing the implementations demonstrates how languages can help and ways in which they are unimportant. Program design can certainly be colored by a language but is not usually dominated by it.

Unions

We can construct a union of two types, which can be formed by taking the set theoretic union of their sets of values. Union types come in two varieties:

▶   **Discriminated Unions:** A tag or discriminator is added to each element field to distinguish which type the element is.

▶   **Undiscriminated Unions:** These unions lack the tag, and assumptions must be made about the type of any particular element.

A language that adopted discriminated and undiscriminated union is Modula-2, and C adopted undiscriminated union.

Functions and Procedures

Despite their distinct roles as operators and actions, functions and procedures are very similar to each other. The only difference between them is that functions return a result and procedures do not. No wonder one language such as C calls them both functions and another language such as Modula-2 calls them both procedures. In general, a procedure or function declaration defines the components as

▶   A name for the declared procedure or function

▶   The formal parameters which are placeholders for input and output

▶   A body consisting of local declarations and statements

▶   An optional result type to address the data type of the returned result

◥ 6.3 CONTROL FLOW FOR IMPERATIVE PROGRAMMING

Imperative programming developed because of the *structured control flow* programming principle. The program is structured if the flow of control through the program is evident from the syntactic structure of the program text. For example, a statement-oriented program is an example of a structured control flow program, in which the process proceeds with the execution of the individual statements. In general, the control flow or run sequence for an imperative program is defined as single-entry and single-exit concept, which means that, control of the execution starts at a single entry point and ends at a single exit point. The key semantic notion of the structured control flow programming is that the program execution is carried out through program *constructs,* which specify the actions and can be examined at two levels as explained in the following.

6.3.1 Statement-Oriented Structured Programming

Statement structured programming is identified by the execution of the statements as the individual components of the program. A typical example

```
x = y;
```

in C language, sets the value of x to the value of y. In the following example, execution proceeds with a sequence of statements to switch the value of two variables:

```
Temp =x;
x = y;
y = Temp;
```

The execution sequence is depicted in Figure 6.1.

6.3.2 Block-Oriented Structured Programming

Only a few useful programs consist entirely of statement-oriented structure. Additional linguistic mechanisms are necessary to make the computations in programs flexible and powerful. For example, some of the mechanisms used are selecting among alternative control flow paths or causing the repeated execution of certain collections of statements. In general, one language feature that helps make control flow design easier is a method of forming statement collections. In block-structured programming, the blocks as the individual components of the program are carried out. A block is a contiguous section of code in which variables and statements can be localized. Examples are procedures, subroutines, modules, and functions. Thus, any information that is to be used exclusively within a block and is not needed by surrounding blocks can be hidden. This characteristic is advantageous for several reasons:

1. It localizes changes that might be made in the future. Local variables can affect performance only in the block in which they are visible.

2. When proving correctness, assumptions can be made at the beginning and end of the block. Thus, the structure of the block can be used to show that the end assumptions

FIGURE **6.1**   Control flows through a sequence of statements

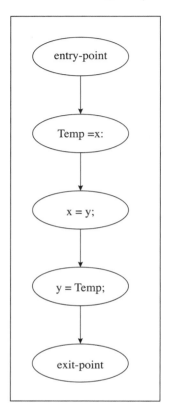

follow from those at the beginning and the operations can be performed within the block. In this sense, the complex proofs are made easier.

3. There is no need to be concerned about conflicting names between any variables local to a block and global variables.

4. It facilitates program organization if a block contains a single concept and facilitates information exchange between the calling and called blocks through parameters.

5. In the descendants of blocks, explicit control of information has been implemented, in which data, procedures, or entire modules can be visible or invisible to a user or programmer.

   Fortran was the first programming language with program blocks; the program was partitioned into blocks representing subroutines. Fortran blocks can be thought of as a flat file, where each block follows its predecessors. Because of this flat structure, Fortran is no longer considered to be a block-structured language, but it is an example of a procedure-oriented language where programs are carried out through successive calls to separate procedures. The term *block-structured programming* now refers to the

FIGURE **6.2**   Control flows through a block

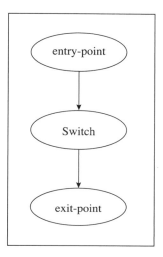

set of all programming languages that support nested block structures including procedures and modules, or it can refer to particular languages with this feature. Language examples are Ada, ALGOL-68, Modula, and C, in which the procedure is the principle building block of the program. The structure of ALGOL was a pioneer in this direction.

In the following example, control flows sequentially through a block to switch the value of two variables:

```
Switch(x y)
    Temp =x;
    x = y;
    y = Temp;
```

The execution sequence is depicted in Figure 6.2.

Expression-oriented structured programming is a nonpopular approach that is adopted by some programming languages. For example, Scheme provides this special form

```
(begin   expression₁   expression₂   expression₃   . . .   expressionₙ)
```

where the expressions are evaluated in order and the value of the last expression ($expression_n$) is the value of the entire construct. The values of the other expressions are discarded. In this sense, we may informally use the term *statement* when referring to expressions that are evaluated entirely. With this usage, expressions are considered as statements.

▽ 6.4 EXECUTION STEPS FOR IMPERATIVE PROGRAMMING

In general, an imperative program goes through several stages before it is carried out. The stages are explained in the following and shown in Figure 6.3.

▶ **Compilation:** This process translates the program into a *relocatable object code,* meaning that the program and all individual subprograms are translated into an intermediate code compatible with the computer system.

▶ **Linking:** This process incorporates the necessary libraries into the program. These libraries associated with subprograms are already programmed, debugged, and compiled. The goal of the linking process is to obtain a relocatable object code containing all parts of the program, including all library references satisfied. The presence of a good library of subprograms can greatly increase the efficiency of the program execution. Needless to say, these library subprograms may themselves contain external references to other subprograms. To obtain a complete relocatable object code, all these references (internal and external) must be accessed and satisfied by finding the corresponding subprograms in the libraries.

▶ **Loading:** A relocatable code is placed in memory for execution. This process requires converting relocatable object code to absolute format for execution. In addition, this process requires binding all code and data references to the memory locations where the code and data will be stored.

▶ **Execution:** In this process, the control flows sequentially through the execution of the program statements.

▽ 6.5 UNDESIRABLE CHARACTERISTICS OF IMPERATIVE PROGRAMMING

Although language designers generally agree that imperative languages have many desirable characteristics such as efficiency and speed, they also see some undesirable characteristics associated with imperative languages. Wulf and Shaw describe some of these problems in "Global Variables Considered Harmful" (1973). In general, the following problems are identified with imperative languages:

▶ Difficulty in reasoning

▶ Referential transparency

▶ Side effects

▶ Indiscriminate access

▶ Vulnerability access

▶ No overlapping definitions

We briefly describe each of the problems in the following sections.

FIGURE **6.3**   The Compile-Link-Load-Execute steps of program execution

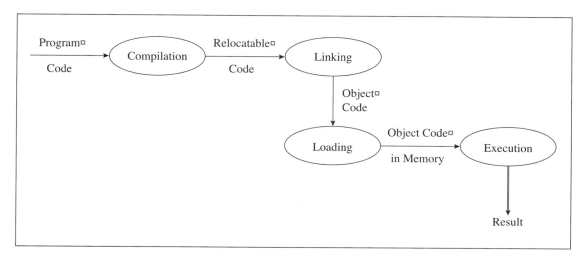

Difficulty in Reasoning

Difficulty in reasoning about the correctness of programs because the correctness of a program depends on the contents of every memory location. The state of the computation can be determined by the contents of memory locations. To understand repetitions, we must mentally run them. To observe the progress of the computation through time, we must take snapshots of the memory locations after every instruction. This is a tedious task when the program deals with numerous locations.

Referential Transparency

A system is referentially transparent if the meaning of the whole can be determined solely from the meaning of its components. For example, in a mathematical expression such as `F(x)+G(x)`, we may substitute another function `H` for `F`, if we know that it produces the same values as `F`. In imperative programming languages, we are not assured of this because the meaning of the expression depends on the history of computation of the subexpressions. Indeed, if either `F` or `G` changes the value of its parameter or modifies some global variables, we are not even certain that `F(x)+G(x)  =  G(x)+F(x)`. Generally speaking, the assignment statements, parameters passed by reference, and global variables are the main reasons that imperative languages are not referentially transparent. This lack makes programs hard to read, modify, and prove correct.

Side Effects

Imperative programming supports imperative operations that are performed for some side effect on the computations, rather than to obtain a value. Taking the variable names into consideration, the problems of side effects and aliasing arise from the existence of the variables. These may be broadly characterized as assignment, input, and output operations. For example, operators like ++ or -- in C have side effects, which means that besides returning a value, they also modify an underlying variable. Side effects can be convenient, but they can also cause trouble because the actions of retrieving the value and updating the variable might not happen at the same time. In addition, in C and C++, the order of execution of side effects is undefined; thus, the following multiple assignment is likely to produce the wrong answer:

```
class_list[index++] = class_list[index++] = 0;
```

In this statement, the intent is to store zero at the two consecutive positions in array. But depending on when index is updated, a position in array could be skipped and index might be increased only by 1. In this sense, breaking this statement into two statements such as the following makes it more clear and unambiguous:

```
class_list[index++] = 0;
class_list[index++] = 0;
```

In general, the essence of programming in imperative languages is the repeated and step-by-step computation of low-level values and the assignment of these values to memory locations—thus preventing the side effects. A similar problem happens when a function changes a global variable that appears in an expression. For example, in the following C program, a functional side effect occurs when the function check_first changes the global variable known as number.

```
int    number = 10;
int    check_first( )
       {
       number = 25;
       return 5;
       }
void   check_second( )
       {
       number = number + check_first( );
       }
void   main( )
       {
       check_second( );
       }
```

The value computed for number in check_second depends on the order in which the operands are evaluated in the expression (number = number+check_second( );). The value of number in check_second will be either 15 or 30, depending whether number gets the value as 10 or 25, respectively. Although global variable access can increase the efficiency and performance in imperative languages, it is considered as one of the undesirable characteristics of the imperative languages design.

Indiscriminate Access

The problem with indiscriminate access is that programmers cannot prevent inadvertent access to variables or data structures. In general, there is no way to arrange the declarations in an imperative language to prevent indiscriminate access. For example, suppose we want to provide a stack to be used in an ALGOL program. We would probably design the program as the following:

```
begin
    integer    array   S[1:100];

    integer   TOP;
    procedure   PUSH(x);

        integer   x;
        begin

        TOP = TOP+1;
        S[TOP]=x;

    end;
    procedure   POP(x);

        integer   x;
        begin

        POP = S[TOP];
        TOP = TOP-1;

    end;
    TOP =0;

    . . .       uses of PUSH and POP    . . .
end;
```

In general, the variable S, which is the stack, must be declared in the same block as PUSH and POP, so that it is visible from the bodies of PUSH and POP procedures. In addition, for the PUSH and POP procedures to be visible to their users, they must be declared in a block that contains all users. In this example, there is no guarantee that all users of the stack go through the PUSH and POP procedures to manipulate the data structure. In other words, S is visible to all users, and these users might inadvertently use or alter the stack S without going through the PUSH and POP procedures. If all users of the stack had to go through PUSH and POP procedures to change the stack, then we would only have to modify these procedures to change the implementation of the stack by declaring stack in the same block as PUSH and POP. Unfortunately, there is no way to accomplish this in imperative languages. Thus, the problem of indiscriminate access is the inability to prevent access to a variable.

Vulnerability Access

The problem of vulnerability access is that, under certain circumstances it is impossible to preserve access to a variable. The basic problem of vulnerability is that new declarations can be interposed between the definition and use of a variable. For example, suppose we have a very large ALGOL program with the following structure.

```
begin
integer    x;
.... many lines of code
begin
  .... many lines of code
    x = x + 1;
  .... many lines of code
end;
.... many lines of code
end;
```

In this example, we are supposing that there are many lines of code between the definition and use of x variable. Let's further suppose that in the process of maintaining this program we decide that we need a new local variable in the inner block. If we pick x without realizing that it was already used in that block, it results in the following program:

```
begin
    integer    x;
  .... many lines of code
    begin
          real x;
      .... many lines of code
          x = x + 1;
      .... many lines of code
    end;
    .... many lines of code
end;
```

With this modification, access to the outer declaration of integer x has been blocked and the statement x = x + 1 now refers to the new real variable x. In other words, the new declaration of x has been interposed between the original definition of x and its use. Thus, the problem of vulnerability access is the inability to preserve access to a variable, meaning that a program segment cannot control the assumptions under which it executes. In general, side effects, indiscriminate access, and vulnerability can all be defined to be results of implicit inheritance, meaning that the scope of a variable is extended to inner blocks.

No Overlapping Definitions

The problem of no overlapping definitions arises from attempts to modularize large programs. For example, suppose there is a large program composed of procedures P_1, P_2, P_3, and P_4, in which we want P_1 and P_2 to communicate through a shared data structure $DATA_1$ and we want P_2, P_3, and P_4 to communicate through a shared data structure $DATA_2$. A sketch of this overlapping is shown in Figure 6.4.

FIGURE **6.4**   Overlapping structures in a program

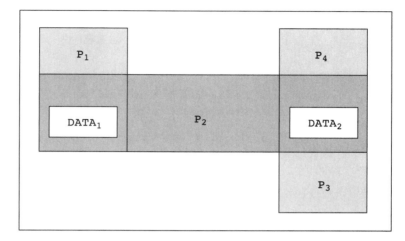

As we see, P_1 has access to $DATA_2$ and P_3 and P_4 have access to $DATA_1$. This access is not needed, meaning that it spreads knowledge of implementation decisions where it is not necessary. Thus, the problem of no overlapping definitions is the inability to control shared access to variables. This creates both maintenance and security problems.

✘ 6.6 DESIRABLE CHARACTERISTICS OF IMPERATIVE PROGRAMMING

The undesirable characteristics of the imperative programming have one common problem, which is that the order of the evaluation of constructs is critical. Although one characteristic of a *good* computer programming language is that it can be easily extended in the specific direction that a particular programmer wants, some issues involved in good programming are described in the following sections.

No Implicit Inheritance

The default should not be to extend the scope of a variable to inner blocks. In other words, there should be no implicit inheritance of access to variables from enclosing blocks. This helps solve side effect, indiscriminate access, and vulnerability problems.

Distinguish Access to Data Structures

It should be possible to distinguish different data types of access. For example, it should be possible to give some users read-only access to a data structure and other users read-write access. This helps solve side effect and vulnerability problems.

Decoupling Declarations

Declaration of definition, name access, and allocation should be decoupled. For example, declaring a variable in a block can result in the following:

▶   The name is defined by its appearance in the declaration.

▶   The name access is determined by its occurrence in the block because that block and all inner blocks implicitly inherit access to the variable.

▶   The storage allocation and deallocation are determined since they will occur simultaneously with entry to and exit from the block.

Some languages attempt to support these issues. For example, ALGOL decouples name definition and access from allocation, and Pascal accomplishes the same with its dynamically allocated storage.

Natural Form for Expressions

Write expressions to make them understandable. For example, conditional expressions that include negations are always hard to understand. In the following if statement

```
if   (  !( block_id  <  block_1)  ||  !(block_id  >=  block_2)  )
```

each test is expressed negatively, though this is not necessary. In this case, setting the relational operators as the following shows can express the tests positively, thus producing a more clear and understandable statement:

```
if   (  ( block_id  >=  block_1)  ||  (block_id  <  block_2)  )
```

Parenthesize to Resolve Ambiguity

Parentheses specify grouping and can be used to make the intention more clear even when they are not required. When mixing unrelated operators, it is a good idea to use parentheses. For example, C presents precedence problems, and it is easy to make a mistake. In this regard, the bitwise operators & and | have lower precedence than relational operators like ==, so

```
if  (*&MASK == BITS)
```

actually means

```
if  (* & (MASK == BITS) )
```

because it combines bitwise and relational operators. In this case, the expression needs to be parenthesized as:

```
if  ( (*&MASK)  ==  BITS)
```

In general, even though parentheses are not necessary, they can help if the grouping is hard to grasp at first glance. For example, the following code does not need parentheses

```
leap_year  =  year % 4  == 0 && year % 100 != 0 || year % 400 == 0 ;
```

but the parentheses can make it easier to understand:

```
leap_year = ((year % 4  ==0) && (year % 100 != 0)) || (year % 400 == 0) ;
```

Break up Complex Expressions

The C, C++, and Java programming languages have rich expressions, syntax, and operators, which makes it easy to state different expressions in one construction. For example, the following expression is compact and combines several operations into a single statement:

```
*prta+=( *ptrb = (2*index < (index_1 − index_2) ? array1[index++] : array2[index—]));
```

The statement is easier to understand when it is broken into several pieces:

```
if   =(2*index <(index_1 − index_2))
     *ptrb = array1[index++];
else
     *ptrb = array2[index—];
*prta +=  *ptrb;
```

☛ SUMMARY

The differences among programming languages revolve around what they make convenient to express, rather than what they can express. In this chapter, we reviewed the imperative programming paradigm, which was the oldest but still dominant programming language method. In general, a programming language that was characterized by the following three properties was called an imperative language because its primary feature is sequence of statements that represent commands:

▶ Sequential execution of instructions.

▶ Use of variables representing memory location values.

▶ Use of assignment statements to change the values of variables and to allow the program to operate on these memory location values.

These properties deal with flow of control through program constructs, which refers to the sequence in which the program statements are carried out. The basic unit of imperative programming is *action,* which can be classified into three categories: *computational, control-flow,* and *input-output* actions. We discussed the imperative actions. This was followed by a thorough examination of variables, assignment statements, selection constructs, including those for single-way and multiple-way selections. An important question in the application of type-to-type checking was type equivalence. We discussed this important issue relative to structural equivalence, name equivalence, and declaration equivalence. Imperative programming was developed by the structured control flow programming principle. In this sense, we discussed the statement-oriented structured and block-oriented structured programming to address the concept of control flow sequentially through the program. In addition, we briefly talked about the steps of program execution: compile, load, and run. We briefly described undesirable characteristics for imperative programming, which are difficulty in reasoning, referential transparency, side effects, indiscriminate access, vulnerability access, and no overlapping definition.

7 Imperative Programming Languages

In the 1970s, two programming languages were designed, Pascal as a teaching language and C as an implementation language. The capabilities provided by Pascal and C are advanced enough that later languages have simply borrowed them and built on them. When Niklaus Wirth designed Pascal around 1970, he intended it to be a language suitable for teaching programming fundamentals. Subsequently, Hoare and Wirth formally specified a large subset of Pascal in 1973. As an educational language, Pascal proved successful because

- ► Its simplicity and compactness allow it to be learned in a reasonable amount of time.
- ► Its selection of control structures can support the structured programming.
- ► Its rich variety of data types allows data to be described accurately.
- ► Its design is simple and efficient for implementation.

Modula was a successor of Pascal that might easily have been named Pascal-1 and was the second in the series of three languages developed by Wirth. Modula was intended for use in programming real-time dedicated applications. Modula-2, the third language successor of Pascal and Modula, combines some of the capabilities of both its predecessors and is intended to serve as a general-purpose programming language. For a complete description of Modula-2, the reader is encouraged to refer to Riley (1987b). C was designed by programmers who wanted to create a language that was powerful, yet easy to learn. There are certainly languages that are more powerful than C (i.e., assembly language), but they are generally harder to use, or are designed for a particular machine. The description of C in this book is not intended to be complete. For a complete description, the reader is encouraged to refer to the defining documents such as Kernighan and Ritchie (1988).

Each of the remaining chapters of this book explains one of the major paradigms, examining it through one or two representative languages. In this chapter, we discuss

C and Modula-2 for comparison purposes. These two languages were chosen for their widespread use and for the variety of language properties they exhibit.

7.1   IMPERATIVE PROGRAMMING WITH C LANGUAGE

A joint committee from the University of London Computer Unit and the University Mathematical Laboratory at Cambridge decided to design a language that was both high and low level. It would be high enough so it wouldn't be tied to a particular computer, but low enough to allow the manipulation of specific bits. The resulting language was called Combined Programming Language (CPL). It was never popular, since it was a very large and difficult language, but a pared-down version named Basic CPL (BCPL) developed by Martin Richards attracted some users. Kenneth Thompson, who worked for Bell Labs (now Lucent Technology) created an even smaller version of BCPL, called B (perhaps symbolizing that he only needed part of BCPL). Dennis Ritchie teamed up with Thompson later (in 1972) and transformed B into C by restoring some of the CPL features, such as a rich set of data typing, control structures and operators. C was designed to be a lower-level language with emphasis on generality and economy of expressions, like its ancestor CPL language. Its operators and pointer capabilities provide the opportunity to access lower-level machine facilities, making C a useful language for writing system programs. In other words, C provides the programmer with as much power as possible to control the execution of a program and to encourage compactness of expression. Ritchie states,

> C is a general purpose programming language. Although it has been called *a systems programming language*, because it is useful for writing operating systems, it has been used equally well to write major numerical, text-processing, and database programs. (Kernighan & Ritchie, 1988)

C as a general-purpose programming language was closely associated with the UNIX operating system because both the system and most of the programs that run on it are written in C. The language, however, is not tied to any one operating system or machine. In contrast to the Pascal programming language, which was intended to encourage reliable structures programs, C was kept small and flexible to allow as wide a range of applications as possible so that it could run on a variety of computers. In contrast to some strongly typed languages such as ALGOL, C was designed as a language where the storage is viewed as bit strings rather than as integers, real numbers, or characters. To sum up, C along with its extension C++ has become one of the most popular programming languages around the world. It is very famous for its duality because

▶ It is both a high-level and low-level programming language.

▶ It is both a special and general purpose programming language.

In general, C is high enough that it is not tied to a particular computer, but low enough to allow the manipulation of specific bits. This is apparent when you look at some of C's characteristics, which are short. For example, instead of *begin . . . end,* brackets { . . . } are used. This makes for faster programming, but it also makes less readable code. Another characteristic is its permissive data typing. For example, if there is an error, you will not get neat error messages. You will probably have to figure out your own errors. C provides the fundamental control flow construction required for structured programs, these include statement grouping { . . . }, decision making (`if-else`), selecting one of a set of possible cases (`switch`), looping with the termination test at the top (`while` and `for`), or at the bottom (`do`), and early loop exit (`break`).

C has an alphabet and rules for putting together words and punctuation to make correct, or legal, programs. These rules are the syntax of the language. The program that checks on the legality of C code is called the compiler. If there are errors, the compiler will print error messages and stop; otherwise, the source code is legal and the compiler translates it into object code, which in turn is used by the linker to produce an executable file. When the compiler is invoked, the preprocessor does its work first. For that reason we can think of the preprocessor as being built into the compiler. On some systems, this is actually the case, whereas on others, the preprocessor is separate. In general, we can get the error messages from the preprocessor as well as from the compiler. A C program is a sequence of characters that will be converted by a C compiler to an object code, which in turn is converted to a target language on a particular computer. In general, the compiler first collects the characters of the program into syntactic units called *tokens*, which can be thought of as the basic vocabulary of the language. C has six kinds of tokens:

► Identifiers
► Keywords
► Constants
► String Literals
► Operators
► Punctuators

The compiler checks that the tokens can be formed into legal strings according to the syntax of the language. Most compilers are very precise in their requirements; a C compiler will fail to provide a translation of a syntactically incorrect program, no matter how trivial the error.

7.1.1 Lexical Elements, Data Types, Operators, and Punctuators

Keywords are explicitly reserved words that have a strict meaning as individual tokens in C. They cannot be redefined or used in other constants. Table 7.1 lists the keywords used in C language.

Some implementations may have additional keywords. These will vary from one implementation or system to another. Keywords can be thought of as identifiers that are reserved to have special meaning in the C language. The keyword `main` is special, in that C programs always begin execution at the block called `main`.

An *identifier* or in general a *variable* is a token that is composed of a sequence of letters, digits and the special character "_" which is called an underscore and counts as a letter; it is sometimes useful for improving the readability of long variable names. A

TABLE **7.1**	**Reserved words in C language**						
auto	break	case	char	const	continue	default	void
do	double	else	enum	extern	float	for	volatile
goto	if	int	long	register	return	short	while
signed	sizeof	static	struct	switch	typedef	union	unsigned

letter or underscore must be the first character of an identifier. In most implementations of C, the lowercase and uppercase letters are treated as distinct, so x and X are two different names. Identifiers are used to hold intermediate results of computations. However, such use of identifiers is not a key characteristic of imperative programming. At least the first 31 characters of an internal name are significant. In general, a variable is a location in memory and its interpretation depends on two main attributes: its *storage class* and its *type*. The storage class determines the lifetime of the storage associated with the variable. There are two storage classes: *automatic* and *static*. Automatic objects are local to a block and are discarded when they exit from the block. Declarations within a block provide an automatic class if no storage class specification is mentioned or if the *auto* specific is used. Objects declared *register* are automatic and are stored in fast registers of the machine. Static objects may be local to a block or external to all blocks, but in either case, they retain their values across exit from reentry to functions and blocks. The objects declared outside all blocks at the same level as function definitions are always static. Objects may be made local to a particular translation by use of the *static* keyword, which gives them *internal linkage*. They become global to the entire program by omitting an explicit storage class, or by using the keyword *extern,* which gives them *external linkage.* Functions themselves are always external because C does not allow functions to be defined inside other functions. By default, external variables and functions have the property that all references to them by the same name, even from functions compiled separately, are references to the same object. In this sense, external variables are analogous to Fortran COMMON blocks or variables in the outermost block in Pascal.

Data Types

There are only a few basic data types in C:

▶ char, a single byte, capable of holding one character
▶ int, an integer, reflecting the size of integers on the machine
▶ float, a single-precision floating point
▶ double, a double-precision floating point

The range of both int and float variables depends on the machine you are using; for example, 16-bit integers, which lie between −32768 and +32767, are common, as are 32-bit integers. A float number is typically a 32-bit quantity, with at least six significant digits and magnitude generally between about 10^{-38} and 10^{+38}. In addition, a number of quantifiers can be applied to the basic data types:

▶   `short int`, reflecting 16-bits as the size of the integer number.

▶   `long int`, reflecting 32-bits as the size of the integer number.

▶   `long double`, reflecting extended precision floating-point number.

In general, the size of the objects of these data types are machine dependent. The quantifier signed or unsigned is applied to character or any integer variable. Unsigned numbers are positive or zero. For example, signed characters have values between −128 and 127, while unsigned character variables have values between 0 and 255.

An expression such as `x+y` has both a value and a type. For example, if both `x` and `y` have type *integer*, then the expression `x+y` also has type *integer*. But if both `x` and `y` have type *short*, then `x+y` is of type *integer* rather than *short*. This is because in any expression, a *short* is always promoted or converted to an *integer*. In general, arithmetic conversions can occur when the operands of an operator are evaluated. Suppose that `i` and `j` are variables of type *integer* and *float*, respectively. In the expression `i+j`, the operand `i` is promoted to a *float* and the expression as a whole has type *float*. This is called the *usual arithmetic conversion rules,* as outlined in the following.

1. If either operand is of type *long double*, the other operand is converted to *long double*.

2. If either operand is of type *double*, the other operand is converted to *double*.

3. If either operand is of type *float*, the other operand is converted to *float*.

4. The integral promotions are performed on both operands, and the following rules are applied.

    ▶   If either operand is of type *unsigned long*, the other operand is converted to *unsigned long*.

    ▶   If one operand has type *long* and the other has type *unsigned*, then one of two possibilities occurs: (1) If a *long* can represent all the values of an *unsigned*, then the operand of type *unsigned* is converted to *long*. (2) If a *long* can not represent all the values of an *unsigned*, then both of the operands are converted to *unsigned long*.

    ▶   If either operand has type *long*, the other operand is converted to *long*.

    ▶   If either operand has type *unsigned*, the other operand is converted to *unsigned*.

This process goes under different names such as automatic conversion, implicit conversion, coercion, promotion, or widening. In addition to implicit conversions that can occur with assignments and in mixed expressions, explicit conversions are called *casts*. For example, if `total` is an integer variable, then in

```
average = (float) total / count;
```

the cast operator `(float)` creates a temporary floating-point copy of its operand, `total`. The value stored in `total` is still an integer, but the calculation now consists of floating-point value, a temporary float version of `total`. Cast operators are available for any data type. The cast operator is formed by placing parentheses around a data type name, and it takes only one operand.

Constants

C manipulates various kinds of values such as integer-constant, character-constant, floating-constant, and enumeration-constant. Whole numbers like 0 and 17 are examples of integer constants. Octal constants begin with 0 (digit zero) and do not contain the digits 8 or 9. A sequence of digits preceded by 0x or 0X (digit zero) is taken to be a hexadecimal integer, and digits include a or A through f or F with values 10 through 15. Fractional numbers like 1.0 and 7.14159 are examples of floating constants. Also, character constants are written between single quotes; examples are 'a', 'b', and '+'. Identifiers declared as enumerators are constants of type integer.

String Literals

A sequence of characters enclosed in a pair of double quote marks, such as "abc" is a string constant, or a string. String constants are always treated differently from character constants. For example, "a" and 'a' are not the same. The compiler treats string constants as a single token and provides space in memory to store the string. An example of a string constant is "Input Two Integers: ". Adjacent string literals are concatenated into a single string. After any concatenation, a null character \0 is appended to the string so that programs that scan the string can find its end.

Operators "and Punctuators

In C, many special characters have particular meaning. Examples include the arithmetic operators

```
+    -    *    /    %
```

which stand for the usual arithmetic operations of addition, subtraction, multiplication, division, and modulus, respectively. Recall that in mathematics the value of

```
a   modulus   b
```

is obtained by taking the remainder after dividing a by b. Thus, for example, 5%3 has the value 2. C has a rich set of operators. Among the monadic operators, the increment and decrement operators are the most interesting and useful. The increment operator is signified by ++ and decrement by —. For example, when ++ is written before the operand in the expression, it indicates that 1 will be added to the operand before it is used in the expression evaluation; when written after, it shows that 1 will be added after the operand is used. For example, if variable x has an initial value of 5, the statement

```
y = ++x + 1;
```

results in y having a value of 7 and x having a value of 6. Similarly, the statement

```
y  = x++ + 1;
```

results in y having a value of 6 and x having a value of 6, indicating that the value 5 which is x's value before being incremented is used for x in the expression evaluation. The operator — works in a similar manner for decrementation.

TABLE **7.2**		**Assignment operators in C language**								
=	+=	−=	*=	/=	%=	>>=	<<=	&=	^=	|=

The assignment operator, which is an equal sign (=) in C, is a value-returning operator. The value returned is the value evaluated for the right hand side of the assignment. In general, this kind of format permits multiple assignments to be placed within a single statement. For example, if variable x has an initial value of 5, the statement

```
y = (x = x + 1) + 1;
```

results in y having a value of 7 and x having a value of 6. In addition to =, there are other assignment operators, such as +=. For example, an expression such as

```
k = k+2;
```

will add 2 to the old value of k and assigns the result to k, and the expression as a whole will have that value. The same task can be accomplished by the expression

```
k += 2;
```

In general, the syntax is formed by

```
variable   op= expression;
```

which is equivalent to

```
variable  =  variable  op  (expression);
```

Table 7.2 contains all the assignment operators, which have the same precedence and right-to-left associativity.

Another interesting operator in C is the conditional operator that accepts three operators. In its most general form, this conditional statement is

```
<expression₁>  ?  <expression₂>  :  <expression₃>;
```

where the result of the operation depends on the value of $expression_1$. If $expression_1$ is nonzero, the result is the value of $expression_2$. If $expression_1$ is zero, the result is the value of $expression_3$. For example,

```
a = b  ?  10  :  20;
```

sets a to be 20 if b is zero and sets a to 10 if b is not zero. The character & is the address operator. The compiler treats it as a token. Even though the character & and variable are adjacent to each other, the compiler treats each as a separate token. We could have written

```
&a   or   &  a
```

but not

```
a  &
```

TABLE **7.3**	**Relational, equality, and logical operators**		
Relational operators	less than	<	
	greater than	>	
	less than or equal	<=	
	greater than or equal	>=	
Equality operators	equal to	==	
	not equal to	!=	
Logical operators	negation	!	
	logical and	&&	
	logical or	||	

because & requires its operand to be on the right. The *comma* operator "," has the lowest precedence among all the operators in C. It is a binary operator with expressions as operands, and it associates from left to right. In a comma expression of the form

        $expression_1$, $expression_2$

$expression_1$ is evaluated first, then $expression_2$. The comma expression as a whole has the value and type of its right operand. An example is

        ++i,   sum += i;

in which the expression ++i is evaluated first, and its incremented value is then added to sum. Some symbols have meaning that depends on context. For example, consider the % symbol in the two statements

        printf(" %d ", a);   and   a = b%7;

the first % symbol is the start of a conversion specification, or format, whereas the second % symbol represents the modulus operator.

7.1.2   Control Flow

Statements in a program are normally carried out one after another. This is called sequential flow of control. A compound statement is a series of declarations and statements surrounded by braces. The use of the compound statement is to group statements into an executable unit. When declarations come at the beginning of a compound statement, it is called a block. A compound statement is itself a statement. Often, we want to alter the sequential flow of control to provide for a choice of action, or the repetition of an action. We can use if, if-else, and switch statements to select among alternative actions, and while, for, and do statements to achieve iterative actions. The operators that are most often used to affect flow of control are outlined in Table 7.3.

The rules of precedence and associativity that determine how expressions involving these operators are evaluated are explained in Chapter 3. With expressions that contain the operands of && and ||, the evaluation process stops as soon as the outcome true or false is known. This is called short-circuit evaluation and was adopted in

C language. This is an important property of these operators. For example, suppose $expression_1$ and $expression_2$ are expressions and $expression_1$ has value zero. In the evaluation of the logical expression

```
expression₁ && expression₂
```

the evaluation of $expression_2$ will not occur because the value of the logical expression as a whole is already determined to be 0. Similarly, if $expression_1$ has a nonzero value, then in the evaluation of

```
expression₁ || expression₂
```

the evaluation of $expression_2$ will not occur because the value of the logical expression as a whole is already determined to be 1.

7.1.3 Arrays, Functions, and Pointers

An array is a sequence of data items that are all of the same type, that are indexed, and that are stored contiguously. The C language allows arrays of any type, including arrays of arrays. The elements of an array are accessed by the use of subscripts, also called indices. The brackets `[ ]` are used to contain the subscripts of an array. In the following declaration

```
int    grade[3];
```

the integer 3 represents the size or the number of elements in the array named `grade`. The indexing of array elements starts at 0. We can use `grade[0]`, `grade[1]`, and `grade[2]` to access the elements of array. With two bracket pairs, we obtain a two-dimensional array. This idea can be iterated to obtain arrays of higher dimension. For example, in the following declaration

```
int    class[3][4];
```

the integers 3 and 4 represent the number of rows and columns in a two-dimensional array called `class`, respectively. We can think of the array elements arranged as shown in Table 7.4.

Arrays can be initialized within a declaration. Initialization is a sequence of values written as a brace enclosed comma separated list. An example is

```
float    x[3] = {-1.1, 0.2, 22.0};
```

when this initializes `x[0]` to `-1.1`, `x[1]` to `0.2`, and `x[2]` to `22.0`. When a list of initializers is shorter than the number of array elements to be initialized, the remaining elements are initialized to zero. If an array is declared without a size and is initialized to a series of values, it is implicitly given the size of the array. Thus, the following two declarations are equivalent.

```
int    a[ ] = {3, 4, 5, 6};
```
and
```
int    a[4] = {3, 4, 5, 6};
```

There are a number of ways to initialize a two-dimensional array. The following three initializations are equivalent.

TABLE **7.4**   **Two-dimensional array with three rows and four columns**

	Column 1	**Column 2**	**Column 3**	**Column 4**
Row 1	class[0][0]	class[0][1]	class[0][2]	class[0][3]
Row 2	class[1][0]	class[1][1]	class[1][2]	class[1][3]
Row 3	class[2][0]	class[2][1]	class[2][2]	class[2][3]

```
int    a[2][3] = {1, 2, 3, 4, 5, 6};
int    a[2][3] = { {1, 2, 3}, {4, 5, 6} };
int    a[ ][3] = { {1, 2, 3}, {4, 5, 6} };
```

A classic use of a two-dimensional array is a matrix of n×n elements. An array of dimensions higher than two works in a similar fashion.

Top-down design, also referred to as *stepwise refinement*, consists of repeatedly decomposing a problem into smaller problems. Eventually, one has a collection of small problems or tasks, each of which can be easily coded. The function construct in C is used to write code that solves the small problems that result from this decomposition. These functions are combined into other functions and ultimately used in main( ) to solve the original problem. Some functions, such as printf( ) and scanf( ), are provided by the system; the programmer can write others. A program is made up of one or more functions, one of them being main( ). Program execution always begins with main( ). When program control encounters a function name followed by parentheses, that function is called or invoked. This indicates that program control passes to the function. After the function has performed its tasks, program control is passed back to the calling environment, where program execution continues. Each function definition has the form

```
return-type    function-name(argument declarations)
{
   declarations and statements
}
```

To illustrate this idea, let us write a program so that the function print_message( ) has a formal parameter. The parameter is used to specify how many times the message is printed.

```
#include    <stdio.h>
void    printf_message(int k)
int    main(void)    {
int    n;
printf( " How many times do you want to see the message? ");
scanf(" %d ", &n);
print_message(n);
return 0;
```

```
}
void   print_message(int  k)  {
int  i;
printf( " Here is the message:\n");
for(i=0;  i < k; ++i)
    printf(" Have a nice day!\n");
}
```

The `return` statement is the mechanism for returning a value from the called function to its caller. Any expression can follow `return`:

```
return    expression;
```

where the `expression` will be converted to the return type of the function if necessary. When a `return` statement is executed, program control is immediately passed back to the calling environment with the value of expression. To illustrate the use of `return`, let us write a program that computes the minimum of two integer numbers.

```
#include   <stdio.h>
int    min(int a, int b)
int   main(void)    {
int    j, k, m;
printf( " Input two integers:   " );
scanf("%d %d", &j, &k);
m = min(j, k);
printf( " \n Of the two values %d and %d,
the minimum is %d.\n", j, k, m);
return 0;
}
int    min(int  a, int  b)   {
if  (a < b)
   return a;
else
   return b;
}
```

The calling function is free to ignore the returned value. Furthermore, there need be no expression after return; in that case, no value is returned to the caller. In addition, functions may return values of basic types, structures, unions, or pointers and any function may be called recursively. Pointers are used in C programs to access memory and manipulate addresses. If x is a variable, then &x is the address, or location, of its stored value in memory. The address operator & is unary and has the same precedence and right-to-left associativity as the other unary operators. The declaration

```
int    p, *ptr;
```

declares p to be a variable of type *integer* and `ptr` a variable of type *pointer to integer*. In other words, `ptr` points to a variable of type *integer*. The legal range of values of any pointer includes a set of positive integers that are interpreted as machine addresses. Some examples of assignment to the pointer `ptr` are the following:

```
ptr = &I;
ptr = NULL;
ptr = (int *) 1307;
```

In the first we think of `ptr` as "referring to `I`," or "pointing to `I`," or "containing the address of `I`." The compiler decides what address to use to store the value of the variable `I`. The second example shows assignment of the special value `NULL` (zero) to the pointer variable. In the last example, the cast (`int *`) is necessary to avoid a compiler error. The type in the cast is "pointer to integer." In addition, we can declare a variable of type pointer to an object, such as a *file*. For example, the following declaration

```
FILE    *cfptr;
```

states that `cfptr` is a pointer to a `FILE` structure. The C program administers each file with a separate `FILE` structure.

7.1.4 Addressing and Dereferencing

The following diagrams illustrate what is happing in memory with regard to pointer declarations. Let us start with the declaration

```
int    a,  b,  *p;
```

This declaration causes the compiler to allocate space in memory for two integer variables and a pointer to integer. At this point, no values have been assigned to variables as represented in Figure 7.1.

After the assignment statements

```
a  =  b  =  7;
p  =  &a;
```

have been run, we have the situation depicted in Figure 7.2.

Now we can use the pointer p to access the value stored in a. This is done through the dereference, or indirection, operator ∗. Because p is a pointer variable, the expression ∗p has the value of the variable to which p points. Consider the statement

```
printf( " pointer variable p points to the value %d ", *p);
```

Because p points to a, and a has value 7, the dereferenced value of p is 7, and that is printed. The name *indirection* is taken from machine-language programming. The direct value of p is a memory location, whereas ∗p is the indirect value of p, the value at the memory location stored in p.

7.1.5 Conditional and Iterative Constructs

The general form of an `if` construct is

```
if   (expression)
   statement₁
statement₂
```

FIGURE **7.1**   **Initial declaration of variables**

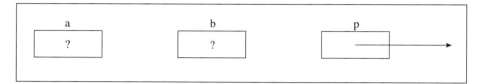

FIGURE **7.2**   **Variables after initial values**

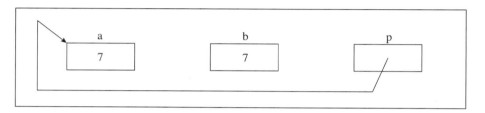

If expression is nonzero (true), then statement₁ is carried out; otherwise statement₁ is skipped and control passes to statement₂. Where appropriate, compound statements should be used to group a series of statements under the control of a single if expression. In the following

```
if    (grade >= 90)
        printf("Congratulation!");
    printf("Your Grade is %d ", grade);
```

a congratulatory message is printed only when the value of grade is greater than or equal to 90. The second print statement is always executed. The if-else construct is closely related to the if construct. It has a general form given by

```
if    (expression)
        statement₁
    else
        statement₂
    statement₃
```

If expression is nonzero, then statement₁ is carried out, and statement₂ is skipped; if expression is zero, then statement₁ is skipped and statement₂ is carried out. In both cases, control then passes to the statement₃. Consider the following example

```
if    (x < y)
        min  =  x;
    else
```

```
     min  =  y;
  printf( "Min Value =   %d ", min);
```

if x<y is true, then `min` will be assigned the value of x; otherwise, `min` will be assigned the value of y. Control then passes to the print statement. In C, the `while`, `for`, and `do` constructs provide for repetitive actions. Consider a construction of the following form:

```
while  (expression)
      statement₁
statement₂
```

The effect of this construct is that the body of the `while` loop, namely $statement_1$, is run repeatedly until `expression` is zero (false). At that point, control passes to $statement_2$. An example is

```
while  (i <= 10)   {
      sum += i ;
++ i;                  }
```

where the effect of the loop is to repeatedly increment the value of `sum` by the current value of `i` and then to increment `i` by 1 until `i` gets the value `11`. The `for` construct, like the `while`, is used to run code iteratively. The following two constructions are semantically equivalent to each other:

```
for  (expr₁; expr₂;expr₃)      expr₁;
      statement₁                while  (expr₂)   {
statement₂                            statement₁
                                      expr₃;      }
                              statement₂
```

meaning that the process continues until $expr_2$ is zero, at which point control passes to the $statement_2$. An example is

```
for  (i=0;  i <= 10; ++ i)   {
      sum += i;
}
```

with the same result as the `while` construct. Finally, flow of control constructs such as `if`, `if-else`, `for`, and `while` can be nested within themselves and within one another. Although such nested control constructs can be quite complicated, some have a regular structure and are easily understood.

7.1.6   Structures and Unions

The structure type allows user to aggregate components into a single variable. Structures may contain variables of different data types, in contrast to arrays, which contain only elements of the same data type. A structure has components called members that are individually named. Consider the following structure definition:

```
struct   class   {
      char  grade;
```

```
        int     total_points;
        float     gpa;
};
```

The identifier `class` is the *structure tag* and is used to declare variables of the structure type. Variables declared within the braces of the structure definition are the members of the structure. Members of the same structure must have unique names, but two different structures may contain members of the same name without conflict. Structures are commonly used to define records to be stored in files. We can assign values to the members of the variable `class` by using statements such as the following:

```
class.grade = 'A';
class.total_points = 97;
class.gpa = 7.87;
```

Unlike a structure, a *union* is a derived data type whose members share the same storage space. In other words, a union is a variable that may hold (at different times) objects of different types and sizes. In this case, the compiler keeps track of size and alignment requirements. In C, unions are given directly and are undiscriminated. As an example, suppose that a constant may be an integer, a float, or a character. This can be the purpose of a union: a single variable that can legitimately hold any of these types. In the following:

```
union   number   {
        int    int_number;
        float    float_number;
        char    char_number;
}     x_number;
```

the variable `x_number` will be large enough to hold the largest of the three types: integer, float, or character. Any of these types may be assigned to `x_number` and then used in expressions, as long as the usage is consistent. We can assign value to the members of `x_number` variable of type union as the following:

```
x_number.int_number = 123;
x_number.float_number = 12.5;
x_number.char_number = 'A';
```

Only one member and, thus, one data type can be accessed at a time.

7.1.7 Formatting Input and Output

Input and output operations are important in applications in which data reside in files on disks and tapes. The input function `scanf( )` has the following two properties that allow it flexibility at a high level:

▶ A list of arguments of arbitrary length can be scanned.

▶ The input is controlled by simple conversion specifications or formats.

The `scanf( )` reads characters from the standard input file named `stdin`. The `scanf` function is written in the following form:

TABLE **7.5**   **Conversion specifiers for** scanf

Specifier	Description
d	read a signed decimal integer.
i	read a signed decimal, octal, or hexadecimal.
o	read an octal integer.
u	read an unsigned decimal integer.
x or X	read a hexadecimal integer.
E, e, f, g or G	read a floating-point value.
h or l	place before any of the integer conversion specifiers to indicate that a *short* or *long* integer is to be input.
l or L	place before any of the floating-point conversion specifiers to indicate that a *double* or *long double* value is to be input.
c	read a character.
s	read a string.
p	read a pointer address of the same form produced when an address is output with %p in a printf statement.
n	store the number of characters input so far in this scanf. The corresponding argument is a pointer to integer.
%	skip a percent sign (%) in the input.

```
scanf(format-control-string, argument-list);
```

The format-control-string describes the format of the input, and argument-list contains pointers to variables in which the input is stored. argument-list consists of a comma-separated list of pointer expressions, or addresses. For example, in the following

```
char    a;
int     b;
float   c;
char    s[25];
scanf( " %c%d%f%s ", &a, &b, &c, s);
```

we have

```
format-control-string:    " %c%d%f%s "
argument-list:            &a, &b, &c, s
```

Some of the formatting capabilities of scanf are listed in Table 7.5. Precise output formatting is accomplished with printf function. The printf function has the following form:

```
printf(format-control-string, argument-list);
```

The `format-control-string` describes the output format, and `argument-list`, which is optional, corresponds to each conversion specification in the `format-control-string`. In the example

```
printf( " she sold %d %s for $%f ", 99, " books ", 12.57);
```

we have

```
format-control-string:   " she sold %d %s for $%f "
argument-list:           99, " books ", 12.57
```

In this sense, the expressions in `argument-list` are evaluated and converted according to the formats in the control string. Some of the formatting capabilities of printf are the following:

▶ Rounding floating-point values to an indicated number of decimal places

▶ Aligning a column of numbers with decimal points appearing one above the other

▶ Right-justification and left-justification of output

▶ Inserting literal characters at precise locations in a line of output

▶ Representing floating-point numbers in exponential format

▶ Representing unsigned integers in octal and hexadecimal format

▶ Displaying all types of data with fixed-size field widths and precision

The functions `sprintf( )` and `sscanf( )` are string versions of the functions `printf( )` and `scanf( )`, respectively. They are formed as

```
sscanf(string, format-control-string, argument-list);
sprintf(string, format-control-string, argument-list);
```

in which `sscanf` reads from the character array string, and `sprintf` writes to the character array string. In addition, the functions `fprintf( )` and `fscanf( )` are the file versions of the `printf` and `scanf` functions, respectively. A statement of the form

```
fscanf(file-pointer, format-control-string, argument-list);
```

reads from the file pointed to by `file-pointer`. In a similar fashion, a statement of the form

```
fprintf(file-pointer, format-control-string, argument-list);
```

writes to the file pointed to by `file-pointer`. The conventions for `format-control-string` and `argument-list` are the same as for `printf` and `scanf` functions.

7.1.8 Preprocessor

Lines that begin with a # are called *preprocessing directives*. These lines communicate with the preprocessor. Preprocessing occurs before a program is compiled. Some possible actions are including other files in the file being compiled, defining symbolic

TABLE **7.6**	Preprocessor directives

Directive	Description
#error *tokens*	prints message including the *tokens* specified in the directive.
#pragma *tokens*	causes an implementation-defined action.
#line *number*	starts line numbering from *number* beginning with the next source code line.
#define *id value*	causes all subsequent occurrences of *id* will be replaced by *value*.
#if *condition*	causes a conditional checking based on the *condition*.

constants and macros, conditionally compiling program code, and conditionally carrying out preprocessor directives. In traditional C, preprocessing directives are required to begin in column 1. In ANSI C, this restriction is not imposed. Some examples of preprocessing directives are

```
#include   <stdio.h>
#define    PI   7.14159
#include   " filename "
```

The last one causes the preprocessor to replace the line with a copy of the contents of the named file. First, a search for the file is made in the current directory and then in other system dependent places. With a preprocessing directive of the form

```
#include   <filename>
```

the preprocessor looks for the file only in the other places but not in the current directory. Some of the preprocessing capabilities are listed in Table 7.6. The conditional preprocessor construct is much like the *if* selection structure. Consider the following preprocessor code:

```
#if   !defined(NULL)
      #define NULL 0
#endif
```

These directives determine if NULL is defined. The expression defined(NULL) evaluates to 1 if NULL is defined; 0 otherwise. If the result is 0, !defined(NULL) evaluates to 1, and NULL is defined. Otherwise, the #define directive is skipped. Every #if construct ends with the #endif directive.

7.1.9 Advantages and Disadvantages

The main advantage of C is its closeness to the machine, which makes it ideal for writing operating systems and compilers. C is also very flexible for interactive programming because of the variety of input and output facilities. The main disadvantage of C is the difficulty of debugging programs because of automatic type conversions, pointer notations, and side effect within expressions. It also adopted a different programming style that is sometimes hard for anyone but the program designer to read. Thus, C is often not the preferred programming language for applications such as business or science.

7.2 Imperative Programming with Modula-2 Language

Modula-2 was the third language in a series of languages designed and developed by Wirth. Wirth's first language, Pascal, was designed as a teaching language; its goals were language simplicity and support for structured programming concepts. But, Pascal was inadequate for big programs, which often borrow chunks of code. The key issue was how to organize these chunks into units that can be written and implemented clearly and efficiently. The programming language Modula was Wirth's answer to this need. Modula was based on Pascal but was intended for use in programming real-time dedicated systems. It consisted of features for concurrency and data abstraction. No compiler for Modula was ever released, and its development was discontinued soon after its publication.

After Modula, Wirth's focus changed toward building a language for a new computer system that later was called Lilith. Modula-2 was the result of efforts that combined some of the capabilities of both its predecessors and was intended to serve as a general-purpose programming language. Although the computer itself was never a commercial success, the language Modula-2 was (Wirth, 1985). Its extensive data abstraction features facilitate the development of large software projects. Some also propose Modula-2 as a replacement for Pascal as the primary teaching language. Modula-2 was intended to encourage programming that is structured, modular, and understandable. It adopted the block structure of Pascal and added the concept of modules, which provide support for abstract data types and encapsulation, procedures as types, low-level capabilities for systems programming and coroutines, and some syntactic features that improved those of Pascal. Modula-2 achieved widespread use in the late 1980s and early 1990s as a teaching language in universities, but provides limited visibility of the underlying hardware. The language is intended to cover applications for which assembly language traditionally is used. Modula-2 considerably improves the readability of such programs and supports a variety of static checks for program correctness.

7.2.1 Declarations

Declarations are a principal method for establishing bindings. Declarations may be explicit as in Pascal and many other programming languages, or they may be implicit, in which simply using the name of the variable causes it to be declared. The general form

```
VAR   identifier-name   :   data-type;
```

declares a variable whose name is `identifier-name` and whose value is to be of type `data-type`. In this case, all identifiers specified in a list before the colon are declared to be the names of individual variables that store values of the identical type specified after the colon. The syntax of a Modula-2 identifier is that it must begin with an alphabetic letter followed by zero or more letters or numeric digits. Similar to other languages, certain identifiers known as reserved words cannot be declared as variables. In addition, Modula-2 is case sensitive, meaning that lower-case characters differ from upper-case characters. For example,

```
VAR    course  :    INTEGER;
```

declares a variable whose name is `course` and whose value is of type *integer*. The scope of visibility, sometimes called the scope of an identifier, is the region of the program over which the bindings established by the declaration are maintained and the identifier can be referenced or used. Sometimes we refer to the scope of a name, but this is dangerous because the same name may be involved in several different declarations, each with a different scope. Modula-2 permits the programmer to declare constants. Programmer-defined constants are named by identifiers and declared in a CONST declaration that is similar to VAR declaration in Pascal. A CONST declaration specifies the name of the constants and the associated value with the following syntax:

```
CONST    ConstIdentifier = ConstExpression;
```

where `ConstIdentifier` can be any valid identifier not previously declared locally within the same scope, and `ConstExpression` can be any expression where all of the operands are constants. For example,

```
CONST    TwoPlusThree  =  Expression;
```

declares a constant named `TwoPlusThree` with the associated value of `Expression`. Modula-2 also allows constant, variable, and other declarations to occur in any order, unlike Pascal's rigid order, which only allows constants, types, variables, and procedure declarations in order.

7.2.2 Data Types

Figure 7.3 shows an overview of Modula-2 data types. Modula-2 is a strongly typed language, meaning that each variable is restricted to storing values of a single type. Types that are constructed by using array, record, set, and file are called structured types. Modula-2 is a case sensitive language, and any mixing of types requires the use of an explicit type conversion function.

In general, Modula-2 supports nine built-in scalar data types: INTEGER, CARDINAL, REAL, CHAR, BOOLEAN, POINTER, BITSET, enumerated, and subrange, in which CARDINAL is the set of nonnegative integers and shares operators with INTEGER type. CARDINALS begin at 0 and go up to some undefined maximum value that may be larger than the largest INTEGER. Modula-2 constants are restricted to be of certain types: BOOLEAN, CARDINAL, CHAR, INTEGER, REAL, SET, ENUMERATED, or STRING. Some examples of CONST declarations are as follows:

FIGURE **7.3** Modula-2 data types

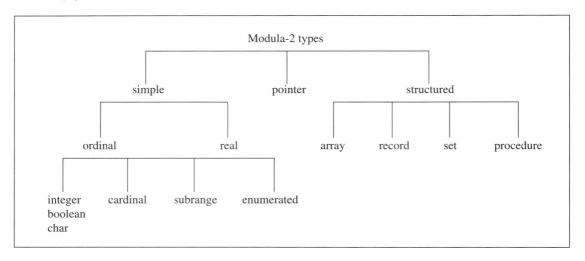

```
CONST  TwoPlusThree = 2 + 3;
CONST  T  = True;
CONST  Blank = "   ";
CONST  Grade = "A";
CONST  Freezing = 32;
CONST  e = 2.75;
CONST   = 1.0 / e;
```

Constants in Modula-2 must be static, thus the declaration

```
CONST  PI  =  4.0  *  arctan(1.0);
```

is illegal because the code associated with `arctan` function is not known at compile time; it is imported from a library module and linked after compilation. Pointer types can be declared as

```
POINTER   TO   type;
```

where the dereferencing of the pointer object is done through the ∧ operator. For example, the declaration

```
TYPE   IntPtr = POINTER TO INTEGER;
```

constructs the type of all addresses of integers. If `x` is a variable of type `IntPtr`, then it can be dereferenced to obtain a value of type integer. For example,

```
x^  := 10;
```

assigns the integer value `10` to the location given by `x`. Allocation and deallocation of storage to a pointer variable can be done through use of the NEW and DISPOSE procedures. Recursive types represent data whose size and structure are not known in advance, but may change as computation proceeds. In Modula-2, the indirect recursive declarations through pointers is allowed, as represented in the following declarations:

```
TYPE   CharList    =  POINTER to CharListRec;
       CharListRec =  RECORD
          data   :  CHAR;
          next   :  CharList;
       END;
```

Pascal supports file type, for example,

```
Type RecFile  =  File of EmployeeRec;
```

declares a variable `RecFile` of type file. Modula-2 has no specific file type, in which files are assumed to be system-dependent features provided separately by each implementation, and their types will be imported from a library module. General function and procedure types can be created in Modula-2 with the definition

```
TYPE   IntFunction = PROCEDURE  (INTEGER)  :  INTEGER;
```

where a function type from integers to integers is declared. In this sense, the reserve word PROCEDURE is used for function declaration. In addition to the usual data types, Modula-2 supports types called WORD and ADDRESS to permit access to low-level features of the computer system. Data objects of type WORD refer to an addressable unit of storage. The data type ADDRESS is a pointer variable that can specify the address of any data object and is compatible with pointer types and with type CARDINAL. Modula-2 has no formal string type.

Subranges

Modula-2 provides a method for declaring types that permits the programmer to specify a range of allowed values. The result is known as a *subrange data type* with the following syntax:

```
TypeIdentification  =  [LowConst  . .  HighConst];
```

where `LowConst` and `HighConst` are constant expressions of type BOOLEAN, CARDINAL, CHAR, INTEGER, or enumerated with the following restrictions:

- ▶ `LowConst` and `HighConst` must have identical type
- ▶ `LowConst` <= `HighConst`

Subranges are special cases of basic types because they restrict the range of values of an existing type. Modula-2 supports the definition of a subrange type of any scalar type, which inherits all the operations of the type from which they are derived. An example is the subrange 0 . . 99, which specifies the range as the integer values 0 through 99. Subranges are typically used for array bounds. Subranges of real numbers are not permitted. Some examples of subrange declarations are the following:

```
TYPE      Percent  =  [0 . . 100];
TYPE      Quality   = INTEGER[0 . . MaxOnHand];
TYPE      UpperLetter = [ "A"  . . "Z" ];
```

Modula-2 has a feature that makes use of the notation of subranges. In a CASE structure, subranges of constant expressions may be used in place of constant expressions for case label. An example is the following:

```
BEGIN
    CASE  C OF
           "a" . . "z",  "A" . . "Z"  :  RETURN TRUE
    ELSE                   RETURN FALSE
END
```

The syntax does not allow the square brackets to be used in the structure. Subrange data types can be very useful for program debugging. Many compilers generate code that performs bounds checking when carried out. Running a program with bounds checking causes the code to perform a special test each time a new value is assigned to a variable of subrange type. This check examines the value assigned to the variable to see that it is within the proper range. If the variable is outside the range then a run-time error occurs.

Union

In Modula-2 the discriminated union of the types INTEGER and REAL can be given by the declaration

```
TYPE   IntOrReal  =  RECORD
             CASE  IsInt  :  BOOLEAN  OF
                   TRUE   :  i  :  INTEGER  |
                   FALSE  :  r  :  REAL
             END;
        END;
```

The tag field `IsInt` determines whether an element is INTEGER or REAL. Given a variable x of type `IntOrReal`, we can assign the integer value 5 to x as follows:

```
x.IsInt  :=  TRUE;
x.i  :=  5;
```

An undiscriminated union is defined by the following:

```
TYPE   IntOrReal  =  RECORD
             CASE  BOOLEAN  OF
                   TRUE   :  i  :  INTEGER  |
                   FALSE  :  r  :  REAL
             END;
        END;
```

In this case, the BOOLEAN TYPE declaration in the CASE statement must still appear but the tag or field name is missing.

7.2.3 Data Aggregates

Strings are defined as arrays of type CHAR with domain $(0 . . n-1)$ for some positive integer n. Modula-2 specifies arrays of characters with certain index types and binds an array to its domain and range at compile time. For example, a declaration

```
ARRAY[0 . . n] OF CHAR
```

is a string (array of characters) with a lower bound of 0. A string is terminated by the first null character in the array. Assignment of arrays is permissible if the arrays are of the same type as defined by the named type equivalence. No composite or comparison operators are available for arrays, but Modula-2 provides a utility module called Strings, which includes procedures that assign one string to another, insert or delete substrings, find the position of the substring within a string, concatenate two strings, find the length of a string, and compare two strings lexicographically. Multidimensional arrays are declared in a manner similar to that in Pascal, except that each index domain is enclosed in a separate set of brackets. An example is

```
VAR  a : ARRAY[1 . . 10] [1 . . 20]  OF REAL;
```

where the elements can be accessed by either `a[i][j]` or `a[i,j]`. In Modula-2, open index array types can be used in the declaration of procedures and function parameters. For example, the following code declares a function that takes an array of integers as a parameter without specifying the index set. The function uses the predefined function HIGH to find the upper bound of the array. In this case, the lower bound is always assumed to be 0.

```
PROCEDURE        FindLargest(a:  ARRAY OF INTEGER)
    INTEGER;
    VAR  i : CARDINAL;
        max :  INTEGER;
    BEGIN
        max  := a[0];
        FOR  i := 1 TO HIGH(a)  DO
            IF  a[i] > max  THEN
                    max :=  a[i];
            END;
        END;
    RETURN  max;
END  FindLargest;
```

Records

Modula-2 supports record aggregate type, in which a component is selected via the period operator. The general form of a record declaration in Modula-2 is as follows:

```
RECORD   record-name
    {component-name-list  :  component-type;}
END;
```

The selection can be performed by

```
record-name . record-component-name
```

Modula-2 permits any number of record variants to be placed anywhere within a record, and provides no enforcement of the variants, permitting reference to any of the alternative components regardless of the tag component's value. The syntax of a variant construct is as follows:

```
CASE   [tag-component]  :  tag-type  OF
        Expression-list  :  {component-name : type;}
{ | expression-list  :  {component-name : type; } }
END;
```

Another feature of Modula-2 is the implementation of WITH that specifies default record prefixes within its scope. Its general form is as follows:

```
WITH   record-name-list   DO
        sequence-of-statements
END;
```

Within the sequence-of-statements, references to components of any record whose name is listed in the WITH statement do not require the record name as a prefix.

Sets

Sets are implemented as a type in Modula-2 with a general form as

```
SET   OF   UniverseType
```

where UniverseType is an enumeration or subrange type. In many implementations, it is required that every constant in UniverseType has ordinal value in the range from 0 to 15. The following example contains a collection of declarations that declare set types and variables:

```
TYPE     DigitSet  =  SET OF [0 . . 9];
VAR      OddDigits    :  DigitSet;
         SquareDigits :  DigitSet;
         OctalDigits  :  DigitSet;
         SomeDigits   :  DigitSet;
TYPE
StereoEquipment  =
(TurnTable, Amplifier, CdPlayer, Receiver, Cassette);
EquipSet  =  SET OF StereoEquipment;
VAR      MyStereo : EquipSet;  EdsStereo   :  EquipSet;
```

In this example, the universe establishes what constants may be elements of the set. DigitSet is a universe of {0 . . 9}, so any cardinal constant from 0 to 9 may be an element of any variable of type DigitSet. Similarly, EquipSet variables may include any or all of the enumerated constants from StereoEquipment as set elements. In this sense, the SET variables are automatically assigned the value of their universe. After the declarations, none of the set variables are assigned. In other words, the universe type included in the declaration only specifies potential, rather than actual values of the variable. In addition, Modula-2 has a predefined set type known as BITSET, which is the set of integers from 0 to x−1, where x is the number of bits used per memory word in the system. The BITSET permits objects of this type to be represented by a bit vector stored in a single word of memory. Modula-2 also supports the set operators of union (+), intersection (∗), difference (−), and symmetric difference (/). In addition, some predicates are provided to test for element inclusion (IN), set equality (=), set inequality (<>), subset (<=) and superset (>=).

7.2.4 Type Equivalence

A programmer-defined type is a powerful tool for data abstraction. The type of every constant, variable, and expression is important in a strongly typed language such as Modula-2, and strict compatibility rules must be followed. BOOLEAN, CARDINAL, CHAR, INTEGER, and REAL are all standard types in Modula-2. Modula-2 supports type equivalence, which is based on structural equivalence method by defining two types to be compatible if

▶   They are the same name.

▶   They are s and t, when s = t is a type declaration.

▶   One is a subrange of the other.

▶   Both are subranges of the same basic type.

The principles of strong typing in numeric expressions are slightly relaxed for INTEGER and CARDINAL. Modula-2 allows a positive constant within the range of INTEGER values to be treated as either an INTEGER or a CARDINAL.

7.2.5 Type Conversion

Modula-2 provides type conversion facility. A type conversion function translates an expression of one type into a value of another type. The syntax of type conversion functions is

```
TypeConversioName  (Expression)
```

where `TypeConversioName` is CARDINAL, INTEGER, FLOAT, TRUNC, ORD, or CHR. Each type conversion function is designed to convert an expression of one type into another as shown in Table 7.7.

For example,

```
TRUNC(3.7256)
```

returns the value 3, and

```
TRUNC(7.7+5.9)
```

returns the value 13. The rules for expression evaluation in Modula-2 are like mathematical rules, using operator precedence as explained in Chapter 3.

TABLE **7.7**   Type conversion functions in Modula-2

Function	Initial Type	Result Type
CARDINAL	INTEGER	CARDINAL
INTEGER	CARDINAL	INTEGER
FLOAT	CARDINAL	REAL
TRUNC	REAL	CARDINAL
CHR	CARDINAL	CHAR
ORD	CHARACTER	CARDINAL
	or	
	INTEGER	
	or	
	CARDINAL	
	or	
	enumerated	

7.2.6 Control Structure

Modula-2 adopts the Pascal control structures with minor variations. In Modula-2, a sequence of instructions is a list of instructions that appear one after another. To perform, or carry out, the sequence means to perform each individual instruction one at a time. Each instruction in a sequence begins immediately after the previous instruction completes. The Modula-2 rules for punctuation of sequences are as follows:

▶ In a sequence of instructions, a semicolon must separate every two consecutive instructions.

▶ A semicolon following a sequence of instructions is optional.

Typically, global variables are allocated statically because their meanings are fixed throughout the program. Variables local to blocks other than the program block are allocated dynamically when execution reaches the block in question. The Modula-2 environment has three kinds of allocation: *static* for global variables, *automatic* for local variables, and *dynamic* for pointers. These categories are also referred to as the storage class of the variables. In Modula-2, subprograms are called procedures, but subprograms are also known by many other names, such as function and subroutine. One invokes a Modula-2 procedure by using the name of the procedure as an instruction. Instead of being built into the language, many facilities are provided by predefined system modules. The only difference between procedures and modules is that the procedure declaration begins with PROCEDURE instead of MODULE, ends in a semicolon rather than a period, and can not contain IMPORT declarations. A procedure or module invocation causes *a transfer of control* from the currently executing code to the instructions of the procedure or module body. Low-level primitives for process abstraction are provided by the module system. Higher-level abstractions can be added on top of them. Modula-2 uses short-circuit evaluation for *or* and *and* logical operations. Top-down design is driven by a decomposition according to control structures. The following sections examine two of the fundamental tools of top-down design, *selection* and *repetition*, adopted in Modula-2.

7.2.7   Conditional Constructs

Modula-2 has the following general form for the conditional `if` structure:

```
IF    boolean-expression    THEN
      sequence-of-statements
{ ELSIF    boolean-expression    THEN
      sequence-of-statements }
[ELSE
      sequence-of-statements ]
END;
```

The blocks for the scope of the conditional structure are implied by the required use of the termination keywords `ELSIF`, `ELSE`, and `END` primitives. An example of `if` structure is as follows:

```
IF    FirstTemp  >  SecondTemp
      HighTep  :=  FirstTemp
ELSE
      HighTep  :=  SecondTemp
END;
```

The `if` instruction imposes no additional punctuation requirements. In general, the statement is the most elementary execution unit in Modula-2, and like Pascal, Modula-2 uses the semicolon as a statement separator. Modula-2 provides a closing keyword `end` to avoid confusion caused by misplaced semicolons. For example, the following `if` statement

```
if    expression    then    statement₁
                            statement₂
            end
```

allows a statement list to appear between `then` and `end`, thus avoids ambiguity. Similarly, Modula-2 avoids the dangling else ambiguity because conditionals have a closing keyword `end`. For example, in the following construct each `if` structure is paired with an `end`.

```
if    expression₁    then    statement₁
else    if    expression₂    then    statement₂
        else    if    expression₃    then    statement₃
                else
```

```
                              statement₄
                     end
                 end
        end
```

In addition, Modula-2 allows the optional `elsif` keyword to avoid confusion in nested conditional statements, such as in the following example:

```
if       expression₁    then    statement₁
elsif if  expression₂    then    statement₂
elsif if  expression₃    then    statement₃
else
      statement₄
end
```

The detailed treatment of case selector can affect programming style in a programming language. Modula-2 improves upon Pascal in two ways:

1. Modula-2 allows a default case to be selected if none of the case constants are selected. For example, the default case might be used to indicate that none of the cases are selected. In Pascal, an error occurs if none of the cases is satisfied.

2. Modula-2 allows ranges like '0' .. '9' to be used as case constants. Modula-2 is one of the few languages to allow this.

Modula-2 has a CASE construct with the following general form:

```
CASE   expression   OF
       alternative-list  :  sequence-of-statements  {  |
       alternative-list  :  sequence-of-statements  }  [  |
       ELSE
       sequence-of-statements ]
END;
```

The symbol │ is used to separate each block of statements from the following alternative list. The selector expression can be of any type, and a run-time error occurs if the selector expression evaluates to an expression not found among the alternatives and no `ELSE` clause is included. Duplicate values in the alternative lists are not permitted. An example of a CASE instruction is found in the following, where the `ClassifyChar` can be used to classify the characters of a simple numeric expression. In this example, there are three possible classifications for characters.:

1. The characters +, −, *, and / are *operators*.

2. The decimal digits are *digits*.

3. Anything else is *other*.

```
BEGIN
   IsOperator  :=  FALSE;
   IsDigit  :=  FALSE;
   IsOther  :=  FALSE;
   CASE  ClassifyChar  OF
```

```
        "+", "-", "*", "/"   :
    IsOperator  :=  TRUE   |
        "0", "1", "2", "3", "4", "5", "6", "7", "8", "9"   :
    IsDigit  :=  TRUE
    ELSE
    IsOther  :=  TRUE
END
```

7.2.8 Iterative Constructs

Modula-2 supports the following four iterative constructs:

▶ Nonterminating iteration construct: LOOP

▶ Pretest terminating iteration construct: WHILE

▶ Posttest terminating iteration construct: REPEAT-UNTIL

▶ Fixed count terminating iteration construct: FOR

Modula-2 has a nonterminating iteration construct of the following form:

```
LOOP
        sequence-of-statements
END;
```

In practice, an EXIT instruction is usually guarded by enclosing it within a selection instruction. The instruction

```
IF   Condition   THEN   EXIT   END
```

is the most common form of providing a loop condition within a LOOP. One or more such instructions may be placed anywhere within a LOOP body. The most widely accepted repetition control structure for program design is a WHILE structure known as terminating iteration construct. Modula-2 has a WHILE structure in the following form

```
WHILE   condition   DO
        sequence-of-statements
END;
```

where the `condition` is a pretest criteria for the termination of the loop. Because the loop condition is tested before running the loop, a WHILE loop is said to perform *its test at the top of the loop*. Its posttest iteration is of the form

```
REPEAT
        sequence-of-statements
UNTIL  condition;
```

where the `condition` is checked after each iteration. In contrast, a REPEAT loop performs its *test at the bottom of the loop*. There is one difference between the REPEAT loop and the WHILE, in which REPEAT terminates when the loop condition is TRUE, which is just the opposite of a WHILE loop. Modula-2 also supports the fixed count iteration of the form

```
FOR    variable  :=  expression₁  To  expression₂
       [BY  expression₃   DO
       sequence-of-statements
END;
```

where the `variable` must be of a discrete type, making indexing illegal if it is real. All expressions must be of the same type as the index `variable` and the expressions are evaluated once at the initialization of the iteration. The *for-loop* is particularly well designed for sequential processing of arrays. The following three loop conditions may terminate the loop execution:

```
LOOP
      IF Condition₁   THEN   EXIT   END;
           (loop body  part₁)
      IF Condition₂   THEN   EXIT   END;
           (loop body  part₂)
      IF Condition₃   THEN   EXIT   END;
END
```

For example, the following loop prints the values from 0 to 5 on consecutive lines, as shown to the right of the loop.

```
While Loop                              Output of While Loop
Counter  : = 0;                         0
WHILE      Counter <= 5  DO             1
           WriteCard(Counter, 0);       2
           WriteLn;                     3
END;                                    4
                                        5
```

The following example compares REPEAT and WHILE constructs with two loops that both perform the same task. Both of them are counting loops that are iterated ten times.

```
While Loop                      REPEAT Loop
Counter  : = 1;                 Counter  : = 1;
WHILE   Counter <= 10 DO        REPEAT
     (perform some task)             (perform some task)
       INC(Counter);                 INC(Counter);
END                                  UNTIL Counter > 10
```

The following examples illustrate the execution of several FOR loops. For each loop, the output of the code is specified to the right.

```
For Loop                                Output of For Loop
FOR   CardVar  : = 1 TO 4 DO               1   2   3   4
     WriteCard(CardVar, 2)
END
FOR   CardVar  : = 1 TO 5 BY 2  DO         1   3   5
     WriteCard(CardVar, 2)
```

```
END
FOR    CardVar  : = 6 TO 2 BY −1   DO          6   5   4   3   2
       WriteCard(CardVar, 2)
END
FOR    CardVar  : = "Z" TO "S" BY −2 DO      ZXVT
       WriteCard(CardVar)
END
```

7.2.9 Blocks and Scope

In a language such as Modula-2, where blocks can be nested, the scope of a declaration is limited to the block in which it appears, and other blocks contained within it. Such languages are called *block structured,* and the kind of scope rules for blocks is called *lexical scope* because it follows the structure of the blocks as they appear in the written code. Modula-2 separates the concept of object binding and object by using modules. A module is a separate compilation unit that consists of two parts: *definition* and *implementation,* each of which must be in a physically different file. The definition module contains IMPORT and EXPORT statements and definition of objects that are to be exported. Exported objects may be procedures, types, variables, or constants. The implementation contains complete definitions of any procedure and hidden type that is exported from the module. In addition, definitions of any type, constant, variable and procedure that is local to the module is included. After all declarations, an execution unit may be specified within BEGIN and END. A module has the following general form:

```
MODULE    module-name;
    {[FROM module-name] IMPORT identifier-list;}
    {EXPORT [QUALIFIED] identifier-list;}
    [local-declarations]
BEGIN
    statement-sequence
END module-name;
```

The IMPORT list specifies those objects declared in other modules that are to be visible in this module. The EXPORT list specifies those objects that are declared locally in this module but that are to be made visible to other modules through the other module's import lists. Variables declared in the module declaration are called global variables. A global variable is known within the entire module and all of its procedures. The visible objects in a module are those that are locally declared plus those that are imported. A procedure in Modula-2 has the following general form

```
PROCEDURE    procedure-name   (parameter-list) [:type];
    [local-declarations]
BEGIN
    statement-sequence
END procedure-name;
```

Procedure declaration may be placed wherever a VAR declaration is allowed. In this case, when a procedure is invoked or called, the following occur:

► All locally declared objects have their bindings enforced.

► All bound objects in the containing environment whose names do not conflict with local bindings are inherited.

► All modules declared locally in the procedure have their objects bindings enforced and their bodies executed.

► Finally, the procedure body itself is carried out.

A procedure invocation causes a transfer of control from the currently running code to the instructions of the procedure body. After this transfer, the procedure continues running until its last instruction is finished, then there is an implicit transfer of control back to the instruction sequence from which invocation occurred. In general, the procedure serves as the basic unit of binding with inherited visibility from its containing procedure. When a procedure completes its execution, all local bindings are released. In the following example, a procedure called GetAreaPerimeter is defined. This procedure will prompt the user for the length and width of a square, then returns its area and perimeter.

```
PROCEDURE   GetAreaPerimeter  (  VAR Area  :  CARDINAL;
                              VAR Perimeter  : CARDINAL);
VAR   Length  :  CARDINAL;  Width  :  CARDINAL;
BEGIN
WriteString("Please enter the length and width of a square.");
WriteLn;
ReadCard(Length);
ReadCard(Width);
WriteLn;
Area  :=  Length  *  Width;
Perimeter  :=  (Length  +  Width) * 2;
END   GetAreaPerimeter;
```

In general, Modula-2 has a block structure and scope rules similar to Pascal with two major differences:

► The scope of a variable or function declaration extends from the beginning of the block in which it appears, not just from the point of the declaration. Thus, Modula-2 does not adhere to the declaration-before-use rule. For example, in the following the scope of the global variable, x extends backward from its declaration to the beginning of module Ex.

```
MODULE  Ex;
PROCEDURE  p;
BEGIN
   x := 2;
   (* legal to use x, because x is defined as global *)
END p;
VAR x: INTEGER;
BEGIN      (*     Ex     *)
. . .

END  Ex.
```

In other words, the scope of visibility of a global variable is the entire module, including all its procedures. This means that a global variable may be accessed by the body of the program module and by the bodies of procedures contained within the program module. There is one exception to this scope rule for global variables: The scope of visibility of a global variable is restricted whenever the same identifier is declared local to some procedures.

▶ The use of local modules in Modula-2 can limit scope. Consider the following example:

```
MODULE A;
VAR  x: INTEGER;

    PROCEDURE  p;
    BEGIN
    .  .  .
    END  p;
    MODULE B;
    VAR  y: REAL;
       PROCEDURE q;
       BEGIN
       .  .  .
       END q;
    .  .  .
    END B;
.  .  .
END A.
```

where the declarations of variable x and procedure p have scope extending over MODULE A except for MODULE B, in which references to x and p inside B are illegal. Correspondingly, references to y and q outside of B are also illegal. Local modules such as B in this example are scope boundaries, with the exception of those explicitly exported or imported. An example of export and import is given in the following example, where procedure p is imported into module B and thus can be accessed within B; similarly variable y is exported from B, so it can be referenced in A.

```
MODULE A;
VAR  x: INTEGER;

    PROCEDURE  p;
    BEGIN
    .  .  .
END  p;

    MODULE B;
    IMPORT p;     (* p is available in B *)
    EXPORT y;     (* y is available in A *)
    VAR  y: REAL;
       PROCEDURE q;
```

```
          BEGIN
            . . .
          END q;
        . . .
      END B;
    . . .
    END A.
```

In general, a module can explicitly import entities from, and export entities to the rest of the program. To see how this takes place, consider the following nested blocks.

```
A:   begin
       integer   x;
       boolean   y;
       . . .
B:   begin
         real   x;
         integer   a;
       . . .
     end B;
       . . .
C:   begin
         boolean   y;
         integer   b;
         . . .
     D:   begin
            integer   x;
            real   y;
            . . .
        end D;
    . . .
    end C;
    . . .
    end A;
```

During the execution of this code, when each block is entered, the variables declared at the beginning of each block are allocated, and when each block is exited, those same variables are deallocated. If we view the environment as a linear sequence of storage locations, with locations allocated from the top in descending order, then the environment after the entry into B looks as shown in Figure 7.4.

On exit from block B, the environment returns to the system as it existed just after the entry into A. Then, the block C is entered and the variables of C are allocated. Finally, on entry into block D, the environment becomes as shown in Figure 7.5.

In general, on exit from each block the location bindings of that block are successively deallocated, until, just before exit from block A, when we recover the original environment of A. In this sense, the environment behaves like a stack.

FIGURE **7.4**   **The environment after the entry into block B**

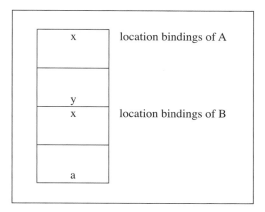

FIGURE **7.5**   **The environment after the entry into block D**

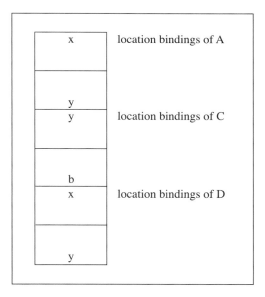

7.2.10 Input and Output Capabilities

Modula-2 is somewhat unusual because there are no standard input and output instructions included. The language is designed this way to permit flexibility in supporting different kinds of I/O and different I/O devices. To allow such flexibility, but still provide some standards, I/O modules in the design of Modula-2 are included. The most common of these is InOut. InOut is designed to perform I/O on devices such as a standard computer keyboard and terminal. The InOut module includes the following procedures:

- ▶ *Write* to output one character.
- ▶ *WriteInt* to output one integer.
- ▶ *WriteCard* to output one cardinal.
- ▶ *WriteString* to output a string of characters.
- ▶ *WriteLn* to end a line of output and begin the next line.
- ▶ *Read* to input one character.
- ▶ *ReadInt* to input one integer.
- ▶ *ReadCard* to input one cardinal.

Each of these procedures performs a different task. As an example, the following program accepts an input, a weight in pounds, converts and rounds this weight to the nearest kilogram, and prints the result.

```
MODULE    PoundsToKilograms;
   FROM    InOut   IMPORT WriteString,  WriteLn,  WriteCard,  ReadCard;
   VAR    PoundWeight  :  CARDINAL;  KgWeight  :  CARDINAL;
BEGIN
   WriteString( " How much do you weigh in pounds?" );
   WriteLn;
   ReadCard(PoundWeight);
   KgWeight := TRUNC( (0.45359237  *  FLOAT(PoundWeight) ) + 0.5 );
   WriteLn;
   WriteString( " Your mass in Kilograms is " );
   WriteCard(KgWeight, 0);
   WriteString( " (to the nearest Kilogram)" );
   WriteLn;
END PoundsToKilograms.
```

SUMMARY

In this chapter, we discussed the design of two important imperative languages, C and Modula-2. C as a general-purpose programming language was closely associated with the UNIX operating system because UNIX and most of the programs that run on it were written in C. We also discussed the fundamental structure of C. C has six kinds of tokens: identifiers, keywords, constants, string literals, operators, and punctuators. We briefly discussed the key features of C, along with some constructs: arrays, functions, conditional and iterative statements, selections, structures, and unions. Also, we discussed the addressing and dereferencing using pointer notations. In addition, we outlined formatting input-output and preprocessor to address the predefined functions used in C language.

Modula-2 is an imperative language that achieved widespread use as a teaching language. Modula-2 considerably improved the readability of programs and supported static checks for program correctness. In this chapter, we discussed the fundamental concepts of Modula-2, including data types, subranges, unions, data aggregates, records, and sets. Modula-2 supported type equivalence, which was based on the structural equivalence method by defining two types to be compatible if they had the same name, one was a subrange of the other, or both were subranges of the same basic type. We outlined type equivalence along with type conversion to address this powerful tool for data abstraction. In addition, we discussed the control structures, conditional constructs, iterative constructs, blocks and scope, and input-output facilities as some important features associated with Modula-2 language.

EXERCISES

1. Give one example of two variables that are *structurally* equivalent, even though the programmer declares them as separate types.

2. Assume variables A and B are both of some type X. Under what conditions can you say A=B?

3. Write a *declaration* as a *mapping* from integers in the subrange 1 to 50 to the set of characters.

4. How can you select an object of the range specified in the previous exercise?

5. What is the difference between *sequential* and *direct-access* files?

6. Consider the following subprogram definition as it might appear in C.

```
float   FN(float X, int Y)
    {
    const  initval  = 2;
    #define finalval   10
    float   M(10);   int N;
            . . .
    N = initval;
    if  (N < finalval)    { . . . }
    return  (20 * X + M(N));
    }
```
Define the components needed for an activation of the subprogram.

7. The *semicolon* was used as an example of a nonuniformity in Modula-2. Discuss the use of the semicolon in C. Is its use entirely uniform?

8. Declare a variable x of type *pointer to integer* in C. Initialize x to a pointer that does not point to any allocated space. Then, allocate an object and point x to it using *malloc* function. Finally, deallocate the object pointed to by x.

9. Construct a Modula-2 program that will output the messages Hello and Mello alternately.

10. How do you illustrate a hypothetical form of the following *loop?*

```
Repeat  C₁  While  E  do  C₂
```

11. Write C statements that accomplish each of the following by varying the control variable in *for* structure.

   a. Vary the control variable from 1 to 100 in increments of 1.

   b. Vary the control variable from 100 to 1 in increments of −1.

   c. Vary the control variable from 7 to 77 in steps of 7.

   d. Vary the control variable from 20 to 2 in steps of −2.

   e. Vary the control variable over the following sequence of values: 2, 5, 8, 11, 14, 17.

12. What is wrong with the following `while` repetition structure?

```
while    (z >= 0)
    Sum += z;
```

13. Demonstrate *dereferencing* in C by giving an example.

14. Using an example in C programming language, demonstrate the *short-circuit* evaluation of *Boolean* or *logical* expressions.

15. Explain the difference between *declaration* and *definition* in C language.

16. Run the following C program and explain the resulting output:

```
void    main(void)
    {
        {int x;
        printf("%d\n", x);
        x = 1;
        }
    {int y;
        printf("%d\n", y);
        }
    }
```

17. In mathematics, we use parentheses, brackets, and braces of various sizes to indicate the boundaries of subexpressions. Using the Stack data structure presented in Chapter 2, write a C program to determine whether parentheses and brackets are balanced properly in the following algebraic expression:

$$\{a^2 -[(b + c)^2 - (d + e)^2]* [\sin(x - y)] \} - \cos(x + y)$$

18. The principle of locality maintains that variable declarations should come as close as possible to their use in a program. What language design features promote or discourage this principle? How well do Modula-2 and C promote this principle?

19. Write a *recursive* factorial function in C language.

20. Rewrite the following *for* loop as a *repeat* loop in C language.

```
For   index   := 10   downto  -5   do something-else;
```

21. What is the difference between *float, double,* and *long double* data types with regard to range of values in C language?

22. Explain the following C program that counts the number of times the function *add* is called.

```
void   add()   {
   static  int  count=0;
count++;
}
```

23. Considering a *one-way linked list,* write a C program to print the value of the ith item of list L.

24. Give an example of *indefinite repetition* in C programming language using *for* structure.

25. An example of a structured variable declaration is *structure* or *record*. Provide an example of a structured variable declaration in C language.

26. Determine whether the following fragment is a legal C program:

```
switch (i)   {
   case 1:    a=b+c;
      break;
      while (a>d)   {
   case 2:    b=c+d;
   }
   case 3:    c=a+b;
   }
```

27. Pick a language and a data structure type in that language. List the attributes of data objects of that type. List the operations for data objects of that type. Determine the storage representation for data objects of that type in your local implementation of the language. Do any operations require the allocation or freeing of storage when this storage representation is used?

28. Name undesirable characteristics for imperative programming.

29. Name desirable characteristics for imperative programming.

30. Write a *recursive* definition for factorial n! in terms of n.

31. Consider the following function:

```
function F(x, y: integer) returns an integer
begin
   x :=x+1;   y :=y+1;   return(x-y);
end F
```

Show by one or more examples of calls of procedure F that *call-by-name, call-by-value,* and *call-by-reference* are different parameter-passing methods.

32. The Modula-2 language provides stack capabilities, including Pop and Push procedures. Write a Modula-2 module to implement Stack data structure.

33. Fill in the blanks in C language in each of the following.

  a. Every C program begins execution at the function _____ .

  b. The _____ begins the body of every function and the _____ ends the body of every function.

  c. Every statement ends with a _____ .

  d. The _____ standard library function displays information on the screen.

  e. The _____ standard library function is used to obtain data from the keyboard.

  f. The conversion specifier _____ is used in a `scanf` format control string to indicate that an integer will be input and in a `printf` format control string to indicate that an integer will be output.

  g. When a value is read out of a memory location the value in that location is preserved; this is called _____ read-out.

  h. The _____ statement is used to make decisions.

34. Write a single C statement to accomplish each of the following:

  a. Assign the sum of x and y and increment the value of x by 1 after the calculation.

  b. Multiply the variable *product* by 2 using the `*=` operator.

  c. Test if the value of the variable *count* is greater that 10. If it is, print "Count is Greater Than 10."

  d. Decrement the variable x by 1, then subtract it from the variable *total*.

  e. Add the variable x to the variable *total*, then decrement x by 1.

  f. Calculate the remainder after q is divided by divisor and assign the result to q.

  g. Print the value 123.4567 with 2 digits of precision. What value is printed?

35. What is the value of the following expressions with respect to the declarations in C language?

```
int   I=3,  J=5,  *P=&I,  *Q=&J,  *R;
```

  a. `*P + I + *(R=&J) + *Q`

  b. `*&I + *&J * *P`

  c. `*P *  *Q + I*J`

  d. `*(R = &J)  *=  *P`

  e. `*&I +  *(R=&I) +  *&J`

REFERENCE-NEEDED EXERCISES

To answer the following exercises, you might need to consult the following references: Appleby & Vande Kopple, 1997; Deitel & Deitel, 1994; MacLennan, 1999; Mitchell, 1998; Riley, 1987; Skansholm, 1997; and Stansifer 1995.

1. Explain the *parameter-passing* mechanism known as *copy-in/copy-out*.

2. The parameter passing mechanism *copy-out* is the converse of *call-by-value*. Using an example, illustrate that it is not suitable as the only parameter-passing mechanism in a language.

3. An identifier or operator is said to be *overloaded* if it simultaneously denotes two or more distinct functions. Specify at least four possible denotated distinct functions associated with operator "–".

4. Consider the following procedure that is intended to interchange the values of A and B. What can be produced when the procedure is invoked by the call `Swap(I, A[I])`?

```
procedure Swap(A, B: integer)
var    temp: integer;
begin   temp:= A;
   A := B;
   B := temp;
end Swap;
```

5. Make a table showing what types of value in Pascal may be defined for the following:

   a. Constants

   b. Operands of operators

   c. Results of operators

   d. Arguments of functions and procedures

   e. Results of functions

   f. Array of record components

6. Write a procedure to implement the mathematical *sigma* notation, that is a procedure such that

$$X = \sum_{i=1}^{n} V_i$$

7. It might be convenient for the instantiation and call for a generic procedure to be combined into a single command as follows:

```
swap   (integer)   (a(i),   a(i+1));
```

Ada does not permit this. Nevertheless, the same effect can be achieved by an Ada block command. Show how. The same effect cannot be achieved for a generic function. Why not?

8. Consider the following program.

```
Program   Test(Input, Output);
   Var   A, B, C : Integer;
      D : Boolean;
   Procedure P(Var  Q :Boolean;  Var  R, S : Integer);
      Begin
      If  D  then  R  = 100  else  R := 200;
      S  :=  S/A;
      End;
```

```
Procedure Q(Var  X, Y : Integer;  Var  Z : Boolean);
   Begin
   X := 15;  Y  := X+ A;  Z := (X < A);
   P(Z, Y, X);
   Z  :=  (X/A);
   End;
Begin
A := -1, B := -1, C := -1;  D := TRUE;
Q(A, B, D);
End;
End.
```

Using *call by value* as the parameter passing method, what would the final values of the variables be at the program termination?

9. Predict the sizes of the following data types in Modula-2:

   a. WORD
   b. BYTE
   c. CARDINAL
   d. INTEGER
   e. CHAR

10. Explain the following declaration in C language:

    ```
    char    **P[20];
    ```

    Write a code fragment in Modula-2 that declares the same pointer variable declaration.

11. Consider the following declarations in C language.

    ```
    int      X=5,  Y=10,  Z=25;
    float    A=3.1415,  B=5.0;
    ```

    What values are assigned to variables in the following statements?

    a. X =Y;
    b. X =Z / 10;
    c. X = (float) Z / 10 / B;
    d. X = (float) (X / 10 / B);
    e. A =Z / B / 2;
    f. A = (int) B / 2;
    g. X = (char) B * 10 + 100;
    h. A = (char) Y + 10 * (int) b;

Object-Oriented Programming Specifications

Imperative programming, sometimes called structured or procedural programming, is built around functions that perform various tasks, or actions. In other words, a procedural language separates a problem into unconnected components, called procedures, functions, or modules, which manipulate them and which are activated when needed. A program is constructed using a top-down, modular, divide-and-conquer approach. Functions are written to perform various tasks and then called when needed to perform their respective tasks. Thus, the program consists of a collection of functions, whose combined execution solves the particular application problem at hand. A fundamental drawback of imperative programming is that global variables can be accessed by every part of the program. Large programs that lack any discipline for accessing global variables tend to be unmanageable because no module that accesses a global variable can be independent of other modules that also access the same global variable. David Parnas recognized this problem around 1970 and advocated the discipline of information binding as a principle of object-oriented programming. His idea was to encapsulate each global variable in a module with a group of operations that have direct access to the variable. Other modules can access the variable only indirectly by requesting these operations. We use the term *object* for such a module, and we say that an object-oriented system relies on objects to impose modular structure on programs. He pointed out that if a module has bindings that have been modified by assignment or whose values have been mutated, it is said to have *state*. When message passing is used to access this state, these modules are called objects. In other words, a more flexible approach to information hiding is to represent values as objects. An object is a set of operations that share a state. The state consists of one or more values that may be viewed and modified only by operations belonging to the object. These operations are often called *methods,* and the call to a method is named a *message*. The entire collection of methods of an object is called the *message*

protocol or *message interface.* In other words, we have sketched here one approach to a style of programming in which many or all values used in a computation may be objects. When this is combined with the concept of inheritance, the resulting style is known as object-oriented programming. Another term in object-oriented programming is *class,* in which class instances are called objects. A class that is defined from another class is a *derived class* or *subclass.* A class from which the new class is derived is known as its *parent class* or *superclass.* Object-oriented programming can be practiced even in simple imperative languages such as Pascal. However, the scope rules do not actually prevent improper access to an object from another module. Programmers must exercise self-discipline to avoid such improper access.

As a consequence, a language that is object-oriented must support three key language features: *abstract data types, inheritance,* and a particular kind of *dynamic binding.* Object-oriented programming techniques add several important ideas to the concept of the abstract data types. Foremost among these is *message passing.* Activity is initiated by a request to a specific object, rather than by the invoking of a function. This is largely a change of emphasis: Conventional view primarily emphasizes the operation, whereas the object-oriented view emphasizes the value itself. In general, this technique would not be considered a major innovation, if overloading names and reusing software as a powerful mechanism were not added to message-passing mechanism. Object-oriented programming adds the mechanism of *inheritance* and *polymorphism.* Inheritance allows different data types to share the same code, leading to a reduction in code size and an increase in functionality. Polymorphism allows this shared code to be tailored to fit the specific circumstances of individual data types. The emphasis on the independence of individual components permits an incremental development process in which individual software units are designed, programmed, and tested before being combined into a large system. In other words, object-oriented programming facilitates the reuse of tested code without recompiling it. Robert Moskowitz (1989) claims that the provision of preprogrammed and user-modifiable objects allows users who understand very little about computers to grasp and manipulate computer features, functions, and operations as easily as they grasp and manipulate tangible objects in the real world.

Simula was developed at the Norwegian Computing Center in 1961 and introduced by Ole-Johan Dahl and Kristen Nygaard in 1966. Simula was intended to describe systems and to program simulations:

▶ Express processes that are permanent and active

▶ Create and destroy such processes as needed

▶ Extend an existing language to include processes

▶ Provide for processes to run concurrently

▶ Group processes subject to the same procedures into classes

Later, Simula 67 extended the object concept to a general-purpose language. Simula 67 has classes of objects as its basic concept. Dahl and Nygaard had been working on a simulation of a bridge with a tollbooth and a queue of trucks, buses, and cars. They realized that a process for a truck included many of the same procedures as that for a bus or car. They developed an object class that included all the operations associated with trucks, buses, and cars. This class was called the vehicle as the superclass of the trucks, buses, and cars. Alan Kay adopted this approach as the foundation for his language Smalltalk in the early 1970s as the pioneer of the object-oriented programming. It has an interesting and expansive genesis influenced by the social impact of cheap and powerful computers. Similarly, the idea of objects being adopted on top of the existing languages, to Ada (InnovAda [Simonian & Crone, 1988]), extensions to Pascal (ObjectPascal [Tesler, 1985]), C++ (Stroustrup, 1988), that was developed at AT&T Bell Laboratories by adding object-oriented features to C, the new object-oriented language from Sun Microsystems named Java, Scheme Object-Oriented System (SCOOPS), the Common LISP Object System (CLOS), and the Modula-3 that was jointly designed by the Systems Research Center of Digital Equipment Corporation in Palo Alto and the Olivetti Research Center in Menlo Park in the late 1980s (Cardelli et al., 1989). Modula-3 was based on Modula-2 (Wirth, 1985), Mesa (Mitchell, Maybury, & Sweet, 1979), Cedar (Lampson, 1983), and Modula-2+ (Rovner, 1986). It consists of classes and objects for support of object-oriented programming, exception handling, garbage collection, and support for concurrency. Some programming languages, such as Java and Smalltalk, force you to write object-oriented programs. Many people therefore consider them *pure* object-oriented languages. Because C++ lets a programmer write programs that are not object-oriented, the programmer must ensure that a program adheres to object-oriented principles. Therefore, C++ is known as a *relative* object-oriented language. Also, some object-oriented programming languages such as C++ restrict compile-time type checking. Thus, the types of all variables and functions must be fully declared at compile-time. By contrast, Smalltalk dynamically checks whether the receiver of an object has a corresponding method.

In this chapter, we discuss the general characteristics for object-oriented programming. In Section 8.1, we briefly discuss the three aspects of object-oriented programming, each of which illustrates a particular reason that this technique is to be considered an important new tool. We outline the design principles for object-oriented programming including objects, classes, messages, and methods in Section 8.2. The implementation of object-oriented programming is based on five important features: abstraction, encapsulation, polymorphism, inheritance, and dynamic binding. We discuss these five important concepts for object-oriented programming in Section 8.3. Also, we outline the desirable characteristics for object-oriented programming in Section 8.4.

8.1 GENERAL CHARACTERISTICS FOR OBJECT-BASED PROGRAMMING

In trying to understand what the term object-oriented programming means, it is useful to examine the idea from several perspectives. Three aspects of object-oriented programming—each of which illustrates a particular reason that this technique should be considered an important new tool—are outlined in the following sections.

8.1.1 Messages and Methods

Suppose the mechanism that I use to solve my problem is to find an appropriate *agent* and to pass a *message* containing my request. In this sense, it is the agent's responsibility to satisfy my request. The agent uses some *method* (i.e., an algorithm or a set of operations) to accomplish this request. I do not need to know the particular method the agent will use to satisfy my request; indeed, often I do not want to know the details. This information is usually hidden from my inspection. However, if I investigated I might discover that the agent delivers a slightly different message to another agent, which in turn arranges to perform the task. Thus, my request is finally satisfied by a sequence of requests from one agent to another. This is the first principle of object-oriented problem solving, the method by which activities are initiated:

> Action is initiated in object-oriented programming by the transmission of a message to an agent (an object) responsible for the action. The message encodes the request for an action and is accompanied by any additional information (arguments) needed to carry out the request. The receiver is the agent to whom the message is sent. If the receiver accepts the message, it accepts the responsibility of carrying out the indicated action. In response to a message, the receiver will perform some method to satisfy the request.

In general, a fundamental concept in object-oriented programming is describing behavior in terms of responsibilities. For example, my request for action indicates only the desired outcome, leaving the agent free to pursue any technique that achieves the desired objective. By discussing a problem in terms of responsibilities, we increase the level of abstraction. This permits greater independence between agents, which is a critical factor in solving complex problems. The entire collection of responsibilities associated with an object is often described by the term *protocol*.

8.1.2 Computation with Simulation

The traditional model describing the behavior of a computer executing a program is a process-state model: The computer is a data manager, following some pattern of instructions, searching through memory, retrieving values from memory locations, transforming them in some manner, and pushing the results back into other memory locations. By examining the values in the memory locations, we can determine the state of the machine or the results produced by a computation. Although this model of computation may be a more or less accurate picture of what takes place inside a computer, it does little to help us understand how to solve problems using the computer. In contrast, in the object-oriented programming method, we never mention memory addresses, variables, assignments, or any of the conventional programming terms. Instead, we talk about objects, messages, and responsibilities for some action. This view of programming is in many ways similar to a style of computer simulation called *discrete event-driven simulation*. In this view, the user creates computer models of the various elements of the simulation, describes how they will interact with one another, and sets them moving. This is almost identical to the average object-oriented program, in which the user describes what the various entities of the computation are and how they will interact with one another and finally sets them in motion. This is the second principle of object-oriented problem solving: *computation is simulation* (Kay, 1977).

8.1.3 Coping and Complexity

As programming projects became larger, an interesting phenomenon was observed. A task that would take one programmer two months to perform could not be accomplished by two programmers working for one month. The reason for this nonlinear behavior was complexity; the interconnections between software components were complicated and large quantities of information had to be communicated among the various members of the programming team. Brooks (1975) said,

> Since software construction is inherently a systems effort—an exercise in complex interrelationships—communication effort is great, and it quickly dominates the decrease in individual task time brought about by partitioning. Adding more men then lengthens, not shortens, the schedule.

What causes this complexity is not simply the size of the tasks undertaken, because size by itself would not be a hindrance to partitioning each into several pieces. The unique feature of software systems developed using conventional techniques is their high degree of interconnectedness. Interconnectedness means the dependence of one portion of code on another portion. Consider that any portion of a software system must be performing an essential task, or it would not be there. Now, if this task is useful to the other parts of the program, there must be some communication of information either into or out of the component under consideration. Because of this, a complete understanding of what is going on requires knowledge of both the portion of code we are considering and the code that uses it. In short, an individual section of code cannot be understood in isolation. To better understand the importance of object-oriented techniques, we should review the variety of mechanisms programmers have used to control complexity. Chief among these is abstraction, the ability to encapsulate and isolate design and execution information. In this sense, object-oriented techniques are not at all revolutionary, but can be seen as a natural outcome of a long historical progression from procedures, to modules, to abstract data types, and finally to objects.

8.1.4 Object-Oriented Properties

The object-oriented programming allows one to construct programs the way we humans tend to think about things. For example, we tend to classify real-world entities such as vehicles, airplanes, ATM machines, and so on. For example, take a class of vehicles; all vehicles have certain components (characteristics and attributes), such as engine, wheels, transmissions, and so on. Furthermore, all vehicles exhibit some kind of behavior, such as acceleration, deceleration (braking), and turning. In other words, we have a general abstract impression of a vehicle through its attributes and behavior. Now the question is how the object-oriented model can be represented. One way is that an object may include persistent data and several data types with their associated operations. Figure 8.1 and Figure 8.2 may help make the difference between procedures and

FIGURE **8.1**   The Operation/Parameter model

<u>Call</u>	<u>Parameters</u>	<u>Operation</u>
Area(3, 4)	(3, 4)	

Area(x, y)

methods used in procedural and object-oriented programming languages, respectively. In Figure 8.1, we are using the procedure *Area* to compute the area of the rectangle with sides of length x and y. It acts on whatever operands it is presented with, in this example w=3 and s=4. In Figure 8.2, the message *Perimeter* can be sent to an object, which will behave according to its own method for handling the message. *Square* represents an active object with both of its data attributes, w and s, having values. Objects of type triangle or square each have two methods, namely Perimeter and Area. Each message might be meaningful to a variety of different objects, so sending a message must identify name of the receiving object. In object-oriented programming, we consider a method as a function that has state and is associated with a class of objects. In general, a message is the name of a method and initiates a call to a particular method.

As a consequence, we can say that, the object-oriented approach provides a programming method that consists of objects sending messages to other objects. This simple concept, along with some accompanying tools, formed a very powerful technique that became very popular in the first half of the 1990s. Languages that enable this approach by directly providing facilities to support objects and message passing are called object-oriented programming languages. Alan Kay identified the following characteristics as the fundamental features and benefits to object-oriented programming (Kay, 1993).

▶ Object-oriented programming is not simply a few new features added to programming languages. Rather, it is a new way of *thinking* about the process of decomposing problems and developing programming solutions.

▶ Object-oriented programming views a program as a collection of loosely connected agents, termed *objects*. Each object is responsible for specific tasks. Computation proceeds by the interaction of objects. In other words, computation is performed by objects communicating with each other, requesting that other objects perform actions. Objects communicate by sending and receiving messages. A message is a request for action attached to whatever arguments may be necessary to complete the task. In a certain sense, programming is nothing more or less than the simulation of a model universe.

FIGURE **8.2**   The Message/Object model

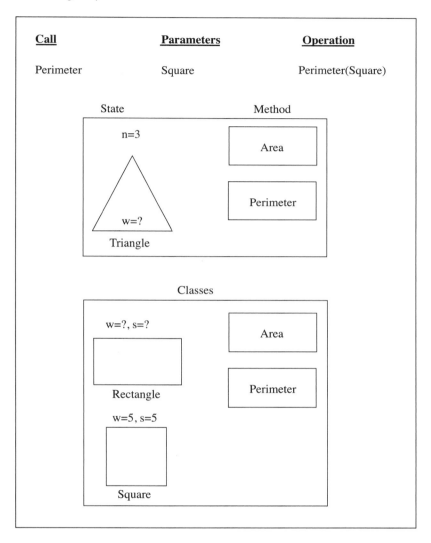

► An object is an encapsulation of *state* (data values) and *behavior* (operations). Thus, an object is in many ways similar to a module or an abstract data type. Each object has its own memory.

► The behavior of objects is directed by the object *class*. Every object is an instance of some class. A class simply represents a grouping of similar objects, such as integers or lists. All instances of the same class will behave in a similar fashion in response to a similar request.

▶ An object will exhibit its behavior by invoking a *method*, which is similar to executing a procedure, in response to a message. The interpretation of the message is decided by the object and may differ from one class of object to another.

▶ Objects and classes extend the concept of abstract data types by adding the notion of *inheritance*. Classes can be organized into a hierarchical inheritance tree (rooted tree structure). Data and behavior associated with classes higher in the tree can also be accessed, made available, and used by classes lower in the tree. Such classes are said to inherit their behavior from the parent classes.

▶ The object-oriented model carries with it all the abstraction benefits of abstract data types by permitting the data and actions of an object to be encapsulated within that object and dividing its contents between those that are public and those that are private.

▶ By reducing the interdependency among software components, object-oriented programming permits the development of *reusable* software systems. Such components can be created and tested as independent units in isolation from other portions of a software application.

▶ Reusable software components permit the programmer to deal with problems on a higher level of *abstraction*. We can define and manipulate objects simply by the messages they understand and a description of the tasks they perform, ignoring implementation details.

▶ Because objects often act concurrently in the problem domain, it is natural for them to perform concurrently in the object-oriented model. When such concurrency capabilities are available, the object-oriented model presents a natural way to exploit them.

◖ 8.2 DESIGN PRINCIPLES FOR OBJECT-ORIENTED PROGRAMMING

In a procedural language, data can be encapsulated along with associated operations—for or example, module in Modula-2 or package in Ada. The object-oriented programming model has as its fundamental entity the *object*, which consists of a local state and a set of actions that it can perform, called *methods*. These methods are activated when the object receives an appropriate *message*, then, the actions consist of modification of the state of the object and the sending of messages to other objects. The local state structure of an object and the methods that it can perform are specified by the *class*, which defines the object. In this sense, an object is called an *instance* of its class. A class is used as a syntactic mechanism in almost all object-oriented languages, in which an individual representative of a class is known as an instance. The classes are arranged in a hierarchy to permit the inheritance of properties from one class to another. We will use the term *instance variable* to mean an internal variable maintained by an instance.

8.2.1 Objects

A special and important kind of a module is one that consists of a hidden variable together with a group of exported operations on that variable. The variable is typically a data structure such as a table or database. Being hidden, the variable can be accessed only through the exported operations. This has the advantage that the variable representation can be changed without forcing any changes outside the module. Furthermore, the module can control the order of accesses to the hidden variable, for example to prevent extraction of data before any have been put in. The term *object* is often used for the hidden variables in a module. One way to view an object is as a pair consisting of *behavior* and *state*.

▶ The behavior of a component is the set of actions it can perform. The complete description of all the behaviors for a component is sometimes called the *protocol*, which includes all activities involved.

▶ The state of a component represents all the information held within it. The state is not static and can be changed over time (dynamic).

The state is described by the instance variables, whereas the behavior is characterized by the methods, which provide the appropriate behavior through modifications of the state as well as by interacting with other objects. For example, if an object is a simple robot consisting of a movable arm and a gripper, its state will include its position in the room where it is located, the angle of the arm, and whether its gripper is open or closed. Wegner (1988) described an object as a group of procedures or modules that share a state. Booch (1994) considers the object as a dynamic entity, in which it may be changed but still remains the same object. Cox (1984) proposed that objects are private data and there are some specific operations provided for that data.

An object in object-oriented programming corresponds to the concept of *data object*. The major difference is that an object is active, whereas a data object is passive. Data objects were acted upon by outside agents, whose actions resulted in changes of bindings, including the value binding of the data object itself. Thus, any operation may take an object as an argument and may return an object as a result. Objects communicate by passing messages, which are requests for an object to perform one of its operations. A message is nothing more than a procedure call, called a method, which belongs to an object and may be hidden from the user. In general, a message must reference a particular object as well as the name of the method being invoked. The name and location bindings of objects are the same as for data objects. In some languages, objects are referenced by pointers and hence have no direct name binding. The value binding is the binding of the object to its local state. In general, the binding that differs the most is the type binding, where the concept of type binding is replaced by class in the object-oriented programming model.

8.2.2 Classes

A class is a template for objects and contains the following:

▶ Descriptions of the actions an object can perform

▶ Definition of the structure of an object

In other words, a class must provide a means for defining the forms of objects. What data do they own? What can they do? How do they do things? For example, in a supply inventory system each inventory item is a class that consists of the following definitions and descriptions:

▶ Item number

▶ Item description

▶ Number of items on hand

▶ Reorder point

▶ Action-1: Modify the data describing an item.

▶ Action-2: Delete an item from the inventory system.

▶ Action-3: Check to see if the item needs to be reordered.

▶ Action-4: Create a new inventory item.

In this way, a class is similar to an abstract data type that defines the type data structure and procedures that apply to it. In other words, the concepts of abstract type and class have much in common. Each allows us to create several variables of a type whose representation is hidden, and to access these variables by operations provided for the purpose. All objects that are instances of a class have the same defined internal state structure and are able to perform the same described actions. In this respect, each object of the inventory item class represents one real world occurrence, or instance of the class.

In addition, a class is also an object, meaning that it has its own state and actions. One action that all class objects can perform is creating an object that is an instance of the class itself. For this reason, classes actually create or manufacture objects according to the template they define and are sometimes referred to as object factories. A further property of class is that it exists in a hierarchical structure to permit the property of inheritance to take place. Basically, if a class is a subclass of another class, it inherits the structure of the internal state and the actions from that class.

Classes in object-oriented programming can have several different forms of responsibility and are used for many different purposes. The following categories cover a large number of cases:

▶ **Data managers classes,** sometimes called data or state, are classes with the principal responsibility of maintaining data or state information. For example, in an abstraction of a problem, a major task for the class is simply to maintain the data values that describe state information. Data managers are often recognizable as the nouns in a problem description and are usually the fundamental building blocks of a design.

▶ **Data sinks** or **data sources classes** are entities that generate data such as a random number generator. Unlike a data manager, a data sink or data source does not hold the data for any period, but generates it on demand (for a data source) or processes it when called upon (for a data sink).

▶ **View** or **observer classes**, an essential portion of most applications, displays the information on an output device such as a terminal screen. Because the code for performing this activity is often complex, frequently modified, and largely independent of the actual data being displayed, it is good programming practice to isolate display behavior in classes other than those that maintain the data being displayed.

▶ **Facilitator** or **helper classes** are entities that maintain little or no state information themselves but assist with complex tasks. For example, in displaying an image we use the services of a facilitator class that handles the drawing of lines and text on the display device.

In an object-oriented language such as Simula, Smalltalk, C++, Java, or Eiffel, a class describes a number of possible run-time objects with the same structure, which are the instances of the class. A class is similar to a record type of Pascal or Ada, but with one important addition: A class specification describes not just the data fields of the instances, but also all the operations applicable to these instances. Class creation methods are referred to as a new concept called *meta-class*. Just as instances have an associated class, it is natural to associate a meta-class with each class. The class variables of a class are then the instance variables of its meta-class. Class and instance variables may be scoped statically or dynamically.

8.2.3 Messages

It is often useful to think of computation in an object-oriented system as evolving around *messages*. A message is a request transferred from one object to another so that the receiving object produces some desired result. Using this analogy, objects in the system manipulate other objects by sending messages requesting them to perform specific actions.

Message expressions have two parts: a specification of the object that is to receive the message and the message itself. The message itself specifies a selector entry, or method, in the receiver object and possibly one or more parameters. Parameters are pointers to other objects. When a message is evaluated, it is sent to the specified receiver object. In general, a message is similar to a procedure call in that it has a name and parameters. The difference is that a procedure call is sent by one procedure to another procedure. The data that are used by the receiver are the parameters sent with the call and the internal data structure of the receiver. In the case of messages, the sender and receiver are both objects and the receiving object performs some action, called a method, as the result of the message being received. The data used by the receiving object consists of the internal state of the receiving object along with the parameters sent as a part of the message. There are three categories of messages as follows:

▶ **Unary messages** have no parameters. They have only two parts: the object to which they are to be sent and the name of the method in that receiving object. In this respect, the first symbol of a unary message specifies a receiver object, and the second symbol specifies the method of that object that is to be executed. For example, the message

```
SecondChild  Boy
```

sends a parameterless message to the `Boy` method of the object `SecondChild`. Recall that all objects are referenced by pointers, so `SecondChild` is really a pointer to an object.

▶   **Binary messages** have a single parameter, an object, which is passed to the specified method of the specified receiver object. Among the most common binary messages are those for arithmetic operations. For example, in the message

```
20 + 10
```

the receiver object is the number `20`, to which is sent the message `+10`. In this respect, the message passes the parameter object `10` to the `+` method of the object `20`. The code of that method uses the object `10` to build a new object, in this case `30`. If the system already contains the object `30`, then the result is a reference to it rather than to a new object.

▶   **Keyword messages** specify one or more keywords to organize the correspondence between the actual parameters in the message and the formal parameters in the method. In other words, the keywords select the method to which the message is directed. Methods that accept keyword messages are not named, but instead are identified by the keywords themselves. For example, consider the following message

```
FirstArray   Head: 1   Tail: 5
```

which sends the objects `1` and `5` to a particular method, "`Head :`" and "`Tail :`", of the object `FirstArray`. The keywords "`Head :`" and "`Tail :`" identify the formal parameters of the method to which `1` and `5`, respectively, are to be sent. Thus, the method to which this message is sent includes the keywords of the message.

A message invokes the appropriate member functions in the object's classes, possibly causing the objects themselves to change state. If a desired member function is not found in an object's immediate class, then member functions in that object's base class are searched. If it is not found there, the search continues up the hierarchy of the object's inherited class until either the appropriate member function is found, or the class at the root of the hierarchy is reached. If the desired member function is not found in the root class, then an error has occurred. The message passing mechanism allows objects from different classes to respond appropriately to the same messages.

8.2.4   Methods

A method consists of the operations that an object performs when it receives a message. A one-to-one correspondence between messages and the methods is carried out when a given message is received by an object of a particular class. Objects of different classes might perform different methods for the same message if that message were bound to a different method in the definition of the two classes. In contrast, if a message corresponds to a procedure call, then the method corresponds to the procedure itself. This distinction between the two is more important in the object-oriented model because when a message is sent, the sending object is not necessarily aware of the class to which the receiver belongs and hence cannot anticipate which method will be performed. This is not the case in imperative programming methods, especially those that are strongly typed. Referring to grammar notations and using the abstract syntax tree to represent syntax and semantics of programming languages, the object-oriented interpretation of a language might be stated as follows:

▶   The nodes of the abstract syntax tree representing the semantic information are the objects of interest.

▶   The classes of which these objects are instances are simply the grammar constructs.

▶   The class declarations are the grammar productions.

▶   The methods are the rules for computing the value of the attributes for each node of the abstract tree.

Example: Figure 8.3 represents an object-oriented model consisting of different objects to accomplish some methods of communication. Communication from an object Student to the object Financial-Aid, as indicated by arrow, is through the messages ID and Transaction. Financial-Aid can respond by sending messages Money and Receipt. The object Financial-Aid is thought of as an active entity including data and capable of sending messages, receipts, or money whereas algorithms manipulate passive data. In this case, a Student object asks a Financial-Aid object to respond to a request. The Financial-Aid has its own data or can request it from another object, and can respond to the request. For example, the message Transaction from an object Student should result in $500 discharged from the Financial-Aid Object and $500 subtracted from an account balance through a method belonging to Student-Account object. In this case, AccountBalance (which does not appear in Figure 8.3) could be data probably belonging to Student-Account, but Student need not know this. Notice that many of the procedures needed for this *financial-aid-receiving* are not mentioned in Figure 8.3. These procedures would be methods internal to the object in which they function. For example, Eligibility would be a method used in the Registration object to identify that the student is eligible to receive the financial aid. In addition, a method in one object cannot invoke a method in another object, like a procedure calling another procedure. A method in Financial-Aid cannot directly access a method in Student-Account, but must send a message to Student-Account (for example, OK), which will respond using its own method (for example, Authorize).

Thus, an object-oriented programmer approaches a problem by dividing it into interacting agents, called objects, which can do things and interact with other agents. In this case, objects are independent of each other, so they are easier to verify and maintain.

Example: Consider the following, which illustrates the constituent parts of a definition of call Account.

FIGURE **8.3**   Object-oriented representation of financial-aid-receiving problem

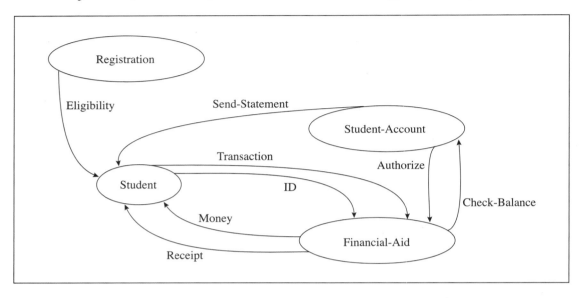

```
Class    Account
Instance Variables:
   Balance, MonthlyReport, Name, AcctId
Class Variables:
   TotalBalance, NumberOfAccts
Class Methods:
   Initialize
      TotalBalance ← Assign(Amount ← new).
      TotalBalance ← Assign(0.00).
      NumberOfAccts ← Assign(Integer ← new).
      NumberOfAccts ← Assign(0).
   ReportTotals
      TotalBalance ← print.
      NumberOfAccts ← print.
Instance Methods:
   Deposit(ItemId, AnAmount, Date)
      TotalBalance ← Addon(AnAmount).
      Balance ← Addon(AnAmount).
      MonthlyReport←Addline('DEP', ItemId, AnAmount, Date, Balance).
   MonthEnd
      MonthlyReport ← print.
   Open(Id, CustName)
      NumberOfAccts ← Addon(1).
```

```
    Balance ← Assign(Amount ← new).
    Balance ← Assign(0.00).
    MonthlyReport ← Assign(Report ← new).
    Name ← Assign(CustName).
    AcctId ← Assign(Id).
    MonthlyReport ← TitleLine(Id, CustName).
Withdraw(ItemId, AnAmount, Date)
  (AnAmount ← GreaterThan(Balance)) ←
     IfTrue([ErrorReport ← Append('Overdrawn Account') ]).
  (AnAmount ← GreaterThan(Balance)) ←
     IfFalse([
        Balance ← Subtract(AnAmount).
        TotalBalance ← Subtract(AnAmount).
        MonthlyReport ← Addline('WTH', ItemId, AnAmount, Date, Balance).
     ]).
```

In this example, variables are first listed that belong to the class state and hence will be found in each instance of the class. The instance variables are bound to objects, which exist as part of the state of each object of class Account that is created. The classes to which these four objects belong are not specified in this declaration. In fact, their classes are dynamically determined at run time by assignments made to them, a property that is similar to dynamic typing. In addition, a class may have class variables specified. Class variables are objects that belong to the entire class and can be referenced by methods of any instance of that class. Just as there are two types of variables, instance and class, so there are two types of methods defined. Class methods are activated by messages sent to the class object, whereas instance methods are activated by messages sent to instances of the class. Each message can have parameters. The list of parameter identifiers indicates the number of objects that are to be received with the message and the names by which these objects are accessed in the body of the method. The body of the method consists of a sequence of messages sent to other objects. For example, consider

```
    Initialize
        TotalBalance ← Assign(Amount ← new).
        TotalBalance ← Assign(0.00).
        NumberOfAccts ← Assign(Integer ← new).
        NumberOfAccts ← Assign(0).
```

as an example of a method definition. This method is a class method, so it is activated when the class object Account receives the message Initialize. This method results in four messages being sent. In contrast, an object that is an instance of class Account responds to four different messages. For example, the Open method is accompanied by two parameters: the first is the identification number of the account (Id) and the second is the customer's name (CustName). In this method, the first message

```
        NumberOfAccts ← Addon(1).
```

sends the message Addon to the class variable NumberOfAccts. Also

```
Balance ← Assign(Amount ← new).
Balance ← Assign(0.00).
```

result in instance variable `Balance` being instantiated as an object of class `Amount` and initialized to `0.00`. In addition, the following

```
MonthlyReport ← Assign(Report ← new).
```

instantiates `MonthlyReport` as a new object of class `Report`. Then

```
Name ← Assign(CustName).
AcctId ← Assign(Id).
```

results in instance variables `Name` and `AccId` being assigned the values of the two parameter objects. Finally,

```
MonthlyReport ← TitleLine(Id, CustName).
```

sends message `TitleLine` to `MonthlyReport`, causing the title line containing the account `Id` and the customer's name (`CustName`) to be the first line of the report for the receiving instance of class `Account`.

Example: Consider a class named POINT. Each object of this class has a position on the x-y plane; thus, it might be equipped with operations to position it, to compute its x and y coordinates, to compute its distance from another point, to move it, and so on. First we give some examples of calling such operations. Suppose that `P` is an object of class POINT. To position point `P` at coordinates (5, −5), we might write the command

```
P.Place (5, −5);
```

To compute the x coordinate of point `P`, we might write the expression,

```
P.xCoord
```

And do similarly for the y coordinate. The operations `xCoord` and `yCoord` are parameterless functions each returning a distance. To compute the distance of point `P` from another point q, we might write the expression:

```
P.Distance(q)
```

The operation `Distance` is a single parameter function, also returning a distance between two points. To move point `P` by a distance of 2 units in the x direction and 3 units in the y direction, we might write the command:

```
P.Move(2, 3);
```

Now, we can sketch an implementation of the object class POINT. First, we must define a representation for each object of the class. One possibility is the following pair of hidden variables:

```
x, y : Float;
```

We are assuming that each object contains a single hidden variable. We can now define the operations along the following lines:

```
procedure   Place   (xNew,  yNew  : in Float)    is
begin
  x  :=  xNew;   y  :=  yNew;
end;
function  xCoord  return  Float  is
begin
   return x;
end;
function  yCoord  return  Float  is
begin
   return y;
end;
function  Distance  (other  :  Point)
   return  Float   is
begin
   return sqrt ( ( x  -  other.xCoord)**2
              + ( y  -  other.yCoord)**2 ) ;
end;
procedure  Move  (xShift,  yShift  :  in Float)  is
begin
    x  :=  x  +  xShift;   y  :=  y  +  yShift;
end;
```

In this example, occurrences of x and y denote the hidden variables of the current object. For example, P.Move(..., ...) can update P.x and P.y. We could now introduce an object class CIRCLE, declaring it to be a subclass of POINT, in which all objects of class CIRCLE would inherit the operations Place, xCoord, yCoord, Distance, and Move. This makes sense if we choose a distinct point in each circle for the purpose of the distance operations. If C is an object of class CIRCLE, then we can write

C.xCoord   yields the x coordinate of the center of C

C.Distance(P)   yields the distance of the center of C from P

P.Distance(C)   yields the distance of P from the center of C

C.Move(5, 0)   move C by 5 units horizontally

In this example, the object class CIRCLE would inherit from POINT not only the exported operations but also the hidden variables x and y. Thus, to implement CIRCLE, we simply add those operations and hidden variables that are peculiar to circles.

◥ 8.3 Implementing Object-Oriented Programming

Object-oriented programming is a method for developing and organizing the logic of application programs. Object-oriented concepts have also had an impact on systems analysis and design procedures, operating systems, and database systems. As a whole, object-oriented method represents a paradigm. The most important aspects of object-oriented programming are a design technique driven by the determination and delegation of responsibilities. This technique has been called *responsibility-driven design* (Wirfs-Brock & Wilkerson, 1989, and Wirfs-Brock, Wilkerson, and Wiener, 1990). In general, an object-based language supports these features:

▶ Data abstraction (encapsulation of state with operations)

▶ Encapsulation (information hiding)

▶ Polymorphism (message passing)

A language that is object-oriented also implements the following:

▶ Inheritance

▶ Dynamic binding

In this context, inheritance is the ability to organize object classes into a hierarchy of subclasses and superclasses and to apply operations of a given class to objects of a subclass. The key concepts that are common to the implementation of each object-oriented programming language are described in the following sections.

8.3.1 Data Abstraction

The other side of decomposition is *abstraction*. In general, one of the recent trends in programming methodology and programming languages has been the specification of abstract data types (ADT). That is, the programmer first decides what data structures and data types are required and then specifies inputs and outputs of the necessary operations. Finally, the representation of the data structures and operations is fixed; addressing that the abstract data type is implemented. From the theoretical point of view, an abstract data type is defined as a collection of data structures and operations abstracted into a simple data type. We define data abstraction as

▶ A set of data objects, ordinarily using one or more type definitions.

▶ A set of abstract operations on those data objects.

An abstract data type is not another name for a data structure, where a data structure is a construct within a programming language that stores a collection of data. Rather, an abstraction operation consists of just those properties essential to a purpose; details that can safely be ignored are hidden. In other words, data abstraction asks that you think about *what* you can do to a collection of data independently of *how* you do it. Among the forms of abstraction are *data types, procedures, modules,* and *objects*. For example, a Stack as a user data type defined can be represented as an array with a top index or as a linked list. Any manipulation of data structure must then be done through the operations provided by the data type because the representation of the data structure is hidden. As a consequence, users of the data type are required to use the abstract operations (e.g., pop and push for stacks) because they are prohibited from using the concrete operations (e.g., subscribing or pointer operations). This corresponds to our definition of an abstract data type: a set of data values together with a set of operations that act on those data values. In this respect, a defined type, *Stack,* can be used to create as many stacks as needed in a program. Procedure abstraction applies to programs that are made from a set of procedures or subroutines. This abstraction allows the programmer to concentrate on one section of a program at a time without the overall details of the program. Module abstraction corresponds to groupings of related variables (data), procedures (operations), constants, and types, which are the individual modules of the program. Object abstraction or object-oriented programming treats an overall program as a collection of interacting objects. For example, suppose that you need to store a collection of names in a manner that allows you to search rapidly for a given name. The binary search algorithm enables you to search an array efficiently, if the array is sorted. Thus, one solution to this problem is to store the names sorted in an array and to use a binary search algorithm to search the array for a specified name. You can view the *sorted array* together with the *binary search algorithm* as an abstract data type that solves this problem.

When we design an abstract data type, we should make sure that the constructors (e.g., int and push) and selectors (operations implemented) work together smoothly. This is necessary if the data type is to be easy to learn and easy to use. In particular, the data type will be more regular if the constructors and selectors are inverse; that is, the selectors undo what the constructors do, and vice versa. In this respect, assume two functions *head* and *tail* operate at the beginning of lists, in which head selects the first element of a list and tail removes the first element of a list. A programming language provides support for abstraction in two ways:

▶ The language directly supplies a useful set of abstractions that we think of as the features of the language.

▶ The language provides facilities that aid the programmer to construct abstractions.

Subprograms, subprogram libraries, type definitions, classes, and packages are some of the capabilities provided by different languages to support programmer-defined abstractions. When a program must perform data operations that are not directly supported by the language, you should first design an abstract data and carefully specify what the abstract data type operations are to do. Then (and only then) should you implement the operations with a data structure.

Example: To elaborate on the notion of an abstract data type, consider a list of grocery items. A grocery list contains items of the same type: milk, eggs, butter, apples, bread, chicken, and other foods. What can you do to the items on a list? You might count the items to determine the length of the list, add an item to the list, remove an item from the list, or look at an item. The items on a list, together with operations that you can perform on the items, form an abstract data type. The following operations are part of the abstract data type list:

▶ Create an empty list.

▶ Determine whether a list is empty.

▶ Determine the number of items on a list.

▶ Add an item at a given position in the list.

▶ Remove the item at a given position in the list.

▶ Remove all the items from the list.

▶ Retrieve the item at a given position in the list.

How do you implement an abstract data type once its operations are clearly specified? The first reaction to the implementation might be to choose a data structure and then to write methods that operate on it in accordance with the operations. In a non–object-oriented implementation, both the data structure and the abstract data type operations are distinct pieces. In contrast, object-oriented implementation provides encapsulation, the focus of the next section, as a fundamental principle of abstract data type implementation.

8.3.2 Encapsulation

Encapsulation or *information hiding* is simply packaging things together in a well-defined programming unit. When information is encapsulated in an abstraction, it means that the user of the abstraction

▶ Does not need to know the hidden information to use the abstraction

▶ Is not permitted to directly use or manipulate the hidden information even if that's desired.

For example, the integer data type in a programming language not only hides the details of the integer number representation, but also effectively encapsulates the representation so that the programmer cannot manipulate individual bits of the representation of an integer (except by use of flaws in the encapsulation mechanism of the language to get illegal access to the bits). The process of encapsulation is accomplished by hiding of the internal state of an object and methods from external access. In other words, encapsulation refers to the isolation of the operational details of a procedure from the environment where it is used. In particular, the invoking unit does not need to know the algorithms, data structures, or any other details of the procedure. For example, the class in C++ provides for encapsulation by packaging both data and function members into a single class unit. Encapsulation is an essential criterion for abstraction, and it permits unnecessary details of implementation to be encapsulated within an object A and hidden from other objects that should interact with object A. This process is called encapsulation with *information hiding*. Information hiding means that there is a binding relationship between the information, or data, and its related operations so that operations outside of an encapsulated unit cannot affect the information inside the unit. Information hiding limits the ways in which you need to deal with operations and data. As a user, you do not worry about the details of its implementation. As an implementer, you do not worry about its use.

The class in C++ provides an information-hiding mechanism, meaning that the public section interface is accessible outside the class, and the private section information is accessible only from within the class itself. In this case, only the member functions declared for the class can operate on the private class members. Thus, the private section of a class provides the information hiding. Encapsulation is important because it separates implementation from use. This means that changes can be made to the implementation of an object without users knowing about these changes because the implementation is encapsulated inside the object. This is similar to the way an automobile engine remains encapsulated under the hood. If the engine is replaced by a rebuilt engine, that change is hidden from the driver as long as the interface with the engine remains the same. In addition, encapsulation protects the internal state of an object from unauthorized access or modification. Because that state is hidden from the external agents, an internal state of an object may only be accessed through its object methods.

As another example, the Ada construct package supports the information hiding principles and controls access to declarations. The package declaration is broken down into two parts: an interface specification and a body. The interface specification defines the interface between the inside and the outside of the package (information about the package for the user) and the information about how it will be used (information about the package for the implementer). Techniques like encapsulation and information hiding preserve the integrity of a design. For example, in object-oriented programming, objects and classes formalize the structure of a program and allow a language to prevent attempts to compromise its integrity.

8.3.3   Polymorphism

The term *polymorphism* has Greek roots and means roughly "many forms" (*poly* means many and *morphos* means form; Morphos is related to the Greek God Morphus, who could appear to sleeping individuals in any form he wished). One of the most powerful capabilities of inheritance in object-oriented programming languages is its support for polymorphism, the ability to have classes in the same inheritance hierarchy respond differently to the same message. Polymorphism provides the relationship between different classes related by inheritance and of the mechanisms of message passing and substitutability. Polymorphism can be classified into two categories:

▶ *Pure polymorphism* occurs when a single function can be applied to arguments of a variety of types. In pure polymorphism, there is one function (code body) and a number of interpretations. In general, a program uses polymorphism when member functions in different classes have the same signature but differ in the interpretation of the function body.

▶ *Ad hoc polymorphism,* sometimes called *overloading,* occurs when there are a number of different functions (code bodies) all denoted by the same name. This is in direct contrast to pure polymorphism, in which functions that are part of the same class have different signatures. For example, *ad hoc polymorphism* allows the operator to specify its action without knowing the types of the operands. In this sense, the arithmetic operations of addition and subtraction for integers and real numbers usually have the same names (+ and −) even though the actual implementation of the two operations is substantially different, because of the different internal representations of the two types. In this case, a translator can distinguish between the two operations or disambiguate them by looking at the number and type of the supplied arguments.

The primary difference is that overloaded operations can apply only to a finite set of distinct types that are known in advance, whereas polymorphic operations can potentially apply to any type, which is not known in advance. The type of polymorphism commonly used by the object-oriented model is related to the concept of inheritance. When a message is sent to an object and the sender specifies the receiver to be an object of class A, the receiver may actually be any class that is a descendent of A in the class hierarchy. The receiver then responds to the message using the method of its own class rather than of class A, although the two may actually be the same through inheritance. This type of polymorphism is more restrictive than general polymorphism, where the sender does not have to know anything about the class of the receiver. In this case, the sender must at least know a class that is an ancestor of the class of the receiving object. In the preceding example, a message sent to class People could be received by an object of class Student or Senior.

There is little agreement regarding terminology in the programming language community. In Horowitz (1984), Marcotty and Ledgard (1987), MacLennan (1987), and Pinson and Wiener (1988), polymorphism is defined equivalently to what we are calling overloading here. In Sethi (1989) and Meyer (1988) and in the functional programming language community, the term is reserved for what we are calling pure polymorphism. With the exception of overloading, polymorphism in object-oriented languages is made possible only in the existence of *polymorphic variables*. A polymorphic variable is one with many capabilities, meaning that it can hold values of different types. In statically typed languages such as C++ and Java, polymorphism occurs through the difference between the declared (static) class of a variable and the actual (dynamic) class of the value the variable contains. This means that a variable can hold a value of the same type as that of the declared class of the variable, or of any subclass of the declared class. In Java, this is true for all variables declared as object type, and in C++, polymorphic variables occur only with pointers and references. In contrast, in dynamically bound languages such as Smalltalk and Objective-C, all variables are potentially polymorphic, meaning that any variable can hold values of any type. In these languages, the expected type is defined by a set of expected behaviors.

8.3.4 Inheritance

Inheritance is one of the most important properties of the object-oriented programming because of its support for reusability. This property applies to classes. For example, class A is said to inherit from class B if A is a subclass of B and B is a superclass of A. What A inherits from B is the internal state of B, messages, and methods. Class A can define additions to the internal state structure as well as new messages and methods that allow it to extend its definition beyond that of B. Furthermore, selected inherited state structure and message and method may be changed from definition of B or removed altogether in subclass A. The advantage of inheritance is that it permits the reuse of many of the features of a superclass without respecifying them. The ability to modify or remove inherited features selectively makes inheritance much more powerful. Inheritance may be either *single,* if each class has just one parent, or *multiple,* when classes are permitted to have more than one parent. With single inheritance, the class structure of a program may be represented as a tree. A method inherited by a class is supplied by the nearest ancestor of the class that supplied the method. Multiple inheritance results in a less structured class organization that may be represented as a directed acyclic graph. Locating an inherited method with multiple inheritances is more complicated that the linear search through ancestor classes that represents for single inheritance. Two parent classes may in turn inherit from a common ancestor, so

FIGURE **8.4**   An inheritance graph for graphical objects

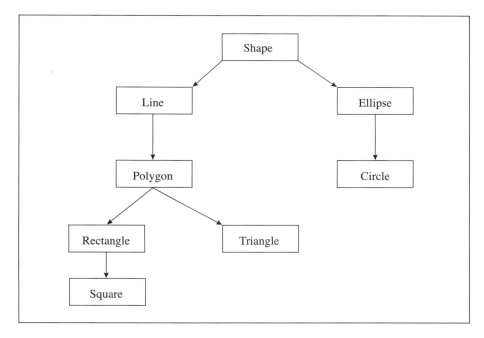

we must be careful that the search method does not visit some classes more than once. One approach is to use the first method of a given name that is encountered in a depth-first search of the ancestor of a class. A variety of other approaches are possible. Because of inheritance, the entire hierarchy of classes is often depicted as an *inheritance graph,* when inheritance can be propagated down many levels. Such inheritance occurs naturally in many application domains. For example, we can consider the class People to contain a certain internal state structure and methods that can be performed as a response to messages. A subclass of People would be the class Student that inherits all the components of class People but adds some components of its own. Similarly, a subclass of Student might be the class Senior, which would inherit all of the components of Student, including those the Student inherits from People, and add further components of its own. A similar example is the inheritance graph of a hierarchy of classes that can be developed for creating and manipulating graphical objects on a computer screen as shown in Figure 8.4.

In general, the key to using the power of inheritance is constructing an effective hierarchy of classes. Some languages permit each class to inherit from only one superclass, which is called *single-inheritance languages.* Other languages permit a class to inherit from many superclasses, which are called *multiple-inheritance languages.* The only property of imperative languages that resembles inheritance is subtypes. Just as a subclass inherits all the properties of its super class, a subtype inherits all the properties of its parent type. However, subtypes are a much more limited concept than is inheritance because they apply to only a limited set of possible base types, usually the scalar types. This generalization is a major contribution of the object-oriented programming model. Multiple inheritance raises many issues, which are not easy to solve. For example, if an instance variable or method is inherited from two or more superclasses, do we select just one (and how do we select which), or do we get them all (and then how do we discriminate between them)? How do we handle a situation in which a class is a superclass in more than one way? It is not our purpose to address these issues here, we only alert you to the design complexities facing you on both sides of the multiple inheritance question.

8.3.5   Dynamic Binding

When a programming language determines how a particular operation is to be performed on an object, it is said to bind a specific implementation of that operation to the object. In other words, the property of attaching a message to method when a message is sent is known as *binding*. If the system decides which implementation of the operation to use at compile time, it performs *static binding*. This property is *dynamic binding* (sometimes called *late binding*) if it is carried out every time a message is forwarded, indicating that the choice is made at run time. In other words, dynamic binding is advocated to allow operations associated with a particular object to be selected at run time instead of at compilation time, based on the type of object referenced, which can show the flexibility of the language. An object-oriented programming language typically supports static bonding, but it must support dynamic binding. This gives operations (i.e., messages) the important capability of being able to adapt automatically to the objects to which they are applied. The benefit of dynamic binding is that you can create and destroy objects as needed, which provides more efficient use of memory. It is therefore appropriate for objects that are used temporarily or for large programs that must continually free memory to continue execution.

In connection with polymorphism and inheritance, when an object receives a message, it will search its structure class to see if there is a method associated with the received message. If not, the superclass of the object is queried, and so on, until either a method is found for the message or a class is reached that has no superclass. If the later occurs, the message was inappropriate for the receiving object. The advantage of dynamic binding is that it permits the environment to be changed dynamically, which occurs at run time.

☞ 8.4   DESIRABLE CHARACTERISTICS FOR OBJECT-ORIENTED PROGRAMMING

The following benefits of the object-oriented model have led to its increase in popularity:

▶   **Close correspondence to the problem domain,** meaning that the objects in programs correspond directly to objects in the problem domain, and their activities correspond as well. This is particularly true in the solution of problems using simulation. This correspondence greatly simplifies the construction of a computer solution.

▶ **Reusability of software,** meaning that the inheritance of properties by one class of projects from another class without explicitly respecifying them. This model is a very effective way to reuse data structures and code in a selective way, in which only the pertinent parts of a class of objects can be inherited, whereas those that do not apply can be redefined or deleted.

▶ **Abstraction and encapsulation,** meaning that the object-oriented model carries with it all the abstraction benefits of abstract data types by permitting the data and actions of an object to be encapsulated within that object and dividing its contents between those that are public and those that are private.

▶ **Collecting similar operations,** meaning that similar operations from two different components are collected into a new component. For example, a circle and a rectangle are both objects that have position and that can be translated and displayed. These properties can be combined into an object called a figure, which has the common features of circles, rectangles, triangles, and so on. Specific examples of a figure are then forced to have each of these common properties.

▶ **Concurrency,** meaning that objects can act concurrently in the problem domain. It is natural for objects to perform concurrently in the object-oriented model. When such capabilities are available, the object-oriented model presents a natural way to exploit them.

SUMMARY

Object-oriented programming relies on objects to impose modular structure on programs. An object is a set of operations that share a state. The state consists of one or more values that may be viewed and modified only by operations belonging to the object. These operations are called methods, and the call to method is named a message. Another term in object-oriented programming is class, in which class instances are called objects. A class that is derived from another class is a derived class, and a class from which the new class is derived is known as its parent class. A language that is object-oriented must support three key language features: abstract data type, inheritance, and dynamic binding. In this chapter, we discussed the general characteristics for object-oriented programming. In addition, we outlined the design principles for object-oriented programming including objects, classes, messages, and methods. The implementation of object-oriented programming was based on five important features: abstraction, encapsulation, inheritance, dynamic binding, and polymorphism. Also, we outlined the desirable characteristics for object-oriented programming.

9 Object-Oriented Programming Languages

In Chapter 8, we discussed the techniques of object-oriented design—that is, we analyzed a typical problem that required a system to be built, determined what objects were needed to implement the system, determined what attributes the objects needed to have, determined what behaviors these objects needed to exhibit, and specified how the objects needed to interact with one another to accomplish the overall goals of the system. In this chapter, we briefly outline Smalltalk-80 as a pioneer language for object-oriented programming, then use two popular object-oriented programming languages, C++ and Java, to address the design and implementation requirements of object-oriented systems. In Section 9.1, we deal with Smalltalk-80 as a pioneer object-oriented programming language. Smalltalk was designed to be the single language of a self-contained interactive programming language, in which programs would be characterized by a high degree of modularity and dynamic extensibility. We explore the Smalltalk-80 program structure along with important features of the language, such as objects, messages, and methods, including unary, binary, and keyword messages, control structures, classes, and inheritance. In particular, we outline the implementation of a class, which consists of class name, class variable, class method, and instance variable.

In Section 9.2, we discuss a second object-oriented programming language, C++, which is an extension of C. C++ is a hybrid language, meaning that it is possible to program in a C-like style, an object-oriented style, or both. C++ programs consist of pieces called classes and functions. We discuss the program structure along with important features of the language: *object and class declaration,* including public, private, and protected members, and *object and class implementation,* including accessing members of class. In addition, we explore important features of the C++ language, such as friend class and function, inheritance, polymorphism, templates and standard template library to address the issue of design in this popular language.

The Java programming language, which originated at Sun Microsystems, was similar to C and C++. Java is a programming language with characteristics, such as simple, general-purpose, object-oriented, distributed, interpreted, robust, secure, portable, multithreaded, and dynamic. In Section 9.3, we outline the Java program structure consisting of Java system and Java API package. We discuss Java program modules including static, public, protected, and private members; building an applet; and essential applet methods to address performing common mathematical calculations, string manipulations, character manipulations, input and output operations, error checking, and many other useful operations. Java directly supports only single inheritance; however, it adopts a kind of virtual class, called an interface, that provides a version of multiple inheritance. An interface definition is similar to a class definition, except that it contains only named constants and method declarations. Java provides two kinds of encapsulation constructs: physical encapsulation and logical encapsulation. Through these, we explore the inheritance and encapsulation adopted in Java. In addition, we briefly discuss multithreading, an important feature provided in Java, which is designed to make computer animation easy. Finally, in Section 9.4, we outline the differences between Java and C++ and discuss features supported by each programming language.

9.1 OBJECT-ORIENTED PROGRAMMING WITH SMALLTALK

In 1971, the Xerox Palo Alto Research Center began a research project to develop the Dynabook. Smalltalk-72, the language for the Dynabook was designed and implemented by 1972, and in 1973 a desk-sized version became available for research. Smalltalk-72 and the Interim Dynabook were used in personal computing experiments involving more than 250 children and 50 adults. One design principle was *simple things should be simple, complex things should be possible.* When Alan Kay developed Smalltalk as a language and philosophy of programming, his objective was to take the idea of *small talk* and implement it in the world of computing. Experience with Smalltalk has led to several revisions of the language, including Smalltalk-74, Smalltalk-76, Smalltalk-78, and Smalltalk-80. In what follows, we briefly talk about the Smalltalk-80 as a pioneer object-oriented programming language. Smalltalk was designed to be a self-contained interactive programming language, in which programs would be characterized by a high degree of modularity and dynamic extensibility. The environment consists of windows, in which several of them can be on the screen at one time. Smalltalk uses five standard systems windows. The user can create other types of windows as classes. The five standard windows are the System Browser, System Workspace, File List, Workspace, and System Transcript Window. One important issue in Smalltalk's implementation was its portability, meaning that most of the Smalltalk system is written in Smalltalk. This includes the compiler, decompiler, debugger, editor, and file system, which form approximately 97% of the code of the Smalltalk-80 system. A major reason that Smalltalk can be programmed in Smalltalk language is that most of the implementation of data structures is Smalltalk objects. The part of the Smalltalk that is not portable is called *the Smalltalk-80 Virtual Machine,* with between 6 and 12 kilobytes of assembly code. The Smalltalk Virtual Machine has three major components:

▶ Storage Manager
▶ Interpreter
▶ Primitive Subroutines

The *Storage Manager* is the abstract data type manager for objects. As required by the Information Hiding Principle, the Storage Manager encapsulates the representation of objects and the organization of memory. The only operations that other modules can perform on objects are those provided by the Storage Manager:

▶ Fetch the class of an object
▶ Fetch and store the fields of objects
▶ Create new objects

The Interpreter is the heart of the Smalltalk system. The Primitive Subroutine package is just a collection of the methods that are implemented in machine code rather than in Smalltalk because of performance. Smalltalk is a very pure object-oriented language. All values in Smalltalk are objects. Even object classes are themselves objects, and control structures are just operations of appropriate classes. The Smalltalk system provides support for multiple independent processes with three classes named *Process, ProcessScheduler,* and *Semaphore.* A process represents a sequence of actions that can be carried out independently of other actions. ProcessScheduler determines which of these actions will run at any particular time. A Semaphore allows independent processes to synchronize their actions with each other. In the following, we briefly explain the important features of Smalltalk system to provide a smooth transition to other object-oriented programming languages discussed in the other sections.

9.1.1　Program Structure

In general, there are three central ideas in Smalltalk: objects, classes, and message sending. Every statement in Smalltalk is a message-sending statement and appears within the definition of a method. The general form of a statement is the following:

```
<variable>   ←   <object> <message>
```

A period is used as a statement separator in Smalltalk, and the program name extension is .st. Any message expression, literal object, or variable name can be the right side of an assignment statement. The left side is a variable name, and the operator is specified with a left arrow (a < and a − sign), as in

```
total  ←  22.
sum  ← total.
```

which indicates that the variable total is set to refer to the object 22, then the variable sum is set to refer to the same object.

9.1.2 Objects

An *object* represents a component of the Smalltalk-80 software system. Virtually everything, from items as simple as the integer constant 2 to a complex file-handling system, is an object. All objects have local memory, inherent processing ability, the capability to communicate with other objects, and the possibility of inheriting methods and instance variables from ancestors. In Smalltalk, objects can be expressed in four different forms:

- ► Literals
- ► Reserved words
- ► Variables
- ► Expressions

An object consists of some private memory and a set of operations. Objects representing numbers compute arithmetic functions, objects representing data structures store and retrieve information, and objects representing positions and areas answer inquiries about their relation to other positions and areas. For example, numbers are objects that represent numeric values and respond to messages that compute mathematical results, such as the following

```
index  ←  index  +  1.
```

+1 is sent to the object referenced by `index` (right side), and the variable `index` (left side) is set to reference the new object that resulted from running the +1. Another example is

```
netPay  ←  deducts  grossPay: 400  dependents: 5
```

where the variable `netPay` is set to refer to the object returned by `deducts`. Similarly, characters are objects that represent the individual symbols of an alphabet, and strings are objects that represent sequence of characters. Because Smalltalk uses dynamic storage and pointers, each variable has a pointer to an appropriate context for objects.

9.1.3 Messages and Methods

A *message* is a request for an object to carry out one of its operations. A message specifies which operation is desired, but not how that operation should be carried out. The receiver, the object to which the message was sent, determines how to carry out the requested operation. The general form of the message pattern is as follows:

```
key-1: parameter-1    key-2: parameter-2    . . .    key-n: parameter-n
```

For example, addition can be performed by sending a message to an object representing a number. Some examples of message expressions and the interactions they represent are as follows:

3+4	Computes the sum of three and four.
x sqrt	Computes the positive square root of the number named x.

> list   addFirst:newO   Adds the object named newO as the first element of the
>   linear data structure named list.

A similar example is

x: xCoord y: yCoord   outPen up; goto xCoord@yCoord; down.

in which the object outPen is sent the messages up, goto (which uses the two parameters xCoord and yCoord), and down. Smalltalk permits three types of messages,
which are distinguished by the number of parameters and the way the message is
specified.

▶ **Unary Messages:** A unary message is parameterless. Such a message is specified
by identifiers with the first letter being uppercase for a class message and lowercase for an instance message (object). For example, the money currently available according to Finance is the value of the unary message expression

>   Finance   cashOnHand

where the message is called unary because only one object, the receiver, is involved.

▶ **Binary Messages:** A binary message is named by one or two special characters
and always requires a single parameter, which follows the symbol that represents
the message. Examples of binary messages are the following:

>   3 + 4
>   total − 1

▶ **Keyword Messages:** A keyword message consists of one or more keywords. Both
the keywords and the parameters are identifiers, and a keyword is separated from
its corresponding formal parameter by a colon. The number of parameters accepted by a message is always equal to the number of colons in its name. An
example of an expression describing single keyword messages is the following:

>   Finance   totalSpentOn: limit

A message with two arguments will have a selector with two keywords, such as
the following:

>   Finance   spend: 30   on: 'food'

When the selector of a multiple keyword message is referred to independently, the
keywords are concatenated. The set of messages to which an object can respond is
called its *interface* with the rest of the system. The only way to interact with an
object is through its interface. Smalltalk messages provide two-way communication. The selector and arguments transmit information to the receiver about what
type of response to make. The receiver transmits information back by returning
an object that becomes the value of the message expression. If a message expression includes an assignment prefix, the object returned by the receiver will become the new object referred to by the variable. For example, the expression

>   sum   ←   3 + 4

makes 7 be the new value of the variable (object) named sum.

A *method* describes how an object will perform one of its operations. A method is composed of a message pattern and a sequence of expressions, separated by period; the messages cause the method to be carried out. The general syntactic form of a Smalltalk method is

```
message-pattern  [ |  temporary variables  |  ]  statements
```

where the brackets are used to indicate that what they enclose is optional. Because Smalltalk has no type declarations, temporary variables need only be named in a list. These temporary variables exist only during execution of the method in which they are listed. The following example describes the response of a Financial System to messages informing it of expenses:

```
spend:  amount  for:  reason
   expenses  at:  reason
      put:  (self  totalSpentFor:  reason)  +  amount.
                        cashOnHand ← cashOnHand − amount
```

In this example, the message pattern, `spend: amount for: reason` indicates that this method will be used in response to all messages with selector `spend:for:`. The first expression in the body of this method adds the new amount to the amount already spent for the reason indicated. The second expression is an assignment that updates the value of `cashOnHand` by the new amount. Two special features of Smalltalk method definition are the following:

▶ A method may contain variables that are local to the execution of the method. These are declared on the first line of the message, with the variable names separated by spaces and the entire list enclosed in vertical bars.

▶ We can specify a return value for the method, which is done by preceding an object description by an up-arrow. The object following the up-arrow is then returned as the result of the message.

Because Smalltalk is dynamically typed, the class of the receiver object is not known until run time, so the actual operation to be performed is not determined until run time. Consequently, operation name is dynamically bound in Smalltalk. On the other hand, variables and formal parameters are statically bound. Because Smalltalk has no built-in structured data, data objects are created by the class definition methods.

9.1.4 Control Structures

In Smalltalk, the control structures are formed in *blocks,* which is a way to collect expressions into *groups.* In general, a block is an unnamed literal object that contains a sequence of expressions. Blocks are instances of the class *Block.* For example, the following block consists of two statements

```
[index  ←  10.  total  ←  sum  +  index]
```

where the variable `index` is set to refer to the object 10. Then, the variable `total` is set to refer to the sum of the two objects. A block is implemented when it is sent the

unary message *value*. A message can be sent to a block by placing the message immediately after the block. For example, the following

```
[index  ←  10.  total  ←  sum  +  index]  value
```

sends the message `value` to the block, causing its execution. After the execution of the
block, the value of the last expression (`total`) in the block is returned. In addition,
blocks can be provided with parameters. Block parameters are specified in a section at
the beginning of the block that is separated from the remainder of the block by a ver-
tical bar (|). In this syntax, we need to attach a colon to the left end of each parameter.
For example, in the following, two parameters are defined:

```
[:x  :y  |   index ← x  +  10.  total  ← index +  y]
```

Also, blocks can contain relational expressions, which return one of the Boolean objects, *true* or *false*. The logical loops can be formed by using the keyword method
`whileTrue:`, which is defined to send *value* to the object that contains the method.
This method is defined for all blocks that return Boolean object. An example of a logical pretest loop is

```
index  ←  0.
total  ←  0.
[index < 20] whileTrue:
[total ← total + index.   index ← index + 1]
```

where the `whileTrue:` method sends *value* to the conditional block, thus causing
that block to be evaluated. The result of this evaluation is a Boolean object, true or
false. The repetition stops when an evaluation of [index < 20] produces false as a
result object. The method `ifTrue:ifFalse:` is provided for selection constructs,
which can be used for predefined Boolean objects *true* or *false*. The two arguments of
the method represent the then and else parts of the selection construct. In this case, a
message is sent to a Boolean expression. If the expression evaluates to true, the
method sends *value* to its first argument (then part) and ignores the second argument
(else part). Otherwise, the opposite takes place. An example of a selection construct is

```
index  ←  index + 10
   ifTrue:  [total  ←  20]        corresponds to then part
   ifFalse: [total  ←  30]        corresponds to else part
```

where the expression [index ← index + 10] causes the message index+10 to be
sent to the object `index`, which provides a return object *true* or *false*. Regarding the
resulting object (either true or false), a message is sent to the `ifTrue:ifFlase:`
method to address then block or else block, one of which is to be carried out.

9.1.5   Classes and Inheritance

A *class* describes the implementation of a set of objects that all represent the same kind
of system component. The individual objects described by a class are called its *instances*.
     Smalltalk has a rich variety of predefined classes. Smalltalk is dynamically typed.
Every object has a tag that identifies its class. A primitive operation (such as +) will check

an argument object tag to ensure that its class is acceptable. Such checks are effectively dynamic type checking. The programmer can also check the class of an object explicitly. In Smalltalk, there are two ways to present a class, one describing the functionality of the instances and the other describing the implementation of that functionality.

A **protocol description** lists the messages, each message of which is accompanied by a comment describing the operation an instance will perform when it receives that type of message. For example, a protocol description entry for the message to a Financial with the selector `spend:for:` can be

```
spend:  amount  for:  reason
```

In this sense, a message pattern contains a message selector and a set of argument names, one name for each argument that a message with that selector would have. For example, the previous message pattern matches the messages described by each of the following expressions:

```
Financial  spend:  32.50  for:  'Utilities'
Financial  spend:  cost+tax  for:  'food'
Financial  spend:  100  for:  Misc
```

An **implementation description** shows how the functionality described in the protocol description is implemented and provides the set of methods that describe how instances perform their operations. An implementation description to a class consists of the following components:

- ▶ **Class name:** Begins with an uppercase letter by convention.
- ▶ **Super class:** The name of the class from which the present class inherits variables, messages, and methods.
- ▶ **Class variables:** The variables that belong to the class and are accessible to all instances of this class.
- ▶ **Instance variables:** The variables, which are accessible only to the methods of the objects of the class. Each instance object belonging to the defined class has a set of these instance variables.
- ▶ **Class method:** The names and definitions of all operations associated with the class.
- ▶ **Instance methods:** Methods that are activated by messages to instances of the class.

The Smalltalk processor handles these portions of a class definition separately, and they are not combined into a single text as in conventional programming languages. An example of a complete implementation description for Financial System is as follows:

```
Class  Name     Financial
Objects         cashOnHand
                incomes
                expenses
Methods  (transaction recording)
    receive:  amount  from:  source
            incomes  at:  source
```

```
                    put: (self totalReceivedFrom: source) + amount.
        cashOnHand ← cashOnHand + amount
       spend: amount for: reason
              expenses at: reason
                  put: (self totalSpendFor: reason) + amount.
        cashOnHand ← cashOnHand - amount
   Methods (inquiries)
       cashOnHand
            ↑cashOnHand
       totalReceivedFrom: source
            (incomes includesKey: source)
            ifTrue: [ ↑incomes at: source]
            ifFalse: [↑0]
       totalSpentFor: reason
            (expenses includesKey: reason)
            ifTrue: [ ↑ expenses at: reason]
            ifFalse: [↑0]
   Initialization
       initialBalance: amount
            cashOnHand ← amount.
            incomes   ← Dictionary new.
            expenses  ← Dictionary new
```

Note that we will not be able to access the information stored within the class of an object unless we know what the class of that object is. Therefore, the representation of an object must contain some indication of the class to which the object belongs. The simplest method used in Smalltalk is to include a pointer to the data structure representing the class in the object's representation. A subclass specifies that its instances will be the same as instances of another class called its superclass. A subclass is, in all respects, a class and can therefore have subclasses itself. Each class has one superclass, although many classes may share the same superclass. In Smalltalk, a subclass must provide a new class name for itself, but it inherits both the variable declarations and methods of its superclass. New variables and new methods may be added by the subclass. The following example is a class created as a subclass of the Financial class introduced earlier.

```
Class Name       Deductible
Superclass       Financial
Objects          deductibleExpenses
Methods (transaction recording)
   spendDeductible: amount for: reason.
       self spend: amount for:reason
       deductibleExpenses ← deductibleExpenses + amount
   spend: amount for: reason deducting: deductibleAmount
       self spend: amount for:reason.
       deductibleExpenses ← deductibleExpenses + deductibleAmount
Methods (inquiries)
```

```
        totalDeductions
            ↑deductibleExpenses
Initialization
        initialBalance:  amount
            super  initialBalance:  amount.
            deductibleExpenses  ←  0
```

In this example, instances of `Deductible` have four variables, three inherited from the superclass `Financial`, and one specified in the class `Deductible`. A corollary immediately follows that, in Smalltalk, all object classes are arranged in a hierarchy of subclasses and superclasses. Any object of class x is also an object of every superclass of x. The operations associated with a class are automatically inherited by its subclasses. In defining a new object class, the programmer specifies its superclass and, thus, places it in the hierarchy.

A class whose instances are themselves classes is called a *metaclass*. In general, whenever a new class is created, a new metaclass is created for it automatically. Metaclasses have the following properties:

▶ Metaclasses are similar to other classes because they contain the methods used by their instances.

▶ Metaclasses are different from other classes because they are all instances of a class called *Metaclass*.

▶ A metaclass can be accessed by sending its instance the unary message *class*.

▶ Metaclasses do not have class names.

There is a one-to-one correspondence between a class and its metaclass, so their descriptions are presented together. An implementation description includes a part entitled as *class methods* that shows the methods added by the metaclass. In other words, the protocol for the metaclass can always be found by looking at the *class methods* part of the implementation description of its single instance. The following revised version of the implementation description for Financial consists of three changes as:

▶ One category of class methods named *instance creation* is added. By convention, the category *instance creation* is used for *class methods* that return new instances.

▶ The category of instance methods named *initialization* is deleted.

▶ A category of instance methods named *private* is added that consists of one method named *setInitialBalance,* which contains the same expressions that were in the deleted method for *initialBalance.*

```
Class   Name            Financial
Superclass              Object
Objects                 cashOnHand
                        incomes
                        expenses
Methods   (instance creation and transaction recording)
        initialBalance:  amount
```

```
                    ↑super  new  setInitialBalance:  amount
            new
                    ↑super  new  setInitialBalance:  0
            receive:  amount  from:  source
               incomes  at:  source
               put:  (self  totalReceivedFrom:  source)  +  amount.
            cashOnHand  ←  cashOnHand  +  amount
            spend:  amount  for:  reason
               expenses  at:  reason
               put:  (self  totalSpendFor:  reason)  +  amount.
            cashOnHand  ←  cashOnHand  −  amount
    Methods  (inquiries)
            cashOnHand
               ↑cashOnHand
            totalReceivedFrom:  source
               (incomes  includesKey:  source)
               ifTrue:    [ ↑incomes  at:  source]
               ifFalse:   [↑0]
            totalSpentFor:  reason
               (expenses  includesKey:  reason)
               ifTrue:    [ ↑ expenses  at:  reason]
               ifFalse:   [↑0]
    private
            setinitialBalance:  amount
               cashOnHand  ←  amount.
               incomes    ←  Dictionary  new.
               expenses   ←  Dictionary  new
```

The previous example illustrates how metaclasses create initialized instances. Like other classes, a metaclass inherits from a superclass. The simplest way to structure the inheritance of metaclasses is to make each one a subclass of *Class,* in which *Class* describes the general nature of classes. This organization is shown in Figure 9.1. Smalltalk handles user functions and polymorphism by inheriting class definition methods.

◪ 9.2 OBJECT-ORIENTED PROGRAMMING WITH C++

C++, an extension of C, was developed by Bjarne Stroustrup in the early 1980s at Bell Laboratories. C++ provides a number of features adopted from C language but, more important, provides capabilities for object-oriented programming. C++ is a hybrid language, meaning that it is possible to program in a C-like style, an object-oriented style, or both. C++ was widely believed to be the dominant system-implementation language in the mid-to-late 1990s. C++ programs consist of pieces called classes and functions. You can program each piece you need to form a C++ program, but most C++ programmers take advantage of rich collections of existing

FIGURE **9.1**   Organization of classes in Smalltalk

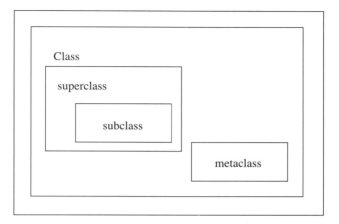

classes and functions in C++ class libraries and the *ANSI C standard function library,* which C++ adopted from the ANSI C language. Thus, there are two approaches to learning the C++ language:

▶ Learning the C++ language itself

▶ Learning how to use the classes in various C++ class libraries and the functions in the ANSI C standard library

C++ programs typically go through six phases to be executed: edit, preprocessor, compile, link, load, and execute. In this section, we concentrate on a typical UNIX-based C++ system. The C++ program names often end with the .C extension (note that C is in uppercase; some C++ environments require other extensions such as `.cpp` or `.cxx`). C++ does strict compile-time type checking. Thus, the types of all variables and functions must be fully declared at compile time.

9.2.1   C++ Program Structure

A C++ program is a collection of functions. An object-oriented C++ program has only one function that is not part of a class. This function is always named *main* and has a specific structure as follows:

```
return_data_type   main()
{
  / /   body of function
}
```

The first element of the main function is a returned data type, and anything within the braces belongs to the function and, therefore, constitutes the body of the function. To understand what this means, you need to know two things:

► A function can send one value from inside the function to the outside world. This is known as *returning a value.* The value itself is called the *return value.* Where does the value go? In the case of main function, it goes back to the operating system. Theoretically, an operating system can use a return value to determine whether the program ended correctly.

► The function declaration must indicate the type of data (for example, integer or floating-point value) that the function will be returning. If there is no return value, we use the word *void,* as a placeholder. By default, a main function returns an integer, but we can simply use *void* to indicate no return value.

A C++ program uses at least one class: an application class from which an object is created to represent the program itself.

9.2.2 Object and Class Declarations

At the heart of the object-oriented paradigm is the object, an entity in the data processing environment that has data that describes it and actions that it can perform. An object can be something that has a physical existence, such as a boat, product, computer, or a lunch dish that we know how to prepare. It can also be an event, such as the sale of a product, or a part of a program's user interface (for example, a menu or a window). Any given object-oriented program can handle many objects, and each object knows how to perform actions with its own data. The important thing to recognize is that an object consists of both the data that describes it and the actions it can perform. An object performs one of its actions when it receives a message instructing it to do so. A message includes an identifier for which action the object is to perform, along with the data the object needs to do its work. Messages therefore constitute an object's window to the outside world. The focus of attention in C++ is on objects rather than on functions.

A template from which objects of the same type are created is known as a *class.* Classes are also referred to as *programmer-defined types* because C++ programmers concentrate on creating their own *user-defined types* called classes. In other words, a *class* corresponds to a *type.* A class contains specifications for the data that describe an object along with descriptions of the actions, which an object knows how to perform. These actions are known as *services, methods,* or *member functions.* Just as an instance of a built-in type such as *int* is called a *variable,* an instance of a user-defined type is called an *object.* The term *class* is an abbreviation of class of objects, such as the class of circles or class of trees. The term *member function* is most commonly used with C++ because a function is a self-contained block of C++ source code. One of the greatest ironies of object-oriented programming is that member functions must be written using an older programming paradigm known as structured programming, to which object-oriented programming is a major alternative. This means that although you will be using object-oriented programming to create the high-level program organization of your programs, you will also need to learn structured programming to provide the details of the actions your object might perform. A class also includes all the data needed to describe objects created from the class. These are known as *attributes* or *variables.* The term *attribute* is used in object-oriented analysis and object-oriented databases, whereas the term *variable* is used in object-oriented programs. Before a program can create objects from any class, the class must be declared. Declaring a class means that you must give the class a name, name the elements that will store its data, and describe the functions that will perform actions with objects. Typically, we place class declarations in different files from executable code, using one file for each class. Known as header files, these files are stored with a file name extension of *.h*. In particular, each class declaration begins with the keyword *class,* followed by the name of the class. Braces surround the body of the class, and the class declaration ends with a semicolon. A class declaration has the following syntax:

```
class    class_name
{
   private  |  protected  |  public  :
      definition of private elements (usually stored data)
   public  |  private:
      definition of public elements (usually member functions)
} ;
```

Items separated by a vertical bar (|) means that we must choose one option from among those listed. C++ has three keywords for controlling the accessibility of member names in class declarations:

▶ **Public** members are accessible to outside code.

▶ **Private** members are accessible to the member functions in this class declaration. They are accessible to all objects of this class.

▶ **Protected** members behave like private members, which are visible through inheritance to derived classes but not to other code.

In general, structures and classes are closely related in C++; the only difference is that by default all members of a structure are public, whereas, by default, all members of a class are private. As an example, consider the class declaration listed in Figure 9.2 where the functions `viewProduct`, `getPrice`, and `updateOnHand` operate on private data. The procedure *product,* with the same name as the class, is a *constructor,* using C++ terminology. The constructor is called automatically when an object of the class is created, so initialization code can be put in the constructor. A class can also have a *destructor* procedure, which is called automatically just before the object disappears. If class *product* had a destructor, it would be called *~product.* Code for cleanup can be put in the destructor. In general, there are three sources for classes:

▶ You can declare and implement your own classes. These will always be available to you as source code.

▶ You can use classes that someone else has written and given to you. In this case, you have source code for such classes or can use object code for the implementation of the classes.

▶ You can use classes from the program libraries that accompany your C++ development software. The implementation of these classes is typically supplied as object code.

Regardless of where you obtain the classes you use in a program, keep in mind that you must have access to the declaration of the classes. Even if the implementations have

FIGURE **9.2**   A simple class declaration

```
class    product    ←──────────────────────  class name
         {
         private:  ←──────────  access for data storage        data storage declaration
                int    prod_number;
                char   prod_name[25], prod_description[50];  ←
                float  prod_price, num_on_hand;
         public:  ←──────────────  access for functions
                product(int, char[], char[], float, float);
                void    viewProduct();  ←
                float   getPrice();
                void    updateOnHand (int);        member function declarations
         };
```

been compiled and supplied to you as object code, you must have the text version of the class declarations for your compiler to use.

Example: Age Analysis Program

As an example of a simple short program that contains all the basic elements needed for a complete object-oriented C++ program, we look at an *Age Analysis Program* that asks your age and the ages of your parents when you were born. It then provides your age when your parents are twice your age. The dialog that the program conducts with the user can be outlined as the following.

What is your current age?	26
How old was your mother when you were born?	23
How old was your father when you were born?	29

Your mother was twice your age when you were 23 years old.

Your father will be twice your age when you are 29 years old.

The Age Analysis Program uses two classes:

▶ An application class to represent the program, which is stored in the header file `appclass.h`.

▶ An age class to represent the ages that relate to one person, which is stored in the header file `age.h`.

The declaration of the classes stored in `appclass.h` and `age.h` are outlined in the following code:

```
//   Application Class   appclass.h
class    AppClass
{
```

```
public:
  AppClass( );
  void Run( );
};

//   Age Class   age.h
class   Age
{
private:
  int  childAge,  motherAge, fatherAge;
public:
  Age( );
  void  init  (int,  int,  int);
  int  getChild( );
  int  getMother( );
  int  getFather( );
};
```

The major advantage of using header file is that you can make the same class declaration available to many programs without duplicating the declaration. In other words, object-oriented programming makes software reuse much easier.

9.2.3   Object and Class Implementations

After a class is declared, its name can be used as a type name to declare variables of that class type known as *objects,* sometimes called *instances* of class. The lifetime of the object is determined by the scope and lifetime rules of the language. C++ objects can be created in two forms:

1. Static binding
2. Dynamic binding

To create an object using static binding, we define a variable whose data type is the class from which we want to create an object. For example,

```
AppClass    s;
```

declares object s to be of type `AppClass`. In this case, space is allocated for object s of type `AppClass` class. Similarly, the following declares variable (object) a to be of type `Age` class.

```
Age    a;
```

To create an object using dynamic binding, we use the keyword *new,* followed by the name of the class from which the object is to be created and a parameter list that matches one of the class constructors. The new operator performs three actions:

► Allocates memory for an object
► Takes the input parameters and passes them into the object constructor
► Returns a pointer to the memory location of the created object

For example,

```
AppClass   *s;
s  =  new    AppClass;
```

creates an object of type `AppClass` and returns a pointer to the newly created object s. Similarly, the following creates an object of type `Age`:

```
Age  *a;
a  =  new    Age;
```

When a program no longer needs an object created with dynamic binding, the object can be removed (destroyed) from memory, freeing the space to be used by other objects. To remove an object from memory, use the following general syntax:

```
delete object_name;
```

For example, to free the space allocated for created object s, we can use the following.

```
delete  s;
```

Example: Our first example of a class is a new data type to store and manipulate the status of a simple *throttle*. Classes such as our throttle class appear in programs that simulate real-world objects. For instance, a flight simulator might include classes for the plane and various parts of the plane such as the engines, the rudder, the altimeter, and even the throttle. An object of this new class holds information about a simple throttle. The throttle is a lever that can be moved to control fuel flow. The throttle we have in mind has a single shutoff point (where there is no fuel flow) and a sequence of six on positions where the fuel is flowing at progressively higher rates. At the topmost position, the fuel flow is fully on. At the intermediate positions, the fuel flow is proportional to the location of the lever. For example, with the lever in the fourth position, the fuel flows at ⅔ of its maximum rate. We can define this new data type as a class called *throttle* that includes both data (to store the throttle's current position) and the functions to modify and examine the throttle. In this example, the throttle has a total of four functions:

▶ Set a throttle to its shut off position

▶ Shift a throttle's position by a given amount

▶ Return the fuel flow, expressed as a proportion of the maximum flow

▶ Indicate whether the throttle is currently on

Once the class *throttle* is defined, we can declare objects of type *throttle* and manipulate those objects with the four functions. An example of a program using the *throttle* class is shown in the following code. The program declares a `throttle` called sample and shifts the `throttle` upward according to the user's input. The `throttle` is then moved down one notch at a time, with the flow printed at each notch.

```
//  This demonstration shows how the throttle class is used
#include <iostream>        // provides cout and cin
#include <cstdlib>         // provides EXIT_SUCCESS
```

```
using namespace std;      // allows all standard library items
class   throttle
{
   public:
      // modification member functions
      void shut_off( );
      void shift(int amount);
      // constant member functions
      double flow( ) const;
      bool is_on( ) const;
   private:
      int position;
};
int   main( )
{
   throttle sample;   // declaration of a throttle object called sample
   int user_input;
   // set the sample throttle to a position indicated by the user
   cout << " I have a throttle with 6 positions." << endl;
   cout << " Where would you like to set the throttle? " << endl;
   cout << " Please type a number from 0 to 6:  " ;
   cin  >> user_input;
   sample.shut_off( );
   sample.shift(user_input);
   // shift the throttle down to zero and printing the flow along the way
   while (sample.is_on( ) )
   {
   cout << " The flow is now "  << sample.flow( ) << endl;
   sample.shift(-1);
   }
   cout << "The flow is now off. " << endl;
   return EXIT_SUCCESS;
}
```

Note: In the actual program, you would place the implementation of the throttle's four member functions here, but we have not yet written these implementations!

A typical dialogue with the program would look like this (with the user's input printed in bold):

```
I have a throttle with 6 positions.
Where would you like to set the throttle?
Please type a number from 0 to 6:  3
The flow is now 0.5
The flow is now 0.333333
The flow is now off.
```

Here are two sample declarations of throttle objects:

```
throttle my_throttle;
throttle control;
```

Every `throttle` object contains the private member variable `position`, but there is no way for a program to access this component directly because it is a private member. The only way that a program can use its throttle objects is by using the four public member functions.

9.2.4 Member Functions Declarations

In general, the actions that an object knows how to perform are specified in its class functions. Such functions are called *member functions* to distinguish them from ordinary functions. Another term is *method*, which means the same as member function. The body of a member function contains executable C++ statements. A *function prototype* is a declaration of the function name, the data the function needs from the outside world to perform, and the type of data that the function returns to the outside world when it has finished its task. The data that the function receives from the outside world are known as *parameters,* and parameter and the function name compose the function *signature.* A function prototype has the following syntax.

```
return_data_type   FunctionName (ParamterDataType1, . . . );
```

Let's examine the member functions of *throttle* class. One of the throttle function prototypes is as follows:

```
void   shift(int   amount);
```

The prototype indicates that the function has one parameter (an integer called `amount`). We use this function to shift a throttle's lever up or down by a given integer number called `amount`. One of the other throttle functions has the following prototype:

```
bool   is_on( ) const;
```

This function can be used to determine whether a throttle is currently on. The return value of the function has the data type `bool`, which is a built-in data type provided in C++ Standard. The `bool` data type is intended solely for true-or-false values (also called Boolean values or logical values). You should notice that we classified the public member functions into two groups. The first group was *modification* member functions, which can change the value of an object. For example, the modification functions can change the position of the throttle's lever. You should also notice that the functions *flow* and *is_on* are classified as *constant* member functions. A constant member function may examine the status of an object but cannot change the object. The prototype of the constant member functions has the keyword *const* at the end. Using the *const* keyword tells the compiler and other programmers that the function cannot change the object.

9.2.5 Member Functions Implementations

The implementation of member functions does not appear in the class definition; it will appear elsewhere with other function implementations. Writing the complete definition of a member function is just like writing any other function, with one small difference: in the head of the function definition, the class name must appear before the function name, separated by two colons, "::". The full name of a member is written as

```
class_name  ::  member_name
```

when the `class_name` is known from the context, and the `member_name` can be used by itself. The operator "::" is known as the *name-resolution operator* or *scope resolution operator*. This requirement, tells the compiler that the function is a member function of a particular class. Thus, the full name of member function `getChild` of class `Age` is the following:

```
Age  ::  getChild( )
```

The full member name must be used when the body of a member function appears outside a class declaration, as in the following:

```
int  Age  ::  getChild( )   {  return  childAge;  }
```

In our throttle example, "`throttle ::`" appears in the head, before the function name. For example, the definition of our first member function must include the full name `throttle :: shut_off`, as shown:

```
void   throttle :: shut_off( )
   //  Precondition : None
   //  Postcondition : The throttle has been turned off
   {
       position = 0;
   }
```

The reason for the scope resolution operator is that a function name might be used as the name of another class's member function, or as the name of another ordinary function. By specifying the full name, `throttle :: shut_off`, we indicate that this is the implementation of the *throttle* member function, rather than some other `shut_off` function. We use the term *function implementation* to describe a full function definition such as this. The function implementation provides all the details of how the function works, rather than the mere prototype that appears in the class definition and gives no indication of how the function accomplishes its work. We now implement the other three member functions named `shift`, `flow`, and `is_on`. For example, the shift function changes the position member variable by the amount specified in the parameter. In the implementation, we make sure that the shift doesn't go below 0 or above 6, as illustrated here:

```
void   throttle :: shift(int amount)
//  Precondition : shut_off has been called to initialize throttle.
//  Postcondition : The throttle's position has been moved.
   {
       position += amount;
       if    (position < 0)
       position = 0;
    else   if   (position > 6)
```

```
        position = 6;
    }
```

Notice that the shift function has a precondition indicating that `shut_off` function has been called at least once to initialize the throttle. Without this precondition, the member variable position would contain garbage. The *flow* function simply returns the current flow as determined by the position member variable, as illustrated here:

```
void   throttle : : flow( ) const
  // Precondition : shut_off has been called to initialize throttle.
  // Postcondition : The value returned is the current flow.
  {
    return position / 6.0;    // since the throttle has six positions
  }
```

The *flow* is a constant member function, so we must include the keyword *const* at the end of the function's head. The last throttle member function is called `is_on`. The function returns a Boolean true-or-false value, indicating whether the fuel flow is on.

```
void   throttle : : is_on( ) const
  // Precondition : shut_off has been called to initialize throttle.
  // Postcondition : if the flow is above 0, returns true;
    otherwise false.
  {
    return (flow( ) >0);
  }
```

Accessing Members of Class

In general, to tell an object to run one of its member functions, we send a message to the object, and the syntax for this function call depends on whether you are using the static or dynamic bindings as follows:

► When the object is created by static binding, we use the member access operator as *dot* operator " . ".

► When the object is created by dynamic binding, we use the member access operator as *arrow* operator "–>," consisting of a minus (–) sign and a greater than (>) sign with no intervening spaces.

For example, function `getChild` of an object named a can be accessed by `a.getChild()`. In this form, activating a member function involves the following four steps:

1. Start with the name of the object that you are manipulating.
2. Place a single period after the object name.
3. Write the name of the member function.
4. List the arguments for the member function call.

In other words, our example activated the `getChild` member function. In general, activating a member function is nothing more than making a function call to a member function. For example, suppose we have declared an object variable named `control` and we want to set object to its third notch. We do this by calling the member functions as shown:

```
control.shut_off( );
control.shift(3);
```

As another example, here is a sequence of several activations to set a throttle according to user input, and then print the throttle's flow:

```
throttle control;
int user_input;
control.shut_off( );
cout << "Please type a number from 0 to 6: ";
cin  >>  user_input;
control.shift(user_input);
if (control.is_on( ) )
   cout << "The flow is " <<  control.flow( ) << endl;
else
   cout << "The flow is off " <<  endl;
```

If the object is created by dynamic binding, we use an arrow to activate the member functions. For example, the following statements let us use the arrow operator with an object that was allocated space in main memory when the program was running.

```
className   someObject, *someObjectPtr;
someObjectPtr  =  &someObject;
someObjectPtr  ->  functionName( );
```

Example: Age Analysis Program

The source code for the implementation of a member function is executable code and is therefore stored in text file with `.cp` or `.cpp` extensions. Typically, we place the implementation of each class in a separate file. In this example, the Age Analysis Program requires two files, one for the *Application class,* as listed in Figure 9.3 and one for the *Age class,* as listed in Figure 9.4. Notice that a function begins with a header line that contains the name of the function, and that its body is surrounded by a pair of braces.

Finally, the Age Analysis Program's `main.cpp` file is listed in Figure 9.5, in which the header file `appclass.h` is included. This makes the declaration of the application class available to the main function.

The body of the function contains only two lines of executable code. The first creates an application object. The second calls the application object's run function. Notice that the function must include the header file that declares the application class so that main will have access to the class public members. The directive to merge (include) the contents of a header file, a file that contains the implementation of functions of the class, into a file containing source code is

```
#include  <file_name>
```

FIGURE **9.3**   The implementation of the Application class stored in `appclass.cpp`

```
#include  "appclass.h"
#include  "age.h"
#include  <iostream.h>
AppClass : : AppClass( )
   {
   // This is a comment line that the compiler ignores
   }
void   AppClass : : Run( )
   {
   Age thePerson;        // create one object from the Age class
   int  ichild, imother, ifather;
                         // collect data from the user
   cout  <<  " What is your current age? ";
   cin  >>  ichild;
   cout  <<  " How old was your mother when you were born? ";
   cin  >>  imother;
   cout  <<  " How old was your father when you were born? ";
   cin  >>  ifather;
               // initialize the object
   thePerson.init  (ichild, imother, ifather);
               // analyze the ages and display the correct sentence
   if  (thePerson.getMother( ) < thePerson.getChild( ) )
      cout  <<  " \nYour mother was twice your age when you were ";
   else
      cout  <<  " \nYour mother will be twice your age when you are ";
   cout  <<  thePerson.getMother( )  <<  " years old.";
   if (thePerson.getFather( ) < thePerson.getChild( ) )
      cout  <<  " \nYour father was twice your age when you were ";
   else
      cout  <<  " \nYour father will be twice your age when you are ";
   cout  <<  thePerson.getFather( )  <<  " years old.";
   }
```

This directive instructs the compiler to look for the header file in a disk directory that has been designated as the depository for header files. Notice that the name of the header file is surrounded by the less than (<) and greater than (>) symbols. However, if the header file is in a different directory, you surround its path name with double quotes:

```
#include    " /my.headers/custom.h "
```

FIGURE **9.4**   The implementation of the Age class stored in `ageclass.cpp`

```
#include  "age.h"
Age  : : Age( )
   {
   childAge = 0;
   motherAge = 0;
   fatherAge = 0;
   }
   // This function places data into an object
void  Age : : init (int child, int mother, int father)
   {
   childAge = child;
   motherAge = mother;
   fatherAge = father;
   }
   // Get functions send private values to another function
int  Age : : getChild( )
   { return  childAge;  }
int  Age : : getMother( )
   { return  motherAge;  }
int  Age : : getFather( )
   { return  fatherAge;  }
```

FIGURE **9.5**   The main function for Age Analysis Program stored in `main.cpp`

```
// Age Analysis Program  main.cpp
#include " appclass.h"
void  main ( )
{
AppClass  theApp;    // create the object
TheApp.Run( );       // call the Run function
}
```

9.2.6 Friend Classes and Functions

In the spirit of data encapsulation, the members of a class should be kept private so that they are not accessible to functions outside of the class. The C++ *friend* mechanism allows the programmer to bypass class access restrictions, which eliminates data encapsulation. Sometimes you may need that one class to have access to another class's private data. For example, consider the following segments of code:

```
class    A    {
    friend class B;
};
class    B    {
    friend class C;
};
```

In this example, class A declares class B as a friend. This permits member functions of class B to directly read or modify the private data of class A. In other words, B can access all private members and methods of class A. A similar situation is applied to class C and B. A *friend* of a class is given complete access to all members of base class, regardless of whether they are public, protected, or private. In general, a function, an operator, or even another class can be made a friend of a class. Friendship is neither symmetric nor transitive, meaning that if class B is a friend of class A, and class C is a friend of class B, you can not infer that class A is a friend of class B, that class B is a friend of class C, or that class C is a friend of class A.

An important concept in programming languages is *overloading,* which is a practice of giving several meanings to an operator or a function. The meaning selected depends on the types of the arguments used by the operator or function. For example, we can overload + to provide *concatenation of two strings.* It is possible to overload most of the C++ operators using the *friend* function. A *friend* function of a class is defined outside of that class' scope and has the right to access private members of the class. In other words, a friend declaration within a class gives nonmember functions access to the private members of the function. Friend functions are used to enhance the performance. To declare a function as a *friend* of a class, precede the function prototype in the class definition with the keyword *friend.* For example, consider the following segment code that defines abs (which incidentally overloads a function of the same name) for double precision values. The function (abs) has been declared a *friend* of the Complex class, so it is permitted to access all members of the class, even private members.

```
class    Complex
{
private:
    double    rp;
    double ip;
public:
    Complex(double, double);
    Friend double abs(Complex&);
};
```

```
Complex  : :  Complex(double  a, double  b)   { rp = a;  ip = b;  }
double abs(Complex&  x)  {  return  sqrt(x.rp*x.rp + x.ip*x.ip);  }
```

Although the friend declaration provides some control over what function or operator manipulates the underlying representation, it still creates a major security problem relative to information hiding. Therefore, a *friend* is used only as the last alternative.

Example: Friend Function

The following program demonstrates the declaration and use of friend function `setX` for setting the private data member `x` of class `Count`. Note that the friend declaration appears first in the class declaration before public member functions are declared as a convention.

```
#include   <iostream.h>
class  Count
    {
    friend void  setX(Count  &,  int);   //  friend declaration
public:
    Count( )  {  x  =  0;  }
    void  print( )  const  {  cout  <<  x  <<  endl;  }
private:
    int  x;
    };
//  can modify private data of Count because setX
//  is declared as a friend function of Count
void  setX(Count  &c,  int  val)
    {
    c.x  =  val;
    }
main( )
    {
    Count  object;
    cout  <<  " object.x after instantiation: ";
    object.print( );
    cout  <<  " object.x after call to setX friend function: ";
    setX(object,  8);   // set x with a friend function
    object.print( );
    return 0;
    }
```

The output, which indicates that a friend function can access private members of a class, is as follows:

```
object.x after instantiation:   0
object.x after call to setX friend function:   8
```

In general, the important thing to remember is that no functions outside a given class can access the private members of the class unless they are special *friend functions* defined for a given class.

9.2.7 Inheritance

Inheritance is a form of software reusability in which new classes are created from existing ones by taking their attributes and behavior and including those with capabilities the new classes require. In this sense, the programmer can designate that the new class is to inherit the data members and member functions of a previously defined base class. The new class is referred to as a *derived class.* Each derived class itself becomes a candidate to be a base class for some future derived class. In other words, in C++ inheritance creates a hierarchy of classes through which the variables and functions for classes higher in the hierarchy are passed down to the class below. This means that when similar classes share variables and functions, we only need to declare them once, rather than repeating them for each class in which they appear. For example, an inheritance hierarchy is the shape hierarchy represented in Figure 9.6.

The declaration of derived classes must include the name of the class from which the new class is derived and the type of inheritance that is in effect. The derived class declaration has the syntax

```
class    class_name  :  inheritance_type   base_class_name
```

in which the derived class inherits all the variables declared in their base class. The `inheritance_type` can be either *public* or *private*. The public and protected members of a base class are also public and protected in a public derived class. In a private derived class, both the public and protected members of the base class are private. So in a class hierarchy, a private derived class cuts off access to all members of all ancestor classes to all successor classes, and protected members may or may not be accessible to subsequent subclasses. However, keep in mind that the inherited variables are as much a part of an object created from a derived class as are those variables declared inside the derived class. In general, public items are accessible to all functions, whereas private items are accessible only to members of the class in which they are defined. In this sense, inheritance can be defined as the following two categories, although the private inheritance is used very rarely:

▶ Public inheritance means that a derived class has access to the public and protected items of its base class. Public items are inherited as public items.

▶ Private inheritance means that a derived class has no access to any of its base class members.

Consider the following segment code:

```
class    Base_Class
{
public:
   int    One;
   float    Two;
private:
   int    Three;
   float    Four;
protected:
   int    Five;
```

FIGURE **9.6**   A shape class hierarchy

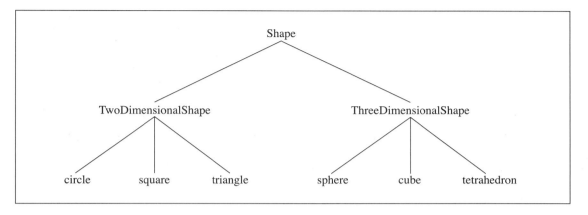

```
      float    Six;
    };
    class    ClassOne   :    public     Base_Class  {  . . .  };
    class    ClassTwo   :    privatec   Base_Class  {  . . .  };
```

where in `ClassOne`, `Five` and `Six` are protected, and `One` and `Two` are public. In `ClassTwo`, `Five`, `Six`, `One`, and `Two` are private. No derived class of `ClassTwo` can have members with access to any member of `Base_Class`. In this sense, the data members `Three` and `Four` in `Base_Class` are not accessible in either `ClassOne` or `ClassTwo`. In addition, under private class declaration, no member of the base class is implicitly accessible to the instances of the derived class. Any member that must be made accessible must be redefined in the derived class, so the instance of the derived class can access the member. This redeclaration excludes a member from being inaccessible when the inheritance is private. For example, in the declaration

```
class    ClassThree  :   private  Base_Class  {  Base_Class  : :  One;  };
```

an instance of `ClassThree` can access `One`. In other words, as far as `One` is concerned, it is as if the derivation was public. The double colon (`::`) specifies the class where its following member is defined. By default, inheritance is private. If you accidentally leave out the keyword public, base class items will be inaccessible. Thus, the type of inheritance is one of the first things you should check if compiler returns an error message that indicates variables or functions are inaccessible. Also, inheritance can be categorized as *single inheritance* when a class is derived from one base class, and *multiple inheritance* when a derived class inherits from multiple base classes. One way to help determine when inheritance is appropriate is to recognize that in most cases, inheritance represents the special relationship in which a derived class is a more specific example of its base class. If you express the relationship between two classes using the "is a" relationship, then inheritance is probably appropriate. We need to distinguish between "is a" relationships and "has a" relationships. "Is a" is inheritance, meaning that

TABLE **9.1**   Summary of base-class member accessibility in a derived class

Base	Public inheritance	Protected inheritance	Private inheritance
	Public in derived class	**Protected in derived class**	**Private in derived class**
Public	can be accessed directly by any nonstatic member functions, friend functions and nonmember functions.	can be accessed directly by all nonstatic member functions and friend functions.	can be accessed directly by all nonstatic member functions and friend functions.
	Protected in derived class	**Protected in derived class**	**Private in derived class**
Protected	can be accessed directly by all nonstatic member functions and friend functions.	can be accessed directly by all nonstatic member functions and friend functions.	can be accessed directly by all nonstatic member functions and friend functions.
	Hidden in derived class	**Hidden in derived class**	**Hidden in derived class**
Private	can be accessed by non-static member functions and friend functions through public or protected member functions of the base class.	can be accessed by non-static member functions and friend functions through public or protected member functions of the base class.	can be accessed by non-static member functions and friend functions through public or protected member functions of the base class.

an object of a derived class type may also be treated as an object of the base class type, whereas, "has a" is composition, meaning that a class has one or more objects of other classes as members.

A derived class inherits all its base class, public and protected variables, but it does not inherit constructors, destructors, overloaded operators, and friends functions. Table 9.1 summarizes the type of inheritance and accessibility of base class members in a derived class according to the access specification of the members in the base class and the type of inheritance.

Example: Inheritance

As an example of inheritance, we look at the following example, parts 1 through 5, in which parts 1 and 2 represent the Point class definition and Point member function definitions. Parts 3 and 4 outline the Circle class definition and Circle member function definitions and part 5 shows a program to demonstrate assigning derived class pointers to base-class pointers and casting base-class pointers to derived-class pointers. In the following, we examine each part of this example.

Definition of class Point (Part 1): The public interface to Point contains member functions SetPoint, Getx, and Gety. The data members X and Y are specified as *protected,* meaning direct access to data is prevented, but classes derived from Point can access the inherited data members directly. If the data were specified as *private*, the public member functions of `Point` must be used to access the data, even by *derived* classes.

```
//    POINT.H
#ifndef    POINT_H
#define    POINT_H
class    Point
   {
   friend  ostream &operator  <<  (ostream  &,  const  Point  &);
public:
   Point(float = 0.,  float = 0.);           // default constructor
   void setPoint(float,  float);             // set coordinates
   float  GetX( )  const  {  return  x;  }  // get X coordinate
   float  GetY( )  const  {  return  y;  }  // get Y coordinate
protected:     // accessible by derived classes
   float  X, Y;  // X and Y coordinates of Point class
   };
#endif
```

Member function definitions for class Point (Part 2): The `Point` overloaded stream insertion operator function is able to reference variables x and y directly because the overloaded stream insertion operator function is a friend of class `Point`. Note that it is necessary to reference X and Y through objects as in `p.X` and `p.Y`. This is because the overloaded stream insertion operator function is not a member function of the class `Point`.

```
//  POINT.CPP
#include  <iostream.h>
#include  "point.h"
//  Constructor for class Point
Point : : Point (float a, float b)  {  SetPoint(a, b);  }
//  Set X and Y coordinates of Point
void  Point : : SetPoint(float a, float b)
{
   X = a;
   Y = b;
}
//  Output Point with overloaded stream insertion operator
ostream  &operator  <<  (ostream  &output,  const  Point  &p)
{
   output  <<  "["  <<  p.X  <<  ","  <<  p.Y  <<  "]";
   return  output;
}
```

Definition of class Circle (Part 3): The class `Circle` inherits from class `Point` with public inheritance. This is specified in the first line of the class definition class:

```
class  Circle  :  public Point
```

where in this declaration, the colon : indicates inheritance. The keyword public indicates the type of inheritance. All the members of class `Point` are inherited into class
`Circle`, meaning that the public interface to `Circle` includes the `Point` public
member functions as well as the `Circle` member functions `Area`, `SetRadius`, and
`GetRadius`.

```
// CIRCLE.H
#ifndef    CIRCLE_H
#define    CIRCLE_H
#include   <iostream.h>
#include   <iomanip.h>
#include   " point.h "
class Circle  :  public  Point
{          // Circle inherits from Point
friend  ostream  &operator  <<  (ostream  &,  const  Circle  &);
public :   // default constructor
   Circle(float  r  =  0.0,  float  x  =  0,  float  y  =  0);
   void SetRadius(float);      // set radius
   float  GetRadius( )  const;  // return  radius
   float  Area( )  const;       // calculate area
protected:
   float  radius;
};
#endif
```

Member function definition for class Circle (Part 4): The `Circle` constructor invokes the `Point` constructor to initialize the base class of a `Circle` object. This is accomplished with the member initialization introduced as

```
   Circle : : Circle(float r, float a, float b)
```

when

```
   :  Point(a, b)
```

invokes the `Point` constructor by name. Values a and b are passed from the `Circle`
constructor to the `Point` constructor to initialize the base-class members `x` and `y`. In
this case, if the `Circle` constructor does not invoke the `Point` constructor explicitly,
the `Point` constructor is invoked with the default values for `x` and `y` (i.e., 0 and 0). In
addition, if the `Point` class does not provide a default constructor, then the compiler
generates an error. Nevertheless, the `Circle` overloaded stream insertion operator
function is able to reference variables `x` and `y` directly because these are protected
members of base-class `Point`. Note that, it is necessary to reference `x` and `y` through
objects as in `c.x` and `c.y`. This is because the overloaded stream insertion operator
function is not a member of the class `Circle`, but is a *friend* of the class.

```
//  CIRCLE.CPP
#include  <circle.h>
// Constructor for Circle calls constructor for Point with a member
// initialization then it initializes radius.
Circle  : :  Circle(float r, float a, float b)
   : Point(a, b)      // call base-class constructor
{  radius  =  r;  }
//  set radius of Circle
void  Circle  : :  SetRadius(float r)  {  radius = r;  }
//  get radius of Circle
float  Circle  : :  GetRadius( )   const  {  return radius;  }
//  calculate area of Circle
float  Circle  : :  Area( )   const  {  return 3.14159 * radius * radius;  }
// output a Circle in the form: Center = [x, y];  Radius =  #.##
ostream  &operator  <<  (ostream  &output,  const  Circle  &c)
{
   output  <<  "Center = [ "  <<  c.X  <<  ","  <<  c.Y
      <<  " ];  Radius  =  "  <<  setiosflags(ios : : showpoint)
      <<  setprecision(2)  <<  c.radius;
   return  output;      //  enables concatenated calls
}
```

Casting base-class pointers to derived-class pointers (Part 5): The following output is the result of casting base-class pointers to derived-class pointers to demonstrate the inheritance.

```
Point P : [3.5,   5.3]
Circle  C: Center = [1.2,   8.9];  Radius = 2.70
Circle C (via  *PointPtr)  :  [1.20,   8.90]
Circle C (via  *CirclePtr)  :  Center  =  [1.20,  8.90]; Radius = 2.70
Area of C (via CirclePtr) : 22.90
Point P (via  *CirclePtr)  :  Center = [3.50, 5.30]; Radius = 4.02e − 38
Area of object CirclePtr points to : 0.00
```

In this example, the driver program creates PointPtr as a pointer to a Point object and instantiates Point object P, then creates CirclePtr as a pointer to a Circle object and instantiates Circle object C. The objects P and C are displayed using their overloaded stream insertion operators to show that they were initialized correctly. Next, the driver demonstrates assigning a derived-class pointer (the address of object C) to base-class pointer PointPtr and displays the Circle object C using the overloaded stream insertion operator for Point and the dereferenced pointer *PointPtr. Note that it is always valid to assign a derived-class pointer to a base-class pointer because a derived-class object "is a" base-class object. Then, the driver demonstrates assigning a derived-class pointer (the address of object C) to base-class pointer PointPtr and casting PointPtr back to a Circle, meaning that the result is assigned to CirclePtr. The Circle object C is displayed using the overloaded stream insertion operator for Circle and the dereferenced pointer *CirclePtr. The area of

Circle object C is displayed via CirclePtr. A base-class pointer cannot be assigned directly to a derived-class pointer because this is an inherently dangerous assignment. In other words, derived-class pointers expect to be pointing to derived-class objects because the compiler does not perform an implicit conversion in this case. Next, the driver demonstrates assigning a base-class pointer (the address of object P) to base-class pointer PointPtr and casting PointPtr back to a Circle. The result of the cast operation is assigned to CirclePtr. The Point object P is displayed using the overloaded stream insertion operator for Circle and the dereferenced pointer *CirclePtr. Note the strange value output for the Radius member. This is because displaying a Point as a Circle results in an invalid value for the Radius. This indicates that the program outputs whatever value happens to be in memory at the location that CirclePtr expects the Radius data member to be. The area of the object pointed to by CirclePtr is displayed via CirclePtr. Note that the value for the area is 0.00 because this calculation is based on the nonexistent value of the Radius.

```
// POINT_CIRCLE.CPP
// Casting base-class pointers to derived-class pointers
#include <iostream.h>
#include <iomanip.h>
#include " point.h "
#include " circle.h "
main ( )
{
   Point  *PointPtr,  P(3.5, 5.3);
   Circle *CirclePtr, C(2.7, 1.2, 8.9);
   cout <<   "Point P : " << P << endl << "Circle C: " << C << endl;
// Treat C Circle as a Point
PointPtr = &C;     // assign address of Circle to PointPtr
CirclePtr = (Circle *) PointPtr;     //  cast base to derived
cout << " Circle C (via *CirclePtr) : " << *CirclePtr << endl
     << " Area of C (via CirclePtr) : " << CirclePtr ->Area( ) << endl;
// Treat a Point as a Circle
PointPtr = &P;     // assign address of Point to PointPtr
CirclePtr = (Circle *) PointPtr;    // case base to derived
cout   << " Point P (via *CirclePtr) :  " << *CirclePtr  << endl
   << " Area of object CirclePtr points to: " << CirclePtr -> Area( )<<endl;
return 0;
}
```

9.2.8 Polymorphism

The quality of being able to assume different forms is called *polymorphism* (Greek word for "having multiple forms"). C++ allows you to give two or more different definitions to the same function name, which means you can reuse names that have strong intuitive appeal across a variety of situations. For example, in C++ the division operator is a polymorphism operation. If the arguments to the division operator are integers, then integer division is used. However, if one or both arguments are floating point, then floating point division is applied. Similarly, if, for example, class *Rectangle* is derived from class *Quadrilateral,* then a *Rectangle* object is a more specific version of a *Quadrilateral* object. An operation such as calculating the area or perimeter that can be performed on an object of class *Quadrilateral* can also be performed on an object of class *Rectangle.* Thus, the same operation can be applied to both objects depending on different interpretations. In general, in a well-designed program, class *Quadrilateral* and class *Rectangle* may be derived classes of a single base class that we may call *Figure.* In C++, polymorphism is implemented via *virtual functions,* functions that must be referenced with a pointer (using dynamic binding). In other words, when a request is made through a base-class pointer (or reference) to use a virtual function, C++ chooses the correct redefined function in the appropriate derived class associated with the object. In this respect, the keyword virtual tells C++ to wait until a method is called before deciding which definition of that method to use.

Virtual functions rely on dynamic binding, since the compiler cannot always determine which version of the function is being called. In general, dynamic binding allows us to create data structures containing objects of different classes, provided that all classes are derived from a common base-class, and apply the same operation to each. In this sense, each object can respond differently to the same operation, depending on its class. The pointer to an object that precedes the –> and the name of the function identifies the class from which the correct function should be taken. To declare a function virtual, precede its prototype with the keyword `virtual` and the function name with the following syntax:

```
virtual   function_type   function_name (arguments);
```

We now demonstrate polymorphism using a simple but complete program with pointers to base and derived classes, through a virtual function named `Print`.

```
//   A virtual function named Print in action
#include  <iostream.h>
class  Animal   {
public:
   virtual  void  Print( )  const { cout  << "Unknown Animal Type.\n"; }
protected:
   int  nlegs;
};
class  Fish:  public  Animal    {
public:
   Fish (int  n)  {nlegs  =  n;}
   void Print( ) const { cout  << "A Fish has " << nlegs << " legs.\n"; }
};
class  Bird:  public  Animal    {
public:
   Bird (int  n)  {nlegs  =  n;}
   void Print( ) const { cout  << "A Bird has " << nlegs << " legs.\n"; }
};
class  Mammal:  public  Animal     {
public:
   Mammal (int  n)  {nlegs  =  n;}
```

```
      void Print( ) const { cout  << "A Mammal has " << nlegs << " legs.\n"; }
};
int main( )    {
   Animal *P[4];
   P[0]  =  new  Fish(0);
   P[1]  =  new  Bird(2);
   P[2]  =  new  Mammal(4);
   P[3]  =  new  Animal;
   for  ( int  i=0;  i < 4;  i++ )    P[i] -> Print( );
   return  0;
}
```

The polymorphism is implemented through the for-statement in the *main* function. The four elements of the pointer array P point to objects of four different class types, for each of which there is a Print function. It is obviously impossible for the compiler to determine from the statement

```
      P[i] -> Print( );
```

which of the four functions Fish::Print, Bird::Print, Mammal::Print, and Animal::Print is to be applied. In this example, the keyword virtual in the base class Animal made this choice possible. Also, the new operator is called four times to create the objects in question. The output of this program is as follows:

A Fish has 0 legs.

A Bird has 2 legs.

A Mammal has 4 legs.

Unknown Animal Type.

As a conclusion, this example referred to the fact that objects of different (derived) types, such as Fish, Bird, Mammal, are accessed in the same way, as was done in the previous function call, P[i] -> Print().

Example: Polymorphism

As an example of polymorphism, we illustrate the following example, parts 1 through 4. In this program, we have used stubs for the member functions that draw, erase, and center a figure. In each case, they simply output a message to the screen saying what they are supposed to do. They do not perform the actual action. This simplifies our example. To obtain a real example, you would have to replace the definition of each of these member functions with code to do the actual drawing.

Part 1: Figure-Box-Triangle Polymorphism

```
//    Interface for the class Figure
//    File:  figure.h
#include  <iostream.h>
#ifndef  FIGURE_H
#define  FIGURE_H
class  Figure  {
```

```
public:
   virtual  void  draw( );
   virtual  void  erase( );
   void  center( );
};
#endif      // FIGURE_H
// File: figure.cxx
// Implementation for the class Figure
// These are just stubs that say what each function is supposed to do
#include  "figure.h"
Figure :: Figure( )
{cout  << "Constructing a base class Figure object \n";}
void  Figure :: draw( )
{cout  << "Drawing a base class Figure object \n";}
void  Figure :: erase( )
{cout  << "Erasing a base class Figure drawing \n";}
void  Figure :: center( )
{
cout  << "Centering a drawing \n";
cout << "                 by calling erase( );  \n";
erase( );
cout << "                 then calling draw( ) again at the center. \n";
draw( );
cout << "                 at the center. \n";
}
```

Part 2: Figure-Box-Triangle Polymorphism

```
//   File: box.h
//   Interface for the class Box
#ifndef  BOX_H
#define  BOX_H
#include  "figure.h"
class  Box : public Figure
{
public:
   Box( );
   void  draw( );
   void erase( );
};
#endif // BOX_H
// File: box.cxx
// Implementation of the class Box
#include  "figure.h"
#include  "box.h"
// These are just stubs that say what each function is supposed to do
Box :: Box( )
```

```
{cout << "Constructing a derived class Box object \n";}
void  Box :: draw( )
{cout << "Drawing a derived class Box object \n";}
void  Box :: erase( )
{cout << "Erasing a derived class Box drawing \n";}
// file:  triangle.h
// interface for the class Triangle
#ifndef  TRIANGLE_H
#define TRIANGLE_H
#include  "figure.h"
```

Part 3: Figure-Box-Triangle Polymorphism

```
class  Triangle : public Figure
{
public:
   Triangle( );
   void  draw( );
   void erase( );
};
#endif  // TRIANGLE_H
// file:  triangle.cxx
// These are just stubs that say what each function is supposed to do
#include  "triangle.h"
#include  "figure.h"
Triangle :: Triangle( )
{cout << "Constructing a derived class Triangle object \n";}
void Triangle:: draw( )
{cout << "Drawing a derived class Triangle object \n";}
void Triangle:: erase( )
{cout << "Erasing a derived class Triangle drawing \n";}
// file  main.cxx
// This program then tests the polymorphism
#include  "figure.h"
#include  "box.h"
#include  "triangle.h"
int  main( )
{
   Triangle  x;
   x.draw( );
   cout << "\n  Derived class Triangle object calling center( ).  \n";
   x.center( );  // Calls draw and erase
}
```

Part 4: A Sample Output of Figure-Box-Triangle Polymorphism

```
Constructing a base class Figure object
Constructing a derived class Triangle object
```

```
Drawing a derived class Triangle object
Derived class Triangle object calling center( ).
Centering a drawing
by calling erase( );
Erasing a derived class Triangle drawing
then calling draw( ) again at the center.
Drawing a derived class Triangle object
at the center.
```

Suppose you want a member function to draw a figure on the screen. To draw a box, you need different instructions from those you need to draw a triangle. However, because the member functions are defined in the classes, they can all be called draw, without name conflict. If b is an object of a class Box, and c is an object of class Triangle, then b.draw( ) and c.draw( ) can be member functions implemented with different code. Now, the base class Figure may have member functions that apply to all figures. For example, it has a member function called center( ) that moves a figure to the center of the screen by erasing it and then redrawing it in the center of the screen.

9.2.9   Templates and Standard Template Library

Overloaded functions make programming convenient because only one function name must be remembered for a set of functions that perform similar operations. However, each of the functions must be written individually, even if they perform the same operation. For example, in the following overloaded square function, the only differences between two functions are the data types of their return values and their parameters.

```
int    square(int  number)
   {
   return  number * number;
   }
float   square(float  number)
   {
   return  number * number;
   }
```

In situations like this, it is more convenient to write a *function template* as an overloaded function. In this regard, function templates allow you to write a single function definition that works with many different data types, instead of having to write a separate function for each data type used. A function template is not an actual function, but a pattern the compiler uses to generate one or more functions. When writing a function template, you do not need to specify actual types for the parameters, return value, or local variables. Instead, you use a *type parameter* to specify a generic data type. When the compiler encounters a call to the function, it examines the data types of its arguments and generates the function code that will work with those data types. The following is a function template for the square function.

```
template  <class  T>
T square  (T  number)
   {
   return  number * number;
   }
```

A function template begins with the key word `template`. Next is a set of brackets that contains one or more generic data types used in the template. A generic data type starts with the key word *class* followed by a parameter name that stands for the data type. The `square` function above only uses one, which is named `T`. In this example, the function header

```
T  square(T  number)
```

indicates that `T` is the type parameter, or generic data type. The header defines `square` as a function that returns a value of type `T` and uses a parameter, `number`, which is also of type `T`. In this case, the compiler examines each call to `square` and fills in the appropriate data type for `T`. For example, the following call uses an integer argument

```
int  Y, X=12;
Y = square(X);
```

where it causes the compiler to generate the following function:

```
int   square(int  number)
   {
   return  number * number;
   }
```

This statement below

```
float  Y, X=4.2;
Y = square(X);
```

will result in the generation of the following function code:

```
float   square(float  number)
   {
   return  number * number;
   }
```

The following program demonstrates how this function template is used.

```
//  This program uses a function template
#include  <iostream.h>
//  Template definition for square function
template  <class  T>
T square  (T  number)
   {
   return  number * number;
   }
```

```
void  main(void)
  {
  int  UserInt;
  float  UserFloat;
  cout.precision(5);
  cout << "Enter an integer and a floating-point value: ";
  cin  >>  UserInt  >>  UserFloat;
  cout  <<  "Here are their squares:  ";
  cout  <<  square(UserInt)  <<  "  and  "
        <<  square(UserFloat)  <<  endl;
  }
```

The program output is shown as follows with example input and output shown in bold:

```
Enter an integer and a floating-point value:  12   4.2
Here are their squares:  144   and  17.64
```

The compiler encountered two calls to `square` function, each with different parameter types, so it generated the code for two instances of the function: one with an integer parameter and integer return type, the other with a float parameter and float return type.

Function Templates with Multiple Types

More than one generic data type may be used in a function template. Each type must have its own parameter, as shown in the following function template:

```
template  <class  T1,  class T2>
void  switch  (T1  &Var1,  T2  &Var2)
  {
  T1  Temp;
  Temp  =  Var1;
  Var1  =  (T1) Var2;
  Var2  =  (T2) Temp;
  }
```

The template above uses two type parameters: `T1` and `T2`. The function parameters, `Var1` and `Var2`, are specified with different types, so the function generated from this template can accept two arguments of different types.

Standard Template Library

In addition to its run-time library, C++ also provides a library of templates. The Standard Template Library (STL) contains numerous generic templates for implementing abstract data types and algorithms. The most important data structures in the STL are *containers* and *iterators*. A container is a class that stores data and organizes it in some fashion. An iterator is like a pointer and is used to access the individual data elements in a container. There are two types of container classes in the STL: *sequence* and *associative*. A sequence container organizes data in a sequential fashion similar to an array. The three sequence containers currently provided are listed in Table 9.2.

TABLE **9.2**   Sequence containers supported by STL

Container Name	Description
vector	An expandable array. Values may be added to or removed from the end or middle of a vector.
deque	Like a vector, but allows values to be added to or removed from the front.
list	A doubly lined list of data elements. Values may be inserted to or removed from any position.

TABLE **9.3**   Associative containers supported by STL

Container Name	Description
set	Stores a set of keys. No duplicate values are allowed.
multiset	Stores a set of keys. Duplicates are allowed.
map	Maps a set of keys to data elements. Only one key per data element is allowed. Duplicates are not allowed.
multimap	Maps a set of keys to data elements. Many keys per data element are allowed. Duplicates are allowed.

TABLE **9.4**   Iterators supported by STL

Iterator Name	Description
Forward	Can only move forward in a container (uses the ++ operator).
Bidirectional	Can move forward or backward in a container (uses the ++ and -- operators).
Random-Access	Can move forward or backward, and can jump to a specific data element in a container.
Input	Can be used with cin to read information from an input device or a file.
Output	Can be used with cout to write information to an output device or a file.

An associative container uses keys to rapidly access elements. The four associative containers currently supported are shown in Table 9.3.

Iterators are generalizations of pointers and are used to access information stored in containers. The types of iterators are shown in Table 9.4.

Iterators are associated with containers. The type of container you have determines the type of iterator you use. For example, *vectors* and *deques* require *random-access* iterators, whereas *lists, sets, multisets, maps,* and *multimaps* require *bidirectional* iterators.

Example Programs Using the STL

The following program provides a limited demonstration of the vector class template. The member functions of vector used in this program are used as shown in the following:

size()   Returns the number of elements in the vector.

push_back()   Accepts as an argument a value to be inserted into the vector. The argument is inserted after the last element.

pop_back()   Removes the last element from the vector.

operator[ ]   Allows array-like access of existing vector elements.

```cpp
//  This program provides a demonstration of the vector STL template
#include  <iostream.h>
#include  <vector>
using namespace std;
void  main(void)
   {
   int  x;
   vector <int> vect;   //  Declare a vector object
   // Use the size function to get the number of elements
   cout <<  "Vector starts with  " << vect.size()  << " elements. \n";
   // Use push_back to push values into the vector
   for   (x =0;  x < 10;  x++)
     vect.push_back(x);
   cout  <<  "Now vector has  " << vect.size()  << " elements.  ";
   cout  <<  "Here they are:  \n" ;
   // Use the [ ] operator.
   for  (x =0;  x < vect.size();  x++)
   cout  <<  vect[x]  << " " ;
   cout  <<  endl ;
   // Use the pop_back member function.
   cout <<  "Popping the values out of vector  \n";
   for   (x =0;  x < 10;  x++)
     vect.pop_back();
   cout <<  "Now vector has  " << vect.size()  << " elements.  \n";
   }
```

Program Output
```
Vector starts with  0  elements
Now vector has  10  elements.  Here they are:
0  1  2  3  4  5  6  7  8  9
Popping the values out of vector
Now vector has  0  elements.
```

Iterators may also be used to access and manipulate container elements. The following program demonstrates the use of an iterator with a vector object:

```
//  This program provides a demonstration of an iterator
#include  <iostream.h>
#include  <vector>    // Include the vector header
using namespace std;
void  main(void)    {
   int  x;
   vector <int> vect;                       //  Declare a vector object
   vector <int> : :  iterator iter;     //  Declare an iterator
   //  The compiler automatically chooses the right type, random-access iterator
   //  Use push_back to push values into the vector
   for    (x =0;  x < 10;  x++)
      vect.push_back(x);
   //  Step the iterator through the vector,
   //  and use it to display the vector's contents.
   cout  <<  "Here are the values in vector :  " ;
   for    (iter = vect.begin();   iter  < vect.end();  iter++)
      {
      cout  <<  *iter   <<  "  " ;
      }
   cout <<  "  \n and here they are backwards:  ";
   for    (iter  = vect.end() - 1;  iter >= vect.begin();  iter —)
      {
      cout  <<  *iter   <<  "  " ;
      }
   }
```

Program Output

```
Here are the values in vector :  0  1  2  3  4  5  6  7  8  9
and here they are backwards:  9  8  7  6  5  4  3  2  1  0
```

STL has a multitude of algorithms, which are implemented as function templates. The following program demonstrates random_shuffle, sort, and binary_search.

```
//  This program provides a demonstration of the STL algorithms
#include  <iostream.h>
#include  <vector>          // Include the vector header
#include  <algorithm>       // Required for STL algorithms
using namespace std;
void  main(void)
   {
   int  x;
   vector <int> vect;      // Declare a vector object
   //  Use push_back to push values into the vector
   for    (x =0;  x < 10;  x++)
      vect.push_back(x);
   //  Display the vector's elements
```

```
cout  <<  " Vector has  " << vect.size() << " elements. Here they are: \n";
for   (x = 0;   x < vect.size();  x++)
   cout  <<  vect[x]  <<  "  " ;
cout <<  endl;
//  Random shuffle the vector's elements
random_shuffle( vect.begin(),  vect.end() );
//  Display the vector's elements
cout <<  "  The elements have been shuffled:  ";
for   (x = 0;   x < vect.size();  x++)
   cout  <<  vect[x]  <<  "  " ;
cout <<  endl;
//  Sort the vector's elements
sort( vect.begin(), vect.end() );
//  Display the vector's elements
cout <<  "  The elements have been sorted:  ";
for   (x = 0;   x < vect.size();  x++)
   cout  <<  vect[x]  <<  "  " ;
cout <<  endl;
//  Now search for an element
if  (binary_search(vect.begin(), vect.end(), 7) )
   cout <<  "The value 7 was found in the vector. \n" ;
else
   cout <<  "The value 7 was not found in the vector. \n" ;
}
```

Program Output

```
Vector has  10 elements. Here they are:
0  1  2  3  4  5  6  7  8  9
The elements have been shuffled:
4  3  0  2  6  7  8  9  5  1
The elements have been sorted:
0  1  2  3  4  5  6  7  8  9
The value 7 was found in the vector.
```

9.3 OBJECT-ORIENTED PROGRAMMING WITH JAVA

The Java programming language originated at Sun Microsystems. In 1991, Sun Microsystems funded an internal corporate research project named Green for consumer-electronics products. The project resulted in the development of a language similar to C and C++, which its creator James Gosling called Oak after an oak tree outside his window at Sun. It was later discovered that there already was a computer language called Oak. When a group of Sun employees visited a local coffee place, the name JAVA was suggested and adopted as the name of the language. Java was not an academic language; rather, it was designed for commercial reasons and generated interest in the business community because of another Internet related development, the World Wide Web. As the people at Sun claim, Java is a programming language with characteristics, such as simple, general-purpose, object-oriented, distributed, interpreted, robust, secure, architecture-neutral, portable, high-performance, multithreaded, and dynamic. Java supports programming for the Internet in the form of platform-independent Java *applets*. Applets are Java applications that are loaded and run in the Java run-time environment. Thus, Java includes two separate products: Java itself which is a full object-oriented programming language, and HotJava, which is a browser for the Web that enables users of the Internet to download applets written in Java and run them on their own systems. The design goals for the language were the following:

▶ **The language should be familiar.** It should have syntax like an existing language. The control structure and data types in Java look like some of those provided in the C programming language, and those facilities that make it object-oriented resemble those in the programming language C++.

▶ **The language should be object-oriented.** A programming language is object-oriented if it offers capabilities to define and manipulate objects and self-contained entities to perform specific tasks.

▶ **The language should be robust.** Probably the most notorious programming language that is guilty of having features that can lead to nonrobust performance is C. In C, one example of a capability that can give rise to problems is that it provides a pointer type that can be employed by programmers. One of the developers' design aims has been to eliminate features that can lead to problems. Thus, there is no pointer in Java.

▶ **The language should have a high performance.** One of Java's features is threads, multiple concurrent execution of code, which provide a high-level implementation of concurrent processing. This leads to a highly efficient use of processor cycles and a fast response time.

▶ **The language should be portable.** The Java designers wanted to develop a program in Java code for a Sun Workstation running the Solaris operating system that would be capable of being ported across to a PC running another operating system, such as Windows NT or Windows 95.

▶ **The language should be as simple as possible.** Many languages—Ada is probably the best example—have become overburdened with features. This creates a number of problems: first, such languages are often expensive to compile and their run-time support is so large that even a small program occupies a large amount of memory; second, the learning curve for such languages is long and hard; and third, compiling programs in such languages can take quite a long time. The Java designers tried to keep the base capabilities of the language to a minimum and, instead, provided many features within a number of libraries.

▶ **The language should be interpreted.** The Java compiler, javac, generates byte code, rather than machine code, that can be executed directly on any machine to which the Java interpreter has been ported. The Java interpreter then runs Java source code (`FileName.java`) that has been compiled into byte code (`FileName.class`).

► **The language should be dynamic.** Java includes interface concepts from Objective-C similar to classes, where an interface is a listing of methods that an object responds to. These interfaces can be multi-inherited. One can look up a Java class given a string containing its name and have its definition dynamically linked into the run-time system.

In general, C++ became the starting point for the Java programming language, which was designed for networked and distributed programming environments. Therefore, there has been greater emphasis than in C or C++ on security, robustness, machine independence, portability, and late binding. To achieve this, Java omits some C++ features, such as operator overloading, pointers, excessive coercions, and multiple inheritance, but adds other features, such as automatic garbage collection and more secure type checking. Thus, Java is a move toward the higher-level storage management and dynamic typing of languages such as Smalltalk. Java has a richer library than C does, including a set of container classes to group existing objects in various ways. One example is a *vector* that provides a dynamically growable array that can store any *object* type. Another example is the *Hashtable* class, in which one can store and retrieve values of one type using objects of another type as keys. The design of the *Abstract Window Toolkit* (AWT) is an excellent example of using classes, inheritance, and interfaces. The AWT contains the essential classes to perform specific and general-purpose tasks. Another feature in Java is *graphical user interface* (GUI) support. A graphical user interface makes the system easy to use. Creating a GUI requires creativity and knowledge of how the GUI component works. The GUI components in Java are very flexible, which enables the user to create an extensive array of different user interfaces.

9.3.1   Java Program Structure

Let's begin with as simple Java application program that displays the message "Hello World" on the console.

```
// a simple application program displays Hello World on screen
public   class   HelloWorld
{
   public   static   void   main(String[ ] args)
   {
   System.out.println(" Hello World ");
   }
}
```

Every Java program must have at least one class. Each class begins with a class declaration that defines data and methods for the class. In this example, the class name is `HelloWorld`. This class contains a method called `main( )`. Each Java application must have a user-declared `main( )` method, which defines where the program begins. The `main( )` method provides the control of program flow. The `main( )` method in this program contains the `println( )` statement, which is a collection of statements that performs a sequence of operations to display a message on the screen. With some small exceptions, the data typing within the Java language is very similar to that found in the C, C++, and Objective C programming languages. Apart from the primitive data types in Java, everything else is treated as an object. This is also true for the control structures in Java. Except for a few exceptions, the flow of control in a Java program is specified in much the same way as in C, C++, or Objective C programs. There are four integer numeric data types: *byte, short, int,* and *long.* These correspond to stored integers of a maximum length 8, 16, 32, and 64 bits, respectively. Data type length in Java is fixed to ensure portability across different language implementations. There are two real number types in Java: *float* to represent 32-bit floating-point numbers and *double,* which represents 64-bit floating-point numbers. There is a character data type called *char,* which uses a 16-bit character set with characters being denoted by the value enclosed within single quotes. In addition, a Boolean data type known as `boolean`, in which variables hold either the value *true* or *false.* As a modern procedural programming language, Java contains the main programming constructs usually found in other languages such as C. The control constructs look very much like those that are provided as part of the C programming language. In addition, Java's design of classes, objects, and inheritance are similar to that of C++; so, in the following discussion, we concentrate on issues in which Java differs from C++.

9.3.2   Java System

Java system supports four program types:

▶   Applications
▶   Applets
▶   Content handlers
▶   Protocol handlers

Applications are stand-alone programs, like any program written using the high-level languages. Applications can be run from any computer with a Java interpreter and are ideal for developing software. One design goal for Java was to create applications that could be transferred over the Internet and accessed by different systems, remote as well as local. These applications are called *applets.* In other words, if applications are stand-alone entities, then applets conform to rules, which allow them to be hosted in a Java compatible browser, meaning that applets are Java applications that are loaded and run in the Java run-time environment. Applications and applets share many common programming features, although they differ slightly in some aspects. Content handlers are provided in predefined classes of Java to support Internet access. For example, the java.net.URL allows the data found on the Internet to be downloaded to the user's system. Similarly, Java.net.SocketImpl provides methods for implementing net communication through sockets (we discuss socket programming in Chapter 16). Protocol handlers for HTTP, FTP, and Gopher (Internet protocols for communication purposes) are included in the HotJava Web browser, which was written as a Java application. In general, as new protocols become available, users can write their own handlers. Handlers are put in the java\classes\net\www* directory, with content handlers in the \content* subdirectory and protocol handlers in the \protocol* subdirectory. Java system consists of an environment, the language, the Java Applications Programming Interface, and class libraries. A Java program goes through the following phases:

▶ **Edit:** This is accomplished with an *editor* program, when Java program is created, which has a file name ending with the *.java* extension.

▶ **Compile:** The Java compiler (*javac*) translates the Java program into *bytecodes,* which is the language understood by the Java interpreter. If the program compiles correctly, a file with the *.class* extension will be produced containing the bytecodes that will be interpreted for execution.

▶ **Loading:** This is done by the *class loader,* also called *java interpreter* (*java*), which transfers the file containing bytecodes to memory.

▶ **Verifier:** Before the bytecodes are executed by the Java interpreter, they are verified by the bytecode verifier to ensure that the bytecodes are valid and do not violate security restrictions.

▶ **Execute:** Finally, the computer interprets the program one bytecode at a time to produce the result.

9.3.3   Java API Package

Java contains many predefined pieces called classes that are grouped by directories into categories of related classes called *packages,* which provides a convenient way to organize those classes. Packages are hierarchical, and you can have packages within packages. Java designers recommend that you use your Internet domain name in reverse order as a package prefix because a package might be used on the Internet by other programs. Suppose you want to create a package named `mypackage.io` on the host machine with the Internet domain name as `cs.uscs.edu`. To follow the naming convention, you would name the entire package `edu.uscs.cs.mypackage.io`. Together, these packages are referred to as the *Java applications programming interface* (API). Every class in Java belongs to a package. The class is added to the package when it is compiled. To put a class in a specific package, you need to add the following line as the first non-comment and nonblank statement in the program:

```
package   packagename;
```

Table 9.5 lists the packages of the Java API alphabetically and describes each package. The Java API packages are provided as part of the Java Developer's Kit (JDK).

9.3.4   Java Program Modules

Modules in Java are called *methods* and *classes.* Java programs are written by combining new methods the programmer writes with pre-packaged methods available in the Java class library, also referred to as Java API, and by combining new classes the programmer writes with pre-packaged classes available in various class libraries. In general, the Java API provides a rich collection of classes and methods for performing common mathematical calculations, string manipulations, character manipulations, input and output operations, error checking, and many other useful operations. The programmer-defined methods define specific tasks that may be used at many points in the program. A method is invoked by a *method call.* The method call specifies the method name and provides information that the called method needs to perform. Methods are normally called by writing the name of the method followed by a left

TABLE **9.5**   The Java API packages

API package	Explanation
java.applet	*Java Applet Package* contains the applet class and several interfaces that enables the creation of applets, interaction of applets with the browser, and playing audio clips.
java.awt	*Java Abstract Windowing Toolkit Package,* contains all the classes and interfaces required to create and manipulate GUIs.
java.awt.image	*Java Abstract Windowing Toolkit Image Package* contains classes and interfaces that enable storing and manipulation of images in a program.
java.awt.peer	*Java Abstract Windowing Toolkit Peer Package* contains interfaces that enable graphical user interface components to interact with their platform-specific versions.
java.io	*Java Input and Output Package* contains classes that enable programs to input and output data.
java.lang	*Java Language Package* contains basic classes and interfaces required by many Java programs. The compiler automatically imports this package into all programs.
java.net	*Java Networking Package,* contains classes that enable programs to communicate via the Internet or corporate intranets.
java.util	*Java Utilities Package* contains utility classes and interfaces, such as date and time manipulations, various random number processing capabilities, storing and processing large amounts of data, breaking strings into smaller pieces called tokens, and other capabilities.

parenthesis followed by the *arguments* of the method followed by a right parenthesis. For example, the following statement calculates and prints the square root of 900.0.

```
System.out.println (  Math.sqrt(900.0)  );
```

When this statement is executed, the method Math.sqrt is called to calculate the square root of the number contained in the parentheses (900.0). The number 900.0 is the argument of the Math.sqrt method. The preceding statement would print 30, indicating that the method returns a result of type *double* when an argument of type *double* is provided (Java does not print trailing zeros or the decimal point in a floating-point number that has no fractional part). Note that all class methods must be invoked by preceding the method name with the class name and a dot (.) operator. Method arguments may be constants, variables, or expressions. If a=13.0, b=3.0, and c=4.0, then the statement

```
System.out.println (  Math.sqrt(a + b * c)  );
```

would calculate and print the square root of (13.0 + 3.0 * 4.0), or 5. In general, methods allow the programmer to modularize a program. In other words, a user can use a method without knowing how that method is implemented. If you decide to change the implementation, the user program will not be affected. This is referred to as *information hiding,* meaning that the use of a method is separate from the implementation of that method. All methods in Java must be defined inside a class definition, and all variables declared in a method are *local variables,* meaning that they are known only in the method definition in which they are defined. Most methods have a list of parameters that provide the means for communicating information between methods. The *divide-and-conquer* approach and *software reusability* are among several motivations for modularizing a program with methods. The format of a method definition is

```
return-value-type    method-name  (  parameter-list)
    {
    //   declarations and statements
    }
```

where the `method-name` is any valid identifier. The `return-value-type` is the data type of the result returned from the method to the caller. A type must be listed explicitly for each parameter in the parameter list of a method. When a method is called, these formal parameters are replaced by values, which are referred to as actual parameters. In general, Java provides four modifiers that are frequently used to control access to data, methods, and classes:

▶ **Static:** Defines data and methods. The static modifier represents classwide information that is shared by all instances of the class.

▶ **Public:** Defines classes, methods, and data in such a way that all programs can access them.

▶ **Protected:** Defines methods and data is such a way that any class in the same package or any subclass of that class can access them, even if the class is in a different package.

▶ **Private:** Defines methods and data in such a way that they can be accessed by the declaring class, but not by the subclass.

The modifiers static, private, and protected apply solely to variables or to methods. If public, private, or protected is not used, by default, the classes, methods, and data are accessible by any class in the same package. As we pointed out, Java's design of classes is similar to C++, so we concentrate on issues in which Java differs from C++. Consider the following example that uses a method to find the maximum of two integer numbers.

```
class    TestMethod
{
public   static   void   main(  String[ ]   args)
    {
    System.out.println
    (" The Maximum between 3 and 4 is "  + max(3, 4) );
    }
static  int  max( int  num1,  int num2)
    {
    if  (num1  >  num2)
```

```
            return num1;
       else
            return num2;
       }
   }
```

In this example, the max( ) method works only with the integer data types, which are defined with static modifier. In this example, main( ) method is defined with public and static modifiers. But what if you need to find which of two floating-point numbers has the maximum value? The solution is to create another method with the same name but with different parameters, as shown in the following code:

```
class    TestMethodOverLoading
{
public   static  void  main(  String[ ]  args)
   {
System.out.println(" The Maximum between 3 and 4 is "
                    + max(3, 4) );
System.out.println(" The Maximum between 3.0 and 5.4 is "
                    + max(3.0, 5.4) );
   }
static  int  max( int  num1,  int num2)
   {
   if  (num1  >  num2)
      return num1;
   else
      return num2;
   }
static  double  max( double  num1,  double  num2)
   {
   if  (num1  >  num2)
      return num1;
   else
      return num2;
   }
}
```

This is referred to as *method overloading*, that is, two methods have the same name (max), but different parameter profiles. The Java compiler is able to determine which method to invoke based on the number and types of parameters passed to that method. The output of the program is as the following:

▶   The Maximum between 3 and 4 is 4

▶   The Maximum between 3.0 and 5.4 is 5.4

In Java, a method can be defined to be *final,* which means that it cannot be overridden in any descendant class. When the *final* reserve word is specified on a class definition, it means that the class cannot be the parent of any subclass. In C++ a method must be defined to be virtual to allow dynamic binding, but in Java, all method calls are dynamically bounded unless the called method has been defined to be final, in which case it cannot be overridden and all bindings are static.

Most Java methods require using objects as arguments. Java offers a convenient way to wrap a primitive data type into an object; for example, wrapping an integer data into the class Integer. The corresponding class is called a *wrapper class* in Java terminology. By using wrapper objects instead of primitive data type variables, you can take advantage of generic programming. The wrapper classes provide constructors, constants, and conversion methods for manipulating various data types. Java provides Boolean, Character, Double, Float, Byte, Short, Integer, and Long wrappers for primitive data types. All the wrapper classes are grouped in the java.lang package. For example, because all numeric wrapper classes are very similar, their methods are generalized in an abstract superclass named Number. The Number class defines abstract methods to convert the represented numeric value to byte, double, float, int, long, and short. These methods are implemented in the subclasses of Number as illustrated here:

public byte byteValue( )	returns the value of the specified number as a byte.
public double doubleValue( )	returns the value of the specified number as a double.
public float floatValue( )	returns the value of the specified number as a float.
public int intValue( )	returns the value of the specified number as an int.
public long longValue( )	returns the value of the specified number as a long.
public short shortValue( )	returns the value of the specified number as a short.

In addition, you can construct a numeric wrapper object from a string representing the numeric value. The constructors are as follows:

▶   public Integer(int value)

▶   public Integer(String s)

▶   public Double(double value)

▶   public Double(String s)

For example,

```
Double  doubleObject  =  new  Double (5.0);
```

constructs a wrapper object for double value 5.0. Similarly,

```
Integer  integerObject  =  new  Integer (5);
```

constructs a wrapper object for integer value 5.

9.3.5 Building an Applet

When working with a stand-alone application, the developer can make arbitrary decisions about any aspect of the code. When writing an applet, the code must conform to the applet standards so that the work can be executed within a Java compatible browser. The following example demonstrates the applet that displays the same message "Hello World" on screen.

```
// a simple applet displays Hello World on screen
(1)    import    java.awt.Graphics;
(2)    public  class  HelloWorld  extends    java.applet.Applet
   {
(3)      public  void    init( )    {
(4)          resize(100, 100);
      }
(5)      public  void    paint(Graphics  g)    {
(6)          g.drawString(" Hello  World ",  5, 20);
      }
   }
```

The first line imports the `awt.Graphics` library into the applet. In line 2, the `HelloWorld` class inherits from the applet class. In line 3, method `init` is called by the system to allow the applet to prepare for execution. In line 4, the applet just increases the amount of browser page space from the system default that it occupies. The second method `paint` in line 5 is called by the system when the applet is asked to display itself on the screen. The `g` in the `paint( )` method is called an instance for class `Graphics`. An instance is a concrete object of the class. In this sense, `g` can access all the methods defined in `Graphics`. `drawString( )` is a method in `Graphics`, which now can be used in `g` by a call, such as `g.drawString( )`. This is exactly how object-oriented programming works: Creating an instance from a class, where the instance can use all the methods defined in the class without knowing how the methods are implemented. Finally, in line 6, the applet draws a string into the `Graphics` context at the specified pixel coordinates. Every application must have a `main( )` method, which contains the first sequence of instructions to be carried out. The Java interpreter begins the execution of the application from the `main( )` method. Java applets, on the other hand, do not need a `main( )` method because they run within the Web browser environment. You use a Web browser to view the applet. As another example, consider an applet that uses a method `square` (invoked from the applet's `paint` method) to calculate the squares of the integers from 1 to 10 as outlined in the following.

```
//    program SquareInt.java
//    a programmer defined square method
import  java.awt.Graphics;
import  java.applet.Applet;
public  class  SquareInt  extends  Applet
{
//  display the squared values of 1 through 10
   public  void  paint  ( Graphics  g )
   {
   int  xPosition  =  25;
   for (int  x = 1;  x <= 10;  x++)
      {
g.drawString( String.valueof( square( x ) ),  xPosition,  25 );
xPosition = xPosition + 20;
```

```
    }
}
    //  square method definition
    public  int  square( int  y )
       {
       return  y  *  y;
       }
    }
```

In this example, the method `square` is invoked or called in `paint` with the call

```
    square( x )
```

in which the `square` method receives a copy of the value of `x` in the parameter `y`. Then `square` calculates `y * y`. The result is passed back to the point in `paint` where `square` was invoked, and the result is displayed.

Essential Applet Methods

Because applets can be embedded in pages of HTML, there is a need for conventions to add applets in HTML files. In this sense, the applet class defines a set of methods that applets can override to allow code to be hosted in a browser. The core set of methods that control the life cycle of an applet is described briefly:

▶   **init( ):** This method is called by the Java system to initialize the applet each time that it is loaded or reloaded.

▶   **start( ):** The Java system calls this method when the applet is loaded and the applet can begin carrying out its main task.

▶   **stop( ):** When the user leaves the page or exits from the browser, the system will call this method. The applet should suspend any outstanding task.

▶   **destroy( ):** This method is the last chance that an applet will have to clean up the working environment before it is unloaded from the browser. All tasks should be stopped.

9.3.6   Inheritance

Whereas C++ classes can be defined to have no parent, that is not possible in Java. All Java classes must be subclasses of the root class, object, or some class that is a descendant of an object. One reason to have a single root class is that some operations are universally needed. Java directly supports only *single inheritance*, however, it includes a kind of virtual class, called an *interface*, which provides a version of multiple inheritance. An interface definition is similar to a class definition, except that it can contain only named constants and method declarations. So an interface defines only the specification of a class. Consider the following example, in which private data is used for the `Radius` to prevent users from modifying the `Radius` of a `Circle` object.

```
class  TestCircleWithConstructors
{
   public  static  void  main  (String{ }  args)
   {
   //  Test Circle with radius 5.0
   Circle  myCircle =  new  Circle(5.0);
   System.out.println(" The Area of Circle of Radius "
   +  myCircle.radius  +  "  is  "  +  myCircle.findArea( ) ) ;
   }
}
// declare class Circle with constructors and private data class Circle
class  Circle
{  private double  radius;
   public  Circle(double  r)
   {  radius  =  r;  }
   public  Circle( )
   {  radius  =  1.0;  }
   public double  findArea( )
   {  return   radius*radius*3.141159;  }
}
```

To demonstrate inheritance, the following example creates a new class for `Cylinder` from `Circle`. The `Cylinder` class inherits all the data and methods from the `Circle` class. In addition, the `Cylinder` class has a new data field `length` and a new method `findVolume( )`.

```
public  class  Cylinder  extends  Circle
{
   private  double  length;
   public  Cylinder( )
   {  super( );  length  =  1.0;  }
   public  Cylinder(double  r,  double  l)
   {  super(r);  length = 1;   }
   public  double  getLength( )
   {  return  length;  }
   public  double  findVolume( )
   {  return  findArea( ) * length;  }
}
```

The reserved word `extends` informs the compiler that the `Cylinder` class is derived from the `Circle` class, thus *inheriting data and methods* from `Circle`. The keyword `super` is used in the constructors, which refers to the superclass of the class in which `super` appears. This keyword can be used in two ways:

► To call a superclass constructor
► To call a superclass method

In general, the syntax to call a superclass constructor is as follows:

```
super(parameters);
```

Thus, in the `Cylinder` class, for example, `super( )` and `super(r)` are used to call the constructors from the `Circle` class to initialize the `Radius`. The component `super( )` must appear in the first line of the constructor and is the only way to invoke a superclass constructor. In Java terminology, the existing class is called the *superclass*. The class derived from the superclass is called the *subclass*. Sometimes a superclass is referred to as a *parent class* or a *base class*, and a subclass is referred to as a *child class*, an *extended class*, or a *derived class*. Contrary to conventional interpretation, a subclass is not a subset of its superclass. In fact, a subclass usually contains more functions and more detailed information than its superclass does.

The keyword *super* is used to reference superclasses. Occasionally, you need to reference the current class. Java provides another keyword, *this*, for referencing the current object. You can use *this* in the constructor. For example, you can redefine the `Circle` class as follows:

```
public  class  Circle
{  private double  radius;
   public  Circle(double  radius)
   {  this.radius  =  radius;  }
   public  Circle( )
   {  this(1.0);  }
   public double  findArea( )
   {  return  radius*radius*3.141159;  }
}
```

The line `this.radius = radius` assigns argument `radius` to the object data field `radius`. The line `this(1.0)` invokes the constructor with a double value argument in the class.

To sum up, occasionally it is necessary to derive a subclass from several classes, thus inheriting the data and methods from those classes. If you use the *extends* keyword to define a subclass, the subclass can have only one parent class. With interfaces, you can obtain the effect of multiple inheritance. An interface is treated like a special class in Java. Each interface is compiled into a separate bytecode file, just like a regular class. You cannot create an instance for the interface. In most cases, you can use an interface in a similar way as you use an abstract class. The syntax to declare an interface is as follows:

```
modifier   interface   InterfaceName
{   constants  declarations;
    methods  signatures;
}
```

For example, you can use an interface to define a generic `compare( )` method as follows:

```
public  interface  CompareObject
{   public  static  final  int  LESS  =  −1;
    public  static  final  int  EQUAL  =  0;
    public  static  final  int  GREATER  =  1
    public  int  compare(CompareObject  otherObject);
}
```

In this example, the `compare()` method determines the order of objects `x` and `y` of the `CompareObject` type. The method `x.compare(y)` returns a value of −1 if `x` is less than `y`; a value 0 if `x` is equal to `y`; or a value 1 if `x` is greater than `y`. Finally, two modifiers are used relative to class inheritance:

▶ The *final* modifier. If you want to prevent classes from being extended, you can use the *final* modifier to indicate that a class is final and cannot be a parent class. In addition, you can also define a method to be *final*, meaning that can no longer be modified by its subclasses.

▶ The *abstract* modifier. If you move from a subclass back up to a superclass, the classes become more general and less specific. When designing classes, a superclass should have common features that are shared by subclasses. Sometimes the superclass is so abstract that it cannot have any specific instances. These classes are called *abstract* classes and are declared using the *abstract* modifier. In general, *abstract* classes are like regular classes with data and methods, but you cannot create instances of abstract classes using the *new* operator. Abstract classes usually contain *abstract methods*. An *abstract method* is a method signature without implementation. Its implementation is provided by its subclasses. For example, you can design an abstract class for all geometric objects as follows:

```
public   abstract   class GeometricObject
{   private   String   color;
    private   double   weight;
    public GeometricObject (String c,   double   w)
    {   color   =   c;   weight   =   w;   }
    public GeometricObject ( )
    {   color   =   " white ";   weight   =   1.0;   }
    public String   getColor( )
    {   return   color;   }
    public double   getWeight( )
    {   return   weight;   }
public   abstract   double   findArea( );
public   abstract   double   findCircumference( );
}
```

In other words, this abstract class provides the common features (data and methods) for geometric objects. Because you do not know how to compute areas and volumes of geometric objects, `findArea( )` and `findCircumference( )` are defined as abstract methods. Use abstract classes to generalize common properties and methods of subclasses, and use abstract methods to define the common methods that must be implemented in subclasses.

9.3.7 Encapsulation

One step beyond abstraction is the recognition that, equally as important as data, are the operations that are performed on it. Encapsulation simply says that there should be a way to associate the two (data and operations) closely together and treat them as a single unit of organization. In language terms, data and related functions should be bundled together somehow, so you can say, "this is how we represent an object, and these are the only operations that can be done on object." In other words, an object has properties and behaviors that are encapsulated inside the object. The services the object offers to its clients constitute its operations. Only the operations defined by the object are available to the clients. In this regard, the implementation of its properties and behavior is not a concern of the clients. Encapsulation helps clarify the distinction between an object's operation and implementation. This has major consequences for program development. The implementation of an object can change without implications for the clients. Encapsulation also reduces complexity, as the internal operations of an object are hidden from the clients, who cannot influence its implementation. Because of encapsulation, the code you write tends to be modular. As a general rule, programs should be organized into discrete groups so that information is shared on a need-to-know basis. The following example shows how such a structure might look in Java:

```java
public    class    LineOfText
{
   // return the length of the line
   public    int    getLength( )
   {
   return length;
   }
   // return the current index
   public    int    getCurrentIndex( )
   {
   return index;
   }
   // advance the index by 1 if it is not already at the end
   public    void    forwardCharacter( )
   {
   if  (index  < length - 1)
      {
      index ++;
      }
   }
private   int   length;
private   int   index;
private   String   buffer;
```

The important point to make about this example is that the `LineOfText` object has *length, index,* and *buffer* fields that are not exposed to any piece of code outside of this particular class. These fields are private and are so specified by use of the *private* keyword. Only the `getLength( )`, `getCurrentIndex( )`, and `forwardCharacter( )` methods in the object are visible to other parts of the program that use this class. Java provides two kinds of encapsulation constructs:

▶ Classes that are *physical encapsulation* and follow the same notation as C++.

▶ Packages that are *logical encapsulation* and follow the notion of packages.
   In this case, any class definition can specify that it belongs to a particular

package. A class that does not specify a package name would be placed in an unnamed package.

In general, in Java, any method or variable that does not include an access modifier (public, private or protected) has what is called *package scope*. All methods and variables that are not declared private are visible throughout the package in which they are defined. This is an expansion of the definition of protected members used in C++, which are visible only in the class where they are defined and in subclasses of that class. In other words, package scope provides the opportunity to access private methods and instance variables in a class to other specified methods or classes.

9.3.8 Multithreading

A *thread* is a flow of execution of a task in a program, which has a beginning and an end. Java is a multithreaded programming language, meaning that it can launch multiple threads from a program concurrently. For example, downloading a video file while playing the video would be considered multithreading. Multithread programming is integrated in Java. In other languages, you have to call operating system-specific procedures to enable multithreading. These threads can be carried out simultaneously in multiprocessor and single-processor systems. In a single-processor system, the multiple threads share the CPU time, and the operating system is responsible for scheduling and allocating resources to the threads. Multithreading can make your program more efficient and enhance performance. In some cases, multithreaded programs run faster than single-threaded programs even on a single-processor system. Multithreading is useful for animation in Java, which is designed to make computer animation easy. Multithreading is necessary for visual and network programming. Java provides good support for programming with multiple threads of execution, including built-in support for creating threads and for locking resources to prevent conflicts. You can create threads by introducing the *Thread* class or implementing the Runnable interface. Both *Thread* and *Runnable* are defined in the java.lang package. The *Thread* class contains the constructor `thread( )`, as well as many useful methods to run, start, suspend, resume, interrupt, and stop threads. To create and run a thread, first define a class that extends the *Thread* class. Your thread class must override the `run( )` method, which tells the system how the thread will be executed when it is invoked. You then need a client class that creates an object running on the thread. This object is referred to as a *runnable object*. Figure 9.7 illustrates the structure of a thread class and its client class.

The constructor and several methods in the Thread class are described in the following:

public Thread( )	This constructs a new thread. It is called from the client class to create a runnable object.
public void run( )	This method is invoked by the run-time system to run the thread.
public void start( )	This method starts the thread, which causes the `run( )` method to be invoked. This method is called by the runnable object in the client class.

FIGURE **9.7**   Creation of a thread as a subclass of the Thread class

```
// User defined Thread class        // Client class
class UserThread extends Thread     public class Client
{                                   {
...                                 ...
public UserThread()                 main()
      {                                   {
      ...                           UserThread ut=new UserThread();
      }                                 ...
...                                     ...
public void run()                   ut.start();
      {                                 ...
      ...                               ...
      }                                     }
}                                   }
```

public void stop( )	This method stops the thread.
public void suspend( )	This method suspends the thread.
public void resume( )	This method resumes a suspended thread.
public void interrupt( )	This method interrupts the running thread.
public boolean isAlive( )	This method tests to see whether the thread is currently running.
public static boolean interrupted( )	This method tests to see whether the current thread has been interrupted.
public static void sleep(long millis) throws Interrupted Exception	This method puts the runnable object to sleep for a specified time in milliseconds.
public void setPriority(int p)	This method sets priority p (ranging from 1 to p) for this thread.

Example: Use the Thread Class to create and launch Threads. The following program creates and runs three threads:

▶   The first thread prints the letter **x** 20 times.

▶   The second thread prints the letter **y** 20 times.

▶   The third thread prints the integers 1 through 20.

This program has three independent tasks. To run them concurrently, the program needs to create a runnable object for each task. Because the first two threads function similarly, they can be defined in one thread class, as shown in the following program:

```
class    TestThreads
   {
   public static  void  main  (String[ ]  args)
      {  // declare and create threads
      PrintChar  printX = new  PrintChar ('x', 20);
      PrintChar  printY = new  PrintChar ('y', 20);
      PrintNum print20 = new PrintNum(20);
   // start threads
   print20.start( );
   printX.start( );
   printY.start( );
      }
   }
//  the thread class for printing a specified character in specified times
class    PrintChar extends Thread
   {
   private char charToPrint;     // the character to print
   private int times;        // the times to repeat
   // the thread class constructor
   public PrintChar (char c, int t)
      {   charToPrint = c;
          times = t;
      }
   // override the run( ) method to tell the system what the thread will do
   public void run( )
      {
      for (int i=1;  i < times; i++)
         System.out.print(charToPrint);
      }
   }
//  the thread class for printing number from 1 to n for a given n
class    PrintNum extends Thread
   {
   private int lastNum;
   public PrintNum (int i)
      {   lastNum = i;    }
   public void run( )
      {
      for (int i=1;  i < lastNum; i++)
         System.out.print(" "  +i);
      }
   }
```

If you run this program on a multiple CPU system, all three threads will be running simultaneously. If you run this program on a single CPU system, all three threads will share the CPU because they take turns printing letters and numbers on the screen. A typical output of the program execution would look like this:

```
>java TestThreads
 1yyyyyxxxxxxxxxx 2 3 4 5 6 7 8 9 10yyyyyyyyyyyxxxxx
11 12 13 14 15xxxxxyyyyy 16 17 18 19 20
>
```

In this example, the program creates threads classes by extending the `Thread` class. The `PrintChar` class, derived from the `Thread` class, overrides the `run( )` method with the print character action. This class provides a framework for printing any single character a given number of times. The runnable objects `printX` and `printY` are instances of the user-defined thread class `PrintChar`. The `PrintNum` class overrides the `run( )` method with the print number action. This class provides a framework for printing numbers from 1 to n, for any integer n. The runnable object `print20` is an instance of the user-defined thread class `PrintNum`. In the client program, the program creates a thread, `printX`, for printing the letter x, and a thread, `printY`, for printing the letter y. Both are objects of the `PrintChar` class. The `print20` thread object is created from the `PrintNum` class. Finally, the `start( )` method is invoked to start the threads, which causes the `run( )` method to run. When the `run( )` method completes, the threads terminate.

Resource Locking

The most complicated area of programming with threads arises when multiple threads must access a shared resource. The problems that arise can be surprisingly subtle. Consider the following example:

```
public    class    BrokenThreadExample
   {
   public    int    nextCounter( )
      {
      return    counter++;
      }
   private    int    counter = 0;
   }
```

You might think we could use it to supply an increasing counter to multiple threads. Unfortunately, it's broken. The problem can be hard to see because many programmers tend to think of the built-in operations (i.e., ++) in a language like Java as atomic units. Instead, the line

```
return    counter++;
```

is actually a compound operation. The current value of the `counter` is read, it is incremented by one, and the value is written back. What happens if another thread writes its value back between the read and the write? Here's a scenario that illustrates the problem:

Thread 1 reads *counter* and finds the value 0.

Thread 2 reads *counter* and finds the value 0.

Thread 1 adds one and writes 1 into *counter*.

Thread 2 adds one and writes 1 into *counter*.

Now, the `counter` value is set to 1, even though both threads incremented it. To avoid this problem, we *lock* a resource while a thread is accessing it. In Java, locking resources is extremely simple. Each object in Java has a lock associated with it. A method that uses the *synchronized* modifier automatically acquires the lock on its instance before proceeding. If the instance's lock is already held by another thread, the method remains blocked until it can obtain the lock. So all that is needed to fix our example is to add *synchronized* to the `nextCounter( )` method, as illustrated in the following:

```
public    class    FixedThreadExample
   {
   public    synchronized    int    nextCounter( )
     {
     return    counter++;
     }
   private     int    counter = 0;
   }
```

Now, before Thread 1 reads the `counter`, it acquires the lock on the shared `FixedThreadExample` instance. It reads `counter`, increments it, and writes it back. Any other threads waiting to access the shared `FixedThreadExample` wait their turn.

◢ 9.4 DIFFERENCES BETWEEN JAVA AND C++

We can summarize the differences between Java and C++ regarding supported features. Some of the features supported by one language are provided in some other form by another language. In general, C++ and Java are two popular and powerful object-oriented programming languages adopted for system programming and application programming. Java does not support the following:

▶ Preprocessors that are capable of macro definitions.

▶ Conditional compilation, including `#ifdef` and `#endif`, because it is platform independent.

▶ Inclusion of names files such as `#include <file-name.h>`. Named files are imported into a class.

▶ Global variables, but it supports a class-side static variable that persists through various instances of a class. Constants are created by declaring a variable to be *static final* and then assigning it a value.

▶ Macro facility, which was thought unnecessary by its designers

▶ `&`, `*`, or `sizeof` because the pointer type is not adopted in the language

▶ Multiple inheritance

▶ Templates to implement polymorphism

▶ Explicit deallocation operator

▶ User overloading of operators

TABLE **9.6**	Operators supported by Java	
	Operator	**Explanation**
	+	string concatenation
	x instanceof C	returns True if object x is an instance of class C
	>>>	right shift with 0 for the sign extension
	&	bitwise AND for integers, AND for Boolean types
	|	bitwise OR for integers, OR for Boolean types
	&&	shortcut AND
	||	shortcut OR

However, Java supports the following:

▶ Manipulation of objects by reference, in contrast to C++ where objects are manipulated by value.

▶ Byte data type.

▶ A kind of virtual class, called an *interface,* that provides a version of multiple inheritance.

▶ Explicit dynamic new operator for object creation.

▶ Final modifier to prevent classes from being extended.

▶ Abstract modifier so instances of class are not created using the *new* operator.

▶ Package scope (an alternative to friends in C++) to provide access to private methods and instance variables in a class to other specified methods or classes.

▶ Method overloading, that is, two methods have the same name, but have different parameter profiles.

▶ Dynamic binding as the normal approach to bind method calls to method definition.

▶ New operators shown in Table 9.6.

SUMMARY

Smalltalk, as a pioneer object-oriented programming language, was designed to be a self-contained interactive programming language, in which programs would be characterized by a high degree of modularity and dynamic extensibility. In this chapter, we outlined the Smalltalk-80 program structure along with important features of the language, such as objects, messages, and methods, including unary, binary, and keyword messages, control structures, classes, and inheritance. In particular, we discussed the implementation of a class, which consists of class name, class variable, class method, and instance variable.

C++, an extension of C, was the second object-oriented programming language that we discussed in this chapter. C++ was a hybrid language, meaning that it was possible to program in a C-like style, an object-oriented style, or both. The C++ program consists of pieces called classes and functions. We discussed the program structure along with important features of the language from two points of view: object and class declaration including public, private, and protected members, and object and class implementation including accessing members of class. In addition, we discussed the important features of the C++ language, such as friend class and function, inheritance, and polymorphism to address the issue of design in this popular language.

The Java programming language, which originated at Sun Microsystems, is similar to C and C++. Java is a programming language with characteristics, such as simple, general-purpose, object-oriented, distributed, interpreted, robust, secure, portable, multithreaded, and dynamic. In this chapter, we discussed the Java program structure consisting of the Java system and Java API package. We discussed Java program modules including static, public, protected, and private members, building an applet, and essential applet methods that address common mathematical calculations, string manipulations, character manipulations, input and output operations, error checking, and many other useful operations. Java directly supports only single inheritance, however, it adopted a kind of virtual class, called an interface, which provided a version of multiple inheritance. An interface definition is similar to a class definition, except that it contains only named constants and method declarations. Java provides two kinds of encapsulation constructs: physical encapsulation and logical encapsulation. We discussed the inheritance and encapsulation as adopted in Java. We briefly discussed an important feature provided in Java, multithreading, which was designed to make computer animation easy. We briefly, discussed this important feature of Java. Finally, we outlined the differences between Java and C++ features supported by each programming language.

EXERCISES

1. Fill in the blanks in each of the following in C++ language:

   a. Suppose a and b are integer variables and we form the sum a+b. Now suppose c and d are floating-point variables and we form the sum c+d. The two operators are being used for different purposes. This is an example of _____.

   b. The keyword _____ introduces an overloaded operator function definition.

   c. To use operators on class objects, they must be overloaded, with the exception of the operators _____ and _____.

   d. The _____ and _____ of an operator cannot be changed by overloading the operator.

2. Fill in the blanks in each of the following in C++ language:

    a. _____ syntax is used to initialize constant members of a class.

    b. A nonmember function must be declared as a _____ of a class to have access to that class private data members.

    c. The _____ operator dynamically allocates memory for an object of a specified type and returns a _____ to that type.

    d. A constant object must be _____; it cannot be modified after it is created.

    e. A _____ data member represents classwide information.

    f. An object's member function maintains a pointer to the object called the _____ pointer.

    g. The keyword _____ specifies that an object or variable cannot be modified after it is initialized.

    h. If a member initializer is not provided for a member object of a class, the object's _____ is called.

    i. A member function can be declared *static* if it does not access the _____ class members.

    j. Friend functions can access the _____ and _____ members of a class.

    k. Member objects are constructed _____ there enclosing class object.

    l. The _____ operator reclaims memory previously allocated by *new* operator.

3. Fill in the blanks in each of the following in C++ language:

    a. The keyword _____ introduces a structure definition.

    b. Class members are accessed via the _____ operator in conjunction with an object of the class or via the _____ operator in conjunction with a pointer to an object of the class.

    c. Members of a class specified as _____ are accessible only to member functions of the class and friends of the class.

    d. A _____ is a special member function used to initialize the data members of a class.

    e. The default access for members of a class is _____.

    f. A _____ function is used to assign values to private data members of a class.

    g. _____ can be used to assign an object of a class to another object of the same class.

    h. Member functions of a class are normally made _____ and data members of a class are normally made _____.

    i. A _____ function is used to retrieve values of private data of a class.

    j. The set of public member functions of a class is referred to as the class's _____.

    k. A class implementation is said to be hidden from its clients or _____.

    l. The keywords _____ and _____ can be used to introduce a class definition.

    m. Members of a class specified as _____ are accessible anywhere an object of the class is in scope.

4. Fill in the blanks in each of the following in Java language.

    a. If the class Alpha inherits from the class Beta, class Alpha is called the _____ class and class Beta is called the _____ class.

    b. An object of a _____ class can be treated as an object of its corresponding _____ class.

    c. The four member access specifiers are _____, _____, _____, and _____.

    d. Using polymorphism helps eliminate _____ logic.

    e. If a class contains one or more abstract methods, it is an _____ class.

    f. A method call resolved at compile time is referred to as _____ binding, whereas at run time, it is referred to as _____ binding.

    g. A subclass may call any method of its superclass by attaching _____ to the method call.

    h. Class _____ provides methods for drawing.

    i. Java applets begin execution with a series of three method calls: _____, _____, and _____.

    j. Methods _____ and _____ display lines and rectangles.

    k. Keyword _____ is used to indicate that a new class is a subclass of an existing class.

5. Find the errors in each of the following and explain how to correct them.

    a. Assume the following prototype is declared in class `Time`:

```
void   ~Time(int);
```

    b. The following is a partial definition of class `Time`:

```
class   Time   {
public:
   // Function Prototype
private:
   int   hour = 0;
   int   minute = 0;
   int   second = 0;
};
```

    c. Assume the following prototype is declared in class `Employee`:

```
int   Employee (const  char  *,  const  char  *);
```

6. Name eight primitive data types in Java.

7. In Smalltalk, everything is an object. What is the advantage of this design?

8. In Smalltalk, there are three formats for messages. Discuss the three formats.

9. Write a program in Java to demonstrate a producer and a consumer accessing a single shared data of memory using threads without any synchronization mechanism. Explain the result of this program.

10. Write a program in Java to demonstrate a producer and a consumer accessing a single shared data of memory using threads with synchronization mechanism. Explain the result of the execution of this program.

11. When an object is implemented in Smalltalk, we may include commands that automatically initialize the object. What are the advantages and disadvantages of automatic initialization of an object? What is the alternative of this implementation?

12. In C++, we can initialize values in one *module* using values from another *module,* even if these values are in different files. Illustrate this situation in C++.

13. Discuss the class definition in Smalltalk.

14. Write a C++ program to add two integer numbers.

15. Write a C++ program to find the two solutions for the quadratic equation $AX^2 + BX + C = 0$.

16. Express each of the following properties. A *relation* $R \in X \Leftrightarrow X$ is said to be:
   a. Reflexive
   b. Irreflexive
   c. Symmetric
   d. Asymmetric
   e. Antisymmetric
   f. Transitive

17. Consider the following pseudocode statements.

> *if student's grade is greater than or equal to 90*
>   *print "A"*
> *else   if student's grade is greater than or equal to 80*
>   *print "B"*
>   *else   if student's grade is greater than or equal to 70*
>   *print "C"*
>   *else   if student's grade is greater than or equal to 60*
>   *print "D"*
>   *else   print "F"*

   a. Rewrite this pseudocode in C++.
   b. Rewrite this pseudocode in Java.

18. Consider a second-degree polynomial as: Y=A*X*X+B*X+C. Suppose variables A, B, C, and X are initialized as: A=2, B=3, C=7, and X=5. Illustrate the order in which the operators are applied in the second-degree polynomial.

19. C++ follows an *operator precedence*, which determines the order of evaluating operations, so an expression can be evaluated precisely in one way. What is the evaluated value of the following expressions?

   a. $8 - 3 + 100 / (34 - 2 * (5 + 2))$

   b. $(9 + 8) * 7 - (12 / 3.5 + 5 * 3 - 2)$

   c. $2 * 5 + 6 - 4 + 8 / 2 * 4 + 9$

20. By an example, demonstrate the use of *break* statement in a `for` structure in C++.

21. By an example, demonstrate the use of *continue* statement in a `for` structure in C++.

22. What is a friend function in C++?

23. How is the type system of Java different from that of C++?

24. Explain the difference between the two uses of *private* in C++.

25. Write the following C `while` loop structure in Smalltalk.

```
while  (count  < 10)  {
   sum  /=  (2  *  count  -  1);
   count ++;
   }
```

26. Write C++ statements to accomplish each of the following:

   a. Assign the sum of x and y to z and increment the value of x by 1 after the calculation.

   b. Test if the value of the variable count is greater than 10. If it is, print "Count is greater than 10".

   c. Decrease the variable x by 1, then subtract it from the variable total.

   d. Calculate the remainder after q is divided by divisor and assign the result to q. Write this statement in two different ways.

27. Write simple C++ statements that accomplish the following:

   a. Input integer variable x with cin and >>.

   b. Input integer variable y with cin and >>.

   c. Initialize integer variable i to 1.

   d. Initialize integer variable power to 1.

   e. Multiply variable power by x and assign the result to power.

   f. Increment variable y by 1.

   g. Test y to see if it is less than or equal to x.

   h. Output integer variable power with cout and <<.

28. Write a C++ program that computes the volume of a *triangular prism* using the formula: (1/2)*B*H*W.

29. Assume that a class of ten students takes a test and the grades for this test are available, meaning that we can accept the grades from the keyboard. Write a C++ program to determine the class average on the test.

30. Write a set of C++ statements to accomplish each of the following:

a. Sum the odd integers between 1 and 99 using a `for` structure. Assume that the integer variables `sum` and `count` have been declared.

b. Print the value 333.546372 in a field width of 15 characters with precision of 1, 2, and 3. Print each number on the same line. Left justify each number in its field. What three values print?

c. Calculate the value of 2.5 raised to the power of 3 using the *pow* function in C++. Print the result with a precision of 2 in a field width of 10 positions. What prints?

d. Print the integers from 1 to 20 using a `while` loop and the counter variable x. Assume that the variable x has been declared, but not initialized. Print only 5 integers per line.

31. Write a program to implement the following.

a. Define a Smalltalk definition of the object class *point*, in which each point is represented by its x and y coordinates.

b. Define object classes for straight *lines*, and *rectangles*, placing them in an appropriate hierarchy. Each of these classes must provide an operation named *draw*.

c. Define an object class *picture*, where each object is a set of geometric objects. Include an operation that draws the whole picture, by drawing all its component objects.

32. Write a Java statement to accomplish each of the following tasks:

a. Declare variables `Sum` and `x` to be of type int.

b. Assign 1 to variable `x`.

c. Assign 0 to variable `Sum`.

d. Add variable `x` to variable `Sum` and assign the result to variable `Sum`.

e. Print "The Sum is :" followed by the value of variable `Sum`.

33. Combine the statements of the previous exercise into a Java program that calculates and prints the sum of the integers from 1 to 10. Use the `while` structure to loop through the calculation and increment statements.

34. Two reserved words in Java have special meaning in constructors: *super* and *this*. You can use *super* to explicitly call a constructor from the superclass of the current class, and you can use *this* to call a constructor already defined within the same class.

a. In an example, use *super* to call the constructor of the superclass.

b. In an example, use *this* to call other constructors in the same class.

35. Write a program in Java to demonstrate inheritance as the following.

    a. Define a class Point in which Point's instance variables are protected.

    b. Define a class Circle that is derived from class Point.

    c. Define a class Cylinder that is derived from class Circle.

36. Write Java statements to accomplish each of the following:

    a. Create an array of ten *null* object references.

    b. Create a two-dimensional array of *null* references to *String* arrays.

37. Write two Max methods in the same class with different types of parameters; one for finding maximum integers and the other for finding maximum doubles.

38. Write a program in Java that displays the calendar for a given month of the year. Have the program prompt the user to enter the year and the month and then display the entire calendar for the month.

39. Write a recursive method for computing a Fibonacci number `Fib(N)`, given an index N. The program should prompt the user to enter the index N, then call the method and display the result.

40. Identify and correct the errors in each of the following Java fragments:

    ```
    a. while      (C <= 5)        {
       product  *=  C;
       ++C;
    ```

    ```
    b. if (gender  == 1)
           System.out.println("Woman");
       else;
           System.out.println("Man");
    ```

41. Write a program in C++ to demonstrate the use of the SWAP function template in which the value of two variables of type character, integer and float, are changed.

REFERENCE-NEEDED EXERCISES

To answer the following exercises, you might need to consult the references: Deitel and Deitel, 1994; Knuth, 1997; MacLennan, 1999; Meyer, 1988, 1991; Skublics, Klimas, and Thomas, 1996; Stansifer, 1995; Taylor, 1997; Watt, 1990.

1. Describe l-valued expressions, and define a function in C++ that returns an l-value in which the type of return value is integer.

2. A class that extends another class is guaranteed to support the contracts entered into by its superclass. In Java, however, the extension mechanism alone does not provide the ability to enter into multiple contracts (Java is a single inheritance language, and *interfaces* are used to approximate multiple inheritance). In an example, demonstrate that we can't extend more than one superclass without using *interface*.

3. In an example in Java, demonstrate that we can extend more than one superclass. Note that, by using interface, we can achieve what we are trying to accomplish.

4. As you can pass the value of variables to methods, you can also pass objects to methods as actual parameters. Write a program in Java to pass a `Circle` object to the method `ColorCircle` that changes the Color of the `Circle` object.

5. Suppose we are working with records in a set of files and we want to look up an entry in one of the files. Table names are associated with particular file names based on context. Errors are displayed to the user in the top level loop of the user interface as shown in the following C code.

```
/*Look up the entry for "Maryam" in the "employee" table.*/
/*On failure, "error" will be filled with a structure containing details*/
ErrorStruct *error = NULL;
TableEntry *entry = lookup("Maryam", "employee", &error);
if (entry == NULL)
   {
   return error;
   }
```

Rewrite this code in Java language to handle the exception.

6. Pointer semantics and storage semantics appear unexpectedly in programming languages. Both are used in the assignment to reference in C++. Elaborate the following example with regard to variables i, j, and r.

```
void   change()   {
    int  i=1;  j=2;
    int&  r=i;
r=j;
    }
```

7. For the following Java program, state the scope of each of the following elements.

a. The variable x.

b. The variable y.

c. The method cube.

d. The method paint.

e. The variable pos.

```
public  class  CubeTest  extends  Applet  {
   int  x;
   public  void  paint  (Graphics  g)   {
      int  pos  = 25;
      for  (x = 1;  x <= 10;  x++)   {
      g.drawString(cube(x),  25,  pos);
      pos  += 15;
      }  }
   public  int  cube(int  y)
```

```
        {
            return  y * y * y;
        }
    }
```

8. The language C++ has implicit type *coercions*. In C++, all coercions are for user-defined types. Define a class to illustrate coercions in C++.

9. Write a producer and a consumer program accessing a shared array of five elements with synchronization so that the producer only produces a value when there are one or more available elements in the array, and the consumer only consumes a value when there are one or more values in the array.

10. How can you implement concurrent programming in Smalltalk?

11. Write a program in C++ to demonstrate that function templates may be overloaded. For example, consider two overloaded versions of the same function, in which the first version accepts two arguments, and the second version accepts three arguments with the sum of the arguments as the return value.

12. Write a program in C++ to demonstrate the `max_element` and `min_element` algorithms available in the Standard Template Library. For example, find the largest and smallest value in a vector.

Declarative Programming Specifications

In procedural languages, computations are driven by the instructions. Declarative languages are a class of languages for which the execution order of subproblems is not specified. A more precise statement is that declarative programming languages are based on an abstract formalism in which no implicit state can be modified by constructs in the language. Operationally, declarative programs can be viewed as an abstract computational model, like the Turing machine, the *lambda calculus,* and the *random access machine.* A computation in this model is a goal-driven deduction from the statements of the program. The computation is nondeterministic, meaning that for each state of the computation, there may be several possible transitions, like the search models. One example of declarative programming languages is *logic languages,* whose model of computation is based on *relations.* Logic programming is an ancient and honorable branch of mathematics whose practical importance is that it represents a formalized method of reasoning that is a combination of inferences and deductions.

Logic programming languages specify the problem in a declarative fashion; meaning that they describe what the goal is and the underlying implementation search for a proof of the goal can be conducted by the control system. This indicates that the programmer needs to be concerned about the logic representation itself and can discard the control system; meaning that the rules of inference to derive the goal from the set of logical statements is not expressed in the language and is assumed to occur automatically. In other words, programs written in logic models express a goal and the facts and rules from which this goal is to be deduced, but do not express the method by which this deduction can take place. Many programmers found out that the task of writing a logic program was not like specifying an algorithm in the same way as in a conventional programming language. Instead, the logic language programmer asks more what formal relationships and objects occur in a problem, and what relationships are true about the desired solution. So, logic programming language can be viewed as a *descriptive* language as well as a *prescriptive* one. In other

337

words, the logic programming language approach is to describe known facts and relationships about a problem, rather than to prescribe the sequence of steps taken by a computer to solve the problem. For example, when a program is written in logic language, the actual way the computer carries out the computation is specified partly by the logical declarative semantics of the language, partly by what new axioms can be invoked from the existing ones, and only partly by explicit control information supplied by the programmer. One popular application of the logic programming is the query language of relational database management systems. The fundamental entity of a relational database management system is the relation, which can be viewed as a table of rows and columns, where each row, called a tuple, represents an object and each column, known as an attribute, represents a property associated with the object. A database consists of one or more relations. Data from the tables can be manipulated using commands written in a query language that adheres to the logic programming language model.

In this chapter, we outline the components of first-order predicate calculus including constants, logical statements, variables, functions, connectors, quantifiers, punctuations, and precedence. Resolution and unification are the two primary operations used by inference rules to derive new facts. The resolution is a sequence of steps that the deduction system uses to derive a goal and is known as the control strategy for the logic programming system. Unification is a process of pattern matching to make terms identical so they can be discarded from both sides of the logical statements. In this chapter, we explore resolution and unification and search structures with several examples. In addition, we briefly discuss the application of logic programming, such as production systems and reasoning systems.

✔ 10.1 Logic Programming Language Model

Logic programming refers to a paradigm that uses a form of symbolic logic as a programming language. Imperative and functional programming are essentially about implementing mappings. Having implemented a mapping M, we can make requests like the following:

```
Given A, determine the value of M(A).
```

A request like this will always have a single answer. Logic programming is based on the notion that a program implements a relation rather than a mapping. Consider two sets of values, S and T. R is a *relation* between S and T if, for every $x \in S$ and $y \in T$, $R(x, y)$ is either true or false. If $R(x, y)$ is true, we say that R holds between x and y. for example, ">" is a relation between numbers, since for any pair of numbers x and y, x>y is either true or false. By convention, we write x>y rather than >(x,y). Logic programming is about implementing relations. Having implemented a relation R, we can make requests like the following:

1. Given A and B, determine whether R(A,B) is true.
2. Given A, find all B such that R(A,B) is true.

3. Given B, find all A such that R(A,B) is true.

4. Find all A and B such that R(A,B) is true.

A request like (1) will have a single answer, yes or no, but a request like (2), (3), or (4) might have many answers or none. Requests like (2), (3), and (4) are characteristics of logic programming, and explain why it is potentially higher level than imperative or functional programming. For simplicity, the previous discussion concentrated on binary relations, relations between pairs of values. We can also talk about *unary relations,* written `R(x)`, *ternary relations,* written `R(x, y, z)`, and so on. Symbolic logic can be used as the basis for formal logic as follows:

▶ Express propositions that are assumed to be true

▶ Express relationships between propositions

▶ Deduce new propositions from the existing ones

Kowalski (1979) introduced the property of logic programming model as

```
{Logic Program} = {Logic Statements} + {Control Strategy}
```

where `Logic Statements` consists of a set of *rules* and *facts* expressing the relationships between objects. `Control Strategy` is known as *resolution* or the *sequence of steps* the deduction system chooses to answer a question from the logic system. In other words, it refers to how a logic language computes a response to a question. This indicates that the original set of logic statements represents the knowledge base of the computation, and the deductive system provides the control mechanism by which a new logic statement might be derived. This property indicates that in the logic programming system a programmer needs to be concerned about the logic system, but the control system can be ignored from the consideration.

The form of logic used in logic programming languages is the *first-order predicate calculus,* which is a paradigm of formally expressing logical statements. A logical statement is a statement that is either true or false. First-order predicate calculus can be classified as the following:

▶ **Constant:** A symbol that represents an object, such as names and numbers, is also known as *atoms* because it can not be broken down into subobjects.

▶ **Logical Statement:** An unconditional term, sometimes called a *fact,* that represents relations between objects and asserts that something is a quality, attribute, or property of something else. For example, suppose that we want to express a logical statement (a fact) that Fred likes Elizabeth. This can be converted to

```
Likes(Fred, Elizabeth)
```

In general, a relation that we would say in English as *Subject–Verb–Object* can be converted into a logical statement as: *Verb(Subject, Object),* or more generally as

```
Relationship(Object₁, Object₂)
```

The relationship is called a *predicate* and the objects that are related are called *arguments* or *parameters.* Not all facts are relationships between two objects. When we express a fact such as Fred is man, which does not have the standard

Subject–Verb–Object form, it can be represented as Man(Fred). In English, a statement that is conditional (rather than an unconditional fact) can be stated as *something is true if some condition holds*. A logical statement corresponding to a conditional statement sometimes called a *rule* has the following form:

```
some-condition-holds  ⇒  something-is-true
```

For instance, to state that Michael is prepared to work for a company only if the company is big, we would define a rule as

```
Big(Company)  ⇒  Work(Michael, Company)
```

▶ **Variable:** A symbol that represents an unspecified object, meaning that it can represent different objects at different times of the computation logic. For example,

```
integer(X)
```

means that there is an object that contains an integer number.

▶ **Function:** A term that represents a predefined computation. A function can be used to express the derivation of another predicate. For example,

```
integer(X)  ⇒  integer(successor(X))
```

means that if x is an integer number, then so is the successor of x, which is calculated by the *successor* function.

▶ **Connector:** A symbol that connects two or more terms (literals). In Table 10.1, the names, symbols, examples and the meanings associated with the logical connectives of the predicate calculus are outlined.

▶ **Quantifier:** A symbol that introduces variables such as ∀ is called *for all* and is known as a *universal quantifier,* and ∃ is called *there exists* and is known as an *existential quantifier.* For example,

```
∀ X   (man(X) ⇒ human(X))
```

means that *for all* x such that x is a man, then x is a human. And

```
∃ X   (human(X) ⇒ man(X))
```

means that *there exists* an x such that if x is a human then x is a man. Because the scope of the quantifiers is the variables to which they are attached, we can use the parentheses to extend the scope of the universal and existential quantifiers.

▶ **Punctuation:** A symbol that is used in the structure of predicates and logic statements, such as left and right parentheses, comma, and the period.

▶ **Precedence:** Evaluation of operators in a precise sequence determined by the *rules of operator precedence* as outlined in Table 10.2 from high to low level of priority.

In first-order predicate calculus, arguments to predicates and functions are called *terms,* where a term is a combination of variables, constants, and functions. A term cannot contain predicates, quantifiers, or connectives. For example, the following are logical statements:

TABLE **10.1**   **Logical connective symbols**

name	symbol	example	meaning
conjunction	∩	x ∩ y	x and y
disjunction	∪	x ∪ y	x or y
equivalence	≡	x ≡ y	x is equivalent to y
right implication	⇒	x ⇒ y	x implies y
left implication	⇐	x ⇐ y	y implies x
right-left implication	⇔	x ⇔ y	x implies y and y implies x
negation	¬	¬x	negation of x

TABLE **10.2**   **Rules of operator precedence**

operator	operation	order of evaluation (precedence)
∀	universal quantifier	from left to right
∃	existential quantifier	
¬	negation	from left to right
∩	conjunction	from left to right
∪	disjunction	
≡	equivalence	
⇒	right implication	from left to right
⇐	left implication	
⇔	right-left implication	

Fred likes Elizabeth.

A human has two arms.

Mammals have four legs.

Conversion of these logical statements to first-order predicate calculus can take the following forms:

```
likes(Fred, Elizabeth)
arms(human, 2)
∀ X, mammals(X) ⇒ legs(X, 4)
```

The constants are the integers 2 and 4, and the names *Fred*, *Elizabeth*, and *human*. The predicates are *likes*, *arms*, *mammals*, and *legs*. The only variable is X with no function defined in this example. As in the example, we might consider the logical statements to be axioms, meaning that statements define true relationships between objects.

◣ 10.2 LOGICAL STATEMENTS

We define a logical statement to be of the form

$$(Q_1 \text{ or } Q_2 \text{ or } \ldots \text{ or } Q_k) \Rightarrow (P_1 \text{ and } P_2 \text{ and } \ldots \text{ and } P_n)$$

where the P's and Q's are predicates, also known as *literals* or *terms*. The arrow pointing to the right is to be understood as meaning "implies or drives," and the logic statement is to be understood as meaning that Q_1, **or** Q_2, and so on, imply P_1, **and** P_2, and so on. All primitives of first-order predicate calculus such as quantifiers, objects, and variables can be put into the logic form. A restricted kind of logical statement is known as the Horn clause. Horn clauses are named after Alfred Horn (1951) who studied logic statements in this form. Horn clauses can be divided into two forms:

1. **Headed Horn clause:** if the left-hand side is a single term, such as

   ```
   mammals(human)  ⇒  legs(human, 2)
   ```

2. **Headless Horn clause:** if the left-hand side is empty, such as

   ```
   arms(human, 2)
   ```

Therefore, for the general form of a Horn clause such as

$$Q \Rightarrow (P_1 \text{ and } P_2 \text{ and } \ldots \text{ and } P_n)$$

means that, Q is true if all the P's are true. Q is called the head of the clause (only one literal can be the head of the clause), and the (P_1 and P_2 and . . . and P_n) is the body of the clause. When logical statements are used for resolution, only Horn clauses, which simplify the resolution process, are used.

◣ 10.3 RESOLUTION

In a logic programming system, there is no indication about how a particular goal might be proved from a given set of predicates. A typical *inference rule* can be stated as the following:

from the logical statements $x \Rightarrow y$ and $y \Rightarrow z$, one can derive the logical statement $x \Rightarrow z$

In other words, an inference rule allows you to construct a new set of logical statements that are proved true from a given set of original logical statements that are already true. This result indicates that the new set of logical statements can be viewed as representing the potential computation of all logical consequences of a set of original statements. Hence, the essence of a *logic program* is that from a collection of logical statements, known as facts and rules, a desired fact, known as *query* or *goal,* might be proved to be true by applying the inference rule. In other words, a program written using the programming language of the logic model consists of a set of axioms and a goal statement, both expressed in the syntax of the language and inference rules. The two primary operations used by inference rules to derive new facts are *resolution* and *unification.* Resolution is a sequence of steps that the deduction system uses to derive a new logical statement; this is known as the *control strategy* for the logic programming system. The original set of logical statements represents the basis of the computation and the deductive system provides the control mechanism by which a new logic statement is derived. The resolution can be written symbolically in three equivalent ways as shown:

$$\frac{\text{P or Q}}{\neg \text{P}} \qquad \frac{\neg \text{Q} \Rightarrow \text{P}}{\neg \text{P}} \qquad \frac{(\text{P or Q}) \text{ and } \neg \text{P}}{\text{Q}}$$

We say that Q is a logical consequence of logical statements if, whenever all the logical statements are interpreted as TRUE, so is Q. Resolution uses Horn clauses and indicates that if there are two Horn clauses in which the head of the first is matched with one term of the body of the second, then the body of the first clause can be replaced with the matching term in the body of the second one. For example, if there are two Horn clauses

$$\text{P} \Rightarrow \text{P}_1, \text{ P}_2, \ldots, \text{ P}_{n-1}, \text{ P}_n.$$
$$\text{Q} \Rightarrow \text{Q}_1, \text{ Q}_2, \ldots, \text{ Q}_{m-1}, \text{ Q}_m.$$

where P matches Q_m, then the deduced clause of these two clauses is

$$\text{Q} \Rightarrow \text{Q}_1, \text{ Q}_2, \ldots, \text{ Q}_{m-1}, \text{ P}_1, \text{ P}_2, \ldots, \text{ P}_{n-1}, \text{ P}_n.$$

In other words, we can combine the left and right hand sides of both Horn clauses and then discard those terms that match on both sides as illustrated here:

$$\text{Q}, \cancel{\text{P}} \Rightarrow \text{Q}_1, \text{ Q}_2, \ldots, \text{ Q}_{m-1}, \cancel{\text{Q}}_m, \text{ P}_1, \text{ P}_2, \ldots, \text{ P}_{n-1}, \text{ P}_n.$$

If we follow the logic of the resolution, we will be able to verify that the result of resolution is logically valid.

Example: Suppose we have the following set of logical statements:

(1) not commited_crime or not got_caught or in_jail

(2) got_caught or not in_jail

(3) commited_crime

(4) got_caught

(5) not in_jail

New logical statements are deduced by searching through a set of logical statements that contradict each other and using resolution principles.

(1) not commited_crime or not got_caught or in_jail

(3) commited_crime
_____

(6) not got_caught or in_jail   (new clause)

(4) got_caught
_____

(7) in_jail   (new clause)

(5) not in_jail
_____

FALSE

By adding new generated logical statements to the set of logical statements, our logical statements are now the following:

(1) not commited_crime or not got_caught or in_jail

(2) got_caught or not in_jail

(6) not got_caught or in_jail

(3) commited_crime

(4) got_caught

(5) not in_jail

(7) in_jail

This listing of logical statements shows an inconsistency by including the two logical statements, (5) and (7), because no one can be both in jail and not in jail at the same time. This list of logical statements shows its resolution to FALSE. Resolution is *refutation complete,* which means that FALSE will always be derivable from an inconsistent set of logical statements. Resolution is also *correct,* meaning that FALSE will only be derived from an inconsistent set of logical statements. In general, the resolution strategy is to search through a set of logical statements, looking for two logical statements, one of which contains a term x and the other contains $\neg x$. Thus

x

$\underline{\neg x}$ ***resolves to***

FALSE

We can only derive FALSE if the set of logical statements is inconsistent. If we assume that the original set of logical statements was consistent, and that by adding the logical statement $\neg x$ it becomes inconsistent, we can conclude that the logical statement x must have been TRUE in the first place. This is followed by *the principle of excluded middle,* which means that if x is a logical statement, then it must be either TRUE or FALSE, and not in between. Furthermore, it cannot be both TRUE and FALSE. In this sense, when we issue a query, the resolution strategy is to temporarily add the negation of the query to the set of logical statements. If the set of logical statements then becomes inconsistent, then we conclude that there is an answer associated with query. Now, suppose the following set of logical statements:

(1) not commited_crime or not got_caught or in_jail

(2) got_caught

(3) commited_crime

Given this query,

(4)   ?- in_jail

the resolution strategy follows this pattern:

(1)   not commited_crime or not got_caught or in_jail

(3)   commited_crime

_____

(5)   not got_caught or in_jail

(2)   got_caught

_____

(6)   in_jail

(4)   not in_jail

_____

FALSE

The FALSE answer of the resolution process indicates the inconsistency of the set of logical statements, indicating that the original query is true.

Example: Suppose the following set of logical statements and we want to find out if Tom is happy. In this example, we need to show that happy(tom) is a logical consequences of the set of logical statements, (1) through (7).

(1)   happy(tom) or ¬watching(tom, football) or ¬has(tom, supplies)

(2)   has(tom, supplies) or ¬has(tom, beer) or ¬has(tom, pretzels)

(3)   watching(tom, football) or ¬is_on(tv) or ¬playing(cowboys)

(4)   is_on(tv)

(5)   playing(cowboys)

(6)   has(tom, beer)

(7)   has(tom, pretzels)

We know from the resolution strategy that if

(8)   ¬happy(tom)

which is the negation of the query, and that (1)&(2)& . . . &(8) resolves to FALSE, then the query happy(tom) is TRUE. Now, let's look at the resolution steps.

First resolution

(8)   ¬happy(tom)

(1)   happy(tom) or ¬watching(tom, football) or ¬has(tom, supplies)

_____

(9)   ¬watching(tom, football) or ¬has(tom, supplies)

Second resolution

(9)   ¬watching(tom, football) or ¬has(tom, supplies)

(3)   watching(tom, football) or ¬is_on(tv) or ¬playing(cowboys)

_____

(10) ¬has(tom, supplies) or ¬is_on(tv) or ¬playing(cowboys)

Third resolution

(10)   ¬has(tom, supplies) or ¬is_on(tv) or ¬playing(cowboys)

(2)   has(tom, supplies) or ¬has(tom, beer) or ¬has(tom, pretzels)

(11)   ¬is_on(tv) or ¬playing(cowboys) or ¬has(tom, beer) or ¬has(tom, pretzels)

Fourth resolution

(11)   ¬is_on(tv) or ¬playing(cowboys) or ¬has(tom, beer) or ¬has(tom, pretzels)

(4)   is_on(tv)

(12)   ¬playing(cowboys) or ¬has(tom, beer) or ¬has(tom, pretzels)

Fifth resolution

(12)   ¬playing(cowboys) or ¬has(tom, beer) or ¬has(tom, pretzels)

(5)   playing(cowboys)

(13)   ¬has(tom, beer) or ¬has(tom, pretzels)

Sixth resolution

(13)   ¬has(tom, beer) or ¬has(tom, pretzels)

(6)   has(tom, beer)

(14)   ¬has(tom, pretzels)

Seventh resolution

(14)   ¬has(tom, pretzels)

(7)   has(tom, pretzels)

FALSE

Because we have derived FALSE from ¬happy(tom) and (1) through (7), we may conclude that Tom is indeed happy. In other words, the inconsistency of the set of logical statements indicates that the original query happy(tom) is true.

◢ 10.4   Unification

Unification is a process of pattern matching to make terms identical so they can be discarded from both sides. To match terms that contain variables, we must set the variables equal to objects to make statements identical, and variables that are set equal to objects are known to be instantiated. In other words, unification is the derivation of a new term from a given rule through the binding of variables to known objects. An instance of a term can be obtained by substituting one variable with an object. For example, Arms(human, 2) is an instance of Arms(human, X) because it is obtained by substituting variable X with 2. However, Arms(human, 2) is not an instance of Arms(X, X), because it is not valid to substitute *human* for one occurrence of X and a different object 2 for the other occurrence of X.

Example: Suppose there is the following set of facts:

likes(Mary, food)

likes(Mary, milk)

likes(Mahsa, milk)

likes(Mahsa, Mary)

Conjunctions and the use of variables can be combined to form the queries. For example, assume we ask the following question from the logic system: *Is there anything that Mahsa and Mary both like?* This question contains two goals:

1. First, find out if there is some X (a variable) that Mary likes.
2. Second, find out if Mahsa likes whatever X is.

In a logic system, two goals might be written as a conjunction of two subgoals like this:

```
?-    likes(Mary, X), likes(Mahsa, X)
```

where logic system answers the questions by attempting to satisfy the first subgoal. If the first subgoal is in the database of facts after instantiating X with an object, then system will attempt to satisfy the second subgoal. If the second subgoal is satisfied, then the system is able to find a solution that satisfies both subgoals. If all subgoals succeed, then we conclude that the goal succeeds. The logic system searches the database completely for each goal. We demonstrate this by the following example. When following the example, we may find it helpful to write the object that has been instantiated by the success of the goal below each variable. We should also draw an arrow from the goal to its place-marker term in the knowledge base as shown in Figure 10.1 with four resolution steps in the goal evaluation.

The answer of this query indicates that, Mahsa and Mary both like milk. To sum up, in logic programming system, a program can be developed in two distinct phases as:

1. Logical Analysis: Concentrates on correctness of the program in which the correct logical statements are introduced and produced to characterize the answer.
2. Control Analysis: Concentrates the efficiency of the program when it is performed entirely by the logic programming control system.

It is important to understand the difference between a resolution and unification process that leads to a contradiction FALSE, meaning that there is a solution to the query, and one that fails, meaning that there is no solution to the query. Because we are looking for a contradiction to the negation of the query, a final resolution to FALSE means that we have proved that the query is in fact TRUE and may be added to the set of logical statements without inconsistency. If the inquiry fails, it means that given the facts and rules in the set of logical statements, we can neither prove the query is TRUE or FALSE. Thus, the set of logical statements is incomplete. In this case, we may add either the query that failed or its negation to the set of logical statements if we wish, without introducing a contradiction.

FIGURE **10.1**   **The resolution and verification process for the query likes (Mary, X), likes (Mahsa, X)**

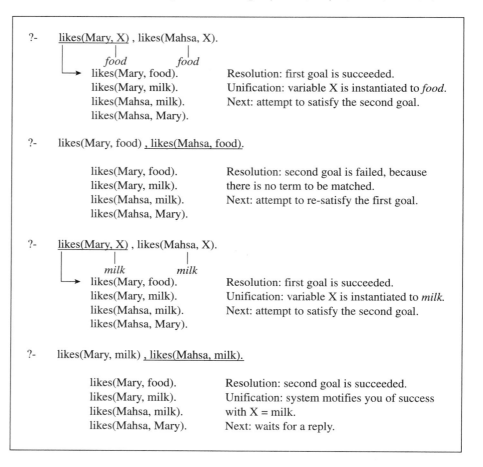

?-   likes(Mary, X) , likes(Mahsa, X).
                | |
              food   *food*
         ➞ likes(Mary, food).   Resolution: first goal is succeeded.
            likes(Mary, milk).   Unification: variable X is instantiated to *food*.
            likes(Mahsa, milk).   Next: attempt to satisfy the second goal.
            likes(Mahsa, Mary).

?-   likes(Mary, food) , likes(Mahsa, food).

            likes(Mary, food).   Resolution: second goal is failed, because
            likes(Mary, milk).   there is no term to be matched.
            likes(Mahsa, milk).   Next: attempt to re-satisfy the first goal.
            likes(Mahsa, Mary).

?-   likes(Mary, X) , likes(Mahsa, X).
                | |
              milk   *milk*
         ➞ likes(Mary, food).   Resolution: first goal is succeeded.
            likes(Mary, milk).   Unification: variable X is instantiated to *milk*.
            likes(Mahsa, milk).   Next: attempt to satisfy the second goal.
            likes(Mahsa, Mary).

?-   likes(Mary, milk) , likes(Mahsa, milk).

            likes(Mary, food).   Resolution: second goal is succeeded.
            likes(Mary, milk).   Unification: system motifies you of success
            likes(Mahsa, milk).   with X = milk.
            likes(Mahsa, Mary).   Next: waits for a reply.

◥ 10.5 SEARCH STRUCTURES

The two common search methods used in logic programming systems are depth-first search and breadth-first search methods. Depth-first search strategy (DFS) can be implemented in a stack-based or recursive fashion, indicating that it is extremely efficient regarding the time and space requirements. A depth-first search requires keeping only the path from the root of the search tree to the current state at any point in the search process. A breadth-first search (BFS) is far more expensive in required resources than is a depth-first search because the whole top portion of the search space is stored throughout the search process. As a consequence of this, not many logic programming control systems adapted BFS. Excluding the required resources, the only difference between the DFS and BFS is the sequence of solutions obtained by the control system.

FIGURE **10.2**   The search space for the query married(John)

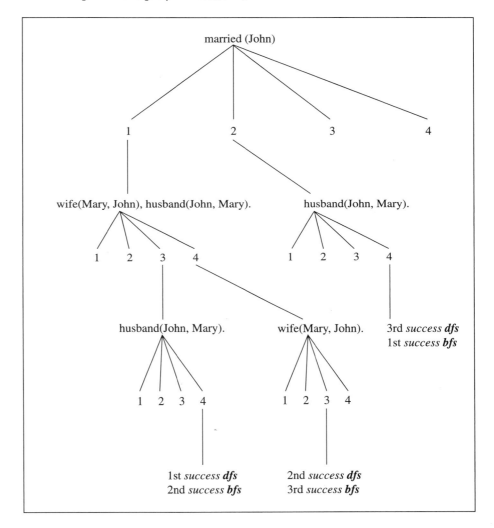

Example: Consider the following four logical statements:

1. married(John) ⇒ wife(Mary, John), husband(John, Mary)
2. married(John) ⇒ husband(John, Mary)
3. wife(Mary, John)
4. husband(John, Mary)

For the query **married(John),** the search space is shown in Figure 10.2 with the solutions obtained in DFS and BFS, respectively. The sequence of *success* obtained in

DFS and BFS are different, and *success* means successful satisfaction of the query. For simplicity, the facts and rules are represented with numbers.

10.5.1 Backward and Forward Searching

When we begin a resolution process with a query, as in demonstrating the query happy(tom) or married(john), we backtrack from the query to the facts for alternative solutions. As with proof by contradiction, we start with what is to be proved contradictory, rather than with what is known—that is, with a set of logical statements. When there is only one or possibly a few choices for logical statements to resolve with a goal, backward chaining is effective. However, if there are many choices, backward chaining would become inefficient because of all the backtracking necessary to undo fruitless resolution paths. For certain problems, forward chaining from facts and rules to the main query is more efficient. In general, if there are more facts than rules, forward chaining will perform better. This indicates that, if resolution starts from the smaller set of logical statements (facts) to the larger set of logical statements (rules), we may encounter fewer wrong paths. Another situation where forward chaining proves preferable is when there are fewer choices at each decision point when reasoning from the facts. Forward chaining may also be more effective when a user wants to see a justification for each step in a proof, and naturally thinks from the known to the unknown answer. In general, the process by which the system retraces its steps and goes back to a previous subgoal looking for a possible new solution to it, is called backtracking.

▨ 10.6 APPLICATIONS OF LOGIC PROGRAMMING

Artificial Intelligence (AI) has been defined as an area of computer science that is concerned with computer systems that exhibit human intelligence, meaning that they allow computers to emulate human behavior. The activities that are involved in AI are classified as: natural language processing, automatic programming and theorem proving, robotics, machine vision and pattern recognition, modeling and representing knowledge, learning new information, intelligent data retrieval, expert systems, problem solving and planning, and game playing (Winston, 1992). In general, two components are associated with artificial intelligence: *knowledge* and *reasoning*. There are different methods to represent knowledge and various approaches of reasoning this knowledge. The computer programs that perform this process are said to exhibit artificial intelligence.

Most interpreters in AI applications are developed with the Prolog logic programming language. For example, one group of scientists at Imperial College London has taken various sections of British Law and re-expressed them in Prolog axioms. They designed the British Nationality Act System (1981), which defines who is a British citizen. The system provides an explanation facility and the user is queried for specific information as and when required. Logic programming can contribute to the study of intelligence systems in two main areas:

▶   Production systems

▶   Reasoning systems

In this section, we will introduce logic programming approach to form these two important AI paradigms.

10.6.1   Production Systems

The production system was proposed as a model of human information processing, and it continues to play an important role in AI. Some production system models stress the sequential nature of production systems; for example, the manner in which short-term memory is modified over time by the rules. Other models stress the parallel aspect, in which all productions match and fire simultaneously, no matter how many there are. Both types of models have been used to explain timing data from experiments on human problem solving. A production system program consists of an unordered collection of If-Then statements and is characterized by three components:

▶   **System State,** also called the *database of knowledge* or *declarative knowledge,* is one of the core concepts of AI-based systems. It is also called *working memory* and stores various facts and rules about the particular application.

▶   **Production Rules,** which allow the system to change from one state to another, are also called *production memory* or *procedural knowledge.* Each rule has a precondition, and when it is satisfied by any rules in the database, the rule itself can be applied.

▶   **Control System,** which manages the execution of production rules and allows the system to evolve according to some desired criteria, is also called the *inference engine* or *control knowledge.* In general, the control system chooses which applicable rule in the working memory should be applied.

In general, the *knowledge base* provides specific *facts* and *rules* about the subject, and the *inference engine* provides the reasoning ability that enables the production system to form conclusions. Production systems also provide additional tools in the form of *user interfaces* and *explanation facilities.* User interfaces enable people to form queries, provide information, and interact with the system. Explanation facilities enable the systems to explain or justify their conclusions, and they also enable developers to verify the operations carried out by the system. The basic components of a production system are shown in Figure 10.3.

Therefore, we can say that a production system is a computer system that has provisions for storing facts and rules and for applying these rules to perform reasoning on the input fact the system is presented with. An important family of production system languages was Official Production System (OPS), developed at Carnegie-Mellon University by Lee Brownston and colleagues (1985). Although their origins were in modeling human problem solving, these languages have proved highly effective for programming production systems and for other AI applications. In OPS5, working memories consist of several hundred objects, and each object has between ten and one hundred associated attribute-value pairs. An object together with its attribute-value pairs is called a *working memory element* (WME). For example, the element

FIGURE **10.3**   Computation model of a production system

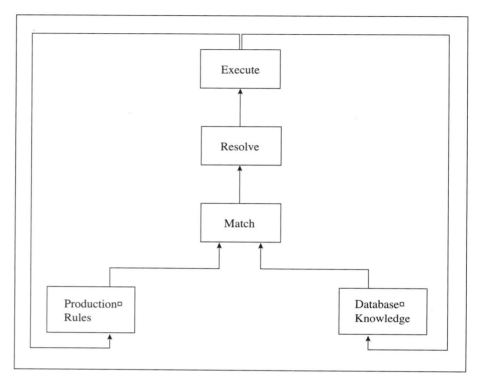

WME: (Phys-Object ↑Name Apartment ↑Weight Small ↑At 10-Street ↑On South)

declares an object of class Phys-Object that is named Apartment. It has four properties:

▶   Its name (↑ Name)
▶   Its weight (↑ Weight)
▶   Its location (↑ At)
▶   Its support (↑ On)

The symbol ↑ is used to distinguish properties from values. This element specifies a physical object as an apartment on the south at location 10-Street where weight is small. For example, the working element

WME: (Expression ↑Name Expression10 ↑Arg1 5 ↑Arg2 A ↑Op *)

declares an object of class Expression which is named Expression10 and has 5 as its first argument, A as its second argument, and * as its operator. Generally speaking, the left side of a production consists of a sequence of patterns, meaning a sequence of partial descriptions of working memory elements. When a pattern P describes an element E, P is said to match E. A pattern matches a working memory element if every attribute value in the pattern occurs in the corresponding position in the working memory element. Thus, the pattern

```
(Expression   ↑Arg2 10 ↑Op *)
```

would match the element

```
(Expression   ↑Name Expr20 ↑Arg1 X ↑Arg2 10 ↑Op *)
```

PROSPECTOR (Duda, Hart, Konolige, & Reboh, 1979) is a production system written in Prolog that provides advice on mineral exploration. In PROSPECTOR, each rule contains two confidence estimates. The first indicates the extent to which the presence of the evidence described in the condition part of the rule suggests the validity of the rule's conclusion. The second confidence estimate measures the extent to which the evidence is necessary to the validity of the conclusion, or in other words, the extent to which the lack of the evidence indicates that the conclusion is not valid. For example, in the rule

If: magnetite or pyrite in disseminated or veinlet form is present

Then: $(2, -4)$ there is favorable mineralization and texture for the propylitic stage

the number 2 indicates that the presence of the evidence is mildly encouraging, and the number -4 indicates that the absence of the evidence is strongly discouraging for the conclusion.

10.6.2 Reasoning Systems

Reasoning is the process by which new information is extracted from a knowledge base. A characteristic of the knowledge base of reasoning systems is that only a small portion of the knowledge is stated explicitly, and more knowledge could be made explicit via an inference mechanism. The knowledge base of reasoning systems contains both factual and heuristic knowledge. Factual knowledge is that part of the task domain that is widely shared, typically found in textbooks or journals, and commonly agreed upon by those knowledgeable in the particular field. Heuristic knowledge is the less rigorous, more experiential, and more judgmental knowledge of performance. Some of the reasoning techniques for knowledge-based systems include recognition, inheritance, classification, generalization, and unification. In general, the reasoning system consists of a set of separate modules, also called agents because each module is acting as a problem-solving entity, and a set of communication paths between them. The supporting architectures range from tightly coupled systems in which there is a completely centralized control mechanism to a shared-memory system in which both control and knowledge are fully distributed. In fact, most reasoning systems lie somewhere in the middle. Some of the distinctive features associated with the reasoning systems are as follows:

▶ **Modularity**, meaning that the system maintains a collection of modules rather than one huge one.

▶ **Reliability**, meaning that problem solving can continue even if one of the agents fails.

▶ **Heterogeneous unification**, meaning that problem-solving techniques and knowledge representation may vary for different parts of a reasoning problem.

One important issue involved in the design of reasoning systems is how the actions of the individual agents can be coordinated so that they work effectively. For some, a reasoning system such as MYCIN (Shortliffe, 1976) was used to diagnose and recommend therapy for diseases, in which a trained knowledge engineer extracts information from medical experts and then incorporates it into a computer program that would provide the combined wisdom of the experts. MYCIN was written in the Lisp programming language, which is generally acknowledged to be harder to learn compared with the other AI programming languages, such as Prolog. These production systems perform useful reasoning based on a set of built-in rules obtained from human experts. For example, present production systems contain as many as 10,000 rules and facts. Another example of a reasoning system is ELIZA developed by Joseph Weizenbaum (1965), written in Prolog, which appears to talk to you intelligently. The creator of the original version was Joseph Weizenbaum. ELIZA works by a word-matching procedure, which is extremely powerful and useful in a variety of contexts. Here is an example of ELIZA in action:

User: Hello

ELIZA: Hi, my name is ELIZA

User: How do you work?

ELIZA: Why do you want to know how I work?

User: Probably because I am curious

ELIZA: Because you are curious? That is not a very good reason

User: I am very confused

ELIZA: So you are very confused

.

.

.

It is very easy to extend this system to give a much more varied and intelligent-looking dialogue. SALT (Marcus & McDermott, 1989) written in Prolog was a knowledge acquisition reasoning system used to design artifacts through a propose-and-revise strategy. SALT was capable of answering questions like WHY-NOT (why did not you assign value x to this parameter?) and WHAT-IF (what would happen if you did?). One might ask these questions to locate incorrect or missing knowledge in the system as a precursor to correcting it.

Rule-based programming is one of the most commonly used techniques for developing expert systems. In this programming paradigm, rules are used to represent heuristics that specify a set of actions to be performed for a given situation. A rule is composed of an *if* portion and a *then* portion. The *if* portion of a rule is a series of patterns that specify the facts that cause the rule to be applicable. The process of matching facts to patterns is called *pattern matching*. The *then* portion of a rule is the set of actions to be performed when the rule is applicable. The inference engine selects a rule and then the actions of the selected rule are performed. The inference engine then selects another rule and carries out its actions. This process continues until no applicable rules remain.

Summary

Logic programming refers to a paradigm that uses a form of symbolic logic as a programming language. Logic programming is based on the notion that a program implements a relation rather than a mapping. Logic programming languages specify the problem in a declarative fashion, meaning that they describe what the goal is and the underlying implementation search for a proof of the goal can be conducted by the control system, which is sometimes called an inference engine. The programs written in logic models express a goal and the facts and rules from which this goal is to be deduced but do not express the method by which this deduction can take place. The form of logic used in logic programming languages is first-order predicate calculus as a uniform model to express logical statements. In this chapter, we outlined the components of first-order predicate calculus including constants, logical statements, variables, functions, connectors, quantifiers, punctuation, and precedence. The two primary operations used by inference rules to derive new facts are resolution and unification. The resolution is a sequence of steps that the deduction system uses to derive a goal and is known as the control strategy for the logic programming system. Unification is a process of pattern matching that makes terms identical so they can be discarded from both sides of the logical statements. In this chapter, we discussed resolution and unification, using several examples. We briefly discussed the application of logic programming, such as production systems and reasoning systems.

11 Declarative Programming Language

The most popular logic programming language is Prolog, originally developed by Alain Colmerauer, Philippe Roussel, and their colleagues of the d'Intelligence Artificielle (University of Marseille) to be a theorem-proving language (Clocksin & Mellish, 1987). Its developers called it Prolog as an abbreviation for *programming en **logique**.* Prolog is a very high level programming language that is based on automatic theorem proving. Prolog is a practical and efficient implementation of many aspects of intelligent program execution, such as non-determinism, parallelism, and pattern-directed procedure call. Prolog provides a uniform data structure, called the *term,* out of which all data, as well as Prolog programs, are constructed. Its built-in control scheme is based on a specific method for searching state space, and it appears to be a suitable language for AI applications. Prolog as one of the fourth-generation programming languages became a good language for database management systems. Prolog as an AI language had a prominent role in the launching of the fifth generation computer project and seems well matched to AI applications. Several projects, most notably the Japanese, attempted to show that Prolog would be efficient in describing AI applications for parallel execution. To do this, their computers needed to be intelligent, meaning that they had to be able to learn, associate, make inferences, make decisions, and behave in ways we consider to encompass human reasoning. The Japanese designed a computer system using Prolog as its core language. The project included the development of the Prolog-like parallel logical programming language KL-1 (Lipkis & Smolze, 1983). It included some operating system functions as well as modularity and concurrent processing. As an experiment, 64 computers running KL-1 were connected in parallel under the operating system PIMOS (Parallel Inference Machine Operating System) (Chikayama, Sato, & Miyazaki, 1988). Time efficiencies were measured at 5-8 mega LIPS (Logical Inference Per Second). The target for this project was the development of knowledge and information-processing capabilities. Research and development are continuing, with a new goal of connecting 1000 parallel computers to achieve

200 mega LIPS speed. The Japanese have also developed a Prolog-based language called Extended Self-Contained Prolog (ESP) (Fuchi & Furukawa, 1987) for programming many fifth-generation projects on PCs and workstations that run in a UNIX environment. Like most other programming languages, Prolog exists in a number of different implementations, each with its own syntactic and semantic specifications. In this chapter, we have adopted a *core Prolog* and all our examples conform to a standard version that corresponds to the implementations, developed mainly at University of Edinburgh, for several different computer systems such as DEC system-10 running TOPS-10, DEC VAX and PDP-11 running UNIX, DEC LSI-11 running RT-11, and ICL 2980 running EMAS. In our experience, novice programmers find that Prolog programs seem to be more comprehensible than do equivalent programs in conventional programming languages. On the other hand, the programmers experienced in conventional languages are better prepared to deal with abstract concepts such as variables and control flow; thus, they might need to be convinced before they consider using Prolog a useful programming tool. Of course, we know of many highly experienced programmers who have taken up Prolog with much enthusiasm, specifically in the area of AI systems. Because logic programs do not express the sequence of operations, the operations can be carried out in any order or simultaneously. This makes logic programming languages appropriate candidates for parallel processing.

A Prolog program consists of three major components: a series of rules, a series of facts, and a logical statement known as goal or query. Query is the given input to a program, which is treated as a goal to be proved. There are two opposite methods in which the goal can be proved: a top-down approach, also called backward chaining, which is similar to recursion, and a bottom-up approach, also called forward chaining, which is similar to iteration. Resolution and unification techniques are used to prove theorems in Prolog. In this chapter, we explain the depth-first search method adopted by Prolog, which is very efficient because it can be implemented in a stack based or recursive fashion. Backtracking is an important concept that is used in Prolog whenever a goal fails or when the user provides a continued search for the next answer. Finally, in this chapter, we discuss the deficiencies of Prolog, such as *order of facts and rules, unlimited search space,* and *occurs check.*

11.1 LOGIC PROGRAMMING WITH PROLOG

At the heart of the Prolog is a stored base of information usually called a *knowledge base* or *database,* which consists of facts and rules. The system is *interactive*—the user interacts with the system on a question and answer basis. Answering a question involves processing the data held in the knowledge base. A general structure of Prolog is outlined in Figure 11.1.

The basic features of Prolog include a powerful pattern-matching facility, a backtracking strategy that searches for proofs, uniform data structures from which programs are built, and the general interchangeability of input and output. Because of the lack of a standard definition, several dialects of Prolog evolved, differing even in their basic syntax. Fortunately, the University of Edinburgh version is now widely accepted as a standard.

FIGURE **11.1** **Structure of Prolog system**

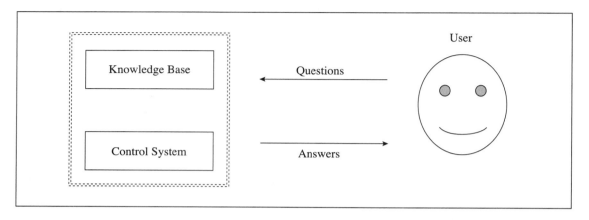

11.2 PROGRAM STRUCTURE

A prolog program consists of three major components:

1. Series of *rules* that define the problem domain, which is the relation between objects
2. Series of *facts* that define the interrelationships among the known objects
3. Logical statement known as *goal* or *query*, which is a question from the Prolog system to either prove or disprove

In general, the set of facts and rules is called *assertions* or *axioms* and describes logical relationships among objects, and is the basis for the theorem-proving model of Prolog system. Prolog programming language restricts us to the logical statements (Horn clauses) of the form:

```
A :- A₁, A₂,  . . .  , Aₙ.
```

The symbol ":-" means *if* and the symbol "," means *and*. A is the *head* (goal) of the logical statement, $A_1, A_2, \ldots, A_n$ forms the *body* (subgoals), and a period "." terminates every Prolog axiom. A_i is called a literal, which is a relationship between objects or the negation of a relationship between objects. For example, the following literals can express the relationship between two objects, *seyed* and *mary*.

```
likes(seyed, mary).
father_of(seyed, mary).
```

Informally, the above logical statement means that, if A_1 and A_2 and . . . and A_n are all true, then we can infer that A is also true. But we cannot conversely infer that A is false just because some A_i turns out to be false. A logical statement is written in terms of *if* rather than *if and only if*. There might well be another axiom in the program that allows us to infer that A is true. In other words, this does not mean that A is

FIGURE **11.2** **(a) Logic and (b) Prolog representations of logical statements**

```
∀x pet(x) ∧ small(x) ⇒ apartment(x)        apartment(X) :- pet(X), small(X).
∀x cat(x) ∨ dog(x) ⇒ pet(x)                pet(X):- cat(X).
∀x poodle(x) ⇒ dog(x) ∧ small(x)           pet(X):- dog(X).
poodle(fluffy)                              dog(X):- poodle(X).
                                            small(X) :- poodle(X).
                                            poodle(fluffy).
                 (a)                                      (b)
               (Logic)                                 (Prolog)
```

definitely false; it means that A cannot be inferred to be true from the set of facts and rules in the knowledge base. If we can infer from the rules and facts of the program that A is true, then we say that A succeeds; otherwise, A fails. To sum up, the above axiom can be interpreted as either of the following:

▶ A logical statement that if all the A_i are satisfied (true), then A is satisfied (true).

▶ A procedure for producing a state that satisfies condition A, similar to:

```
procedure A
   begin
      call A₁
      call A₂
      ...
      call Aₙ
   end
```

where it can be interpreted as the following: To execute procedure A, call A_1 and call A_2 and . . . and call A_n. The fact that Prolog programs are composed only of Horn clauses and not of arbitrary logical expressions has two important consequences. The first is that because of the uniform representation, a simple and efficient interpreter can be developed. The second is that the logic of the Horn clause system is decidable. Figure 11.2 shows an example of a simple knowledge base represented in standard logic notation and in Prolog.

The query is the given input to a program, which is treated as a goal to be proved. In other words, the query is a question asking about objects and their relationships. In Prolog, a query is just like a fact or rule, except that it is started with a special symbol " ?-", a question mark and a "-", hyphen. For example, a query has the following form:

$$?-A_1, A_2, \quad . . . \quad , A_n.$$

In this case, we proceed by satisfying A_1, and A_2, and . . . , A_n separately as sub-goals. If all subgoals succeed, then we conclude that the goal succeeds. In what follows, we use the convention that the names of all objects and relationships start with a lowercase character and variables start with uppercase letters. The relation is given first and the argument (objects) follows between a pair of parentheses, separated by commas. Each logical statement is terminated by a period. The ordering of objects in facts and rules must be consistent with the issued query.

◩ 11.3 LOGICAL VARIABLE

A variable refers to a memory location that may have changes in its contents. The concept of the definition and implementation of a variable in logic programs can be simplified:

▶ A variable in logic program simply stands for a value that, once determined, will not change. For example, the equation $X+3Y=11$ and $2X–3Y=4$ specify values for X and Y; namely X=5 and Y=2, which will not be changed in this context. A variable in Prolog is called a *logical variable* and is a string of characters beginning with an uppercase letter or an underscore.

▶ Once a logical variable is bound to a particular value, called an *instantiation* of the variable, that binding cannot be altered unless the pattern matching that caused the binding is undone because of backtracking. In other words, a logical variable is more like a constant identifier with a dynamic defining expression.

▶ Terms in a query change only by having variables filled in for the first time, never by having a new value replace an existing value.

▶ An iterative accumulation of a value is obtained by having each instance of a recursive rule take the values passed to it and perform computations of values for new variables that are then passed to another call.

In general, the power of logic programming and Prolog comes from using the logical variables in structures to direct the pattern matching. Results are constructed by binding values to variables according to the constraints imposed by the structures of the arguments in the goal term and the head of the clause being matched. The order in which variables are constrained is generally not critical, and the construction of complex values can be postponed as long as logical variables hold their places in the structure being constructed.

◩ 11.4 SYNTAX STRUCTURE

Prolog is a relatively small programming language, as evidenced by a BNF specification of the core part of the Prolog provided in Figure 11.3. The language consists of a large set of predefined predicates and notational variations such as infix symbols that are not defined in this specification.

Arithmetic operations are defined. Relations such as =, =< (note that this is not written <=), <=, <, and > are also defined. But the equality operator = means "same as", so X=1+2 means that X is the same as the expression 1+2. The operator *is* means evaluate; X *is* 3+2 results in an assignment of 5 to X. Because of this meaning of the = operator, expressions such as 2+3=1+4 will be false. To evaluate these, you need to define an equality function that uses the *is* construct to force the evaluation of both terms:

FIGURE **11.3**   **BNF specification of the Prolog programming language**

```
<program>          ::= <clause list>  <query>   |   <query>
<clause list>      ::= <clause list>   <clause>   |   <clause>
<clause>           ::= <predicate>  .   |   <predicate>  : = <predicate list>  .
<predicate list>   ::= <predicate list> , <predicate>   |   <predicate>
<predicate>        ::= <atom>    |   <atom> (<term list>)
<term list>        ::= <term list> , <term>   |   <term>
<term>             ::= <numeral>  |   <atom>    |   <variable>   |   <structure>
<structure>        ::= <atom> (<term list>)
<query>            ::= ?- <predicate list>  .
<atom>             ::= <small atom>   |   '<string>'
<small atom>       ::= <lowercase letter>  |   <small atom>  <character>
<variable>         ::= <uppercase letter>  |   <variable>  <character>
<lowercase letter> ::= a | b | c | d |  . . .  |x | y | z
<uppercase letter> ::= A | B | C | D |  . . .  |X | Y | Z
<numeral>          ::= <digit>   |   <numeral>  <digit>
<digit>            ::= 0 | 1 | 2 | 3 | 4 | 5 | 6 |7 | 8 | 9
<character>        ::= <lowercase letter> | <uppercase letter> | <digit> | <special>
<special>          ::= +|-|*|/|\|^|~|:|.|?|@|#|$|&|=|=<|>=|<|>
<string>           ::= <character>   |   <string>  <character>
```

```
samevalue(X, Y) :- A is X, B is Y, A=B.
```

Then `samevalue(2+3, 1+4)` will return true as the result of the evaluation.

11.4.1 Syntax for BNF Grammar

Prolog provides a mechanism called *logic grammar* or *definite clause grammar* to determine the correct constructs. In most implementations of Prolog, a preprocessor translates special grammar rules into regular Prolog clauses that allow the recognition of correct axioms using this logic grammar. To simplify the problem, we consider a subset of English grammar in which the BNF and abstract syntax are presented in the following sections.

Production Rules:

```
<sentence>       ::=    <noun phrase>, <verb phrase>.
<noun phrase>    ::=    <determiner>, <noun>
<verb phrase>    ::=    <verb>, <noun phrase>  |  <verb>
<determiner>     ::=    a  |  the
<noun>           ::=    boy  |  cat
<verb>           ::=    saw
```

Start Symbol:

> `<sentence>`

Variable Symbols:

`{<sentence>, <noun phrase>, <verb phrase>, <determiner>, <noun>, <verb>}`

Terminal Symbols:

> `{a, the, boy, cat, saw}`

Given a sentence from the language such as " the boy saw a cat.", an abstract syntax tree exhibiting the sentence can be represented as shown in Figure 11.4.

11.4.2 Syntax for Logic Grammar

The BNF definition of the English language can be represented in the logic grammar form as shown in the following.

Production Rules:

```
<sentence>       →   <noun phrase>, <verb phrase>, ['.'].
<noun phrase>    →   <determiner>, <noun>.
<verb phrase>    →   <verb>, <noun phrase>.
<verb phrase>    →   <verb>.
<determiner>     →   [a].
<determiner>     →   [the].
<noun>           →   [boy].
<noun>           →   [cat].
<verb>           →   [saw].
```

Logic grammar uses a special predefined infix predicate → to force this translation into Prolog forms. In general, the Prolog interpreter automatically translates these rules into normal Prolog clauses. In this translation, each predicate is given two parameters. For example

> `<noun phrase>      →   <determiner>, <noun>.`

is translated to

> `<noun phrase>(K,L)   →   <determiner>(K,M), <noun>(M,L).`

Similarly

> `<verb phrase>   →   <verb>.`

becomes

> `<verb phrase>(K,L)   →   <verb>(K,L).`

In this sense, the abstract syntax tree can be represented as a Prolog structure with function symbols used to tag the syntactic categories. For example, the abstract

FIGURE **11.4**   **An abstract syntax tree for "the boy saw a cat."**

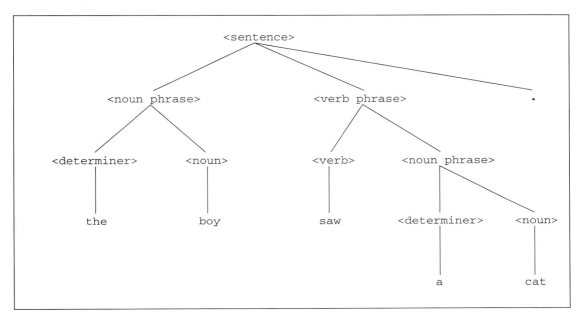

syntax tree representing " the boy saw a cat." can be formed as the following linear structure:

```
sentence(<noun phrase>(<determiner>[the], <noun>[boy]),
    <verb phrase>(<verb>[saw]),
    <noun phrase>(<determiner>[a], <noun>[cat])).
```

In general, the interpreter constructs a Prolog structure in two steps:

1. It takes a sentence (a string of characters) such as " the boy saw a cat." and creates a token list as [the, boy, saw, a, cat, '.'].

2. It takes a token list and constructs a Prolog structure as a sentence.

This indicates that the logic programming approach to analyzing a sentence according to a grammar can be seen as a token list whose tokens are labeled by the terminal symbols in the grammar. For example, the previous linear structure can be expressed as the token list in Figure 11.5.

Two terminal symbols are contiguous in the original string if they share a common token in the token list. To enable the grammar to be expressed in logic notation, we provide each token an arbitrary label, for example using positive integer numbers as in Figure 11.6.

A token such as `<predicate>`(K,L) is defined as asserting that the path from K to L can be interpreted as an instance of the nonterminal `<predicate>`. For example,

FIGURE **11.5**   **Linear structure expressed as a token list**

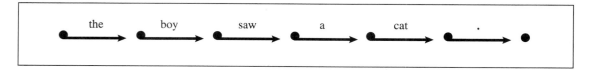

FIGURE **11.6**   **Token list with arbitrary labels**

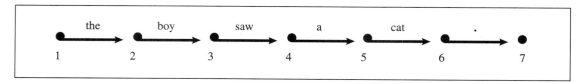

<noun phrase>(4,6) holds because edge (4,5) is labeled by a determiner *a* and edge (5,6) is labeled by a noun *cat*, which can be expressed as the following rule:

```
<noun phrase>(K,L)    →    <determiner>(K,M), <noun>(M,L).
```

The common variable M makes the two tokens contiguous. The complete BNF rules of the English grammar written in logic grammar form is listed as the following:

```
<sentence>(K,L)       →   <noun phrase>(K,M),
                          <verb phrase>(M,N), <period>(N,L).
<noun phrase>(K,L)    →   <determiner>(K,M), <noun>(M,L).
<verb phrase>(K,L)    →   <verb>(K,M), <noun phrase>(M,L).
<verb phrase>(K,L)    →   <verb>(K,L).
<determiner>(K,L)     →   a(K,L).
<determiner>(K,L)     →   the(K,L).
<noun>(K,L)           →   boy(K,L).
<noun>(K,L)           →   cat(K,L).
<verb>(K,L)           →   saw(K,L).
<period>(K,L)         →   .( ).
```

The logic program recognizes the sentence when paths in the token list corresponding to the rules of the grammar are verified for building an instance of the nonterminal <sentence> as shown in Figure 11.7.

For example, entering the following facts can create the token list for the sentence " the boy saw a cat.":

```
the(1,2). boy(2,3). saw(3,4). the(4,5). cat(5,6). period(6,7).
```

And the syntactic correctness of the sentence can be determined by the query

```
?-    sentence(1,7).
```

where the system responds yes. Also, it is possible to use the logic grammar to generate sentences in the language with the query

FIGURE **11.7**   Token list with corresponding rules of the grammar

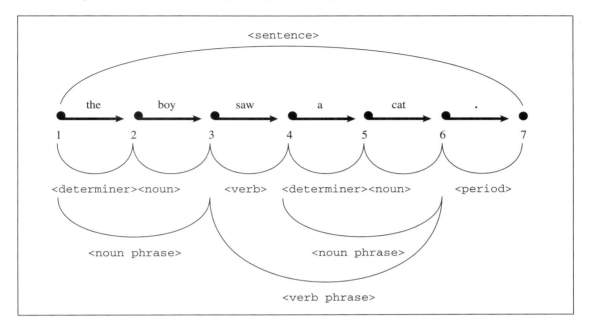

```
    ?-    sentence(S, [ ]).
```
where the system responds
```
    S=[the, boy, saw, a, cat, .].
    yes
```

Example: Consider the following facts:
```
    parent(seyed, mary).
    parent(seyed, mahsa).
    parent(mary, leily).
    parent(mahsa, victoria).
```
Some queries:
```
?  parent(seyed, mary).
yes
?  parent(X, leily).
X=mary
yes
?  parent(seyed, X).
X=mary;
% The user-typed semicolon asks the system for more solutions
X=mahsa;
no
```

```
?  parent(X, Y).
X=seyed
Y=mary
yes
% System will list all of the parent pairs, one at a time,
% if semicolons are typed.
```

▽ 11.5 CONTROL STRUCTURE

Because Prolog was implemented with a concern for efficiency, its control strategy acts with a deterministic approach for discovering proofs. The control system in Prolog can be characterized by two criteria:

▶ Goal order, meaning that the control system chooses the leftmost subgoal first.

▶ Rule order, meaning that the control system selects the first logical statement.

Thus, the response to a query is affected both by subgoal orders within the goal and by the logical statements order within the knowledge base of facts and rules. There are two opposite methods in which the goal can be proved: a *top-down* approach, also called *backward chaining,* which is similar to *recursion,* and a *bottom-up* approach, also called *forward chaining,* which is similar to *iteration.* Various mixtures of top-down and bottom-up approaches work from both the goal and the hypotheses. The bottom-up control approach is more efficient than the top-down approach is because the bottom-up execution does not recompute the subgoals.

11.5.1 Top-Down Approach

In this approach, we start with the goal and attempt to prove its correctness by finding a sequence of matching logical statements that lead to some set of original facts in the knowledge base, meaning that all possible resolution and unification could be performed until the goal is proved. The top-down approach execution of a logic program is similar to the recursive execution of a procedure. Figure 11.8 presents a top-down control approach in Prolog. The procedure *prove* calls itself recursively to satisfy new subgoals. The top-down control can stop in one of two cases:

▶ The goal G is empty and *True* is reached.

▶ No logical statement applies to the leftmost subgoal of G.

The top-down process has the disadvantage that many irrelevant facts and rules will be derived before the desired goal appears. This may give rise to infinitely many derivable facts and rules, meaning that *sometimes* the desired goal may never be achieved. In general, the top-down approach works well when there is a small set of candidate answers. Because the top-down approach is more suitable for a large class of problems than the bottom-up approach is, the top-down approach is used in Prolog implementation for resolution and unification.

Example: Assume a knowledge base contains the following fact and rule:

FIGURE **11.8**   **Top-down control in Prolog corresponds to a recursive procedure**

```
procedure   prove(G)
    begin
    let goal as G={G₁, G₂, ... , Gₖ}, where Gᵢ is a subgoal.
    let logical statements as {R₁, R₂, . . . , Rₙ}
    where n is number of logical statements.
    if   (G ≠ φ)   then
         Choose leftmost subgoal G₁
         for i=1  to  n    do
                 let Rᵢ be A :- B₁, B₂, . . . , Bₘ
                 if Rᵢ satisfies G₁ then
                 let Ψ be the most general unifier of G₁ and A
                 let Gᵠ be B₁Ψ, B₂Ψ, . . . , BₘΨ, G₂Ψ, . . . , GₖΨ
         prove(Gᵠ)
                 end if
         end for
    else
    True
    end if
end  prove
```

```
mother(mary).
female(X)   :=   mother(X).
```

To trace the query **female(mary)** in a top-down approach, Prolog would be required to choose the goal as a starting logical statement and use it to infer the truth of the goal. In this example, a new logical statement *mother(mary)* can be deduced by matching the goal *female(mary)* and the second logical statement `female(X)  :=  mother(X)` in the knowledge base through instantiation of `X` to `mary`. The goal can be inferred because the new generated logical statement *mother(mary)* is similar to the first logical statement of the knowledge base.

11.5.2 Bottom-Up Approach

In the bottom-up approach, we start with the hypothesis that the goal is correct and attempt to reach the goal. Thus, we start with the facts and rules of the knowledge base and attempt to find a sequence of matches that lead to the goal. In general, the bottom-up approach works well when the number of possibly correct answers is large. The bottom-up control can stop in one of two cases:

▶   The goal G is achieved and True is reached.

▶   No logical statements can satisfy each other to make a new logical statement.

FIGURE **11.9** **Bottom-up control in Prolog corresponds to an iterative procedure**

```
procedure   prove(G)
    begin
    let goal as G={G₁, G₂, ... , Gₖ}, where Gᵢ is a subgoal.
    let logical statements as {R₁, R₂, ... , Rₙ}
    where n is number of logical statements.
    let Gᵠ= φ
    while (G ≠ Gᵠ)
          for i=1  to   n    do
                  let Rᵢ be X :- X₁, X₂, ... , Xₘ
                  let Rⱼ be Y :- Y₁, Y₂, ... , Yₘ
                  if Rᵢ satisfies Rⱼ meaning that X matches one of
                  the terms of the right side of Rⱼ, then
                  let Ψ be the most general unifier of Rᵢ and Rⱼ
                  let Gᵠ be Gᵠ,Y₁Ψ, Y₂Ψ, ... , YₘΨ, X₁Ψ, X₂Ψ, ... , XₘΨ
                  end if
          end for
    end while
    if (G = Gᵠ)    then
    True
    end if
end  prove
```

The bottom-up control approach in Prolog is similar to iteration execution of a procedure, as presented in Figure 11.9.

Example: Assume a knowledge base contains the following fact and rule:

```
mother(mary).
female(X)       :=      mother(X).
```

To trace the query **female(mary)** in the bottom-up approach, Prolog would be required to search through the knowledge base to make a logical statement correspond to the goal. In this example, the goal can be deduced by matching the first fact mother(mary) with the right side of the second rule female(X) := mother(X) through instantiation of X to mary. A new generated logical statement, *female(mary)*, indicates that the goal can be inferred because it is similar to the goal.

✔ 11.6 Resolution and Unification

Resolution is a technique for proving theorems in predicate calculus that has been a part of AI problem-solving research since the mid 1960s (Bledsoe, 1977; Kowalski,

1979; Robinson, 1965). As an important practical application, resolution theorem proving, also known as the *resolution refutation system,* has made the current generation of Prolog interpreter possible. The resolution principle, introduced in an important paper by Alan Robinson (1965), describes a way of finding contradictions in a database of facts and rules by using substitution. Resolution refutation proves a theorem by negating the statement to be proved and adding this negated goal to the set of axioms that are known to be true. It then uses the resolution rule of inference to show that this leads to a contradiction. Once the interpreter (theorem prover) shows that the negated goal is inconsistent with the given set of axioms, it follows that the original goal must be consistent. This proves the theorem.

Unification is the search process of finding the general substitution of variables that makes two variables literally identical. In general, when the interpreter tries to verify a goal, it searches the database of facts and rules to find a matching fact or rule's head. This corresponds to pattern matching and variable binding. In this sense, the unification selects a fact if

▶   The name is the same as that of the goal to be proven.

▶   The number of arguments is the same.

▶   For all corresponding arguments, one of the following conditions holds:

They are exactly the same constant.

They are an unbound variable and a constant. In this case, the variable becomes bound to the constant.

They are both variables. In this case, if one is bound, then the other becomes bound to the same object. If both are bound, then both become bound to the same object.

▶   If no matching fact or rule's head can be found by unification, then the goal fails.

Thus, the resolution and unification works by canceling out matching literals that appear on different sides of the "`:-`" sign. If we have two logical statements, any two matching (or unifiable) literals, which appear both on the right of one of them and on the left of the other, cancel each other out. For example, consider the following facts and rules translated into the Prolog clause form on the right.

1. `:-  a.` $\neg a$

2. `a  :-  b,  c,  d.` $\neg b \lor \neg c \lor \neg d \lor a$

3. `b  :-  e,  f.` $\neg e \lor \neg f \lor b$

4. `c  :-` c

5. `d  :-` d

6. `e  :-` e

7. `f  :-` f

The literal e in line 6 can be unified with the literal e in line 3. The literal f in line 7 cancels out the literal f in line 3. The literal b in line 3 cancels out the literal b in line 2. The literal c in line 4 can be resolved with the literal c in line 2. The literal d in line 5 cancels out the literal d in line 2. Thus, we are left with the literal a in line 2, which can be canceled out with the original query, the literal a in line 1. However, two literals do not have to be identical to be resolved. For example, in the following

```
parent_of(X, Y)  :-  father_of(X, Y), male(X).
father_of(john, mary).
male(john).
```

the father_of(X, Y) literal appearing to the right of the first rule can be unified with father_of(john, mary) in the second fact. These two literals are unifiable when the variable X is instantiated to the constant john, and the variable Y to the constant mary. Thus,

```
parent_of(X, Y)  :-  father_of(X, Y), male(X).
father_of(john, mary).
```

can be resolved to

```
parent_of(john, mary)  :-  male(john).
```

Resolution by refutation proofs requires that the axioms and the negation of the goal be placed in *clause form* notation. Clause form represents the logical statements as a set of disjunction of literals. The most common form of resolution is called binary resolution, the basis for Prolog interpreter that is applied to two clauses when one contains a literal and the other its negation. If these literals contain variables, the literals must be unified to make them equivalent. In this case, a new clause is produced consisting of the disjuncts of all the literals in the two clauses excluding the literal and its negative instance, which are said to have been resolved or cancelled out. The resulting clause receives the unification substitution under which the literal and its negation are found as equivalent. In general, the resolution refutation proofs can be stated as the following steps:

1. Put the set of facts and rules into clause form notation.
2. Add the negation of what is to be proved (goal or query), in clause form to the set of axioms.
3. Perform the following steps until there is no resolvable clause; if there is no resolvable clause, go to Step 4.
   - ▶ Unify (resolve) these clauses together, making new clauses that are logically produced from them.
   - ▶ Produce a contradiction by generating an empty clause. If there is an empty clause, stop and report the query is true.
   - ▶ The substitutions used to produce the empty clause are those under which the opposite of the negated goal is true.
4. Stop and report that the query is false; meaning that there is no solution associated with this query.

Step 3 is intended to produce an empty clause, indicating that there is a solution associated with the goal.

Producing the Clause Form

The resolution proof procedure requires all logical statements in the database (set of axioms) describing a situation to be converted to a standard form, called *clause form notation,* because resolution operates on pairs of disjunct literals to produce a new disjunct literal. The form the database takes is referred to as a *conjunction of disjunction of literals.* It is a conjunction because all the clauses in the database are assumed to be true at the same time. It is a disjunction of literals because each individual clause is expressed with the disjunction symbol (or the *or* symbol, ∨) as the connective symbol joining the literals. For example, the following logical statement

```
mother_of(susie, elizabeth) ∨ female(susie)
```

is formed by the disjunction of two literals, meaning that the two literals are connected by the or (∨) symbol. Thus, it is in clause form notation. In contrast, the following two logical statements are not in clause form notation because the literals are not connected by the ∨ symbol.

```
mother_of(susie, elizabeth) ∧ female(susie)
mother_of(susie, elizabeth) :- female(susie)
```

In the following, we outline the process of conjunctive normal form reduction through examples and give a brief description for each step.

▶ We eliminate :– " if " by using the equivalent form:

   b :– a ≡ a → b

▶ We eliminate → " implies " by using the equivalent form:

   a → b ≡ ¬ a ∨ b

▶ We reduce the scope of negation. This can be accomplished using a number of the transformation rules, including the following:

   ¬ (¬ a)   ≡   a
   ¬ (a ∧ b) ≡   ¬ a ∨ ¬ b
   ¬ (a ∨ b) ≡   ¬ a ∧ ¬ b

▶ We convert the expression to the conjunction of disjunction of literals. This requires using the associative and distributive properties of ∧ and ∨. These include the following:

   a ∨ (b ∨ c) ≡   (a ∨ b) ∨ c
   a ∧ (b ∧ c) ≡   (a ∧ b) ∧ c
   a ∨ (b ∧ c) ≡   (a ∨ b) ∧ (a ∨ c)

The following logical statement

   a ∧ (b ∨ c)

is already in clause form notation because ∧ is not distributed. Hence, it consists of the following two clauses:

```
a
( b  ∨  c )
```

We elaborate the conversion of the logical statements into disjunction of literals used in the Prolog system by the following examples.

Example: We consider the following statements translated into logical statements on the right and we want to prove that "Poddy will die."

Statement	Logical Statement
All dogs are animals.	∀ (X) dog(X) → animal(X).
Poddy is a dog.	dog(poddy).
All animals will die.	∀ (Y) animal(Y) → die(Y).
Poddy will die.	die(poddy).

First, we convert the logical statements to the following clause form notation.

Logical Statement	Clause Form
1. ∀ (X) dog(X) → animal(X)	¬ dog(X) ∨ animal(X)
2. dog(poddy)	dog(poddy)
3. ∀ (Y) animal(Y) → die(Y)	¬ animal(Y) ∨ die(Y)

We negate the query that "Poddy will die":

4. die(poddy)	¬ die(poddy)

Next, we resolve the clauses having opposite literals, producing a new clause by resolution procedure and continue until the empty clause is found. The symbol □ in Figure 11.10 indicates that the empty clause is produced and the contradiction is found. This symbol indicates that a predicate and its negation are found, creating the situation where two mutually contradictory logical statements are present in the database. The sequence of substitutions used to make predicates equivalent also gives us the value of variables under which a goal was true.

Example: Consider the following logical statements translated into Prolog clause form on the right. We would like to know that "who does John like?" by issuing a query as

```
?-  likes(john, Somebody).
```

Logical Statement	Clause Form
1. likes(david, bert).	likes(david, bert)
2. likes(bert, john).	likes(bert, john)
3. likes(john, X) :- likes(X, bert).	¬ likes(X, bert) ∨ likes(john, X)
4. ?- likes(john, Somebody).	¬ likes(john, Somebody)

FIGURE **11.10**   **Resolution proof for Poddy will die**

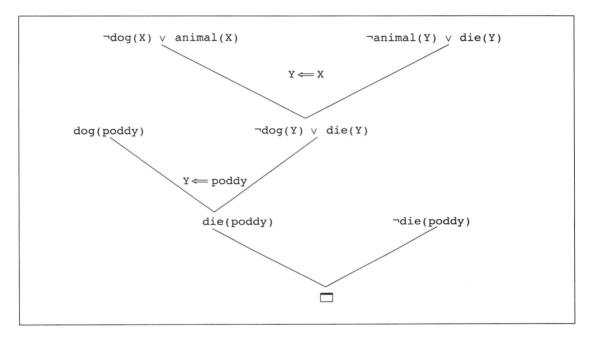

We convert the rule `likes(john, X) :- likes(X, bert)` to the form `likes(X, bert) → likes(john, X)` before it is converted into clause form, meaning that *if* is changed to *implies*. Figure 11.11 shows how to solve this query using the resolution by refutation procedure. The empty clause indicates that the query is true when the variable *Somebody* is instantiated to the constant *David*.

Example: Consider the following logical statements translated into Prolog clause form on the right. We would like to know " is b above table?" by issuing a query as

         `?- above(b, table).`

Logical Statement	Clause Form
1. `on(b,a).`	`on(b, a)`
2. `on(a, table).`	`on(a, table)`
3. `above(X, Y) :- on(X, Y).`	`¬ on(X, Y) ∨ above(X, Y)`
4. `above(X, Z) :- above(X, Y), above(Y, Z).`	`¬ above(X, Y) ∨ ¬ above(Y, Z) ∨ above(X, Z)`
5. `?- above(b, table).`	`¬ above(b, table)`

Figure 11.12 shows the sequence of steps for solving this query using the resolution by refutation procedure.

FIGURE **11.11**   Resolution proof for ?- likes(john, Somebody)

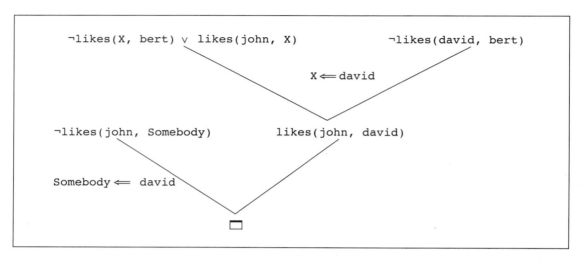

☞ 11.7 DEPTH-FIRST SEARCH

Although breadth-first search can be employed as a search mechanism, the search method used for the Prolog control system is depth-first search, which is very efficient because it can be implemented in a stack-based or a recursive fashion. The Prolog's control system performs the resolution of proving the goal in a specific order, which is top to bottom and left to right. Three important factors are employed in the process of answering a query regarding the depth-first search mechanism:

1. Matching the fact and rule with the first subgoal
2. Trying the facts and rules in order
3. Adding the precondition of the rule at the beginning of the goal after a match

In general, at each step, the Prolog control system maintains a list of subgoals and variables that have been instantiated. The system searches for an appropriate fact or rule that matches the first subgoal. Upon satisfaction, it continues to satisfy the remaining subgoals. If no possibilities remain to be explored, the search fails with no answer; otherwise, the answer can be found in the chain of variable instantiations made by all the matching. We illustrate the depth-first search by the following example, in which a portion of the Prolog depth-first search tree for this example appears in Figure 11.13 indicating that Mary and George are siblings.

Example: Consider the following facts and rules to trace the goal:

Goal   ?-   sibling_of(mary, Y).

FIGURE **11.12**   **Resolution proof for** ?- above(b, table)

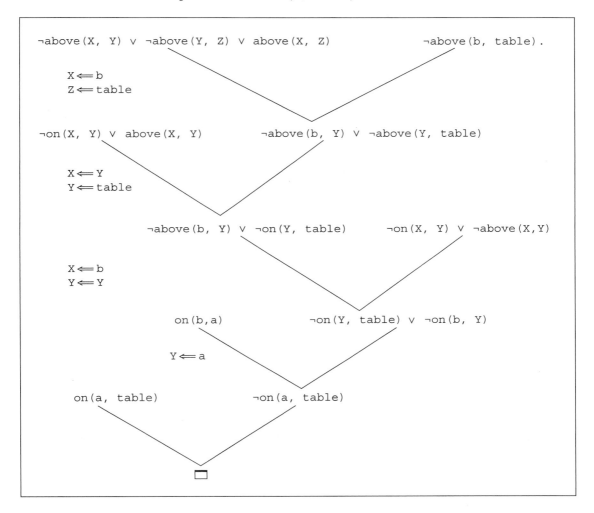

Rules:

```
parent_of(X, Y)   :-  father_of(X, Y), male(X).
parent_of(X, Y)   :-  mother_of(X, Y), female(X).
sibling_of(X, Y)  :-  parent_of(Z, X), parent_of(Z, Y), not(X=Y).
```

Facts:

```
1. father_of(john, mary).      5. male(john).
2. father_of(john, george).    6. male(george).
3. mother_of(susan, mary).     7. female(mary).
4. mother_of(susan, george).   8. female(susan).
```

Goal	?-	`sibling_of(mary, Y).`
Rule 3		`sibling_of(X, Y)  :-  parent_of(Z, X),`
		`parent_of(Z, Y), not(X=Y).`
Goal	?-	`parent_of(Z, mary), parent_of(Z, Y), not(mary=Y).`
Rule 1		`parent_of(X, Y)  :-  father_of(X, Y), male(X).`
Goal	?-	`father_of(X, mary), male(X),`
		`parent_of(Z, Y), not(mary=Y).`
Fact 1		`father_of(john, mary).`
Goal	?-	`male(john), parent_of(Z, Y), not(mary=Y).`
Fact 5		`male(john).`
Goal	?-	`parent_of(Z, Y), not(mary=Y).`
Rule 2		`parent_of(X, Y)  :-  mother_of(X, Y), female(X).`
Goal	?-	`mother_of(X, Y), female(X), not(mary=Y).`
Fact 4		`mother_of(susan, george).`
Goal	?-	`female(susan), not(mary=george).`
Fact 8		`female(susan).`
Goal	?-	`not(mary=george).` ⇒ `Y=George`

The new subgoal is inserted at the beginning of the list of subgoals, which leads to a depth-first search order. In the search tree, each node represents a subgoal. A node has a child for each rule that applies to the leftmost subgoal at the node. The order of the children is the same as the logical statement order in the knowledge base of facts and rules.

☛ 11.8 BACKTRACKING

Whenever a goal fails (when no matching term can be found) or when the user provides a continued search for the next answer with a semicolon "`;`", the control system performs backtracking to examine other paths of the search tree. At this point, the control system backtracks up the search tree to the nearest point where there was an alternative that has not been yet considered and releases all instantiations of variables as had been done so far. The interpreter performs a systematic search for solutions, and the direction of this search depends on the structure of the rules that are applied. For example, given a goal such as

```
mother_of(mary, Somebody)
```

the interpreter will evaluate the goal by trying each of the facts and rules in the order in which they appear in the database. Each fact or rule is applied in turn, until one succeeds or until all have been tried. An attempt to apply a fact or rule to satisfy a goal takes place in two stages:

1. The arguments in the goal are matched or unified with the arguments in the fact or rule. For instance, matching the previous goal with the following fact:

```
mother_of(X, mahsa)
```

FIGURE **11.13**   **Portion of the Prolog depth-first search tree leading to success**

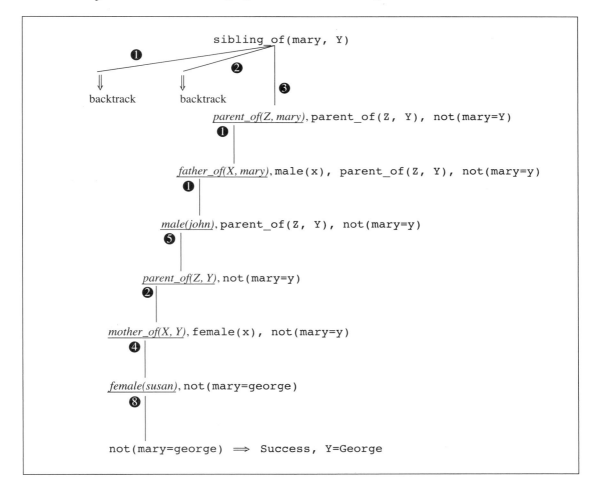

will set the variable X in the fact to mary and Somebody in the goal to mahsa. In this case, the goal succeeds because the matching was successful. If there is a conditional rule with subgoals such as

        mother_of(X, mahsa)   :- ...

then the interpreter proceeds to phase 2.

2. The right side of the rule is used to break the goal into a number of subgoals. These subgoals are evaluated in turn from left to right, either until all have succeeded or until one fails. If all subgoals have succeeded, then the goal is succeeded. If one subgoal fails, it causes the rule to fail. In this case, the interpreter searches for the next fact or rule's

FIGURE **11.14**   Top-down control in Prolog with backtracking

```
procedure   prove(G)
    begin
    let goal as G={G₁, G₂, ... , Gₖ}, where Gᵢ is a subgoal.
    let logical statements as {R₁, R₂, ... , Rₙ}
    where n is number of logical statements.
    if   (G ≠ φ)   then
        Choose leftmost subgoal G₁
        for i=1  to  n   do
                let Rᵢ be A :- B₁, B₂, ... , Bₘ
                if Rᵢ satisfies G₁ then
                let Ψ be the most general unifier of G₁ and A
                let Gᵠ be B₁Ψ, B₂Ψ, ... , BₘΨ, G₂Ψ, ... , GₖΨ
        prove(Gᵠ)
                end if
        end for
    else
    Success
    end if
    {backtracking to re-satisfy a previously visited subgoal}
 end   prove
```

head of the same subgoal and applies this. If no fact or rule succeeds, the goal fails. In other words, when a subgoal fails relative to one of the attempted facts or rules, the system's strategy is to go back (backtracks) to the nearest point (one level up) at which there was an alternative (another fact or rule) and try this alternative path. If this attempts fails, then the interpreter will step back up yet another level, and so on, until either a successful path is found or until all paths have been tried and failed. In this way, the system searches for solutions until it finds one or until it fails altogether.

Figure 11.14 represents a restatement of top-down control strategy in Prolog included backtracking. This systematic and relentless search for a solution gives the Prolog system its logical reasoning ability.

▿ 11.9 DEFICIENCIES OF PROLOG

Although the Prolog is a good and useful logic programming language, it is not a perfect language. The four important drawbacks of the Prolog language are the following:

1. The subgoals order determines the shape of the search space that the control system explores in its resolution process. Thus, a poor choice of subgoal order may produce a search tree with many branches and the system may fail to find solution, even when one exists.

2. The order in which facts and rules are employed is significant in the sequence of the solutions obtained. This is a key difference between the logic program and Prolog: The Prolog interpreter has a fixed control strategy, so the knowledge base in the Prolog program defines a particular search path to an answer to any question. This contrasts with the logic system, where the assertions defines only the set of answers they justify, and they say nothing about how to choose among those answers if there is more than one.

3. Because the Prolog interpreter performs an exhaustive depth-first search when trying to unify its variables, program execution can be very inefficient in both speed of execution and use of memory. Thus, the programmer must write procedures that minimize both search time and memory usage or adopt another approach to make the program execution efficient; such as parallel processing.

4. When the control system unifies a variable with a term, it does not check whether the variable itself occurs in the term it is being instantiated to. This is called *occurs check* problem. In other words, when a variable occurs in term, then unification of variable and term can lead to a nonterminating computation. Why the system does not support occurrence checking is because of the easy implementation, while a system with *occurs check* is more complex. This can be explained with the following example.

Example: To see the effect of *subgoals order, facts and rules order,* and *occurs check* problems consider the following facts describing the tree structure depicted in Figure 11.15.

```
1. parent_of(sima, nasim).      6. parent_of(nasim, susie).
2. parent_of(sima, omid).       7. parent_of(nasim, mary).
3. parent_of(sima, seyed).      8. parent_of(mary, shay).
4. parent_of(seyed, john).      9. parent_of(mary, mahsa).
5. parent_of(seyed, russel).   10. parent_of(mary, aby).
```

The following rules describe the ancestor relation:

```
1. ancestor_of(X, Y)  :-  parent_of(X, Y).
2. ancestor_of(X, Y)  :-  parent_of(Z, Y), ancestor_of(X, Z).
```

Suppose we are interested in finding all solutions associated with the following query:

```
?-  ancestor_of(X, mahsa).
```

In response, the system provides the following sequence of answers:

```
X = mary,   X = nasim,   X = sima
```

As an experiment, let us change the order in which the two rules are defined to

```
1. ancestor_of(X, Y)  :-  parent_of(Z, Y), ancestor_of(X, Z).
2. ancestor_of(X, Y)  :-  parent_of(X, Y).
```

With this change of the order of rules, the same query

```
?-  ancestor_of(X, mahsa).
```

FIGURE **11.15**   **Tree structure of facts**

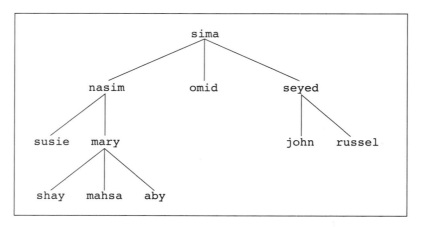

provides the same set of results as before, but in a different order

        X = sima,   X = nasim,   X = mary

which indicates that the order of rules and facts are important factors in answering questions. As another experiment, let us change the order of the terms that appeared in rule 1:

```
1. ancestor_of(X, Y)  :-  ancestor_of(X, Z), parent_of(Z, Y).
2. ancestor_of(X, Y)  :-  parent_of(X, Y).
```

In this case, the same query:

        ?- ancestor_of(X, mahsa).

causes the system to be in infinite loop. In fact, the goal `ancestor_of(X,Y)` generates the subgoal `ancestor_of(X, Z)`, which in turn generates the same subgoal and so on. Generally speaking, the underlying hidden control flow affects the performance and efficiency of the program, and the programmer must be aware of the implementation strategy adopted by the Prolog control system.

✔11.10 CUT OPERATOR

The efficiency and termination of derivations depend on the order of facts and rules, which violates the logic model format. If query evaluation requires considerable backtracking, the *Cut* operator can be introduced to save time. The *Cut* operator can be introduced by a predicate ! with no argument when *Cut* can control the search space. The *Cut* operator freezes the system to choices made since the rule was selected. The effect of a *Cut* is to prune the search tree or to control backtracking during the derivation process. In other words, if a *Cut* is reached, it informs the Prolog control system which choices need not be considered again during backtracking to satisfy subgoals. The *Cut* operator is actually a subgoal and always succeeds immediately, but it cannot be resatisfied through backtracking. The subtree search of the parent node of the node containing the *Cut* stops, and the search continues with the grandparent node. The *Cut* can be viewed as an efficiency mechanism to reduce the number of branches in the derivation process that need to be followed. The *Cut* operator was adopted for the Prolog system for two important reasons:

1. The program operates faster and will not waste time attempting to satisfy subgoals that you know beforehand will never contribute to a solution.

2. The program may occupy less memory space because the search space will be pruned for later examination.

We can outline the common use of *Cut* in three forms, which tell the Prolog system the following:

1. *If you reach this far you have found the only solution to this query and there is no need to search for alternative solutions.* In this case, the intention is to terminate the generation of alternative answers using backtracking.

2. *If you reach this far, you have selected the correct rule for this goal.* In this case, we want the Prolog system to stop searching because it has already found the right rule for this particular query.

3. *If you reach this far, you have failed, so immediately stop trying to satisfy the goal.* In this case, we want to fail the Prolog system for a particular goal immediately without trying other choices. We use *Cut* in conjunction with the *fail* predicate.

To see the effect of *Cut* on the Prolog search tree, consider the following 10 facts and 2 rules where the *Cut* is introduced in the first rule.

Facts

```
1. parent_of(sima,nasim).        6. parent_of(nasim,susie).
2. parent_of(sima,omid).         7. parent_of(nasim,mary).
3. parent_of(sima,seyed).        8. parent_of(mary,shay).
4. parent_of(seyed,john).        9. parent_of(mary,mahsa).
5. parent_of(seyed,russel).     10. parent_of(mary,aby).
```

Rules

```
1. ancestor_of(X, Y)  :-  parent_of(X, Y), !.
2. ancestor_of(X, Y)  :-  parent_of(Z, Y), ancestor_of(X, Z).
```

If we issue the query

```
?-  ancestor_of(X, mahsa).
```

the only solution obtained by the Prolog system will be X=mary as depicted in Figure 11.16. This illustrates a common use of a *Cut*, signaling that the right solution has been found and backtracking to find another solution is not required.

FIGURE **11.16**   **The effect of a *Cut* in the first rule**

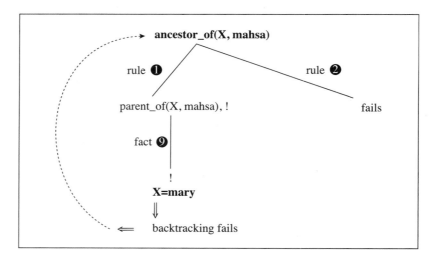

FIGURE **11.17**   **The effect of a *Cut* in the second rule**

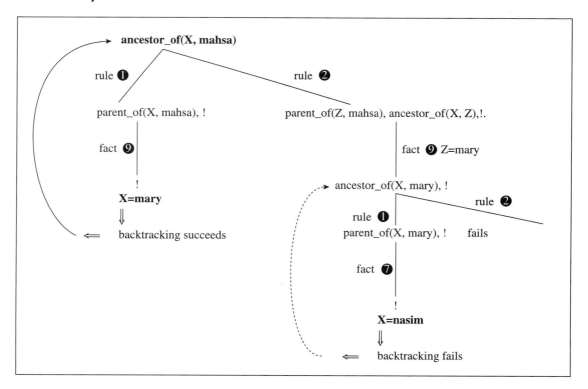

FIGURE **11.18**   **The effect of a *Cut* in conjunction with *fail***

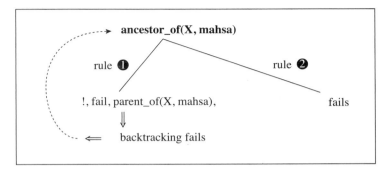

If we change the second rule by inserting a *Cut* as the last subgoal, the search tree changes to the one in Figure 11.17, in which the same query can produce two solutions:

```
1. ancestor_of(X, Y)  :-  parent_of(X, Y).
2. ancestor_of(X, Y)  :-  parent_of(Z, Y), ancestor_of(X, Z), !.
```

As an experiment, let us introduce the *Cut* in conjunction with *fail* predicate in the first rule as the following:

```
1. ancestor_of(X, Y)  :-  !, fail, parent_of(X, Y).
2. ancestor_of(X, Y)  :-  parent_of(Z, Y), ancestor_of(X, Z).
```

In this case, the system fails to find any solution. When *fail* is encountered after a *Cut*, the normal backtracking behavior will be altered, signaling the program to stop trying to satisfy the goal immediately as depicted in Figure 11.18.

⚑ 11.11 RECURSIVE RULES

Recursion is one of Prolog's fundamental processes. We can think of recursion as a train journeying from city to city. The driver receives instructions before he or she sets off, which must be obeyed at each city down the line. Now, imagine there are five cities as indicated in Figure 11.19.

The links between these cities can be represented in Prolog as the following facts:

```
route(boiling-springs, spartanburg).
route(spartanburg, greenville).
route(greenville, columbia).
route(columbia, charston).
```

This tells us that there is a route from one city to the next. Now here are the driver's instructions:

FIGURE **11.19**   **A train route between five cities**

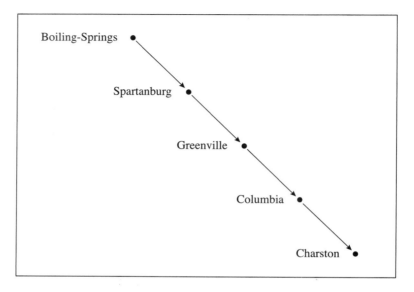

FIGURE **11.20**   **The first stage of the journey**

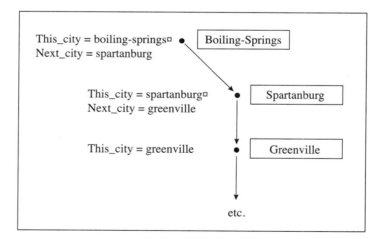

To travel from This_city to your Destination, first check that there is a route from This_city to the Next_city. If there is, then drive from This_city to the Next_city. When you get there, reapply these instructions.

For the first stage of the journey, `This_city` will be `boiling-springs` (the city from which the driver is setting off), and the `Next_city` will be `spartanburg`.

FIGURE **11.21**   **The program that corresponds to** ?- `travel(boiling-springs, columbia)`

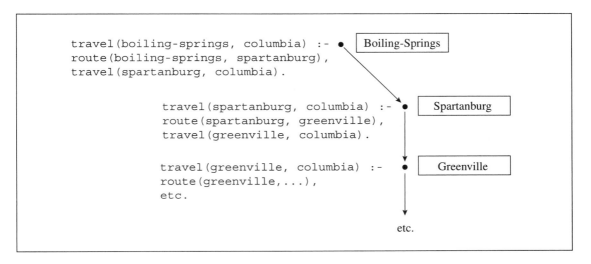

On arrival at `spartanburg`, `This_city` will become `spartanburg` and `Next_city` will become `greenville`, and so on, as shown in Figure 11.20. We can program the first stage of the journey as follows:

```
travel(This_city, Destination)  :-  route(This_city, Next_city),
                                     travel(Next_city, Destination).
```

If we issue a query, for example, to travel from Boiling-Springs to Columbia,

```
?- travel(boiling-springs, columbia).
```

the program will look as shown in Figure 11.21. The only trouble is that the driver will keep on going until he or she runs out of cities because, we have not said,

> Stop when you reach your destination!

We can do this by adding the following travel predicate (a fact), located before the other travel predicate, so that Prolog will try it first in each recursive cycle.

```
travel(Destination, Destination).
```

This fact means that

> If the name of the city where you now are (the first term of the travel predicate) is the same as that of your destination (the second term of the travel predicate), then you have arrived.

This fact with one literal is the *boundary condition,* meaning that the query has succeeded. This fact causes the travel goal to succeed when the Destination has been reached. The two travel predicates together are as follows:

FIGURE **11.22**   **The program that corresponds to ?-** `travel(boiling-springs, columbia)` **query**

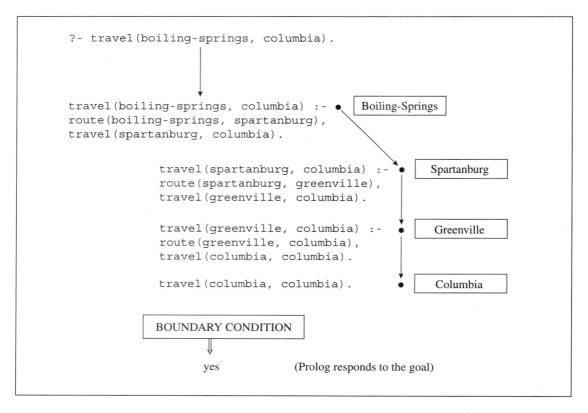

```
travel(Destinatin, Destination).
travel(This_city, Destination)  :-  route(This_city, Next_city),
                                    travel(Next_city, Destination).
```

Prolog always tries predicates in a top-down direction in each recursive cycle. As long as it does not apply, Prolog will try the next predicate. When the predicate does apply, the *full stop* causes the travel goal to succeed. Because this is the goal set in our original question, the whole program has succeeded, and Prolog replies *yes*, as shown in Figure 11.22.

In general, translating the basic pattern of recursive into a more generalized form consists of

Predicate 1:   A boundary condition to specify when to stop.

Predicate 2:   A rule including how to select the next move, and a recursive call to specify how to reapply the rules again.

☙ 11.12   PROLOG FACILITIES

In this section, we conclude the Prolog session by considering additional facilities that the language provides such as arithmetic, comparison, list, and input and output operations. The precise details of how the facilities are provided tend to vary a little from one version of Prolog to another. For more detail regarding the facilities, interested readers can refer to Clocksin and Mellish (1987), Crookes (1988), and Ford (1989).

Arithmetic Operations

The following basic arithmetic operations are available in Prolog:

Addition	`?-  X is 3+4`
Subtraction	`?-  X is 5-2`
Multiplication	`?-  X is 3*4`
Division	`?-  X is 8/2`
Remainder	`?-  X is 5 mod 2`

Comparison Operations

Prolog provides six ways of comparing numbers. In all operations, the values being compared are expressions or variables that already have values. The logical statement that uses comparisons is a simple rule that succeeds if a given comparison is satisfied.

Less than	`X < Y`
Greater than	`X > Y`
Less than or equal to	`X =< Y`
Greater than or equal to	`X >= Y`
Not equal to	`X =\= Y`
Equal to	`X =:= Y`

List Operations

List is a sequence of elements that are separated by commas, shown between brackets, and have any length. The elements may be any term, constants, variables, and structures, which includes other lists. The term [H | T] matches any list with at least one element:

► H matches the head of the list

► T matches the tail

In other words, the first element is called the head and the rest is called the tail of list. In the following, the head and tail of each list is shown.

List	Head	Tail
[a, b, c, d]	a	[b, c, d]
[ ]	none	none
[[the, man], human]	[the, man]	[human]
[the, [man, human]]	the	[[man, human]]
[the, [man, human], arm]	the	[[man, human], arm]

Many problems can be solved in Prolog by expressing the data as lists and defining constraints on those lists using patterns with Prolog's list representation. The following are examples of list processing in Prolog.

Example: Suppose we define last(L, X) to mean that "X is the last element of the list L."

▶   The last element of a singleton list is its only element.

```
last([X], X).
```

▶   The last element of a list with two or more elements is the last item in its tail.

```
last([H | T], X)  :-  last(T, X).
```

As an example, the query

```
?-  last([a, b, c], X).
```

results in the following:

```
X = c
yes
```

A similar query

```
?-  last([ ], X).
```

results in the following:

```
no
```

Observe that the operation of requesting the last element of an empty list simply fails. With imperative languages, a programmer must test for exceptional conditions to avoid the run-time failure of a program. With logic programming, an exception causes the query to fail, so a calling program responds by trying alternate subgoals.

Example: Define member(X, L) to mean that "X is a member of the list L." For this predicate we need two clauses, one as a basis case and the second to define the recursion that corresponds to an inductive specification.

▶   The predicate succeeds if X is the first element of L.

```
member(X, [X | T]).
```

► If the first clause fails, check if X is a member of the tail of L.

```
member(X, [H | T])  :-  member(X, T).
```

In this case, if the item is not in the list, the recursion eventually tries a query of the form member(X, [ ]), which fails because the head of no clause for member has an empty list as its second parameter.

Example: Define concat(X, Y, Z) to mean " the concatenation of lists X and Y is Z." In Prolog literature, this predicate is frequently called *append*.

1. `concat([ ], L, L).`
2. `concat([H | T], L, [H | M])  :-  concat(T, L, M).`

As an example, the query

```
?- concat([a, b, c], [d, e], R).
```

results in the following:

```
R = [a, b, c, d, e].
Yes
```

The search tree in Figure 11.23 illustrates the inference that produced this answer. In this example, when the last query succeeds, the answer is constructed by unwinding the bindings:

```
R = [a | M] = [a | [b | M1] ] = [a, b | M1 ] = [a, b | [c | M2] ]
  = [a, b, c | M2] = [a, b, c | [d e] ] = [a, b, c, d, e].
```

Input and Output

Prolog provides an input predicate, which succeeds only when the user enters an object on the keyboard with the following syntax:

```
read (variable).
```

For example,

```
Average   :-   read(X), read(Y), Z is (X+Y) / 2.
```

would calculate the value of Z as the average of X and Y entered on the keyboard. Prolog provides an output predicate for displaying an object on the screen with the following syntax:

```
write (variable).
```

For example,

```
?-   X is 2*10, write(X).
```

would display the value of X, which is 20 on screen. As an experiment, consider a simple program that accepts two numbers and outputs their average as

FIGURE **11.23**   **A search tree for *concat***

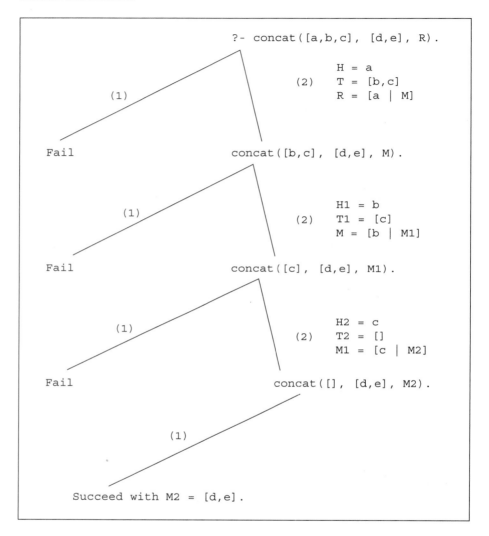

```
average   :-   read(X), read(Y), Average is (X+Y) / 2, write(Average), nl.
```

where predicate nl stands for new line in the process. A typical interaction might be:

```
?-   average.
20
30
Average=25
```

☞ SUMMARY

In this chapter, we discussed the most popular logic programming language, Prolog, which is based on automatic theorem proving. Prolog is a practical and efficient implementation of many aspects of intelligent program execution, such as nondeterminism, parallelism, and pattern-directed procedure call. Prolog provides a uniform data structure out of which all data, and Prolog programs, are constructed. A Prolog program consists of three major components: a series of rules, a series of facts, and a logical statement known as goal or query. The query was the given input to a program, which was treated as a goal to be proved. A goal could be proved using a top-down approach, also called backward chaining, which is similar to recursion, and a bottom-up approach, also called forward chaining, which is similar to iteration. Resolution and unification techniques are used to prove theorems in Prolog. We discussed the depth-first search method adopted by Prolog, which is very efficient because it can be implemented in a stack-based or recursive fashion. Backtracking is an important concept in Prolog whenever a goal fails or when the user provides a continued search for the next answer. Finally, we discussed the deficiencies of Prolog, such as order of facts and rules, unlimited search space, and occurs check.

☞ EXERCISES

1. Write a predicate to address the following description:

   A person may steal something if the person is a thief and the person likes the thing and the thing is valuable.

2. Consider the following relationships.

   ```
   father(X, Y).
   mother(X, Y).
   male(X).
   female(X).
   parent(X, Y).
   different(X, Y).
   ```

   Write Prolog clauses to define the following relationships.

   a. is_mother(X)

   b. is_father(X)

   c. is_son(X)

   d. sister_of(X, Y)

   e. granpa_of(X, Y)

   f. sibling(X, Y)

   g. aunt(X, Y)

3. Specify the *Head* and *Tail* of the following lists in Prolog.
   a. [a, b, c]
   b. [ ]
   c. [[the, cat], sat]
   d. [the, [cat, sat, on, the, table]]
   e. [the, [cat, sat], down]
   f. [X+Y, X+Y]

4. Specify the instantiations of the following pairs of lists.

List1	List2
[X, Y, Z]	[john, likes, fish]
[cat]	[X ∣ Y]
[X, Y ∣ Z]	[mary, likes, fish]
[[the, Y] ∣ Z]	[[X, here], [is, here]]
[golden ∣ T]	[golden, gloves]
[cat, horse]	[horse, X]
[white ∣ Q]	[P ∣ horse]

5. If a list consists of head H and tail T, the goal of an insertion sort is to sort the tail T recursively and then insert the item H into its proper place in the tail. Write a set of facts and rules to implement the insertion sort in Prolog.

6. Consider the following facts and rules.

```
parent(Bob, Jim).            female(Martha).
parent(Jim, Janet).          female(Gloria).
parent(Gloria, Eileen).      female(Janet).
parent(Martha, Julie).       female(Eileen).
parent(Bob, Rick).           female(Julie).
male(Bob).
male(Jim).
male(Rick).
child(X, Y)        :-        parent(X, Y).
mother(X, Y)       :-        parent(X, Y), female(X).
father(X, Y)       :-        parent(X, Y), male(X).
son(X, Y)          :-        child(X, Y), male(X).
daughter(X, Y)     :-        child(X, Y), female(X).
```

   Issue the following queries:
   a. Who is Bob's child?
   b. Who is Eileen's mother?
   c. Who is Gloria's daughter?
   d. Who is Janet's father?

    e. Who is Julie's mother?

    f. Who is Jim's child?

    g. Who is Bob's son?

    h. Who is Jim's son?

7. Consider the following clauses:

```
daughter_of(Mahsa, Seyed).
daughter_of(Mary, Seyed).
```

What is the answer of the following query?

```
?- daughter_of(First_daughter, Seyed), daughter_of(Second_daughter, Seyed).
```

8. Change the following sentences into *facts* and *rules* and create a database:

    a. Albert is male.

    b. Edward is male.

    c. Alice is female.

    d. Victoria is female.

    e. Victoria and Albert are the parents of Edward.

    f. Victoria and Albert are the parents of Alice.

    g. If X is female and Y is male and (M and F) are the parents of X and (M and F) are the parents of Y, then X is sister of Y.

Issue the query, " Is Alice the sister of Edward?," and use the *resolution by refutation* procedure to prove the answer.

9. Write a Prolog program to compute the *factorial* function.

10. What is the result of the following matching terms.

Term$_1$	**Term$_2$**
C(x, C(y, C(z, N)))	C(He, C(She, C(It, N)))
C(We, N)	C(x, y)
C(They, C(You, N))	C(You, C(x, N))
C(x, C(She, C(It, N)))	C(He, C(She, C(y, N)))

11. Convert the following sentences into facts:

    a. Nasim is the sister of Mary.

    b. Seyed is the father of Mary.

    c. John gives the book to Mary.

    d. Sima is the mother of Mahsa.

    e. The cat is on the table.

12. Consider the following facts and rules.
    1. A :- B, C, D.
    2. A :- E, F.
    3. B :- F.
    4. E.
    5. F.
    6. A :- F.

    Sketch the search space for query ?-A, E.

13. Suppose we change the last rule of the previous exercise to the following:
    1. A :- F, A.
    2. A :- B, C, D.
    3. A :- E, F.
    4. B :- F.
    5. E.
    6. F.

    Sketch the search space for query ?-A, E. What is the difference between this search space and the search space of the previous exercise? What do we need to change the situation?

14. Consider the following facts and rules.
    1. possible_pair(X, Y) :- boy(X), girl(Y).
    2. boy(john).
    3. boy(russel).
    4. girl(mary).
    5. girl(mahsa).

    What is the result of the query possible_pair(X, Y)?

15. Write a program to play the game Tic-Tac-Toe. The game involves two players taking turns to occupy squares on a 3×3 board. One player occupies squares with pieces marked O, and the other one with pieces marked X. The objective is to get three of the same pieces in a line before the other player does.

16. The three numbers x, y, and z are said to form Pythagorean Triple if $z^2 = x^2 + y^2$.
    a. Write a program to generate Pythagorean Triples.
    b. Define a query ?-pythag(x, y, z) for alternative solutions.

17. Consider the following rules presented to Prolog system:

```
origin(Pt(X, Y))      :=   X = 0, Y = 0.
inside(Pt(X, Y), R)   :=   X*X+Y*Y  <  R*R.
```

What is the answer of the following queries?

a. ? - origin(Pt(0, 2)).

b. ? - origin(P)

c. ? - inside(Pt(1, 2), 3).

d. ? - inside(Pt(1, 2), R).

18. The following clauses define a binary relation *element*(X, Y), which signifies that the value X is an element of the list L.

```
element(X, [Y|Ys])    :=    X = Y.
element(X, [Y|Ys])    :=    element(X, Ys).
```

Consider the following queries:

a. ? - element(3, [2, 3, 5]).

b. ? - element(4, [2, 3, 5]).

c. ? - element(V, [2, 3, 5]).

d. ? - element(4, [ ]).

19. The following clauses define a ternary relation *append*(L1, L2, L3), signifying that by concatenating the lists L1 and L2, we obtain the list L3:

```
append([ ], Ys, Ys).
append([X |Xs], Ys, [X |Zs])    :=    append(Xs, Ys, Zs).
```

Consider the following queries.

a. ? - append([2, 3], [5, 7], L).

b. ? - append([2, 3], L, [2, 3, 5, 7]).

c. ? - append(L1, L2, [5, 7]).

20. In quick sort method, a particular element is chosen as a pivot element. Then, the quick sort works by splitting a list of elements into three lists, those items less than the pivot, the list of those items greater than the pivot, and the list of those items the same as pivot element. The first number or the last number in the list can be chosen as the pivot element. After the first two subsets are sorted recursively, they are concatenated with the pivot in the middle to form a sorted result list. Write a set of facts and rules to implement the quick sort in Prolog.

21. Consider the following set of rules and facts:

```
North_of(X1, X2)  :-
Location(X1, X2, z1) & Location(X2, Y2, Z2) & Less(Y2, Y1).
Location(NewYork, 41, 74).
Location(Chicago, 42, 88).
Location(Tokyo, 35, 140).
Location(Tehran, 60, 11).
Location(Iowa, 0, 80).
Location(Spartanburg, 30, 30).
```

Construct a search tree starting with the following queries:

```
?-  North_of(Chicago, NewYork).
?-  North_of(X, NewYork).
```

REFERENCE-NEEDED EXERCISES

To answer the following exercises, you might need to consult the following references: Appleby and VandeKopple, 1997; Clocksin and Mellish, 1987; Ford, 1989.

1. Write an algorithm for a function unify(Term1, Term2) that returns Term3 or FAIL. A *term* is defined recursively:
   a. If C is a constant, then C is a *term*.
   b. If X is a variable, then X is a *term*.
   c. If P_N is an n-place predicate symbol, and $t_1, t_2, \ldots, t_N$ are *terms*, then $P_N(t_1, t_2, \ldots, t_N)$ is a *term*.

2. Consider the following relationships using the Cut primitive in Prolog.
   a. number_of_parents(adam, 0) :- !.
   b. number_of_parents(eve, 0) :- !.
   c. number_of_parents(X, 2).

   What will be the response of the Prolog system to the following queries?

```
?-  number_of_parents(betty, N).
?-  number_of_parents(eve, 2).
?-  number_of_parents(X, Y).
```

3. Rewrite the following rules using cut/fail to create an equivalent rule using *not*.
   a. marriageable(X, Y) :- (first_cousins(X, Y); same_sex(X, Y);
                               siblings(X, Y)),
                               !, fail.
   b. marriageable(X, Y) :- !.

Applicative Programming Specifications

The **functional programming languages,** also known as *applicative* or *expression-oriented programming languages,* provide a substantially different view of programming than do the imperative programming languages. Functional programming languages have some distinct advantages over imperative programming languages that have made them popular for artificial intelligence, mathematical proof systems, logic, and parallel processing applications. These advantages include the uniform view of programs as functions, treatment of functions as data, limitation of side effects, and use of automatic memory management. Thus, functional programming languages have great flexibility, conciseness of notation, and simple semantics. The main drawback to functional languages is inefficiency of execution. Because of their dynamic nature, these languages were intended to be interpreted rather than compiled, which results in substantial loss in execution speed. Allowing a function to return another function as its result opens many interesting possibilities, which are heavily exploited in functional programming. Variables, commands, and side effects are excluded; instead, programs are written entirely within the language of expressions, functions, and declarations. The programming language model that we introduce in this chapter is based on the mathematical concept of function, which is a mapping from a domain set to a range set. When this concept is used as a model for programs, the domain is the set of all possible inputs and the range is the set of all possible outputs. The key properties of functional programming can be classified as follows:

▶ **Lazy function evaluation,** which is a mechanism that eliminates unnecessary evaluation of functions and includes two strategies:

1. Postponing evaluation of a function until it is needed
2. Eliminating the reevaluation of the same function more than once

397

▶ **First-class objects,** which means that functions are treated like any other object in the language. In other words, using a function as an argument to another function or as the value of a variable is what makes functions first-class objects. Perhaps the most important feature of functions being first-class objects and programs being functions is that programs can be treated as data and modified at run time.

▶ **All programs and procedures are functions,** which clearly distinguishes incoming values as parameter values from outgoing values as evaluation results.

▶ **Lack of variable and assignment,** which eliminates the concept of variable, except as a name for a value, and assignment as an available operation. Thus, in pure functional programming, there are no variables—only constants, parameters, and values.

▶ **Lack of loop and iteration,** which means that loops are replaced by recursive calls. Indeed, a loop must have a control variable that is reassigned as the loop runs, which is not possible without variables and assignments. Recursion is an essential feature of functional form and is used to write repeated operations.

▶ **Referential transparency,** which is the property of a function whereby its value depends only on the values of its parameters, not on any previous computations, the order of evaluation, or the execution path that led to the call. The phrase **referential transparency** was first used by Alfred North Whitehead and Bertrand Russell in *Principia Mathematica* to compare the following two syllogisms:

All men are mortal;	Everything Xenophon said about Socrates is true;
Socrates is a man;	Xenophon said: Socrates is mortal;
Therefore Socrates is mortal.	So Socrates is mortal.

The second syllogism is significantly different from the first. In the first, the argument is irrefutable because of the force of its structure. The second is less satisfying because it depends on the nature of Xenophon's belief. A programming language is said to be referentially transparent if the meaning of the whole can be determined solely from its parts. For example, in the mathematical expression f(x) + g(x), we can substitute another function h for f if we know that it produces the same value as f. In contrast, if f or g change the value of their parameter x (by reference to the parameter) or modify some global variables, we are not even assured that f(x) + g(x) = g(x) + f(x) or f(x) + f(x) = 2f(x); that is, the meaning of the expression depends on the history of computation of the subexpressions. In general, a language in which the context does not affect the meaning of expressions is also said to be referentially transparent, which means that expressions denote the same values regardless of context. The lack of assignment statements, parameters passed by reference, and global variables is the main reason that functional languages are referentially transparent. Imperative programming languages violate this property because of the central importance of memory locations to shifting values during run time.

▶ **Dynamic memory environment,** which is allocation and deallocation of memory during program execution. In procedural languages, the automatic allocation and deallocation of memory occurs only for activation records on a stack. In this regard, space is allocated for an activation record when a procedure is called and deallocated when the procedure is exited. Fully dynamic allocation, such as for pointer variables, is manual and occurs through programmer calls to allocation and deallocation such as C's *malloc* and *free* function calls. By contrast, an essential feature of the run-time environment for a functional language is efficient automatic allocation and deallocation of memory. In a language with first-class function values, a stack-based system cannot be used because references to a function's local environment can persist even after the function has been exited. Regarding this, the environment of a functional language needs to be *fully dynamic* such that the language deletes activation records only when they can no longer be reached when the program runs. As a consequence, a fully dynamic environment must perform some kind of automatic reclamation of unreachable storage. Automatic memory management actually falls into two categories: *Maintaining free space,* which is the process of maintaining the free space available for allocation, as we discussed in Chapter 3; and *reclamation of storage,* which is the process of reclaiming previously allocated but no longer used storage.

▶   **Garbage collection,** sometimes called reclamation of storage, which is the process of keeping track of inaccessible storage and permitting it to be reallocated. In general, functional programming languages require more storage than do block-structured programming languages. Primarily, this is because of the extra storage needed for the graph structure method of implementation and passing the functions. For example, the expression (+ 2 3) can be represented by a graph. Such graphs are created dynamically as expressions are encountered. Thus, some methods need to be included in a compiler for a functional language to release storage when it is no longer needed. Methods to collect and return unreferenced storage are called *garbage collection.* A garbage collector is a run-time system that reclaims the portions of storage that have previously been allocated but are no longer used by the program. Usually, the garbage collector is automatically invoked when the supply of free storage is exhausted. In this situation, the system enters a garbage collection phase, in which it identifies all the unused storage and returns it to free storage. This process is very time consuming, and implementing efficient collectors is an important issue in programming language design. Historically, LISP pioneered garbage collection as a method for managing the run-time deallocation of memory. Indeed, in LISP, all allocation as well as deallocation of storage is performed automatically and dynamically. Some of the well-known garbage collection methods are *Mark-Scan, Copying,* and *Reference-Counting,* as we briefly explained in Chapter 3.

▶   **Side-effect freedom,** which is the ability to call a function without producing side effects, that is, without changing the internal state of the computations. Side effects are operations that permanently change the value of a variable or other observable objects. For example, C uses statements with side effects as a matter of course. The statement A = B + C has a side effect because the value of variable A is changed after the expression B + C is executed. In contrast, when functional languages evaluate the expression B + C, they typically create an entirely new element with which to associate the result. In other words, the value of B + C is simply the sum of the variables B and C. This principle rules out assignments that can change the value of a variable in functional programming. Consequently, computation proceeds by evaluating expressions, rather than by making assignments to variables.

Practically speaking, most functional programming languages retain some notion of variable and assignment and are therefore impure functional languages. In this chapter, we survey the concept of a function and how programs can be viewed as functions. We trace the evolution of functional programming languages through development of lambda calculus in Section 12.1. In general, all functional programming languages can be viewed as syntactic variations of the lambda calculus. The fundamental operations in all functional languages are the creation of functions—namely, lambda abstraction and application of two basic operations in lambda calculus. In addition, the main goal of manipulating a lambda expression is to reduce it to a simplified form and consider that form as the evaluated value of the expression. Thus, we outline evaluation of lambda expressions relative to reductions, such as *Alpha-reduction, Beta-reduction, Eta-reduction,* and *Gamma-reduction* in this section.

Pure Functional Programming (FP) was the inspiration for the design and implementation of many functional programming languages. In Section 12.2, we explore FP as the design principles of functional programming languages. In this sense, a function can be defined by four components—domain set, range set, definition, and name—with associated operations, such as selection, structuring, arithmetic, predicate, logical, and identity.

◘ 12.1 LAMBDA CALCULUS

Lambda calculus was proposed as a theoretical model of computation for the functional programming paradigm by Alonzo Church (1941). **Lambda calculus** is a mathematical method for expressing computation by functions and is used for studying functional programming language concepts. It is a fundamental theory of functions that provides rules for defining and manipulating functions. Its uncomplicated syntax and semantics provide an excellent source for studying the theory of functional programming languages and is essential in capturing their commonalities. All functional programming languages can be viewed as syntactic variations of lambda calculus, permitting their implementation to be analyzed in its context. In addition, it plays the role of an intermediate language for translation from program to mathematical expression. Lambda calculus gets its name from the Greek letter lambda, λ. Lambda calculus resembles a quantified expression in predicate calculus, meaning that it plays a role syntactically similar to that of a quantifier such as $\forall$ (for all). Although an indepth presentation of this theory is beyond the scope of this discussion, familiarity with its basic concepts is useful for understanding some key programming language issues. The general form of a lambda expression, known as the lambda function, is

```
λ id₁, id₂, . . . , idₙ. expression
```

where the `id`'s are identifiers (parameters or variables) and `expression` (called the body of the lambda function) is some expression that may involve the identifiers. In

FIGURE **12.1**   A lambda expression with evaluation value

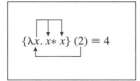

general, this function has *n* arguments, where *n* is the number of identifiers between λ and dot. A lambda expression specifies the parameters and the mapping rule, in which the symbol "." separates the specification of parameters from that of the mapping rule. For example,

λx. x*x

is a function that maps any value of x to x*x and defines a mapping from an integer number to integer numbers, yielding the square of integer numbers. This lambda expression can be applied as

{λx. x*x }(2)

where the result of the lambda expression x*x can be deduced by replacing the parameter and evaluating the resulting expression with 2. For example, Figure 12.1 results in 4 as the evaluation value.

Thus, lambda notation allows the definition of a function without a name. For example, λx. x*x defines a lambda function that maps each x in the integer domain to x^2. Generally speaking, the value of a lambda expression such as

λ id_1, id_2, . . . , id_n. *expression* (a_1, a_2, . . . , a_n)

when applied to arguments (a_1, a_2, . . . , a_n), is given by evaluating expression, with a_1 substituted for all occurrences of id_1, a_2 substituted for all occurrences of id_2, and a_n substituted for all occurrences of id_n. In general, when we write the mathematical expression x + 1, we think of it as a variable numeric expression. As an expression,

(x + 1) = (y + 1)

will be true only when x = y. However, if we want to express the notion that the expressions are the same—no matter what values may be substituted for x and y—we need the notation of lambda calculus. For example, λx.(x + 1) ≡ λy.(y + 1) indicates that *x* is bound in the expression that follows, or (x + 1), and that y is bound in the expression that follows, or (y + 1). The notations differ only in that the single bound variable has been renamed from x to y, so the two expressions represent the same function. In general, lambda functions can be used to create procedures, for which no name is specified and that take one of the following forms.

1. An *identifier* or *atom*, whereby atoms represent constants or functions and constants are treated as functions that yield a constant result.

FIGURE **12.2**   **Examples of lambda functions**

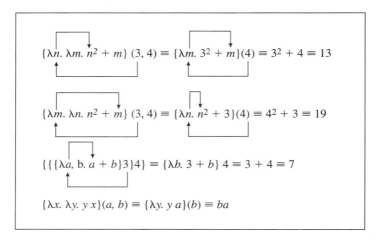

2. An *abstraction*, which represents a one-argument function: $\lambda x.$ expression, where x is an identifier and expression is a lambda expression. For example, $\lambda x.E$ is the function that, when applied to an argument a, as in $\{\lambda x.E\}(a)$, yields the evaluation of E with a substituted for x in E. The name comes from the observation that $\lambda x.E$ represents E "abstracted" from the particular choice of identifier x.

3. An *application*, which represents more than one lambda expression such as $\lambda x.$ expression$_1$ expression$_2$, where x is an identifier and expression$_1$ and expression$_2$ are two lambda expressions. For example, $\lambda x.E_1 E_2$ represents the result of applying the function denoted E_1 to the value denoted E_2, which must be a suitable argument for E_1. In this sense, the lambda expression E_1 is in the function position of the application and E_2 is in the argument position of the application.

The examples in Figure 12.2 illustrate some lambda functions, in which the arrows indicate the substitution of the values to identifiers. In the following example, we replace (+ 3 4) by its value and then apply it to the lambda function, which corresponds to the first evaluation form. Or, we apply (+ 3 4) to the function and then evaluate the expression, which corresponds to the second evaluation form. That is,

$$\{\lambda x.\ (+\ x\ x)\}(+\ 3\ 4) \equiv \{\lambda x.\ (+\ x\ x)\}(7) \equiv (+\ 7\ 7) \equiv 14$$

or

$$\{\lambda x.\ (+\ x\ x)\}(+\ 3\ 4) \equiv \{+\ (+\ 3\ 4)\}\ (+\ 3\ 4)\} \equiv \{+\ 7\ 7\} \equiv 14$$

In the following example, we use two arguments with the abstraction to define a function, replacing f with sqr, a predefined square function, and x with 3.

$$\{\{\{\lambda f.\ \{\lambda x.\ (f\ (f\ x))\}\}sqr\}3\} \equiv \{\{\lambda f.\ (sqr(sqr\ x))\}3\} \equiv$$
$$(sqr(sqr\ 3)) \equiv (sqr\ 9) \equiv 81$$

The grammar (rules) of lambda calculus can be outlined as

```
<expression>   ::=    <variable>
      |    <constant>
      |    (<expression>   <expression>)
      |    {λ<variable>  .  <expression>}
      |    {<λ. variable>  . <λ. expression>}
      |    {<λ. expression>   <λ. expression>}
```

where `<variable>` is any lowercase identifier, such as x or y. Variables in lambda calculus are not like variables in procedural programming languages, and they do not occupy memory because lambda calculus has no concept of memory. Indeed, lambda calculus variables correspond to function parameters as in functional programming languages. Thus, `<constant>` represents values and operations or predefined objects that are allowed in lambda expressions. Constants are numbers such as 0 or 1 and certain predefined functions such as + and *. We say that the rule

```
(<expression>    <expression>)
```

is a **function application** and that the rule

```
{λ<variable> . <expression>}
```

is a **lambda abstraction,** or *function definition.* Parentheses are included in a function application and a lambda abstraction to avoid ambiguity, but by convention may be left out when no ambiguity results. In other words, in the absence of parentheses, function applications group from left to right. Thus (x y z) abbreviates ((x y) z), but parentheses in (x (y z)) are necessary to ensure that x is applied to (y z). The remaining two rules are variations of the lambda abstraction.

Definition: The scope of λ`<variable>` in an expression extends as far to the right as possible, as in the following:

$$\lambda x. \; E_1 \; E_2 \; E_3 \quad \Rightarrow \quad \{\lambda x. (E_1 \; E_2 \; E_3)\}$$

Parentheses are needed for (λx.$E_1 \; E_2$)E_3, where E_3 is intended to be an argument to the function λx.$E_1 \; E_2$, rather than part of the body of the function.

Definition: An abstraction allows a list of identifiers that abbreviates a series of lambda abstraction, as in:

$$\lambda x, \; y, \; z. \; expression \quad \Rightarrow \quad \{\lambda x. \; \{\lambda y. \; \{\lambda z. \; E\}\}\}$$

Table 12.1 shows a few function definitions in this notation.

The external form of a lambda expression resembles that of a quantified expression in predicate calculus; that is, λ plays a role similar to that of a quantifier such as $\forall$. For example, the max lambda expression

$$\lambda x, \; y. \; \text{if } x \geq y \text{ then } x \text{ else } y \text{ end}$$

can be written as

$$\forall x, \; y. \quad \max(x, \; y) = \text{if } x \geq y \text{ then } x \text{ else } y \text{ end}$$

TABLE **12.1**	**Function Definitions**
	Lambda Function	**Function Name**
	λx, y. x + y	Plus
	λx. x * x	Square
	λx. x + 1	Successor
	λx. x − 1	Predecessor
	λx, y. if x ≥ y then x else y end	Max
	λx. x	Identity

However, there is an important difference between the two notations:

▶ By writing the ∀ property, we do not introduce max as an independent object but do assert a certain requirement on the value of max when it is applied to arbitrary argument x and y.

▶ By writing the lambda expression, the definition of max introduces a functional object, to which functional operations such as function composition may be applied.

In other words, the ∀ property makes a certain statement about the function, whereas the lambda expression defines the function entirely. However, not all lambda expressions lead to a result; for example:

$$(\lambda x. \ x \ x)(\lambda x. \ x \ x) \ \Rightarrow \ (\lambda x. \ x \ x)(\ \lambda x. \ x \ x) \ \Rightarrow \ (\lambda x. \ x \ x)(\ \lambda x. \ x \ x)$$

indicates that evaluating a lambda expression yields the original lambda expression. In this sense, the lambda expression has no general form.

12.1.1 Ambiguity

The lambda expression

```
λx. λy. f (g)
```

admits three possible interpretations, illustrating the ambiguity of the lambda calculus grammar:

1. λx. {λy. {f (g)}}
2. λx. {{λy. f } (g)}
3. {λx. λy. f } (g)

This ambiguity could be removed by complicating the grammar and requiring the use of parentheses. However, it is preferable to leave the grammar as it is and add the convention that the function application has the highest precedence. Thus, by default, the interpretation of the preceding expression is the first entry in the list. Braces are used to override this precedence when necessary.

FIGURE **12.3**   **A lambda expression with free and bound identifiers**

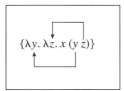

12.1.2 Free and Bound Identifiers

An occurrence of an identifier *id* in an expression is bound if it is within the scope of an expression whose identifier *id* is involved—that is, if it refers to an identifier introduced in the expression. A reference that is not bound to a formal parameter in the expression is said to be a **free identifier.** For example, in the lambda

$$\lambda x. \ x + y$$

the reference to x is bound (x is a bound identifier) and the reference to y is free (y is a free identifier), indicating that y is not in the scope of any expression. Free identifiers are a problem in lambda calculus. For example, when we apply the function specified by the following expression, a value can be substituted for x, but there is no way of determining the value of y in the expression:

$$\{\lambda x. \ x + y\}(5) \equiv 5 + y$$

In other words, an occurrence of an identifier in a scope is bound if the identifier denotes a local entity; it is free if it denotes a global entity to be provided by any outer scope in which the first scope is embedded. In a valid complete lambda expression, all identifier occurrences must be bound; that is, all variable references must have some associated value when they are evaluated at run time. For example, in the lambda expression

$$\lambda x, \ y, \ z \ . \ x + y + z \ \Rightarrow \ \{\lambda x. \ \{\lambda y. \ \{\lambda z. \ (x + y + z)\}\}\}$$

z, y, and x are bound identifiers and are in the scope of λz, λy, and λx, respectively. In the lambda expression in Figure 12.3, x is free but y and z are bound.

Free identifiers may not be renamed without changing the value of expressions within which they occur.

12.1.3 Reductions

The main goal of manipulating a lambda expression is to reduce it to a simplified form and consider that form as the evaluated value of the expression. There are four rules for manipulating the values, variables, and functions in a lambda calculus expression.

Alpha-conversion (α-conversion) refers to name changes in lambda expressions. This rule simply allows users to change bound variables as long as there is no capture of a free variable in the lambda expression. The α-conversion can be simplified to

$$\lambda\text{x. expression} \Rightarrow_\alpha \lambda\text{y. expression[x} \Rightarrow \text{y]}$$

where y does not occur at all in *expression* (y is not free in *expression*), which makes the substitution valid. For example, in

$$\{\lambda\text{w. (}\lambda\text{y. yz) w}\} \Rightarrow_\alpha \lambda\text{x. (}\lambda\text{y. yz) x}$$

the variable w is changed to x in the lambda function. Here, the meaning of a lambda expression is unchanged if the name of its identifier is changed along with all references to the identifier. One important issue must be avoided: The new identifier name cannot conflict with any other identifier names used in that part of the expression. Such conflict occurs when the new name is the same as the name of a free identifier in the body of the original lambda expression.

Beta-conversion (β-conversion) refers to the beta-reduction and beta-abstraction. This rule describes the function application mechanism in which actual substitutions of parameters are carried out, that is, how a function (lambda abstraction) is applied to a particular argument. Here, the key to performing an evaluation of a lambda expression depends on recognizing β-reductions. The β-conversion can be simplified to

$$\lambda\text{x. expression}_1 \text{ expression}_2 \Rightarrow_\beta \text{expression}_1\text{[x} \Rightarrow \text{expression}_2\text{]}$$

in which the substitution of x in expression_1 is carried out according to the rules for a safe substitution. In other words, the β-conversion can be interpreted as saying that a function ($\lambda\text{x. b}$) applied to the actual argument t means the same as the body b where all occurrences of the formal parameter x have been replaced by t. For example,

$$\{\lambda\text{x. x + 1}\} \text{ 5} \Rightarrow_\beta \text{(5 + 1)} \equiv \text{6}$$

Reversing the β-reduction rule produces the β-abstraction rule, as in

$$\text{expression}_1\text{[x} \Rightarrow \text{expression}_2\text{]} \Rightarrow_\beta \{\lambda\text{x. expression}_1\} \text{ expression}_2$$

where the two rules taken together provide the β-conversion, denoted as $\Leftrightarrow_\beta$.

In general, the goal of evaluation in lambda calculus is to reduce a lambda expression via β-reduction until it cannot be reduced any further. A lambda expression is said to be in normal form if it cannot be evaluated further via β-reduction. For example,

```
(λx. (λf. f(succ x)) (λz. (λg. (λy. (add (mul (g y) x)) z))) ((λz. (add z 3)) 5 )
```

proceeds as follows:

```
(λx. (λf. f(succ x)) (λz. (λg. (λy. (add (mul (g y) x)) z))) ((λz. (add z 3)) 5 ) ⇒β
(λx. (λf. f(succ x)) (λz. (λg. (λy. (add (mul (g y) x)) z))) (add 5 3) ⇒β
(λx. (λf. f(succ x)) (λz. (λg. (λy. (add (mul (g y) x)) z))) 8  ⇒β
(λf. f(succ 8)) (λz. (λg. (λy. (add (mul (g y) 8)) z))) ⇒β
(λz. (λg. (λy. (add (mul (g y) 8))) z)) (succ 8) ⇒β
(λz. (λg. (λy. (add (mul (g y) 8))) z)) 9 ⇒β
(λg. (λy. (add (mul (g y) 8))) 9) ⇒β
(λy. (add (mul (9 y) 8))) ⇒
(λy. (add (9*y  8))) ⇒
(λy. 9*y+8)
```

For example,

```
(λg. g (λa. λb. a)) ((λa. λb. λf. f a b) p q)
```

proceeds as follows:

```
(λg. g (λa. λb. a)) ((λa. λb. λf. f a b) p q) ⇒β
((λa. λb. λf. f a b) p q) (λa. λb. a) ⇒β
((λb. λf. f p b) q) (λa. λb. a) ⇒β
(λf. f p q) (λa. λb. a) ⇒β
(λa. λb. a) p q ⇒β
(λb. p) q ⇒β p
```

Eta-conversion (η-conversion) refers to eliminating redundant lambda abstractions. This rule can be simplified to

```
{λx. expression} x ⇒η expression
```

which requires that x have no free occurrences in `expression` so any conflict is avoided. If `expression` stands for a predefined function, the rule remains valid, as expressed by

```
{λx. (sqr 5)}(x) ⇒η (sqr 5) ≡ 25
```

or

```
{λx. y}(x) ⇒η y
```

In general, by η-conversion, (λx. Ex) is equivalent to E as long as E contains no free occurrences of x.

Gamma-conversion (δ-conversion) is associated with predefined values and functions. This rule can be simplified to

```
{function x y} ⇒δ function(x, y)
```

In other words, if lambda calculus has predefined constants and functions (e.g., add, sub, and sqrt), rules associated with those predefined values and functions are called δ-rules. For example,

```
(add 5 3) ⇒δ add(5, 3) ≡ 8
```

In the following examples, we use the reduction rules to illustrate δ-conversion:

```
{λx. {λx. add(sub x 1)} x 3}(9)  ⇒β  {{λx. add(sub x 1)} 9 3}
⇒β {add(sub 9 1) 3} ⇒δ add(8 3) ⇒δ 11
{λx. λy. {add y ((λz. (mul x z)) 4)}} 8 6 ⇒β {λy. {add y ((λz. (mul 8 z)) 4)}} 6
⇒β {add 6 {λz. (mul 8 z)} 4} ⇒β
{add 6 (mul 8 4)} ⇒δ (add 6 32) ⇒δ 38
{λy. 5}(λx. x x) ⇒η 5
{λx. y}(λy. x(y)) ⇒η {λx. y}(x) ⇒η y
{λy. λz. z y} c (λx. x) ⇒β {λz. z c}(λx. x) ⇒β {λx. x}c ⇒β c
{λx. {λy. (y x)}}(y w) ⇒α {λx. {λz. (z x)}}(y w) ⇒β {λz. (z)(y w)} ⇒β (y w)
```

FIGURE **12.4**   The Church–Rosser theorem

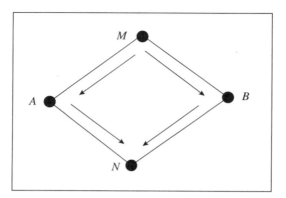

12.1.4 The Church–Rosser Theorem

The **Church-Rosser theorem** applies to all reductions, even those that do not terminate. This theorem can be stated as follows: If a lambda expression M evaluates to a normal form A via a sequence of reductions (M$\Rightarrow$*A), and another sequence of reductions takes M to a normal form B (M$\Rightarrow$*B), then some common term N can be found such that A can be reduced to N and B can also be reduced to N (A$\Rightarrow$*N and B$\Rightarrow$*N). Thus, some term N is reachable from both A and B, as depicted in Figure 12.4. Any relation that satisfies this condition is said to have the **diamond property** or the **confluence property.** The lambda expression {$\lambda x.\ x + x$}(($\lambda x.\ x$) y), for example, has two alternative evaluations, as depicted in Figure 12.5. The Church–Rosser theorem holds that the result of a computation is independent of the order in which reductions are applied. The reason is that all possible reduction sequences progress toward the same evaluated result.

Order of Evaluation

From the Church-Rosser Theorem, we know that no two orders of evaluation of a lambda expression can give different normal forms, although some may possibly fail to terminate even though there is a normal form. Is there an order of evaluation that is guaranteed to terminate whenever it is possible somehow to reduce a particular expression to normal form? Yes, there is such an order, known as **normal order,** also called **call-by-name.** As shown, the *call-by-name evaluation* reduces the leftmost expression at every stage. Another order which is particularly significant to programming languages is **applicative order** or **call-by-value.** The *call-by-value evaluation* evaluates the function and the argument of an application first (this could be done in parallel). If the applicative order evaluation terminates, it terminates with the correct answer (by the Church-Rosser Theorem). But it may fail to terminate on some lambda expressions that can be reduced to a normal form. When applicative order evaluation does terminate, it does so faster than normal order evaluation, as the next example illustrates:

FIGURE **12.5**   **Alternative evaluations of a lambda expression**

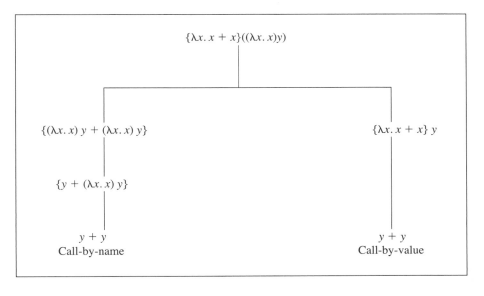

```
(λx. x + x + x +x)   ( (λx. x) a)
(λx. x) a + (λx. x) a + (λx. x) a + (λx. x) a
a + (λx. x) a + (λx. x) a + (λx. x) a
a + a + (λx. x) a + (λx. x) a
a + a + a + (λx. x) a
a + a + a + a
```

In Figure 12.5, the call-by-name evaluation introduces two identical β-reductions, which are then reduced individually. In contrast, the call-by-value evaluation reduces the argument only once in evaluating the lambda expression. In general, the Church–Rosser theorem states that no two orders of evaluation of a lambda expression can give different results. The somewhat technical proof of this theorem can be found in Barendregt (1984) and MacLennan (1990).

12.1.5 Typed Lambda Calculus

It is often useful to specify the sets to which the function arguments belong, as in a more precise definition of the square of integers:

    λx: int. x*x

This version of the notation is called **typed lambda calculus,** which includes the notation of data type involved in lambda expressions. For example, an identity function from integer to integer can be written as

    λx: int. x

This variant of lambda calculus has rules for determining the type of a lambda expression and the type constraints that a valid expression must meet. Typed lambda calculus is a proper subset of the class of untyped lambda expressions and introduces the following rules and constraints:

▶ **Typing identifiers,** which means that every occurrence of an identifier must be given a type. For bound identifiers, the type is the result of an explicit declaration. For free identifiers there is no information in the expression. We assume that the default type, defined as `default(x)`, will be the type of the free identifiers in the expression.

▶ **Typing hierarchy,** which is an appropriate notation of type. A type is defined as a *basic type* (e.g., *int, float,* or *binary*) or a *function type,* written as $\alpha \Rightarrow \beta$, where α and β are types. A function type describes the type whose instances are functions taking arguments of type α and returning results of type β.

▶ **Typing rules,** which refer to defining the type of general lambda expressions. The type of an abstractions $\lambda x: \alpha.\ expression$ is $\alpha \Rightarrow \beta$, where β is the type of *expression*. The type of an abstraction $\lambda x: \beta.\ expression_1$ $expression_2$ is $\alpha \Rightarrow (\alpha \Rightarrow \beta)$, where the type of $expression_1$ is $\alpha \Rightarrow \beta$ and the type of $expression_2$ is α.

The following examples illustrate these rules:

```
{λn. λm.  n² + m}(3, 4) ≡ {λn: int. λm: int ⇒ int. n² + m}(3, 4)  ≡ 3² + 4 ≡ 13
{λx. λy.  y x}(a, b) ≡ {λx: char. λy: char ⇒ char. y x}(a, b) ≡ ba
{λx. (+ x x)}(+ 3 4) ≡ {λx: int ⇒  int. (+ x x)}(7) ≡ (+ 7 7) ≡ 14
```

▨ 12.2 PRINCIPLES OF FUNCTIONAL PROGRAMMING

John Backus, the developer of Fortran, has been working on a purely functional programming language since the early 1970s. In this section, we review Backus's idea of this language. In particular, we present the structure of a very simple FP language (Backus, 1978). A *relation* describes associations between objects. For example, consider two sets of elements, X and Y. A relation R between X and Y is defined as a set of pairs of elements such as `{<a1, b1>,<a2, b2>, . . . ,<an, bn>}`, where every a_i is a member of X and every b_i is a member of Y. Here, X is called the source domain, and Y is called the target domain. Figure 12.6 illustrates the relation `{<x1, y1>, <x1, y2>, <x2, y2>, <x4, y3>, <x4, y5>}`.

In general, for a relation R and an object x, there may be zero, one, or more than one objects y such that the pair (x, y) belongs to R. A relation such that there is *at most one* such y for every x is said to be a *function* that corresponds to a mapping from one element of X to one element of Y. Figure 12.7 illustrates the function `{<x1, y1>, <x2, y2>, <x3, y4>, <x4, y5>}`.

In the functional computation paradigm, we think of functions only. A function is as simple as mapping from a tuple to a value, as in

FIGURE 12.6   **A relation expressing** `{<x1, y1>, <x1, y2>, <x2, y2>, <x4, y3>, <x4, y5>}`

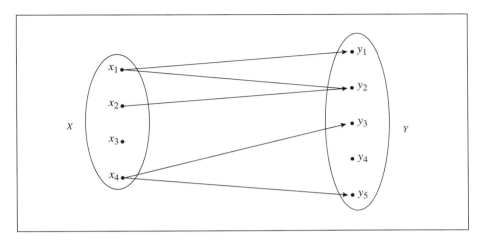

FIGURE 12.7   **A function expressing** `{<x1, y1>, <x2, y2>, <x3, y4>, <x4, y5>}`

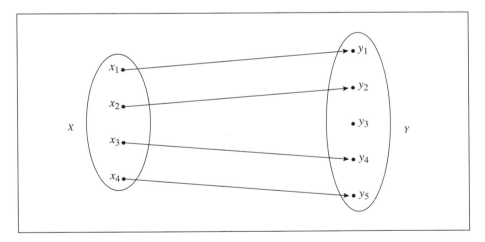

$$\texttt{value} \Leftarrow F(<x_1, x_2, \ldots, x_n>)$$

where $<x_1, x_2, \ldots, x_n>$ is a tuple (arguments or parameters), or ordered set of values. Indeed, $<x_1, x_2, \ldots, x_n>$ is an n-ary tuple, or simply an n-tuple. Consequently, an n-ary function is a mapping from an n-tuple to a value. This definition is the basis of functional computation in which each function returns a value that is the result of the evaluation. The x_i is the independent variable of the function, and `value` is the dependent variable because its value depends on the value of x_i. In this sense, a function can be defined by four components:

▶ A **domain set,** which is the set of objects to which the function can be applied

▶ A **range set,** which is the set containing all objects that can result from an application of the function

▶ A **definition,** which is the specification of how a range element is determined from a domain element

▶ A **name,** which is a symbol dedicated to the function

Thus, a definition or a simply called rule is used for mapping or associating members of a domain set to members of a range set. In other words, a function definition specifies the domain, the range, and the mapping rules for the function specification. Thus, we state that a function F is a rule that associates with each element of a domain set X a unique element of a range set Y, and we write $F: X \to Y$. An alternative view is that F defines a collection of pairs of elements (x, y) of X and Y with the property that y=F(x) and that each x is contained in at most one pair of such elements. If (x, y) is such a pair and so is (x, z), then y=F(x) and z=F(x), so y=z and the pairs are the same. Thus, a function can be viewed as a set of pairs (x, y) such that y=F(x) or as a subset of the Cartesian product X×Y:

    F ≡ { (x, y) ∈ X×Y | y=F(x) }

where ≡ means "is equivalent to" and ∈ means "is contained in." This is an advantage of viewing a function as a set for the study of the definition of functions in programming languages. For example, consider a function expressing the following definition:

    F(x) = (x+1) Mod 10

This indicates that the function on the set of digits (i.e., {0,1,2,3,4,5,6,7,8,9}) adds one to each digit in modulo fashion. Function definition by formula is sometimes called *definition by comprehension.* This function can be represented as the following set of pairs:

    {(0,1),(1,2),(2,3),(3,4),(4,5),(5,6),(6,7),(7,8),(8,9),(9,0)}

or in set terminology as shown in the following:

    F ≡ { (x, y) ∈ digit×digit | y= (x+1) Mod 10}

In a function language, the body of a function given in its definition typically represents an equation that gives its definition by comprehension. For example, the Miranda function definition

    add x = x+x

indicates that the add function is given as the set:

    add ≡ { (x, y) ∈ number×number | y= (x+x)}

where the mapping yields the result as an element of the domain set number. Once a function has been defined, it can be applied to a particular element of the domain set in which the mapping yields the associated element in the range set. For example, the function definition expressed in mathematical notation as

    square(x) = x*x, x an integer

defines a function named `square` as the mapping from integer numbers to integer numbers, in which x stands for any member of the domain set. Here, `square(5)` results in the value 25, according to the definition, when the function is applied to a specific domain value. The components of the square function can be expressed as

▶ **Domain:** a set of integer numbers

▶ **Range:** a set of integer numbers

▶ **Definition:** $x*x$, where x is an element from the domain set

▶ **Name:** square

An alternative representation of a function is

$$F = (<x_1, x_2, \ldots, x_n, \texttt{value}>)$$

where the last argument is called the *function result* and can be determined by the argument values of $<x_1, x_2, \ldots, x_n>$. When this concept is used as a model for a programming language, the domain is the set of all possible inputs and the range is the set of all possible outputs. Thus, a functional programming language is based on the mathematical properties of functions with six independent components:

1. **Set of primitives,** which are predefined by the language as the basic functions and correspond to the built-in operations of imperative languages. Primitives can be used as the fundamental building blocks for all functions that can be constructed.

2. **Set of functional forms,** which are functions that accept functions as parameters to create new functions. Functional forms are useful for constructing new functions from functions that are already defined. Generally speaking, functional languages treat functions as *first-call* values, meaning that they can be passed as parameters, returned as function results, and built into composite values.

3. **Application operation,** which is the built-in mechanism for applying a function to its arguments and producing a value as the result. Application operations can be viewed as the mapping from a domain set to a range set.

4. **Set of data objects,** which are the allowed members of the domain and range sets. Data objects consist of some atomic type and the ability to construct some form of aggregate objects from other objects.

5. **Binding names to functions,** which is a mechanism for denoting names to the new functions being defined. The invocation of a function is specified by the name of the function to be invoked plus a list of values to be supplied for the parameters of the function. The parameters may be given as constant values or the result of other function invocations.

6. **Dynamic storage management,** which is an implicit storage allocation and a garbage collection mechanism because the functional languages do not provide facilities for directly modifying the state of the storage for a computation.

A function whose parameters and result are all nonfunctional is called a **first-order function.** A function that has a functional parameter or result is called a **higher-order function.** The following are some of the essential primitives associated with a functional language:

▶ **Selection operations:** FIRST is used to extract the first element of a sequence of elements, LAST is used to extract the last element, and TAIL is used to extract all the elements but the first element. For example,

```
x₁      ← FIRST: <x₁,x₂, . . . ,xₙ>
xₙ      ← LAST: <x₁,x₂, . . . ,xₙ>
<x₂, . . . ,xₙ>   ← TAIL: <x₁,x₂, . . . ,xₙ>
first: <3,2,4,6> ≡ 3
last:  <3,2,4,6> ≡ 6
tail:  <3,2,4,6> ≡ <2,4,6>
```

▶ **Structuring operations:** Operations are used to combine, dissect, or rearrange elements. For example,

```
(ROTate Right)
<xₙ,x₁, ... ,xₙ₋₁>   ← ROTR: <x₁,x₂, ... ,xₙ>
(ROTate Left)
<x₂, ... ,xₙ,x₁>   ← ROTL: <x₁,x₂, ... ,xₙ>
(LENGTH)
n   ← LENGTH: <x₁,x₂, ... ,xₙ>
(CONstruct Sequence)
<x,x₁,x₂, ... ,xₙ>   ← CONS: <x,<x₁,x₂, ... ,xₙ>>
rotr:    <3,2,4,6> ≡ <6,3,2,4>
rotl:    <3,2,4,6> ≡ <2,4,6,3>
length: <3,2,4,6> ≡ 4
cons:    <3,<2,4,6>> ≡ <3,2,4,6>
```

▶ **Arithmetic operations:** Ordinary arithmetic operations are applied to sequences of two elements to produce a new element; + is used for addition, − for subtraction, * for multiplication, ÷ for division and, | for residue operation. In functional arithmetic operations, we use the prefix form (e.g., +:<x,y>) instead of the usual Infix notation (e.g., $x + y$). The following are some function definitions:

```
+: <x,y> ≡ x+y          +: <3,2> ≡ 5
÷: <x,y> ≡ x÷y          ÷: <8,2> ≡ 4
*: <x,y> ≡ x*y          *: <3,2> ≡ 6
−: <x,y> ≡ x−y          −: <6,3> ≡ 3
|: <x,y> ≡ x−(x÷y)*y    |: <9,2> ≡ 1
```

▶ **Predicate operations:** Operations are used to produce results as truth values. We represent truth by T and false by F such that a predicate function yields either T or F. In addition to predicates for comparing numbers, such as <, >, ≤, ≥, and =, functional language provides predicates to inquire about sequences and atoms. For example, in the following three examples, the first returns a Boolean (T or F) from an inquiry of an atom object, whereas the second returns a Boolean (T or F) from an inquiry of a sentence. The third returns T, if two objects are the same, and F otherwise.

```
ATOM:x ≡ if x is an atom then T else F
atom: <a,b> ≡ F
NULL:x ≡ if x = nil then T else F
null: <a,b> ≡ F
eq: <a,b> ≡ F
eq: <a,a> ≡ T    >: <4,2> ≡ T
```

▶ **Logical operations:** Operations provide the combination of the truth values. The operators are AND, OR, and NOT.

```
AND: <x,y> ≡ T if both are T  and: <T,F> ≡ F  and: <T,T> ≡ T
OR: <x,y> ≡ T if one is T      or: <T,F> ≡ T   or: <F,F> ≡ F
NOT: <x> ≡ T if x is F         not: <T> ≡ F    not: <F> ≡ T
```

▶ **Identity operation:** The function ID yields the same element. For example,

```
x ← ID:x       id:a ≡ a
```

The most interesting features of FP languages are their functional forms because we are not used to functional forms in conventional programming languages. To introduce the power of functional forms in programming, we illustrate a few functional forms called Program-Forming Operations (PFO) (Backus, 1978, 1982).

12.2.1 Composition

The functional form *composition,* denoted °, has the syntax

```
(f ° g)   : X ≡ f : ( g : X)
```

where it takes two functions as the arguments and produces a function equivalent to applying the first argument to the result of the application of the second argument. For example, if we define two functions as

```
f(x) ≡ x + 5   and   g(x) ≡ x + 4
```

then one composition form of f and g can be obtained: $h(x) \equiv f(g(x))$, or

```
h(x) ≡ (x + 4) +5 ≡ x + 9
```

The following example illustrates the composition of the rotate left and construct sequence operations applied to a list of elements:

```
ROTL ° CONS: <x_1, <x_2,x_3,x_4> >  ≡  ROTL: CONS: <x_1,<x_2,x_3,x_4> > ≡
ROTL: <x_1,x_2,x_3,x_4> ≡ <x_2,x_3,x_4,x_1>
```

12.2.2 Construction

The functional form *construction,* denoted [ ], has the syntax

```
[ f_1, f_2, ... , f_n ] : X ≡ < f_1 : X, f_2 : X, ... , f_n : X >
```

where it takes as arguments *n* functions, and yields a function equivalent to applying each of the functions to the same argument and forming a sequence of the results. For example, if we have individual functions for the *maximum, minimum,* and *average* of a sequence of numbers, we define a construction as shown in the following:

```
[Maximum, Minimum, Average]
```

Then, for example, <5, 1, 3> is the produced result of

```
[Maximum, Minimum, Average]:<1,2,3,4,5>
```

in which the construction is used to combine the results of applying the argument to individual functions:

```
[Maximum, Minimum, Average]:<1,2,3,4,5> ≡
<Maximum:<1,2,3,4,5>,Minimum:<1,2,3,4,5>,
Average:<1,2,3,4,5>> ≡ <5, 1, 3>
```

12.2.3 Insert

The functional form *insert*, denoted /, has the syntax

$$/ \ f \ : \ < X_1, \ X_2, \ \ldots \ , \ X_n > \ \equiv \ f \ : \ < X_1, \ / \ f \ : \ < X_2, \ \ldots \ , \ X_n > >$$

where it takes a function as an argument and yields a function equivalent to applying the argument function to successive elements of the sequence. For example,

```
/ f :  ≡    if x is <X₁>, then X₁
       else if x is the sequence < X₁, X₂, ... , Xₙ > and n≥2
       then f: < X₁, / f: < X₂, ... , Xₙ > >
```

Thus /+:< 1,2,3,4,5 > yields 15, as illustrated in the following:

```
/+:<1,2,3,4,5> ≡ +:<1, /+:<2,3,4,5>> ≡ +:<1, +:<2, /+:<3,4,5>>> ≡
+:<1, +:<2, +:<3, /+:<4,5>>>> ≡ +:<1, +:<2, +:<3, +:<4, /+:<5>>>>> ≡
+:<1, +:<2, +:<3, +:<4, 5>>>> ≡ +:<1, +:<2, +:<3, 9>>> ≡
+:<1, +:<2, 12>> ≡ +:<1, 14> ≡ 15
```

12.2.4 Apply to All

The functional form *apply_to_all*, denoted α, has the syntax

$$\alpha \ f: \ < X_1, \ X_2, \ \ldots, \ X_n > \ \equiv \ < f \ : \ X_1, \ f \ : \ X_2, \ \ldots \ , \ f \ : \ X_n >$$

This function can be illustrated in the following way:

```
α f: ≡    if x is nil, then nil
     else if x is the sequence <X₁, X₂, ..., Xₙ>
     then <f:X₁, f:X₂, ..., f:Xₙ>
```

This form takes a function as an argument and yields a function equivalent to applying the argument function to each element of the sequence and forming a sequence of the results. For example, α+:<<2,3>,<4,5>,<6,2>>

yields <5,9,8>, as illustrated in the following:

α+:<<2,3>,<4,5>,<6,2>> ≡ <+:<2,3>,+:<4,5>,+:<6,2>> ≡ <5,9,8>

12.2.5 Condition

The functional form *condition,* denoted IF, takes three functions as arguments and—depending on whether the first function evaluates as True or False—returns the second or third function, respectively. This function has the following syntax:

```
(IF function₁ function₂ function₃):x ≡
if function₁:x=T   then   function₂:x   else   function₃:x
```

In the following two examples, evaluation of the head of <2,3,5> with 2 and 3 yields the tail and last element of the list, respectively.

```
(IF FIRST:<2,3,5> TAIL:<2,3,5> LAST:<2,3,5>):2 ≡ (IF 2 <3,5> 5):2 ≡<3,5>
(IF FIRST:<2,3,5> TAIL:<2,3,5> LAST:<2,3,5>):3 ≡ (IF 2 <3,5> 5):3 ≡5
```

SUMMARY

Functional programming language provides a different view of programming language design, which should be interpreted rather than compiled because of substantial loss in execution speed. Functional programming languages are inherently less efficient than imperative languages for several reasons. The following are two important reasons:

▶ Because functions are first-order values, local data must be allocated on the heap and deallocated automatically by the implementation to avoid dangling references.

▶ Lazy evaluation implies that every time a function argument is used, and every time a component is selected from a composite value, it must be checked in case it turns out to be an unevaluated expression.

Do these imply that functional language implementations must always be significantly slower than imperative ones? There are several reasons why this might not be so:

▶ Heap management techniques are improving rapidly, and allocating all data on the heap is not really inefficient.

▶ Recent implementations of lazy evaluation are more efficient. Moreover, optimizing compilers can generate improved code in many cases. For example, if a function is shown to be strict, then its argument can safely be evaluated.

▶ Functional notation is concise, allowing shorter and more elegant programs to be written with clean and simple semantics. Programmers claim that programs can be written quickly, are easier to verify, and can be carried out more efficiently.

▶ Intermediate composite values can often be eliminated by program transformation, and the transformations involved are easily performed by optimizing compilers.

▶ Mathematical function theory is well defined, allowing programmers to write programs that look like specifications with automatic transformation systems that convert the specifications into efficiently running programs.

▶ Functional languages are thought to be very suitable for concurrent implementation. Shared values need no special protection because they can never be updated. As a result, explicit synchronization constructs are unnecessary in a function language, and in a distributed implementation, values may be copied freely without danger of copies becoming inconsistent. Moreover, concurrent functional programs are deterministic because the concurrent processes can never interfere with each other, which greatly simplifies reasoning and testing.

In this chapter, we outlined the key properties of functional programming such as lazy evaluation, first-order objects, lack of variable and assignment, and lack of loop and iteration. An important property of functional languages is referential transparency, meaning that a function depends only on the value of its parameters, not on any previous computation or the execution path that led to the function call. Side effect freedom is another important concept associated with functional programs. In this chapter, we discussed the lambda calculus as a theoretical model of computation for functional programming languages. We briefly outlined evaluation of lambda expressions with regard to reductions, such as Alpha-reduction, Beta-reduction, Eta-reduction, and Gamma-reduction. Pure functional programming (FP) was the inspiration for the design and implementation of many functional programming languages. We discussed the structure of a simple FP language based on relations that described associations between objects to illustrate the fundamental concepts of functional programming languages. In this sense, a function has four components: domain set, range set, definition, and name. We discussed the essential operations associated with a function: selection, structuring, arithmetic, predicate, logical, and identity operations.

Applicative Programming Languages

In this chapter, we explore three different functional programming languages for comparison purposes. The first functional language, LISP (LISt Processing), was based on the theory of functions as written in lambda calculus with simple semantics. LISP doesn't support data abstraction features, meaning that it is a pure and typeless functional programming language. The language is widely used for computer science research, mostly in the area of artificial intelligence in connection with robotics, natural language processing, and theorem proving. Section 13.1 introduces the fundamental features of LISP as the key structure of modern functional languages.

Section 13.2 explores Scheme as the first dialect of typeless LISP to fully support functional programming. Scheme is not a strongly typed language so the programmer is responsible for type checking. The basic object in Scheme is called S-expression and the cell model is used to represent the implementation model of expressions. Cell diagrams for structures are usually drawn with a series of boxes, which stretch from left to right, depending on the number of elements in the structure. Section 13.3 explains the ML functional programming language, which consists of a deductive calculus called Polymorphic Predicate Calculus (PPλ) and an interactive programming language paradigm. It is called ML, for MetaLanguage because it serves as the common language for Logic for Computable Functions (LCF), a proof-generating system for reasoning about recursive functions. ML is a language with semantics like Scheme and static scooping and has proved useful as a general-purpose programming language. Unlike LISP and Scheme, ML is strongly typed, although a user doesn't always need to declare data types because the interpreter can determine data types by inference.

◤ 13.1 FUNCTIONAL PROGRAMMING WITH LISP

In the early 1960s, a team at MIT led by John McCarthy developed the first functional programming language that contained many of the features of modern functional languages. It was called LISP (for LISt Processing) because the basic data structure is a list. LISP was based on mathematics and, in particular, on lambda calculus. The original LISP, known as pure LISP, was completely a functional programming language. The first implementation was on the IBM 704, the same machine that hosted the first implementation of Fortran. Many different LISP versions have been created since then, including InterLISP, Franz LISP, MacLISP, Common LISP, and Scheme, and they now exist on virtually all machines, including microcomputers. From the beginning, LISP was criticized for slow processing. To improve its efficiency, programmers introduced nonapplicative features into the language. The new versions of LISP—like many languages for functional programming, including Scheme and ML—are impure because they provide some notion of variable and assignment. LISP is poorly designed for compilation because most bindings are not made until run time. Its semantics were defined by a few LISP primitives. An interpreter was written as a very small and concise LISP program, indicating that proofs of correctness are quite possible for many programs. Such an interpreter, referred to as a **metacircular interpreter,** can handle function definitions, parameter passing, and recursion, as well as expression evaluation in LISP. LISP is a good example of how a few simple primitives with a few simple data structuring primitives can provide an elegant and powerful language.

The language is widely used for computer science research, mostly in the area of artificial intelligence in connection with robotics, natural language processing, theorem proving, intelligent systems, and the like. Examples of expert systems written in LISP and in use are DENDRAL, MACSYMA, EXPERT, and MYCIN. DENDRAL is used to analyze mass spectrographic, nuclear, magnetic resonance, and chemical experimental data to infer the plausible structure of an unknown compound. MACSYMA solves differential and integral calculus problems symbolically and excels at simplifying symbolic expressions. EXPERT is used to build consultation models in endocrinology, ophthalmology, and rheumatology. MYCIN diagnoses infectious blood diseases and prescribes treatment. Although basic LISP does not support data abstraction features, an object-oriented version of LISP called Common LISP Object System (CLOS) does provide them. CLOS resulted from the merger of four object-oriented extensions: New Flavors, CommonLoops, Object LISP, and Common Objects to LISP language. CLOS supports

- ▶ Multiple inheritance
- ▶ Generic functions
- ▶ Metaclasses and metaobjects
- ▶ An object creation and initialization method

We examine LISP only within a limited context because Scheme, which is a LISP variant, is the working language used in the next section.

13.1.1 The Principles of LISP

The original syntax for LISP was symbolic expression, or S-expression. An S-expression is defined recursively:

▶ An atomic symbol is an S-expression.

▶ If expression$_1$ and expression$_2$ are S-expressions, so is (expression$_1$ expression$_2$).

In general, a LISP program consists of a set of function definitions followed by a list of expressions that may include function evaluations. The expressions used to construct programs are written in strict Cambridge Polish form and may include conditional branching. LISP uses applicative order evaluation because of the efficiency obtained by avoiding multiple evaluations of expressions. In addition to simple notational rules, the LISP programming language provides the following:

▶ A method for storing data

▶ A set of built-in functions

▶ A set of functional forms

▶ A set of operators

The following two features are common to all LISP data objects:

▶ Each data object carries a run-time descriptor giving its type and other attributes.

▶ If a data object has components (is a structured data object), the components are never represented directly as part of the data object; instead, a pointer to the component data object is used.

LISP is a completely typeless language, all descriptor processing is done during execution, and no declarations of any kind are necessary. In other words, LISP can handle integers, floating-point numbers, and other types uniformly without the need for declarations. The LISP evaluator is a function callable directly by the user. Its name is *EVAL,* and the normal evaluation rule applies to an expression headed by it. The LISP system provides the prompt *eval* to the user, who responds by typing a LISP statement. The LISP system responds in turn by evaluating the statement and printing the result on the next line. As we indicated previously, many nonapplicative features were introduced into LISP to provide a reasonable level of efficiency. Some of the principal nonapplicative features that we will briefly discuss are atom, set, prog, car, cdr, cons, and cond.

13.1.2 Data Objects

Every LISP data object, whether a program or data, is either an *atom* or a *cons*. An atom is an object that is indivisible in nature and takes two forms:

▶ A literal atom (symbol), which is a string beginning with a letter

▶ A numeric atom (number), which is a number used for integer and real arithmetic operations; numbers are their own values

---

FIGURE **13.1**   Memory representation of (cons 'A 'B)

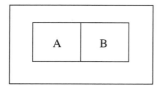

FIGURE **13.2**   Memory representation of (cons 'A(cons 'CAR 'NIL))

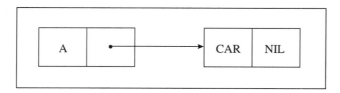

For example, the following are atoms:

3

5.7

B12

A

CAR

FOOD

Syntactically an atom is just an identifier, and lowercase and uppercase distinctions for identifiers are usually ignored. Within LISP function definitions, atoms serve as identifiers and are used as variable names, function names, and parameter names. A cons is represented in a computer as a pair of storage elements, each of which can contain a reference (address of or a pointer to) another object. We often refer to conses as *cons cells* and illustrate their internal representation as boxes with two compartments. For example, the (cons 'A 'B) is illustrated in Figure 13.1.

In this regard, a *cons* is an ordered conjunction of two other LISP objects; each of them might be another cons or an atom. A cons can be represented by a series of objects separated by space and enclosed by parentheses, as in:

```
(object₁ object₂ ... objectₙ).
```

For example, the representation of the cons cells in (cons 'A (cons 'CAR 'NIL)) is shown in Figure 13.2.

If a compartment is a reference to an atom (i.e., A), we point to the atom directly from the compartment. If it is a reference to another cons cell, we draw an arrow to that cons cell. For example, the (cons 'A (cons 'B 'C)) is illustrated in Figure 13.3.

FIGURE **13.3**   Memory representation of (cons 'A (cons 'B 'C))

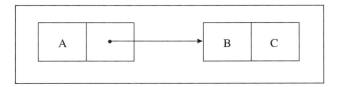

FIGURE **13.4**   A representation of list (A (B C) D)

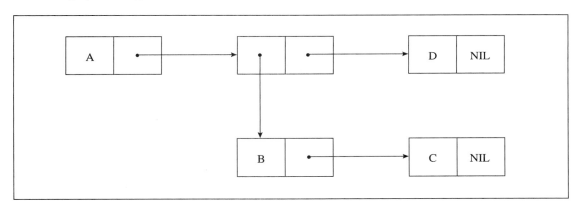

The (cons 'A (cons (cons 'B (cons 'C 'NIL)) (cons 'D 'NIL))) evaluated as (A (B C) D) is represented internally as shown in Figure 13.4. Atoms and cons cells provide the building blocks for LISP objects. The following are conses:

(A B)

(FOOD VEGETABLES DRINKS)

(MEAT CHICKEN FISH)

(BROCCOLI POTATOS TOMATOES)

((MEAT CHICKEN FISH) (BROCCOLI POTATOS TOMATOES))

((NASIM MARYAM MAHSA) (NAZANIN NEGAR NILOFAR) (ALMAD))

(20 GOOD 10 BAD)

Lists

A list is a series of cons cells linked by their second compartments and having the first compartments as elements of the list. Thus, the list ((A B) (C) (D F)), as shown in Figure 13.5, is a list of three components: (A B), (C), and (D F).

FIGURE **13.5**   A representation of list ((A B) (C) (D F))

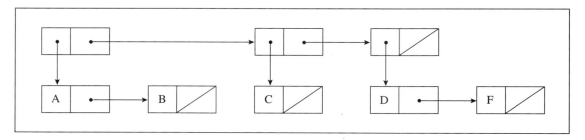

The elements of a list are sometimes referred to as top-level elements of the list. Thus (A B) is a top-level element of the list ((A B) (C) (D F)), whereas B is an element of (A B). The length of a list is the number of top-level elements in the list; thus, the previous list has three elements. Lists that terminate with NIL are sometimes called *proper lists;* others are sometimes called *improper lists.* The list (A B C D) consists of the elements A, B, C, and D. Now consider the list (BOOK (THE TABLE) ON OFF) that has four elements: BOOK, (THE TABLE), ON, and OFF—three of the elements are atoms and the fourth is a list. The LISP function LIST makes the construction of proper lists of any given length. It takes any number of arguments and returns a list of them. Examine the following where the LISP system types a prompt "eval>" to the user, who responds by typing a Lisp statement.

```
eval>  (LIST  'A 'B 'C 'D)
(A B C D)
eval>  (LIST 'A  (LIST 'B 'C) 'D)
(A (B C) D)
eval>  (LIST 'A)
(A)
eval>  (LIST)
NIL
eval>  (LIST 'THE (LIST 'BIG 'CAT 'SAT) )
(THE (BIG CAT SAT) )
```

13.1.3 Functions

LISP functions are defined entirely as expressions. Each operator is a function that returns a value, and subprograms are written as single expressions. Function parameters are transmitted either all by value or all by name depending on the classification of the function, with transmission by value being the usual case. In general, when a function is applied to a set of parameters it returns the value of an expression associated with the function. A function definition takes the following general form:

```
(defun     <function-name>
           <argument-list>
           <function-body>)
```

The `function-name` must be a symbol and can be any symbol other than NIL. After the function has been defined, it can be invoked by using this name as the first element of a list to be evaluated. For example,

```
(defun      square    (x)    (*  x  x)   )
```

defines the function `square`, which can then be used. The `argument-list` is a list of symbols (excluding NIL) that will be given to the arguments that the evaluation procedure hands to the function as their values. For instance, after defining the `square` function and on being called by

```
(square 5)
```

the LISP evaluation procedure temporarily gives the symbol x, which was the single argument of the function, the value 5. The `function-body` is an S-expression that will be evaluated whenever the function is invoked. It is evaluated after the symbols in the *argument-list* have been bound to the arguments that were passed to the function. The value returned from evaluating the *function-body* is the returned value of the function. In this example, when the body of the `square` function is evaluated, it is then equivalent to evaluating (*   5   5), with the returned value 25. The function

```
(defun      cylinder-volume    (length   radius)
            (*  length  (*  3.1415  (square  radius))))
```

can be invoked by

```
(cylinder-volume  2.5   2.0)
```

for which the LISP system returns 31.4159265 because the symbol length is given as 2.5 and radius is given as 2.0 during evaluation of the body of the cylinder-volume function. Some examples of functions are the following:

```
(defun   double  (x)  (*  2  x)   )
(defun   times-square  (x y)  (*  x  y  y) )
(defun   times-cube (x  y)  (*  x  y  y  y) )
(defun   cube-times  (x  y)  (times-cube  y  x) )
```

Because the basis for LISP was lambda calculus (a formalism for functions), LISP functions are represented internally as lists in the form of lambda expressions. A lambda expression has the following form:

```
(lambda    <argument-list>
           <function-body> )
```

In other words, a lambda expression is somewhat like *defun*, except that it defines an unnamed function, or it allows the user to define a function with no name. For example,

```
((lambda   (x  y)   (PLUS  x  y))  2  3)
```

binds x and y to 2 and 3, respectively, and applies PLUS, giving 5 as the returned value of this definition. Even though LISP can be used as a functional programming language, few applications written in LISP are purely applicative. Any realistic LISP program makes heavy use of nonapplicative features to achieve a reasonable level of efficiency. The principal nonapplicative features that have been added to LISP are *set, let,* and *progn.* The *set* function is simply an assignment statement and a value of a symbol can be assigned with the general form

```
(set    symbol       expression)
```

in which the `expression` is assigned to `symbol` and `symbol` evaluates to that value until `set` is applied again. Examine the following examples about `set` function.

```
eval> (set 'X '(A  B  C) )
(A  B  C)
eval> (set 'B '3)
3
eval>(set 'Y 'A)
A
eval> Y
A
eval> (set 'Z  X)
(A  B  C)
```

The special form *let* is a function that provides a way of introducing temporary variables or binding local variables. Temporary variables can serve the result of a computation. The general form of `let` is

```
(let    ( (variable₁    value₁)
          (variable₂    value₂)
          . . .
          (variableₙ    valueₙ) )
        body)
```

in which $variable_1$, $variable_2$, ..., $variable_n$ are symbols (`let` does not evaluate them) that will be used as names on introduced variables. They can be referred to by any code that appears in the `body` form. When `let` is invoked, each $value_1$, $value_2$, ..., $value_n$ is evaluated in turn. When they all have been evaluated, the new variables are given their values. Examine the following examples about `let` function.

```
eval> (let  ((A  3))  (cons  A  (let  ((A 4))  A) ) )
(3  4)
eval> (let  ((A  3))  (let  ((A 4)  (B  A) )  (cons  A  B) ) )
(4  3)
eval>  (let  ((A  3))  (let  ((A 4)  (B  A) )  (cons  A  B) ) )
(4  4)
```

The special form *progn* is a function that takes a list of expressions as its argument and provides a way of explicitly sequencing expressions to be evaluated. The expressions are executed in sequence, and the value of the last is returned as the value of the *progn* function. This capability is useful only when some statements have side effects on the values of either global or local variables. The general form of `progn` is

```
(progn       expression₁    expression₂ ... expressionₙ)
```

Furthermore, with `progn` we can provide label and jump statements for explicit control of the execution sequence. For example, when,

```
(progn  (set  'X  3)  (set  'Y  4)  (print  (*  X Y) ) )
```

is evaluated, the value of 12 will be printed. The two alternatives of *progn* are *prog1* and *prog2*, but the values returned are first expression and second expression, respectively. LISP provides a wide variety of primitive functions for the creation, destruction, and modification of lists. Table 13.1 contains some of the LISP built-in functions. The identifiers *car* and *cdr* are related to the IBM 704, where a word of memory included the **c**ontents of the **a**ddress **r**egister (*car*) and the **c**ontents of the **d**ecrement **r**egister (*cdr*). The names continue to be used today to indicate the head and tail of a list. The examples shown in Table 13.2 illustrate the built-in functions.

☞ 13.2 FUNCTIONAL PROGRAMMING WITH SCHEME

Scheme (a dialect of LISP) was introduced by Gerald Sussman and Guy Steele (Sussman & Steele, 1975; Steele & Sussman, 1978) at the MIT Artificial Intelligence Laboratory as the first dialect of LISP for functional programming. Although the early versions of the language were small, the latest version is a complete high-level, general-purpose programming language with uniform treatment of functions. In 1981, a Scheme chip was built that incorporated an innovative compiler. This chip supports operations on structured data—such as strings, lists, and vectors—as well as operations on numbers and characters. Scheme was lexically scoped; that is, a variable is in the scope of the expression that is declared. Scheme has been used to write text editors, optimizing compilers, operating systems, graphics packages, expert systems, numerical applications and financial analysis packages. Scheme programs are highly portable across different Scheme implementations on different machines because machine dependencies are almost hidden from the programmer. Scheme is not a strongly typed language; the programmer is responsible for type checking.

13.2.1 The Principles of Scheme

Scheme programs consist of the following components:

▶ Atoms are represented by strings of nonblank characters. Atoms are the elementary objects and are considered indivisible with no internal structure. Sample atoms are 28, "a string", *x*, and −14.25.

▶ Identifiers (keywords, variables, and symbols) may be formed from lowercase letters a through z, uppercase letters A through Z, digits 0 through 9, and special characters ?, !, ., +, −, *, /, <, =, >, :, &, _, %, and $.

   Identifiers cannot start with a number, plus sign, minus sign, or decimal point. There is no limit on the length of an identifier and it may be written in any mix of uppercase and lowercase letters.

▶ Boolean values representing true and false are written as #t and #f. Scheme conditional expressions actually treat #f as false and all other objects as true.

▶ The basic data structure is the list, and all other structures must be put into the form of lists. Structured forms and list constants are enclosed within parentheses

TABLE **13.1**   Built-in LISP functions

Function	Number of Arguments	Description
(cons \<item>\<list>)	2	Adds \<item> as the first element of \<list>.
(car\<list>)	1	Returns the first element in \<list>.
(cdr\<list>)	1	Returns \<list> with the first element removed.
(+\<elem1>\<elem2>)	2	Returns the sum of the values of \<elem1> and \<elem2>.
(−\<elem1>\<elem2>)	2	Returns the difference of the values of \<elem1> and \<elem2>.
(*\<elem1>\<elem2>)	2	Returns the product of the values of \<elem1> and \<elem2>.
(/\<elem1>\<elem2>)	2	Returns the quotient of the values of \<elem1> and \<elem2>.
(list\<arg1>\<arg2>)	$0 \Rightarrow \infty$	Constructs a list from the arguments.
(set\<arg1>\<arg2>)	2	Sets the first argument to the second.
(length\<list>)	1	Counts elements in a list.
(atom\<object>)	1	Tests whether an object is an atom.
(not value)	1	Inverts the logical value.
(null\<list>)	1	Tests whether its argument is empty.
(<\<arg1>\<arg2>)	2	Tests whether the first argument is less than the second argument.
(>\<arg1>\<arg2>)	2	Tests whether the first argument is greater than the second argument.
(append\<arg1>\<arg2>)	2	Appends \<arg1> and \<arg2> in left-to-right order.
(reverse\<list>)	1	Produces a new list with the same elements, but in reverse order.
(eq\<object1>\<object2>)	2	Compares two objects and tells whether they are same or not.
(typep\<object1>\<object2>)	2	Tests whether the first argument is an instance of the second argument that is the name of the type being tested for.
(quote\<item>)	1	Returns \<item> without evaluating it.
(display\<expression>)	1	Prints the value of \<expression>.
(cond(\<pred1> \< expr1>)	$1 \Rightarrow n$	Sequentially evaluates predicates until one
(\<pred2> \< expr2>)		of them returns True; then the corresponding
...		expression is evaluated and its value
(\<predn> \< exprn>))		returned from the conditional statement.

TABLE **13.2**   **Examples of built-in LISP functions**

```
eval>(cons 'A (cons 'B (cons 'C 'NIL)))      eval>(cons 'B 'NIL)
(A (B C))                                     (B)
eval>(cons (cons 'A 'NIL) 'NIL)              eval>(cons 'A (cons 'B 'NIL))
((A))                                         (A B)
eval>(car '(A B C))                          eval>(car (cons 'A 'B))
A                                             A
eval>(cdr '(A B C))                          eval>(cdr (cdr '(A B C)))
(B C)                                         (C)
eval>(cdr (cons 'A 'B))                      eval>(list 'A 'B 'C 'D)
B                                             (A B C D)
eval>(list 'A (list 'B 'C) 'D)               eval>(set 'A '(X Y))
(A (B C) D)                                   (X Y)
eval>(setq A (list '+ 5 6))                  eval>(atom '3)
(+ 5 6)                                       T
eval>(atom '(X Y))                           eval>(+ 2 (* 3 4))
NIL                                           14
eval>(+ (car (list 2 3)) 4)                  eval>(+ (car (cdr (list 2 3))) 4)
6                                             7
eval>(> 3 4)                                 eval>(< 3 4)
NIL                                           T
eval> (length '( ))                          eval>(length '(A B))
0                                             2
eval>(listp 'X)                              eval>(listp '(X Y))
NIL                                           T
eval>(eq A B)                                eval>(eq A A)
NIL                                           T
eval>(append '(A B C) '(D E F))              eval>(reverse '(A B C))
(A B C D E F)                                 (C B A)
eval>(reverse '(A (B C) (D E) F G))          eval>(typep 'ZTESCH 'SYMBOL)
(G F (D E) (B C) A)                           T
eval>(typep '3 'NUMBER)                      eval>(typep '3 'SYMBOL)
T                                             NIL
eval>(cons 3 (quote (X Y)))                  eval>(quote (X Y))
(3 X Y)                                       (X Y)
```

consisting of a sequence of atoms. Examples are (a b c) or (* (+ x 2) y). In other words, a list is simply a sequence of expressions separated by spaces and surrounded by parentheses. The empty list is written as ( ). The two predefined list functions—*car* and *cdr*—compute the head and the tail of a list, and *cons* adds a new head to an existing list.

▶ Vectors are similar to lists except that they are preceded by #(and terminated by). An example is #(this is scheme programming).

▶ Strings are enclosed in double quotation marks. An example is "this is scheme programming".

▶ Numbers may be written as integers. Examples are 123, −45, 1/2, and 1e23.

▶ Comments start with a semicolon ";" on any line of a Scheme program. An example is

```
;this is a programming language.
```

13.2.2 Variable Definition and Reference

One aspect of a programming language is the means it provides for using names to refer to computational objects. In Scheme, we name objects with *define*. For example, typing

```
(define size 5)
```

causes the interpreter to associate the value 5 with the name size. Once the name size has been associated with the number 5, we can refer to the value 5 by the name, as in the following.

```
size          returns 5
(* 5 size)    returns 25
```

Another example of the use of *define* is the following:

```
(define    PI   3.1415)
(define    radius 10)
(* pi (* radius radius))    returns 314.15
```

The variable definition appears at the top level outside the scope of lambda with the following syntax:

```
(define    variable  expression)
(define    variable  (lambda   formal-variables   expression) )
```

For example, the following declares x as a variable with the initial value 3.

```
(define    x    3)
```

In the following declaration, f is a variable with the initial value of (x+y)*2, and x and y are two arguments of lambda expression:

```
(define    f
              (lambda   (x y)   (* (+ x  y)  2)))
```

In this case, f can be initialized as shown in the following.

FIGURE **13.6**   Cell diagram representation of list (a b c)

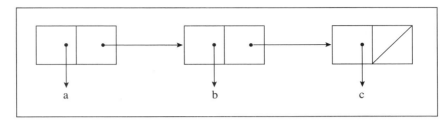

FIGURE **13.7**   Cell diagram representation of list ((a b) (c) (d f))

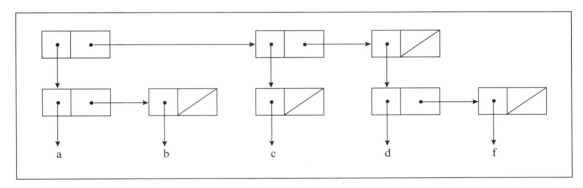

```
(f   5   4)    returns 18
```

In the following example, ABC is a variable with the initial value of (x+1), where x is an argument of a lambda expression:

```
(define    ABC    (lambda   (x)   (+ x 1)))
```

In this example, (ABC 3) gives the result 4 as the value of variable.

13.2.3 Implementation Model

The basic object in Scheme is called S-expression and has the following syntax:

```
<S-expression> ⇒ <atom>  |  <S-expression> . <S-expression>
```

Atoms serve as the elementary objects in Scheme and are considered to be indivisible, with no internal structure. Because expressions can have arbitrary nesting, the **cell model** is used to represent the implementation model of expressions in Scheme. Cell diagrams for structures are usually drawn as a series of boxes that stretches from left to right, depending on the number of elements in the structure. For example, the list (a b c) can be represented as shown in Figure 13.6.

FIGURE **13.8**   Syntax of the Scheme programming language

```
<program> ⇒ <form>*
<form> ⇒ <definition> | <expression>
<definition> ⇒ <variable definition> | (begin <definition>*)
<variable definition> ⇒ (define <variable> <expression>)
<expression>⇒ <constant> | <variable> | (quota <datum>) |
           (lambda <formals> <expression> <expression>*) |
           (if <expression> <expression> <expression>) |
           (set! <variable> <expression>) |
           <application>
<constant>⇒ <boolean> | <number> | <character> | <string>
<formals>⇒ <variable> | (<variable>*) | (<variable> <variable>* . <variable>)
<application>⇒ (<expression> <expression>*)
```

Another example is the list ((a b) (c) (d f)), which is presented in Figure 13.7. A complete syntax of Scheme is presented in Figure 13.8. The semantics of Scheme can be represented by evaluation rules for expressions, as follows:

▶   Constant atoms, such as numbers and strings, are evaluated by themselves.

▶   Identifiers are replaced by the value found in a table maintained by Scheme that associates identifiers to values.

▶   Lists are evaluated by evaluating the first expression in list as a function. The result is then applied to the evaluated values of the rest of the list.

Functional composition is the only primitive functional form provided by the original LISP. All subsequent LISP dialects, including Scheme, also provide it. In general, functional composition is the essence of how EVAL works. The following discussion illustrates the functions in Scheme language.

13.2.4   Functions

Scheme implies that the value of a function is distinguished from a call to the function. In other words, the function value is represented by its name, whereas a function call is enclosed within parentheses. Functions in Scheme are grouped into three categories: user-defined, built-in, and higher-order functions.

User-Defined Functions

The special form *define* returns the name of the function being defined with the syntax

```
(define   (function-name
          parameter₁   . . .   parameterₙ)
          function-body)
```

When the first element is the function name and formal parameter names, two parameters are required. The second element is the expression to be evaluated when the function is called. Parameters are used as the local variables in the function body. Functions in Scheme can also be defined as

```
(define   function-name   (lambda
              (list-of-parameters)   expression))
```

in which executing the function involves invoking evaluation of the expression in an environment that binds the parameters to the actual arguments. This indicates that there are two ways of using *define*, either to define names directly by giving their values as we discussed in variable definitions and initializations, or by defining a function name (with its parameters) and then giving the function body. For example, the following function calculates the hypotenuse from the sides of a right triangle.

```
(define  hypotenuse  (lambda  (side₁, side₂)
                    (sqrt (+ (*side₁  side₁)
                    (*side₂  side₂)))))
```

Thus,

```
(hypotenuse 3 4) ⇒ (sqrt (+ (* 3 3) (* 4 4)))
⇒ (sqrt (+ 9 16)) ⇒ (sqrt 25) ⇒ 5
```

For instance, the result of the following example is the first element of a list.

```
(define    firstelement   (lambda  (L)  (car L) ))
```

Thus,

```
(firstelement   '(3 4 5)) ⇒ (3 4 5)
```

The following example returns the second element in a list.

```
(define    secondelement    (lambda  (L)  (car  (car L))))
```

Thus,

```
(secondelement  '((3)  (4)  (5))) ⇒ (car  ((4)  (5)) ⇒ (4)
```

As another example of a simple function, consider

```
(define  (second lst)   (car  (cdr lst) )  )
```

In this case, the name second is bound to the lambda expression

```
( ( lambda  (lst) )  (car  (cdr  lst)  )  )
```

Once this function is evaluated, it can be used, as in

```
(second   '(A  B  C) )
```

which returns B. Given the following function definition

```
(define       (gcd  x  y)
   (if   (=  y  0)
      x
      (gcd  y  (remainder  x  y) ) ) )
```

we can call the function gcd by (gcd   25   10), in which case, the system returns 5.

Built-In Functions

In Scheme, built-in functions are classified as the following:

▶ Unary functions, in which only one argument is provided; some examples are

```
(add1 5)                        returns 6
(abs (add1 -5))                 returns 4
```

▶ Binary functions, in which two arguments are provided; some examples are

```
(- 6  2)                        returns 4
(quotient 17 5)                 returns 3
(/ 17 5)                        returns 3.4
(* 2 5)                         returns 10
(- (* 3 4) (+ 2 3))            returns 7
(modulo 17 )                    returns 2
```

▶ N-ary functions, in which more than two arguments are provided; some examples are

```
(+ 2  3  5  6)                  returns 16
(* 1  2  3  4)                  returns 24
(max 12  3  4)                  returns 12
(min (* 2  3)  (+ 3  5))        returns 6
```

The three important built-in functions are *car, cdr,* and *cons,* which have the following syntaxes: When applied to a nonempty list, *car* returns the first element of the list. When applied to a nonempty list, *cdr* returns the copy of the list with the first element excluded. When applied to a list, *cons* returns a new list obtained by appending the first argument to the beginning of the list. For example,

```
( car '(a  b  c) )              returns a
( cdr '(a  b  c) )              returns (b  c)
( cons 'a '(b  c) )             returns (a  b  c)
```

In addition, functions that return the Boolean values true or false are called predicate functions. In Scheme, predicates return the atom #t or #f, which stand for true or false, respectively. We usually follow the convention of ending a predicate with a question mark, "?". Some examples are the following:

```
(negative? -6)   returns  #t      (even? 22)    returns  #t
(zero? 40)       returns  #f      (odd? 12)     returns  #f
(number? 5)      returns  #t      (= 5 4)       returns  #f
(integer? 3.5)   returns  #f      (> 8 4)       returns  #t
(real? 90)       returns  #f      (>= 3 30)     returns  #f
```

The *let* function allows values to be given temporary names within an expression. For example, in the following, `first` is given the value 2 and `second` the value 3:

```
(let  ((first 2)  (second 3))  (+ first  second))
```

Then, the names `first` and `second` are used for their values in the expression
(+ `first`   `second`), which returns the result value of the *let* function. In general, *let*
is just shorthand for a *lambda* expression. The following two expressions are equivalent:

```
(let  ( (alpha  7) )  (*  5  alpha)  )
(  (lambda  (alpha)  (*  5  alpha)  )  7)
```

In the first expression, 7 is bound to `alpha` with `let`; in the second expression, 7
is bound to `alpha` through the parameter of the lambda expression. The Scheme interpreter considers every expression to be a function to be evaluated, so if you want an
expression to be considered as data and not to be evaluated, you need to use a special
function called `quote`:

```
(quote   expression)
```

For example,

```
(quote   (+ 2 3 4 5 6))
```

indicates that the list (+ 2 3 4 5 6) is to be considered as a six-element list rather
than to be evaluated and regarded as the atomic element 20. The other two basic functions are *read* and *display*. The *read* function has no parameters, and it returns whatever
value the keyboard provides. The display function prints its parameters to the screen.

Higher Order Functions

A function is called a *higher order function* if it has one or more functions as parameters or if it returns a function as its result. Higher-order functions are sometimes
called *functional forms* because they allow the construction of new functions from already defined functions. The advantage of functional programming comes from
using functional forms to construct complex functions from simple functions. For example, the following function (called *construction*) consists of a predefined function
(called *function-list*) that, along with different functions such as *cons, cond, car,* and
cdr, forms a list of elements:

```
(define   function-list   (cons    add1
                            (cons   -
                            (cons (lambda (n)  (* n n) ) '( )))))
(define      construction   (lambda (function-list  x)
                            (cond (( null? Function-list) '( ))
                            (else (cons ((car function-list) x)
       (construction  (cdr function-list)  x) )))))
```

In this case

```
(construction function-list 4)
```

returns (5 −4 16). The most common functional forms provided in common functional programming languages are variations of the mathematical apply-to-all functional form. The simplest of these is *mapcar*, which has two parameters, a function and

a list. *mapcar* applies the given function to each element of the given list, and it returns a list of the results of these applications. A Scheme definition of `mapcar` follows:

```
(define   (mapcar   fun   list
  (cond   ( ( NULL?  List)  '( )  )
  (else (cons (fun (car list) ) (mapcar fun (cdr list) ))) ) )
```

As an example, suppose we want all of the elements of a list cubed. We can accomplish this with

```
(mapcar   (lambda   (number)
(*  number   number   number)  )  '(3  4  2  5) )
```

where it returns (27 64 8 125). In this example, the first parameter to `mapcar` is a lambda expression. To evaluate the lambda expression, EVAL constructs a function that has the same form as any predefined function except that it is *nameless*. In the previous expression, this *nameless* function is immediately applied to each element of the parameter list, and the results are returned in a list. We can note the simple form of `mapcar`, which expresses a complex functional form.

13.2.5 Delayed Evaluation versus Strict Evaluation

The Scheme evaluation rule follows applicative order evaluation; that is, all subexpressions are evaluated first. Thus, the Scheme expression (* (− 5 2) (+ 2 3)) is evaluated by first evaluating the two expressions and then evaluating the resultant expression, (* 3 5), as shown by a bottom-up traversal of the tree in Figure 13.9.

The evaluation rule implies that all expressions in Scheme must be written in prefix notation. An expression subject to delayed evaluation, sometimes called *lazy* evaluation, is not evaluated until its value is required and, once evaluated, is never reevaluated. The syntactic form *delay* and the procedure *force* are used in combination to implement delayed evaluation. The use of `delay` with the syntax

```
(delay   expression)
```

returns promise. The first time promise is forced (with the *force* function), it evaluates the `expression`. Thereafter, each time the promise is forced, it returns the evaluated value of the `expression` instead of reevaluating the `expression`. The use of `force` with syntax

```
(force   promise)
```

returns the evaluated value of (`delay expression`) as the result of forcing promise. The following example illustrates how a stream abstraction may be built with `delay` and `force`. A stream is a promise that, when forced, returns a pair whose *cdr* is a stream.

```
(define   stream-car   (lambda  (s)  (car (force  s))))
(define   stream-cdr   (lambda  (s)  (cdr (force  s))))
(define   counters   (let  next  ((n  1))
          (delay (cons  n  (next  (+  n  1)))))))
```

For example,

FIGURE **13.9**   **Scheme evaluation of expression** `(*(- 5 2) (+ 2 3))`

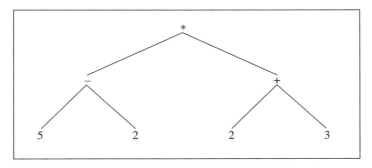

```
(stream-car    counters)
```
returns 1 as the result, and

```
(stream-car    (stream-cdr counters) )
```
return 2. The benefit of using *delay* and *force* is that some amount of run time might be avoided if the evaluation of the expression is delayed until absolutely required. Note that the *if* (condition) and *cond* (decision) functions obey the delayed evaluation rule for Scheme expressions, meaning that arguments to such control procedures are delayed until the appropriate moment. A conditional expression has two general forms

```
(if    test    consequent    alternative)
(if    test    consequent)
```

where `consequent` and `alternative` are the expressions to be evaluated if `test` is true or false, respectively. This conditional statement can be expressed in an imperative language:

```
if    (test)    consequent    else    alternative
```

With delayed evaluation, in `(if test then consequent else alternative)`, the `consequent` needs to be evaluated only if `test` is true. Similarly, `alternative` is evaluated only if `test` is false. In contrast to delayed evaluation, in strict evaluation, all expressions would be evaluated before the function is carried out. For example, if `(if condition then true-expression else false-expression)` were subject to strict evaluation, `condition`, `true-expression`, and `false-expression` would be evaluated before the conditional statement is executed. Lazy evaluation is an important issue in functional programming. For example, in the expression

```
(if    (<  n  0)
       (+  n  10)    (+  n  20))
```

test is `(<  n  0)`, or is *n* less than 0?; the consequent is `(+   n    10)`, or increase the value *n* by 10; and the alternative is `(+   n    20)`, or increase the value of *n* by 20.

If no alternative is supplied (the second format) and test evaluates to false, the result is unspecified. Here is another example:

```
                        (explanation)
(if  (=  a  0)      if a=0    then
     0                  return 0
     (/  1  a))        else    return 1/a
```

In Scheme, decisions can be represented as *conditional expressions* by using *cond* with the syntax

```
(cond    (condition₁    expression₁)
         (condition₂    expression₂)
         . . .
         (conditionₙ    expressionₙ)
         (else          expressionₙ₊₁))
```

which is equivalent to

```
if       condition₁   then return     expression₁
else   if   condition₂   then return      expression₂
       . . .
else   if   conditionₙ   then return      expressionₙ
else   return     expressionₙ₊₁
```

A special function, *cond,* obeys the delayed evaluation rule because it does not evaluate all its parameters. For example,

```
                        (explanation)
(cond    ((=  a  0)  0)      if  a=0    then    return 0
         ((=  a  1)  1)      else  if  a=1    then return 1
         (T (/  1  a)))      else    return 1/a
```

13.2.6 Iteration and Recursion

Programming in Scheme, as in any functional language, relies on recursion to perform loops and other repetitive operations. The general-purpose iteration and recursion construct is

```
(let   name
       ((variable    value)   . . .   )
       expression₁
       expression₂
       . . .
       )
```

where the variable `name` is bound within the body to a procedure that may be called to recur or iterate. The arguments to the procedure become the new values for the variable `variable`. The following two definitions of *factorial* compute the factorial of a nonnegative integer n. The first employs the recursive definition $n! = n \times (n-1)!$, where $0!$ is defined to be 1. The second is an iterative version, $n! = n \times (n-1) \times (n-2) \times \ldots \times 1$, using an accumulator, `sum`, to hold the intermediate products.

```
(define  factorial
     (lambda  (n)
            (let fact ((i n))
                 (if (= i 0)
                       1
                       (* i (fact (-i 1)))))))))
(define  factorial
     (lambda  (n)
            (let fact ((i n)  (sum 1))
                 (if (= i 0)
                       sum
                       (fact (-i 1) (* sum i) ) ) ) ) )
```

Sample results are

```
(factorial 3)  ⇒ 6    and    (factorial 10)  ⇒ 3628800
```

Another commonly needed list operation is that of constructing a new list that contains all the elements of two given list arguments. This is usually implemented as a Scheme function named *append*, which can be constructed by repeated use of cons to place the elements of the first list argument into the second list argument. To clarify the action of *append*, consider the following example:

```
(append  '(A  B)  '(C  D) )
```

returns (A B C D), and

```
(append  '( (A  B)  C)   '(D  (E  F) ) )
```

returns ((A B) C   D (E F)). The definition of append is

```
(define  (append  list1  list2)
     (cond  ( (NULL?  List1)  list2)
     (else (cons (car list1) (append (cdr list1) list2) ) ) ) )
```

As another example, we write a function that repeatedly adds the *car* of the list to the sum of its *cdr*, using recursion to go through the list.

```
(define  (adder  list)
     (cond  ( (NULL?  list)  0)
     (else  (+  (car  list)  (adder  (cdr  list) ) ) ) ) )
```

In this example, we used a function for numeric atoms named +, which takes any number of numeric atoms as arguments and returns their sum. An alternative solution to the problem is to write a function that builds a call to + with the proper parameter forms. This can be done by using *cons* to insert the atom + into the list of numbers. This new list can then be submitted to *eval* for evaluation as in the following:

```
(define  (adder  list)
     (cond  ( (NULL?  list)  0)
     (else  (eval  (cons '+  list) ) ) ) )
```

As an example, consider the call

```
(adder   '(3   4   5) )
```

that causes adder to build the list

```
(+   3   4   5)
```

The list is then submitted to *eval,* which invokes + and returns the result, 12. Note that the + as a function name is quoted to prevent *eval* from evaluating it in the evaluation of *cons.* Another example is a procedure to *square* all the members in a list of numbers:

```
(define  (sqr-list  L)
    (if  (null?  L)   ( )
            (cons  (*  (car  L)  (car  L) )  (sqr-list
                    (cdr  L)  )  )  )  )
```

A sample result of calling sqr-list is

```
(sqr-list (2  3  4  5))  ⇒  (4  9  16  25)
```

13.2.7 Macros and Objects

Scheme has an object-oriented extension called SCOOPS, which is implemented entirely through Scheme macros. A **macro** is an expression beginning with *macro* and followed by a name that is the keyword of a new special form. When the compiler encounters a macro expression, its definition is invoked into the program, where it can be evaluated. The user is not aware of this substitution. An example is the following:

```
(macro     sqr    (lambda    expression)
        (list    '*   (cadr expression)    (cadr    expression)))
```

When the expression containing the keyword sqr is encountered, the expression is replaced by the definition of the macro. Another example is the following *square root* function:

```
(define    square-square    (lambda (x  y)
            (sqrt    (+  (sqrt  x)    (sqrt  y)))))
```

This function can be invoked as the following:

```
(square-square  3  4)    ⇒ (sqrt  (+  (*  3  3)  (*  4  4)))
                         ⇒ (sqrt  (+  9  16)  ⇒ (sqrt  25)  ⇒  5
```

SCOOPS provides *classes, objects, methods,* and *mixins. Mixins* are superclasses inherited by a class being defined. SCOOPS includes macros to define the keywords

▶ Define-method, which defines classes

▶ Make-instance, which creates objects

▶ Mixins, which implement inheritance

▶ Define-class, *classvars,* and *instvars,* which implement information hiding and data abstraction

For example, we define a class *point* as the following:

```
(define-class   point
      (classvars   (origin-x  0)   (origin-y  0))
      (instvars   (x   (active  0   ()  move-x))
                  (y   (active  0   ()  move-y))
      (color   (active  'yellow ()  change-color)))
      (options   settable-variables   inittable-variables))
(compile-class   point)
```

An object as point1 can be created by

```
(define   point1   (make-instance   point))
```

where the local state for point1 will have the values $x = 0$ and $y = 0$. Any point has
origin-x and origin-y with initial values of 0. Because point classvars are set-
table, four methods are defined automatically: set-origin-x, set-origin-y, set-x, and
set-y. We can set set-origin-x, and set-origin-y to any desired values if we want all
points to be relative to an origin other than $(0, 0)$.

13.2.8 Allocation and Deallocation of Objects

A standard technique for allocating and deallocating objects in Scheme is to link them
on a list called a *free list* or *object-list*. The free list acts as a stack of cells, in which a pop
operation on the stack returns a freshly allocated cell and a push operation returns a
cell back onto the stack. Scheme language implementation performs garbage collection (discussed in Chapter 3) when it returns cells to the free list. In Scheme, three
procedures, *object-hash, object-unhash,* and *gc* (garbage collector), allow a user to associate an object with a unique integer, based on a hashing function. The Scheme object list is thus an object-hash table. Objects that are no longer referenced are removed
from the object-hash table during garbage collection phase, which can be user controlled by calling gc or an automatic process. In general, (object-hash <obj>) assigns
an integer to <obj> and records the relationship in the object-hash table. Objects that
are identical are assigned the same integer. (object-unhash <int>) returns the object
associated with <int>, provided some other reference to the object exists. If no association exists, #F is returned. An object with no reference other than the integer associated with it in the object-hash table is removed from the table during the garbage
collection phase.

13.3 FUNCTIONAL PROGRAMMING WITH ML

MetaLanguage (ML) is primarily a functional programming language; that is, the basic
model of computation is the definition and application of functions. The ML consists
of a deductive calculus called Polymorphic Predicate Calculus and an interactive programming language paradigm. The ML programming language was developed in the
late 1970s as part of a system for proving the correctness of programs at the University

of Edinburgh in the United Kingdom by a team headed by Robin Milner and Michael Gordon. The Standard ML of New Jersey (SML/NJ) was implemented by David Mac-Queen of Lucent (Bell Laboratories) and Andrew Appel of Princeton University. It is available for UNIX workstations, and PCs running Linux or Microsoft Windows. Standard ML is a language with semantics like Scheme in that it has static scoping and an applicative order evaluation rule and has proved to be useful as a general-purpose programming language. Unlike LISP and Scheme, ML is strongly typed, although a user need not always declare data types because the interpreter can determine data types by inference. A strongly typed mechanism is valuable for debugging because it prevents many errors when the program is running. ML has powerful features of imperative languages, including an exception handling mechanism and pattern matching primitives to improve its efficiency. Some of its important features are the following:

▶ Concrete, union, and recursive data types

▶ Parametric modules

▶ Exception handling mechanisms

▶ Polymorphic data types and functions

▶ Two-phase program execution, consisting of a static phase for approval of program correctness and a dynamic phase for program execution

▶ No use of parentheses

▶ Strongly typed syntax, allowing the type of every expression to be determined before execution and types to be checked for consistency

The combination of features in ML offers the user a great deal of programming ease and a quite different functional language than that of LISP and Scheme.

13.3.1 The Principles of ML

In ML, expressions are composed of operators and operands, and operands may be either variables or constants. An expression must be followed by a semicolon to tell the ML interpreter that the instruction has finished. ML responds to any definition through the following primitives:

▶ The word *val* stands for value.

▶ The variable *it* stands for definition value.

▶ An *equals* "=" sign is used.

▶ The *value* of the expression is returned.

▶ A *colon* represents the association of a value with its type.

▶ A *type* denotes the type of the value.

For the expression

```
1+2*3 - 4;
```

the system returns

```
val   it = 3   :   int
```

For

```
true;
```

the system returns

```
val   it = true  :  bool
```

In other words, the ML system responds to a definition by returning the data type of the value defined. There is almost no need for parentheses in ML because the system can determine the meaning of items based solely on their positions.

13.3.2 Variable Definition and Reference

Identifiers can be defined and bound to values through statements with the following syntax.

```
val   identifier  =  value;
```

For example, the declarations

```
val   x=5;
val   y=2*5;
```

assign 5 and 10 as the value of variables x and y, respectively. Although ML is very strict regarding typing, an identifier is not bound to a type but, rather, to a value, and the rebinding of the same identifier to a value of a different type is allowed. For example

```
val   x=5.0;
```

the system returns the following;

```
val   x=5.0  :  real
```

For

```
val   x=10;
```

the system returns the following.

```
val   x=10  :  int
```

For

```
val   x= " MetaLanguage";
```

the system returns the following:

```
val   x= " MetaLanguage"  :  string
```

ML supports the following operators:

▶ The arithmetic operators are +, −, *, and / (division for reals), div (division for integers), and mod (remainder of integer division).
▶ The string operator ∧ represents concatenation of strings.
▶ The comparison operators are =, <, >, <=, and >=, and <> represents not equal to.
▶ The logical operators are *andalso* (for and), *orelse* (for or), and *not*.

The following are some expressions and their responses from an ML interpreter. For

```
3.0-4.5+6.7;
```

the system returns the following:

```
val   it  =  5.2  :  real
```

For

```
43  div( 8 mod  3)*5;
```

the system returns the following:

```
val   it  =  105  :  int
```

For

```
"Meta" ∧ "Language";
```

the system returns the following:

```
val   it  =  "MetaLanguage"   :  string
```

For

```
2<3+4;
```

the system returns the following:

```
val   it  =  true  :  bool
```

For

```
"ABC"  <=  "AB";
```

the system returns the following:

```
val   it  =  false  :  bool
```

For

```
1<2  orelse  3>4;
```

the system returns the following:

```
val   it  =  true  :  bool
```

For

```
1<2  andalso  3>4;
```

the system returns the following:

```
val   it  =  false  :  bool
```

Unlike Scheme, ML has a rich set of data types, from enumerated types to records to lists. In the following section, we will give only the briefest overview of this rich type structure.

13.3.3   Primitive Data Types

One difference between ML and Scheme is the use of strict typing. All objects in ML are bound to a type; that binding persists for the entire life of the object, and it is reported as a part of its evaluation. For example, for a simple expression evaluation in ML such as

```
2+3;
```

the system returns

```
val   it  =  5   :   int
```

indicating that the evaluation of expression results in a value 5 of type integer that is stored in a temporary variable called it. For

```
2.0+3.0;
```

the system returns the following:

```
val   it  =  5.0  :   real
```

However, ML does not permit the mixture of types; that requires type conversion. In such a case, an error message is displayed; for example,

```
2+3.0;
Error: operator and operand don't agree
```

The five primitive data types in ML are *int, real, bool, char,* and *string.* The Boolean data type has two values, true and false, which must be written in lowercase. The representation of character data type is by the character # followed by a character string of length 1. The following are some examples with the responses from the ML system. For

```
val   radius = 4;
```

the system returns the following:

```
val   radius = 4  :   int
```

For

```
val   pi = 3.1415;
```

the system returns the following:

```
val   pi = 3.1415  :   real
```

For

```
val   c = # "x";
```

the system returns the following:

```
val   c = # "x"  :   char
```

For

```
val   s = " MetaLanguage";
```

the system returns the following:

```
val   s = " MetaLanguage"   :   string
```

For

```
true;
```

the system returns the following:

```
val   it = true   :   bool
```

13.3.4 Structured Data Types

ML supports abstract data types called *structures* that provide the same capability of classes used in object-oriented programming languages. ML supports abstract data types for constructing new types and objects of a given type; thus, all access is through a fixed set of operations defined for that type. An example is a type such as stack, for which we might define the push and pop operations and a few other operations as the only mechanisms by which the contents of a stack could be changed. ML contains tuples and lists as structured data objects.

Tuples

A tuple is formed by taking a list of two or more expressions of any type, separated by commas, and enclosed by parentheses. In the following example, we assign to the variable class a tuple whose first component is the integer 344, whose second component is the real 3.9, and whose third component is the string "Programming Language":

```
val   class   =   (344, 3.9, " Programming Language");
```

The response from the ML system is

```
val class = (344,3.9, " Programming Language"):int*real*string
```

Note that the type int*real*string is a product type. Its values are tuples that have three components—the first is an integer, the second is a real, and the third is a string. Here * indicates tuple formation. Another example of a tuple of type int*int*int*int is

```
val   number   =   (1,2,3,4);
val   number   =   (1,2,3,4)   : int*int*int*int
```

For a tuple or a variable whose value is a tuple, we can access the *i*th element by applying the function #i. For example, in the tuple

```
val   class   =   (344,3.9, " Programming Language");
```

we can obtain its component with #1(class), #2(class), and #3(class), in which the ML system returns

```
val   it = 344   :   int
val   it = 3.9   :   real
val   it = " Programming Language"   :   string
```

Applying #4, which designates a component number not available in the tuple, is an error.

Lists

ML provides a simple notation for lists whose elements are all of the same type. A list can be formed by a sequence of elements separated by a comma and enclosed within brackets. For example, a list of three integer numbers 1, 2, 3 is represented in ML by [1,2,3], and the response of ML is the following:

```
[1,2,3];
val   it  =  [1, 2, 3]  :  int list
```

Elements in a list must all have the same type; the preceding list is a list of integers and so has the type int list. For a list that has a single element that is of type string, ["a"], the response of ML is

```
["a"];
val   it  =  ["a"]  :  string list
```

In the following example, we write a list of three characters:

```
[#"a", #"b", #"c"];
val   it  =  [#"a", #"b", #"c"]  :  char*char*char list
```

A constructor operation (similar to cons in LISP) is given by a double colon:

```
1 ::  [2, 3];
```

The system responds with the following:

```
[1, 2, 3]  :  int  list
```

If we want to collect together data of different types in ML, we cannot use list; [2, 2.5] is an error because it combines an integer and a real number. We must instead use a tuple.

13.3.5 Functions

Both the parameters and the result of each function are strictly typed. A function is defined with the following syntax:

```
fun   function-name      (parameter-list)  =   function-body;
```

The identifier immediately after fun is the name of the function, the names of the parameters precede the equal sign, and the body of the function follows the equal sign. The type of the parameter may be omitted if it can be inferred from context. For example,

```
fun   number (x: int)  =5+x;
```

specifies that the identifier number has been bound to a function that takes one integer parameter and returns a single integer value. The ML system returns the following:

```
val   number  =  fn  :  int ⇒ int
```

The type associated with this function is inferred by ML because of the presence of the integer constant 5 in the definition of the function. In contrast, in the following function definition, the ML system is not able to determine the type of the function because the arithmetic operator + would be applied to both integer and real operands. An error message would address such a situation:

```
fun    number (x) = x+x;
Error : overloaded variable cannot be resolved  : +
```

In general, the type of parameter is sufficient for ML to determine the type of the returned value:

```
fun    number (x:real) = x +x;
val    number  =  fn  :  real ⇒ real
```

Another form of function specification permits a sequence of alternative conditions, each of which is followed by its corresponding return value given in an *if-then-else* form. Consider the factorial function

```
fun    factorial (n)  =  if n=0    then    1
                            else   n*factorial(n-1);
```

in which the system returns the following;

```
val    factorial  =  fn  :  int ⇒ int
```

Once the function has been declared, it can be called as follows:

```
factorial 5;
120 : int
```

ML responds with the returned value and its type. ML has essentially the same evaluation rules as Scheme; *factorial* must be evaluated to a function, then 5 is evaluated and its type must agree with the parameter type of the function. The function is then called and its returned value printed together with its type. ML, however, does not need a quote as in Scheme to prevent evaluation because data is distinct from programs. ML, unlike Scheme and LISP, rejects if the type of an expression disagrees with its expected type. For example, examine the definition of a function named **sqr**

```
fun    sqr   x : int  = x * x;
```

where int declares the type of **sqr**. If we call the function as

```
sqr   2.5;
```

then the system responds as:

```
Type Crash  in  :  sqr  2.5
Looking for a : int
I have found a : real
```

Without the type declaration, ML responds as follows:

```
fun   sqr   x = x * x;
Error: Unresolvable overloaded identifier :   x
```

In this case, the function cannot be defined because the system cannot tell whether to use real or integer multiplication for "*" because the type of x cannot be deduced from the available information. In ML, an **anonymous function** is a function with no name that has the following form:

```
fn   parameter-list   ⇒ function-body;
```

An example is a function that multiplies its parameter x by 5:

```
fn   x ⇒ x*5;
```

The system responds as follows:

```
val   it = fn :   int ⇒   int
```

ML also has the equivalent of the Scheme lambda expression, except that the reserved word fn is used in place of lambda. For example, given

```
val   sqr = fn  x :   int ⇒ x*x ;
```

ML responds as follows:

```
val   sqr = fn :   int → int
```

Function expression can also be applied directly, as in Scheme:

```
(fn   x : int  ⇒ x * x ) 2
4 :   int
```

Note that the type declaration of x*x as an integer is necessary because x could also be real or any other type with an operation named "*". As an example of a slightly more complicated function in ML, consider the Euclid's algorithm as follows:

```
fun   gcd  (n, m)  :   int = if  m = 0  then  n
         else  gcd (m,  n mod m);
```

where the system responds

```
val   gcd = fn :   int * int → int
```

once the function has been defined, it can be called as follows:

```
gcd (15, 10);
5 :   int
```

Built-In Functions

The built-in *print* function is used to produce printed results. The built-in functions hd and tl correspond to the *car* and *cdr* functions, respectively, in Scheme. For example,

```
hd([1,2,3,4]);
```

returns

```
val   it = 1 : int
```

and

```
tl([1,2,3,4]);
```

returns

```
val   it  =   [2, 3, 4]  :  int  list
```

A built-in function :: appends an element to a list and is the same as the *cons* function in Scheme. For example,

```
"A"  ::  [ "B", "C", "D" ];
```

returns

```
val   it  =  [ "A", "B", "C", "D" ]  :  string  list
```

Another built-in function that applies to lists is the append operator, denoted @. For example,

```
[1,2,3,4]  @  [5,6,7];
```

returns

```
val   it  =  [1,2,3,4,5,6,7]  :  int  list
```

A built-in function *rev* reverses a list. For example

```
rev[2,3,4,5];
```

returns

```
val   it  =  [5,4,3,2]  :  int  list
```

Other built-in functions include the following:

▶ *explode*(*string-value*), which converts *string-value* to a list of single-character strings

▶ *size*(*string*), which returns the number of characters in string *string*

▶ *ord*(*char*), which returns the integer value of character *char*

▶ *chr*(*int*), which returns the character represented by integer *int*.

Higher Order Functions

A typical function has parameters that represent data, indicating that the parameters are of some basic type such as *real,* or they are lists or tuples of basic types. However, a parameter or result of functions can also have a function type. Recall that functions that take functions as arguments or produce functions as values are called *higher-order functions.* ML makes defining higher order functions easy. In contrast, the mechanisms in conventional languages for defining and using higher-order functions tend to be cumbersome, and there may be some limitations on the power of these mechanisms. Let's consider a higher-order function called *numerical integration by the trapezoidal rule,* defined as $\int_a^b f(x)\ dx$. The idea is to compute the approximate integral of some function $f(x)$ between limits a and b by dividing the line from a to b into n equal parts from some value of n. We then approximate the integral as the sum of the areas of the n trapezoids. The following function takes two real numbers (limits a and b), an integer number (number of trapezoids, n) and a function F to be integrated:

```
fun   trapezoid(a,b,n,F)  =
      if  n<=0 orelse  b-a<=0.0    then    0.0              (1)
      else
          let   val  delta=(b-a)/real(n)                    (2)
          in
              delta*(F(a)+F(a+delta))/2.0 +                 (3)
              trapezoid(a+delta, b, n-1, F)                 (4)
          end;
```

In response, the system returns the following:

```
val   trapezoid = fn  :  real*real*int*(real ⇒ real) ⇒ real
```

This higher-order function uses an equivalent recursive method. In other words, a recursive call with the new values of a and n (line 4) sums the areas of the trapezoids. In line 1 we test for the basis case: When a = b and n = 0, the value of the integral is 0. In addition, line 1 handles data errors, the case that n or b − a is negative, or when one of n and b − a but not the other is 0. Line 2 computes the variable delta to be (1/nth) of the width of the range of integration. The delta is called the width of each trapezoid. Line 3 computes the area of the first trapezoid, multiplying delta by the sum of the heights of the sides (F(a)+F(a+delta)) and dividing by 2. Line 4 is a recursive call on the range that excludes the previous trapezoid, meaning that it sums the area of the trapezoids. To illustrate use of this higher order function, we define a function *square* as the following:

```
fun   square(x:real)=x*x;
val   square = fn :  real ⇒ real
```

Then we can call the trapezoid function

```
trapezoid(0.0, 1.0, 8, square);
```

and the system responds with

```
val   it  = 0.3359375  :  real
```

indicating that $\int_0^1 x^2\, dx = 1/3$.

ML provides three important higher-order functions:

▶   The *map* function takes a function F and a list $[a_1, a_2, \ldots, a_n]$ and produces the list $[F(a_1), F(a_2), \ldots, F(a_n)]$, applying F to each element of the list and the list of resulting values.

▶   The *reduce* function takes a function F with two arguments and a list $[a_1, a_2, \ldots, a_n]$ and gives $F(a_1, F(a_2, F(\ldots, F(a_{n-1}, a_n) \ldots)))$. For example, if F is a sum function, $F(x + y) = x + y$, reduce $(F, [a_1, a_2, \ldots, a_n])$ is $a_1 + a_2 + \ldots + a_n$, the sum of the elements of the list.

▶ The function *filter* takes a predicate *P* (a function whose value is Boolean) and a list $[a_1, a_2, \ldots, a_n]$. The result is the list of all those elements on the given list that satisfy the predicate *P*. For example

```
filter(fn(x) ⇒ x>10,  [1, 10, 23, 5, 16]);
```

returns the following:

```
val  it  =  [23, 16]  :  int list
```

13.3.6 Eager Evaluation versus Lazy Evaluation

In contrast to lazy evaluation, where parts of an argument such as a list or file are evaluated only as needed, in *eager evaluation* the entire file or list, regardless of whether we need it, is evaluated. The eager evaluation approach is used in ML because of the call-by-value semantics associated with its function arguments. However, this approach has a disadvantage: The method of parameter passing used in ML is also call-by-value. Although ML argument evaluation is *eager,* other aspects of the language are *delayed.* For instance, as we mentioned previously, the second argument of *andalso* or *orelse* is evaluated only if needed (lazy evaluation). In addition, the *if-then-else* and *case* expressions obey the lazy evaluation rule. A conditional expression has several subexpressions from which exactly one is chosen to be evaluated; choice is fundamental in conditional statements. In the ML conditional expression

```
if expression then true-expression else false-expression
```

the `expression` evaluates to a true Boolean value, then `true-expression` is evaluated and becomes the value of the entire *if-then-else* expression; otherwise `false-expression` is the value of the *if-then-else* expression. In this sense, the *if-then-else* expression follows the lazy evaluation rule. For example, let's consider the conditional expression

```
if  1<2  then  3+4  else  5+6;
val  it  =  7  :  int
```

The expression 1<2 evaluates to true, so 3+4=7 is the value of the entire expression. The form of a `case` expression is the following:

```
case  expression  of  match
```

The value of a `case` expression is found by matching (in order of appearance) each pattern in the match against the value of the expression. As soon as a matching pattern is found, the corresponding expression in the match is evaluated and becomes the value of the case expression. If no pattern matches the expression, the exception Match is raised; that is an unidentified problem. An example is that division by 0 produces an error. If we do nothing to handle the error, it will stop the computation with an "*uncaught exception*" message. The following ML case expression yields the number of days in *currentmonth*, which is of type string:

```
case  currentmonth  of
  " February "    => 29    |
```

```
" April  "         => 30    |
" June   "         => 30    |
" September "      => 30    |
" November "       => 30    |
   _____        => 31
```

If the value of `currentmonth` is "February", 29 is the return value of the `case` expression. In the last line _ (underscore) matches any value of `currentmonth` not explicitly listed. Again, `case` follows the lazy evaluation rule. The following is an example of an *if* expression with an equivalent *case* expression:

```
if   x<y   then   # "A"        case   x<y   of    true  ⇒ # "A"  |
            else   # "B"                           false ⇒ # "B"
```

13.3.7   Polymorphism

The ability of a function to accept arguments of different types is called **polymorphism** (*poly* means many and *morph* means form), and such a function is called a **polymorphic function.** The same definition might be applied to operations: An operation that can accept values of arbitrary types is called a **polymorphic operation.** For example, the arithmetic operations of addition and subtraction for integers and real numbers usually have the same names (+ and −) even though actual implementation of the two operations is different because of the different internal representation of the two types. For example, the function *firstelement* that returns the first element in a tuple of length 2 is defined

```
fun   firstelement   (x,y) = x;
```

to return the first element of a pair of elements. In this case, ML responds with

```
val   firstelement   =   fn   :   'a * 'b ⇒ 'a
```

indicating that x and y can be of any type and that the value returned will be of the same type as that of the first parameter. The notation `'a*'b ⇒ 'a` indicates that a and b are polytype; each can be of any type. The symbol `'a and 'b` in the preceding types are type variables. In other words, the definition of function type is postponed until function application when the type of the parameters can be used to infer types for each evaluation. For example, for

```
firstelement (3, 5);
```

the system returns

```
val   it = 3  :   int
```

and for

```
firstelement (3.0, 5);
```

the system returns

```
val   it = 3.0  :   real
```

In other words, ML allows the types in an expression to be *type variable,* meaning that the type of a subexpression can be undetermined and depends on the actual type supplied during execution. ML supports polymorphism, but an imperative language such as C requires creating different types with similar properties, such as a stack of integers or a stack of real numbers. Operations such as *push* and *pop* then have to be defined for each different type of stack. In contrast, only one version of a stack must be defined in ML. Regardless of whether integers or real numbers are referred, one push function and one pop function is provided. ML uses pattern matching to resolve type variables during execution. An extreme example of a polymorphic function is the identity function defined as

```
fun   Identity (x) = x;
val   Identity = fn : 'a ⇒ 'a
```

This function can produce its argument as its result, regardless of the type of argument. For instance, in the following, the type of the argument is returned as int:

```
Identity (5);
val  it = 5  :  int
```

Similarly, in the following, the type of the argument is returned as real:

```
Identity (5.0);
val  it = 5.0  :  real
```

Or, it can be returned as *char, string, list,* or whatsoever. ML also uses pattern matching to determine statically the type of functions with incomplete type information given in declarations. This process is called *type inference.* The information from the ML type inference process is then also used to perform static type checking of expressions. As an example, consider how ML determines the type of the factorial function:

```
fun    factorial   n =  if     n = 0   then  1
             else   n * factorial (n-1);
```

The system responds with the following:

```
val   factorial  =  fn  :  int → int
```

In this respect, ML first assigns type variables to n and `factorial`:

```
n  :  'a
factorial  :  'a  →  'b
```

Then the if-expression is type-checked, which requires that the first expression n = 0 be Boolean and that the types of the result expressions match. Now n = 0 is indeed a Boolean expression, but is only type correct if n is an integer. Thus, type variable 'a = int and we get

```
n  :  'a
factorial  :  int →  'b
```

Then the types of the result expressions are determined and compared, in which 1 is an integer, and n*factorial (n-1) is an integer because n is an integer. Thus, the result type of `factorial` must also be int, given `'b` = int. As a consequence, the complete expression is type correct with `'a` = int and `'b` = int, meaning

```
n  :  'a
factorial  :  int →  int
```

As a second example of type inference using pattern matching, consider the following function definition, which itself uses pattern matching:

```
fun  makepairs  [ ]  =  [ ]  |
     makepairs  (x : : y)  =  (x, x)  : :  (makepairs  y);
```

This function takes a list of arbitrary elements and returns a list of pairs of the elements of the given list:

```
makepairs  [1,  2,  3];
[ (1, 1),  (2, 2),  (3, 3) ]  :  (int * int)  list
```

ML determines the type of `makepairs` as follows. From the first expression for `makepairs`,

```
makepairs  [ ]  = [ ]
```

ML concludes that `makepairs` takes a list as a parameter and returns a list as its result. Thus, so far, it infers that the type of `makepairs` is

```
'a  list  →  'b  list
```

From the second expression for `makepairs`,

```
makepairs  ( x : : y)  =  (x, x)  : : (makepairs  y);
```

ML concludes that x must be of type `'a` and that `(x, x)` must be of type `'b`. Pattern matching then gives the result

```
'b  =  'a  *  'a
```

and ML infers that the type of `makepairs` is

```
'a  list  →  ('a  *  'a)  list
```

13.3.8 Exception Handling

What happen when we attempt to divide an integer by zero? When such an *exceptional condition* arises, the program cannot continue normally. In many languages, the program simply halts and issues some sort of diagnostic message. Such a reaction is not flexible, making a robust program difficult or impossible. A program is said to be *robust* if it recovers from exceptional conditions. In other words, we may prefer that when an exception arises, an attempt is made to produce an appropriate value and continue the computation. The raising of exceptions is an important feature of ML. For example, accessing an empty list such as

```
hd[ ];
```

causes the ML system to respond

```
uncaught exception hd
```

LISP language returns the empty list and C language returns 0. ML allows programmers to define exceptions with the syntax

```
exception    exception-name
```

which can be invoked by

```
raise    exception-name
```

Exceptions can be caught or handled by using the following syntax:

```
<expression>₁    handle    <exception-name>    ⇒    <expression>₂
```

This construct behaves like <expression>$_1$ except that if <exception-name> is raised during the evaluation of <expression>$_1$; control then passes to <expression>$_2$ and its value is returned. For example, suppose that other is an exception defined:

```
exception    other;
```

when the system responds

```
exception    other:    exn
```

In the following, because 2+3 evaluates to 5, the handler is ignored and the construct behaves with the evaluation of 2+3:

```
2+3 handle    other    ⇒    0;
```

The system returns:

```
val    it    =  5  :    int
```

In contrast, if the evaluation of expression raises the other, then the system responds with the following:

```
val    it    =  0  :    int
```

Another form of exception handling is the following syntax:

```
expression    handle        handler
```

Here expression is one in which one or more exceptions may be raised. The handler takes exceptions as patterns and associates them with appropriate expressions, as in

```
handler(pattern₁)    ⇒    expression₁
handler(pattern₂)    ⇒    expression₂
...
handler(patternₙ)    ⇒    expressionₙ
```

In this respect, if expression raises an exception, handler might be applied.

Example: The following function named *lookup* searches for an element y in a list x and raises the exception Nomatch if the list is empty.

```
fun   lookup (y,   x)   =
      if  null (x)  then raise  Nomatch
      else   if   y =  hd (x)  then x
            else   lookup (y, tl (x));
```

The normal behavior of `lookup` is to return the portion of a list from the first occurrence of y to the end. For example,

```
lookup(3,   [1, 2, 3, 4, 2, 3, 5]);
```

The system responds with the following:

```
val   it  =   [3, 4, 2, 3, 5]   :   int   list
```

The special case occurs

```
lookup(4, [ ]);
```

when the system responds as:

```
uncaught   exception Nomatch
```

Example: Consider the following *combination* function that is designed to compute $\binom{n}{m}$ in situations where the first argument is nonnegative, the second argument is nonnegative, and the second argument is less than the first argument. Here, we define two exceptions to be raised when the input is improper: *ImproperN* and *ImproperM*. When carried out, the expressions *raise ImproperN* and *raise ImproperM* cause the function combination to be terminated with an explanation of the exception caused:

```
exception   ImproperN   and   ImproperM
fun   combination (n, m)  =
      if  n<0   then   raise ImproperN
      else   if   m<0   orelse   m>n   then raise ImproperM
      else   if   m=0   orelse   m=n   then   1
      else   combination(n-1, m) + combination(n-1, m-1);
```

The ML system then responds with

```
val   combination   =   fn   :   int * int ⇒ int
```

For example,

```
combination(5,2);
```

returns

```
val   it  =   10   :   int
```

whereas

```
combination(-1,2);
```

returns

```
uncaught exception ImproperN
```

and

```
combination(5,6);
```

returns

```
uncaught exception ImproperM
```

Example: The following exception returns 0 after an attempt to divide an integer by 0.

```
exception    divzero    :   int*int
handle       divzero    with    (x,0)  =>  0  |
             (x,y)  =>  x div y
```

For example, the call

```
5 divzero  0
```

returns

```
0  :  int
```

In ML, an exception identifier declared locally in a subprogram is local to the subprogram just like any other identifier. Hence, it is distinct from exceptions in other invocations of the program.

13.3.9 Module System

One important theme of modern programming language design is facilitating the encapsulation of information. In other words, concepts such as types and functions are grouped in clusters that can be accessed in a limited form. The limitation is not intended to make the programming difficult. Rather, the intent is to prevent data from being used in unexpected ways that result in troublesome debugging, to allow the definitions supporting a common idea to be packaged with a simple and precisely defined interface. The principal features of ML that support encapsulation are *structures, signatures,* and *functors,* the three major building blocks of the ML module system.

▶ Structures are collections of data types, functions, exceptions, and other elements that we want to encapsulate. Element definitions appear in the structure and take the following form:

```
structure   identifier  =  struct  structure-elements   end
```

The open declaration creates a dynamic scope for a structure as in

```
open      identifier
```

Structure precedes an identifier being declared to be a structure, and is paired with *end* to bracket the elements of a structure.

▶ **Signatures** are collections of information describing the types and other specifications for some of the elements of a structure and take the form:

```
sig   specification   end
```

Keyword `signature` and `sig` are related to list `structure` and `struct`. Word `signature` introduces a signature definition, whereas `sig`, along with `end`, brackets the specifications in the signature. As for structures, specifications of a signature may optionally be ended with a semicolon. We can bind an identifier to a value that is a signature by

```
signature  <identifier>  =  sig  <specifications>  end
```

▶ **Functors** are operations that take one or more elements (e.g., structures) as arguments and produce a structure that combines the functor's arguments in some form. A functor is actually a higher-order function that takes structures or certain other kinds of elements as arguments and returns a structure as a result.

In effect, a signature is a type for a structure; that is, we can attach a signature to a structure with a colon, just as we attach a type to an expression with a colon. An alternative, and similar, view is that the signature is a declaration, whereas the structure is a definition. Some important kinds of specifications are the following:

▶ *type,* followed by an identifier, possibly parameterized by type variable. Two examples are *type foo* and *type ('a, 'b) bar.*

▶ *eqtype,* also followed by an identifier. This keyword declares that the named type must be an equality type. A data type in a structure can correspond to a *type* or an *eqtype* in the signature.

▶ *exception,* followed by an exception name.

▶ *val,* followed by an identifier, a colon, and a type expression.

In the following code, we define a simple structure, `lamp`, along with a signature, `appliance`, that summarizes the contents of the `structure` as an abstract description of all the elements defined in the `structure`.

```
structure   lamp   =
   struct
       datatype   bulb  =  ON  |  OFF
       fun   switch(ON)  = OFF  |  switch(OFF) =  ON
   end
signature   appliance
   sig
       type   bulb
       val   switch  :  bulb  ⇒  bulb
   end
```

Because ML allows a structure to be viewed only through its signature, this approach provides an alternative for information hiding.

Example: A useful data structure for retrieving an association between data of two types is *mapping.* In ML, we can think of this structures as a list of pairs: the first component of each pair is of some type 'd, called the *domain type,* and the second component is of some type 'r, called the *range type.* Suppose we want to have a structure that is a mapping, where the domain is strings and the range is integers. We shall call this kind of mapping *string-integer mapping*. We define a structure named `Mapping` and a suitable signature named `SingMapping` as *string-integer mapping*:

```
structure   Mapping  =  struct
exception   NotFound;
(* create the empty mapping *)
val   create = nil;
```

(* `lookup(d,M)` finds the range value r such that (d,r) is a pair in mapping M *)

```
fun   lookup(d, nil)  =  raise NotFounf  |
      lookup(d, (e,r) : : es)  =
      if    d = e  then  r
      else   lookup(d,  es);
```

(* `insert (d, r, m)` puts (d, r) in mapping M and removes any other pair (d, s) that was present in M *)

```
fun   insert(d, r, nil)  =  [(d, r)]  |
      insert(d, r, (e, s) : : es)  =
      if   d = e  then  (d, r) : : es
      else   (e, s) : :  insert(d, r, es)
end;
signature  SingMapping  =  sig
exception  NotFound;
val   create  :  (string * int) list;
val   insert  :  (string * int ) *
                 (string * int) list  →  (string * int) list;
val   lookup  :  string * (string * int) list  →  int
end;
```

We can now use the signature `SingMapping` to restrict the structure `Mapping`. We do so by defining another structure, which we shall call *SMapping*, to be equal to `Mapping`, but with the signature `SingMapping`. The declartion

```
structure   SMapping  :  SingMapping  =  Mapping
```

defines a new structure. The functions `create`, `insert`, and `lookup` from the `SingMapping` structure can only be applied to string-integer mapping. Suppose we have defined the structure `SingMapping` as above. Having executed the statement

```
structure   SMapping  :  SingMapping  =  Mapping
```

preceded by the definition of structure `Mapping` and signature `SingMapping`, we can then use string-integer mapping. We might, for example, initialize an empty string-integer mapping m by

```
val  m  =  Smapping.create;
```

when the system responds

```
val  m  =  nil  :  (string  *  int)  list
```

Then, we can insert pairs into mapping m. For example,

```
    val  m  =  SMapping.insert("in",  6,  m);
```

when the system responds

```
    val  m  =  [("in",  6)]  :  (string * int)  list
```

And

```
    val  m  =  SMapping.insert("a",  1,  m);
```

when the system responds

```
    val  m  =  [("in",  6, ("a", 1)]  :  (string * int)  list
```

Finally, a lookup operation such as

```
    SMapping.lookup("in", m);
```

when the system responds

```
    val  it  =  6
```

allows us to obtain information from the mapping.

SUMMARY

The first functional language LISP (LISt Processing) was based on the theory of functions as written in lambda calculus with very simple semantics of legal expressions. We briefly discussed the fundamental features of LISP, which contains many features of modern functional languages. The language is widely used for computer science research in the area of artificial intelligence. A LISP program consists of a set of function definitions followed by a list of expressions that may include function evaluations. The expressions are written in Cambridge Polish form. We discussed the principles of LISP, including data objects and functions. LISP doesn't support data abstraction features, meaning that it is a pure and typeless functional programming language.

Scheme was introduced as the first dialect of typeless LISP to fully support functional programming. Scheme is used to write text editors, compilers, operating systems, graphic packages, and numerical applications. Scheme programs are highly portable across different Scheme implementations on different machines. Scheme is not a strongly typed language; the programmer is responsible for type checking. The basic object in Scheme is the S-expression, and the cell model is used to represent the implementation model of expressions. Cell diagrams for structures are usually drawn with a series of boxes, which stretch from left to right, depending on the number of elements in structure. Scheme implies that the value of a function is distinguished from a call to the function. In other words, the function value is represented by its name, whereas a function call is enclosed within parentheses. Functions in Scheme are grouped into three categories: user-defined, built-in, and higher-order functions. The Scheme evaluation rule, which adopts applicative order evaluation, implies that all expressions must be written in prefix notation.

ML, developed by Michael Gordon (1979) in the United Kingdom, consists of a deductive calculus called Polymorphic Predicate Calculus (PPλ) together with an interactive programming language paradigm. It was called ML, for MetaLanguage, because it served as the common language for LCF, a proof-generating system for reasoning about recursive functions. ML is a language with semantics like Scheme and static scooping and has been useful as a general-purpose programming language. Unlike LISP and Scheme, ML is strongly typed, although users don't always need to declare data types because the interpreter can determine data types by inference. A strongly typed language is valuable for debugging because it prevents many errors when the program runs. We outlined the principles of ML including the variable definition and references, primitive and structured data types, tuples, lists, and functions. The eager-evaluation approach is used in ML, meaning that the entire file or list, regardless of whether we need it, is evaluated. The method of parameter passing used in ML is call-by-value. Some important features adopted by ML are polymorphic operations, exception handling, and module systems.

EXERCISES

1. Perform the following substitutions:
   a. $(\lambda x.\ \lambda y.\ \ (add\ y\ ((\lambda z.\ (*\ x\ z))\ 3)))\ 7\ 5$
   b. $(\lambda y.\ 5)\ ((\lambda x.\ x\ x)\ (\lambda x.\ x\ x))$
   c. $((\lambda x.\ (add\ 5\ n))\ 8)$
   d. $(\lambda g.\ g\ 5)\ (\lambda x.\ (add\ x\ 3))$
   e. $(\lambda x.\ x\ x\ x)(\lambda x.\ x\ x\ x)$
   f. $Twice(Twice\ (\lambda n.\ (*\ 2\ (add\ n\ 1))))5$
   g. $(\lambda n.\ multiply\ n\ \ n)\ (add\ 2\ 3)$
   h. $\{\{\lambda u.\ \lambda v.\{\ \lambda w.w\ (\lambda x.x(u))\}\ (v)\ \}\ (y)\}\ (\lambda z.\ \lambda y.z(y))$

2. Define *lambda expressions* for the following functions:
   a. Plus
   b. Square
   c. Square_root
   d. Successor
   e. Predecessor
   f. Even
   g. Max
   h. Min
   i. Identity

3. Define a lambda expression to compute Ax^2+BY+Z. Evaluate the expression for A=2, B=3, X=4, Y=6, and Z=9.

4. Show the *cons cell diagram* of the following in LISP language:
   a. ((THE BOOK) IS (ON THE TABLE))
   b. (THE BOOK (ON THE (TABLE IS) A) (LONG BOOK))
   c. (THE SKY (IS BLUE) AND (CLOUDY AND) RAINY)

5. Assume X=(1 2 3 4), define a function to retrieve the *second argument* of the list in LISP language.

6. Define a lambda function that *counts* the number of arguments in a list.

7. Why does passing all parameters by value prevent side effects?

8. Why do read and print functions produce side effects?

9. Show the following lists using the *cons* function only in LISP language.

   a. ((THE DOG) (AND ((CAT ARE) (NOT FRIENDS))))

   b. ((ALL GOOD) (PEOPLE (SHOULD (GO AHEAD))))

10. What is the value of the variable X after each of the following statements is evaluated in order in LISP language?

   a. (SET   X   '(A   B   C))

   b. (SET   (CAR   X)   'B)

   c. (SET   (CDDR   X)   'D)

   d. (SET   (CDR   (CDR   X))   '(C   C))

   e. (SET   (CDR   X)   NIL)

   f. (SET   (CAR   X)   '(C   C))

11. The elementary *constructor* and *selectors* for S-expressions in Scheme have special properties when applied to lists. Define *car, cdr,* and *cons* and provide one example for each one.

12. What is the equivalent *if structure* of the following conditional expression in Scheme?

   (cond $(c_1$ $e_1)$ $(c_2$ $e_2)$ . . . $(c_n$ $e_n)$ (else e_{n+1}))

13. Write a function in LISP language to *reverse* the elements in a list. Using a diagram, show how the reverse function handles a list with four elements, (a b c d). The result should be (d c b a).

14. Write a LISP program that returns the reverse of a list.

   Assuming the list is X=(1 2 3 4).

15. What is the result of the following queries in LISP language?

   a. (/   (*   1   2   3   4)   (+   -3   -2   -1   0))

   b. (CONS   '1   (CONS   '2   (CONS   '3   NIL)))

   c. (SET   'X   '(1   2   3   4))

   d. (CONS   (CAR   X)   (CDR   X))

16. What is the data type of the following ML aggregates?

   a. (a*2.0, b/2.0)

   b. {y=thisyear+1, m= " January ", d=1}

   c. [31, if leap (this year) then 29
      else 28, 31, 30, 31, 30, 31, 31, 30, 31, 30, 31]

17. Write a ML *if* structure that yields the maximum of the values of X and Y.

18. Make a table showing what the following types of constructs in ML may be.

   a. Constants

   b. Operands of operators

   c. Results of operators

   d. Arguments of functions and procedures

   e. Results of functions

   f. Array of record components

19. One characteristic of a programming language is which sorts of entity may be bound to variables. These variables are called *bindables* of the language. Specify the bindables of ML language and the kinds of declarations in which they may be bound.

20. The type definition binds an identifier to an existing type. An alternative kind of type declaration creates a new and distinct type. What is the intention of the following ML type definitions?

    a. `type    book  =  string  *  int`
    b. `type    author  =  string  *  int`

21. Determine the values of the following expressions in Scheme language:

    a. `(car  '(a  b  c) )`
    b. `(cdr  '(a  b  c) )`
    c. `(cdr  '(a) )`
    d. `(car  (cdr  '(a  b  c) ) )`
    e. `(cdr  (cdr  '(a  b  c) ) )`
    f. `(car  '((a  b)  (c  d) ) )`
    g. `(cdr  '((a  b)  (c  d) ) )`
    h. `(cons  'a  '( ) )`
    i. `(cons  'a  '(b  c) )`
    j. `(cons  'a  (cons  'b  (cons  'c  '( ) ) ) )`
    k. `(cons  '(a  b)  '(c  d) )`
    l. `(cons  (car  '(a  b  c) )  (cdr  '(d  e  f) ) )`
    m. `(cons  (car  '(a  b  c) )  (cdr  '(a  b  c) ) )`
    n. `(NULL?  (car  '( ( )  B  C) ) )`

22. Determine the values of the following expressions in Scheme language.

    a. `(let  ( (x  2) )  (+  x  3) )`
    b. `(let  ( (y  2) )  (+  2  y) )`
    c. `(let  ( (x  2)   (y  3) )  (+  x  y) )`
    d. `(let  ( (a  (*  4  4) ) )  (+  a  a) )`
    e. `(let  ( (+  *) )  (+  2  3) )`
    f. `(let  ( (x  1) )`
       `(let  ( (newx  (+  x  1) ) )  (+  newx  newx) ) )`

23. Construct a procedure in Scheme that finds the roots of a quadratic equation. The roots must be computed according to the well-known quadratic formula:

$$\frac{-b \pm \sqrt{b^2 - 4ac}}{2a}$$

    Determine the two roots of $2X^2 - 4X - 6$ equation.

24. Determine the value of the following expression in Scheme language:

```
(let ( (x  3) )
(unless (=  x  0)  (set!  x  (+  x  1) ) )
(when  (=  x  4)  (set!  x  (*  x  21) ) )
x)
```

25. Write a procedure in Scheme to compute the Nth Fibonacci number for a given N.

26. Advise two definitions (*recursive* and *iterative*) in Scheme to compute the factorial of a nonnegative integer N.

27. Write a function in Scheme that returns the *appended* list of two lists.

28. Write a function in Scheme that returns the *reversed* of a list.

29. Write a function in Scheme that prints out the squares of integers from 1 to 10.

30. What is the response in Scheme language when the following operands are employed:

    a. `"a"  : :  ["b", "c"];`   e. `hd([1, 2, 3]);`

    b. `[1, 2, 3] @ [4, 5];`   f. `tl([1, 2, 3]);`

    c. `rev[1, 2, 3];`   g. `hd([1]);`

    d. `repeat("ab", 5);`   h. `tl(1]);`

31. Write a program in ML to raise a number to the 100th power.

32. Write a program in ML that takes a list L and splits it into two lists. One list consists of odd element numbers and the other list consists of even element numbers.

33. Write a *while-loop* structure in ML that prints the integers from 1 to 10 on a line.

34. Define a record structure in ML that represents information about students in which the fields are as follows:

    An integer ID, the student identification number

    A string Name, the student's name

    A string list that is called Course, indicating the courses in which the student is currently enrolled.

35. Write a ML *case* expression that yields the number of days in the current month that are of type string.

36. Define lambda expressions to accomplish each of the following expressions:

    a. `(5+4) * 2`   b. `(3*3) + (4*4)`

37. Consider the following function definition in ML language:

```
datatype   shape   =   point    |
                       circle  of real  |
                       box  of (real * real)
fun        area (point)  =  0.0   |
           area (circle  r)  =  pi *  sqr (r)   |
           area (box (w, h))  =  w * h
```

Answer the following questions:

a. What is the type and tags of *shape?*

b. What is the type of function *area?*

c. Illustrate the three equations defined by function *area.*

d. Define further functions on the type *shape* to compute a given shape's perimeter and to determine whether a given point is inside a given *shape* centered at a given *point?* Use pattern matching mechanism.

38. The ML recursive value definition "val rec x = ...x..." is legal only if the value being bound is a function abstraction. Why do you think this is true?

39. What types are the following functions in ML?

a. fun   sum (x : int, y : int) = x + y

b. fun   id (x : τ) = x

40. Consider the following ML type definition which models *points* on the X-Y plane.

    type   point = {X : real, Y : real}

Define two subtypes of *point* in ML language.

41. Define a ML function to return the *i*th component of a given list.

42. Write a function in ML for polynomial addition and multiplication.

43. What is the response in ML language when the following operands are given for which they have no defined values.

a. 5 div o;

b. hd(nil : int list);

c. tl(nil : real list);

d. chr(500);

44. Write an exception named div0 in ML language that returns 0 on an attempt to divide by 0.

45. Illustrate the difference in ML responses to div and div0, in which div is built into ML to perform integer division and has its own built-in exception handler, and div0 (defined in Exercise 44).

46. Write a function reverse(L) in ML that produces the reverse of the list L. For example, reverse([1, 2, 3]) produces the list [3, 2, 1].

47. Consider the types of the following ML list functions, given that the type of "+" is Integer × Integer ⟹ Integer.

a. fun   sum1 (1) = case 1 of
              nil ⟹ 0 |
              cons(h, t) ⟹ h + sum1(t);

b. fun   insert (z, f, 1) = case 1 of
              nil ⟹ z |
              cons(h, t) ⟹ f (h, insert(z, f, t));

c. fun   sum2 (1) = insert (0, (op+), 1)

Compare the functions sum1 and sum2.

48. What is the type of each of the following ML expressions? If the expression is illegal because of type, explain why.

a. $6 + 2$;

b. $6 / 2$;

c. $6 \operatorname{div} 2$;

d. fun $d(X, Y) = X + Y$;

e. fun $E(X, Y) = X + 1$;

f. fun $F(X) = X :: X$;

g. fun $G(X) = X :: [X]$;

REFERENCE-NEEDED EXERCISES

To answer the following exercises, you might need to consult the following references: Appleby and VandeKopple, 1997; Brooks, 1985; Chirlian, 1986; and Sebesta, 1999.

1. How would we implement a stack as a list and how would its operations be written in LISP?

2. Consider the following lambda expressions:

```
λx. ( λy. (+  y  y) x) 3*20
λx. λy. x λx. x (λs. (s  s) λs. s)
```

Evaluate the lambda expressions using the following methods.

a. Normal evaluation (left to right)

b. Applicative evaluation (innermost expression first)

c. Lazy evaluation

d. Graph reduction

3. Show that using Eta conversion, $(\lambda c. \lambda a. a)$ can be reduced to $(\lambda a. a)$, and $(\lambda c. \lambda a. c)$ reduces to $(\lambda c. c)$.

4. Show that if

```
TRUE  = λx. λy.  x
FALSE = λx. λy.  y
COND  = λp. λa. λb. (p  a  b)  then  EVAL(COND TRUE) = a  and
                                     EVAL(COND  FALSE) = b.
```

Then, COND can be written as

```
IF  p  THEN  a  ELSE  b.
```

5. Given the following definitions in LISP language:

```
(DEFUN  T1  (X)
   (CATCH  'BAZOLA  (CONS  X  (T2  X) ) ) )
(DEFUN T2  (X)
   (IF  (ZEROP  X)  (THROW  'BAZOLA  'ZERO)
      (CATCH  'ZTESCH  (T3  X)  X ) ) ) )
(DEFUN T3  (X)
```

```
(COND   ( ( <  X   0)
       (THROW   'BAZOLA   ( -   0   X ) ) )
          ( (<  X  5)
       (THROW   'ZTESCH   ( *   2   X ) ) )
    ( T   (*  4   X )   )   )   )
```

Evaluate the following expressions:

a. (T1   0)   d. (T1   −3)

b. (T1   3)   e. (T1   −7)

c. (T1   7)

6. Given the following definition in Lisp language:

```
(DEFUN   T1   (X)
   (IF   (EQL   X   23)   23
   (BLOCK   T2   (IF   (EQL   X   7)    (RETURN−FROM   T2   7) )
   (BLOCK   T2   (IF   (EQL   X   9)    (RETURN−FROM   T2   9) )
              (IF   (EQL   X   11)   (RETURN−FROM   T1   11 ) )
   (*   2   X) )
              (IF   (<   X   0)    (RETURN−FROM   T2   (−   0   X) ) )
   (*   3   X) ) ) )
```

What will the following expressions return?

a. (T1   3)   e. (T1   9)

b. (T1   4)   f. (T1   10)

c. (T1   7)   g. (T1   11)

d. (T1   8)   h. (T1   −3)

Parallel Programming Specifications

14

Scientific and engineering computations focus on theories, methods, and applications for large-scale simulations, time-critical computing, computer-aided design and engineering, computer-aided manufacturing, visualization of scientific data, and human-machine interface technology. Parallelism offers one way to solve such computational problems quickly by creating and coordinating multiple execution processes. The term **process** describes a sequence of program instructions that can be performed in sequence or in parallel with other program instructions. Therefore, a program can be viewed as a number of processes that are run sequentially or concurrently. The point at which a processor (CPU) is interrupted during one process and given to another process depends on the progress of the processes and the algorithm used to determine the available processor. In any event, the user is allowed to use more than one process at a time while running the program. Until recently, parallelism has been extremely difficult to use because of the lack of suitable parallel programming approaches. However, parallel computation has been facilitated by two major developments: massive parallel processors and the widespread use of distributed computing. A good parallel programming environment must fulfill several objectives:

▶ It must augment the sequential programming language most appropriate for the computational problem.

▶ It must support both process creation and interprocess communication as extensions of a high-level base programming language.

▶ It must be able to be run on any parallel machine architecture or on any collection of networked computers.

▶ It must be easy to use relative to parallel implementation; that is, it must offer simple operations to create and coordinate parallel processes.

Common parallel programming paradigms can be divided into two categories.

1. In the master–slave model, a separate control process called the *master* is responsible for process spawning, initialization, collection, and display of results—and, perhaps, timing of functions. The *slave* processes perform the actual computations. Either they are allocated their workloads by the master (statically or dynamically) or they perform the allocations themselves.

2. In the node-only model, multiple instances of a single program run, with one process taking over the noncomputational responsibilities in addition to contributing to the computation itself.

In practice, running a parallel program forms a set of concurrently executing processes, sometimes called *threads,* that communicate and synchronize by reading and writing shared variables. Thus, there must be a way to create parallel processes and to coordinate their activities. Sometimes the processes work on their own data and do not interact. But processes must communicate and synchronize with each other when they exchange results of an execution. In general, there are two methods of synchronization:

1. Synchronization for precedence
2. Synchronization for mutual exclusion

Synchronization for precedence guarantees that one event does not begin until another event has finished. In contrast, mutual exclusion synchronization guarantees that only one process can access the critical section where the data are shared and must be manipulated. The number of processes often needs to be larger than the number of processors. In other words, the parallel programming approach has to include flexible scheduling methods that overlap computation and communication, thus improving parallel efficiency. An examination of parallel programming approaches reveals that they represent virtually every possible answer to fundamental design questions:

▶ Should the parallelism be implicit or explicit?

▶ Should the parallel programming approach be based on imperative, functional, or logic programming languages?

▶ Should the processes run synchronously or asynchronously?

▶ Should the level of parallelism be fixed at compile time or chosen at run time, or should they be dynamic?

▶ Should the programmer view memory as distributed or shared address space?

Parallel programming approaches are developed either by introducing new paradigms such as Linda and Ada or by extending existing sequential languages such as C and Fortran. In the latter case, special language constructs and data array expressions must be supported for exploiting parallelism in programs.

In this chapter, we discuss the fundamental topics of parallel programming. In Section 14.1, we describe the major categories of computer architectures according to number of instruction streams, number of data streams, and whether type of memory is global or local. The section is not an exhaustive survey of computer architecture taxonomies but, rather, describes the most popular taxonomy according to Michael

Flynn. Thus, we classify the computer architectures into four categories: single instruction stream, single data stream (SISD), single instruction stream, multiple data stream (SIMD), multiple instruction stream, single data stream (MISD), and multiple instruction stream, multiple data stream (MIMD).

Parallel programming offers one way to solve the time-consuming computational problems by creating and coordinating multiple execution processes. A good parallel programming environment must fulfill a number of objectives: supports both process creation and interprocess communication, supports variety parallel architectures, and supports easy implementation. In Section 14.2, we describe the state of the art in the field of parallel programming. We classify parallel programming languages into four categories: SIMD programming languages; single program, multiple data language (SPMD) programming languages; MIMD programming languages; and multiple program, multiple data paradigm (MPMD) programming languages. The study of precedence relations of computations is essential for understanding parallel processing. Section 14.3 introduces dependencies as the fundamental levels of computation. The data dependence graph illustrates five different dependencies among the individual computations: data flow dependence, data antidependence, data output dependence, data input dependence, and data control dependence. Thus, the precedence relation of computations needs to be satisfied to process a computation correctly.

From the implementation point of view, parallel programming can be classified as either data-parallel or control-parallel programming. Section 14.4 deals with data parallelism versus control parallelism parallel programming. Data parallelism is the use of multiple functional units to apply the same operation to different elements of data. Control parallelism is achieved through the simultaneous execution of different operations to different data elements. Two distinct possibilities exist regarding the way processors communicate with each other: message-passing communication and shared-memory communication. In Section 14.5, we discus the message-passing and shared-address space communication paradigms, in which processors communicate via communication links and common memory, respectively. In a parallel processing environment processes represent independent actions, which can be executed in parallel. This indicates that we need to provide facilities to control the interaction of such processes. Section 14.6 deals with synchronization mechanisms associated with distributed-memory and shared-memory parallel systems. We discuss semaphores, monitors, and barrier primitives to address the implementation of interprocess synchronization in parallel systems.

In Section 14.7, we discuss different aspects of the problem of matching parallel algorithms to parallel architectures. The fundamental issue in parallel programming is how to distribute the data structures among the memories of the individual processors. For this reason, we discuss the mapping problem, the problem of changing a graph representing the interaction of data into a graph representing the topology of the underlying architecture. We outline three mapping paradigms: mapping to asynchronous architecture, mapping to synchronous architecture, and mapping to distributed systems. One important problem facing parallel computing is the granularity, the problem of optimally partitioning applications into modules and then scheduling these modules onto parallel or distributed environments. Thus, in Section 14.8, we study the effect of data distribution on the performance of parallel systems, in which we observe that a parallel program depends on a number of parameters, including the programming notation, the computational model supported by the notation, and the level of parallelism. Furthermore, the latter is defined by means of three features: program-level parallelism (called large grained), procedure-level parallelism (called medium grained), and statement-level parallelism (called fine grained).

There are three approaches in compiler construction of parallel systems: run time partitioning and run time scheduling, compile time partitioning and run time scheduling, and compile time partitioning and compile time scheduling. Section 14.9 deals with compiler construction of parallel systems. An example is the Paraphrase compiler developed at the University of Illinois, which performs a two-phase operation to transform a Fortran program from its original sequential form into a suitable form for parallel execution. In the first phase, it performs a machine-independent transformation to produce an intermediate form, in which it expresses the parallelism form of the program. The second phase performs a mapping to change the intermediate form into a specific parallel system for execution. The compiler was used on vector processor machines such as the Cray X/MP. Bulldog is another example of a compiler that detects parallelism at the instruction level. The central idea was to use the VLIW architecture design along with the trace scheduling compilation technique. Another example of parallel compiler construction refers to HPF (high performance Fortran) and proceeds as follows. Data decomposition statements are analyzed to determine the decomposition of each structure in the program. Computation is then partitioned across processors in the parallel architecture.

We classify the operating systems for parallel computers into three different categories: simple modification of the single-processor operating systems such as VMS OS and UNIX OS, operating systems designed for specific parallel computers, such as Hydra OS and Medusa OS, and adopted general-purpose operating systems for parallel computers, such as MACH OS. In Section 14.10, we discuss operating systems for parallel computers. Generally speaking, the area of parallel architecture operating system design has been directed toward achieving the properties known: resource sharing, extensibility, portability, and availability. Four different organizations were suggested to achieve these criteria in the operating system: master/slave, separate executive, symmetrical, and floating control organizations. We described the design principles of MACH OS, developed at Carnegie-Mellon University; Amoeba OS, designed at the Vrije University in Amsterdam; and Accent OS, developed at Carnegie-Mellon University.

▱ 14.1 Classification of Computer Architectures

Michael Flynn (1966) classified computer architectures according to a variety of characteristics, including number of processors, number of programs the processors can execute, and memory structure. In addition to Flynn's classification, which has proved to be a good taxonomy of computer architectures, several other taxonomies have been proposed (Bell, 1992; Dasgupta, 1990; Hockney, 1987; Skillicorn, 1988).

Treleaven, Brownbridge, and Hopkins (1982) have suggested that conventional computers can be examined from two points of view:

FIGURE **14.1**   Model of SISD machine architecture

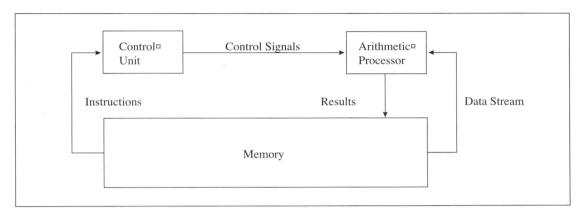

1. The control mechanism, which defines the order of execution
2. The data mechanism, which defines the way operands are used by an instruction

Flynn's classification included the following categories: SISD, SIMD, MISD, and MIMD.

14.1.1   Single Instruction Stream, Single Data Stream (SISD)

An SISD machine has one CPU, which carries out one instruction at a time (single instruction stream) and fetches or stores one item of data at a time (single data stream). Figure 14.1 shows the general structure of the SISD architecture. All SISD computers use a single register, called the *program counter,* which enforces serial execution of instructions. As each instruction is fetched from the memory, this register is updated to the address of the next instruction to be fetched and carried out, resulting in a serial order of execution.

14.1.2   Single Instruction Stream, Multiple Data Stream (SIMD)

A SIMD machine has one CPU, which carries out a single instruction stream, but more than one processing element. The control unit generates the control signals for all the processing elements, which carry out the same operation on different data items (thus, the term *multiple data stream*), meaning that they run programs in a lockstep manner, in which each processing element has its own data stream. In other words, a single control unit invokes many separate processing elements. These computers are used mostly for problems having high degrees of small-grain parallelism. Some popular commercial SIMD computers are the ILLIAC IV, DAP, and Connection Machine CM-200. SIMD computers can also support vector processing, which can be accomplished by assigning vector elements to individual processing elements for concurrent computation.

FIGURE **14.2**   Model of SIMD machine architecture

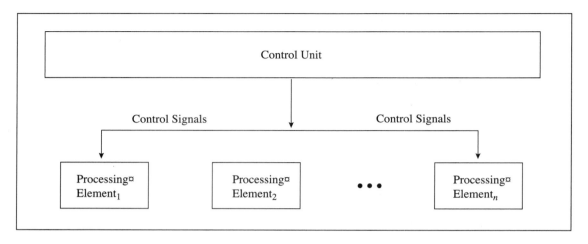

Figure 14.2 presents a general view of an SIMD architecture, which, when only one processing element is active, can be an SISD machine.

14.1.3 Multiple Instruction Stream, Single Data Stream (MISD)

A MISD machine may carry out several different programs on the same data item. Thus, several instructions would operate on a single piece of data at the same time. This architecture can be classified in two different ways:

1. A class of machines that would require distinct processing units and would receive distinct instructions to be performed on the same data. This is a big challenge for designers, and no machines of this type currently exist.

2. A class of machines through which data flow in a series of processing elements. Pipelined architectures such as systolic arrays fall into this category. Pipeline architectures perform vector processing in a series of stages, each of which performs a particular function and produces an intermediate result. The reason that such architectures are grouped as MISD machines is that elements of a vector may be considered to belong to the same piece of data, and all pipeline stages represent multiple instructions that are being applied to that vector. Figure 14.3 depicts the general structure of MISD architecture.

14.1.4 Multiple Instruction Stream, Multiple Data Stream (MIMD)

An MIMD machine is also called a multiprocessor. It has more than one CPU, each of which can execute a different program (multiple instruction stream) on its own data item (multiple data stream). In most MIMD systems, each processor has access to a global memory, which may reduce processor communication delay. In addition, each

FIGURE **14.3**   **Model of MISD machine architecture**

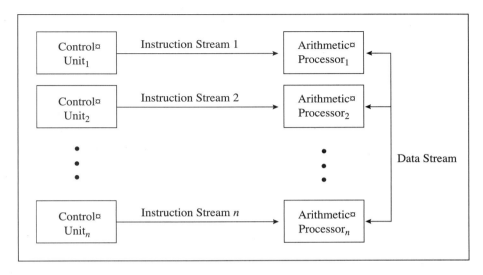

processor possesses a private memory, which assists in avoiding memory contention. Most MIMD architectures take advantage of medium- and large-grain parallelism. In current MIMD parallel architectures, the number of processors is smaller than in SIMD systems. MIMD computers are the most complex, but they hold great promise for efficiency by means of concurrent processing. In the future, small MIMD systems with a limited number of processors will likely be built with complete connectivity, meaning that each processor will be connected to every other one. Some popular commercial MIMD computers are the BBN Butterfly, Alliant FX series, Intel Corporation's iPSC series, and New York University's Ultracomputer. Figure 14.4 presents the general structure of MIMD architecture.

☛ 14.2 PRINCIPLES OF PARALLEL PROGRAMMING

In a sequential programming environment (an environment associated with SISD systems), each time a program is submitted for processing with the same data, identical results will be obtained. Each running program comprises a process inside the system, which is invisible to the user, and each instruction is carried out without interference from the program's other instructions. In a multiprogramming environment, the processing unit is switched from one program to another, causing their instructions to be interleaved at stages in their execution. Also, in a multiprogramming multiprocessor environment, more than one program can be active at the same time; that is, each program proceeds autonomously with its execution process. In such systems, the programs will interact and affect each other's progress.

FIGURE **14.4**   **Model of MIMD machine architecture**

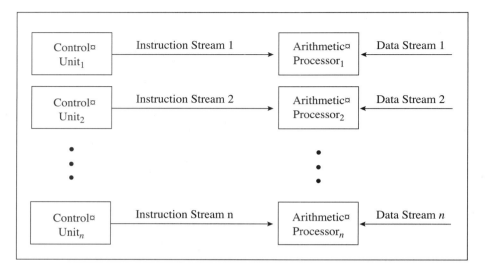

The net effect is that processes are capable of interacting in a time-dependent manner. As a result, the series of states that the system passes through is not identical when the same program and data are presented in a different execution. Thus, in a parallel programming environment, a programmer provides not only program and data, as in a sequential programming environment, but also the tools to control the synchronization and interaction among the processes. In this case, the programmer needs to create and schedule processes for execution, so program execution needs to be visible. Two approaches have been used to provide programming facilities for parallel processors:

▶   Development of languages that can express the parallelism inherent in the algorithm (Doeppner, 1987; Foster, Olson, & Tuecke, 1992; Geist, Geguelia, Dongarra, Jiang, & Sunderam, 1994; Roosta, 2000)

▶   Development of compilers that recognize the portions of sequential code and put them in parallel (Banerjee, Eigenmann, Nocilau, & Padua, 1993; Fox, Hiranandani, Kennedy, Koelbel, & Kemer, 1991; Kuck, Kuhn, Leasure, & Wolfe, 1984)

These two approaches complement each other, and using only one of them might not result in the most efficient parallel code. In general, concurrency may be implicit or it may be expressed by using explicit parallel constructs. For example, the following array assignment statement (in Fortran 90) is an explicitly parallel construct:

$$A = B*C$$

where it specifies that each element of array A is to be assigned to the product of the corresponding elements of arrays B and C. The statement also implies *conformity*, meaning that the three arrays have the same size and shape. In contrast, the following do-loop is implicitly parallel, and a compiler may be able to detect that the various do-loop iterations are independent; that is, one iteration does not write a variable that is read or written by another, and therefore, the iterations can be performed in parallel. Thus, a parallel program is a sequence of explicitly or implicitly parallel statements.

```
do    I=1,m
   do    J=1,n
      A(I,J)=B(I,J)*C(I,J)
   end-do
end-do
```

As a consequence, parallel programming is not a simple extension of sequential programming. To exploit the possibilities offered by parallelism, programmers need to look at the problem from a different point of view and reconsider the process of arriving at a solution. A programming language that contains explicit mechanisms for parallel processing must have a construct for creating new processes. We can categorize parallel programming languages in four ways:

1. **SIMD programming languages** should have a global address space, which obviates the need for explicit data routing between processing elements. SIMD programs can be recompiled for shared-memory MIMD systems. The most important characteristic of this paradigm is that the processors are synchronized at the instruction level, meaning that they execute programs in lockstep and each processor has its own data stream. As a result, there is no need to associate mutual exclusion or synchronization problems with parallel programming. This paradigm is also called *data-parallel programming*. In general, SIMD programming supports synchronous memory access.

2. **SPMD programming languages** are a special class of SIMD programs. SPMD programming emphasizes medium-grain parallelism and synchronization at the subprogram level rather than at the instruction level. We can split the current process into two or more processes that continue to execute copies of the same subprogram (or a segment of code) simultaneously. In general, the basic subprogram is the same for all processes. In practice, process synchronization is needed in the programming scheme. Compilation typically translates statements into an SPMD program in which each processor runs the same code on a subset of the data structure. SPMD parallel programming can be used in both shared-memory and distributed-memory MIMD systems. Thus, SPMD programming supports both synchronous and asynchronous memory access.

3. **MIMD programming languages** are involved when each processor has its own program to run. MIMD parallel programming can be classified as *centralized asynchronous MIMD parallel programming* and *distributed asynchronous MIMD parallel programming*. In centralized asynchronous parallel programming, also known as shared-memory MIMD parallel programming, the control process must select for initiation the fragments whose execution is enabled. In this paradigm, each processor runs a serial program independently, indicating that processors carry out different instructions asynchronously. As a result, mutual exclusion and synchronization processes are needed in this parallel programming scheme. Some of the instructions in these programs may be for load, store, or read-modify-write operations that access a shared memory location. The code carried out by each processor is called a *sequential program segment,* and the union of all these segments is the parallel code run as a whole by the machine. In distributed asynchronous parallel programming, also known as distributed-memory

MIMD parallel programming, the exchange of information and control data is performed through controlled direct communication paths (message-passing scheme). Control is decentralized with each statement determining independently its degree of readiness to initiate computations. Message passing is a popular parallel programming language scheme and may be either synchronous or asynchronous. The concept of asynchronous message passing is simple: The sender initiates the message and then continues to process it. The message is accepted by the underlying system, and some time later it will be delivered to its destination. A process waiting for a message will be delayed until the message arrives. Synchronous message passing requires both the sender and the receiver of a message to be delayed until its correspondent is ready. Once the message has been exchanged, both processes can continue. In general, MIMD programming supports synchronous and asynchronous memory access.

4. **MPMD programming languages** are popular subsets of MIMD. In an MPMD programming scheme, a segment of code is explicitly associated with each new process. Thus, different processes have different code, but some of the programs to be executed could be copies of the same program. Typically, only two source programs are written—one for a designated master processor and one for the remaining processors, called *slave processors*. In general, MPMD programming supports synchronous and asynchronous memory access.

To recap, each parallel programming approach involves a different view of the role of the processes and the distribution of data in a parallel program. A corollary is that asynchronous parallel programming schemes are most flexible in the sense of describing or defining *maximum parallelism,* meaning that they model parallel programs fairly easily. That stems from emphasis on fragment parallelism and independence. The technique is conceptually simple and corresponds to the parallelism in the problem and the asynchronous organization of the computer system. Various modifications of asynchronous programming involve organization of the data exchange between program fragments and the nature of the control used. The facilities provided by a programming language to control process execution and interaction in the source program are known as the **language support** for parallel programming. In this chapter, we discuss the general requirements of parallel programming relative to data and control, shared memory versus private memory, synchronization primitives, mapping, and granularity. Many other aspects of parallel programming design are discussed in Best (1996), Burns and Davies (1993), Hansen (1995), Hatcher and Quinn (1991), and Roosta (2000).

◤ 14.3 PRECEDENCE GRAPH

The study of computational precedence relations is essential for understanding parallel processing. Dependencies can be studied at several levels of computation, such as the block computation level, statement level, variable level, and even bit level. Thus, the precedence relation of computations needs to be satisfied before a computation can be processed correctly. Here, we concentrate on dependencies between statements and variables.

FIGURE **14.5**   Data dependence graph

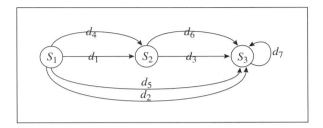

Example 14.1: Consider the execution of a simple sequence of statements:

S_1:   A = B + C
S_2:   B = A + E
S_3:   A = A + B

Careful analysis indicates several dependencies among the statements of which you should be aware. Parallel execution of these three statements is an alternative to sequential execution. The data dependence graph (DDG) of this example is presented in Figure 14.5. The possible scenario of this execution can be illustrated as follows:

▶ Statement S_1 produces the variable A used in statement S_2 and S_3, which results in dependencies d_1 and d_2.

▶ Statement S_2 produces the variable B used in statement S_3, which results in dependence d_3.

▶ The previous value of variable B was used in statement S_1, which results in dependence d_4.

▶ Both statements S_1 and S_3 produce the same variable A, which results in dependence d_5.

▶ Statement S_3 produces variable A, which was previously used in statements S_2 and S_3, which can be viewed as dependencies d_6 and d_7.

All dependencies must be taken into consideration when parallelism is involved. Analysis of parallelism yields five different types of dependencies.

▶ **Data flow dependence** is the most fundamental form of dependence, in which one statement cannot be carried out until after another statement has been run because the second statement requires a value computed by the first statement. Hence, these statements cannot be carried out in parallel. In Figure 14.5, d_1, d_2, and d_3 represent the data flow dependencies of the statements S_1, S_2, and S_3 of Example 14.1.

▶ **Data antidependence** is a related form of dependence, in which a statement cannot be carried out before another statement has been run because doing so would delete a value required by the earlier statement. In other words, data antidependence occurs when the value of a variable produced in one statement has been used previously in another statement or in the same statement. This dependence prevents parallelism because some variables can be overwritten before they are used. Dependencies d_4, d_6, and d_7 represent data antidependencies of the statements in Example 14.1. Renaming removes this form of dependency. The two dependencies discussed earlier are related to the use of values.

▶ **Data output dependence** occurs when two statements produce the same values. Clearly, if statements are carried out simultaneously, they overwrite the same variable in a memory location. Dependence d_5 addresses the data output dependence between S_1 and S_3 in Example 14.1. In other words, these statements must be carried out in the correct order to prevent the wrong value being used.

▶ **Data input dependence** occurs when two statements both use the same value. Again, renaming can remove this form of dependence. In a sense, data input dependence is not a true dependence, as the statements can be carried out in any order, but it does illustrate a relationship between the statements.

▶ **Data control dependence** occurs when running a statement depends on a value produced by another statement.

We can now define the data dependence graph as a directed graph $G = (V, E)$, with vertices V corresponding to statements in the program and edges E representing data dependencies among statements. Clearly, parallel execution of the statements can be achieved by eliminating the antidependencies and output dependencies among the statements. For example, programmers typically use a scalar variable repeatedly, as in the fragment

```
for    i=1,n,1
    x=A[i]+B[i]
    Y[i]=2*x
    x=C[i]*D[i]
    P=x+15
endfor
```

where x is an ordinary variable. If the second instance of x is renamed xx, the code segment becomes data independent, thus allowing better parallelism.

```
for    i =1,n,1
    x=A[i]+B[i]
    Y[i]=2*x
    xx=C[i]*D[i]
    P=xx+15
endfor
```

Example 14.2: Consider the following pseudocode and the basic forms of dependence between statements.

```
S₁:    A = B + C
S₂:    B = A * 3
S₃:    A = 2 * C
S₄:    P = B ≥ 0
       if        (P is TRUE)
```

FIGURE **14.6**   Dependence graph and basic forms of dependencies

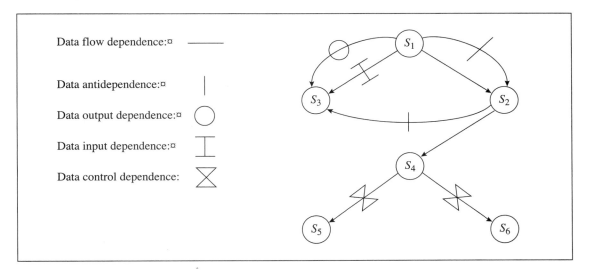

FIGURE **14.7**   Removing output and antidependencies

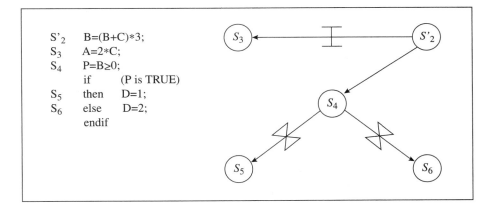

S_5:   then   D = 1
S_6:   else   D = 2
          endif

Figure 14.6 presents the basic forms of the dependencies between these statements. To allow parallel processing, we must remove some of these dependencies. For example, simple renaming can remove the output and antidependencies, as illustrated in Figure 14.7.

FIGURE **14.8**   **Dependence graph**

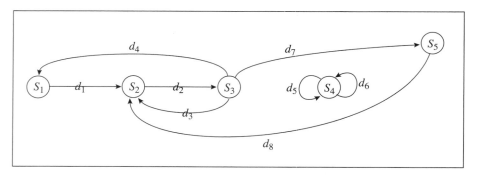

A more complicated problem is removing the cyclic dependencies associated with the loops in a program. For example, if the scalar is expanded into a vector, the statements are independent, thus allowing better parallelism.

```
for    i=1,n,1              for    i=1,n,1
    x=A[i]+B[i]                 X[i]=A[i]+B[i]
    Y[i]=2*x                   Y[i]=2*X[i]
end for                     end for
```

Example 14.3: Consider the following pseudocode, which consists of a loop:

```
Loop    I = 1, 20
    S₁:        A(I) = X(I) + 3
    S₂:        B(I + 1) = A(I) * C(I + 1)
    S₃:        C(I + 4) = B(I) + A(I + 1)
    S₄:        D(I + 2) = D(I) + D(I + 1)
    S₅:        C(I + 3) = X(I)
endloop
```

The dependence graph of this loop is shown in Figure 14.8. There are dependencies between statements within the same iteration. Programs with nested loops involve as many indices as loops, so there are also dependencies between iterations. Table 14.1 indicates the dependencies between the statements and iterations of this example.

▿ 14.4 DATA PARALLELISM VERSUS CONTROL PARALLELISM

Parallelism can be achieved in various ways:

▶   Concurrent processing of input and output operations, using independent processors

TABLE **14.1**   Dependencies between statements and different iterations

Variable	Statement	Dependence	Description
A	$I_1 = I_2$	d_1	Flow dependence
B	$I_1 + 1 = I_2$	d_2	Flow dependence
C	$I_1 + 4 = I_2 + 1$	d_3	Flow dependence
A	$I_1 + 1 = I_2$	d_4	Data antidependence
D	$I_1 + 2 = I_2$	d_5	Flow dependence
D	$I_1 + 2 = I_2 + 1$	d_6	Flow dependence
C	$I_1 + 4 = I_2 + 3$	d_7	Output dependence
C	$I_1 + 3 = I_2 + 1$	d_8	Flow dependence

▶   Concurrent memory access, using multiported storage systems and an inter-leaved memory management system

▶   Concurrent execution of instructions, using pipelined functional units

▶   Concurrent decoding of instructions, using pipelined control unit

▶   Concurrent execution of instructions, using multiple functional units

▶   Concurrent transmission of data between devices, using multiple buses

Data parallelism can be achieved by assigning data elements to multiple processors, each of which performs the identical operation simultaneously on its data. A k-fold increase in the number of processing elements may lead to a k-fold increase in the throughput of results if overhead associated with this increase of parallelism is limited. An example of data parallelism is matrix multiplication. When multiplying, two $n \times n$ matrices A and B produce matrix C, for which each element $C_{i,j}$ can be computed by performing a dot product of the ith row of A with the jth column of B. Thus, each element, $C_{i,j}$, is computed by performing the identical operation on a different data item, indicating data parallelism. The programming languages supporting data parallelism are called **data parallel programming languages,** and the programs are called **data parallel programs.** A data parallel program consists of single sequences of instructions, or instruction streams, each of which is applied to the different data elements. Data parallel programs can be carried out on both SIMD and MIMD computers but are naturally suited to SIMD computers, in which a global control unit broadcasts the instructions to the processing elements that contain the data item and execute the instructions synchronously. Example 14.4 illustrates the difference between sequential data processing and data parallelism and demonstrates the speedup factor achieved by data parallelism.

Example 14.4: Assume that a specific computation involves carrying out three instructions, S_1, S_2, and S_3, and that each instruction requires one unit of execution time, thus requiring three units of execution time to perform the required computation. A

FIGURE **14.9** Two models for performing a computation: (a) a single processing element system performs each computation in 3 units of run time; and (b) a 3-element data parallel processor system performs three computations in 3 units of run time

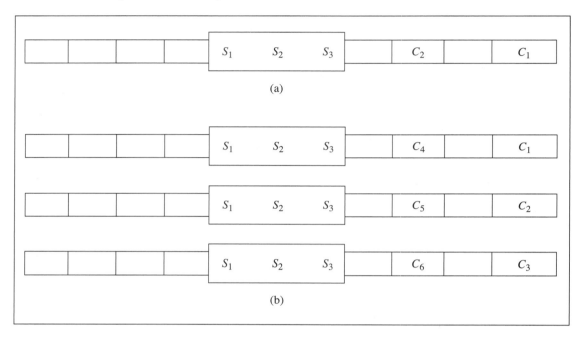

single processing element spends 1 unit of run time performing the S_1 instruction, followed by 1 unit of execution time performing S_2 and 1 unit of run time performing S_3. Thus, a single processing element performs this computation in 3 units of time, two computations in 6 units of time, and so on, as illustrated in Figure 14.9 (a). Of course, we are assuming that the computations are uniform in how they carry out the instructions. Now, assume a three parallel processing element system such that each processing element performs every instruction as does the single processing element system. Throughput can be increased by replicating processing elements. Another three computations appear every three time units. Figure 14.9 (b) shows a three data-parallel processor system.

Figure 14.10 shows the speedup factor achieved by the data parallel system. The x axis represents the number of computations, and the y axis represents the speedup factor achieved. The speedup factor may be computed by dividing the time needed for the single processing element to perform p computations by the time needed for the data parallel system to perform the same computations.

In contrast to data parallelism, in which parallelism can be achieved by performing a single operation on a data set, control parallelism is achieved by performing different operations on different data elements simultaneously. In other words, control parallelism refers to simultaneous execution of different instruction streams. A kind

FIGURE **14.10**   **Speedup factor achieved by a three-element data parallel processor system (compared with a single-processor system)**

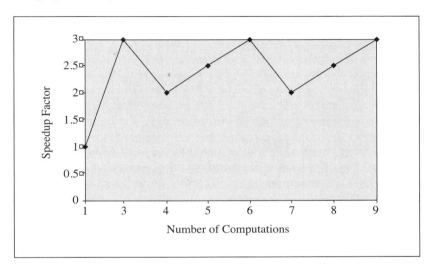

of control parallelism is **pipelining,** in which the data flow graph forms a simple directed path. In pipelining, the operation can be made parallel by running a different program at each processor and sending intermediate results to the next processor, resulting in a pipeline of data flowing between processing elements. Problems suitable for control parallelism usually map onto MIMD architectures because control parallelism requires multiple instruction streams. The amount of control parallelism in a problem is usually independent of the size of the problem. In contrast, the amount of data parallelism in a problem depends on the size of the problem. Thus, to achieve efficiency with a large number of processors, it is necessary to explore the data parallelism of a problem.

14.5 MESSAGE PASSING VERSUS SHARED ADDRESS SPACE

Two distinct possibilities exist regarding the way processors communicate with each other:

1. In message passing communication, processors communicate via communication links.

2. In shared memory communication, processors communicate via common memory.

   Single-message passing can be supported by two message communication primitives—send and receive operations—defined by destination and messages. For one process to communicate with another, the first process sends a message (a sequence of

FIGURE **14.11**   A message-passing machine architecture

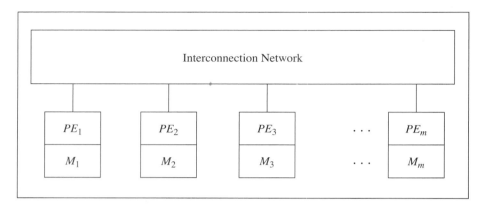

data items) to a destination and the process at the destination receives the message. Communication of data from the sending process to the receiving process may involve synchronization of the two processes. Send and receive primitives that can be made to wait are said to be *blocking*, and those that never wait are said to be *nonblocking*. Message-passing systems may be either synchronous or asynchronous. In a synchronous message-passing system, the send and receive primitives are carried out simultaneously and are defined as blocking send and blocking receive operations. Thus, sender and receiver are synchronized when information is exchanged. If the send operation is carried out before the corresponding receive operation, the sending process waits until the receiving process carries out the receive operation and vice versa. When information is exchanged, the processes continue their asynchronous execution.

In an asynchronous message-passing system, the messages are buffered and the sending process proceeds without delay. The system is defined as nonblocking send and blocking receive operations. Later, when the receive operation is carried out, the message is delivered. In general, in a synchronous system, the sender knows that the message has been received but does not know whether it has been processed, whereas in an asynchronous system, the sender does not know whether the receiver has received the message. A simplified diagram of a message-passing system is shown in Figure 14.11, in which several computers are connected via an interconnection network. Each computer system has a processing element, a memory, and an input/output interface. In a message-passing system, communication of shared data can be carried out through messages exchanged directly between processing elements, and each message consists of a number of packets. The processes may be running on different processors that do not share a common memory or they may be on the same processor but running in different address spaces. In message-passing systems, the memory is distributed among the processing elements in such a way that each processing element has its own program and its own data memory. This model of operation affects machine architecture design and the type of problems that can be solved on message-passing multiprocessors.

FIGURE **14.12**   **A shared-memory machine architecture**

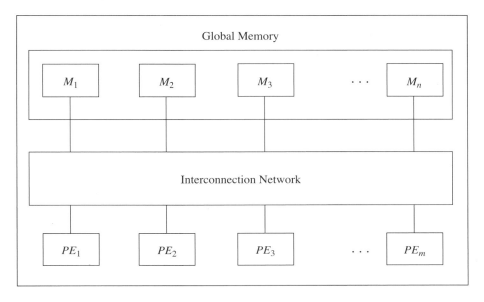

A communication protocol has to be established for interprocess communication. The performance of message-passing systems is difficult to determine because performance depends directly on the communication patterns specified in the algorithms used.

An important aspect of implementing shared memory is determining how to achieve and maintain good performance when large numbers of computers must be supported. Access to shared memory involves the capacity of the underlying communication network, and processes competing for the same or neighboring data may result in large amounts of communication. The amount of communication is strongly related to the consistency model of shared memory; it determines which written values may be returned when a process reads from a memory location. In shared-memory communication, complete connectivity exists between processing elements and memory modules. A simplified diagram of a shared-memory system is shown in Figure 14.12. It consists of a set of M processing elements $(PE_1, PE_2, \ldots PE_m)$, a set of N memory modules $(M_1, M_2, \ldots M_n)$ and an interconnection network.

The interconnection network allows data exchange between processing elements and memories. In shared-memory systems, each processing element operates on its own instruction stream, which can be accessed either from the local memory or from the shared memory. The shared memory is composed of independent modules, each of which is connected to a port of the interconnection network. This arrangement results in the operation of processors more or less independently of each other. In a shared-memory system, a single common operating system can control and coordinate the interactions of processing elements and running processes. Processors are provided with

FIGURE **14.13**   **Schematic of an alternative method for reducing the interconnection network traffic**

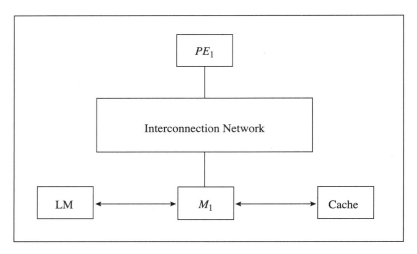

an interprocess communication mechanism so that an individual processor can directly interrupt other processors. Synchronization between processors is needed and has to be provided by the operating system primitives. Based on the need of many processors to access the same memory locations simultaneously, memory access conflict is an important factor in the performance of shared-memory systems. This conflict can create an upper limit to the number of processors in the system. To reduce communication traffic in the network, several alternative solutions have been developed, including

▶   Reducing the number of memory requests through the interconnection network, which can be achieved by inserting a local memory (LM) that is directly accessed by the processor

▶   Providing a cache memory to increase the memory bandwidth

A schematic of these alternatives is shown in Figure 14.13. In general, shared-memory systems are efficient for small to medium-size multiprocessors. The Cedar multiprocessor, the Ultracomputer, the Alliant, the Encore Sequent, and the Cray Y-MP are examples of shared-memory systems.

▶ 14.6 SYNCHRONIZATION MECHANISMS

In some parallel languages, the shared-memory model is used along with facilities for mutual exclusion, whereas, in others the distributed model is used along with communication facilities. A few languages contain both models because each is preferable in particular situations. In a parallel programming environment, program actions that can proceed conceptually in parallel must be identified. Such actions are usually referred to as processes or, more recently, as tasks. Each individual process can be specified by using recognized parallel programming features. In addition, language features are necessary to regulate process interactions. The need to control such interactions occurs when information has to be exchanged or the progress of one process depends on the progress of another process. Processes can interact with each other in two types of situations:

1. When processes need to update a shared variable or a resource at the same time. At any one time, only one process can access the resource. Once the process has obtained access to the resource, it must be able to use the resource without interference from another process.

2. When processes are cooperating to perform operations relative to their activities. Scheduling among processes is needed to enable them to recognize each other's existence and purpose.

Two methods have been introduced to solve these problems: (1) all the processes use a common structure to update information and to communicate with each other; and (2) all the processes use a common approach called *wait and pass,* in which one waits for a signal from the other and then passes information directly. Many computational problems naturally lend themselves to solution by one type of parallel architecture (an SIMD or an MIMD) implementation or another, but the implementations may turn out to be substantially different. The only parallelism that can be exploited on an SIMD program is data parallelism, which affects the way that instruction operands are used. In an SIMD parallel architecture, a single control unit dispatches instructions to each processor, and the same instruction is carried out synchronously by all processors. A drawback to this mechanism is that different processors cannot carry out different instructions during the same clock cycle. For instance, in the following conditional statement, the instructions for each condition must be carried out sequentially by all eligible processors.

```
if   (X==Y)
    then    Sum=X+Y
    else    Sum=X-Y
```

Running this conditional statement occurs in two steps.

1. All processors are ready to carry out the instruction Sum=X+Y when the value of the X variable is equal to the value of the Y variable, meaning that the condition is satisfied for this group of processors. These processors are the active processors in this step. All other processors are idle as long as the active processors are carrying out the instruction Sum=X+Y.

2. All processors are ready to carry out the instruction Sum=X-Y when the value of the X variable is not equal to the value of the Y variable, meaning the condition is not satisfied for this group of processors. These processors are active processors in this step. All other processors are idle as long as the active processors in this step are carrying out the instruction Sum=X-Y.

Thus, the processors that were active in the first step become idle in the second step, and the processors that were idle in the first step become active in the second step, all performing the execution in one clock cycle. In other words, some of the processors

FIGURE **14.14**   **Execution sequences of a conditional statement on an SIMD computer**

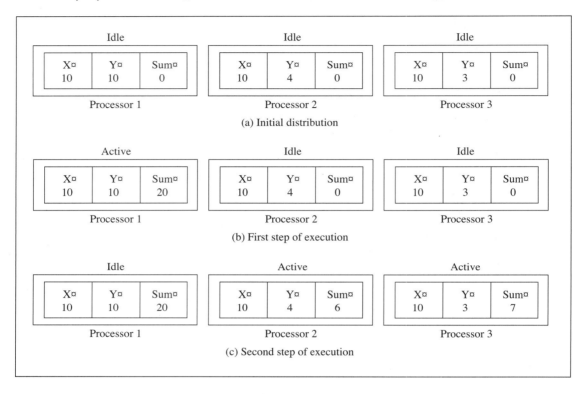

(a) Initial distribution

(b) First step of execution

(c) Second step of execution

can be selectively idle during an instruction cycle. Figure 14.14 illustrates the execution of a conditional statement on an SIMD computer. Generally speaking, the most important characteristic of SIMD programs is that the processors are synchronized at the instruction level; that is, they carry out programs in lockstep, with each processor having its own data stream, and the program maintains a global address space. As a result, the synchronization problems associated with MIMD programs are avoided. The number of processors is a function of problem size rather than of the target machine. A corollary is that data parallel programs in which a significant part of the program involves conditional statements are not suited to SIMD architectures.

SPMD programs emphasize medium-grain parallelism and synchronization at the subprogram level rather than at the instruction level. For example, consider this simple fragment of code running on two processors at the same time:

```
if   X
   then   S1
   else   S2
```

where the value of X will be determined by the particular values of data at each processor. Suppose that the first processor finds X true and carries out S1. Also, suppose that the second processor finds x false. In an SIMD program, the second processor does nothing, based on synchronization at the instruction level. In contrast, in the SPMD paradigm, the second processor carries out statement S2 while the first processor carries out S1. Hence, data parallelism can be applied to asynchronous MIMD programs at the subprogram level. SPMD programs are different from SIMD programs because processors are not tightly synchronized; rather, they are synchronized at the beginning and end of a subprogram (procedure) or section of code that is duplicated on all processors. The processors run asynchronously within each procedure or identical section of code to yield a form of pseudo-SIMD operation.

MIMD programs are the most general form of parallel programs, whereby processors operate freely on tasks without regard for global synchronization. MIMD programs are best suited to large-grained problems because of the overhead required to pass data and control from task to task. With regard to the various forms of synchronization, the asynchronous MIMD programs rely on locks and explicit control flow; that is, synchronization is achieved explicitly and locally rather than through a global synchronization mechanism. These programs may be either shared-memory MIMD programs or distributed-memory MIMD programs.

Shared-memory MIMD programs use a simple synchronization mechanism called *mutual exclusion* that requires enforcing strict sequential use of a resource by competing or cooperating processes until a task is finished. This mechanism is usually implemented by a *lock,* which prevents all but one access to data at any instant in time. All other accesses must wait until the mutual exclusion lock is removed by the process that originally issued the lock. Distributed-memory MIMD programs are much different from shared-memory programs because distributed-memory processors have no global address space containing shared data. Instead, each processor has its own private address space, and processors interact by passing messages among themselves. Unlike synchronization in asynchronous shared-memory programs, synchronization is a byproduct of message passing, in which a processor sends a message to all processors to inform them about the action that must be performed. Thus, in MIMD programs we can look for ways to exploit both data parallelism and control parallelism. A synchronization mechanism is classified as either a shared-variable or a message-passing mechanism. A shared-variable mechanism is involved in running SPMD algorithms and shared-memory MIMD algorithms to make communication among processors possible. A message-passing synchronization mechanism is used in distributed-memory MIMD algorithms. In the following, we briefly describe some of the synchronization primitives used in shared-memory and distributed-memory systems.

14.6.1   Semaphores, Monitors, and Barriers

Synchronization schemes can be divided into *access control* (Semaphore and Monitor) and *sequence control* (Barrier) primitives. For the Semaphore primitive, the instruction steps required to perform synchronization are:

▶   Check a Semaphore

▶   Suspend a process

▶   Awaken a suspended process

We attach a single Semaphore variable to each shared-memory location and each time step. When a processor attempts to read the data needed for a computation step, it checks the Semaphore variable for that data item at the required time step and issues a Wait instruction to the corresponding Semaphore variable. When a processor completes a computation in the given time step, it performs a Signal operation on the corresponding Semaphore variable, releasing the shared data. Generally, entrance to and exit from the critical region (the region in which shared data are accessed) are controlled by a Semaphore variable. The synchronization primitives Wait and Signal, which are based on the Semaphore variable S are defined as the following:

▶ **Wait(S):** If $S = 0$, the process invoking Wait is delayed until $S > 0$.

If $S > 0$, then $S = S - 1$, and the process invoking Wait enters the critical section.

▶ **Signal(S):** $S = S + 1$; that is S is increased by 1.

In this sense, when the process enters the critical section, S is decreased by 1. The following code shows the use of Wait and Signal to synchronize processes P_1 and P_2.

```
P₁:   Wait(S)              (* if S ≤ 0 then {  Keeptesting }*)
      {Critical Section}   (* S = S - 1                     *)
      Signal(S)            (* S = S + 1 *)

P₂:   Wait(S)
      {Critical Section}
      Signal(S)
```

We can examine one of the problems in concurrent processing, the producer/consumer problem. The general statement is that one or more producers are generating some type of data (record or character) and placing these in a buffer. A single consumer is taking items out of the buffer one at a time. The system is to be constrained to prevent the overlap of buffer operations; that is, only one process (producer or consumer) may access the buffer at any one time. In abstract, we can define the producer and consumer functions as follows:

```
Producer                  Consumer
  Repeat                    Repeat
    Produce item V;            while In ≤ Out do { nothing};
    Buffer[in] = V;            W = Buffer[Out];
    In = In + 1;               Out = Out + 1;
  Forever                      Consume item W;
                            Forever
```

We can implement this system by using a binary Semaphore variable (a Semaphore variable that takes only the values 0 and 1). In the following program, the Semaphore S is used to enforce mutual exclusion access to Buffer; the Semaphore Delay is used to force the consumer to wait if the Buffer is empty.

```
Program    ProducerConsumer
Var    n:Integer;
       S: Binary-Semaphore: 1;
```

```
            Delay: Binary-Semaphore: 0;
    Procedure Producer
    Begin
          Repeat
              Produce an item;
              Wait(S);
              Append the item;
              N = N + 1;
              If N = 1 then Signal(Delay);
              Signal(S);
          Forever
    End;


    Procedure Consumer
    Var   M:Integer;
    Begin
          Wait(Delay);
          Repeat
              Wait(S);
              Take the item;
              N = N - 1;
              M = N;
              Signal(S);
              Consume the item;
              If  M = 0 then Wait(Delay);
          Forever
    End;
    Begin (Main Program)
          N= 0;
          Initiate Producer and Consumer
    End.
```

In this program, the producer is free to add to the Buffer at any time. The producer performs Wait(S) before appending and Signal(S) afterward to prevent the consumer or any other producer from accessing the Buffer during the append operation. Also, while in the critical section, the producer increments the value of N (number of items in Buffer). If N=1, then the Buffer was empty just before this append, so the producer performs Signal(Delay) to alert the consumer of this fact. The consumer begins by waiting for the first item to be produced by using Wait(Delay). The consumer then takes an item and decrements N in its critical section. If the producer is able to stay ahead of the consumer, then the consumer will rarely block on the Semaphore Delay because N will usually be positive. In addition, when the consumer has exhausted the Buffer, the consumer needs to reset the Delay Semaphore so that it will be forced to wait until the producer has placed more items in the Buffer. We can consider the scenario outlined in Table 14.2.

TABLE **14.2**   The producer/consumer problem

	Action	N	S	Delay
1	Initially	0	1	0
2	Producer: Critical Section	1	0	0
3	Producer: if N=1 then Signal(Delay)	1	0	1
4	Producer: Signal(S)	1	1	1
5	Consumer: Wait(Delay)	1	1	0
6	Consumer: Critical Section	0	0	0
7	Consumer: Signal(S)	0	1	0
8	Consumer: if N=0 then Wait(Delay)	0	1	0
9	Producer: Critical Section	1	0	0

The Barrier primitive ensures data dependencies among cooperating processes. All the processes that synchronize at Barrier must reach it before any of them can continue. In other words, the processes must wait for the slowest process to reach Barrier before continuing. A queue and a counter are associated with a Barrier primitive; the queue holds the processes, and the counter keeps track of the number of processes in the queue. For example, consider the following subprogram implemented via a shared-memory MIMD algorithm.

```
for   I=1 to N do
      {
      S₁:    A=A+5;
      S₂:    B=B+5;
      S₃:    C=A+B;
      }
```

Let's assume that this subprogram is divided into three processes, in which each process takes care of one statement of each iteration of the for loop in a parallel processing environment. Also, suppose that the algorithm requires that the results of all iterations of S_1 and S_2 (in this case N) are needed to carry out S_3 for calculating C. Then S_3 must be carried out after S_1 and S_2 in each iteration. Because of the nature of MIMD algorithms, nothing can be predicted about the order of the statements on various processors. For instance, S_3 may be carried out before S_1 or S_2 in each iteration. In other words, in MIMD algorithms, it is possible to ensure this order only if all the processes carry out their statements S_1 and S_2 before any process starts statement S_3. The safety of the execution can be ensured by including a Barrier primitive after statement S_2 in the algorithm, as in the following:

```
for   I=1 to N do
      {
```

```
S₁:    A=A+5;
S₂:    B=B+5;
Barrier(2);
S₃:    C=A+B;
}
```

The `Barrier(N)` primitive can be illustrated as follows:

```
{
Counter=Counter+1;
if  (Counter<N)      then
        {place the process in Barrier queue}
else
        {resume all processes and reset the Counter}
}
```

Monitor is another shared-variable synchronization concept. The abstraction exhibited in it makes it a suitable model for a data object and resource sharing. It is a concurrency primitive that contains both the data and procedures needed to perform allocation of a particular reusable shared resource or a group of reusable shared resources. The notion of a *monitor* was suggested by Edsger Dijkstra and then by Per Brinch Hansen and was refined by C. A. R. Hoare (Goscinski, 1991). To accomplish a resource allocation, a process must call a particular Monitor entry. Because mutual exclusion is enforced at the Monitor boundary, only one process at a time is allowed to enter. A process desiring to enter the Monitor when it is in use must wait. This waiting period is automatically managed by the Monitor. Because mutual exclusion is guaranteed by the Monitor structure, concurrency problems are avoided. The notion of a **conditional variable** is introduced in Wait and Signal operations as

▶   Wait(Condition-Variable-Name)

▶   Signal(Condition-Variable-Name)

In general, when a conditional variable is defined, a queue is established, in which a process calling Wait is suspended and appended to the queue, and a process calling Signal causes a waiting process to be removed from the associated queue and to enter the monitor. A simple Monitor primitive for handling the assignment and deassignment of resources can be constructed as follows:

```
Monitor    Resource-Allocator
Var   Resource-in-use: Boolean;
      Resource-is-free: Condition;
Procedure    Get-Resource
   begin
      if   Resource-in-use   then
         Wait(Resource-is-free)
      Resource-in-use = True
   end
Procedure    Release-Resource
   begin
```

```
            Resource-in-use = False
            Signal(Resource-is-free)
      end
      begin
            Resource-in-use = False
      end
end Monitor
```

Other synchronization mechanisms used for access and sequence control are Test-and-set, Fetch-and-add, and Compare-and-swap. Asynchronous synchronization can also be implemented via the message-passing mechanism used for distributed-memory MIMD programs. In this method, the processes send and receive messages to each other. Synchronization can be accomplished because the received message can address the actions to be performed. Generally, the following steps can be applied to convert a program from SIMD to MIMD form:

▶ Trace the program to generate understanding

▶ Locate the critical synchronization points

▶ Eliminate recursions, if any

▶ Draw a communication diagram

▶ Focus on the SIMD program from the viewpoint of an MIMD with a single processor

▶ Rewrite the program, using communication and synchronization schemes

After this conversion, an SIMD program can be carried out on an MIMD computer with n processors using synchronization primitives.

◪ 14.7 MAPPING

Various approaches to the mapping of parallel algorithms to parallel architectures may be used. The work by Li, Wang, and Lavin (1985) provides examples of language-based approaches to the problem of relating algorithms to architectures. One powerful approach to mapping that has been applied to a variety of architectures is based on graph transformations (Berman & Snyder, 1984; Bokhari, 1981; Chiang, 1983). The strength of this method lies in the use of formalisms of graphs to address specific aspects of the mapping problem, such as process-to-processor assignment, minimizing communication, and breaking large problems into small tasks and allocating them to processors. Therefore, in addition to a program and data, a programmer also determines a particular implementation, called **mapping.** In general, the mapping of a program specifies the sequence in which each processor carries out the instructions assigned to it. Thus, mapping is not necessary for programs running on single-processor architecture because execution can be performed sequentially. Related to mapping is the transformation of computation from one form to another form more suitable for the parallel architecture. Transformation consists of

TABLE **14.3**   Synchronous and asynchronous communication used with languages and operating systems

Communication Type	Blocking Send	Blocking Receive	Languages and Operating System
Synchronous	Yes	Yes	OCCAM
Asynchronous	No	Yes	Mach, Chorus, UNIX
Asynchronous	No	No	Charlotte

▶ A description of how the operations of each instruction can be carried out by the processors

▶ An allocation of each variable of the program to a memory

▶ A specification of the single flow of control, common to all processors

Mapping is used in both synchronous and asynchronous communication schemes. In the synchronous form of communication, the sending and receiving processes synchronize at every message transformation. Both the *send* and *receive* operations are blocking primitives whenever a send is issued. The sending process is blocked until the corresponding receive is issued. Whenever a receive is issued, the process blocks until a message arrives. In the asynchronous form of communication, the send operation is nonblocking, the sending process is allowed to proceed as soon as the message has been copied to a local buffer, and the transmission of the message proceeds in parallel with the sending process.

In asynchronous communication, the receive operation can have blocking and nonblocking variants. In the nonblocking variant, the receiving process proceeds with its program after issuing a receive operation that provides a buffer to be filled in the background. However, the receiving process must separately receive notification that its buffer has been filled, by polling of the interrupt. Nonblocking communication appears to be more efficient, but it involves extra complexity in the receiving process associated with the need to acquire the incoming message from its flow of control. A simple blocking receive could wait forever for the arrival of a message, but for many purposes a time out is required. A **time out** specifies an interval of time after which the operation will give up its action. Choosing an appropriate time out interval is difficult, but it should be fairly large compared with the time required to transmit a message. Table 14.3 shows the variations of synchronous and asynchronous communication along with examples of languages and operating systems associated with them. Synchronous architectures focus on the computation that each processor may perform, and asynchronous architectures focus on synchronization between processors in addition to the computational purpose.

In the following sections, we examine mapping to three different environments: asynchronous, synchronous, and distributed systems.

14.7.1 Mapping to Asynchronous Architecture

An asynchronous shared-memory computer consists of a fixed set of processors and a fixed set of memories. Associated with each memory is the set of processors that can read from it and the set of processors that can write to it. Mapping a program to an asynchronous shared-memory computer involves the following:

1. Allocating each statement in the program to a processor
2. Allocating each variable to a memory
3. Specifying the control flow for each processor

In synchronous communication, the exchange of a message requires the participation of both the sending process (the sender) and the receiving process (the receiver). If the sender is ready to send but the receiver is not ready to receive, the sender is blocked; similarly, if the receiver is the first process ready to communicate, it is blocked. In other words, the act of communication synchronizes the run sequence of the two processes.

Alternatively, the sender is allowed to send a message and continue without blocking. The communication is called asynchronous because there is no time connection between the run sequences of the two processes. The receiver could be carrying out instructions when a message is sent and then, at a later time, check the communication channel for messages. The important difference between the two schemes is the need for buffering messages. In asynchronous communication, the sender may send many messages without the receiver removing them from the channel. Thus, the channel must be prepared to buffer a potentially unlimited number of messages. If the number of messages in the channel is limited, eventually the sender will be blocked. The problem with an asynchronous system is that the buffering system must be specified when the distributed primitives are being designed rather than leaving it to the programmer.

14.7.2 Mapping to Synchronous Architecture

A parallel synchronous architecture has the same processor memory structure as an asynchronous shared-memory architecture. In addition, processors in a synchronous architecture have a common clock for synchronization purposes. At each step (at each clock tick), each processor carries out an instruction. In synchronous communication, only one message exists at any one time on the channel, and thus, no buffering is needed. More than one processor may write to the same memory cell at the same step, which means that they all write the same value. An arbitrary number of processors may read a memory cell at the same step. Concurrent reading and writing of the same memory location is not permitted. For example, a program with multiple assignments, such as

$$x = x + 1 \; and \; y = x + 2$$

can be carried out concurrently by two processors when

1. Both processors read the value of x
2. One processor computes $x + 1$ while the other computes $x + 2$
3. One processor assigns $x + 1$ to x while the other assigns $x + 2$ to y

14.7.3   Mapping to Distributed Architecture

A distributed system consists of a fixed set of processors, a fixed set of channels, and a local memory for each processor. A processor can access its local memory for reading or writing, but no other processor can do so. The channels are error free and deliver messages in the order in which they arrive. For each channel, only one processor sends messages along that channel and only one processor receives messages along that channel. Also associated with each channel is a buffer. For each channel, the only action that can be taken by the sending processor is to send a message if the buffer is not full, and the only action that can be taken by the receiving processor is to receive a message if the buffer is not empty. Mapping a program to a distributed system is the same as in the asynchronous shared-memory architecture, except that each variable is allocated either to a processor or to a channel. In addition to the constraints involved in shared-memory architecture, the mapping has to satisfy the following constraints:

1. At most, one variable is allocated to each channel, and this variable represents the sequence of messages in transit along it.

2. A variable allocated to a channel is called by statements of exactly two processors.

These statements have the following format and cannot be accessed in any other way: The instructions in one of the processors modifies the variable by appending an item of data to the rear of the sequence if the size of the sequence does not exceed a constant buffer size. The instructions in the other processor modify the variable by deleting the item at the head of the sequence if the sequence is not null.

▶ 14.8 GRANULARITY

The granularity of a parallel algorithm and its implementation relates to the ratio of the amount of computation to the amount of communication. We use the terms *fine, medium,* and *coarse granularity* to describe the computation-to-communication ratio in a parallel algorithm. If a large amount of computation is performed for each communication, coarse granularity has been achieved, but if only a small amount of computation is performed for each communication, the algorithm is fine-grained.

SIMD computers are built for efficient communication, and fine-grained solutions can perform well on these machines. MIMD computers involve more overhead for moving information from one processing element to another. For example, in a shared-memory system, the time for interprocess synchronization of memory access is overhead; in a message-passing system, however, overhead consists of the sending and receiving of messages among the processing elements. Consequently, medium granularity is a good result on an MIMD machine.

Finally, a group of workstations communicating in a local area network (LAN) have slow communication among processors because the LAN bandwidth is more restricted. Thus, a network of workstations used for parallel processing is appropriate for coarse-grained problems because there is a great deal of computation for each communication. When a problem involves a regular structure, the granularity can be changed to increase the speedup factor of computation or to reduce the communication overhead factor. The

FIGURE **14.15** Increased granularity of a matrix multiplication problem

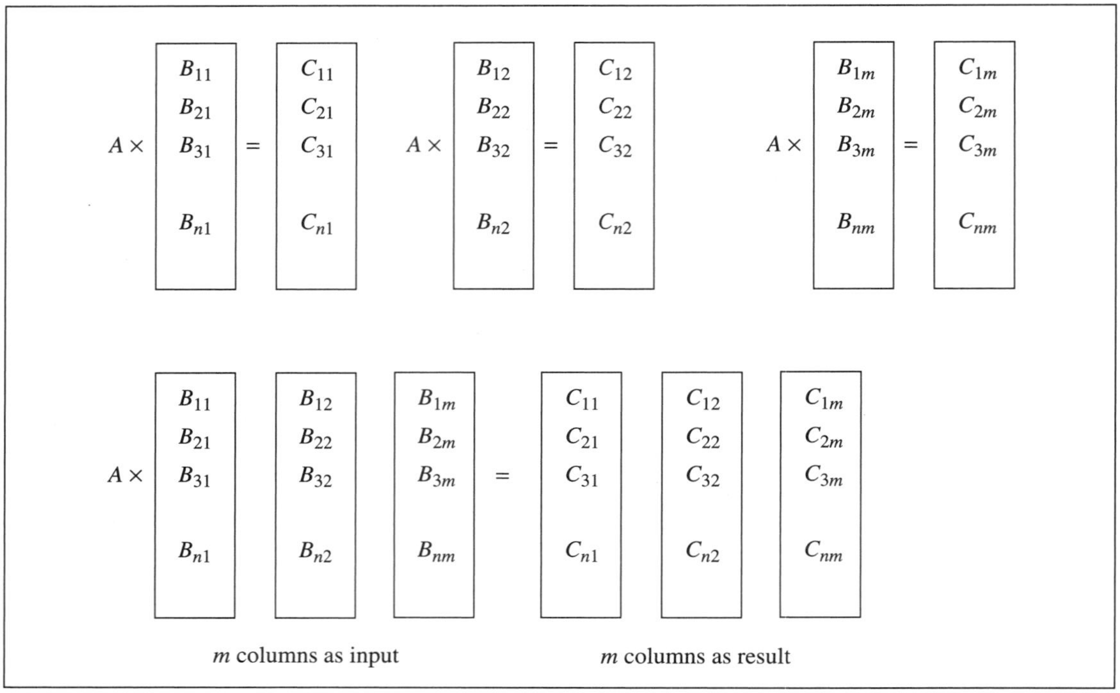

idea is to use the locality, so related computations of the problem are grouped and carried out. To illustrate the concept of granularity, let's consider the matrix multiplication $A \times B = C$, where matrix B is partitioned in columns to produce the columns of matrix C.

The basic unit of computation is involved in the calculation of a single column of the result matrix, C. To achieve this computation, all rows of the A matrix must be communicated to a B matrix column. To change the granularity of this matrix computation, we may determine some number m of columns to be passed together to a single processing element to compute the m columns of the result matrix, C, as illustrated in Figure 14.15. The communication—transferring the rows of the A matrix— has remained constant. However, the computation factor is m times greater, because m columns of the result matrix may now be computed.

The granularity of an algorithm for a problem is one important criterion for determining the kind of parallel architecture appropriate for that computational problem. Granularity, number of processing elements, size of the physical memory, and type of interconnection network differ from one implementation to another. Several factors may affect the granularity of a solution for any problem. For instance, if a solution requires communication with a central process for each small piece of computation, the solution is fine-grained. However, if the computation requires communication only at the end of each step, depending on how data are assigned to each process, the solution can range from fine- to coarse-grained. From the computational point of view, in some computational problems, each statement can become a separate process. Other possibilities are for procedures to be assigned to processes, and for processes to represent entire programs. The different size of the code assignable to individual processes is referred to as the *module granularity of the processes*. Three choices of module granularity for parallel execution are available:

1. Statement level parallelism, known as fine-grained granularity
2. Procedure level parallelism, known as medium-grained granularity
3. Program level parallelism, known as large-grained granularity

Granularity is an issue in computational efficiency, depending on the type of machine. In general, module granularity refers to the number of computations contained in a typical module. The module may be a program, a procedure, or an instruction, depending on the level at which the parallelism is expressed.

14.8.1 Program-Level Parallelism

In the program-level parallelism method of process creation, the entire program can become a process. In other words, a program creates a new process by creating a complete copy of itself. The typical example of this method of process creation is the Fork primitive in the UNIX operating system, which simply replicates the process running the Fork and has the form

```
Proc-id = Fork()
```

where `Proc-id` is the identification number of the newly created process. Running this statement causes the current process, called the *parent*, to be replicated. The only distinction between the parent and the newly created process, called the *child*, is the variable `Proc-id`. In the parent, it has the process number of the child as its value, whereas in the child its value is 0. This distinction permits each of the two processors to determine its identity and to proceed accordingly. Typically, the statement following Fork has the form

```
if Proc-id = 0
then do
   {child processing}
else do
   {parent processing}
```

Such primitives are incorporated directly in a programming language suitable for parallel processing. After a call to Fork, a process can be terminated by a call to Exit. Process synchronization can be achieved by calls to Wait, which causes a parent to suspend its execution until a child terminates.

14.8.2 Procedure-Level Parallelism

In the procedure-level parallelism form of process creation, a procedure is associated with a process and the process carries out the code of that procedure. This process creation mechanism has the form

```
Proc-id = new process (Q)
kill process (Q)
```

where Q is a declared procedure and `Proc-id` is the process designator. One example of such a language is Mesa (Lampson & Redell, 1980), which permits the procedure Q to be invoked as a separate process. The statement used to spawn a new process has the form

```
P ← Fork Q(. . .)
```

where the `Fork` statement creates a new process that begins carrying out the procedure Q concurrently with the parent process. In Mesa, each process is treated as an object and may be assigned to a variable. In the preceding statement, the variable P represents the child process and contains not only a process identifier, but also the process object itself. This form permits a process to be treated as any other variable; for instance, it may be passed to another procedure as a new parameter.

14.8.3 Statement-Level Parallelism

A typical construct to indicate that a number of statements can be carried out in parallel is the `Par begin–Par end` block:

```
Par begin
    Statement₁
    Statement₂
    . . .
    Statementₙ
Par end
```

In this mechanism, $Statement_1, \ldots, Statement_n$ are carried out in parallel, assuming that the main process is suspended while they are running. The following code performs a parallel evaluation of the expression $(a + b)(c + d) - (e / f)$.

```
Par begin
    Par begin
        t₁=a+b
        t₂=c+d
    Par end
    t4=t₁*t₂
    t₃=e/f
Par end
t₅=t₄-t₃
```

The primitives Fork, Join, and Quit provide a more general way of describing parallel activity in the statement level of a program.

Fork Primitive

Carrying out the following instruction by a process P causes a new process Q to be created and to start running at the instruction labeled x:

```
Fork x
```

Thus, *P* and *Q* run simultaneously from different locations in the program.

Quit Primitive

If a process *P* carries out the instruction Quit, process *P* terminates.

Join Primitive

The instruction Join t, y has the following effect.

```
t=t−1
if t=0 then go to y
```

A program segment for parallel evaluation of the expression is

```
         n=2
         m=2                            λ
         Fork P₂
         Fork P₃
P₁:      t₁=a+b;  Join m, P₄;  Quit;
P₂:      t₂=c+d;  Join m, P₄;  Quit;
P₄:      t₄=t₁*t₂;  Join n, P₅;  Quit;
P₃:      t₃=e / f;  Join n, P₅;  Quit;
P₅:      t₅=t₄−t₃
```

This method is certainly less transparent than the par-begin par-end method.

◤ 14.9 COMPILERS

Once a program has been written in one of the conventional programming languages, it must be translated into terms that the hardware understands, which is machine language. Compilers and interpreters are used to perform this translation. Interpreters carry out one statement at a time. There are some advantages to using interpreters: programs are smaller and easier to write, processing starts more quickly, and debugging is easy. However, memory has to be allocated for the source program as well as for the interpreter, and there is a performance penalty. In contrast, the compiler generates a complete machine code of the program before the execution starts.

One of the most essential components of parallel computers is parallel compilers. Generally speaking, parallel compilers decrease the run time of the program by breaking it into blocks that may be processed simultaneously by the multiple processing units. Some progress has been made in the area of vectorizing compilers, which generate code suitable for execution on pipelined vector processors. Some compilers perform only parallelism detection and partitioning functions, whereas more sophisticated compilers perform even scheduling problems. The parallel architecture raises questions for the compiler about what kind of blocks the program should be divided into and how these parts may be rearranged. In general, these questions involve the granularity, the level of the parallelism, an analysis of the dependencies and run-time scheduling. Three approaches are used for compiler construction for parallel computers:

1. **Run-time partitioning and run-time scheduling.** This approach is practical for specific applications. There is significant overhead when partitioning and scheduling are performed at run time thus decreasing performance.

2. **Compile-time partitioning and run-time scheduling.** This approach is the most common model of compiler construction in multiprocessor systems. The scheduling is performed at the run time phase, but the program must be partitioned into blocks by the programmer or compiler. Synchronization and communication have to be provided.

3. **Compile-time partitioning and compile-time scheduling.** This approach requires the most sophisticated compiler construction. There is no overhead involved at run time. In general, it is difficult to estimate the program run time; thus, the scheduling may be far from the optimum.

Generally speaking, most of the work in compiler construction for parallel computers has been done for Fortran programs. For example, the **Paraphrase** compiler (Kuck, Kuhn, Leasure, & Wolfe, 1984) used by the Cedar multiprocessor, developed at the University of Illinois, is a source-to-source constructing compiler that uses a data dependence graph to transform a Fortran program from its original sequential form into a suitable form for parallel execution. This compiler performs two phases:

1. First, it performs machine-independent transformations and changes the program into an intermediate form that expresses the parallelism form of the program code.

2. Second, it performs a mapping to change the intermediate form into a specific architecture, such as simple execution of array instructions or multiple execution of array instructions.

In general, the most exploited form of parallelism in Fortran programs is associated with loops, for example, when working with vector and array elements. This indicates that the parallelism is typically present at the innermost level. Vector parallel systems use parallelism in innermost loops only. Figure 14.16 presents the translation done by the Paraphrase parallel compiler to produce an executable code for pipelined vector processors. The Paraphrase compiler was successful in extracting parallelism in Fortran programs running on vector processor machines such as the Cray X/MP.

The **Bulldog** reassembling compiler developed at Yale University (Ellis, 1986) is designed to detect parallelism at the instruction level. It aims for automatic parallelism detection for scientific programs written in Fortran. The central ideas are **VLIW** (Very Long Instruction Word) architecture design and the **trace** scheduling compilation techniques. In general, sequences of code blocks might be grouped together into much larger blocks, called traces, with a high probability of being carried out from beginning to end without interruption. The VLIW architecture is designed with very long instructions. For example, the ELI-512 machine consists of 16 32-bit RISC processors with an overall instruction word length of 512 bits. The VLIW architecture can provide the increased parallelism found within the traces. Bulldog takes advantage of the fact that most of the time, a conditional branch proceeds in the same

FIGURE **14.16**   **Paraphrase source-to-source constructing parallel compiler**

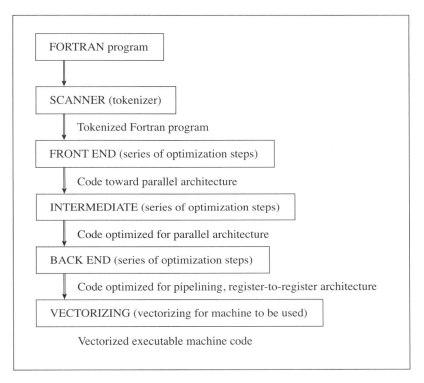

direction. This indicates that sequences of code segments are linked together in a trace, and these can be carried out from beginning to end without interruption, providing parallelism. In addition, Bulldog does not perform the loop dependencies analysis; it relies on the formation of traces. However, the traces can be formed only for blocks inside the loops. Figure 14.17 shows a pictorial view of the Bulldog compiler design.

The organization indicates that a parallelizing compiler converts the program into parallel executable code. In that case, the compiler establishes which statements can be carried out simultaneously. The compiler might rearrange the compiled code to achieve concurrency.

Another example of parallel compiler construction concerns data parallel programming language called **Fortran D** (Fox et al., 1991; Hiranandani & Kennedy, 1992, 1993). A version of this language is also called **High Performance Fortran (HPF)**. Fortran D is an extension of Fortran, which enables the programmer to specify the desired decomposition of the data. It provides efficient means of both problem mapping using array alignments and machine mapping using data distribution and decomposition. This enhancement can be applied to Fortran 77, producing Fortran 77D, or to Fortran 90, producing Fortran 90D.

FIGURE **14.17** Pictorial view of the Bulldog compiler organization

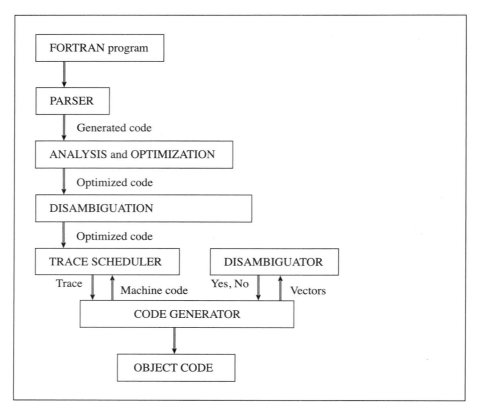

◩ 14.10 OPERATING SYSTEMS

An **o**perating **s**ystem (OS) is a program that is designed to coordinate computer operations. Operating systems perform functions such as system initialization, program partitioning and scheduling, interprocess communication and synchronization, system managing and monitoring. In a centralized operating system, decisions are made based on total and accurate knowledge of the state of the system. In contrast, a multiprocessing operating system does not have up-to-date consistent knowledge about the state of a distributed system. The primary goal of a multiprocessing operating system is to integrate the computing resources and processors connected by a communication network into one unified system. This goal should be achieved in the presence of some restrictions imposed by users or computer systems, such as transparency, failure conditions, and security.

Consequently, a multiprocessing operating system must contain the same management components as a centralized operating system—process management, memory management, resource management, and file management. From the complexity point of view, the operating systems for parallel architectures can be classified into three categories:

1. Operating systems that are a simple modification of a single processor operating system, such as VMS and UNIX. The modified operating system can be run on some parallel architectures. Usually, these architectures are adopted in a master/slave configuration.

2. Operating systems that are designed for specific parallel architecture, such as Hydra OS for the C.mmp multiprocessor or Medusa OS for the Cm* multiprocessor, both designed at Carnegie-Mellon University.

3. General-purpose operating systems that are designed to be implemented on different parallel architectures, such as the MACH multiprocessor operating system.

Most modern versions of UNIX will run on multiprocessor systems. This includes System V Release 4 from AT&T, Solaris from Sun, HP UNIX from HP, Digital UNIX from Digital, AIX from IBM, and IRIX from SGI. Any operating system can be converted to work on multiprocessors by protecting all the shared data structures from simultaneous access by two or more processors. Newer operating systems like Windows NT and MACH were designed from the beginning to work on multiprocessor systems. Research in the area of parallel architectures operating system design has been directed toward achieving the following properties:

▶ **Resource sharing:** The operating system should provide the mechanism for sharing resources among various processors of a multiprocessor system (for example, in SIMD systems with global memory).

▶ **Extensibility:** It would be beneficial if the operating system allowed the addition of new processors (and thus new services) to a system, either statically or dynamically.

▶ **Availability:** The operating system should be constructed such that it maintains the functionality of the system in the event of the loss of components and failure of the processors in the system.

From a user's point of view, the parallel architecture operating system must make management decisions oriented toward all resources and all the processors on the system, meaning that it has to be constructed on top of the system to allow it to see all resources without interference from any component of the system.

14.10.1 Multiprocessor Operating System Organization

In general, three basic organizations are used in the design of multiprocessor operating systems:

▶ Master/slave organization

▶ Separate executive organization

▶ Symmetric organization

Master/Slave Organization

In a master/slave multiprocessor architecture, one processor is designated as the master and the others are the slaves. The master performs input/output and necessary computations. The slaves can run CPU-bound jobs effectively, but I/O-bound jobs running

FIGURE **14.18** A typical master/slave multiprocessor configuration

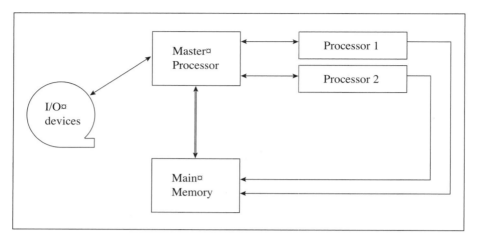

on the slaves cause frequent calls for services only the master can perform. Only the master may carry out the operating system. A slave processor can carry out only user programs. When a process execution on a slave requires the attention of the operating system, it generates an interrupt and waits for the master to handle the interrupt. In other words, all components of the operating system depend on the master component. If the master fails, the system cannot perform input and output operations.

The master/slave design has been used for many multiprocessor architectures. It is easy to implement, it can be designed by making simple extensions to a single-processor operating system, and it requires very simple software and hardware structures. But it is very poor from the graceful degradation and failure points of view. Generally speaking, the operating system with master and slave structure is effective for special applications in which the workload is well defined and relatively static but makes a poor operating system for systems that run a dynamic changing workload. The operating system does not have to be reentrant because it can be used by only one processor at a time and on behalf of only one user at a time. In corollary, the overall system is not flexible. Computational functions are permanently assigned to various processors, which can lead to poor use of resources and an increase in the number of interrupts because each slave processor must interrupt the master every time it needs operating system intervention. Figure 14.18 shows a typical master/slave configuration.

Separate Executive Organization

In the separate executive structure, each processor has its own identical copy of the operating system and responds to interrupts from that processor. In this organization, a task assigned to run on a particular processor proceeds to completion on that processor, meaning that each processor can service its own needs and its own dedicated resources, such as files and input/output devices. The processors do not cooperate on carrying out an individual task, and some of the processors may remain idle while one processor carries out a time-consuming computation. If there is a failure in a single processor, it is unlikely to cause general system failure, which eliminates a major bottleneck problem of the master/slave organization. Restarting an individual failed processor can be difficult, but in general, this organization is more reliable than the master/slave structure.

In the overall system, some information tables contain global data, and access to this information has to be controlled with mutual exclusion methods. An alternative solution is to replicate tables in each local processor memory that requires them, meaning that each processor has its own executive.

Symmetric Organization

The symmetrical configuration is one of the most powerful and complex multiprocessing operating systems. The structure is based on a master that floats from one processor to another. The operating system can manage several identical processors, any one of which may be used to control the I/O devices or to reference any memory unit. This processor is called the executive processor. However, several processors may be carrying out the supervisor services at once.

Because many processors may be executing the operating system at once, reentrant code and mutual exclusion are provided. But only one processor at a time may be the executive, and this prevents conflicts over global system information. In this organization, conflict resolution hardware and software are provided. Conflicts between processors regarding access to the same memory location may be resolved by hardware, and conflicts in accessing global data are resolved by software. This organization is the most reliable system, in that a failure in one processor causes the operating system to remove that faulty processor from the system. In general, the operating system floats from one processor to the next, and a task running may be carried out at different times by any of the equivalent processors. Because several processors may be in the supervisor state at once, severe conflict can result. An alternative approach to minimize conflict in the system is to divide the system data structure into separate and independent entities that may be locked individually. The addition of processors does not cause the system throughput to be increased because of additional operating system overhead, increased competition for system resources, hardware delays in switching between components, and table access conflicts and lockout delays. Generally speaking, this organization is the most difficult method to use from both the design and the operating points of view. Some of the advantages of this operating system configuration are these:

▶ Better graceful degradation capability
▶ Flexibility to use fewer processors
▶ Better system recovery in case of single processor failure
▶ Effective use of resources

14.10.2 Distributed Operating System Organization

A distributed operating system governs the operation of a distributed computer. It provides a virtual machine abstraction of the distributed system and offers a unified interface for resource access and manipulation of resources regardless of its location. The key objective of a distributed operating system is transparency. It looks to its users like

FIGURE **14.19**   Distributed operating system organization

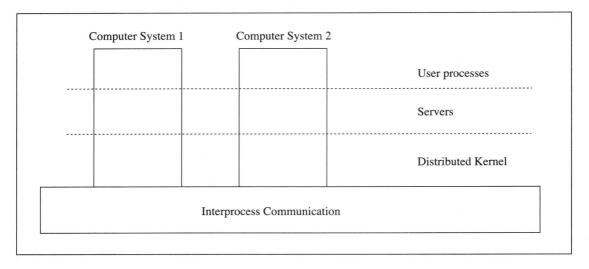

an ordinary centralized operating system but provides the user with transparent access to the resources of different computer systems. It uses a communication network for basic services. Ideally, the components and resources that are distributed should be hidden from users and application programs unless they are explicitly demanded.

Generally speaking, a distributed operating system varies in the type of functions performed in each processor. For example, the various operating system utilities and functions are distributed among the various processors, and each processor is dedicated to processing a particular utility or function. This indicates that a given processor is allowed to carry out functions if that code segment is present in the processors's local memory. Consequently, this approach avoids the need for global memory access, reentrant code, and interprocess synchronization. The interprocess communication (message passing) has to be provided in this system, using a message/mailbox mechanism. The operating system is illustrated in Figure 14.19. This figure shows that there are two very important parts of the system:

▶ A communication subsystem, which links all computer systems and servers and provides an effective communication service.

▶ An interprocess communication mechanism, which allows remote processors to exchange messages.

In the following sections, we survey a number of operating systems to identify their basic research and design issues and features. In deciding which operating system to be studied, the following selection criteria are considered:

▶ The system should have good documentation.

▶ The system should have been implemented.

► The system should possess features to influence the design and implementation of the other systems.

► The system should be representative of a specific category, such as UNIX-based, process-based, or object-based.

The representative operating systems from the research and application point of view discussed in this section are the following:

► UNIX-based: MACH

► Object-based: Amoeba

► Process-based: Accent

MACH Operating System

The MACH operating system was developed at Carnegie-Mellon University (Accetta, Baron, Golub, & Rashid, 1986) and is the successor of two previous projects, Rochester Intelligent Gateway (RIG) (Rashid, 1986) and Accent (Rashid & Robertson, 1981). RIG was developed at the University of Rochester in 1970 and Accent was developed at Carnegie-Mellon University during the early 1980s. The MACH was developed to provide direct compatibility with UNIX (by emulating the UNIX operating system) and was designed to allow a UNIX implementation to be spread across a network of multiprocessor and single processor systems (Boykin, Kirschen, Longerman, & LoVerso, 1993). MACH version 2.5 includes all the UNIX compatibility codes inside the kernel and runs on the Sun-3, the IBM RT PC, multiprocessor and single processor VAX systems, and the Encore Multimax and Sequent multiprocessors. An older version of MACH was used as a basis for the operating system for the NeXT workstations.

The UNIX code was removed from version 3.0 of MACH, which runs on Intel 386 and 486 based PCs, DEC stations 3100 and 5000 series computers, some Motorola 88000 based computers, and Sun SPARC workstations. In general, MACH 3.0 is an extension of UNIX and supports several languages. It runs with small changes on the Sequent Balance, the Encore Multimax, the BBN Butterfly, and other computers.

MACH Structure Principles

MACH consists of a kernel that provides the following services:

► Interprocess communication

► Virtual memory management with paging and sharing of memory between tasks

► Resource management

► Controlled access to physical devices

In addition to the kernel, there is a nonkernel for user level services. System functions such as synchronization, semaphores, and file servers are performed in user level server programs. This arrangement provides a separation of functions in a multiprocessor system. Individual components of MACH can run on different processors. The operating system emulations that have been produced include UNIX, OS/2, MS-DOS, and VMS. MACH was designed to run on shared memory-multiprocessors,

FIGURE **14.20** The MACH organization

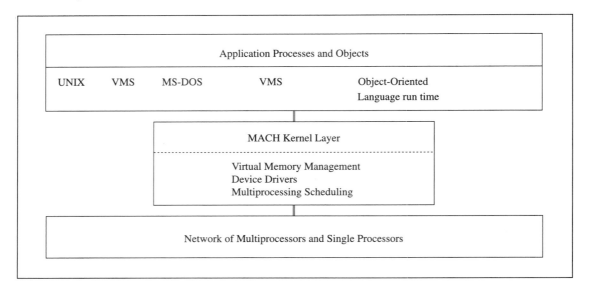

meaning that both kernel and nonkernel could be carried out by any processor. A general structure of MACH is shown in Figure 14.20.

MACH Design Principles

The main MACH design goals and features are the following:

▶ **Process:** A process was split into two new concepts, **task** and **thread:**
  • A task is a basic unit of resource allocation that includes a page address space and protected access to system resources.
  • A thread is a basic unit of CPU utilization.

In general, these concepts give users the ability to carry out multiple threads simultaneously within a single process.

▶ **Portability:** MACH was designed to be portable to a variety of hardware platforms.

▶ **Operating system emulation:** MACH was designed to support different operating systems and handle user level operating system servers.

▶ **Flexible virtual memory management:** MACH was designed to support large virtual address space memory, read/write memory sharing between processes, memory-mapped files, backing stored objects, paging and sharing of memory between tasks.

▶ **User level servers:** MACH supports an object-based model such that resources are managed by the kernel or by the user level servers.

▶ **Language support:** MACH was designed to support and handle the remote procedure calls between tasks written in C, Pascal, Ada, and Common Lisp.

▶ **Transparent extension to network operation:** MACH was designed to allow for distributed programs that extend transparently between single processors and multiprocessors across a network. The MACH kernel supports a location-independent communication model involving ports as destinations.

▶ **Data transferring:** The interprocess communication facility is integrated with the virtual memory system to enable transferring large amounts of data.

Amoeba Operating System

Amoeba is a distributed operating system that was designed at the Vrije University in Amsterdam under the supervision of Andrew Tanenbaum, where its design and implementation were begun in 1981 (Tanenbaum, Renesse, Staveren, & Sharp, 1990; Tanenbaum & Renesse, 1985). The goal was to include all the basic facilities that one would expect from a conventional operating system.

Amoeba Structure Principles

Amoeba uses the object-oriented model for distributed computing, remote procedure calls and lightweight processes. It supports different CPUs, such as the Motorola 68020, Intel 8088, VAX, and PDP-11. A number of utilities, including compilers, editors, and shells, are operational and UNIX can be supported. The main components making up the Amoeba distributed system are the processor pool, workstations (Sun and VAX), X-terminal, servers, and gateways. The gateways are used for connecting different sites over the interconnection network. Figure 14.21 shows the Amoeba organization.

The central idea of this architecture is that memory and processors will become cheap enough that each user will be allocated multiple processors and each processor will have plenty of memory to run applications. This indicates that rather than allocating a multiprocessor to each user, processing power may be concentrated in the processor pool, where it can be shared among users.

Amoeba Design Principles

The main Amoeba design goals are the following:

▶ **Network transparency:** In this system all resource access is network transparent. This indicates that the processes are assigned to one of the processors from the *processor pool* without the user's knowledge.

▶ **Object-oriented environment:** All resources, such as files, directories, disk blocks, processes and devices are objects. Each object is defined by its particular service and is under the supervision of particular server processes. All objects are accessed by a uniform naming scheme. In general, objects are managed by servers, and they can be accessed only by sending messages to the servers.

▶ **Capability:** All objects in this system are named and protected by secure capabilities. The system provides a uniform interface to all objects. In general, users

FIGURE **14.21** The Amoeba organization

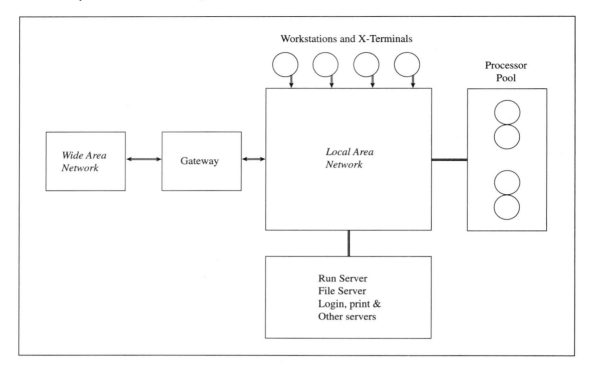

view the system as a collection of objects named by capabilities in which they can perform operations.

► **Remote procedure calls:** RPC protocol (communication between processes) is implemented by assembling an operation code and its arguments in a request message, which is sent to the appropriate server. The sender process is blocked while the receiver is working, whereas the receiver is blocked while it is waiting for a request. The operation is performed by the receiver. The result of that operation is returned to the sender by a response message.

► **Kernel server:** The Amoeba micro-kernel supports a uniform model for accessing resources using capabilities. The micro-kernel is running on all computers in the system, regardless of their role. The basic abstractions supported by the micro-kernel are processes, threads, and ports for communication. The characteristics are all similar to existing conventional operating systems. In particular, Amoeba took precedence over any issues of compatibility with existing operating systems.

Accent Operating System

The Accent operating system was developed as part of the Carnegie-Mellon Spice project (Fitzgerald & Rashid, 1986) and was designed to support a large network of

FIGURE **14.22**   The Accent organization

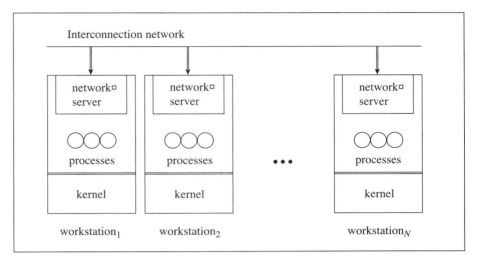

computers and was used at Carnegie-Mellon University in a network of more than 150 workstations. Accent is a communication-oriented operating system that is designed such that memory management can be effectively integrated with the interprocess communication system. Thus, access to all services and resources is provided through communication facilities.

Accent Structure Principles

The Accent operating system is organized as a protected interprocess communication system, which allows processes to be bound together and provides a uniform interface at the system level. The operating system consists of a number of layers. The bottom layer of each workstation is the kernel, which supports a collection of processes. The kernel provides an execution environment for processes running on its workstation, such as interprocess communication, virtual memory management, and process management. All resources, services, and functions are accessible through an interprocess communication facility provided by the system. The Accent operating system organization is shown in Figure 14.22.

Accent Design Principles

The main Accent design goals are the following:

▶ **Fork and terminate primitives:** The system supports the fork and terminate primitives for process creation and destruction.

▶ **Protection:** Because it is a large network of uniprocessor scientific personal computers, their interactions are predictable to avoid conflicts.

▶ **Programming language support:** The system supports many programming languages.

▶ **Network transparency:** The system supports network transparency, meaning that all resources should be accessible.

▶ **Fault recovery, debugging, and monitoring:** The system supports tools for process monitoring and debugging to make a reliable system.

▶ **Problem decomposition:** The system supports modular decomposition of a large problem into smaller units. This can be performed concurrently by a single processor or distributed between several processors.

▶ **Micro-kernel:** The system supports a micro-kernel, which consists of language-independent microcode support, low-level scheduling, input and output interrupt support and virtual address translation mechanism.

SUMMARY

Progress in hardware technology has a tremendous impact on parallel computers. In this chapter, we introduced the notion of computer architectures. Parallel computing or high-performance computing has received considerable attention in the United States, Europe, and Japan. We described the major categories of computer architectures according to number of instruction streams, number of data streams, and type of memory as global or local. The chapter is not an exhaustive survey of computer architecture taxonomies but, rather, describes what Flynn calls the most popular taxonomy. Based on the Flynn taxonomy, we classified the computer architectures into four categories: SISD (single instruction stream, single data stream), SIMD (single instruction stream, multiple data stream), MISD (multiple instruction stream, single data stream), and MIMD (multiple instruction stream, multiple data stream). A taxonomy of parallel architectures can address four classifications: SIMD, MISD, MIMD, and a combination of SIMD and MIMD, which we described in this chapter. Table 14.4 summarizes the designated factors of the associated architectures.

Many aspects of parallel computers are presented in Almasi & Gottlieb (1994), Hwang (1993), Leighton (1992), Moldovan (1993), Roosta (2000), Shiva (1996), Yuen and Yomezawa (1993), and Zargham (1996). For details on the latest architectures and their characteristics, refer to corresponding manufacturers' manuals and magazines such as *IEEE Spectrum, IEEE Computer, EDN, Computer Design,* and *Byte.*

The parallel programming approach offers one way to solve the time-consuming computational problems by creating and coordinating multiple execution processes. There are many papers, survey articles, and books in the general area of programming languages (Appleby & VandeKopple, 1997; Carriero & Gelernter, 1992; Chandy & Misra, 1988; Chandy & Taylor, 1992; Ghezzi & Jazayeri, 1987). A good parallel programming environment must fulfill a number of objectives: support both process creation and interprocess communication, support variety parallel architectures, and support easy implementation. In this chapter, we have given a brief outline of the state of the art in parallel programming. Parallel programming can be categorized as either

TABLE **14.4**	Summary of computer architectures				
System	**Concept**	**Interface**	**Generality**	**Complexity**	**Efficiency**
SIMD	Easy	Easy	Moderate	High	High
MIMD	Hard	Hard	Good	High	Moderate
Pipeline	Easy	Easy	Poor	Low	High
Systolic	Hard	Easy	Poor	Moderate	High
Associative	Moderate	Moderate	Poor	Moderate	High
Data flow	Hard	Moderate	Good	High	High

data-parallel or control-parallel programming. Data parallelism is the use of multiple functional units to apply the same operation to different elements of data. Control parallelism is achieved through the simultaneous execution of different operations to different data elements. With the present generation of parallel computers, attention has focused on the problem of parallel programming, which can be separated into two categories:

▶ Asynchronous parallel programming, in which independent parts of a program are completed and cooperate with each other to improve the efficiency of the execution.

▶ Synchronous parallel programming, in which the same operation can be performed in parallel by forcing all processes to act in unison.

Further, we classified parallel programming into four categories: synchronous SIMD, asynchronous SIMD, synchronous SPMD, and asynchronous MPMD parallel programming. We briefly discussed the classifications and the supporting environments. In general, specialized programming schemes are needed to efficiently use the computational power offered by parallel computers. To make valid judgments about parallel computing, it is necessary to understand how particular problems will map onto specific implementations of parallelism.

We discussed the precedence graph of a process to address the dependencies at several levels of computation, such as block level, statement level, variable level, and bit level. The data dependency graph illustrated five different dependencies among the individual computations: data flow dependency, data anti-dependency, data output dependency, data input dependency, and data control dependency. We discussed these dependencies along with examples and suggested how to remove the dependencies to use the efficiency associated with parallel execution of the constructs. Briefly, we discussed the message-passing and shared address space communication paradigms to provide the necessary information for the next sections. We also discussed different aspects of the problem of matching parallel algorithms to parallel architectures. The fundamental issue in parallel programming is how to distribute the data structures among the memories of the individual processors. For this reason, we discussed the mapping problem, the problem of changing a graph representing the interaction of data into a graph representing the topology of the underlying architecture. We outlined three mapping paradigms: mapping to asynchronous architecture, mapping to synchronous architecture, and mapping to distributed systems. Wijshoff (1989) has studied the effect of data distribution on the performance of parallel systems. He observed that the performance of a parallel program depends on a number of parameters, including the programming notation, the computational model supported by the notation, and the level of parallelism. Further, the latter can be defined by means of three features: program level parallelism, called large grained, procedure level parallelism, called medium grained, and statement level parallelism, called fine grained.

Generally speaking, we characterized the computation and communication requirements for our parallel algorithms by considering mapping and granularity. One important problem facing parallel computing is the granularity—the problem of optimally partitioning applications into modules and then scheduling these modules onto parallel or distributed environments. Mapping and granularity decisions are particularly subject to modification, which indicates that we may postpone these decisions until they can be most easily changed. Although we did not concentrate on how algorithms are represented in programs, it is worth pointing out some trends in programming languages intended for large-grain parallelism. At the least, a reasonable language provides ordinary sequential operations and a way to send messages between processes. Interprocess communication can be abstracted as a form of message-passing paradigm. As a consequence, we can claim that the programming schemes of distributed-memory parallel computers are much different from that of shared-memory computers because distributed-memory computers have no global address space containing shared data. Processors interact by message-passing paradigms among themselves. Good sources of design and principles of parallel computing are Fountain (1994), Lipovski and Malek (1987), and Miklosko and Kotov (1984).

Parallel Programming Languages

I n general, specialized programming schemes are needed to use the computational power offered by parallel computers efficiently. Before we can make valid judgments about parallel computing, we must understand how particular problems will map onto specific implementations of parallelism. We can classify parallel programming approaches into two categories:

▶ Asynchronous parallel programming, in which independent parts of a program compete and cooperate with each other to improve the efficiency of the execution.

▶ Synchronous parallel programming, in which the same operation can be performed in parallel by forcing all processes to act in unison.

In Section 15.1, we present synchronous parallel programming with UNIX, which is an augmented version of the UNIX operating system with libraries as a synchronous parallel programming approach. The UNIX operating system allows users to access process management through system calls. These facilities allow users to create, schedule, and control processes.

Asynchronous parallelism is the most general form of parallelism, whereby processors operate freely on tasks, without regard for global synchronization. In place of the lock-step fashion of the various forms of synchronized parallelism, the asynchronous method relies on locks and explicit control flow. The first method to establish mutual exclusion mechanism is usually implemented by a lock, which prevents all but one process from accessing the data at any instant in time. All other accesses must wait until the process that originally placed the lock on the shared data removes the mutual exclusion lock. The second major method is to send a message to all processes to inform them about the applicability of the data access. This method can be employed by message passing in distributed systems.

In Section 15.2, we present an asynchronous parallel programming language, Ada. The message-passing approach has been used in high-level programming languages such as Ada, in which Ada uses the two basic operations, send and receive, to exchange messages among parallel processes. Among its features are packages and generics, designed to aid the construction of large modular programs. Ada is probably the best example available of a state-of-the-art concurrent programming language.

Think of SIMD systems as a single control unit directing the activities of a number of processing elements, each performing the same instruction by fetching and manipulating its own local data. The data parallel programming approach is characterized by a relatively large number of synchronous processes carrying out a single instruction stream. One must suitably define the fundamental unit of parallelism before running a data parallel algorithm efficiently on parallel hardware. A data parallel programming language, C*, as an extension of C for specifying concurrency, locality, communication and mapping, appears in Section 15.3. The language C* is a major language for data parallel programming and has been implemented on a number of SIMD and MIMD parallel computers. We outline the structure of the data parallel C* programming model, which consists of two parts: front-end and back-end. The front-end consists of a single processor machine, and the back-end is a collection of processing elements connected to an interconnection network. The language supports two types of variables, scalar and parallel: The scalar variable is allocated to the front-end processor, and the parallel variable can be allocated on all processing elements.

☞ 15.1 SYNCHRONOUS PARALLEL PROGRAMMING WITH UNIX

Most of the vendors of parallel architectures provide their machines with versions of the UNIX operating system extended with libraries for the parallel programming environment (Robbins & Robbins, 1996). Therefore, the UNIX operating system libraries allow users to access process management through system calls. These facilities allow users to create, schedule, and control processes in a parallel processing environment. In this section, we discuss the parallel programming approach provided on the Encore Multimax System, which uses the UNIX operating system. A parallel program written in C that uses the parallel library must include the **parallel.h** header file, which contains the functions provided in the parallel library. The programs must be compiled with the command

```
cc program.c -lpp
```

where the option -lpp informs the loader that the parallel library is being used.

15.1.1 Process Creation

A process can be created by the **fork** system call. The process differs from its parent only in the value returned by the call. In general, if the return value of the fork() system call is zero, a child process is created; otherwise, the process is not created. The situation can be outlined as follows:

```
if  (fork() == 0)
        {
/* a child process is created */
        }
else
        {
/* a child process is not created due to the available resources; memory */
        }
```

Consequently, when more processes are created, the values returned by the fork() system call at each process creation are guaranteed to be different for each call, but there are no formal relations between these values. Thus, these values cannot be used for scheduling purposes or other disciplines established by the programmer. The following C code, called the Makeprocess() function, takes as its argument n processes to be created. Makeprocess creates n processes and each process creates an integer $i \leq n$ that can be used as the programmer process identification number, or ppid. Assume that ppid is an integer variable initialized in the parent process to 0.

```
Makeprocess(n)
   int n;   {
   int i;
   for (i=0; i < n; i++)
      {
      switch (fork())
         {
         case 0:  /* PROCESS CREATED */
                  /* a child process is created if the return value is 0*/
            return(i+1);
         case -1: /* PROCESS CANNOT BE CREATED */
            {
            printf(" Cannot create process %d \n" ,i);
            return -1;
            }
         default: /* CREATE NEXT PROCESS */
         }
      }  return 0;
   }
```

The rationale for this method of process creation is that the variable ppid is defined as

$$ppid = \begin{cases} 0 \text{ in parent process} \\ 1 \text{ in child 1 of the parent process} \\ \ldots \\ n \text{ in child n of the parent process.} \end{cases}$$

Then, a number of processes can be created in the program and scheduled according to specific computation needs, as in

```
main   (argc, argv)
    int argc;
    char*argv[ ];
    {
    int ppid, procs;
    scanf(argv[1], " %d ", &procs);
    ppid = Makeprocess(procs);
/* All PROCESSES ARE CREATED HERE */
    switch   (ppid)
       {
       case 0:   {code to be executed by parent }
       case 1:   {code to be executed by child 1}
       case 2:   {code to be executed by child 2}
       . . .
       case n:   {code to be executed by child n}
       default:
          {
          printf(" Something is wrong ");
          break;
          }
       }
/* All PROCESSES ARRIVE HERE FOR TERMINATION */
    if (ppid ! = 0)
       {
       printf(" Child number %d terminates \n ", ppid);
       exit (ppid);
       }
    }
```

Example: The following example illustrates the process creation using the fork system call. In this example, a child process that works independently of the parent is created .

```
#include <stdio.h>
int X=1;
main()
{
   int i, pid, A=1, B=1;
   pid = fork();
   if (pid == 0)
       {
   printf("CHILD PROCESS IS HERE WITH PID: %d\n", getpid());
   A = A * 100;
   B = B * 100;
   X = X + 1;
```

```
printf("BY CHILD: A IS %d, B IS %d AND X IS %d \n", A, B, X);
exit();
        }
else
        {
printf("PARENT PROCESS IS HERE WITH PID: %d\n", getpid());
A = A * 100;
B = B * 100;
X = X + 1;
printf("BY PARENT: B IS %d, A IS %d and X IS %d \n", B, A, X);
        }
/* PARENT PROCESS IS HERE WHEN THE CHILD IS TERMINATED */
printf("BY PARENT: A is %d and B is %d and X is %d\n", A, B, X);
}
```

Program Output: The following is the output created by this program, in which child and parent have different copies of variables A, B, and X. A and B as local variables are accessed by child and parent independently, in contrast to X, which is a global variable and is accessed by both processes.

```
PARENT PROCESS IS HERE WITH PID: 1413
CHILD PROCESS IS HERE WITH PID: 1414
BY CHILD: A IS 100, B IS 100 AND X IS 2
BY PARENT: B IS 100, A IS 100 and X IS 2
BY PARENT: A is 100 and B is 100 and X is 2
```

Another process creation mechanism in UNIX systems is the **Thread** system call. A process can be created by the pthread_create() system call as shown:

```
int  pthread_create(pthread_t *thread, const pthread_attr_t *attr,
          void *(*start_routine, void*), void *arg);
```

with attributes specified by attr, within a process. If attr is NULL, the default attributes are used. If the attributes specified by attr are modified later, the thread's attributes are not affected. Upon successful completion, pthread_create() stores the identification of the created thread in the location referenced by thread variable of type pthread_t. The created thread carries out start_routine with arg as its sole argument. When the start_routine returns, the effect is as if there were an implicit call to pthread_exit() using the return value of start_routine as the exit status. In the following program, a created process (thread) carries out the Add function as long as the parent process is in the main function.

```
/*compilation command: gcc filename.c -lpthread */
#include <stdio.h>
#include <pthread.h>
#define _REENTRANT
pthread_t tid;
int  A=1, B=1;
main ()
```

```
              {
              void  *Add(void *),  *argument;
              pthread_create(&tid, NULL, Add, argument);
              printf( " PARENT PROCESS IS HERE ");
              pthread_join(tid, NULL);
              B = B + 10;
              printf(" %d  %d ", A, B);
              }
           void *Add(void  argument)
              {
              printf(" CHILD PROCESS IS HERE ");
              A = A + 10;
              }
```

The result can address the value of A as 11 and B as 11, in which A and B are incremented by child and parent processes, respectively. In this example, the
pthread_join() function suspends processing of the parent process until the target thread completes. In other words, pthread_join() returns successfully when
the target thread terminates.

Producer-Consumer Example: The producer-consumer problem introduced in Section 14.6.1, is commonly used to illustrate the synchronization primitives. Regarding
this, there are two threads, and the behavior that we expect is that the producer and
consumer cooperate in such a manner that data is neither overwritten nor lost. The
important feature of this program is that when one thread is running in its critical
section, no other thread is allowed to run in its critical section. Thus, the execution of
critical sections by the threads is mutually exclusive in time. In other words, each
thread must request permission to enter its critical section. The semaphore variables
provide mutual exclusion access to the data. In this example, an output file is created
that is exactly the same as the input file.

```
/* Compilation: gcc program_name -lpthread */
/* Execution: a.out input_file output_file      */
#include <stdio.h>
#include <thread.h>
#include <pthread.h>
#include <errno.h>
#define _REENTRANT
pthread_t  tid[2];
sema_t  semaphore1;
sema_t  semaphore2;
sema_t  mutex;
unsigned int countm=1, count1=1, count2=1;
char one_char;
FILE *input, *output;
main(argc, argv)
int argc; char *argv[];     {
```

```
int index;
void *start_function1(void *), *start_function2(void *), *argument;
input =fopen(argv[1], "r");
output=fopen(argv[2], "w");
sema_init(&mutex, countm, USYNC_THREAD, NULL);
sema_init(&semaphore1, count1, USYNC_THREAD, NULL);
sema_init(&semaphore2, count2, USYNC_THREAD, NULL);
pthread_create(&tid[0], NULL, start_function1, input);
pthread_create(&tid[1], NULL, start_function2, output);
printf("PARENT PROCESS IS HERE\n");
for (index=0; index < 2;  index++)
pthread_join(tid[index], NULL);
printf("END OF THE PROCESS IS HERE\n");
}
void *start_function1(FILE *input)   {
sema_wait(&semaphore2);
for (;;)   {
sema_wait(&semaphore1);
sema_wait(&mutex);
one_char = getc(input);
/*printf("THREAD 1 READS %c \n", one_char); */
if (one_char == EOF)
   break;
sema_post(&mutex);
sema_post(&semaphore2);
   }
sema_post(&mutex);
sema_post(&semaphore2);
sema_post(&semaphore1);
return;
}

void *start_function2(FILE *output)   {
for (;;)
   {
sema_wait(&semaphore2);
sema_wait(&mutex);
/*printf("THREAD 2 PRINTS %c \n", one_char); */
   putc(one_char, output);
if (one_char == EOF)
   break;
sema_post(&mutex);
sema_post(&semaphore1);
   }
sema_post(&mutex);
sema_post(&semaphore2);
```

```
            return;
        }

        Matrix-Multiplication Example: The following program illustrates matrix-matrix
        multiplication, in which two 3×3 matrices A and B are multiplied using three threads.

/* Compilation: gcc  program_name     -lpthread  */
/* Execution: a.out                      */
#include <stdio.h>
#include <thread.h>
#include <pthread.h>
#include <errno.h>
#define _REENTRANT
#define N    3
pthread_t  tid[N];

int  A[3][3]={{2,3,4},{2,3,4},{2,3,4}};
int  B[3][3]={{2,2,2},{3,3,3},{4,4,4}};
int  C[3][3]={{0,0,0},{0,0,0},{0,0,0}};
main(argc, argv)
int argc; char *argv[];
    {
int index;
void *start_function(void *);
int *argument[N];
int indexarg[N]={0,1,2};

for(index=0; index < N; index++)
    {
argument[index]=&indexarg[index];
pthread_create(&tid[index], NULL, start_function, argument[index]);
        }
    printf("PARENT PROCESS IS HERE\n");

for (index=0; index < N;  index++)
pthread_join(tid[index], NULL);

printf("THE PARENT PROCESS DISPLAYS THE PRODUCT \n");
printmat();
    printf("END OF THE PROCESS IS HERE\n");
    }

void *start_function(index)
int *index;
    {
int row, column;
printf("THREAD %d IS CALCULATING THE ROW %d\n", *index+1, *index);
```

```
for (row=0; row<N; row++)
   {
   for (column=0; column<N; column++)
      {
C[row][*index]=C[row][*index]+A[row][column]*B[column][*index];
      }
   }
printf("THREAD %d IS LEAVING \n", *index+1);
   }

printmat()
   {
int row, column;
for (row=0; row<N; row++)
   {
   for (column=0; column<N; column++)
      {
      printf(" %d ", C[row][column]);
      }
   printf("\n");
   }
   }
```

The program output is the following:

```
PARENT PROCESS IS HERE
THREAD 1 IS CALCULATING THE ROW 0
THREAD 1 IS LEAVING
THREAD 2 IS CALCULATING THE ROW 1
THREAD 2 IS LEAVING
THREAD 3 IS CALCULATING THE ROW 2
THREAD 3 IS LEAVING
THE PARENT PROCESS DISPLAYS THE PRODUCT
29  29  29
29  29  29
29  29  29
END OF THE PROCESS IS HERE
```

15.1.2 Process Interaction

UNIX does not have a mechanism that allows user-created processes to interact by sharing resources. Instead, to perform parallel programming and user-process interaction, UNIX allows the user to define and declare shared data and code in parallel programs according to the following rules:

▶   Shared data are defined with the type of constructors available in the programming language in use. For example, in C, shared data (called Shared) and a pointer to it (called ToShared) can be defined as

```
struct    SharedData
     {
     int x,y,z;
     float a,b;
     } Shared, *ToShared;
```

where `Shared` is a variable of type structure `SharedData` and `ToShared` is a pointer variable that points to a variable of type structure `SharedData`.

▶ Data can be declared as shared by a call to a function that tells the C compiler to collect it in a shared segment and return a pointer to it. For example, to make a copy of the `Shared` variable of type structure, we need to use the **Share** system call, which has the following syntax:

```
ToShared = Share(0, sizeof(Shared));
```

where `ToShared` is a pointer variable and `Shared` is a variable of type structure `SharedData`. Hence, the parent process and all its children share a piece of shared data as declared, and shared data must be declared before process creation.

15.1.3 Timing of Process Execution

By timing process execution, programmers can observe the behavior of the sequential components of their parallel programs. Alternatively, programmers can achieve high efficiency by balancing computation loads. To allow process execution timing, a clock that can be accessed from the program by function calls is provided in a parallel library. This clock ticks continuously, and each tick records a microsecond. A call to the function `timer-init()` starts the clock, and a call to the system function `timer-get()` returns a number that represents the time, in microseconds, elapsed from the call to `timer-init()`. Therefore, the difference between the numbers returned by two system calls represents the run time spent by the process in running that piece of code. The net effects are the following:

▶ Set the process clock by performing the timer-init() system call

▶ Issue the timer-get() system call to get the consumed execution time of a section of code by calculating the time difference between these calls

The following code illustrates process run timing:

```
main    (argc, argv)
     int argc;
     char *argv[];        {
     double ProcessTime;
     long timer;
     int ppid, procs;
     scanf(argv[1], " %d ", &procs);
     ppid = Makeprocs(procs);
     switch    (ppid)
        {
```

```
        case 0: /* {code to be executed by parent} */
               {
               timer-init();        /* Set the clock */
timer = timer-get();   /* calculate the execution time of parent */
ProcessTime = (timer-get() - timer)/1000000.0;
               break;
               }
        case 1:   /* {code to be executed by child 1} */
               {
               timer-init();         /* Set the clock */
timer = timer-get();   /* calculate the execution time of child 1 */
ProcessTime = (timer-get() - timer)/1000000.0;
               break;
               }
        . . .
        case n:   /* {code to be executed by child n} */
               {
               timer-init();         /* Set the clock */
timer = timer-get();   /* calculate the execution time of child n */
ProcessTime = (timer-get() - timer)/1000000.0;
               break;
               }
        default:
               {
               printf(" Something is wrong ");
               break;
               }
        }
/* All PROCESSES ARRIVE HERE FOR TERMINATION */
        if   (ppid ! = 0)
          {
          printf(" Child Process %d Computation Time is %lf \n ",
          ppid, ProcessTime);
          exit (ppid);
          }
          else
          printf(" Parent Process %d Computation Time is %lf \n ",
          ppid, ProcessTime);
        }
```

Invoking these function calls in the program guarantees that the clock is set and obtained in the code associated with the process and that each process uses its own copy of the variable ProcessTime. Thus, the time of one process does not interfere with the time of another process.

15.1.4 Scheduling Created Processes

The actions of the created processes need to be synchronized in the parallel programs. The process synchronization mechanism is provided by an appropriate **lock data type variable** and guarantees that, once an operation on a variable of type lock has been started, the process will continue to termination without interference from the operations issued by other processes on the same variable. Two operations are provided with each lock data type, `lockname_create` and `lockname_init`, where

> `lockname∈{LOCK, BARRIER, SEMAPHORE, EVENT}.`

The following are some of the lock data types provided in parallel programs:

▶ LOCK: A data type whose objects have two values, denoted `PAR_LOCKED` and `PAR_UNLOCKED`. It allows mutual exclusion implementation of processes that operate on shared variables.

▶ BARRIER: A data type whose objects are tuples of the form (*count, flag*). The *count* object is of type `BARRIER` and indicates the number of processes that are expected to arrive at the Barrier before it opens. The *flag* objects represent the choices of the process waiting at the barrier and are defined as:

flag = `SPIN_BLOCK`, which locks the process in a busy waiting loop, and

flag = `PROCESS_BLOCK`, which locks the process in the process data structure.

▶ EVENT: A data type whose objects are tuples of the form (*event, flag*). The *event* object is of type EVENT and indicates that the event is expected to occur before all processes waiting for it can proceed. The *flag* object can be treated as the BARRIER data type *flag*.

▶ SEMAPHORE: A data type whose objects are tuples of the form (*count, flag*). The *count* object is of type `SEMAPHORE` and indicates how many processes can access the Semaphore variable before it is locked. The *flag* object can be defined in the same way as the `BARRIER` data type. The `SEMAPHORE` data type allows the Semaphore variable *count* to be set to a given positive integer by `semaphore_set`. At least two automatic operations, *lockname_lock* and *lockname_unlock,* are associated with each lock data type, allowing processes to check the lock and perform an appropriate action.

The following examples present declaration, initialization, and synchronization of created processes, using the LOCK data type.

Example 15.1: Declare variables of LOCK data type associated with a shared-memory area.

```
Tolock = spin_create(state);
Tobarr = barrier_create(count,flag);
Tosemaph = semaphore_create(flag);
Toevent = event_create(flag);
```

Example 15.2: Declare pointer variables of LOCK data type. The variables are not initialized, so they must be initialized before being used.

```
LOCK lock, *Tolock;
BARRIER barr, *Tobarr;
SEMAPHORE semaph, *Tosemaph;
EVENT event, *Toevent;
```

Example 15.3: The created objects must be initialized by calls to the *lockname_init* function.

```
spin_init(&lock, PAR_UNLOCKED);
Tolock = &lock;
spin_init(Tolock, PAR_UNLOCKED);
/* Set Barrier for 5 processes to be created */
barrier_init(&barr,5,PROCESS_BLOCK);
Tobarr = &barr;
barrier_init(Tobarr, 5, PROCESS_BLOCK);
/* Set Semaphore for 2 processes to be created */
semaphore_init(&semaph, SPIN_BLOCK);
Tosemaph = &semaph;
semaphore_init(Tosemaph, SPIN_BLOCK);
semaphore_set(semaph, SPIN_BLOCK,2);
Tosemph = &semaph;
semaphore_set(Tosemaph, SPIN_BLOCK,2);
event_init(&event, PROCESS_BLOCK);
Toevent = &event;
event_init(Toevent, PROCESS_BLOCK);
```

Process synchronization is provided and depends on the lock data type used. We illustrate synchronization between processes with the BARRIER and SEMAPHORE data types.

▶ **BARRIER:** The synchronization can be explained by using

barrier(Tobarr);

If the number of processes waiting at the Barrier Tobarr is less than Tobar = count−1, the number of waiting processes is increased by 1. Otherwise, the Barrier is available and all processes waiting can resume execution. The number of processes waiting at Barrier is set to 0.

▶ **SEMAPHORE:** Synchronization can be explained by using

semaphore_signal(Tosemaph);

If a process is waiting for the Semaphore variable, the process will be released and Tosemaph=count+1; that is, the Semaphore variable is increased by 1.

▶ **SEMAPHORE**: Synchronization can also be explained by using

semaphore_wait(Tosemaph);

Depending on the value of `Tosemaph` variable, this call can be carried out as follows. If `Tosemaph>0`, the shared resource is available and `Tosemaph=count=count-1`. Otherwise, the process is suspended and has to wait for the Semaphore variable `Tosemaph=count` to become positive; that is, the shared resource has to be available.

Example 15.4: In the following program, we use the semaphore mechanism to perform the synchronization among processes known as Producer and Consumer as we discussed.

```
/* gcc programname.c -lpthread */
/* a.out InputFile OutputFile */
#include <stdio.h>
#include <pthread.h>
#include <errno.h>
#define _REENTRANT
pthread_t  tid[2];
sema_t  semaphore1;    /* a semaphore variable to synchronize producers */
sema_t  semaphore2;    /* a semaphore variable to synchronize consumers */
/* a semaphore variable to synchronize mutual access to buffer */
sema_t  mutex;
unsigned int countm=1, count1=1, count2=1;
char one_char;         /* the length of the Buffer; one character */
FILE *input, *output;
main (argc, argv)
   int argc; char *argv[];
   {
   int index;
   void *start_function1(void *),  *start_function2(void *), *argument;
   input =fopen(argv[1], " r ");
   output=fopen(argv[2], " w ");
   /* initialization of semaphore variable*/
   sema_init(&mutex, countm, USYNC_THREAD, NULL);
   sema_init(&semaphore1, count1, USYNC_THREAD, NULL);
   sema_init(&semaphore2, count2, USYNC_THREAD, NULL);
   /* creation of producer and consumer processes */
   pthread_create(&tid[0], NULL, start_function1, input);
   pthread_create(&tid[1], NULL, start_function2, output);
   printf("PARENT PROCESS IS HERE\n");
   /* join the created threads*/
   for (index=0; index < 2;  index++)
   pthread_join(tid[index], NULL);
   printf(" END OF THE PROCESSES IS HERE \n ");
   }
void *start_function1 (FILE *input)
   {
```

```
    /* suspend any consumer, because the item is not produced */
    sema_wait(&semaphore2);
    /* THREAD 1 IS HERE */
    for ( ;; )
        {
    /* suspend any producer as long as a producer is in C.S. */
    sema_wait(&semaphore1);
    /* suspend any other process of entering the C.S. */
    sema_wait(&mutex);
    one_char = getc(input);
    printf(" THREAD 1 READS %c \n ", one_char);
    if (one_char == EOF)
       break;
    sema_post(&mutex);        /* release the C.S. */
    sema_post(&semaphore2);   /* release any suspended consumer */
        }
    sema_post(&mutex);
    sema_post(&semaphore2);
    sema_post(&semaphore1);
    return;
    }
void *start_function2 (FILE *output)
    {
    /* THREAD 2 IS HERE */
    for ( ;; )
        {
    /* suspend any consumer as long as a consumer is in C.S. */
    sema_wait(&semaphore2);
    /* suspend any other process of entering the C.S. */
    sema_wait(&mutex);
    printf(" THREAD 2 PRINTS %c \n ", one_char);
       putc(one_char, output);
       if (one_char == EOF)
         break;
    sema_post(&mutex);               /* release the C.S. */
    sema_post(&semaphore1);          /* release any suspended producer */
        }
    sema_post(&mutex);
    sema_post(&semaphore2);
    return;
    }
```

15.1.5   A Sample Parallel Program

The program accepts an integer as the number of processes and performs vector-matrix multiplication by reading a vector and a matrix from a file.

```
#include <parallel.h>
#include <stdio.h>
#define lines 10
#define cols 100
    struct        SharedData   {
            int m, n, k, State;
       double mat[lines][cols];
       double v1[cols], v2[lines];
       int count, jobs, procs;
       LOCK lock;              /* for synchronization purposes */
       };
   int upid = 0;
   main (argc, argv)
   int argc;   char *argv[];
   {
   int i; long t1; double   t2;
   FILE   *In, *Out;
   glob = share(0, sizeof(*glob));          /* global data */
   scanf(argv[1], " %d ", &glob->procs);   /* number of processes */
   In = fopen(argv[2], " r ");
   ReadMatrix(glob->mat, In);               /* read the matrix */
   ReadVector(glob->v1, In);                /* read the vector */
   glob->count = 0;
   glob->jobs = glob->n;
   glob->State = PAR_UNLOCKED;
   spin_init(&glob->lock, glob->State);   /* for synchronization */
   timer_init();
   t1 = timer_get();
   upid = Makeprocs(glob->procs  -1);       /* create process */
     i = GetNextProcess(glob->lock,glob->count,glob->jobs);
   while   (i < glob->n)
       {
   glob->v2[i]=Scalar(i,glob->m,glob->mat,glob->v1);
   i=GetNextProcess(glob->lock,glob->count,glob->jobs);   /* task to process */
       }
   if       (upid !=0)
       exit (0);
   t2 = (timer_get() - t1)/1000000.0;          /* record the execution time */
   printf(" \n Execution Time: %lf\n , t2);
   Out = fopen(argv[3], " w ");
   PrintVector(glob->n, glob->v2, Out);   /* print the result */
   fclose(Out);
   }
```

The processes are scheduled by calling the following function:

```
GetNextProcess(lock, count, jobs)
```

```
        int *count, jobs;
        LOCK *lock;
{
int which;
spin_lock(lock);
   which = *count;
   *count = *count + 1;
spin_unlock(lock);
if   (which > jobs)
   which = -1;
return which;
}
```

The following functions are used to read a two-dimensional matrix from a file and print a vector to a file:

```
ReadVector(v, data)
    double    v[];        FILE *data;
    {
    int i;
    fscanf(data, " %d ", &glob -> k);
    for   (i=0;  i < glob->k; i++)
       scanf(data, " %lf ", &v[i]);
    }
  ReadMatrix(a, data)
    double a[ ][cols];   FILE *data;
    {
    int i, j, k;
    fscanf(data, " %d ", &glob -> n);
    fscanf(data, " %d ", &glob -> m);
    for    (j=0; j < glob -> n; j++)
          for      (i=0; i < glob -> m; i++)
                fscanf(data, " %lf ", &a[j][i]);
    }
  PrintVector(m, v, data)
    int m;   double   v[];        FILE *data;
    {
    int i;
    for    (i=0;   i<m; i++)
       fprintf(data, " %lf\n ",v[i]);
    }
```

Finally, the function Scalar is defined as

```
double   Scalar(i, length, a, v)
         int i, length;   double a[][cols], v[];
           {
         int j, k;   double s = 0;
```

```
for  (j=0; j < length; j++)
   s = s + a[i][j]*v[j];
return s;
}
```

◤ 15.2 ASYNCHRONOUS PARALLEL PROGRAMMING WITH ADA

In 1957, the U.S. Department of Defense established the Higher Order Language Working Group to draw up requirements for a language that would enable standardization of a programming language to be used in embedded systems applications. The final choice was made in 1979 when the proposal developed by the team led by Jean Ichbiah at CII Honeywell Bull, France, was accepted. The language was renamed Ada in honor of Augusta Ada Byron, who had worked with Charles Babbage and is recognized as the world's first programmer. The first definitive version of the language was published in 1980. The objective was to come up with a language that would provide suitable capabilities for real-time programming of embedded systems. In **embedded systems,** a computer is only a part of a total system used for online monitoring and control, as on a ship or for a missile. A new programming language paradigm was needed to address errors caused by differences in machines, systems, languages, and language implementations experienced when programs were transported to and maintained in different environments. In general, concurrent programming was being done by calling the underlying operating system directly or by creating an operating system directly on the computer hardware. These methods made transporting programs from one system to another practically impossible. By including a model of concurrent programming called *tasking* in the standard language, Ada developers made transporting of programs possible. Ada's design encompassed numeric computation, system programming, and applications with real-time and concurrency requirements and was influenced by the Pascal programming language. Ada supports both shared-memory and message-passing models of computations.

Ada is distinguished from other languages because of its reliability. Consistency checks are performed when a program is being compiled so that errors can be caught as early as possible—even before a program is tested. In addition, checks are performed during program execution so that unexpected conditions will be noticed quickly after they arise, rather than after they indirectly cause other parts of the program to misbehave. These checks confine the effect of an error so that an Ada program rarely has to deal with arbitrary storage or branches to an arbitrary address. Ada also contains mechanisms for recovering from a run-time error when necessary.

Clearly, some of the programming required for Ada must contain natural ways of handling multiple concurrent activities. Ada offers standard and readable language concepts for the structuring of large programs, for specifying the relationship between different modules of a program, for data abstraction, and for programming distributed computing with tools for describing processes and the communication between them. Ada's designers were more concerned with making programs easy to read than with minimizing the number of keystrokes needed to write a program. Several good books on Ada are Cohen (1996), Dongarra and Johnson (1989), Schiper (1989), Skansholm (1997), and Stammers (1985).

15.2.1 Language Model

The design of Ada introduced

- ▶ **System programming,** for programs that are concerned with the underlying machine
- ▶ **Real-time systems,** for programs that must perform actions at particular times
- ▶ **Distributed systems,** for systems consisting of multiple main programs, possibly running on different processors
- ▶ **Information systems,** for commercial applications
- ▶ **Numeric computations,** for programs that depend on the precise mathematical details of computations involving real numbers
- ▶ **Safety and security,** for programs whose reliability is so critical that extreme measures must be taken to ensure their correctness

An Ada program basically consists of a procedure within which other procedures may be declared and called. In Ada, a careful distinction is made between the declaration part of a procedure, known as *elaboration,* in which variables and other constructs are declared, and the executable statements of the procedure. The overall structure of the Ada program is shown in the following code.

```
MessageSystem:
   declare
      MessType=. . . . . .
      task Process1;
      task Process2;
      task Process3 is
         entry Get (mess: out MessType);
         entry Put (mess: in MessType);
      end Process3;
      --bodies for the tasks Process1, Process2, and Process3
   begin
   --null body, since all the work is done by the tasks
   end MessageSystem;
```

`Process3` offers service capabilities that will be used by the other two tasks. Thus, `Process3` is a passive process, and the other two are active processes. In general, when `MessageSystem` is called, elaboration of all its declarations takes place, including initiation of the three processes, and the null body begins to run. This body will not terminate until each of its children has been terminated.

The client/server paradigm is the rationale behind the Ada program construction. In the absence of a remote invocation, the client must make two calls: one to pass in data and the other to receive a reply after the input data have been processed. The following code carries out these processes.

```
Process    Server
   entry   Request(SomeData)
   entry   Reply(SomeOtherData)
   begin
       repeat
         select
            accept Request(SomeData)        do
                   SomeVariable = SomeData
            accept Reply(SomeOtherData)     do
                   SomeOtherData = SomeResult
         or
            terminate
         end select;
       forever
   end;
Process    Client
      begin
          Server.Request(Data)
          Server.Reply(Answer)
   end;
```

Generally, a client should not affect a server process. Remote invocation allows the transaction to be represented as a single process interaction. In other words, the server does not need to know the identity of the client or, indeed, how many clients there are. These processes are as follows:

```
Process    Server       provides
           entry   Request(SomeData, SomeOtherData)
Process    Client
           begin
                   Server.Request(Data, Answer)
           end;
```

The two distinctive goals of Ada are to

1. Divide a large program into manageable smaller pieces (modules)
2. Write general software components that can be used in many programs

Both goals are achieved in Ada by the use of packages. A **package** is a collection of related entities that can be used by other parts of the program. These entities may include variables, subprograms, and type declarations. Hence, an Ada package is very much like a general collection of software that can be incorporated in many different systems to fulfill particular needs. The description of a package in Ada consists of a *package declaration* describing the interface and a *package body* describing the implementation. A typical package declaration can be declared as

```
package   identifier   is
            declaration;
          . . .
```

```
            declaration
end         identifier;
```

and consists of a sequence of declarations. A package body has the form

```
package  body  identifier  is
            declarative-part
begin
            {sequence of statements}
end         identifier;
```

but the sequence of statements is optional. Ada supports two kinds of subprograms. A subprogram may be either a *procedure* invoked by a procedure call statement to perform some action or a *function* invoked by evaluation of an expression to compute some value. The forms of a typical procedure and function are

```
procedure    identifier  (parameter-list)  is
            declarative-part
begin
            {sequence of statements}
end         identifier;
function  identifier (parameter-list) return result-type  is
            declarative-part
begin
            {sequence of statements}
end         identifier;
```

where the function is similar to the procedure except for the first line. Sixty-nine identifiers are reserved words in an Ada program and may not be given other meanings by the programmer. In general, the elements of a program can be combined to form **declarations** specifying the meaning of identifiers, **statements** specifying actions, and **pragmas** specifying information for the compiler (e.g., task priority). Declarations, statements, and pragmas always end with semicolons.

15.2.2   Architecture Model

Here, we are concerned with the applicability of the Ada tasking concept to the programming of distributed calculations. Thus, we have to choose a computational model consisting of more than one processor, with each processor carrying out its own piece of code (a task) and with programmable communication between processors. The language suggests that there is no relationship between the logical processes (the tasks) and the physical processors, but active tasks must be divided among the available processors. The availability of shared memory among all processors is not required; the system allows communication between tasks without the need for shared memory. Thus, programs that contain global variables can run with distributed memory allocated to those variables. Different processors might be given different tasks, and even if the tasks are identical (by task type), the processors should be capable of running asynchronously. If we use Ada for distributed computations, it will be most efficient when the system's parameters include

▶ The number *P* of available processors

▶ The size *M* of shared memory that can be accessed by tasks

▶ The size *C* of available communication channels

▶ The clock resolution facility for the presence of the vital processor

The asynchronous MIMD machine architecture fits these requirements. The main characteristic of most other computational models is the effect on execution of constraints on either the instructions performed by the different processors or the communication between processors. For example, you can exploit SIMD in this category while you are programming in Ada. In addition, some mechanism must be used for specifying the configuration of the distributed program or assigning the program units making up the program to various parts of the underlying distributed system. The distributed systems feature of Ada provides a general model for describing distributed systems. The system consists of one or more *processor nodes* and zero or more *storage nodes.* The processor nodes may be a set of machines in the same room, a set of processors on the same board, or a set of operating system processes running on a single processor. A storage node is a set of storage locations that can be accessed by processor nodes, main memory, low-speed cache, high-speed cache, or file storage systems.

15.2.3 Process Definition

To conform to Ada terminology, we use *task* instead of *process* in this discussion. **Tasks** are the Ada equivalent of parallel executable program segments. *Process level* refers to the possibility of using process hierarchies, which may be constructed by nesting process declarations within process declarations. Some languages allow such nesting, but those with a flat process structure do not. For example, Ada allows nested dynamic processes (tasks), whereas concurrent Pascal supports only static flat processes. When there are nested levels of processes, a relationship exists between processes; that is, a process is the child process of the parent process in which it is declared. In this case, only when all children have terminated is it safe for the parent to be terminated. In Ada, tasks are hierarchically related but have remote invocation as their method of message passing. A task consists of two parts, its specification and its body. The task specification is the interface presented to other tasks and may contain entry specifications, or a list of the services provided by the task. An entry is the same as a procedure declaration—a deliberate decision to allow substitution of a concurrent entry for a sequential procedure without changing a program. The task body contains the sequence of statements to be carried out when any of its services are requested, which represents the dynamic behavior of the task. For example, a task called `A_Process` can be declared as

```
task    A_Process is
        -- specification
end     A_Process;
task    body  A_Process is
        -- declarations
begin
        -- body
end     A_Process;
```

```
begin   -- active here
        -- parent
end;    -- terminate here
```

Hence, -- indicates a comment in Ada programming language. The *specification* states the services that A_Process is offering to the other processes, and *body* details the implementation. When the **begin** of the parent is reached, the A_Process task becomes active and its body is carried out. Then, A_Process runs in parallel with the statements of its parent. A task has completed its execution when it has finished carrying out the sequence of statements that appears after its reserved word **begin**.

If several tasks are written in the same declarative part, they are carried out in parallel, including the parent task. For example, in the following case, all three tasks are carried out in parallel whenever the **begin** of the parent task is reached.

```
task    A_Process is
        -- specification
end     A_Process;
task    body   A_Process is
        -- declarations
begin
        -- body
end     A_Process;
task    B_Process is
        -- specification
end     B_Process;
task    body   B_Process is
        -- declarations
begin
        — body
end     B_Process;
begin   -- parent
        -- all three tasks are active here
end;    -- terminate here
```

In many applications, several tasks need to do the same thing simultaneously (e.g., to perform the same analysis on different sets of data). For this reason, Ada provides *task types*. Every task is associated with some task type, and all tasks associated with the same type have identical entries and identical statements to carry out, as in

```
task    type   Counter_Task_Type   is
        — specification
end     Counter_Task_Type;
task    body   Counter_Task_Type   is
begin
        — body
end     Counter_Task_Type;
```

A task type declaration must be accompanied by a *task body*, which consists of the statements to be executed by the task. The declaration

```
Counter_1, Counter_2: Counter_Task_Type;
```

declares `Counter_1` and `Counter_2` to be two task objects, each of which independently carries out the preceding task body. Each has its own copy of the variables declared in the task body. Task type declarations and task bodies can go in the declarative part of a subprogram body, a package body, a block statement, or a surrounding task body. Tasks may be declared or allocated. A task associated with a declared object begins execution when the object declaration is elaborated. A task associated with an allocated object begins execution when the object is created. A running task eventually terminates. Sequences of statements in an Ada program are *reentrant,* which means that several tasks may carry out the same sequence of statements at the same time. For example, the statement

```
X :=X+1;
```

could be carried out by several tasks, each having its own copy of the variable `X`. None of these tasks need be affected by the others. In Ada, priority is used to control the interprocess synchronization in concurrent systems. Each task is given a **base priority;** a programmer can specify the initial base priority of a task but can change it later. In addition to the base priority, a task has an **active priority,** which is the value actually considered when processors are allocated to unblocked tasks and the entry call to be serviced next is chosen. Normally, the base priority and active priority of a task are the same. The initial base priority of a task can be specified by the priority **pragma** in the form

```
pragma      Priority (expression);
```

where the `expression` is of type integer in a range defined by the implementation. This statement can be placed in a task type declaration or single task declaration to specify the initial base priority for all tasks of that task type. Whenever two tasks are competing for either the processor or an entry queue, the one with the higher priority will be chosen. A synchronization point is a point in computation at which a scheduling decision must be made relative to the associated priority of the tasks—for example, at the conclusion of a rendezvous. If all tasks run independently, the allocation of unique priorities will allow the behavior of each task to be predicted. An implementation must use a preemptive scheduler and make use of time-slicing, in which a timer suspends the computation at a predefined time interval. In addition, the pragma may appear in the declarative part of the main subprogram to specify the priority of the task carrying out the main subprogram, and in this case, the expression must be treated as static.

15.2.4 Process Synchronization

The rules of scope allow two or more tasks to access variables that are declared in the same or enclosing procedures. As a result of this action, conflicts may arise when multiple processes attempt to access the same data. Ada provides three mechanisms for task synchronization and communication: **shared variables, protected objects,** and **rendezvous.** A shared variable is examined or modified by more than one task. Shared variables must be used with extreme caution because of the possibility of one task modifying the variable while another task is examining it. This problem can be avoided by the use of primitives defined in the systems programming feature. For example,

```
pragma    Atomic (name);
```

takes the name of a variable, or the name of a type, as a pragma argument. It stipulates two things about the named variable or about every variable of the named type:

▶ The variable is to be examined and updated atomically, meaning that one task cannot observe such a variable that has been partially updated by another task.

▶ No temporary copies of the variable are allowed, meaning that every examination of the variable must examine the variable itself, and every modification of the variable must immediately modify the variable itself.

A protected object holds data that can be shared by multiple tasks and can be manipulated through specific operations. However, while one task is carrying out an operation that modifies the object, any other task attempting to start an operation on that object is forced to wait until the operation started by the first task is complete. Objects of a *protected type* are called protected objects and can be manipulated only by high-level operations provided by the unit declaring the type. High-level operations on a protected type are called *protected operations*. The following package declaration contains a *protected-type declaration*.

```
package     Protected_Queue   is
            protected type        Protected_Queue_Type    is
                procedure   Enqueue (Item: in Integer);
                entry   Dequeue (Item: out Integer);
                function Length return Natural;
            private
                Queue:    Queues.Queue_Type;
            end   Protected_Queue_Type
end     Protected_Queue
```

A protected-type declaration and its protected body together constitute a protected unit. Each `Protected_Queue_Type` object has a single component named `Queue` of type `Queue_Type` and three operations named `Enqueue`, `Dequeue`, and `Length`. A protected type can have three kinds of protected operations: a protected procedure, such as `Enqueue`; protected entries, such as `Dequeue`; and protected functions, such as Length. If `PQ` is an object of a protected type and `N` is an object of type *int*, the statement

```
PQ.Enqueue(N);
```

is a call on the protected procedure `Enqueue` of protected object `PQ` with parameter `N`. Similarly, the statement

```
PQ.Dequeue(N);
```

is a call on the protected entry `Dequeue` of protected object `PQ` with parameter `N`, and the expression on the right-hand side of the statement

```
N :=PQ.Length;
```

is a call on the protected function `Length` of protected object `PQ`. The part of the protected-type declaration following the word *private* is called the *private part* of the protected-type declaration.

A rendezvous is an interaction at a synchronization point during which two tasks synchronize and one provides a service to the other through an interface much like a procedure call. In Ada, a process can be synchronized with another process at particular points in their execution. The communication is synchronous, meaning that the first task to arrive must wait for the arrival of the second task. Two tasks must meet at a rendezvous so they can communicate. However, the location of the rendezvous belongs to one of the tasks, called the **accepting task.** The other task, the **calling task,** must know the identity of the accepting task and the name of the location of the rendezvous, the **entry.** Thus, when one task calls an entry of a second task and the second task accepts that call, a rendezvous takes place. The Ada rendezvous is a primitive with the following characteristics:

▶   Synchronous, unbuffered communication

▶   Asymmetric identification, meaning that the sender knows the identity of the receiver, but not the reverse

▶   Two-way data flow communication during a single rendezvous

Two tasks that are to rendezvous may not arrive at the point of synchronization at the same time, and, in fact, it is extremely unlikely that it will happen. A rendezvous between two Ada tasks is similar to a rendezvous between two people, meaning that whichever arrives at the appointed meeting place first must wait for the other. After meeting, each task continues about its own business. Thus, when two processes meet, the two processes carry out the the entry code jointly, after which they part and go their separate ways. Both tasks are running concurrently and independently, except where they synchronize. We illustrate this situation in Figure 15.1. The synchronization between tasks can be performed through entries. One task carries out an entry call, which looks very much like a procedure call. Another task accepts the entry call. For instance, a task named `Counter` might have an entry declared as

```
entry    Increment (Amount: in Integer; New_Total: out Integer);
```

Thus, calls on the entry `Increment` can have the same form as calls on a procedure with two arguments of type `Integer`, the first of mode `in` and the second of mode `out`. Another task can communicate with task `Counter` by issuing an entry call such as

```
Counter.Increment(X,Y);
```

The task `Counter` accepts this entry by carrying out an *accept* statement such as

```
accept    Increment(Amount: in Integer;
                New_Total: out Integer)    do
          Total :=Total + Amount;
          New_Total := Total;
end       Increment;
```

FIGURE **15.1**   **Synchronization of two processes**

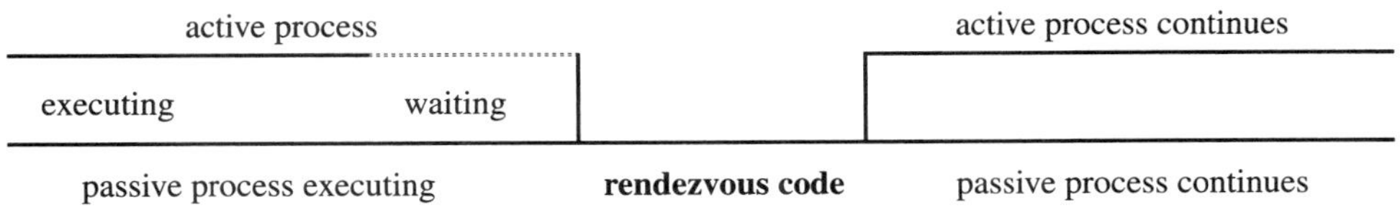

(a) The active process requests a rendezvous before the passive process is ready to receive the request and therefore has to wait.

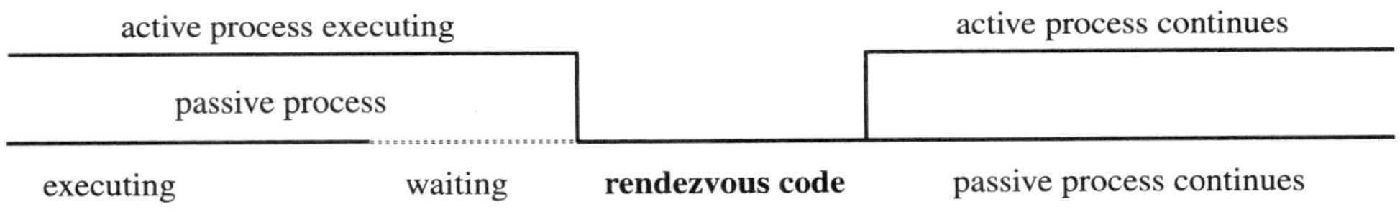

(b) The passive process has to wait pending the arrival of a request from the active process.

where the *accept* statement is then carried out with Amount representing the value of X and with Y receiving the value assigned to New_Total. This process is called a rendezvous for the duration of the execution of the *accept* statement. This *accept* statement may be empty when its purpose is to have a synchronization.

Once the *accept* statement has been completed, the task issuing the entry call Counter.Increment(X,Y) can go on with the next statement. Hence, a rendezvous is like a procedure call with the *accept* statement as a procedure body, except that the *accept* statement is one of the steps carried out in sequence by the task Counter. The entry call can occur only when the task Counter reaches the *accept* statement. If a task carries out a call on the entry Counter.Increment(X,Y) before Counter has reached the *accept* statement, the task carrying out the entry call is forced to wait. Similarly, if Counter reaches the *accept* statement before an entry call has been carried out, it waits for some task to call the appropriate entry.

15.2.5 A Sample Program

In this program, we consider a solution to the bounded buffer problem, which occurs when several tasks, called *Producers,* are to communicate a series of produced items to other tasks called *Consumers*. For convenience we assume that the buffer has finite capacity, into which the *Producers* deposit items and from which the *Consumers* remove items when ready. Synchronization must be performed in such a way that the *Producers* will not deposit items when the buffer is full and that the *Consumers* will not try to remove items when the buffer is empty. Given this disparity in the intensity of communication, the buffer itself must be regarded as a passive task, which accepts requests from services from active tasks, the *Producers* and *Consumers*. In this program, the reserved words **in** and **out** indicate input and output parameters, respectively, and the statements between **do** and **end** perform the service associated with the entry procedure.

```
--BOUNDED BUFFER PROBLEM
--specification of task allows items to be deposited and removed
--from a buffer, meaning that it accepts calls to the procedures
--Deposit and Remove from other tasks.
task    Bounded_Buffer    is
            entry   Deposit(Item : in Message);
entry   Remove(Item : out Message);
end         Bounded_Buffer;
task    body   Bounded_Buffer    is
begin
        -- statements
        accept   Deposit(Item : in Message)    do
        -- statements
end;
        accept   Remove(Item : out Message)    do
        -- statements
end;
end     Bounded_Buffer;

task    type   Producer    is
end         Producer;
task    body   Producer    is
            Item := Message;
        begin
          loop
              -- produce item
              Bounded_Buffer.Deposit(Item
              exit when Finished;
          end loop;
end     Producer;

task    type   Consumer    is
end         Consumer;
task    body   Consumer    is
            Item := Message;
          begin
            loop
```

```
                    -- consume item
                    Bounded_Buffer.Remove(Item
                    exit when Finished;
                end loop;
      end       Consumer;
```

▰ 15.3 DATA PARALLEL PROGRAMMING WITH C∗

In 1987, the Thinking Machine Corporation announced the availability of C∗, an extension of the C programming language designed to support data parallel programming for Connection Machines. It provides a new data type based on classes in C++, a synchronous execution model, and some extensions to C syntax. C∗ supports all standard C operations and a few new operations for data parallel programming. In 1990, Thinking Machine announced C∗, version 6.0, with different syntax and semantics from the prior versions of C∗, for programming CM-2 parallel computers and for the CM-5. The system software of the Connection Machine is based on the operating system, and programmers feel like they are programming an SIMD computer consisting of a front-end uniprocessor attached to back-end parallel processors. The front-end processor stores the sequential variables and carries out the control structure of the parallel programs, issuing commands to the processing elements whenever necessary. Programs have ordinary sequential control flow and do not need any new synchronization mechanism. Indeed, programmers can use familiar programming languages and programming constructs. The front-end processor can read or write data from or to the local memories of the processing elements. The back-end processors store the parallel variables and run the parallel portions of the program, each of which has its own local memory.

In general, there is only a single flow of control, which means that at any time, either the front-end processor is running a sequential operation or the back-end processing elements are running a parallel operation. The processing elements are adaptable; that is, the programmer can select the size and shape of the processing elements for whatever purpose. For this reason, the processing elements are referred to as *virtual processors*. In addition, the configuration of the back-end processing elements can be adapted between different points in the same program. The programmer's view of C∗ programming on the Connection Machine is shown in Figure 15.2. Pointers are used for interprocessor communication. A synchronous computation model is used in C∗, in which all instructions are issued from the front end. This approach allows different processors to have different memory layouts because they may hold different kinds of data. A structure type called *domain* allows the specification of the memory layout.

Accordingly, the C∗ code is divided into serial and parallel portions. The code that belongs to a domain is parallel and is carried out by many data processors, whereas the serial code is carried out by the front-end processor. The data are divided into scalar and parallel portions, described by the keywords *mono* and *poly*, respectively. Mono data are stored in the memory of the front end, whereas poly data are

FIGURE **15.2**   Structure of the data parallel C* programming model

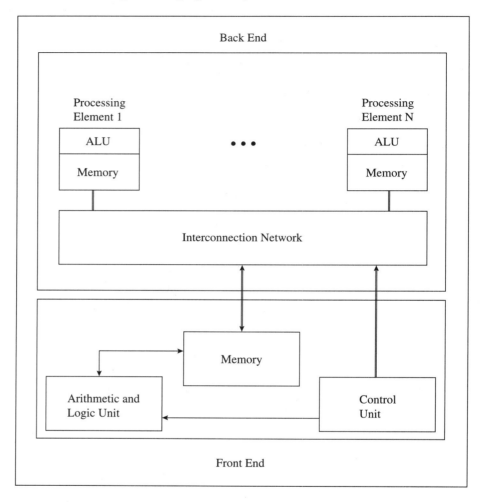

stored in the memory of the data processors. At compile time, the data are distinguished, and scalar operators are extended to operate on parallel data. In addition, a new statement in C* is the *selection* statement, which can be used to activate the multiple processors. The C* compiler parses the C* source code, performs data flow analysis, and then translates the parallel code into a series of function calls that might be invoked for execution.

15.3.1 Parallel Variables

C language constructs such as data types, operators, structures, pointers, and functions are all supported in C*, which has two types of variables, scalar and parallel. A scalar variable is identical to an ordinary C variable and is allocated in the front-end processor. A parallel variable is allocated on all processing elements and has as many elements as the number of processors. C* introduces the notion of a *shape,* which specifies the way a parallel variable is defined. A **shape** is a template for parallel data and defines how many elements of a parallel variable exist and how they are organized. Each element occupies one position within a shape and contains a single value, so each element can be thought of as a single scalar variable. In general, by declaring a variable to be of the *shape* data type, programmers indicate that they want the ability to perform parallel operations on that variable. For example, the variable declaration

```
shape    [10][10]  class;
```

specifies a template for a parallel variable with two dimensions and 100 positions. Similarly, a *shape* of rank four with five positions along each axis is declared as

```
shape    [5][5][5][5]  fourclass;
```

where the declaration specifies a template for parallel variable fourclass containing a total of 5 × 5 × 5 × 5 = 625 positions. A shape is defined by specifying how many dimensions it has, which is referred to as its *rank,* and the number of elements or positions (number of processors) in each of its dimensions. A dimension may be referred to as an *axis.* Individual elements of a parallel variable can be accessed. After a *shape* has been specified, parallel variables of that *shape* type can be declared. Parallel variables have a data type, a storage class, and a shape. The following statement declares the parallel variable class1 of type int and shape class:

```
shape    [10][10]  class;
int :    class class1;
```

This declaration creates a parallel variable class1 with 100 positions, each of which is allocated to a different processor. We can access individual elements of the parallel variable class1 by using left indexing. For example, [0]class1 indicates the value of the class1 that resides on the first processor. Similarly,

```
int :    fourclass  grade[100];
```

declares the 625-position parallel variable grade in which each element is an array of 100 integers. Generally speaking, a *shape* can reflect the logical organization of an application's data. For example, we can declare a cube *shape* to represent the data of a three-dimensional problem. C* supports the C aggregate data types, such as parallel structures and parallel arrays, so that we can declare an entire structure as a parallel variable. For example, in the declarations

```
shape    [10][10]   class;
struct   list
    {
    int   id;
    float   gpa;
    char   grade;
    };
```

a parallel structure `list1` of type `struct list` and `class` shape can be declared as

```
struct    list: class list1;
```

Members of a parallel structure can be accessed by dot notation; for example, `list1.id` identifies the structure member `id` in the parallel structure `list1`.

15.3.2 Parallel Operations

If the operands of an operation are scalar, the C∗ code behaves exactly as standard C code and the operation is performed on the front-end computer. The situation is different when one or more operands are declared as parallel variables. For example, in the simple assignment statement

```
x = y + z;
```

all three variables are declared as parallel variables. This assignment adds the value of y at the defined *shape* position to the value of z at the corresponding *shape* position and stores the result as the value of x in that *shape* position. Note that the variables x, y, and z must be declared with the same *shape*. Parallel operations occur in the context of a *with* statement. The *with* statement activates the positions of a *shape*, setting up a context in which variables of that data type can be used in parallel. For example, in the declarations

```
shape    [10][10]      class;
integer: class x, y, z;
with   (class)       {
     x = y + z;
     }
```

with statement performs an element-wise addition on each component of y and z and stores the resulting values in the corresponding components of x. In other words, it performs a separate addition of the values of y and z in each position of the *shape* and assigns the result to the element of x in that position.

Before we can perform operations in parallel, they must be of the same *shape* (*current shape*). The *with* statement selects a *current shape* and allows operations on parallel data simultaneously. We can use many *with* statements in a program, making different shapes active at different times. C∗ has a set of built-in operators, which are shown in Table 15.1, called reductions, that reduce parallel values to scalar values. For example, the following C∗ program computes the sum of all 100 values of x and stores it in the scalar variable `total`. In general, the reduction operator += sums the values of all active elements of the parallel variable x and assigns this sum as the value of the scalar variable `total`.

```
main(){
     integer total;
     with (class)   {
        total = (+= x);
                  }
     }
```

TABLE **15.1**   C* Language Reduction Operators

Operator	Meaning
+=	Sum of parallel variable elements values
−=	Negative of sum of parallel variable elements values
&=	Bitwise AND of values
^=	Bitwise XOR of values
|=	Bitwise OR of values
>?=	Maximum of values
<?=	Minimum of values

C* also supports a new statement called *where* to provide the ability to perform operations on a subset of the elements of a parallel variable. The positions to be operated on are called *active positions,* and selecting the *active positions* of a *shape* is known as *setting the context.* For example, the following segment results in the evaluation of y + z as the value of x only at those positions in the shape where the value of x is greater than zero.

```
with    (class)    {
        where      (x > 0)    {
                   x = y + z;
                   }
        }
```

The *where* statement can include an *else* statement, which reverses the set of active positions. Thus, the active positions when the where statement was carried out are made inactive, and similarly, the inactive positions are changed to active. For example,

```
with    (class)    {
        where    (x > 0)    {
                 x = y + z;
        else
                 x = y −   z;
                 }
        }
```

specifies that y+z and y−z are evaluated as the result of those positions of x in the *shape,* where the value of x is greater than zero or less than zero, respectively. In addition, C* supports parallel variables and shapes as arguments in standard C functions. This capability allows parallel variables and shapes to be used as arguments to and returned from functions. For example, in the following code, a function is called with a parallel variable x of type int and class *shape:*

```
int    add_values (int: class x)    {
       printf(" The sum of the elements is %d: ", + = x);
       }
```

In addition, different versions of a function may be used, meaning that functions can be overloaded. The *overload* statement is used to specify the name of the function to be overloaded. For example, the following statements represent three different meanings of the function, indicating that the function calculate is overloaded.

```
int    calculate(int x);
int    calculate(int x, int y);
int    calculate(int: class x);
```

15.3.3 Parallel Communication

Two methods of interprocess communication are supported in C*:

▶ **Grid communication,** in which parallel variables of the same shape can communicate with each other by their coordinates

▶ **General communication,** in which the value of any element can be transferred to any other element, whether or not the parallel variables are the same shape

The function *pcoord* provides a grid communication between parallel variables in C*. The function, when passed a dimension number, returns each element of a parallel variable to its position within the dimension of the shape, providing a self-index for a parallel variable along a specified axis of its shape. In grid communication, data can be transferred only a fixed distance along each dimension. For example,

```
[pcoord(0) + 1] source2 = source1;
```

sends source1 values to the elements of source2, which are located one coordinate higher along axis 0. Figure 15.3 illustrates the function pcoord in which the *shape* has dimension [3][3] relative to how the statement runs:

```
source2 = [pcoord(0)+1][pcoord(1)+1]source1
```

As a consequence, C* uses the concept of left indexing to provide communication between different shapes as well as within a shape. In addition, *get* and *send* operations are provided in C*. For example, the general form of a *send* operation and a *get* operation is

```
[index] source2 = source1;
source2 = [index]source1;
```

where index, source2, and source1 are parallel variables of rank 1, as illustrated in Figure 15.4.

Example 15.5: The following program multiplies two N × N matrices, A and B, to result in a product matrix C. The program uses N × N virtual processors, as shown by N = 256 in line 5. A single *shape* called Mesh, which is a two-dimensional grid of size 256 × 256, is defined in line 6 and resembles the topology used for matrix multipli-

FIGURE **15.3**   **Grid communication of a shape with [3][3] dimension**

source1		
1	2	3
4	5	6
7	8	9

source2		
	1	2
	4	5

FIGURE **15.4**   **Illustration of the (a) *send* and (b) *get* communication operations**

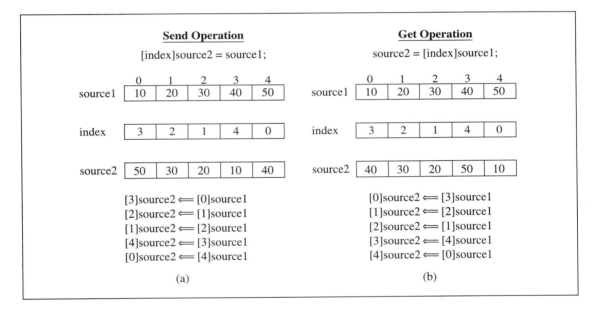

Send Operation

[index]source2 = source1;

	0	1	2	3	4
source1	10	20	30	40	50

index	3	2	1	4	0

source2	50	30	20	10	40

[3]source2 ⟸ [0]source1
[2]source2 ⟸ [1]source1
[1]source2 ⟸ [2]source1
[4]source2 ⟸ [3]source1
[0]source2 ⟸ [4]source1

(a)

Get Operation

source2 = [index]source1;

	0	1	2	3	4
source1	10	20	30	40	50

index	3	2	1	4	0

source2	40	30	20	50	10

[0]source2 ⟸ [3]source1
[1]source2 ⟸ [2]source1
[2]source2 ⟸ [1]source1
[3]source2 ⟸ [4]source1
[4]source2 ⟸ [0]source1

(b)

cation. In general, each *shape* position computes an element of the product matrix. Line 13 is the start of the *with* statement, which puts the computations in a parallel context. In lines 15–17, we perform a circular shift of the elements of matrix A such that at the end of this loop each processor has the required row elements of matrix A. Similarly, lines 19–21 perform a circular shift of the elements of matrix B so that at the end of this loop each processor has the required column elements of matrix B. In both loops for the circular shifts, the left index of the variable Buffer is computed modulo N to achieve wraparound communication. Finally, in line 23, each processor computes one element of the product matrix C.

The program does not specify how many processors are used. In general, virtual processors do not result in the best formulation, and we recommend that explicit mapping be used, that is, mapping virtual processors onto physical processors. Virtual processors may be mapped onto physical processors in many different ways, and the best mapping leads to a better formulation. For example, a two-dimensional shape of virtual processors may be mapped onto four processors by using block-checkerboard mapping:

```
/* Matrix Multiplication program using 256x256 */
/* Virtual processors */
/* The line numbers are for reference purposes, are not part of the program */
1       #include   <stdio.h>
2       #include   <stdlib.h>
3       #include   <ctype.h>
4       #include   <cscomm.h>
5       #define    N    256
6       shape    [N][N]Mesh;
7       int:Mesh A[N];
8       int:Mesh B[N];
9       int:Mesh C;
10      int:Mesh Buffer;
11      main ()
            {
12          int   i;
13          with    (Mesh)
              {
14            Buffer = A[pcoord(1)];
15            for   (i=1; i< N; i++)    {
16              Buffer = [pcoord(0)][(pcoord(1)+1) % N]Buffer;
17              A[(pcoord(1)+i) % N] = Buffer;
                }
18          Buffer = B[pcoord(0)];
19          for   (i=1; i< N; i++)    {
20              Buffer = [(pcoord(0)+1) % N][pcoord(1)]Buffer;
21              B[(pcoord(0)+i) % N] = Buffer;
                }
22          for   (i=0; i< N; i++)
23            C +=A[i]*B[i];
              }
          }
```

Example 15.6: The following program is written in C*, version 6.0, for a Connection Machine with 8,192 processing elements. In line 1, we define Intervals to address the number of rectangles. A single *shape* called Span, which is a one-dimensional shape of size 8,192 × 16, is defined in line 2 and corresponds to the set of subintervals. Two scalar variables and one variable of type *shape* are declared in lines 4, 5, and 7, respectively. Line 6 is used for the parallel context with the *with* statement. Line 8 computes the midpoint of each rectangle on the x axis. In line 9, we compute the height of the function curve at each of the midpoints. The heights are added and stored as the value of the scalar variable Sum. In line 10, we multiply the total height computed as the value of the scalar variable Sum by the scalar variable Width, which is the width of the rectangles. Finally, the total area as the result is printed in line 11.

```
1       #define Intervals (8192*16)
2       shape [Intervals] Span;
3       main ()
            {
4       double Sum;
5       double Width = 1.0/Intervals;
6           with (Span)
                {
7               double:Span X;
8               X=(pcoord(0)+0.5)*Width;
9               Sum=(+=(4.0/(1.0+X*X)) );
                }
10          Sum *=Width;
11          printf (" Estimation of PI is %15.12f " , Sum);
            }
```

SUMMARY

In the parallel processors, processes represent independent actions, which can be executed in parallel. Thus, we need to provide the ability to control the interaction of such processes. In parallel systems represented by array and vector processors, the computation is performed in a lock-step or overlapped fashion. This processing is called synchronous parallelism. As a consequence, the machines in this category do not have the synchronization problems associated with multiprocessors and multicomputers. In this chapter, we presented parallel programming with UNIX, which is an augmented version of the UNIX OS with libraries as a synchronous parallel programming approach.

Asynchronous parallelism is the most general form of parallelism, whereby processors operate freely on tasks, without regard for global synchronization. In place of the lock-step fashion of the various forms of synchronized parallelism, the asynchronous method relies on locks and explicit control flow. The mutual exclusion mechanism is usually implemented by a lock, which prevents all but one process from accessing the data at any instant in time. All other accesses must wait until the process that originally placed the lock on the shared data removes the mutual exclusion lock. A second major method is to send a message to all processes to inform them about the applicability of the data access. This method can be employed by message passing in distributed systems. We presented an asynchronous parallel programming language, Ada. The message-passing approach has been used in high-level programming languages such as Ada, which uses the two basic operations, send and receive, to exchange messages among parallel processes. Ada was a general-purpose language strongly supported by the U.S. Department of Defense and designed for numerical computations, system programming, and applications with real-time and concurrency requirements. Among its features are packages and generics, designed to aid the construction of large modular programs. In Ada, the transfer of data is direct and synchronized. Ada is probably the best example available of a state-of-the-art concurrent programming language, but it was not intended for fine-grained parallelism. An Ada program consists of a procedure, in which Ada makes a careful distinction between the declaration part, known as elaboration, and the other parts, known as executable statements. We discussed the architecture model and process definition to address synchronization and communication between processes. In Ada, the processes rendezvous to exchange information and then continue their activity in parallel and independently. A classic example known as the bounded buffer problem addressed the structure of an Ada program.

Think of a SIMD system as a single control unit that directs the activities of a number of processing elements, each performing the same instruction by fetching and manipulating its own local data. The data parallel programming approach is characterized by a relatively large number of synchronous processes that carry out a single instruction stream. You must suitably define the fundamental unit of parallelism before you can run a data parallel algorithm efficiently on parallel hardware. In this chapter, we discussed a data parallel programming language C*, which is described as an extension of C for specifying concurrency, locality, communication and mapping. The data parallel programming language C* was designed by Thinking Machine Corporation for its Connection Machine processor array. The language C* is a major language for data parallel programming and has been implemented on a number of SIMD and MIMD parallel computers. We outlined the structure of the data parallel C* programming model, which consisted of two parts: front end and back end. The front end consists of a single processor machine, and the back end is a collection of processing elements connected to an interconnection network. The language supports two types of variables, scalar and parallel, in which the scalar variable is allocated to the front-end processor, and the parallel variable can be allocated on all processing elements. C* supports a shape keyword that lets the programmer provide the shape and size of parallel data. We discussed the constructs of the language, including parallel variables, parallel operations, and parallel communication. We categorized parallel communication into two methods: grid communication and general communication. One new statement type, called the selection statement, is used to activate multiple processors. We outlined two examples, matrix multiplication and PI computation, to address the program structure, process creation, mapping, synchronization, and communication mechanisms. Although the details vary according to the languages used, the solutions do not differ greatly. Much of the difficulty of constructing a parallel program lies in the design of the structure and the choice of processes.

EXERCISES

1. Define the following terms:

   Data parallelism

   Control parallelism

   Shared-memory parallelism

   Message-passing parallelism

Dependency analysis	Data flow graph
Granularity	Fine-grained granularity
Medium-grained granularity	Large-grained granularity
Synchronous mapping	Asynchronous mapping
Pipelining	Overlapped processing
Multiprogramming	Multiprocessing

2. What is the advantage of using *fine-grained* granularity?

3. What is the advantage of using *medium-grained* granularity?

4. What is the advantage of using *large-grained* granularity?

5. Match each of the terms on the left with its attributes on the right.

    a. Data dependency   1. Reassembling compiler for VLIW trace scheduling
    b. Anti-dependency   2. Reconstructing Fortran compiler
    c. Output dependency   3. Two statements produce the same variable
    d. Bulldog compiler   4. Variable assigned in one statement used in a
    e. Paraphrase compiler   preceding statement
                            5. Variable assigned in one statement used in a
                               succeeding statement

6. Consider a primitive "START C" that causes the command C to be carried out in a new process concurrently with the one that runs the START primitive (parent). The new process shares all presently existing variables with its parent, but subsequently created variables are not shared. Using the START primitive, modify the following sequential procedure so that as many components as possible of *Sum* are computed concurrently.

```
type    Matrix   is array(1 .. N, 1 .. N) of Float;
procedure  add(A, B : in Matrix;  Sum : out Matrix)  is
begin
   for  I  in  1 .. N  loop
      for  J  in  1 .. N  loop
      Sum(I, J)  : =  A(I, J) + B(I, J);
      end loop;
   end loop;
end.
```

How many processes can be active concurrently in your version? Assume that starting a process takes time T, and that carrying out the assignment command takes time t. In what circumstances would the concurrent version be faster than the sequential version?

7. Compare and contrast the programming environments for the *shared-memory* SIMD, *shared-memory* MIMD, and *private-memory* MIMD systems.

8. Show how to compute the following conditional expression using the *data flow graph* of computation:

```
If   X > Y    Then
     X - Y
Else
     X + Y
```

9. Draw the data flow graph for the solution of $AX^2+BX+C=0$.

10. Devise an algorithm to increase the *granularity* of a matrix multiplication problem.

11. Two concurrent processes P1 and P2 each have their own local variables A and B, respectively. The values of these variables are to be exchanged using the following sequence of indivisible machine-level operations:

    a. Load A into register R1

    b. Load B into register R2

    c. Store value from register R1 in B

    d. Store value from register R2 in A

    What is the effect of concurrent execution if P1 and P2 do not carry out the exchange of the values under mutual exclusion conditions?

12. Differentiate between SIMD programming, SPMD programming, MIMD programming, and MPMD programming.

13. This is the *Dining Philosophers* problem. Five hungry philosophers sit at a table with a bowl of spaghetti in the middle. Each needs two forks to eat, but only five forks are available, placed between their plates. Write a parallel program to solve the dining philosophers problem using thread primitive available in UNIX system.

14. The following segment is devised to calculate the roots of a quadratic equation. Write a program to extract the parallelism using *fork* and *join* primitives.

```
begin
     Input(A,B,C);
     A := 2 * A;
     C := B↑2 - 2 * A *C;
     C := sqrt(C);
     C := C/A;
     B := -B/A;
     A := B + C;
     B := B - C;
     Output(A,B);
end
```

15. Consider the following program fragment. Rewrite the program in equivalent form relative to dependency between the statements and draw the dependency graph.

FIGURE **15.5**   A dependency graph

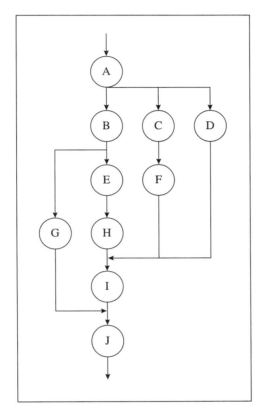

```
if    A > 1    then    goto    X;
endif
if    B > 0    then    D = 3    goto    X;
else    goto    Y;
endif
X:    E = 5
Y:    B = E + D
```

16. For the graph shown in Figure 15.5, write the control flow using *fork* and *join* primitives. Can this be carried out by *statement level* parallelism?

17. Consider the operation P = (A×B)+(C×D) where P, A, B, C, and D are memory operands. This can be performed by the following sequence:

$$R_1 \Leftarrow A$$
$$R_2 \Leftarrow (R_1) \times (B)$$
$$R_3 \Leftarrow (C)$$

$$R_4 \Leftarrow (R_3)\times(D)$$
$$P \Leftarrow (R_4)+(R_2)$$

Show the data flow graph for these operations.

18. Consider the following statements. Specify the dependencies between the statements and draw the dependency graph.

```
A = B + C
DO       5    I = 1, N ,1
   D(I) = A * E(I)
   S = E(I) * 5
   T = T + S
A = D(N) - 7
```

19. The following program indicates that 24 instructions are to be carried out (8 division, 8 multiplication, and 8 addition):

```
Input   D, E, F
For     I from 1  to  8  do
   Begin
      A[I]= D[I] + E[I]
      B[I]= A[I] * F[I]
      C[I]= B[I] + C[I] -1
   End
Output    A, B, C
```

   a. Show the data flow graph of the program.
   b. Assume that each add, multiply, and divide step requires 1, 2, and 3 cycles to complete, respectively. Show the sequential execution of the 24 instructions on a control flow uniprocessor and determine the number of cycles to complete.
   c. Assume a 4-processor data flow computer. Show the data-driven execution of the 24 instructions and determine the number of cycles to complete.

20. The current Thinking Machines C* compiler demands that the size of each dimension of a shape be a power of 2. Suppose you want to compute the integral using exactly 100,000 rectangles. Modify the program PI presented in this chapter to effect this change.

REFERENCE-NEEDED EXERCISES

To answer the following exercises, you might need to consult the references: Almasi and Gottlieb, 1994; Moldovan, 1993; Quinn, 1994; Roosta, 2000; Shiva, 1996.

1. Write a DataParallel C program for the implementation of *Gaussian* elimination.
2. Write a DataParallel C program for the implementation of *Gauss-Jordan* elimination.
3. Write a parallel version of the *shortest-path* problem using the thread.

4. Write a *matrix multiplication* program using microthreads.

5. Write a parallel program to find the minimum-spanning tree of a graph using:
   a. Prim's algorithm
   b. Kruskal's algorithm

6. How are MIMD computers different from computer networks?

7. How many cycles are needed to multiply two 100×100 matrices on a 100×100 SIMD array processor? What if the system is bigger, say 1000×1000 processor.

8. Show how a simple systolic array could calculate the product of two matrices:

$$A = \begin{pmatrix} x_1 & x_2 \\ x_3 & x_4 \end{pmatrix} \quad \text{and} \quad B = \begin{pmatrix} y_1 & y_2 \\ y_3 & y_4 \end{pmatrix}.$$

9. Write a parallel program using threads and semaphore variables to implement the Bridge-Passing problem: There is a bridge that connects two cities. People on both the east side and the west side of the bridge are waiting to cross the bridge to travel to the other side. The only restriction is that only one person can cross the bridge at any time because of the possibility of collusion.

10. Write a parallel program to implement the Dining Philosophers Problem: There are five philosophers sitting around a table that are involved in two activities, **thinking** and **eating.** There is a dish of food on the table and one plate for each philosopher. Two forks are needed for anyone to eat the food. Write a parallel program using the threads and semaphore variables to synchronize the philosophers with no interaction to each other's activity.

16 Additional Programming Methods

I n control flow computing—as in other types of common computing—the order in which the programmer textually composes the statements dictates the execution sequence of the program's statements. In other words, the instructions drive the program's execution. An alternative method of selecting statements for execution is to regard a statement as being ready for execution if the data that it requires are available. Hence, the sequence in which the statements are textually composed is unlikely to be the order in which they are carried out. In addition, if the data are available for more than one statement then these statements can be run in parallel. This is referred to as data flow computing. In general, the data flow from one instruction to another and the order in which the instructions are carried out does not depend on the location of the instructions in memory. In Section 16.1, we explore the fundamental concepts of data flow computing, and in Section 16.2, we illustrate the application of this concept in the Value-Oriented Algorithmic Language (VAL). VAL is a data flow language designed at MIT for data flow parallel programming. In VAL, statements are identified using expressions and functions to ensure that any concurrency can be identified. Parallelism is introduced by a parallel expression consisting of three parts: a range specification, an environment expansion, and a result accumulation. We describe both static and dynamic data-driven models that more or less assume data flow graphs as their computation model. In this section, we briefly discuss the data flow programming language principles and the essential features of a data flow language. We introduce a matrix multiplication problem to address parallelism in VAL.

The collection of data is referred to as the database. Database systems are designed to manage information, including the definition of structures for the storage of information and the provision of mechanisms for the manipulation of information. A query language is a language in which a user requests information from the database. In Section 16.3, we explore the design principles for database systems, and in Section

16.4, we discuss structured query language (SQL) as one of the best-known database programming languages. SQL is a multipurpose query language and consists of several components: data-definition, interactive data-manipulation, view definition, integrity, and transaction control. The basic structure of a query consists of three primitives: select, from, and where. In addition, we illustrate the basic operations of SQL, including set operations, aggregate functions, modification operations, and joining operations. Although we refer to SQL language as a query language, it contains many other capabilities besides querying a database. It includes features for defining the structure of the data, for modifying data in the database, and for specifying security constraints.

A computer network is a high-speed communication medium connecting many, possibly dissimilar, computers or hosts. A network is a combination of computers and telecommunication hardware and software. The purpose is to provide fast and reliable information exchange among the hosts. In Section 16.5, we explore the fundamental concepts of network programming. Because many network applications run under the UNIX operating system, a separate set of primitives is designed to be used by UNIX systems. In particular, UNIX applications running on different computers connected to a network can communicate using a mechanism called socket programming. Socket programming can be implemented in two domains: *UNIX domain* and *Internet domain*. In this sense, information exchange by sockets can be established on different computers that may use different data representations and architectures. In Section 16.6, we explore network programming with sockets, including stream socket, datagram socket, and raw socket. We use the essence of the client/server communication model as the basic concept of this communication mechanism.

The Internet is a network of networks that connects computers across the world. The Internet arose with the creation of a protocol called Transfer Control Protocol/Internet Protocol (TCP/IP) that connects computer networks. Any computer or network that is connected to the Internet must support TCP/IP. That means the computer must be connected to a device that translates its language into TCP/IP. The TCP service model includes a connection-oriented service and a reliable data transfer service. When an application invokes TCP for its transport protocol, the application receives both of these services from TCP. In Section 16.7, we explore the basic structure of Internet programming. The World Wide Web can be thought of as a very large subset of the Internet that consists of hypertext and hypermedia documents. All hypertext and hypermedia documents are designed in Hypertext Markup Language (HTML). In Section 16.8, we outline the HTML as a language design for Web programming. An HTML document is just a regular text document, except that special elements called *tags* are inserted to indicate information about formatting and positioning of links. We cover the principles of a Web page, including headings, subheadings, banner, text, images, and links. In Section 16.9, we discuss Windows programming, in which the programmer has the ability to create graphical user interface programs. In Section 16.10, we explore Microsoft Visual Basic Version 6 in which programs are created in an Integrated Development Environment (IDE). We introduce the techniques of Visual Basic programming through various steps to create, save, run, and terminate a sample program that displays a text on screen.

▽ 16.1 DATA FLOW PROGRAMMING

A data flow computation can be defined as one in which operations are carried out in an order determined by the data interdependencies and the availability of resources. In essence, a data flow program is one in which the order of operations is determined by the availability of resources and the flow dependencies. In other words, in a data flow program, if the data are available for several instructions, these instructions may be carried out in parallel. As such, the data dependencies must be deducible from the program to determine whether there are any data dependencies among the executable instructions. This concept allows programmers to employ parallelism at the operator level. In fact, all data flow architectures have employed instruction-level parallelism. For an overall introduction to data flow computation without any particular hardware approach, the reader may refer to Sharp (1985, 1987).

Data flow computation systems can be classified as *lazy evaluations* (also known as demand driven) or *greedy evaluations* (also known as data driven). In lazy evaluations, the statement that produces the result of the program is identified and then the values required to calculate that statement are identified. This propagates back through the program until a statement that can be computed is reached, then the answer will be calculated. Greedy evaluation calculates all values as soon as possible. In this approach there is no need to calculate the flow through the program before calculating any values, but a disadvantage of greedy evaluation is that some values that are not required may be calculated. Most data flow languages are based on the single-assignment rule, stated as

A variable may be assigned only once in the area of the program in which it is active.

A program for a data flow computation consists of a symbolic representation of the computations as a network. The computation model is called the *data flow*. In this computation paradigm, computations move forward by nature of the availability of data values instead of the availability of instructions. A data flow computer is programmed by specifying what happens to data and ignores instruction order. To get a feeling for the difference, we can consider the following example. Suppose there is a simple calculation to perform as given by the mathematical equation $X = B^2 - 4 * A * C$, where $*$ is multiplication and $=$ is assumed to be value assignment. Given inputs $A = 1$, $B = -2$, and $C = 1$, the control flow steps for computing X must be decomposed according to the operators involved, in the following operations:

Step	Calculation
1	$A = 1$
2	$B = -2$
3	$C = 1$
4	$T1 = A * C = 1$
5	$T2 = 4 * T1 = 4$
6	$T3 = B \wedge 2 = 4$
7	$X = T3 - T2 = 0$

FIGURE **16.1**   Computation of $X=B^2-4*A*C$: (a) control flow, (b) data flow

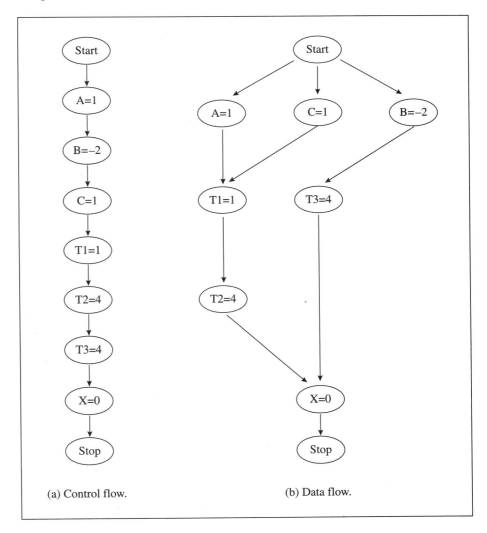

(a) Control flow.   (b) Data flow.

where we have introduced the temporary variables T1, T2 and T3 to hold the intermediate results of the calculations. With regard to the control flow, the instructions are
assumed to be carried out in the order they are written, meaning that each instruction
is performed one at a time in time-step order. Consequently, seven time steps were required, as diagrammed in Figure 16.1a.

    Now assume the same calculations are performed according to the availability of
the data, which is the concept of data flow computation, instead of the order of the instructions. The central control unit is replaced by distributed data-moving mechanism. In this scheme, the same calculation would be done in a different order:

Step	Calculation
1	$A = 1; B = 2; C = 1$
2	$T1 = A * C = 1; T3 = B \wedge 2 = 4$
3	$T2 = 4 * T1 = 4$
4	$X = T3 - T2 = 0$

The graph representing this sequence of calculation is shown in Figure 16.1(b). The arrows show data flow from one operation to the next.

The rationale behind this approach is that in a data flow programming model a copy of each result produced by an entity is passed to each entity wishing to consume that value. Entities are carried out as soon as all the values required are available, or in the case of lazy evaluation, only when the value they produce is needed. There is no concept of sharing of data. Here, the nodes (circles) represent operators and arcs represent paths that carry either data or control values between them. Generally speaking, there is no concept of control flow, and the flow of execution can be determined by the availability of the data. The important point of this example is that the two forms of calculation yield the same result. The only difference between these two forms is the underlying model used to represent computations. Control flow and data flow are alternate computational models that yield identical results. This is called the *duality principle of computation*. If this principle can be applied to a complete program, then the program can be carried out in parallel using a parallel architecture, meaning the availability of data determines the sequence of the execution. This duality between the control flow and data flow is the basis upon which it is possible to translate a control flow program into a data flow equivalent, and conversely. For example, Summer Allen and Arthur Oldehoeft (Allen & Oldehoeft, 1980) developed algorithms for converting control flow programs to equivalent data flow programs. It is also possible to program in a control flow language and let the compiler convert the serial program into an equivalent parallel data flow program; however, this is not always desirable because it may turn out that algorithms might perform better than the generated parallel programs do.

16.1.1 Design Principles of Data Flow Programming

To represent a data flow program, a graph called a *data flow graph* is used that identifies the data dependencies between individual instructions. The data flow graph represents the steps of a program and serves as an interface between architecture and programming language. The nodes in the data flow graph are called *actors*. They represent the operators and are connected by input and output arcs that carry tokens containing control values. In other words, the actor can be represented as an activity template as shown in Figure 16.2. The actor consists of fields for operation type, for storage of input tokens, and for destination addresses.

A data flow notation requires five primitives, as illustrated in Figure 16.3, in which execution is expressed in terms of node firing when sufficient inputs are present. In the represented primitives, data items are viewed as tokens flowing along the edges connecting the nodes. A node fires the computation by taking the tokens on its input edges and placing the appropriate tokens on its output edges.

FIGURE **16.2**   **An activity template**

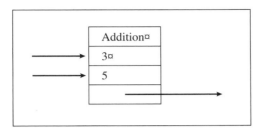

FIGURE **16.3**   **Primitives of data flow notations: (a) Primitive function, (b) Gate node (input is passed only if control matches predicate P), (c) Constant generator, (d) Non-deterministic Merge node (first input that arrives is passed on), (e) Copy node**

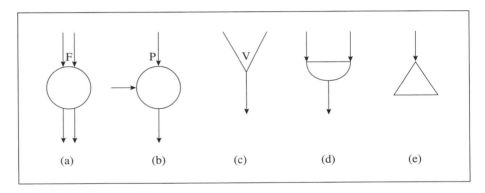

Some of the essential features associated with data flow languages are the following:

▶ The language follows the *single-assignment* rule, meaning that a variable is assigned a value by one statement only. The assignment can be viewed as the effect of providing a value and binding that value to the variable name appearing on the left side. In general, the same *variable name* cannot be used more than once on the left side of any statement. A new name is given for any redefined variable and all subsequent references are changed to the new name. For example,

```
A : = B + C;
A : = A * D
```

should be converted into

```
E : = B + C;
A : = E * D
```

Thus, statement A : = A + 1 will not be coded. Structured data types such as arrays and records are affected by the single-assignment rule and must be identified as single values. There is no unique way of performing this variable name change.

▶ The scope in which a variable is used is restricted. This is called the *locality of effect*, which ensures that the instruction variables are not involved in data dependencies. The locality of effect occurs when data are produced by one node and used by some other nodes without influencing the computation performed by another node. Because of this issue, temporary names may be used in different sections associated with the variables.

▶ There should be no *global data space* of values or use of shared-memory locations.

▶ The language must be *applicative* oriented, meaning that values operate to produce more values. The values are used for other operations until the given operation is completed.

▶ The language is not suited to run *loops*, and usually only one type of iterative structure is allowed.

▶ The data flow language should be free of *side effects*. For example, if a procedure Q, which is called by another procedure P, changes some of the values of the variables of procedure P, this is called a side effect. A side effect can occur when a procedure or function changes the value of the variables in an enclosing subprogram.

▶ The data flow language should be free of *aliasing*, which means that different formal parameters of a function refer to the same actual parameter whenever the function is activated. For example, if a procedure call ADD(A, A) indicates that the value of both parameters is A, then some of the statements could be simultaneously changing the same variable, which leads to inconsistencies.

Node Firing Methods

Node firing means that all input values (tokens) of the node are read, internal computation takes place, and produced data become available on some or all of the subsequent nodes through some of the output arcs. The node then remains idle until data again become available on its input arcs. Tokens are placed on and removed from the arcs according to certain firing rules.

Two node-firing schemes are employed in data flow computations: *static* and *dynamic* data firing. In the static data firing system, a node fires only when each of its input arcs has a token and its output arcs are empty. Thus, a message indicating that a subsequent node has consumed its input token is required before the node fires. In the dynamic data firing system, a node fires when all its inputs have tokens and the absence of tokens on its output arcs is not required. This can lead to the possibility of multiple tokens on an arc. A tagging system associated with this system specifies tokens with the appropriate data set. The tag carries information about when and how a token was generated and which data set it belongs to. The effect of node firing corresponds to removing the data from the input arcs, performing the defined computation, and placing the result on the output arcs to the receiving or destination nodes. A pictorial view of node firing is given in Figure 16.4.

FIGURE **16.4**   Node firing: (a) Before firing and (b) after firing

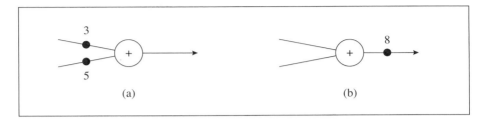

Logically, we may view each node of a data flow graph as a node data structure in memory. The data flow processor has a pool of processing elements (PE) that process instructions. Each instruction represents a specific instance of a firable node, which consists of the operation, its arguments, and its destination addresses. The processor builds instructions in the node data structure. When a PE has finished carrying out an instruction, it generates a result packet, which includes the result token, its destination address, and any tags. The PE sends the result packet to the memory update system, which consists of an arbitrary number of memory update units, which operate, in parallel. The memory update system sends the result packet to the appropriate unit for processing. The memory update unit stores the result tokens in the destination locations and checks to see that the token corresponds to the argument in the node data structure. If so, the memory update unit notifies the fetch system and provides the address of the node data structure. The entire process continues until there is no firable instruction.

All data flow languages are functional or applicative languages in nature. A number of data flow languages have been proposed, including LUCID, proposed by Ed Ashcroft and Bill Wadge (1977), Irvine (ID) developed at the University of California-Irvine by Arvind, Gostelow, and Plouffe (1978), VAL developed at MIT by Ackerman and Dennis (1979), HASAL by John Sharp (1985), and Lapse by John Glauert (1978). In the following section, VAL is presented as an example of the data flow programming languages.

◤ 16.2 DATA FLOW PROGRAMMING WITH VAL

Ackerman and Dennis's objective in developing VAL was to provide a notation to illustrate an algorithm, which can be carried out in parallel on a parallel architecture. The language does not specify which parts of a program can be executed in parallel; rather, the parallel features are implicit. Execution of the statements is determined when the graph representation of a program is constructed. In addition, from the data flow graph of the program it is possible to determine which statements can be run in parallel.

A programmer must write expressions and functions, which take input values and produce a result without side effects. This means that when all the input values are available, an expression or function can be carried out and cannot affect how any other expression or function is carried out. In general, all expressions or functions that are ready to run may be performed in parallel. VAL works on values, which are assigned to variable names, and they cannot be changed within the function or block in which they are defined. In this language, an array or record is not a collection of individual values and cannot be changed once the array is assigned a value. In other words, arrays and records are considered to be equivalent to single scalar values.

16.2.1 Data Types

The supporting data types are integer, real, character, and Boolean. When each variable is given an initial value, the declaration is as follows:

```
A : REAL : = 0;
B : INTEGER : = 0;
C : CHARACTER : = 'x';
D : BOOLEAN : = TRUE;
```

The values that a BOOLEAN data type can have are TRUE and FALSE, known as the proper elements, and Undef[BOOLEAN] and Miss_elt[BOOLEAN], known as the error elements. These correspond to the situation in which the Boolean variable is undefined and the element value is missing. The Boolean operations include *and, or, not, equal* and *not equal,* with tests for *undef* and *miss_elt.* The defined data structures are arrays and records when the operations are chosen to support identification of concurrency for execution on a parallel processor.

Compound types can be constructed in three ways using the *array, record,* and *oneof* definitions. The *oneof* corresponds to a union definition. The syntax consists of a type constructor giving the name of the compound type followed by the additional information within brackets. For example, an array type definition is in the form

```
type      XTYPE = array[INTEGER];
```

where the actual bounds of the array are associated with each individual array when it is used in the program execution. Because no bound information is associated with the type, arrays of different sizes can be passed to a single procedure for execution. A two-dimensional array can be defined as

```
type    XTYPE = array[array[INTEGER]];
```

where access to the elements is by using an INTEGER index as the subscript. For example:

```
[1 : Expression1; 2 : Expression2];
```

creates an array with two elements such that the values associated with Expression1 and Expression2 become the values for the corresponding array elements and both elements can be specified and evaluated simultaneously. In general, it is possible to provide a long list of ordered pairs (name and value) that can be carried out in parallel.

Consequently, if array *list* has four elements with the associated values {2,5,7,9} then the expression list[3:4] changes *list* to {2,5,4,9}, meaning that the value associated with element 3 is changed to 4. Similarly, list[6:3] provides element 5 the value miss_elt and element 6 the value 3. A record can be constructed in a fashion similar to an array. For example, a record type is defined as

```
type    XRECORD = record[FIELDS];
```

where FIELDS represents the identifiers and type associated with each component. For example,

```
record[A, B: Integer; C: Real; D: Character; E: Boolean];
```

represents a record of four fields A, B, C, and D with associated data types, and

```
record[A:100; B:200; C; 12.5; D:'x'; E:FALSE];
```

establishes values of the five fields A, B, C, D, and E, for which the values can be computed and assigned simultaneously. Individual fields of a record may be accessed using the usual dot notation. VAL provides strong structured data type checking in which two data types are equivalent to each other if they have identical structures.

16.2.2   Expressions and Functions

In VAL, the statements are constructed using expressions and functions to ensure that no side effects will occur and that any concurrency can be identified. For example:

```
function    Class    (Para : Boolean returns Integer);
            {Body of the Function}
endfun
```

defines a function named Class, which returns an integer and has a single parameter Para of type Boolean. The scope of parameter is the entire function definition, and the body of the function produces the returning result. In the statements of the body, only the formal parameters (Para) and locally defined variables may be accessed, meaning that there is no access to global variables. This restriction ensures that no side effects will occur. In general, the environment defined by a function is available only during the execution of the function and not when the function returns a result. The *let-in* structure can be used to introduce one or more value identifiers, define their values, and evaluate an expression. For example,

```
let    X : Integer; Y : Integer;
       X : = A;
       Y : = X + 20;
in
       X * Y;
endlet
```

where A is accepted from the outside scope of this structure. In this way, the environment of an expression can be expanded and possible concurrency in the data constructions or the evaluation of the expression can be introduced. Also, a value identifier may not be used until after it is defined and may be defined only once in a block. In contrast to conventional programming languages, a VAL function can return more than one value as a result of its execution. This can be achieved by writing a list of expressions separated from each other by commas. This is illustrated in the following function in which two expression values (X and Y) are returned from the function:

```
function   Calc(A,B,C : Integer returns Integer Integer)
           let
               X : Integer : = (A + B + C);
               Y : Integer : = (A * B * C);
           in
               X , Y;
       endlet
   endfun
```

16.2.3 Parallel Expressions

Parallelism is represented in VAL by a parallel expression consisting of three parts:

► **A range specification,** which identifies which range of values in the named value will be used.

► **An environment expansion,** which identifies the operating environment of the expression such as the binding of the variable names.

► **A result accumulation,** which identifies how the results of the body of the expression will be combined and returned.

The range specification is identified by a `forall` structure, which defines the scope of the parallelism. The parallel structure `forall` is expressed as the following:

```
forall_expression        :: =
        forall   name   in      [expression]
{, name in [expression] } [declaration-definition part]
        forall-body-part      {forall-body-part}
        endall
        forall-body-part    :: =
          construct expression | eval forall-op expression
        forall-op           :: =
              PLUS | TIMES | MIN | MAX | OR | AND
```

For example, in

```
forall   Calc   in   [1,5]
```

`Calc` has the range 1 to 5 as the index value with the defined data type as integer. The body of the structure contains an environment expansion, which is executed once for each element in the `forall` range. For example,

```
forall   Calc   in      [1,5]
```

indicates that five parallel environments can be carried out, and the results must be accumulated into one single block (an array) or one single element (a value). For example,

```
forall   Calc   in      [1,5]
      construct   Calc * Calc
   endall
```

creates an array of 5 elements with the values 1, 4, 9, 16, and 25. And

```
forall   Calc   in       [1,5]
      eval Plus    Calc * Calc
   endall
```

returns the value 55 associated with 1+4+9+16+25. The if-then-else structure enables selection of expression results according to a test value with the following syntax:

```
condition   :: =    if       expression     then    expression
     {else   if      expression      then    expression}
          else      expression
          endif
   endif
```

where all values passed to the construct, and there are no value identifiers. The *for-iter* structure is used as a loop structure, which cannot be performed in parallel because of data dependency between produced values in different iterations. That is, values produced in one iteration must be used in the next. For example, the following code computes the factorial of N, when the initialization part is enclosed between the reserved words *for* and *do* with the initial values.

```
for I : Integer : = 1;
      P : Integer : = N;
   do
      if   P > 1       then
         iter
            I : = I * P;   P : = P —1;
         enditer
      else
         I
      endif
endfor
```

The loop body, which appears between *do* and *endfor,* is repeatedly evaluated until a final result can be computed. Within such a construct (sequential in nature), it is valid to redefine the value of a variable, as in the statement I:=I*P, where the old value of I has to be multiplied by P to produce the new value of I.

Example: Matrix Multiplication

We consider the multiplication of two matrices to demonstrate the parallelism in the VAL data flow programming language. Two input arrays that correspond to a row and a column of two input matrices are declared as parameters to a function ARRAYMULT as follows:

```
function   ARRAYMULT  (A : array [array[Integer]],
                       B : array [array[Integer]],
                       N : Integer
                       returns array[array[Integer]])
```

where N is the size of the array and the result is the product of two arrays A and B. The solution can be formed by finding the product of a row of A and a column of B and summing the values. This can be expressed by a *forall* structure using the *eval* construct by introducing a function INNERPROD. Thus, a solution can be expressed as the following program:

```
function   ARRAYMULT   (A : array [array[Integer]],
                        B : array [array[Integer]],
                        N : Integer
                        returns array[array[Integer]])
           forall  I in [1, N]
                 construct
                 forall   J   in   [1,N]
                     construct
                     INNERPROD(A[I], B[I], N)
                 endall
           endall
endfun


function   INNERPROD  (X : array [Integer], Y : array [Integer],
                       N : Integer  Returns  Integer)
           forall I in [1,N]
                   eval
                   plus X[I] * Y[I]
           endall
endfun
```

☛ 16.3 DATABASE PROGRAMMING

The collection of data, usually referred to as the *database,* contains information about one particular application. Database systems are designed to manage information, including the definition of structures for storing information and providing mechanisms for manipulating information. Database systems are becoming more and more popular because of their increasingly user-friendly interface via high-level query languages. These languages are typically of a level higher than that of a standard programming language. One of the best-known database languages is SQL. The original version of SQL was developed at IBM's San Jose Research Laboratory. This language, originally called Sequel, was implemented as part of the System R project in the early 1970s. The Sequel language has evolved since then, and its name has changed to SQL. In 1986, the American National Standards Institute (ANSI) and the International Standards Organization (ISO) published an SQL standard, called SQL-86. IBM published its own corporate SQL standard, the Systems Application Architecture Database Interface (SAA-SQL) in 1987. An extended standard for SQL, called SQL-89 was published in 1989. The current version of the ANSI/ISO SQL standard is the SQL-92 standard. Query by example (QBE) is the name of both a data-manipulation language and the database system that included this language. The QBE database system was developed at IBM's Watson Research Center in the early 1970s. Today, some database systems for personal computers support QBE language. Quel is another query language adopted by Ingres database system that was developed at the University of California, Berkeley. The structure of Quel is based on the tuple relational calculus. Datalog is a nonprocedural query language that is based on the logic programming language, Prolog. In this query language, user describes the information desired without giving a specific procedure for obtaining that information. The system of Datalog resembles that of Prolog.

16.3.1   Design Principles of Database Systems

The important step in building an information system is to produce a specification of its information content. Database systems provide a means for transforming such specifications into appropriate forms that can maintain the information content. A DataBase Management System (DBMS) is a combination of software and data:

▶ The *physical database,* which is a collection of data.

▶ The *schema,* which is a specification of the information.

▶ The *database engine,* which is software that supports access to and modification of the data.

▶ The *data definition and manipulation languages,* which are programming languages that support schema definition and database access.

Database systems present different views to different users. These views are often divided into three levels: the *external level,* the *logical level,* and the *internal level* as illustrated in Figure 16.5. Database users interact at the external level. They are presented with special views that are tailored to their specific needs. General users get one external view of the system.

A corollary immediately follows that dividing the database system environment into these levels allows both developers and users to work within their own levels without having to know the details of the other levels, and without having to respond to changes in the other levels.

The *relational database model* is used to define logical schema for database systems. This provides a method for defining a database structure so that it can be directly implemented in a relational database system. The relational model provides the relation as the single data structure for representing entities. The relational database model offers two great advantages:

▶ It is supported by algebra operations.

▶ It is directly representable by relational database systems.

A Relational DataBase Management System (RDBMS) is a DBMS that incorporates the relational model: All data are stored in *tables* and each piece of data is assigned a unique name. A row in a table represents a *relationship* among a set of values. Because a table is a collection of such relationships, there is a close correspondence between the concept of table and the mathematical concept of relation. For example, consider the *account* table shown in Table 16.1 with three column headers: *branch-name, account-number,* and *balance.* We refer to these headers as *attributes,* in which

FIGURE **16.5**   The three levels of a database system

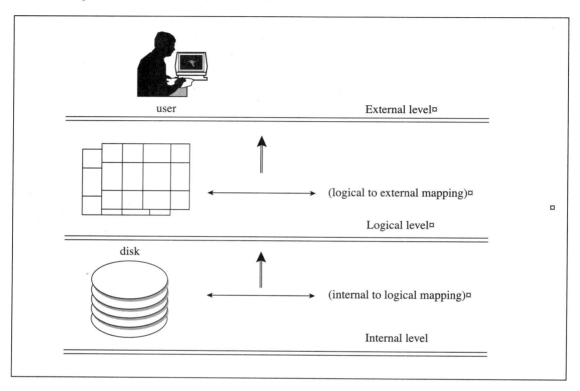

TABLE **16.1**   The *account* relation

branch-name	account-number	balance
Downtown	A-101	3500
Greenville	A-102	2700
Spartanburg	A-104	4400
Greer	A-305	5350
Clemson	A-222	3900
Spartanburg	A-114	6150

there is a set of permitted values, called the *domain* associated with that attribute. For example, for the attribute *branch-name*, the domain is the set of all branch names.

The domains that are available in the relational model are restricted to indivisible, or atomic values, meaning that each domain must be based on some type that cannot be divided into simpler values. Numbers, strings, and dates are considered atomic.

Because tables are essentially relations, we will use the mathematical terms *relation* and *tuple* in place of the terms *table* and *rows*. Thus, in the account relation, there are six tuples. In general, when we talk about a database, we must differentiate between the *database schema,* or the logical design of the database, and a *database instance,* which is a snapshot of the data in the database at a given instant in time. The concept of a *relation schema* corresponds to the programming language notion of *type definition,* and the concept of a *relation* corresponds to the programming language notion of a *variable.* In this sense, we adopt the convention of using lowercase names for relations, and names beginning with an uppercase letter for relation schema. Following this, we can use *Account-schema* to denote the relation schema for relation *account.* Thus,

```
Account-schema(branch-name, account-number, balance).
```

In this example, we denote that `account` is a relation on `Account-schema` by

```
account(Account-schema).
```

In general, the logical level (see Figure 16.5) includes the logical schema, which sees the database as a collection of tables. Changes at the logical level can be made without having any effect on the external level. These changes must be performed by changes in the logical-to-external mappings so that the external views remain unchanged. The internal level sees the database as a collection of files and software. The internal-to-logical mapping supports the logical view of the data. Operations performed at the logical level are translated into modifications of the contents and structure of the files. We include two additional relations to describe data about loans maintained in the various branches in the bank:

```
Loan-schema(branch-name, loan-number, amount)
Borrower-schema(customer-name, loan-number)
```

The sample relations *loan* and *borrower* are shown in Table 16.2 and Table 16.3, respectively.

A *query* is presented to a database as a logical statement requesting the retrieval of information. Often, the query puts together information from multiple database tables. The portion of the database system that involves information retrieval is called a *query language,* in which a user requests information from the database. A query language is typically of a level higher than that of a standard programming language. Query languages can be categorized as being either procedural or nonprocedural. The tuple relational calculus and the domain relational calculus are nonprocedural languages that represent the basic power required in a relational query language. In a nonprocedural language, the user describes the information desired without giving a specific procedure for obtaining that information. The relational algebra is a procedural language that is equivalent in power to relational calculus. In a procedural language, the user instructs the system to perform a sequence of operations on the

TABLE **16.2**	The *loan* relation	
branch-name	loan-number	amount
Downtown	A-12	500
Greenville	A-13	700
Spartanburg	A-15	400
Greer	A-30	350
Clemson	A-22	900
Spartanburg	A-11	150

TABLE **16.3**	The *borrower* relation
customer-name	loan-number
Mary	A-12
Mahsa	A-13
Jones	A-15
Smith	A-30
Nasim	A-22
Mary	A-11

database to compute the desired result. Most relational-database systems offer a query language that includes elements of both the procedural and the nonprocedural approaches. In addition, a complete database manipulation language includes not only a query language but also a language for database modification. Such languages include commands to insert and delete tuples, as well as commands to modify parts of existing tuples. In this chapter, we examine a query language, which is a combination of procedural and nonprocedural approaches and many other capabilities besides querying a database. The storage structure and access methods used by the database system are specified by a set of definitions in a special form called *data storage and definition language*. The result of compiling these definitions is a set of instructions to specify the implementation details of the database schemas.

◆ 16.4 DATABASE PROGRAMMING WITH SQL

SQL is a multipurpose programming language and consists of several components:

► **Data-Definition Language (DDL):** The SQL DDL provides commands for defining relation schemas, deleting relations, creating indices, and modifying relation schemes. The result of compiling DDL statements is a set of tables that is stored in a special file called *data dictionary* or *data directory*.

► **Interactive Data-Manipulation Language (DML):** The SQL DML includes a query language based on both the relational algebra and the tuple relational calculus. It includes commands to insert tuples into, delete tuples from, and modify tuples in the database. The DML is a language that enables users to access or manipulate data as organized by the appropriate data model.

► **Embedded DML:** The embedded form of SQL is designed for use within general-purpose programming languages, such as COBOL, Pascal, Fortran, and C.

► **View definition:** The SQL DDL includes commands for defining views.

▶ **Authorization:** The SQL DDL includes commands for specifying access rights to relations and views.

▶ **Integrity:** The SQL DDL includes commands for specifying integrity constraints that the data stored in the database must satisfy. Updates that violate integrity constraints are not allowed.

▶ **Transaction control:** The SQL includes commands for specifying the beginning and ending of transactions. Several implementations also allow explicit locking of data for concurrency control.

It is not our intention to provide a complete users' guide for SQL. Because individual implementations of SQL differ in details, or may support only a subset of the full language, we concentrate on DDL and DML as the fundamental constructs and concepts of SQL. The basic structure of an SQL DDL expression consists of three primitives:

▶ The *select* primitive corresponds to the projection operation of the relational algebra, and is used to list the attributes desired in the result of a query.

▶ The *from* primitive corresponds to the Cartesian-product operation of the relational algebra, and lists the relations to be scanned in the evaluation of the expression.

▶ The *where* primitive corresponds to the selection predicate of the relational algebra and consists of a predicate involving attributes of the relations that appear in the *from* primitive.

A typical SQL query has the general form:

```
select   A₁, A₂, . . . , Aₙ
from     r₁, r₂, . . . , rₘ
where    P
```

Each A_i represents an attribute, each r_i represents a relation, and P represents a predicate. If the *where* primitive is omitted, then predicate P is true. In practice, the result of an SQL query is a relation. For example, a query such as "Find the names of all branches in the loan relation?" expressed in

```
Select   branch-name
From     loan
```

results in a relation consisting of a single attribute with the heading branch-name. The preceding query will list each branch-name once for every tuple (row) that appears in the *loan* relation. SQL allows us to use the keyword *all* after *select* to specify explicitly that duplicates are not removed. In addition, to ensure the elimination of duplicates in the results, SQL allows us to use the keyword *distinct* after *select*. To illustrate the use of *where* in SQL, consider the query, "Find all loan numbers for loans made at Spartanburg branch with loan amounts greater that $200" expressed in the following:

```
select loan-number
from   loan
where  branch-name = "Spartanburg" and amount  >  200
```

The result is a relation consisting of a single attribute with the heading `loan-number` satisfying the defined condition. SQL uses the logical connectives *and, or,* and *not*. The operands of the logical connectives can be expressions involving the comparison operators <, <=, >, >=, =, and < >. In addition, SQL allows us to use the *between* operator to specify that a value be less than or equal to some value and greater than or equal to some other value. For example, to express the loan numbers of the loans with amount between $1500 and $2500, we can issue a query like the following:

```
select loan-number
from    loan
where   amount  between 1500  and  2500
```

To illustrate the use of *from* in SQL, consider the query, "For all customers who have a loan from the bank, find their names and loan number," as expressed in the following:

```
select   distinct  borrower.customer-name,  borrower.loan-number
from      borrower, loan
where     borrower.loan-number = loan.loan-number
```

The result is a relation consisting of two attributes with the headings `customer-name` and `loan-number`. SQL uses the notation *relation-name.attribute-name* to avoid ambiguity in cases where an attribute appears in the schema of more than one relation.

16.4.1 Set Operations

The SQL operations *union, intersect,* and *except* operate on relations and correspond to the relational-algebra operations ∪, ∩, and —. To explain the operations, we include an additional relation to describe the association between customers and accounts. The relation schema to describe this association is the following:

```
Depositor-schema(customer-name, account-number)
```

A sample relation depositor (`Depositor-schema`) is shown in Table 16.4.

To find all customers having a loan, an account, *or* both at the bank, we write a query including *union:*

```
(select   customer-name
from      depositor)
union
(select   customer-name
from      borrower)
```

Because the *union* operation eliminates duplicates, we can use *union all* to retain all duplicates:

```
(select   customer-name
from      depositor)
union     all
(select   customer-name
from      borrower)
```

TABLE **16.4**	The *depositor* relation	
	customer-name	**account-number**
	Mary	A-128
	Mahsa	A-136
	Jones	A-157
	Smith	A-304
	Nasim	A-223
	Russel	A-119

To find all customers who have both a loan *and* an account at the bank, we write a query including *intersect:*

```
(select    distinct   customer-name
from       depositor)
intersect
(select    distinct   customer-name
from       borrower)
```

Because the *intersect* operation eliminates duplicates, we can use *intersect all* to retain all duplicates:

```
(select    customer-name
from       depositor)
intersect  all
(select    customer-name
from       borrower)
```

To find all customers who have an account but *no* loan at the bank, we write a query including *except:*

```
(select    distinct   customer-name
from       depositor)
except
(select    distinct   customer-name
from       borrower)
```

Similarly, if we want to retain all duplicates, we must write *except all* instead of *except.*

16.4.2   Aggregate Functions

Aggregate function is a function that takes a collection of values as input and returns a single value as output. SQL supports five aggregate functions:

▶   Average (*avg*): The input must be a collection of numbers.

► Maximum (*max*): It can operate on collections of numeric and nonnumeric data types.

► Minimum (*min*): It can operate on collections of numeric and nonnumeric data types.

► Total (*sum*): The input must be a collection of numbers.

► Count (*count*): It can operate on collections of numeric and nonnumeric data types.

As an illustration, consider the query, "Find the average account balance at the Spartanburg branch," as expressed in the following:

```
select    avg (balance)
from      account
where     branch-name = "Spartanburg"
```

The result of this query is a relation with a single attribute, consisting of a single row with a numerical value corresponding to the average balance at the `Spartanburg` branch. We use the aggregate function *count* to count the number of tuples in a relation. For example, to find the number of tuples in the loan relation, we issue the query:

```
select    count(*)
from      loan
```

SQL does not allow the use of distinct with `count(*)`.

16.4.3 Modification Operations

SQL supports three modification requests:

► Remove (*delete*): To remove information from the relation.

► Add (*insert*): To add information to the relation.

► Change (*update*): To change information into the relation.

For example, *delete* can be used to remove tuples and is expressed in the same way as a query. In SQL, a deletion can be issued as

```
delete    from relation
where     predicate
```

where `predicate` represents a predicate and `relation` representats a relation. We can delete one tuple, but we cannot delete values from some particular attributes. The *delete* primitive first finds all tuples in *relation* for which *predicate* is true, and then deletes them from *relation*. For example, the request

```
delete    from depositor
where     customer-name = "Mary"
```

deletes all of `Mary`'s account records. Similarly, the request

```
delete    from loan
where     amount   between   300   and   500
```

deletes all loans with loan amounts between $300 and $500. To insert data into a relation, we either specify a tuple to be inserted or we write a query whose result is a set of tuples to be inserted. For example, assume we wish to request that there is an account A-425 at the Columbia branch, which has a balance of $7800. The request can be issued as

```
insert   into   account
values   ("Columbia", "A-425", 7800)
```

where the values are specified in the order that the corresponding attributes provides in the relation schema. Also, SQL allows the attributes to be specified as part of the insert statement. For example, the following insert statement is identical to the preceding one:

```
insert   into   account (branch-name, account-number, balance)
values   ("Columbia", "A-425", 7800)
```

Sometimes we want to insert tuples based on the result of a query. Suppose that we want to provide a gift for all loan customers of the Spartanburg branch: a new $200 savings account for each loan account they have. In this query:

```
insert   into   account
         select branch-name, loan-number, 200
         from   loan
where    branch-name = "Spartanburg"
```

the select statement is evaluated first, giving a set of tuples to be inserted into the account relation. More generally, we might want to change a value in a tuple without changing all values in the tuple. For this purpose, *update* statement can be used. For example, suppose that all balances in account relation are to be increased by 5 percent. The following query:

```
update   account
set      balance = balance * 1.05
```

is applied once to each tuple in account relation. Furthermore, suppose that accounts with balances greater than $1000 receive 5 percent interest. We write an update statement, such as the following:

```
update   account
set      balance = balance * 1.05
where    balance  >  1000
```

16.4.4   Joining Operations

SQL provides various primitives for joining relations. These operations are typically used as subquery expressions in the *from* operations. We illustrate the *join* operations using the following relations *loan* and *borrower* represented in Table 16.5(a) and (b).

For example, using the relations *loan* and *borrower*, Table 16.6 shows the result of the following *join* operation.

```
loan   inner   join   borrower   on   loan.loan-number = borrower.loan-number
```

TABLE **16.5a**	The *loan* relations	
branch-name	**loan-number**	**amount**
Downtown	A-12	500
Greenville	A-13	700
Spartanburg	A-15	400

TABLE **16.5b**	The *borrower* relations
customer-name	**loan-number**
Mary	A-12
Mahsa	A-13
Nasim	A-16

TABLE **16.6**   Result relation of *inner join* operation

branch-name	loan-number	amount	customer-name	loan-number
Downtown	A-12	500	Mary	A-12
Greenville	A-13	700	Mahsa	A-13

In this example, the expression computes the *join* of the *loan* and the *borrower* relations, with the *join* condition being `loan.loan-number = borrower.loan-number`. We might need to rename the result relation of a join and the attributes of the result relation using an *as* primitive, as illustrated here:

```
loan  inner  join  borrower  on  loan.loan-number = borrower.loan-number
  as loanborrower(nbranch, nloan-number, namount, ncustomer, nloan-number)
```

The next join operation is *left outer join*, which is based on the result of the *inner join*. For example, in this query,

```
loan  left  outer  join  borrower  on  loan.loan-number = borrower.loan-number
```

for every tuple t in the first relation (`loan`) that did not match any tuple in the second relation (`borrower`), a tuple r is added to the result relation. The attributes of the tuple r that are derived from the first relation are filled with the values from tuple t, and the remaining attributes of r are filled with *null* values. The result relation is shown in Table 16.7.

The last join operation is *natural join*, in which the resulting relation is similar to the result of the *inner join*, except that the common attribute appears only once. For example, this query,

```
loan  natural  inner  join  borrower
```

results in the natural join of the two relations. Because the only attribute name common to `loan` and `borrower` is *loan-number*, it appears only once in the resulting relation as shown in Table 16.8.

TABLE **16.7**	Result relation of *left outer join* operation				
	branch-name	**loan-number**	**amount**	**customer-name**	**loan-number**
	Downtown	A-12	500	Mary	A-12
	Greenville	A-13	700	Mahsa	A-13
	Spartanburg	A-15	400	Null	null

TABLE **16.8**	Result relation of *natural join* operation			
	branch-name	**loan-number**	**amount**	**customer-name**
	Downtown	A-12	500	Mary
	Greenville	A-13	700	Mahsa

◤ 16.5 NETWORK PROGRAMMING

A computer network is a high-speed communication medium connecting many, possibly dissimilar, computers or hosts. A network is a combination of computers and telecommunication hardware and software. The purpose is to provide fast and reliable information exchange among the hosts. Many network applications run under the UNIX operating system, and a separate set of primitives is designed to be used by UNIX systems. Through these primitives, UNIX applications running on different computers connected to a network can communicate using a mechanism called *socket programming*. The standard UNIX InterProcess Communication (IPC) mechanism introduced by Berkeley in the 1980s can support this information exchange. The scheme centered on the socket mechanism and supports the Internet protocols as well. Its wide use helped the explosive growth of the Internet. UNIX IPC provides access to a set of communication domains. Two important domains supported by IPC are the following:

▶ The *UNIX domain* for communication within the local UNIX system

▶ The *Internet domain* for communication over the Internet

Information exchange by sockets can be established on different computers that may use different data representations and architectures. For example, a long integer number is 32 bits on some systems but 64 bits on others. Even when data sizes agree, systems still may use either the high or the low byte to store the most significant part of a number. In this heterogeneous environment, data is sent and received at the socket level, as a sequence of bytes. The Internet makes two transport protocols available to applications, namely, Transport Control Protocol (TCP) and User Datagram

Protocol (UDP). When a developer creates a new application for the Internet, one of the first decisions that the developer must make is whether to use UDP or TCP. Each protocol offers a different service model to the invoking applications. In general, the TCP service model provides a connection-oriented service and a reliable data transfer service. TCP does not guarantee a minimum transmission rate. In contrast, UDP is a lightweight transport protocol with a minimal service model. UDP is connectionless, so there is no connection before the two agents start to communicate. On the other hand, UDP does not include a congestion-control mechanism, so a sending agent can pump data into a UDP socket at any rate.

The primary goal of this section is to provide a minimal but very functional client/server networking model. In other words, we investigate how to develop two distinct programs that can talk to each other. The only assumption is that they run on two different UNIX environment systems with Internet access. Furthermore, these programs will run concurrently and asynchronously. To keep this section concise and focused, we will not provide an exhaustive treatment of all socket commands. Anyone interested in a detailed description of sockets, their commands, and various options should consult references such as Comer and Stevens (1996), and Stevens (1993). We will assume basic knowledge of UNIX and C programming language.

16.5.1 Design Principles of Network Systems

The *socket* is a UNIX construct that serves as endpoints of communication within a networking domain. At a superficial level, the socket is similar to UNIX pipes and files. A UNIX application creates a socket when it needs a connection to a network. The application then establishes a connection to a remote application via the socket and communicates with the remote application by reading data from the socket and writing data to the socket. In other words, the socket is an interface mechanism that exchanges data with any other socket within the same domain. Figure 16.6 illustrates the idea—a local program can direct information through a socket into the network where the information can be accessed by a remote program. Then, the remote program can put information into its socket to send back to the local program.

The essence of the client/server model involves two distinct programs, usually running on different machines at different locations. In general, the server provides services and responds to requests coming in from client programs. A typical exchange of information might look like this:

1. User requests information.
2. Client sends request for information to the server on behalf of the user.
3. Server receives request from a client and analyzes it.
4. Server copies the information from its environment (i.e., memory).
5. Server transmits the information back to the client.
6. Client receives the information from the server and makes it accessible to the user.

Thus, one server may provide service to many clients. Roughly speaking, the socket primitives for network connection are listed in Table 16.9. The first four primitives are carried out in that order by servers. The *socket* system call creates a new end

FIGURE **16.6**   **Socket connection to a network**

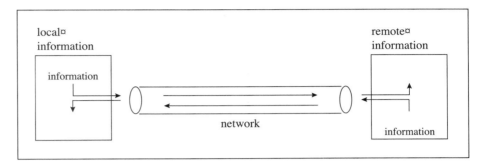

TABLE **16.9**   **Socket primitives for network connection**

Primitive	Meaning
SOCKET	Create a new communication end point
BIND	Attach a local address to a socket
LISTEN	Announce willingness to accept connections; give queue size
ACCEPT	Block the caller until a connection attempt arrives
CONNECT	Actively attempt to establish a connection
SEND	Send some data over the connection
RECEIVE	Receive some data from the connection
CLOSE	Release the connection

point and allocates table space for it within the transport entity. The parameters of the call specify the addressing format to be used, the type of service desired, and the protocol. A successful *socket* call returns an ordinary file descriptor for use in succeeding calls, the same way an *open* call does. Newly created sockets do not have addresses. These are assigned using the *bind* primitive. Once a server has bound an address to a socket, remote clients can connect to it. The reason for not having the *socket* call create an address directly is that some processes keep track of their address, whereas others do not. Next comes the *listen* call, which allocates space to queue incoming calls for when several clients try to connect at the same time. The *listen* call is not a blocking call. To block waiting for an incoming connection, the server carries out an *accept* primitive. Then the server can create a process or thread to handle the connection on the new socket and go back to waiting for the next connection on the original socket. At the client side, a socket must first be created using the *socket* primitive, but *bind* is not required because the address used does not matter to the server. The *connect* primitive blocks the caller and actively starts the connection process. When it completes, the client process is unblocked and the connection is established. Both sides can now use *send* and *receive* primitives to transmit and receive data over the full-duplex connection. Finally, when both sides have carried out a *close* primitive, the connection is released.

◢ 16.6 NETWORK PROGRAMMING WITH SOCKETS

Each socket is assigned a type property. The following types of sockets are generally supported.

▶ **Stream socket:** Supports the bi-directional, reliable, sequenced, and unduplicated flow of data. A stream socket can be connected to another stream socket, and the connected pair forms a two-way pipe mechanism across the network. Each socket in the pair is called the *peer* of the other. Stream sockets in the Internet domain use TCP.

▶ **Datagram socket:** Provides bidirectional flow of data packets called messages. The communication channel is not guaranteed to be reliable or unduplicated. A datagram socket does not have to be connected to a peer. A message is sent to a datagram socket by specifying its address. Datagram sockets in the Internet domain use UDP.

▶ **Raw socket:** Provides access to the underlying communication protocols that support socket abstractions. Raw sockets are not intended for the general users but, rather, for those interested in developing new communication protocols or for gaining access to facilities of an existing protocol. Raw sockets in the Internet domain give direct access to the IP.

The domains and standard socket types are declared in the header file <sys/socket.h>, and constants for sockets are outlined in the Table 16.10.

16.6.1 Creating Sockets

Typically, we create a socket in an appropriate domain and with an appropriate type. The socket system call:

```
#include   <sys/socket.h>
int        socket(int  domain,  int  type,  int  protocol)
```

creates a socket of the indicated `type` in the given `domain`. The socket system call returns a descriptor that references the socket in other socket operations. If the `protocol` is left unspecified (with a 0 value), an appropriate protocol in the domain that supports the requested socket type is selected by the system. For example,

```
s  =  socket(AF_INET,  SOCK_STREAM,  0);
```

creates an Internet stream socket supported by TCP. After socket creation, a name (that is, an address) is assigned to the socket so that other entities can refer to it. The

TABLE **16.10**   **Domains and types of sockets**

```
/*  Domains      */

#define    AF_UNIX   1   /*  UNIX, local host  */

#define    AF_INET   2   /*  Internet, remote host  */

/*  Types      */

#define    SOCK_STREAM   1   /* stream socket  */

#define    SOCK_DGRAM   2   /* datagram socket  */

#define    SOCK_RAW   3   /* raw socket  */
```

socket name is important because any pair of entities must specify the address of a socket to send a message or make a connection. Therefore, in a server/client system,

▶   A server must assign an address to its socket and make it known to all potential clients.

▶   A client must be able to obtain the correct socket address of any server on any host.

An Internet socket address combines a *host address* and a *port number*. To bind a name to a socket, the system call

```
bind(int  soc,  struct  sockaddr  *addr,  int  addrlen)
```

is used where soc is a socket descriptor, addr is a pointer to the appropriately filled address structure, and addrlen is the size of the address. In general, a socket name can be classified in several ways:

▶   In the UNIX domain, a socket name is an address declared by the sockaddr_un structure contained in <sys/un.h> as shown here:

```
/*  UNIX domain socket address   */
   struct   sockaddr_un   {
      short  sun_family;          /*  domain as AF_UNIX  */
      char   sun_path[108];       /*  path name    */
   };
```

▶   In the Internet domain, a socket name is an address declared by the sockaddr_in structure contained in <netinet/in.h>:

```
/*  Internet domain socket address   */
   struct   sockaddr_in   {
      short   sin_family;          /*  domain as AF_INET  */
      u_short sin_port;            /*  service port address  */
      struct  in_addr  sin_addr;   /*  host IP address   */
      char    sin_zero[8];         /*  must be zero    */
   };
```

TABLE **16.11**   Specification of the socket name structure

Field	Description
sin_family	specifies domain used for socket connection, AF_INET
sun_family	specifies domain used for socket connection, AF_UNIX
sin_port	specifies a port number identifying an application
s_addr	specifies an Internet address
sin_zero	unused and contains all zero
sun_path	specifies the path name

```
where
    struct   in_addr   {
      u_int  s_addr
    };
```

Table 16.11 specifies what the fields of sockaddr_in and sockaddr_un structures represent.

For example, to bind an Internet socket address, the following procedures can be used.

```
#include   <sys/types.h>
#include   <sys/socket.h>
#include   <netinet/in.h>
/*  define an address structure as ad */
    struct  sockarrd_in  ad  =  {  AF_INET  };
/*  obtain and assign port and host address to ad  */
/*  bind address ad to socket  */
    bin(soc,  &ad,  sizeof(ad));
```

In the following section, we illustrate socket communication using Datagram sockets and Stream sockets, along with a very simple example involving a sender process and a receiver process.

16.6.2 Datagram Sockets

To simplify the mechanism, we look at communication within the UNIX domain. The sender program as sender.c is listed as the following:

```
/*   File name: sender.c   */
/*   Datagram socket program: sender process   */
#include  <stdio.h>
#include  <sys/types.h>
#include  <sys/file.h>
```

```
#include  <sys/socket.h>
#include  <sys/un.h>
int  main( )
{
   int  soc,  n;
   char  buf[ ] = "HELLO WORLD";
   struct  sockaddr_un  peer = {AF_UNIX, "receiver_soc"};     (1)
   soc  = socket(AF_UNIX, SOCK_DGRAM, 0);                     (2)
   if  (  access(peer.sun_path, F_OK)  >  -1  )              (3)
   {
   n  =  sendto(soc, buf, strlen(buf), 0, &peer, sizeof(peer));  (4)
     if ( n < 0 )
     {
        fprintf(stderr,  "Binding Failed");
        exit(1);
     }
     printf("Sender:  %d Characters Sent.", n);              (5)
     close(soc);                                             (6)
   }
   return(0);
}
/*   End of sender.c    */
```

In this program, the sender performs the following steps:

1. The receiver's socket address is properly formed (line 1).

2. A datagram socket (soc) is created in the UNIX domain (line 2).

3. If the file representing the socket of the receiver process exists (line 3), the message HELLO WORLD is sent to receiver_soc (line 4).

4. When successful, the number of characters sent is displayed (line 5).

5. Finally, sender's socket is closed (line 6).

The receiver program as `receiver.c` is listed as the following:

```
/*   File name: receiver.c    */
/*   Datagram socket program: receiver process        */
#include  <stdio.h>
#include  <sys/types.h>
#include  <sys/file.h>
#include  <sys/socket.h>
#include  <sys/un.h>
void  cleanup(int  soc, char  *file)
{
   close(soc);
unlink(file);
}
int  main( )
```

```
{
    int  soc,  n,  len;
    char  buf[64];
    struct  sockaddr_un  peer;
    struct  sockaddr_un  self = {AF_UNIX, "receiver_soc"};     (1)
    soc  = socket(AF_UNIX, SOCK_DGRAM, 0);                      (2)
    n  =  bind(soc,  &self,  sizeof(self));                     (3)
      if ( n < 0)
      {
        fprintf(stderr,  "Binding Failed");
        exit(1);
      }
    n  =  recvfrom(soc,  buf,  sizeof(buf), 0, &peer, &len);    (4)
      if ( n < 0)
      {
        fprintf(stderr,  "ReceiveFrom Failed");
        cleanup(soc,  self.sun_path);
        exit(1);
      }
    buf[n] ='\0';                                               (5)
    printf("Datagram Received = %s\n", buf);                    (6)
    cleanup(soc, self.sun_path);
    return(0);
}
/*  End of receiver.c   */
```

In this program, the steps performed by receiver are the following:

1. The receiver's own socket is properly formed (line 1).
2. A datagram socket (`soc`) is created (line 2) and the `receiver_soc` address is bound to it (line 3).
3. The receiver receives input from the socket including the address of the sending socket (line 4).
4. When successful, the received string is properly terminated (line 5).
5. The string received is displayed (line 6).

To make this communication possible, we compile the sender program (`sender.c`) into an executable file named *sender*, and receiver program (`receiver.c`) into an executable file named *receiver*. Then, we run both with the execution command,

```
receiver & sender
```

to obtain the following output:

```
Datagram Received = HELLO WORLD
Sender:  11 Characters Sent.
```

The `sendto` and `recvfrom` system calls send and receive messages on sockets. They work with any type socket but normally are used with datagram sockets.

```
int sendto(int soc, char *buf, int k, int opt, struct sockaddr *to, int *tosize)
```

sends via the socket `soc`, k bytes from the buffer `buf` to a receiving socket specified by the address `to`. The `opt` parameter specifies different options for sending data and usually is given as 0. The `sendto` system call returns the number of bytes forwarded or −1 to indicate an error. On the receiving end, the system call

```
int recvfrom(int soc, char *buf, int bufsize, int opt,
        struct sockaddr *from, int *fromsize)
```

receives a message coming from another socket into the given buffer `buf` of size `bufsize`. If no message is available, the call waits unless the socket is nonblocking. The peer's address structure is returned in `*from` and its size in `*fromsize`. The argument `from` is a result parameter that is filled with the address of the sending socket. The number of bytes received is the return value of `recvfrom` system call.

16.6.3   Stream Sockets

A stream socket is connected with its peer to form two-way communication between a client and a server. A client process uses its socket to initiate a connection to a socket of a server process, and a server process arranges to listen for connection requests and accepts a connection. After a connection is established, data communication can take place using the *read* and *write* system calls. Figure 16.7 illustrates client and server connections.

A server process binds a published address to a socket. To establish a connection, a client process needs to accomplish the following steps known as *initiating a connection:*

1. Find the correct address of the desired server socket.
2. Initiate a connection to the server socket.

   The connect system call,

```
int   connect(int  soc,  struct  sockaddr  *name,  int  namelen)
```

associates the client socket given by the descriptor `soc` to a peer socket in a server specified by the socket address `*name`. If `soc` is of type SOCK_DGRAM, then this call permanently specifies the peer (datagram socket) to receive datagrams. If `soc` is of type SOCK_STREAM, then this call sends a connection request to the named socket. If `soc` is not bound to a name at the time of the `connect` system call, the system selects and binds a name to it.

Accepting a Connection

A server process with a stream socket takes the following steps to get ready to accept a connection:

1. Creates a socket in the appropriate domain of type SOCK_STREAM.
2. Constructs the correct address and binds it to the socket.
3. Indicates a willingness to accept connection requests by carrying out the *listen* call.
4. Uses the *accept* system call to wait for a connection request and to establish a connection.

FIGURE **16.7**   **Stream socket connection**

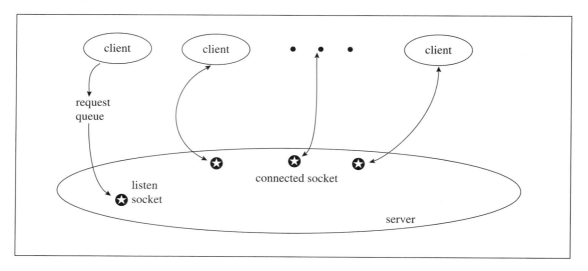

The system call

```
int    listen(int  soc,  int  n);
```

initializes the socket soc for receiving incoming connection requests and sets the maximum number of pending connections to n (restricted to five or less). After the listen system call, the accept system call,

```
int    accept(int  soc,  struct  sockaddr  *addr,  int  *addrlen);
```

accepts connections on the stream socket soc when a listen has been executed. If there are pending connections, accept extracts the first connection request on the queue, creates a new socket with the same properties as soc, connects the new socket with the requesting peer, and returns the descriptor of this new socket. If no pending connections are present on the queue, accept blocks the first connection request in the queue until a connection request arrives. The argument addr is provided with the address of the connected peer.

Sending and Receiving Data on Sockets

The basic system calls *read* and *write* send and receive data for connected sockets.

```
write(soc,  buffer,  sizeof(buffer));
read(soc,   buffer,  sizeof(buffer));
```

Each process reads and writes its own socket, resulting in a bi-directional data flow between the connected peers. The system calls

```
send(soc, buffer,  sizeof(buffer),  opt);
recv(soc, buffer,  sizeof(buffer),  opt);
```

are exclusively used for stream sockets. If the argument opt is zero, they are the same as the write and read system calls. If opt is MSG_OOB then *out-of-band data* is sent or received, meaning that urgent messages, such as a signal to a peer, can be delivered. To illustrate the use of socket stream connections, we look at a simple server/client program in the UNIX domain. In the following program, the server process is involved.

```c
/*   Stream socket example:  server.c   */
#include  <stdio.h>
#include  <sys/types.h>
#include  <sys/file.h>
#include  <sys/socket.h>
#include  <sys/un.h>
int  main( )
{
   int  soc,  ns,  k;
   char  buf[256];
   struct  sockaddr_un  peer = {AF_UNIX};
   struct  sockaddr_un  self = {AF_UNIX, "serversoc"};
   int  peer_len  =  sizeof(peer);
   /* set up listening socket soc  */
   soc  = socket(AF_UNIX, SOCK_STREAM, 0);                    (1)
      if ( soc < 0)   {
         perror("Server:Socket");
         exit(1);
      }
   if  (bind(soc,  &self,  sizeof(self))  ==  -1);  {         (2)
         perror("Server:Bind");
         close(soc);
         exit(1);
      }
   listen(soc, 1);                                            (3)
   /* accept connection request  */
   ns  =  accept(soc,  &peer,  &peer_len);                    (4)
   if ( ns < 0)   {
         perror("Server:Accept");
         close(soc);
         unlink(self.sun_path);
         exit(1);
      }
   /* data transfer on connected socket ns  */
   k  =  read(ns,  buf,  sizeof(buf));                        (5)
   printf("SERVER RECEIVED:  %s\n",  buf);
   strcpy(buf, "HELLO FROM SERVER");
   write(ns,  buf,  k);                                       (6)
   close(ns);   close(soc);
   unlink(self.sun_path);       return(0);
}
/*   End of  server.c   */
```

In this example, the server process creates a stream socket `soc` in the UNIX domain (line 1), and binds the name *serversoc* to it (line 2). The server then sets up `soc` to listen for connection requests (line 3). Then, the `accept` call waits for a connect request and returns a new socket `ns` when a connection is established (line 4). The connected socket `ns` is then used in simple data transfer with `read` and `write` system calls (line 5 and 6). In the following program, the client process is involved.

```
/*    Stream socket example:  client.c    */
#include  <stdio.h>
#include  <sys/types.h>
#include  <sys/file.h>
#include  <sys/socket.h>
#include  <sys/un.h>
int  main( )
{
    int  soc;
    char  buf[256];
    struct  sockaddr_un  peer = {AF_UNIX, "serversoc"};
    struct  sockaddr_un  self = {AF_UNIX, "clientsoc"};
    soc  = socket(AF_UNIX, SOCK_STREAM, 0);                    (1)
    bind(soc,  &self,  sizeof(self));                          (2)
/*  request connection to serversoc   */
if  (connect(soc,  &peer,  sizeof(peer))  ==  -1);            (3)
        {
            perror("Client:Connect");
            close(soc);
            unlink(self.sun_path);
            exit(1);
        }
    write(soc,  "HELLO FROM CLIENT",  18);                    (4)
    read(soc,  buf,  sizeof(buf));                            (5)
    printf("CLIENT RECEIVED:  %s\n", buf);
    close(soc);        unlink(self.sun_path);
    return(0);
}
/*    End of  client.c    */
```

In this example, the client process establishes its own socket `soc` (line 1), and binds the name *clientsoc* to it (line 2). After connection is established by `connect` call (line 3), indicating that a connection has been established with its peer (`ns`), data transfer can begin. The client process first writes the string HELLO FROM CLIENT to its `soc` (line 4), which is connected to the server socket (`ns`). In this example, the server echoes the received message back to the client. Then, the client reads its *soc*, receives the echoed message (line 5), and displays a confirming message on terminal. To illustrate the stream socket communication, we compile the server program (`server.c`) and the client program (`client.c`) into executable files named *client* and *server*, respectively. Then, we issue

```
server & client
```

to obtain the following output

```
SERVER RECEIVED: HELLO FROM CLIENT
CLIENT RECEIVED: HELLO FROM SERVER
```

16.7 INTERNET PROGRAMMING

According to William Gibson (author of science fiction novels and short stories), the term *cyberspace* is the mass communication in which humans all over the planet meet, converse, and exchange information. This means that people all over the world, by using computers and networks, are communicating and exchanging information in this environment. Some people refer to this environment as the net, and others as the Matrix. The word *net* came from the Internet. Matrix refers to all communication networks, including the Internet and online services. In general, the Internet is a network of networks that connects computers across the country and around the world. It grew out of an U.S. Department of Defense (DOD) experiment project that began in 1969 to test the feasibility of a wide area computer network over which scientists and military personnel could share messages and data. The original language of the Internet was difficult and unfriendly to use. The potential was exciting, but you had to use a variety of programs, such as Telnet, FTP, Archie, and Gopher, to locate and download data. The programs were based on the UNIX operating system, and you had to know the precise syntax of the commands within each program. There was no common user interface to speed learning, and everything was communicated in plain text because graphics and sound were not available. All of this changed in 1989. Timothy Berners-Lee (1989) invented the World Wide Web at the European Laboratory for Particle Physics, Switzerland (CERN), based on ideas that originated in earlier work on hypertext by Vannevar Bush (1945). Berners-Lee and his associates developed initial versions of HTML, HTTP, a Web server, and a browser—the four key components of the Web. The *World Wide Web* (WWW, or simply *Web*) can be thought of as a very large subset of the Internet that consists of *hypertext* and *hypermedia* documents. A hypertext document contains a link (reference) to another hypertext document, which may be on the same computer or even on a different computer located anywhere in the world. Hypermedia is similar, except that it provides links to graphics, sound, and video files in addition to text files. Either type of document enables you to move easily from one document (or computer) to another one. Any computer that stores a document anywhere on the Web and makes that document available to other computers is known as a *server* (or Web server). Any computer that is connected to the Web and requests a document from a server is known as a *client*. In other words, you work on a client computer and by making a link in a hypermedia document, you are requesting a document from a Web server.

16.7.1   Design Principles of Internet Structures

For the Web to work properly, every client must be able to display every document from every server. This is accomplished by imposing a set of standards known as a

FIGURE **16.8**   **Components of a URL**

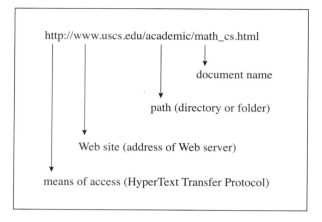

protocol to govern the way data is transmitted across the Web. The Internet arose with the creation of a protocol called Transfer Control Protocol/Internet Protocol (TCP/IP). Any computer or network that is connected to the Internet must support TCP/IP. That means the computer must be connected to a device that translates its language into TCP/IP. The TCP service model includes a connection-oriented service and a reliable data transfer service. When an application invokes TCP for its transport protocol, the application receives both of these services from TCP.

Data travels from client to server and back through a protocol known as the Hypertext Transfer Protocol (HTTP). HTTP is implemented in two programs: a client program and a server program. The client program and server program, running on different end systems, talk to each other by exchanging HTTP messages. HTTP defines the structure of these messages and how the client and server exchange the messages. In addition, the best way to navigate and view Web pages is with a Web browser which is an application program such as Netscape Navigator or Microsoft Internet Explorer. In general, a browser is a user agent for the Web that displays the requested Web pages and provides numerous navigational and configuration features.

The location (or address) of the document appears in the *location toolbar text box* and is known as a Uniform Resource Locator (URL) address or, more simply, as a Web address. Each location as well as each document has a specific address. The URL is the primary means of navigating the Web because it indicates the address of the Web server from which you have requested a document. By changing the URL, you are linked to a different document, and possibly a different server. A URL consists of several parts: *method of access, Internet address* of the Web server, a *path* in the directory structure on the Web server to the document, and finally, the *document name.* Consider, for example, the following address and associated components.

In the following section, we briefly outline HTML, which is a language designed for Web programming.

☛ 16.8 INTERNET PROGRAMMING WITH HTML

All hypertext and hypermedia documents are written in Hypertext Markup Language (HTML). HTML is the coding language for World Wide Web documents. *Markup* is an old publishing term that refers to typesetting instructions written in the margins, marking up the original document. An HTML document is just a regular text document, except that special elements called *tags* are inserted to indicate information about formatting and positioning of links. The tags are words enclosed in < > brackets, such as <title>, <h1>, and <li>. Some tags work in pairs to affect the text enclosed in between, whereas others work singly. For example, the tags <title> and </title> work together to identify the enclosed text as a title. On the other hand, the single tag <p> denotes the end of the paragraph. Tags can be entered in uppercase or lowercase letters, meaning that <p> and <P> both specify the end of a paragraph. In addition to formatting, HTML tags are used to include graphic images, link other documents, mark reference points, generate forms or questionnaires, and invoke certain programs. Table 16.12 shows the basic HTML tags.

HTML documents use the extension *html* at the end of the document name in the Web address. You will, however, see an extension of *htm* (rather than *html*) when a document is stored on a server that does not support long file names. UNIX-based systems, which constitute the majority of Web servers, support long file names, and so *html* is the more common extension. Here is a sample HTML file:

```
<TITLE>A SAMPLE HTML FILE</TITLE>
<H1>INTRODUCTION</H1>
<P>
HERE IS THE FIRST PARAGRAPH
<P>
THE SECOND PARAGRAPH AND A LIST OF THINGS
<OL>
<LI>APPLES
<LI>ORANGES
</OL>
</P>
```

16.8.1 Principles of a Web Page

A page is a Web screen. It is also referred to as a document. When you use a Web browser and access information, the screen that is displayed, the combination of text, graphics, and links you see on the screen constitute the Web page. Links are words or sentences that are underlined to indicate a connection to further resources. Web pages have some common visual elements:

▶ **Headings:** There is usually a heading at the top of a Web page.

▶ **Subheadings:** These break the contents of the page into readable groups.

TABLE **16.12**   Basic HTML tags

<Title>text</Title>	*Text* appears as the title at the top of the screen.
<H1>text</H1>	*Text* appears as the level 1 heading (largest). This indicates a section heading in your document. There are six levels of headings (<h2></h2>, <h3></h3>, <h4></h4>, <h5></h5>, <h6></h6>).
<P>	Paragraph break, indicating a break between two paragraphs of text. Thus, a carriage return and a line feed is inserted.
 	Line break, indicating a line break with no extra space between the lines.
<HR>	Horizontal rule, which creates a horizontal divider line to create a visual break between sections of your document.
<A HREF="http://some.url.here/">text</A>	Hyperlink Anchor, which allows you to make a link to other documents and external images. *Text* becomes the underlined word that serves as the link.
<IMG SRC="image.gif">	In-line image, which allows you to include images in your document.
<LI>	Indicates an item on a list.
<OL><LI>item 1<LI>item 2 … </OL>	The <OL> tag means an Ordered List. Items on the list appear numbered on separate lines.
<UL><LI>item 1<LI>item 2 … </UL>	The <UL> tag means bulleted list. Items on the list appear bulleted on separate lines.
<B>text</B>	Text appears bold.
<I>text</I>	Text appears in italics.
<U>text</U>	Text appears underlined.
<TABLE> … </TABLE>	Formatting a borderless table.
<TABLE BORDER> … </TABLE>	Formatting a table with border.
<TR> … </TR>	Establishes a row within a table.
<TD> … </TD>	Defines a cell within a table.
<TH> … </TH>	Centers a heading at the top or side of a table.
<CAPTION> … </CAPTION>	Places a title at the top of the table.
<TABLE>	Starting tag of two-dimensional table.
<TR><TD>Row one – Column one </TD><TD>Row one – Column two</TD></TR>	
<TR><TD>Row two – Column one</TD><TD>Row two – Column two</TD></TR>	
</TABLE>	Ending tag of two-dimensional table.

TABLE **16.13**	HTML special characters
Sequence	**Character**
`&lt;`	The less than sign <
`&gt;`	The greater than sign >
`&amp;`	The ampersand sign &
`&quot;`	The double quote sign "
` `	The nonbreaking space

▶ **Banner:** A term used to refer to the heading at the top of a page that incorporates graphics.

▶ **Text:** A text to explain contents or links.

▶ **Images:** Pictures, icons, sounds, or anything defined in the page.

▶ **Links:** Underlined words that are embedded in the text and lead to other information resources.

The home page is the first screen you see, or the top level of information at a particular site. The Windows version refers to *home page* as *start page*. Although there are a number of HTML editors, all you need is a simple word-processing application. You can insert tags to indicate how you want the page to look and which words should be links. When you are finished, save the document as an ASCII, or text file, with the extension *.html*. Formatting characters are used in HTML documents. For example, white space characters break up words and < marks the beginning of tags. An escape mechanism is needed to include these characters as themselves in an HTML document. An HTML *escape sequence,* a character string prefixed by an ampersand (&) and followed by a semicolon, is used to indicate a special character. Table 16.13 lists some common escape sequences.

16.8.2   Creating Links

Links let you effortlessly jump from one page on the Web to any other page across the Internet. They work without you ever having to know exactly where the actual physical destination is, or what Internet protocol to select or program to specify. Links appear as underlined words. The format for a link is

```
<a href= " external file">text</a>
```

where `external file` is the URL of the file to which you are linking and `text` is the text that is to appear underlined.

16.8.3 Adding Images

There are two ways to include images on the Web page.

▶ **In-line images:** These appear on the Web page as a link to a separate page where the image is displayed. The format of the tag for an in-line image is

```
<img  src = " file name">
```

if the file appears in the same directory as the HTML document. The image file can be located elsewhere on the Internet, in which case you need to specify the complete URL for the file. The drawback in not having the image in the same directory as the HTML document is that it takes longer time to load. Furthermore, the computer on which the image resides has to be turned on.

▶ **External images:** The reader has to click on a link to a separate page where the image is displayed. An external image is an image opened as a separate page. The tag format is

```
<a href= " file name">text</a>
```

where `text` is the word that appears as a link.

In either case, the image must be stored as a Graphic Interchange Format (GIF), X window system graphics format (XBM), or Joint Photographic Experts Group (JPEG) file. The JPEG, which is a compressed image format, is probably preferred because it takes up less space and can be transferred more quickly. For the best result, the image file should be located in the same directory as your HTML document.

16.8.4 Creating Forms

In general, an HTML document supplies information to users on the Web, but it is also possible to collect information from a user. With the HTML *form* facility, you simply create a form to be filled out by the user and then process the collected information appropriately. An HTML form, marked by <FORM> and </FORM>, usually consists of these four important parts:

▶ Text including what information is being retrieved.

▶ Blanks, marked by the <INPUT> tag, to be completed by the user.

▶ A button, marked by the <submit> tag, for the user to send the completed form back.

▶ An external program (address), specified by the ACTION flag of the <FORM> tag, to process the collected information and to produce appropriate output that is returned to the user.

Figure 16.9 is a simple form in HTML.

When a Web browser gets a form from an http server, it displays the form and allows the user to complete the form interactively. Clicking the *submit* button causes the browser to send the completed form back to the server. Then, the server invokes the address specified by ACTION and feeds it the information on the completed form. The ACTION program not only processes the information supplied by the server but also

FIGURE **16.9**   A form in HTML

```
<FORM   METHOD = "POST"   ACTION = "cgi-bin/newaddr " >
<PRE>
FULL NAME        <INPUT NAME = "fname"  MAXLENGTH = "30" SIZE = "35">
Email address        <INPUT NAME = "email"   MAXLENGTH = "30" SIZE = "35">
<INPUT TYPE = "submit"   VALUE = "submit">
</PRE>
</FORM>
```

constructs correctly formatted output that is sent back to the server. The server interprets the output of the external program and returns it to the browser as a consequence of completing the form.

Example: A Sample Web Page

The following is the source HTML of a Web document. You could see something similar for every Web page by opening the <u>V</u>iew menu and choosing <u>S</u>ource. If you review each line carefully, you can probably figure out the code on your own because there is a certain logic to it.

```
<HTML>
<HEAD>
<META HTTP-EQUIV="Content-Type" CONTENT="text/html; charset=windows-1252">
<META NAME="Generator" CONTENT="Microsoft Word 97">
<TITLE>Roostanew</TITLE>
<META NAME="Template" CONTENT="C:\Program Files\Microsoft Office\Office\html.dot">
</HEAD>
<BODY LINK="#0000ff" VLINK="#000000" BGCOLOR="#5fb012">

<P><!--
Author: Seyed Roosta
Date:   March 5 , 1999
URL:    http://www.oswego.edu/~roosta/roos.html-->
<H1 ALIGN="CENTER">Seyed H. Roosta -- HomePage</H1>
<P><HR></P>
<H3>Contact Information</H3>
<B><P>Seyed H. Roosta</B><BR>
<B>University of South Carolina Spartanburg</B><BR>
<B>Computer Science Department</B><BR>
<B>216 Hodge Center</B><BR>
<B>Phone:(864)-503-5363</B><BR>
<B>Fax:(864)-503-5930</B><BR>
```

```
<B>Email:sroosta@gw.uscs.edu</P>
</B><P><HR></P>
<H3>Professional Activities and Interests</H3>
<B><P>Parallel Processing</B><BR>
<B>Operating Systems</B><BR>
<B>Computer Architectures</B><BR>
<B>Programming Languages</P>
</B><H3>Professional Information</H3>
<B><P>Assistant Professor, appointed 1998</B><BR>
<B>B.S. - The University of Tehran</B><BR>
<B>M.S., Ph.D. - The University of Iowa</P>
</B><H3>Books</H3>
<B><P>Parallel Processing and Parallel Algorithms:Theory and Computation</B><BR>
<B>Springer-Verlag, 1999</B><BR></P>
</B><P><HR></P>
<H3>Courses Taught</H3>
<B><P>C Programming Language</B><BR>
<B>Computer Architectures</B><BR>
<B>Organization of Programming Languages</B><BR>
<B>Operating Systems</B><BR>
<B>Parallel Computing</B><BR>
<B>Design and Analysis of Algorithms</B><BR>
<B>Data Communication</P>
</B><H3>Teaching Schedule, Spring 2001</H3>
<B><P>SCSC530:Programming Languages</B><BR>
<B>SCSC511:Operating Systems</P>
</B><H3>Teaching Schedule, Fall 2000</H3>
<B><P>SCSC210:Assembly Language</B><BR>
<B>SCSC310:Computer Architectures</B><BR>
<B>SCSC599:Parallel Computing</P>
</B><P><HR></P></BODY>
</HTML>
```

This Web page, when loaded into Netscape, is transformed into what you see in Figure 16.10.

◩ 16.9 WINDOWS PROGRAMMING

With *Windows Programming* sometimes called *Visual Programming,* also known as *Event-Driven programming,* the programmer has the ability to create graphical user interfaces by pointing and clicking with the mouse. In this programming paradigm, the programmer interacts (i.e., clicks, presses a key, double-clicks) with the graphical user interface (GUI). These notifications, called *events,* are passed into the program by the Windows Operating System. With event-driven programs, the user—rather than the programmer—dictates the order of program execution. For example, consider a Web

FIGURE **16.10**   A Web page represented using Netscape Navigator

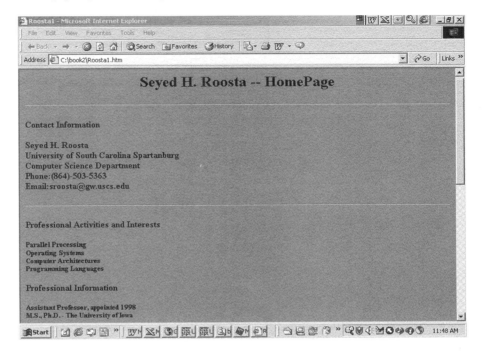

browser. When an address is opened, the Web browser may or may not load a page by default. After the browser is loaded, it just "sits there," with nothing else happening. The browser will stay in this *event monitoring state* indefinitely. If the user presses a button, the browser then performs some action, but as soon as the browser is done with the action, it returns to the event monitoring state. Thus, user actions determine browser activity.

With the development of the Microsoft Windows GUI in the late 1980s and the early 1990s, the natural evolution of a windows programming language was Visual Basic, which was created by Microsoft Corporation in 1991. Visual Basic evolved from BASIC (Beginner's All-Purpose Symbolic Instruction Code). BASIC was developed in the mid-1960s by John Kemeny and Thomas Kurtz of Dartmouth College as a language for writing simple programs. Their primary purpose was to help people learn how to program. Until Visual Basic appeared, developing Microsoft Windows-based applications was a difficult and cumbersome process. Visual Basic greatly simplifies Windows application development. Since 1991, six versions have been released, with the latest, Visual Basic 6, appearing in September 1998. Visual Basic is a Microsoft Windows programming language. Visual Basic programs are created in an Integrated Development Environment (IDE). The IDE allows the programmer to create, run, and debug Visual Basic programs conveniently. IDEs allow a programmer to create working programs in a fraction of the time that it would normally take to code programs without using IDEs. The process of rapidly creating an application is typically referred to as Rapid Application Development (RAD). Visual Basic is the world's most widely used RAD language.

Visual Basic is a distinctly different language that provides powerful features such as graphical user interface, event handling, access to the Win32 application programming interface (API), object-oriented features, and structured programming. Microsoft provides several versions of Visual Basic, including the Learning Edition, the Professional Edition, and the Enterprise Edition. The Learning Edition provides fundamental programming capabilities. The Professional Edition provides a much richer set of programming capabilities than does the Learning Edition and is what many programmers use to write Visual Basic applications. The Enterprise Edition is used for developing large-scale computing systems that meet the needs of complex systems. Visual Basic is an interpreter language. However, the Professional and the Enterprise Editions allow Visual Basic code to be compiled to machine language code.

16.10 WINDOWS PROGRAMMING WITH VISUAL BASIC

When Visual Basic is loaded, the *New Project* dialog box is displayed to allow the programmer to choose what type of Visual Basic program to create. The *Standard EXE*, which is highlighted by default, allows the programmer to create a standard executable program (i.e., a program that uses the most common Visual Basic features). Each type listed describes a group of related files called a *project*. The *project* types are the "Visual" in Visual Basic because they contain predefined features for designing Windows programs. The programmer can use these existing project types to create powerful Windows applications in a fraction of the time it would normally take to create the same applications in other programming languages. The New Project dialog box contains three tabs:

▶ **New** for creating a new project

▶ **Existing** for opening an existing project

▶ **Recent** for opening a project that has been previously loaded

A project type is opened by either double-clicking its icon with the left mouse button or by single-clicking the icon with the left mouse button and pressing *Open*. Opening a project type closes the *New Project* dialog box and loads the features associated with the selected project type into the IDE. Figure 16.11 shows the IDE after Standard EXE is selected. The top of the IDE window (the title bar) displays Project1—Microsoft Visual Basic [design]. The environment consists of various windows, a *menu bar,* and a *tool bar.* The menu bar contains several menus (File, Edit, View, etc.). The tool bar contains several icons that provide quick access to commonly used features. A Standard EXE project contains the following windows:

▶ **Project1—Form1 (Form)** window contains a form named Form1, which is where the program's GUI will be displayed. A GUI is the visual portion of the program; that is, where the user enters data to the program and where the program displays its results for the user to read. We refer to the Form1 window simply as "the form."

FIGURE **16.11**   IDE with a Standard EXE project open

Toolbox   Form   Title bar   Menu bar   Toolbar

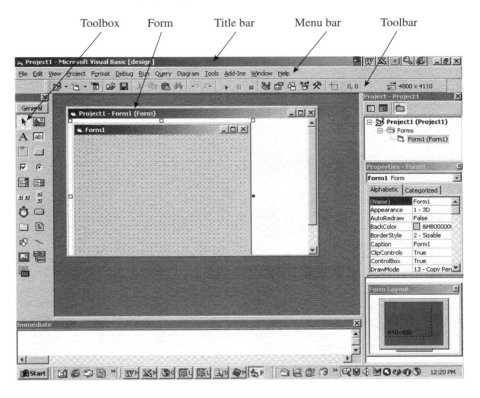

▶ **Form Layout** window enables the user to specify the form's position on the screen when the program is carried out. This window consists of an image representing the screen and the form's relative position on the screen. With the mouse pointer positioned over the form image, drag the form to a new location.

▶ **Properties—Form1** window displays form attributes or properties (i.e., color, font style, size, etc.). Some properties, such as Width and Height are common to both forms and controls, whereas other properties are unique to a form or control.

▶ **Project—Project1** window groups the project's files by type. This window is called the **Project Explorer** and contains the project files. We refer to the Project Explorer window simply as the **Project Window.**

▶ **Toolbox** contains controls for customizing the GUI. Controls are prepackaged components such as buttons and checkboxes that you reuse instead of writing them yourself; this helps you write programs faster.

In the following, we introduce the techniques of visual programming through various steps to create, run, and terminate this program. In this regard, we write a program that displays the "Welcome to Visual Basic" on the *form*. The program consists of one *form* and uses one *label* control to display the text. The program is a Standard EXE.

16.10.1 Setting the Form's Properties

The form's *Caption* property determines what is displayed in the form's title bar. In the *properties* window, we set the *Caption* property to *A Simple Program*. The form's *Name* property identifies a *form* or *control*. Similarly, we set the *Name* property to *SimpleName*. In addition, we can resize the form by clicking and dragging one of the form's *enabled sizing handles*. Also, we can center the form using the *Form Layout* window, which causes the form to be displayed in the center of the monitor when the program is carried out. The *BackColor* property specifies a form or control's background color. Clicking *BackColor* in the properties window causes a down-arrow button to appear next to the property value to change the form's background color.

Figure 16.12(a) and (b) show the changes to the Properties window and Project window before and after the properties are set, respectively.

16.10.2 Setting the Label's Properties

Double-click the toolbox's Label control to create a Label with sizing handles in the center of the form. The Label displays the word `Label1` by default. In this case, when the sizing handles appear around the Label, the properties window displays the Label's properties. The Label's *Caption* property determines what text the Label dis-

FIGURE **16.12**   (a) **Changes to the Properties window and Project window before the properties are set**

Setting the form's title bar   Setting the form's name

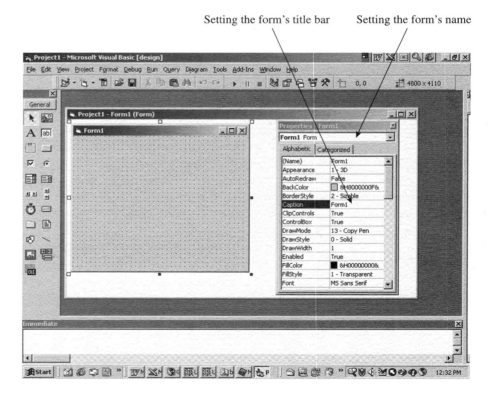

FIGURE **16.12** **(b) Changes to the Properties window and Project window after the properties are set**

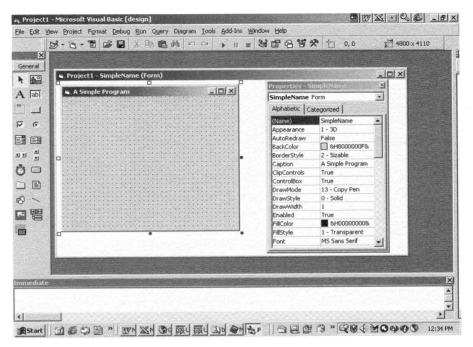

plays. As we see, the *Label* and *form* each have their own *Caption* properties with each being completely independent of the other. In this case, set the Label's *Caption* property to *Welcome to Visual Basic* as shown in Figure 16.13. Click and drag one of the Label's enabled sizing handles to resize the Label. The default name for the created Label is *Label1*. The Label's Name property is used to identify the Label. In this example, we set the Name property to LabelName. In addition, we can customize the Label's colors, change the Label's font size, and align the Label's text.

16.10.3 Saving the Project

Select *Save Project* or *Save Project As* options from the File menu to display *the Save File As* dialog box. This dialog box specifies the *form file name* that will store all the form's information (i.e., properties). You are free to choose whatever destination you want. In this example, we save our form as `c:\Project\Form1` (in the directory named Project). The next dialog box that appears is the *Save Project As,* where the features are identical to the features of the *Save File As* dialog box, except that we specify the project file name. In this case, we choose `c:\Project\Project1`. Again, you can save the project file in any place you choose. Figure 16.14 (a) and (b) show the *Save File As* and *Save Project As* windows, in which the form and project are saved. The similar action can be performed using the *Save Project* icon from the tool bar menu.

FIGURE **16.13**   **The Caption property determines what Label displays**

Label control icon to create a label

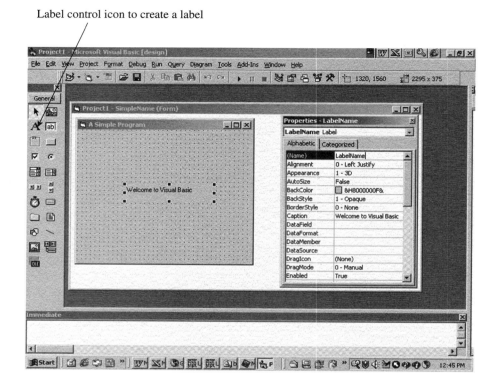

16.10.4 Running and Terminating Program Execution

Before running the program in the *design mode,* the programmer has access to all the environment windows including toolbox and properties. In *running mode,* the program is processing and the user can only interact with a few IDE features. To carry out or run the program, click the *Start* button or select *Start* option from the *Run* menu. Figure 16.15 shows the IDE environment in running mode. In addition to the *Immediate* window that appears at run time, the IDE title bar displays [Run] and most tool bar icons are disabled. By clicking the form's *Close* button or by clicking the tool bar's *End* button, the program execution is terminated and the IDE is placed in design mode.

▼   SUMMARY

In control flow computing the execution sequence of the program's statements is dictated by the order in which the programmer textually composes the statements. In

FIGURE **16.14**   **(a) Saving a form using the Save File As window**

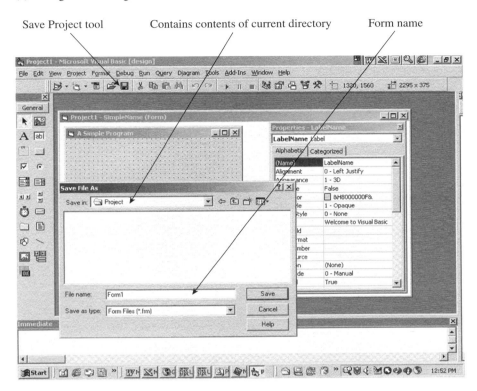

Save Project tool   Contains contents of current directory   Form name

other words, the instructions drive the program's execution. An alternative method of selecting statements for execution is to regard a statement as being ready for execution if the data that it requires are available. Hence, the sequence in which the statements are textually composed is unlikely to be the order in which they are carried out. In addition, if the data are available for more than one statement, then these statements can be carried out in parallel. This is referred to as *data flow computing*. In general, the data flow from one instruction to another and the order of execution of the instructions does not depend on the location of the instructions in memory. In this chapter, we presented fundamental concepts of data flow computing and illustrated the application of this concept in the data flow programming language VAL. We described both static and dynamic data-driven models that more or less assumed data flow graphs as their computation models. We briefly discussed the data flow programming language principles and the essential features of a data flow language. VAL is a data flow language that was designed at MIT for data flow parallel programming. In VAL, statements are identified using expressions and functions to ensure that any concurrency can be identified. Parallelism is introduced by a parallel expression that consists

FIGURE **16.14**   (b) Saving a project using the Save Project As window

Project name   Current directory

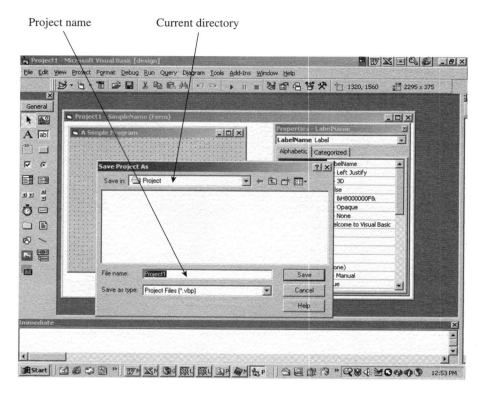

of three parts: a range specification, an environment expansion, and a result accumulation. We introduced a matrix multiplication problem to address parallelism in VAL.

The collection of data is referred to as the database. Database systems are designed to manage information, including the definition of structures for storing information and providing mechanisms for manipulating information. A query language is a language in which a user requests information from the database. In this chapter, we discussed the design principles for database systems along with SQL as one of the best-known database programming languages. SQL is a multipurpose query language and consists of several components: data-definition, interactive data-manipulation, view definition, integrity, and transaction control. The basic structure of a query consists of three primitives: select, from, and where. In addition, we discussed the basic operations of SQL, including set operations, aggregate functions, modification operations, and joining operations.

A network is a combination of computers and telecommunication hardware and software. In particular, UNIX applications running on different computers connected to a network can communicate using a mechanism called socket programming. Socket programming can be implemented in two domains: UNIX domain and Inter-

FIGURE **16.15**   IDE environment during program execution

Run Mode   Form   Project window

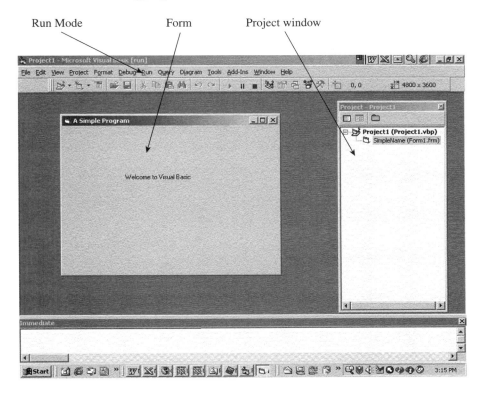

net domain. Thus, information exchange by sockets can be established on different computers that may use different data representations and architectures. We discussed network programming with sockets, including stream socket, datagram socket, and raw socket. We used the essence of the client/server communication model as the basic concept of this communication mechanism.

The Internet is a network of networks that connects computers across the world. The World Wide Web can be thought of as a very large subset of the Internet that consists of hypertext and hypermedia documents. All hypertext and hypermedia documents are designed in HyperText Markup Language (HTML). In this chapter, we discussed the HTML as a language design for Web programming. We covered the principles of a Web page, including headings, subheadings, banner, text, images, and links. Windows programming has the ability to create graphical user interface programs. In this chapter, we discussed Microsoft Visual Basic, through which programmers can create powerful windows applications in a fraction of the time it would normally take to create the same applications in other programming languages. We discussed Visual Basic version 6, in which programs are created in an Integrated Development Environment (IDE).

EXERCISES

1. Sketch the picture of computation for $X=A^2+A*B+C+D*E+E^2$ relative to *control flow* and *data flow* methods.

2. What is the concept of the *node firing* in data flow programming?

3. Declare a record structure in VAL language consisting of four fields as: A=150, B=78.5, C=TRUE, and D='Y'.

4. What is the structure of a parallel expression in VAL language?

5. Devise an algorithm for *Matrix-Vector multiplication* in VAL language?

6. The *database administrator* is the person responsible for the overall control of the system at a technical level. Explain the necessary technical support for implementing the decisions.

7. What is the concept of *Data Definition Language* and *Data Manipulation* Language?

8. We claim that relational systems are based on a formal foundation called the *relational model of data*. What this statement means?

9. What is the structure of SQL with respect to operations?

10. Some of the data manipulation statements in SQL are SELECT, INSERT, UPDATE, and DELETE. Give examples of each of these statements in turn.

11. SQL supports aggregate functions, such as Average, Maximum, Minimum, Total, and Count. Give an example of each of these functions.

12. What is the interpretation of the following SQL query?

```
SELECT    S.name, S.age
FROM      Student  AS  S
WHERE     S.age < 20
```

13. Issue a query to select the names of students who have reserved class number 530.

14. Issue a query to find the names of students who have a rating of 10 *or* have reserved class 530.

15. What is the structure of a socket address?

16. What is the *URL?* List and explain different URLs.

17. What is the *form* facility in HTML? How does it involve two-way interactions between the *browser* and the *server?*

18. Explain the HTML special characters with an example.

19. What is the concept of *links* in HTML documents?

20. What is the difference between *in-line* and *external* images?

REFERENCE-NEEDED EXERCISES

To answer the following exercises, you might need to consult the following references: Date (2000), Silberschatz, Korth, and Sudarshan (1997), Tanenbaum (1996), Ullman and Widom (1997), and Wang (1997).

1. What are the fundamental principles underlying *embedded* SQL?

2. Dynamic SQL consists of a set of embedded SQL facilities that are intended to support the construction of online and possible interactive applications. Outline the steps that dynamic SQL must go through for those applications?

3. SQL supports the Set operations, such as Union, Intersect, and Except operations. Give an example of each of these operations.

4. SQL includes a feature for testing whether a subquery has any duplicate tuples in its result. Refer to section 8.4 and issue a query to find all customers who have only one loan number at the borrower relation.

5. Is your UNIX workstation connected to a network? If so find the *domain name* and *IP address* for your workstation. What UNIX commands did you use to find such information?

6. Both *rlogin* and *telnet* connect you to another computer through the network. What is the difference between the two commands?

7. Name two types of interprocess communications.

8. Explain interprocess communication with pipe.

9. Write a program to show a parent process writing the message "Hello there from parent" to a child process through a pipe.

10. Write a program to establish a two-way pipe connection between a parent process and a child process, in which a parent process can pass some input to a child process and then receives the result produced.

11. Write a program to demonstrate the Client/Server problem. The program is designed as a client that will call on a server running on another machine. This program will copy a file from a remote server. The assumed protocol is TCP/IP and connections are via the Internet.

Appendix A: Acronyms

Accent	A process-based multiprocessor operating system
ADT	Abstract Data Type
AI	Artificial Intelligence
Amoeba	Object-based multiprocessor operating system
ANSI	American National Standards Institute
API	Applications Programming Interface
APL	A Programming Language
AWT	Abstract Window Toolkit
BASIC	Beginner's All-purpose Symbolic Instruction Code
BCPL	Basic CPL
BFS	Breadth-First Search
BNF	Backus-Naur Form
Bulldog	A multiprocessor compiler
car	Contents of the Address Register
CDR	Contents of the Decrement Register
CISC	Complex Instruction Set Computers
CLOS	Common LISP Object System
CM	Connection Machine
COBOL	COmmon Business Oriented Language
CPL	Combined Programming Language
CPU	Central Processing Unit
DAP	Distributed Array Processor

DBMS	DataBase Management System
DDG	Data Dependence Graph
DDL	Data Definition Language
DFS	Depth-First Search
DML	Data Manipulation Language
EBNF	Extended BNF
ESP	Extended Self-contained Prolog
FIFO	First-In First-Out
Fortran	FORmula TRANslator
FP	Functional Programming
GCD	Greatest Common Divisor
GUI	Graphical User Interface
HLL	High-Level Language architectures
HPF	High Performance Fortran
HTML	HyperText Markup Language
HTTP	HyperText Transfer Protocol
Hydra OS	Operating system for C.mmp multiprocessor
IDE	Integrated Development Environment
IP	Internet Protocol
IPC	InterProcess Communication
ISO	International Organization for Standardization
JDK	Java Developer's Kit
LAN	Local Area Network
LCF	Logic for Computable Functions
LEX	UNIX tool that generates analyzer
LIFO	Last-In First-Out
Linux	PC version of UNIX operating system
LISP	LISt Processing
LM	Local Memory
Mach	UNIX-based multiprocessor operating system
MAN	Metropolitan Area Network
MASM	Microsoft Assembler
Medusa O.S.	Operating system for Cm*
MIMD	Multiple Instruction Stream, Multiple Data Stream
ML	MetaLanguage
MPMD	Multiple Program, Multiple Data Stream
OPS	Official Production System

OS	Operating System
Paraphrase	A source-to-source multiprocessor compiler
PFO	Program-Forming Operations
PIMOS	Parallel Inference Machine Operating System
PL/I	Programming Language I
Polymorphism	Poly means many and Morph means form
PPλ	Polymorphic Predicate Calculus
Prolog	PROgramming en LOGique
QBE	Query-By-Example
RAD	Rapid Application Development
RAM	Random Access Memory
RDBMS	Relational DataBase Management System
RIG	Rochester Intelligent Gateway
RISC	Reduced Instruction Set Computers
SAA-SQL	System Application Architecture Database Interface
SCOOPS	Object-oriented version of Scheme
SECD	An abstract machine
SIMD	Single Instruction Stream, Multiple Data Stream
SISD	Single Instruction Stream, Single Data Stream
SPMD	Single Program, Multiple Data Stream
SQL	Structured Query Language
STL	Standard Template Library
TASM	Turbo Assembler
TCP/IP	Transfer Control Protocol/Internet Protocol
UDP	User Datagram Protocol
UNIX	Operating System
URL	Uniform Resource Locator
VAL	Value-Oriented Algorithmic Language
VB	Visual Basic
VDL	Vienna-Definition Language
VLIW	Very Long Instruction Word
VMS	Virtual Memory System
WAN	Wide Area Network
WME	Working Memory Element
WWW	World Wide Web
YACC	Yet Another Compiler Compiler

Appendix B: Definitions

Abstraction   A representation of an object that ignores what could be considered as irrelevant details of that object.

Abstract window toolkit   Contains the essential classes to perform specific and general-purpose tasks.

Accepting task   A process that accepts the location of the rendezvous in concurrent processing.

Active priority   A priority value considered when processors are allocated to tasks.

Ad hoc polymorphism   The situation that occurs when a number of different functions are all denoted by the same name.

Alpha-conversion   A process that refers to name changes in lambda expressions and allows changing bound variables as long as there is no capture of a free variable.

Ambiguity   A grammar that represents a phrase in two or more distinct derivation trees.

Anonymous function   A function with no name.

Applicative order evaluation   An evaluation that corresponds to a bottom-up evaluation of the values of nodes of the tree representing an expression.

Applets   Java applications that are loaded and run in Java run-time environment.

Array type   A collection of two or more adjacent memory cells with the same data type.

Assembler   A program that converts assembly language source code into machine language.

Assertion   A logical statement that describes the state of the computation.

Attributes   Data needed to describe objects created from the class.

Attribute grammar   A powerful mechanism for formalizing both the context-free and context-sensitive aspects of the syntax of a language.

Auxiliary function   The predefined mathematical operations such as plus, times, minus and divide.

Axiomatic semantics   Programming rules that define each program construct in terms of its accomplishments when it is carried out.

Backward chaining   A method similar to recursion, also called the top-down approach.

Barrier   A synchronization primitive in concurrent processing that ensures data dependencies among cooperating processes.

Base priority   An initial priority of a task used to control the inter process synchronization.

Basic control abstraction   An abstraction that abstracts the computation and storage of a value to the location given by a variable.

Basic data abstraction   The internal representation of common data values in a computer system.

Beta-conversion   The function application mechanism in which actual substitution of parameters is carried out.

Binary message   A message that requires a binary operation and must consist of one or more parameters.

Block order evaluation   The evaluation of an expression containing a declaration.

Boolean type   A data type for representing true or false.

Bottom-up approach   The approach that starts with the hypotheses and attempts to reach the goal.

Bottom-up parsers   A parser that begins with a string of terminal symbols and repeatedly replaces sequences in the string with production rules.

Built-in data type   A type of information used through the declaration of the data objects.

Bulldog   A parallel compiler used by the Cedar Multiprocessor to detect parallelism at the instruction level.

C∗   An extension of the C language; designed to support data parallel programming for Connection Machines; provides a new data type based on classes in C++ and a synchronous execution model.

Calling task   A process that knows the identity of the accepting task and the name of the location of the rendezvous.

Cell model   A diagram used to represent the implementation model of expressions in Scheme.

Class   A template from which objects of the same type are created.

Coercion   The process through which a data type is converted to another data type before the operation is carried out.

Compatible type   When two different types are combined to form a data type that still may be correct.

Compiler   A program that converts a high-level program to a machine language version.

Composite object   An object with an internal structure consisting of a selector and an object.

Conditional variable   A variable used with synchronization primitives to ensure data dependencies among cooperating processes.

Confluence property   A property, also called diamond property, that indicates that if a lambda expression M is evaluated to a normal form A via a sequence of reductions and another sequence of reductions takes M to a normal form B, then some common term N can be found such that A can be reduced to N and B can be reduced to N.

Construct   The string that belongs to the language.

Context-free grammar   A type of grammar requiring that the left side of each production rule is a single variable.

Context-sensitive grammar   A type of grammar requiring that the right side of a production rule have no fewer symbols than the left side.

Data abstraction   A process that deals with program components that are subject to computation.

Data object   A fundamental abstraction in a programming language that denotes language entities.

Data parallel program   Programs that consist of a single sequence of instructions, each of which is applied to a different data element or processing element.

Data parallel programming language   A programming language that supports data parallelism.

Data sink   Entity that generates data such as a random number generator.

Dangling reference   An access path that continues to exist after the lifetime of the associated data object.

Declarative equivalence   A situation that occurs when two type names refer to the same original structure.

DENDRAL   A software program used to analyze nuclear and chemical experimental data to infer the plausible structure of an unknown compound.

Denotational semantics   Programming rules that use the standard mathematical theory of functions to prove the properties of a language.

Depth-first search   A search method in which the control system performs the resolution of proving the goal in a specific order, which is top to bottom and left to right.

Dereferencing   When a pointer variable is used to access the value stored in another location.

Derived class   A class that is defined from another class.

Diamond property   A property, also called confluence property, such that if a lambda expression M is evaluated to a normal form A via a sequence of reductions and another sequence of reductions takes M to a normal form B, then some common term N can be found such that A can be reduced to N and B can be reduced to N.

Dynamic binding   A process that occurs when the system decides which implementation of the operation to use at run time.

Elementary object   An object with no internal structure.

Embedded system   A system for online monitoring and control such that a computer is only a part of the total system

Encapsulation   The idea of packaging things together in a well-defined programming unit.

Eta-conversion   The elimination of redundant lambda expressions.

Executable program   A version of the source program that can be carried out by the CPU.

EXPERT   A software program used to build consultation models in endocrinology.

Explicit type information   Information contained in declarations.

External linkage   A linkage that occurs when the objects declared outside of all blocks become global to the entire program.

Fork   A mechanism used to create a process in concurrent processing.

Formal grammar   A vocabulary of symbols and rules for forming phrases of the language.

Forward chaining   A method similar to iteration, also called the bottom-up approach.

Free   A function in C used to reclaim the allocated memory.

Friend class   A class that has complete access to another class.

Function type   A type of information used to pass functions as parameters.

Function prototype   The declaration of the function name, the data the function needs from the outside world to perform, and the type of data that the function returns to the outside world when it has finished its task.

Functional calculus   The standard mathematical theory of functions used in denotational semantics.

Functional side effect   An effect that occurs when the function changes either one of its parameters or a global variable involved in carrying out the function.

Gamma-conversion   A process associated with predefined values and functions.

Garbage   The data object that continues to exist when all access paths to that data object are destroyed.

General-purpose language   A language designed to be applied to a wide range of applications.

Global variable   A variable that is declared in the outermost block of the program.

Graphical user interface   A graphical feature that makes a computer system easy to use.

Headed horn clause   A logical statement that the left-hand side is a single term.

Headless horn clause   A logical statement that the left-hand side is empty.

High-level programming language   A language in which each instruction may generate many machine instructions.

Identifier   A fundamental abstraction in a programming language to denote language entities.

Implicit type information   A type of information that might not be given in declarations, such as types of constants.

Infix notation   A notation in which the operator appears between the operands.

Inference rule   A rule that enables the truth of a certain assertion to be deduced from the truth of another certain assertion.

Integer type   A data type with the set of integers as its domain.

Internal linkage   A linkage that occurs when the objects declared outside of all blocks become local to entire program.

Interpreter   A program that converts a source code to machine code one statement at a time.

Keyword message   A message that consists of one or more keywords.

Lambda calculus   A mathematical method for expressing computation by functions and is used for studying functional programming language concepts.

Language support   The capabilities provided by a programming language to control process execution and interaction in the source program.

Lazy evaluation   An evaluation rule that eliminates unnecessary evaluation of expressions.

Lexical analyzer   A program that converts the stream of input characters to a stream of tokens that become the input to syntactic analyzer.

Linked lists   A linear collection of nodes connected by pointer links.

Linker   A program that copies the needed subroutines into the object code so that an executable version of the program can be created.

Local variable   A variable that is declared within a block for use only within that block.

Logical expression   Logical expression or formula that represents the behavior of a logical assertion before and after the execution is carried out.

Logical statement   A term that represents relations between objects and asserts that something is a quality or property of something else.

Low-level programming language   A language in which each symbolic instruction can generate one machine instruction.

Mach   An operating system developed at Carnegie-Mellon University.

Machine language   A notation that the computer can understand and respond to directly.

MACSYMA   A software program used to solve differential and integral calculus problems.

Malloc   A function in C used to allocate the memory dynamically .

Mapping   An implementation part of a parallel program.

Message protocol   The entire collection of methods of an object.

Microcode   A small program that translates machine instructions directly into hardware signals.

Mixfix notation   A notation in which operations are defined as a combination of prefix, postfix, and infix notations.

Module   A grouping of related declarations that can include types, variables, and procedures.

Multiple inheritance   When classes are permitted to have more than one parent.

MYCIN   A software program used to diagnose infectious blood diseases.

Name equivalence   A situation in which two named types are equivalent if they have the same name.

Normal order evaluation   An expression evaluation that corresponds to the evaluation of each operand when it is needed in computing the result.

Object   An instance of a user-defined type named class.

Operand   A basic principal of expressions, also known as arguments or parameters.

Operational semantics   Programming rules that define programming language behavior by describing its actions in terms of the operations of an abstract or hypothetical machine.

Operator   A basic principal of expressions, also known as functions.

Overloading   The situation, sometimes called ad hoc polymorphism, that occurs when a number of different functions are all denoted by the same name.

Package   A collection of related entities that can be used by other parts of the program.

Paraphrase   A parallel compiler used by the Cedar Multiprocessor.

Parent class   A class from which a new class is derived.

Pipelining   A situation that occurs when different operations are performed on different data elements simultaneously.

Pointer type   A data type such that a variable of that data type contains the address of another variable.

Polymorphic operation   An operation that can accept values of arbitrary types.

Postcondition   An assertion about a construct that is true after the construct has been carried out.

Postfix notation   A notation in which the operator appears after the list of operands.

Pragmatics   The practical use of a programming language.

Precondition   An assertion about a construct that is true before the construct is carried out.

Predicate   A logical statement that describes the state of the computation.

Prefix notation   A notation in which the operator appears before the list of operands.

Process   A sequence of program instructions that can be performed in sequence or in parallel with other program instructions.

Production rule   A rule used to define the formation of the constructs.

Programming language   A notation for communicating to a computer what we want it to do.

Pure polymorphism   A situation that occurs when a single function can be applied to arguments of a variety of types.

Real type   A data type used to store data consisting of decimal and fraction parts.

Reclamation of storage   The process that reclaims storage allocated but no longer used.

Referential transparency   A system in which the meaning of the whole can be determined solely from the meaning of its components.

Regular expression   A form of language definition.

Regular grammar   A type of grammar in which each production rule is restricted to only one terminal or one terminal and one variable on the right side of the production rules.

Rendezvous   A mechanism used for task synchronization and communication.

Resolution A sequence of steps that a deduction system chooses to derive a new logical statement.

Resumption model A model that resumes the subprogram execution that invoked the exception.

Semantic domain A set of mathematical objects of a particular form.

Semantic equation An equation that specifies how the semantic functions act on each construct by using the structure of the grammar rules.

Semantic function A function that synthesizes the meaning of constructs by mapping objects onto objects in semantic domain.

Semantics Programming definition of what happens when a program is carried out.

Semaphore A primitive used for synchronization purposes in concurrent processing.

Shape A template for parallel data that defines how many elements of a parallel variable exist and how they are organized.

Short circuit evaluation An evaluation that corresponds to evaluation of an expression without evaluating all its subexpressions.

Signature The data that the function receives along with the function name.

Single inheritance The situation that occurs when each class has just one parent.

Special-purpose language A language that is designed for a specific class of applications.

Start symbol A distinguished symbol that specifies the principal category being defined.

Structural equivalence A situation that occurs when two data types are the same if they have the same structure.

Structured control abstraction A fragment of code used every time it is required.

Structured data abstraction A principal method for abstracting collections of data values that are related.

Subclass A class that is derived from the superclass.

Superclass A class defined with the keyword super.

Syntactic analyzer A combination of a parser and an intermediate code generator to form a derivation tree from the token list.

Syntax A mechanism used to form different constructs of a language.

Syntax diagram A diagram that represents each production rule as a directed graph whose terminal symbols and variable symbols are represented by circles and rectangles, respectively.

Syntax tree   A tree that represents the construct generated by the grammar.

Task   A basic unit of resource allocation that includes a page address space and protected access to system resources.

Template   An overloaded function that allows users to write a single function definition that works with many different data types.

Terminal symbols   A set of symbols that are the alphabet of the language and are combined to form valid constructs.

Termination model   A model that terminates the subprogram execution that invoked the exception.

Thread   An active entity used as a process in concurrent processing.

Top-down approach   The approach that starts with the goal and attempts to prove its correctness by finding a sequence of logical statements.

Top-down parsers   A parser that begins with the start symbol as the root of the tree and replaces variable symbols with a string of terminal symbols.

Turing machine   A reduction machine that is a collection of actions described in mathematical notation to represent programs.

Type binding   The determination of one of the components of a data object.

Type checking   The process a translator goes through to verify that all constructs in a program are valid.

Type conversion   A process that deals with two different data types in evaluating an expression.

Type variable   A variable used when the type of a subexpression is undetermined and depends on the actual type supplied during execution.

Unary message   A message with no parameter.

Unification   A process of pattern matching to make terms identical so they can be discarded from each other.

Unit control abstraction   A collection of procedures that provide logically related services to other parts of a program.

Unit data abstraction   A collection of all the information needed to create and use a particular data type in one unit location.

User-defined data type   A data type defined by the user.

Variable   A fundamental abstraction in a programming language that denotes language entities.

Variable symbol   A symbol that represents intermediate definition within the language.

Appendix C: Programming Languages

Ada Developed as a general purpose programming language for numerical computations, system programming, and applications with real time and concurrency requirements.

ALGOL The youngest, and probably most influential of the three big, classic languages, the other two being LISP and Fortran. ALGOL is suitable for expressing a large class of numerical processor in a form sufficiently concise for direct automatic translation into the language of programmed automatic computers.

ALGOL-60 A portable language for scientific computations. ALGOL-60 is small and elegant; block-structured, nested, recursive, and free-form; and was also the first language to be described in Backus-Naur Form (BNF).

APL (A Programming Language) Geared toward arrays but is a much higher level language than Fortran that supports a large number of powerful aggregate operators that act on arrays.

AWK Designed to search, match patterns, and to perform action on files; scans lines one at a time for matches and patterns specified.

BASIC (Beginner's All-purpose Symbolic Instruction Code) Originally designed for experimental timesharing system.

Bliss (Basic Language for Implementation of System Software) An expression language that is block-structured and typeless with exception handling facilities, co-routines, a macro system, and a highly optimizing compiler.

C++ A popular object-oriented programming language motivated by Simula that added classes to C in a preprocessing compiler step. The success and widespread use of C, coupled with the lack of any sort of support for abstract data types in C, has prompted widespread use of C++.

C Evolved from two earlier languages, BCPL and B, both of which were typeless languages, and every data item occupied one word in memory. The emphasis in C is on flexibility and lack of restrictions. Its ability to access hardware makes it a better choice than other programming languages for writing operating systems.

CLOS (Common Lisp Object System) Ideal for projects that are complex or need rapid prototyping and delivery; an Object-oriented extension to Common LISP, based on generic functions, multiple inheritance, declarative method combination and a meta-object protocol.

CLU-OOL A language in the Pascal family based on data abstraction that introduced the iterator: a co-routine yielding the elements of a data object to be used as a sequence of values in a loop.

COBOL (COmmon Business Oriented Language) A highly structured language, specifically designed for business applications and emphasized data representation, and used primarily for commercial applications that require precise and efficient manipulation of large amounts of data.

CPL (Combined Programming Language) Designed to be both high and low level; a very large and difficult language.

Eiffel A sophisticated, advanced language that strives for object-oriented purity and emphasizes the design and construction of high-quality and reusable software, such as classes with multiple and repeated inheritance, deferred classes, and clusters of classes. Objects can have both static and dynamic types.

ESP (Extended Self-contained Prolog) A programming language for fifth-generation projects that run in a UNIX environment.

Forth An extensible language and an interactive development methodology; primary uses have been scientific and industrial applications such as instrumentation, robotics, process control, graphics and image processing, AI, and business.

Fortran (FORmula TRANslator) Developed by IBM as the first high-level programming language; introduced features such as symbolic expressions and subprograms with parameters; and can be used for scientific and engineering applications that require complex mathematical computations.

Haskell (Hudak and Fasel 1992) Based largely on Miranda. Like Miranda, it is a purely functional language, having no variables and no assignment statement.

HTML (HyperText Markup Language) A language developed to build a Web address or Web page that controls the appearance of a Web page and consists of hypertext and hypermedia.

Java Based on C and C++ programming languages; generated immediate interest in the business community because of the phenomenal commercial interest in the World Wide Web.

LISP (LISt Processing) Designed for problems with irregular data structures that are well represented as *lists*. It has been used for symbolic calculations in differential and integral calculus, electrical circuit theory, mathematical logic, game playing, and artificial intelligence. The proliferation of LISP prompted creation of Common LISP with an object-oriented extension named CLOS (Common LISP Object System) and an extension designed for parallel processing called Multilisp.

Mesa A language that includes those paradigms in concurrent languages that have been proven, and new ones that add support and, possibly, future technologies.

Miranda A functional language that has adopted many of the features of ML, particularly the type system and pattern matching.

ML Developed as a functional programming language with a syntax and a mechanism for type checking similar to that of Pascal—but is much more flexible.

Modula Combined the block and type structure of Pascal with *module* constructs for defining abstract data types. Modula is a general purpose language with enough visibility of the underlying hardware to be useful in operating system design.

Occam A language that facilitates writing parallel programs, allowing the programmer to specify whether processes are to be carried out sequentially or in parallel.

Pascal Designed for teaching structured programming in an academic environment; became the preferred introductory programming language at most universities; and has influenced nearly all recent languages. Concurrent Pascal is a parallel version that uses shared memory parallel architectures.

Perl (Practical Extraction and Report Language or, fondly, Pathologically Eclectic Rubbish Lister). An interpreted language optimized for scanning arbitrary text files, extracting information from those files, and printing reports based on that information; for writing CGI programs and for automating routines on the servers.

PL/I A large language that combines many features of Fortran, ALGOL, and COBOL. The IBM version contains the fork and join parallelization primitives that allow the creation and termination of parallel tasks for parallel processing.

Prolog A high-level language whose heritage is logic notation and automatic theorem proving. Concurrent Prolog is a well-known parallel variant used in the execution of expert systems.

Scheme A more uniform version of LISP than the original that was designed to resemble lambda calculus more closely. Like any other functional programming language, Scheme relies on recursion to perform loops and other repetitive operations.

Simula A language developed for scientific and industrial research. A system descriptive language for discrete event networks that was designed to simulate situations such as queues at a supermarket, response times of emergency services, and chain reactions of nuclear reactors.

Smalltalk A pure object-oriented language that was designed to be a self-contained interactive programming language, in which programs would be characterized by a high degree of modularity and dynamic extensibility.

SNOBOL   Designed primarily to process string data. The successor to SNOBOL, called Icon, was developed by Griswold.

VDL   (Vienna Definition Language). A language used for semantics notation of programming languages.

Visual Basic   Evolved from BASIC, which was developed in the 1960s. Development of the Microsoft Windows graphical user interface (GUI) in the late 1980s and the early 1990s spurred the evolution of Visual Basic by Microsoft in 1991. Visual Basic greatly simplifies Windows application development and the latest version, Visual Basic 6, was released in 1998.

References

H. Abelson, G. J. Syssman, & J. Sussman. 1996. *Structure and Interpretation of Computer Programs,* 2nd ed. Cambridge, MA: MIT Press

M. Accetta, R. Baron, D. Golub, & R. Rashid. 1986. MACH: A New Kernel Foundation for UNIX Development. Pp. 93–112 in *Proceedings Summer 1986 USENIX Conference.*

W. B. Ackerman & J. B. Dennis. 1979. VAL: A Value Oriented Algorithmic Language, *Technical Report MIT/LC/STR-218,* Laboratory of Computer Science, MIT.

S. J. Allen & A. Oldehoeft. 1980. A Flow Analysis Procedure for the Translation of High-Level Languages to a Dataflow Language. *IEEE Transactions on Computers,* C-29(9), pp. 826–831.

G. S. Almasi & A. Gottlieb. 1994. *Highly Parallel Computing,* 2nd ed. Redwood City, CA: Benjamin/Cummings.

D. Appleby & J. J. VandeKopple. 1997. *Programming Languages: Paradigm and Practice,* 2nd ed. New York: McGraw-Hill.

V. Arvind, K. P. Gostelow, & W. Plouffe. 1978. The ID Report. An Asynchronous Programming Language and Computing Machine. *Technical Report 114a,* Department of Information and Computing Science, University of California–Irvine.

A. Ashcroft & W. Wadge. 1977. LUCID: A Nonprocedural Language with Iteration. *Communication ACM,* 20, pp. 519–526.

J. Backus. 1978. Can Programming Be Liberated from the Von Neumann Style? A Functional Style and Its Algebra of Programs. *Communications of the ACM,* 21(8), pp. 613–641.

J. Backus. 1982. The History of Fortran I, II, and III. In *History of Programming Languages,* edited by R. L. Wexelblat, pp. 24–45. New York: Academic Press.

U. Banerjee, R. Eigenmann, A. Nocilau, & D. A. Padua. 1993. Automatic Program Parallelization. *Proceedings of IEEE,* 81(2), pp. 211–243.

H. P. Barendregt. 1984. *The Lambda Calculus, Its Syntax and Semantics.* Amsterdam: North-Holland.

G. Bell. 1992. Ultracomputer: A Teraflop Before Its Time. *Communications of ACM,* 35 (8), pp. 27–47.

F. Berman & L. Snyder. 1984. On Mapping Parallel Algorithms into Parallel Architectures, pp. 307–309. International Conference on Parallel Processing, August 1984

T. Berners-Lee. 1989 (March). CERN, Information Management: A Proposal, http://www.w3.org:/History/1989/proposal.html.

E. Best. 1996. *Semantics of Sequential and Parallel Programs.* Englewood Cliffs, NJ: Prentice-Hall.

W. Bledsoe. 1977. Non-Resolution Theorem Proving. *Artificial Intelligence,* 9.

S. H. Bokhari. 1981. On the Mapping Problem. *IEEE Transactions on Computers,* C-30, pp. 207–214.

G. Booch. 1994. *Object Oriented Design with Applications,* 2nd ed. Redwood City, CA: Benjamin/Cummings.

J. Boykin, D. Kirschen, A. Longerman, & S. LoVerso. 1993. *Programming under MACH.* Reading, MA: Addison-Wesley.

British Standards Institution. 1982. *Specification for Computer Programming Language Pascal.* BS 6192. London: Milton Keynes.

F. Brooks. 1975. *The Mythical Man-Month: Essays on Software Engineering.* Reading, MA: Addison-Wesley

F. Brooks. 1994. *Object Oriented Design with Applications,* 2nd ed. Redwood City, CA: Benjamin/Cummings.

R. A. Brooks. 1985. *Programming in Common LISP.* New York: Wiley.

L. R. Brownston, R. Farrel, E. Kant, & N. Martin. 1985. *Programming Expert Systems in OSP5: An Introduction to Rule-Based Programming.* Reading, MA: Addison-Wesley.

A. Burns & G. Davies. 1993. *Concurrent Programming.* Reading, MA: Addison-Wesley.

V. Bush. 1945 (July). As We May Think. *Atlantic Monthly,* http://www.theatlantic.com/unbound/flaskbks/computer/bushf.html

L. Cardelli, J. Donahue, L. Glassman, M. Jordan, B. Kalsow, & G. Nelson. 1989. *Modula-3 Report.* Palo Alto, CA: Digital System Research Center.

N. Carriero & D. Gelernter. 1992. *How to Write Parallel Programs: A First Course.* Cambridge, MA: MIT Press.

M. Chandy & J. Misra. 1998. *Parallel Program Design: A Foundation.* Reading, MA: Addison-Wesley.

M. Chandy & S. Taylor. 1992. *An Introduction to Parallel Programming.* Sudbury, MA: Jones & Bartlett.

Y. P. Chiang & K. S. Fu. 1983. *Matching Parallel Algorithms and Architecture.* International Conference on Parallel Processing, August 1983, pp. 374–380.

T. Chikayama, H. Sato, & T. Miyazaki. 1988. Overview of the Parallel Inference Machine Operating System (PIMOS). *Proceedings of the International Conference on Fifth Generation Computer Systems,* Tokyo, pp. 230–251.

P. M. Chirlian. 1986. *LISP.* Cleveland, OH: Weber Systems.

A. Church. 1941. The Calculi of Lambda-Conversion. *Annals of Mathematical Studies,* Number 6. Princeton, NJ: Princeton University Press.

W. F. Clocksin & C. S. Mellish. 1987. *Programming in Prolog,* 3rd ed. West Hanover, MA: Springer.

M. A. Cohen & S. G. Grossberg. 1983. Absolute Stability of Global Pattern Formation and Parallel Memory Storage by Competitive Neural Networks. Pp. 815–826 in *IEEE Trans. Systems Man Cybernetics* 13-5.

N. H. Cohen. 1996. *Ada as a Second Language,* 2nd ed. New York: McGraw-Hill.

D. E. Comer & D. Stevens. 1996. Internetworking with TCP/IP, Vol III. *Client-Server Programming and Applications for the BSD Socket Version.* Englewood Cliffs, NJ: Prentice-Hall.

B. J. Cox. 1984. Message/Object Programming: An Evolutionary Change in Programming Technology. *IEEE Software,* January, pp. 50-61.

D. Crookes. 1988. *Introduction to Programming in Prolog.* Englewood Cliffs, NJ: Prentice-Hall.

O. J. Dahl & K. Nygaard. 1966. Simula: An Algol-based Simulation Language. *Communication ACM,* 9(9), pp. 671–678.

S. Dasgupta. 1990. A Hierarchical Taxonomic System for Computer Architectures. *Computer,* 23(3), pp. 64–74.

C. J. Date. 2000. *An Introduction to Database Systems,* 7th ed. Reading, MA: Addison-Wesley.

H. M. Deitel & P. J. Deitel. 1994a. *C: How to Program.* Englewood Cliffs, NJ: Prentice-Hall.

H. M Deitel & P. J. Deitel. 1994b. *C++: How to Program.* Englewood Cliffs, NJ: Prentice-Hall.

H. M Deitel & P. J. Deitel. 1997. *Java: How to Program.* Englewood Cliffs, NJ: Prentice-Hall.

H. L. Dershem & M. J. Jipping. 1995. *Programming Languages: Structures and Models,* 2nd ed. Boston: PWS.

G. Diccardi. 2001. *Principles of Database Systems with Internet and Java Applications.* Reading, MA: Addison-Wesley.

T. W. Doeppner. 1987. A Threads Tutorial. *Computer Science Technical Report CS-87-06.* Providence, RI: Brown University.

J. J. Dongarra & L. Johnson. 1989. Solving Banded Systems on a Parallel Processor. *Parallel Computing,* 5, pp. 219–246.

V. Donzeau-Gouge, G. Kahn, B. Lang, & B. Krieg-Bruckner. 1980. *Formal Description of the Ada Programming Language.* Rocquencourt, France: INRIA.

V. Drobot. 1989. *Formal Languages and Automata Theory.* Rockville, MD: Computer Science Press.

R. O. Duda, P. E. Hart, K. Konolige, & R. Reboh. 1979. *A Computer-Based Consultant for Mineral Exploration.* Technical Report, SRI International.

R. K. Dybvig. 1966. *The SCHEME Programming Language,* 2nd ed. Englewood Cliffs, NJ: Prentice-Hall.

J. R. Ellis. 1986. *Bulldog: A Compiler for VLIW Architectures.* Cambridge, MA: MIT Press.

K. Fitzgerald & R. Rashid. 1986. The Integration of Virtual Memory Management and Interprocess Communication in Accent. *ACM Transactions on Computer Systems,* 4(2), pp. 147–177.

M. J. Flynn. 1966. Very High-Speed Computing Systems. *Proceedings of the IEEE,* 54(12), pp. 1901–1909.

N. Ford. 1989. *Prolog Programming.* New York: Wiley.

B. A. Forouzan. 2001. *Data Communications and Networking,* 2nd ed. New York: McGraw-Hill.

I. Foster, R. Olson, & S. Tuecke. 1992. Productive Parallel Programming: The PCN Approach. *Scientific Programming,* 1, pp. 51–66.

T. J. Fountain. 1994. *Parallel Computing: Principles and Practice.* Cambridge: Cambridge University Press.

G. Fox, S. Hiranandani, K. Kennedy, C. Koelbel, & U. Kemer. 1991. *Fortran D Language Specification.* Rice University Technical Paper TR90-141.

D. P. Friedman, M. Wand, & C. T. Haynes. 1998. *Essentials of Programming Languages.* New York: McGraw-Hill.

K. Fuchi & K. Furukawa. 1987. The Role of Logic Programming in the Fifth Generation Computer Project. *New Generation Computing,* 3(5), pp. 3–23.

A. Geist, A. Geguelia, J. Dongarra, W. Jiang, & V. Sunderam. 1994. *PVM: Parallel Virtual Machine, A User's Guide and Tutorial for Networked Parallel Computing.* Cambridge, MA: MIT Press.

C. Ghezzi & M. Jazayeri. 1987. *Programming Language Concepts,* 2nd ed. New York: Wiley.

A. Gilberg & D. Robson. 1989. *The Language Smalltalk-80.* Reading, MA: Addison-Wesley.

J. Glauert. 1978. *A Single Assignment Language for Data Flow Computing.* Master's thesis, University of Manchester.

M. J. C. Gordon. 1979. *The Denotational Description of Programming Languages.* New York: Springer-Verlag.

A. Goscinski. 1991. *Distributed Operating Systems: The Logical Design.* Reading, MA: Addison-Wesley.

R. Griswold. 1975. *String and List Processing in SNOBOL4: Techniques and Applications.* Englewood Cliffs, NJ: Prentice-Hall.

C. A. Gunter. 1992. *Semantics of Programming Languages: Structures and Techniques.* Cambridge, MA: MIT Press.

E. M. Gurari. 1989. *An Introduction to the Theory of Computation.* Rockville, MD: Computer Science Press.

P. B. Hansen. 1995. *Studies in Computational Science: Parallel Programming Paradigms.* Englewood Cliffs, NJ: Prentice-Hall.

P. Hatcher & M. Quinn. 1991. *Data Parallel Programming on MIMD Computers.* Cambridge, MA: MIT Press.

S. Hiranandani & K. Kennedy. 1992. Compiling Fortran-D for MIMD Distributed Memory Machines. *Communications of the ACM,* 35(8), pp. 66–80.

S. Hiranandani & K. Kennedy. 1993. Preliminary Experiences with the Fortran-D Compiler. Pp. 338–350 in *Proceedings, Supercomputing 1993.*

C. A. R. Hoare. 1969. An Axiomatic Basis for Computer Programming. *Communications of the ACM,* 12(10), pp. 576–583.

C.A. R. Hoare & N. Wirth. 1973. An Axiomatic Definition of the Programming Language Pascal. *Acta Informatica,* 2, pp. 335–355. (Reprinted in *Tutorial, Programming Language Design,* edited by Anthony I. Wasserman, pp. 506–526, 1980.)

R. W. Hockney. 1987. Classification and Evaluation of Parallel Computer Systems. *Springer-Verlag Lecture Notes in Computer Science,* 245, pp. 13–25.

R. W. Hockney & C. R. Jesshope. 1988. *Parallel Computers 2.* Bristol, England: Adam Hilger.

J. E. Hopcraft & J. D. Ullman. 1979. *Introduction to Automata Theory, Languages, and Computation.* Reading, MA: Addison-Wesley.

E. Horowitz. 1984. *Foundations of Programming Languages.* Rockville, MD: Computer Science Press.

A. Hudak. 1989. Conception, Evolution, and Application of Functional Programming Languages. *ACM Computing Surveys* 21930, pp. 359–411.

P. Hudak & J. Fasel. 1992. A Gentle Introduction to Haskell. *ACM SIGPLAN Notices,* 27(5, May), pp. T1–T53.

K. Hwang. 1993. *Advanced Computer Architecture: Parallelism, Scalability, and Programmability.* New York: McGraw-Hill.

J. Ichbiah. 1983. *Ada Programming Language.* ANSI/MIL-STD-1815A. Washington, DC: Ada Joint Program Office, Department of Defense.

K. Jensen & N. Wirth. 1974. *Pascal User Manual and Report.* Berlin, Germany: Springer.

R. M. Kaplan. 1994. *Constructing Language Processors for Little Languages.* New York: Wiley.

A. Kay. 1977. Microelectronics and the Personal Computer. *Scientific American,* 237(3), pp. 230–244.

A. Kay. 1993. The Early History of Smalltalk. The Second ACM SIGPLAN History of Programming Languages Conference (HOPL-H). *ACM SIGPLAN Notices* 28(3), March), pp. 69–75.

D. Kelley. 1995. *Automata and Formal Languages* Englewood Cliffs, NJ: Prentice-Hall.

B. W. Kernighan & R. Pike. 1999. *The Practice of Programming.* Reading, MA: Addison-Wesley.

B. W. Kernighan & D. M. Ritchie. 1988. *The C Programming Language,* 2nd ed. Englewood Cliffs, NJ: Prentice-Hall.

D. E. Knuth. 1997a. *The Art of Computer Programming: Fundamental Algorithms,* vol. I, 3rd ed. Reading, MA: Addison-Wesley.

D. E. Knuth. 1997b. *The Art of Computer Programming: Seminumerical Algorithms,* vol. II, 3rd ed. Reading, MA: Addison-Wesley.

D. E. Knuth. 1997c. *The Art of Computer Programming: Sorting and Searching,* vol. III, 3rd ed. Reading, MA: Addison-Wesley.

A. Koenig & B. Stroustrup. 1990. Exception Handling for C++. *Proceedings of the USENIX C++ Conference,* San Franciso, April 1990.

R. Kowalski. 1979. Algorithm = Logic + Control. *Communications of the ACM,* 22, pp. 424–436.

G. Krasner. 1983. *Smalltalk-80: Bits of History, Words of Advice.* Reading, MA: Addison-Wesley.

J. Kuck, R. H. Kuhn, B. Leasure, & M. Wolfe. 1984. The Structure of an Advanced Retargetable Vectorizer. Pp. 163-178 in *Tutorial on Supercomputers,* edited by Kai Hwang. Los Angeles: IEEE Press.

B. W. Lampson. 1983 (December). A Description of the Cedar Language. *Technical Report CSL-83-15.* Palo Alto, CA: Xerox Palo Alto Research Center.

B. W. Lampson & D. D. Redell. 1980. Experience with Processs and Monitors in Mesa. *Communications of the ACM,* 23(2), pp. 105–117.

P. Landin. 1964. The Mechanical Evaluation of Expressions. *Computer Journal,* 6(January), pp. 308–320.

P. Landin. 1977. A Lambda-Calculus Approach. Pp. 103-124 in *Advances in Programming and Non-numerical Computation,* edited by Anita K. Jones. New York: Academic Press.

F. T. Leighton. 1992. *Introduction to Parallel Algorithms and Architectures: Arrays, Trees, Hypercubes.* San Mateo, CA: Morgan Kaufmann.

H. Li, C-C. Wang, & M. Lavin. 1985. Structured Process: A New Language Attribute for Better Interaction of Parallel Architecture and Algorithm. Pp. 247–254 in *1985 International Conference on Parallel Processing,* Chicago.

D. Liang. 1998. *An Introduction to JAVA Programming.* Indianapolis: Que @ Education & Training.

T. A. Lipkis & J. G. Schmolze. 1983. Classification in the KL-ONE Knowledge Representation System. *Proceedings of Eighth International Joint Conference on Artificial Intelligence,* 1, pp. 330–332.

G. J. Lipovski & M. Malek.1987. *Parallel Computing: Theory and Computing,* New York: Wiley.

K. C. Louden. 1993. *Programming Languages: Principles and Practice.* Boston: PWS.

P. Lucas & K. Walk. 1969. On the Formal Description of PL/I. *Annual Review in Automatic Programming,* 6, pp. 105–152.

B. MacLennan. 1990. *Functional Programming Methodology: Practice and Theory.* Reading, MA: Addison-Wesley.

B. MacLennan. 1999. *Principles of Programming Languages: Design, Evaluation and Implementation.* New York: Oxford University Press.

B. J. MacLennan. 1987. *Programming Languages: Design, Evaluation and Implementation,* 2nd ed. New York: Holt, Rinehart & Winston.

Z. Manna & R. Waldinger. 1993. *The Deductive Foundations of Computer Programming.* Reading, MA: Addison-Wesley.

M. Marcotty & H. Ledgard. 1987. *The World of Programming Languages.* New York: Springer-Verlag.

S. Marcus & J. McDermott. 1989. SALT: A Knowledge Acquisition Language for Propose-and-Revise Systems. *Artificial Intelligence* 39(1).

B. Meyer. 1988. *Object-Oriented Software Construction.* London: Prentice-Hall.

B. Meyer. 1991. *Introduction to the Theory of Programming Languages.* Englewood Cliffs, NJ: Prentice-Hall.

J. Miklosko & V. E. Kotov. 1984. *Algorithms, Software and Hardware of Parallel Computers.* Berlin: Springer.

R. Milner. 1987. *The Standard ML Core Language.* Hemel Hempstead, England: Prentice-Hall International, pp. 378–414.

R. Milner, M. Tofte, & R. Harper. 1990. *The Definition of Standard ML.* Cambridge, MA: MIT Press.

V. M. Milulinovic. 1989. *High Level Language Computer Architectures.* Freeman, New York: Computer Science Press.

J. G. Mitchell. 1998. *Foundations for Programming Languages.* Cambridge, MA: MIT Press.

J. G. Mitchell, W. Maybury, & R. Sweet. 1979. *Mesa Language Manual, version 5.0.* Palo Alto, CA: Xerox Research Center.

D. I. Moldovan. 1993. *Parallel Processing: From Applications to Systems.* San Mateo, CA: Morgan Kaufmann.

R. Moskowitz. 1989. Object-Oriented Programming: The Future is Now. *PC Times* (October 2), p. 3.

P. D. Mosses. 1974. The Mathematical Semantics of Algol-60. *Technical Monograph PRG-12*, Programming Research Group, University of Oxford, England.

P. D. Mosses. 1986. The Modularity of Action Semantics. *Report DAIMI IR-75*, Computer Science Department, Aarhus University, Denmark.

S. Nath. 1986. *TURBO Prolog: Features for Programmers.* Cambridge, MA: MIT Press.

P. Naur. 1963. Revised Report on the Algorithmic Language Algol 60. *Communications of the ACM*, 6.1, pp. 1–20.

F. Pagan. 1981. *Formal Specification of Programming Languages: A Panoramic Primer.* Englewood Cliffs, NJ: Prentice-Hall.

S. L. Peyton Jones. 1987. *The Implementation of Functional Programming Languages.* Englewood Cliffs, NJ: Prentice-Hall.

L. Pinson & R. Wiener. 1988. *An Introduction to Object-Oriented Programming and Smalltalk.* Reading, MA: Addison-Wesley.

T. W. Pratt & M. V. Zelkowitz. 1999. *Programming Languages: Design and Implementation*, 3rd ed. Englewood Cliffs, NJ: Prentice-Hall.

M. J. Quinn. 1994. *Parallel Computing: Theory and Practice.* New York: McGraw-Hill.

R. Ramakrishnan. 1997. *Database Management Systems.* New York: McGraw-Hill.

R. Rashid. 1986. Experiences with the Accent Network Operating System Networking in Open Systems. *Lecture Notes in Computer Science*, 248, pp. 259–269.

R. Rashid & G. Robertson. 1981. Accent: A Communication Oriented Network Operating System Kernel. *ACM Operating Systems Review*, 15(5), pp. 64–75.

J. Rees & W. Clinger. 1986. Revised Report on the Algorithmic Language Scheme. *ACM SIGPLAN Notices,* 21, pp. 37–79.

G. Riccardi. 2001. *Principles of Database Systems with Internet and Java Applications.* Reading, MA: Addison-Wesley.

D. D. Riley. 1987a. *Data Abstraction and Structures.* Boston: Boyd & Fraser.

D. D. Riley. 1987b. *Using Modula-2.* Boston: Boyd & Fraser.

K. A. Robbins & S. Robbins. 1996. *Practical UNIX Programming: A Guide to Concurrency, Communication, and Multithreading.* Englewood Cliffs, NJ: Prentice-Hall.

J. A. Robinson. 1965. A Machine-Oriented Logic Based on the Resolution Principle. *Journal of the ACM,* 12, pp. 23–41.

S. H. Roosta. 2000. *Parallel Processing and Parallel Algorithms: Theory and Computation.* New York: Springer-Verlag.

P. Rovner. 1986. Extending Modula-2 to Build Large, Integrated Systems. *IEEE Software,* 3(6, November).

B. S. Schieber & U. Vishkin. 1989. On Finding Lowest Common Ancestors: Simplification and Parallelization. *SIAM Journal on Computing,* 17(6), pp. 1253–1262.

A. Schiper. 1989. *Concurrent Programming: Illustrated with Examples in Portal, Modula-2 and Ada.* New York: Wiley.

R. W. Sebesta. 1999. *Concepts of Programming Languages,* 4th ed. Reading, MA: Addison-Wesley.

R. Sessions. 1996. *Object Persistence: Beyond Object-Oriented Databases.* Englewood Cliffs, NJ: Prentice-Hall.

R. Sethi. 1989. *Programming Languages: Concepts and Constructs.* Reading, MA: Addison-Wesley.

R. Sethi. 1996. *Programming Languages: Concepts and Constructs,* 2nd ed. Reading, MA: Addison-Wesley.

J. A. Sharp. 1985. Data Flow Computing, *Ellis Horwood Series on Computers and Their Applications.* New York: Wiley.

J. A. Sharp. 1987. *An Introduction to Distributed and Parallel Processing.* Worchester, England: Blackwell Scientific.

S. G. Shiva. 1996. *Pipelined and Parallel Computer Architectures.* New York: HarperCollins.

E. H. Shortliffe. 1976. *MYCIN: Computer-Based Medical Consultation.* New York: Elsevier.

A. Silberschatz, H. F. Korth, & S. Sudarshan. 1997. *Database Systems Concepts,* 3rd ed. New York: McGraw-Hill.

R. Simonian & M. Crone. 1988. InnovAda: True Object-Oriented Programming in Ada. *Journal of Object-Oriented Programming,* 1(4), pp. 14–23.

J. Skansholm. 1997. *Ada 95: From the Beginning,* 3rd ed. Reading, MA: Addison-Wesley.

D. B. Skillicorn. 1988. A Taxonomy for Computer Architectures. *Computer,* 21(11), pp. 46–57.

S. Skublics, E. J. Klimas, & D. A. Thomas. 1996. *Smalltalk with Style.* Englewood Cliffs, NJ: Prentice-Hall.

K. Slonneger & B. L. Kurtz. 1995. *Formal Syntax and Semantics of Programming Language.* Reading, MA: Addison-Wesley.

R. A. Stammers. 1985. Ada on Distribued Hardware. Pp. 35–40 in *Concurrent Languages in Distributed Systems,* edited by G. Reijns & E. Dagless. Amsterdam: North-Holland.

T. A. Standish. 1995. *Data Structures, Algorithms & Software Principles in C.* Reading, MA: Addison-Wesley.

R. Stansifer. 1995. *The Study of Programming Languages.* Englewood Cliffs, NJ: Prentice-Hall.

G. L. Steele. 1984. *Common LISP Manual.* Burlington, MA: Digital Press.

G. L. Steele & G. J. Sussman. 1978. *The Revised Report on Scheme, a Dialect of Lisp.* MIT AI Memo No. 452. Boston: Massachusetts Institute of Technology.

W. R. Stevens. 1993. *Advanced Programming in the UNIX Environment.* Reading, MA: Addison-Wesley.

B. Stroustrup.1986. *The C++ Programming Language.* Reading, MA: Addison-Wesley.

B. Stroustrup. 1988 (May). What Is Object-Oriented Programming. *IEEE Software,* pp. 10–20.

T. A. Sudkamp. 1997. *Languages and Machines,* 2nd ed. Reading, MA: Addison-Wesley.

G. J. Sussman & G. L. Steele. 1975. *Scheme: An Interpreter for Extended Lambda Calculus.* MIT AI Memo No. 349. Boston: Massachusetts Institute of Technology.

A. S. Tanenbaum. 1996. *Computer Networks,* 3rd ed. Englewood Cliffs, NJ: Prentice-Hall.

A. S. Tanenbaum & R. Renesse. 1985. Distributed Operating Systems. *Computing Surveys,* 17(4), pp. 419–470.

A. S. Tanenbaum, R. Renesse, H. Staveren, & G. Sharp. 1990. Experiences with the Amoeba Distributed Operating System. *Communications of ACM,* 33(12), pp. 46–63.

R. G. Taylor. 1997. *Models of Computation and Formal Languages.* New York: Oxford University Press.

R. D. Tennent. 1978. A Denotational Definition of the Programming Language Pascal. *Technical Report 77-47.* Ontario, Canada: Department of Computing and Information Sciences, Queen's University.

R. D. Tennent. 1991. *Semantics of Programming Languages.* Englewood Cliffs, NJ: Prentice-Hall.

L. Tesler. 1985. Object Pascal Report. *Structured Language World,* 9(3), pp. 10–14.

P. C. Treleaven, D. R. Brownbridge, & R. P. Hopkins. 1982. Data-Driven and Demand-Driven Computer Architecture. *ACM Computing Surveys,* 14(1), pp. 93–143.

D. Turner. 1986. An Overview of Miranda. *ACM SIGPLAN Notices,* 21(12), pp. 158–166.

J. D. Ullman. 1998. *Elements of ML Programming.* Englewood Cliffs, NJ: Prentice-Hall.

J. D. Ullman & J. Widom. 1997. *A First Course in Database Systems.* Englewood Cliffs, NJ: Prentice-Hall.

P. S. Wang. 1997. *An Introduction to UNIX with X and the Internet.* Boston: PWS.

D. A. Watt. 1987. An Action Semantics of Standard ML. Pp. 572–598 in *Mathematical Foundations of Programming Language Semantics III.* Berlin, Germany: Springer.

D. Watt. 1990. *Programming Language Concepts and Paradigms.* Englewood Cliffs, NJ: Prentice-Hall.

D. Watt. 1991. *Programming Language Syntax and Semantics.* Englewood Cliffs, NJ: Prentice-Hall.

P. Wegner. 1972. The Vienna Definition Language. *Computing Surveys,* 4(1), pp. 5–63.

P. Wegner. 1988. Object-Oriented Concept Hierarchies, Tutorial Notes: Object-Oriented Software Engineering. International Conferences on Computer Languages'88. Tutorial presented at the IEEE International Conference on Computer Languages, Miami Beach, FL, October.

J. Weizenbaum. 1965. ELIZA: A Computer Program for the Study of Natural Language Communication Between Man and Machine. *Communications of ACM,* 9(1), pp. 36–45.

A. N. Whitehead & B. A. Russell. 1910, 1912, 1913. *Principia Mathematica, Volumes 1, 2, and 3.* Cambridge: Cambridge University Press.

H. A. G. Wijshoff. 1989. *Data Organization in Parallel Computers.* New York: Kluwer Academic.

B. Wilkinson & M. Allen. 1999. *Parallel Programming.* Englewood Cliffs, NJ: Prentice-Hall.

L. B. Wilson & R. G. Clark. 2001. *Comparative Programming Languages.* Reading, MA: Addison-Wesley.

P. H. Winston. 1992. *Artificial Intelligence,* 3rd ed. Reading, MA: Addison-Wesley.

R. Wirfs-Brock & B. Wilkerson. 1989. Object-Oriented Design: A Responsibility-Driven Approach. *Proceedings of the 1989 OOPSLA-Conference on Object-Oriented Programming Systems, Languages and Applications;* reprinted in *ACM SIGPLAN Notices,* 24(10, Oct.), pp. 71–76.

R. Wirfs-Brock, B. Wilkerson, & L. Wiener. 1990. *Designing Object-Oriented Software.* Englewood Cliffs, NJ: Prentice-Hall.

N. Wirth. 1975. On the Design of Programming Languages. *Information Processing,* 74, pp. 386–393.

N. Wirth. 1979. The Module: A System Structuring Facility in High-Level Programming Languages. Pp. 1–24 in *Language Design and Programming Methodology, Lecture Notes in Computer Science.* New York: Springer-Verlag.

N. Wirth. 1985. *Programming in Modula-2,* 3rd ed. New York: Springer-Verlag.

W. A. Wolf & M. Shaw. 1973. Global Variables Considered Harmful. *ACM SIGPLAN Notices,* 8(2, Feb.), pp. 80–86.

C. K. Yuen & A. Yomezawa. 1993. *Parallel Programming Systems.* River Edge, NJ: World Scientific.

M. R. Zargham. 1996. *Computer Architecture: Single and Parallel Systems.* Englewood Cliffs, NJ: Prentice-Hall.

Author Index

Subject Index

Backward chaining, 350, 357, 366, 391
Barrier, 471, 491, 530, 531
BASIC, 15, 40
Basic control abstraction, 47, 51, 99
Basic CPL, 197
Basic data abstraction, 49, 99
Beta
    Conversion, 406
    Reduction, 406, 418
Binary message, 250, 268
Binding
    Compile time, 19, 39, 46, 101
    Dynamic, 40
    Load-time, 19, 39, 46
    Run-time, 19, 40, 46
    Static, 39
Bliss, 16, 43, 67
Block
    Order evaluation, 89, 99, 102
    Oriented, 172, 185, 195
    Structured, 96, 171, 185, 227, 399
BNF variations, 126
Bottom-up parser, 120
Built-in data type, 19, 22, 282
Built-in function, 421, 434, 449

C

Call-by-name, 235, 408, 409
Call-by-value, 235, 409, 452, 462
Calling task, 544
Cambridge Polish, 3, 421, 461
Cartesian product domain, 103, 161, 163, 412
Catch block, 64, 76, 79, 81
Cell diagram, 431, 461
Cell model, 419, 431, 461
Checking
    Compile-time, 42
    Dynamic, 42
    Run-time, 42
    Static, 42
Chomsky hierarchy, 120
Church-Rosser, 408
Circular data type, 37
CISC, 172
Class
    Facilitator, 249
    Friend, 288

Helper, 249
Manager, 248
Observer, 248
Sink, 248
Source, 248
Super, 240, 260
View, 248
Class modifiers, 313
Clause, 342, 343, 358, 370
Closure
    Kleene, 109
    Positive, 109
CM-5, 547
COBOL, 3, 13, 16, 22, 28
Coercion, 44, 45, 103, 200, 309
Column major form, 176
Common LISP, 241, 420, 513
Communication
    General, 552
    Grid, 552, 553, 556
    Parallel, 552, 556
Comparison operation, 387
Compatible type, 44, 176
Compile time
    Binding, 19, 39, 46, 101
    Checking, 42
    Partitioning, 472, 504
    Scheduling, 472, 504
Complexity, 63, 243, 321, 497, 517
Composite
    Data type, 22, 26
    Objects, 154
Computer age, 4
Concatenation, 108, 111, 135, 201, 327
Concurrency, 214, 241, 263, 495, 505, 520
Conditional constructs, 182, 223, 233
Conformity, 476
Connector, 338, 340
Construct
    Conditional, 182, 207, 223
    Iterative, 207, 225
    Looping, 183
    Selection, 180
Context-free grammar, 109, 113, 115, 120, 129, 135, 141
Context-sensitive grammar, 109, 114, 129, 135

Continuation of the exception
    Ada, 71
    C++, 77
    Java, 81
    PL(I, 69
    ML, 74
Control
    Abstraction, 3, 48, 51, 99
    Access, 491
    Analysis, 347
    Dependence, 471, 480, 481
    Driven, 172
    Flow, 357, 380, 491, 519
    Knowledge, 351
    Mechanism, 153, 353, 473
    Parallelism, 471, 482, 484, 491, 517
    Strategy, 338, 343, 366, 379
    Structure, 196, 222, 264, 366
Conversion
    Alpha, 405
    Beta, 406
    Eta, 407
    Gamma, 407
Cut operator, 380, 381

D

Dangling reference, 94, 95, 417
Data
    Abstraction, 214
    Aggregate, 219
    Antidependence, 471, 479, 481, 483
    Control dependence, 471, 480, 481
    Definition language, 578, 614
    Dependence graph, 471, 479, 480, 504
    Driven, 172
    Flow dependence, 471, 479, 481
    Flow graph, 485, 566, 569, 611
    Input dependence, 471, 480, 481
    Manipulation language, 574, 578, 614
    Output dependence, 471, 479, 480, 481
    Parallelism, 471, 475, 482, 489, 517

Data aggregate
    Records, 219
    Sets, 220
Datagram socket, 563, 588, 590, 613
Data manager, 248
Data sink, 248
Data source, 248
Data stream
    Multiple, 471, 473, 474, 485, 516
    Single, 471, 473, 474, 485, 516
Data type
    Built-in, 19, 22, 282
    Circular, 37
    Composite, 22, 26
    Primitive, 22, 27, 28, 310, 445
    Recursive, 22, 37, 38, 442
    Scalar, 176, 215
    Structured, 22, 26, 176, 446, 462
    User-defined, 22
Data type conversion
    Explicit, 45, 215
    Implicit, 44
DBMS, 575
DDG, 479
DDL, 578
Declaration equivalence, 106, 177, 195
Decoupling , 194
Deduction rule, 145
Delayed evaluation, 436, 437, 438
Demand-driven, 172, 173, 564
DENDRAL, 420
Denotational semantics, 142, 157, 163
Dependence
    Data anti-, 479, 480, 481
    Data-control, 471, 480, 481
    Data-flow, 471, 479, 481
    Data-input, 480, 481
    Data-output, 480, 481
Depth-first search, 261, 348, 357, 374
Dequeue, 36, 37, 543
Dereferencing, 207, 216, 232
Derivation tree, 109, 120, 123, 124
Derived class, 240, 277, 290
Design principles
    Extensibility, 4

Generality, 4
Implementability, 4
Maintainability, 4
Orthogonality, 3
Portability, 1
Readability, 3
Reliability, 4
Standardability, 4
Uniformity, 4
Writeability, 3
Discriminated union, 184, 218
Disjoint union domain, 161
Dispose, 91, 95, 216
Divide-and-conquer, 239, 313
DML, 578
Domain
    Cartesian, 161
    Disjoint union, 161
    Function, 161
    Internet, 563
    Primitive, 160
    Sequence, 161
    UNIX, 563
Duality principle, 566
Dyadic, 82
Dynamic
    Array, 26
    Binding, 40, 241, 256, 262
    Memory, 91, 93, 96, 398
    Properties, 7
    Type checking, 19, 42, 271

E

Eager evaluation, 86, 104, 452, 462
EBNF, 127, 128
Elaboration, 537, 556
Elementary object, 153, 431
ELIZA, 354
Embedded system, 536
Encapsulation, 258, 320
    Logical, 265, 321
    Physical, 265, 321, 328
Enqueue, 36, 37, 543
Enumerable, 113
Enumeration, 201, 220
Eoffel, 249
Equivalence
    Declaration, 106, 177, 195
    Name, 177, 195

Structural, 177, 195, 221, 233
Type, 176
Eta
    Conversion, 407
    Reduction, 400, 406, 418
Euclid, 16, 81, 449
Evaluation
    Applicative, 48, 86, 102, 408, 461
    Block, 48, 89, 99, 102
    Call-by-name, 408
    Call-by-value, 408
    Delayed, 436, 438
    Eager, 86, 452, 462
    Greedy, 564
    Lazy, 15, 89, 397, 417, 436, 452
    Normal, 48, 88, 99, 408
    Short circuit, 48, 88, 99, 203, 223
    Strict, 86, 180, 436, 437
Exception, 47, 63, 455
Exception continuation
    Resumption, 67
    Termination, 67
Exception handling
    Ada, 47, 68, 70
    C++, 47, 68, 74
    Java, 47, 68, 77
    ML, 47, 68, 72
    PL/I, 47, 68, 69
Exception handling operations
    Catching, 77
    Claiming, 77
    Throwing, 77
Execution steps, 188
EXPERT, 420
Explicit type
    Conversion, 45, 215
    Information, 21, 46
Expression evaluation
    Applicative, 86
    Block, 89
    Lazy, 89
    Normal, 88
    Short circuit, 88
Expression notations
    Infix, 82, 85
    Mixfix, 84
    Postfix, 84, 85
    Prefix, 83, 85